Foreword by Edward Woodward OBE.

It is quite astounding how much our country has to offer the visitor these days. Whether you are after some time away from it all, a chance to delve into Britain's history, or the opportunity to walk amongst some of the many areas of outstanding natural beauty, rural or urban, we really do have it all, whether we get the chance to appreciate it or not!

I have stayed in most parts of Britain at one time or another. There is nothing more frustrating than the inevitable conversation shortly after you have returned from an area which makes you aware of what you have missed. You know the sort of thing; an assumption that you cannot possibly have visited such a town without seeing the superb orchards, ancient remains or perhaps modern shopping village. By then it is too late, and you silently vow to be much better prepared before future visits. I have made that promise many times, but seldom kept it!

I like the series of guides of which you are now holding a volume simply because they represent an attempt to give any visitor a comprehensive reference work for what can be found in a given area, but without sticking to dry facts alone. After all, what do you remember most about a particular visit, be it for work or holiday? Every town, city and village has its own atmosphere, its own stories from past and present, and its own unique setting in our equally varied countryside. The most famous attraction may be the most remembered, but any two people will describe it differently, focusing on their own preferred details. When I hear mention of a particular town or city it is often a hotel room that comes to mind, or a certain street, theatre, or restaurant.

The authors of the Four Seasons Guides have put some real flavour into what they have written; a mixture of personal comment, recollection and opinion with the solid base ingredients necessary to any guide book; relevant and up to date information about attractions, places to visit and to stay in. So many places are covered, but each has retained some of its individuality even in the midst of such a multitude.

These are books into which you can dip now and then for a little entertainment or information. You may then find yourself reading for longer than you at first intended, as one anecdote, piece of folklore or description leads you onto another. Any book which can make you smile at one moment, and at the next form a determination in your mind to visit somewhere new, must be a welcome addition to the bookshelf, or travelling bag.

Edward Woodward OBE.

The Four Seasons Discerning Visitor
About This Guide

This guide is designed to be user-friendly, each featured hotel etc., has either a full or half dedicated page, together with a Quick Reference Panel, including the tariff. Each county is separated into chapters, making it easy to find the area, or activity of particular interest to the user. The chapters commence with a summary of the area, including potted history, folklore, anecdotes etc. places to visit, attractions, and activities, all with telephone numbers, opening times etc., (where available).

*To locate a particular destination, turn to the main index
at the back of the book on pages 510-514 ...*

*For quick reference to locate a particular venue
turn to the index to selected venues in this section on pages vi-viii .....*

To locate a particular region turn to the index to chapters in this section on page v ....

*To plan a day out, a scenic tour, or a specific activity, turn to the chapter indices,
these appear at the start of each chapter. Should the activity of your choice not
appear within the chapter, at the back of the guide there is a glossary listing more places
to visit etc.*

Whilst every precaution has been taken in selecting venues for this guide, the publishers can not accept responsibility if you are not satisfied, To ensure standards are maintained, your comments(good or otherwise) would be appreciated, and passed onto the venue concerned.

For possible inclusion in future editions, should you find a venue that you have enjoyed, not featured in this guide, that you may wish to tell us about, we would be extremely grateful.

*To book accommodation contact the venue directly, or for convenience e-mail the publishers,
(kingsley@hotels.u-net.com), telephone 01752 559999, fax 01752 558888, your enquiry
will be passed to the venue of your choice.*

WHEN BOOKING PLEASE MENTION THIS GUIDE, THANK YOU.

Please remember, a booking made on the telephone or by any other method, renders you liable for the cost of the accommodation. It is a wise precaution to insure against unforeseen circumstances. Most hotels etc., are reasonable if genuine reasons prevent you from arriving on the due date. (We do not accept deposits, charge a booking fee, or accept any responsibility with regard to the booking or any other facet). The venues featured in this guide have been selected to ensure that your stay or meal, is both pleasurable and value for money.

Please turn to the back of the guide for readers comments page 516. To order guides in this series please turn to page 515.

Please write to:-
KINGSLEY MEDIA LTD., FREEPOST PY2100. PLYMOUTH PL1 3BR.
(Your name and address will not be used other than as stated above, or sold to any other organisation)

CONTENTS

Chapter One: Ship Shape and Bristol Fashion
(Bristol - Clifton - Clevedon - Portishead)

Chapter Two: The Circus is Always in Town
(Bath - Keynsham - Frome)

Chapter Three: Of Steam Trains and Cider, Beaches and Cliffs
(Weston-Super-Mare - Minehead - Taunton - Bridgwater - The Quantocks)

Chapter Four: A Royal Forest and Much Moor
(Porlock - Dulverton - Lynton & Lynmouth)

Chapter Five: The Smallest City and the Largest Street
(Cheddar - The Mendips - Wells - Glastonbury - Yeovil - Wincanton)

Chapter Six: The Old, the New and Raking for the Moon
(Malmesbury - Swindon - Cheltenham - Avebury - Devizes)

Chapter 7: The Plain and the Extraordinary
(Salisbury - Stonehenge - Pewsey - Wilton)

Chapter 8: The West Beckons
(Bournemouth - Poole - Wareham - Swanage - Wimborne)

Chapter 9: The Heart of Hardy's Wessex
(Dorchester - Bridport - Weymouth - Portland - Lyme Regis)

Chapter 10: North Past the Giant and a Multitude of Villages
(Blandford - Sherborne - Shaftesbury)

Index to Selected Venues

Aaron Lodge	Bristol	48
Acorn Inn	Evershot	502
Almondsbury Int'change	Almondsbury	33
Alum Grange	Alum Chine	389
Alveston House	Alveston	34
Anchor Hotel & Ship Inn	Porlock Weir	175
Anchor Inn	Dulverton	176
Anchor Inn	Ham Green	49
Angel Inn	Heytesbury	333
Anglebury House	Wareham	390
Applegates	Bradford On Avon	283
Apsley House	Bath	81
Arches Hotel	Bristol	49
Ardene	Boscombe	391
Ashwick C/House	Dulverton	177
Bales Mead	West Porlock	178
Bason Bridge Inn	East Huntspill	143
Bath Lodge	Norton St Philip	82
Bath Spa Hotel	Bath	83
Beechfield House	Beanacre	284
Beechleas	Wimbourne Minster	392
Belfield Guest House	Shepton Mallet	244
Bell Inn	Buckland Dinham	101
Bell On The Common	Broughton Gifford	296
Belmont	Warminster	350
Bennett Arms	Semley	503
Berkeley Sq Hotel	Bristol	35
Beryl	Wells	223
Bishopstrow House	Warminster	334
Black Horse	Clapton In Gordano	36
Black Swan	Langport	245
Boltons (The)	Neighbourne Oakhill	224
Bond's Hotel & Rest.	Castle Cary	225
Bossington Farm	Appleford	179
Bowlish House	Shepton Mallet	226
Box Tree House	Westbury Sub Mendip	245
Bradford Old Mill	Bradford On Avon	285
Bridge House Hotel	Beaminster	445
Broadview Gardens	Crewkerne	227
Brook House	Semington	350
Burton Cliff Hotel	Burton Bradstock	446
Cambridge Arms	Bristol	50
Camelot	Blue Anchor	131
Carnarvon Arms	Dulverton	180
Casterbridge Hotel	Dorchester	447
Castle Hotel	Porlock	181
Castle Inn	Castle Combe	286
Castle Inn	West Lulworth	393
Cat Head	Stoke Sub Hamdon	228
Chilvester Hill House	Calne	287
Chimneys G. House	Chideock	454
Clench Farmhouse	Clench	296
Cleveland Hotel	Westbourne	394
Cloisters Restaurant	Wells	246
Combe Grove Manor	Monkton Combe	84
Connaught Hotel	Bournemouth	395
Cottage Garden	Compton Dando	85
Cottage Hotel	Porlockweir	182
Coxley Vineyard	Coxley	229
Cromwell House	Lulworth Cove	396
Crown At Wells	Wells	246
Crown Hotel & Rest.	Marnhull	510
Crown Hotel	Alvediston	335
Crown Hotel	Exford	183
Curdon Mill	Williton	132
Deverill End	South Veny	336
Devon Hotel	Uplyme	448
Downfield	Watchet	191
Downlands House	Bristol	37
Drusillas Inn	Wimborne	409
Dundry Inn	Dundry	50
Durley Court Hotel	Bournemouth	397
Eagle House	Bathford	86
Earlham Lodge	Bournemouth	398
Eastbury Hotel	Sherborne	504
Eden Vale	Beckington	87
Elm Tree Inn	Langton Herring	449
Failand Inn	Failand	51
Fairfield House	Williton	143
Farthings Hotel	Hatch Beauchamp	230
Fishermans House	Mildenhall	297
Fountain Inn	Wells	247
Franklyns Farm	Chewton Mendip	247
Frog Street Farm	Beercrocombe	248
Frome Way	Radstock	88
Gables	Dunster	133
Gables	East Chinnock	248
Gaggle Of Geese	Buckland Newton	455
Galley Restaurant	Swanage	410
George & Dragon	Pensford	38
Gervis Court	Bournemouth	399
Globe Inn	Appley	134
Grange Hotel	Sherborne	510
Grasmere House	Salisbury	337
Green Lane House	Hinton Charterhouse	89
Griffs Hotel	Bournemouth	400
Harveys Restaurant	Bristol	39
Hawaiian	Bournemouth	401
Hayburn Wyke	Salisbury	338
Haydon House	Bath	101
Heatherleys	Bristol	51
Heddons Gate	Parracombe	184
Hemsworth Manor	Witchampton	410
Henbury Lodge	Henbury	52
Hermitage	Box	297
Highbury Vaults	Bristol	40
Higher Combe Farm	Dulverton	192
Higher Dipford Farm	Trull	144
Highways G. House	Poole	411
Hinton Grange	Hinton	90

Index to Selected Venues

Holly Lodge	Bath	91
Home Park Farm	Blue Anchor	144
Homewood Park	Hinton Charterhouse	92
Hopewell	Wimborne	411
Hotel Alexandra	Lyme Regis	450
Hotel Washington	Bournemouth	402
Howards House	Teffont Evias	339
Howards	Hotwell	52
Hunstrete House	Hunstrete	41
Infield House	Wells	231
Innlodge	Yatton	42
Irondale House	Rode	102
Kemps House	Wareham	403
Kimberley Court	Bournemouth	404
King John's Hunting Lodge	Lacock	298
Kings Arms	Montacute	232
L'Arivee	Weston Super Mare	145
La Bisalta	Frome	102
La Fleur De Lys	Shaftesbury	511
Lamb At Weare	Lower Weare	249
Lamb On The Strand	Semington	351
Lamperts Cottage	Sydling St Nicholas	456
Lana	Westbury Sub Mendip	233
Langford Manor	Five Head nr Taunton	234
Langley House	Wiveliscombe	135
Langton Arms	Tarrant Monkton	405
Les Parisiens	Warminster	351
Limpey Stoke Hotel	Lower Stoke	93
Lodge (The)	Standerwick	94
London House	Pewsey	340
Longhope Hotel	Melksham	288
Longwater Park Farm	Erlestoke	352
Lorna Doone (The)	Porlock	185
Lucknam Park	Colerne	289
Lutteral Arms	Dunster	136
Lynch (The)	Somerton	235
Manor Hotel	West Bexington	451
Manor House	Piddlehinton	456
Manor Lodge	Keynsham	103
Market Cross Hotel	Cheddar	249
Marquis Of Lorne	Nettlecombe	457
Middlewick Farm	Wick	236
Midway Cottage	Farleigh Wick	298
Mill House	Berwick St James	352
Milton Farm	East Knoyle	341
Miners Arms	Priddy	237
Monkton Inn	West Monkton	145
Morris' Farmhouse	Baverstock	353
Neston Country Inn	Neston	299
Newton House	Sturminster Newton	511
No 3	Glastonbury	238
Old Bank	Marnhull	512
Old Brew House	Langton Long	512
Old Farmhouse	Buckland Newton	457
Old Manor	Trowle	342
Old Rectory	Winterbourne Steepleton	452
Old Stagecoach Inn	Crewkerne	239
Old Stores	Westbury Sub Mendip	240
Paradise House	Bath	95
Pecking Mill Inn	Shepton Mallet	241
Pembroke Arms	Favant	343
Periton Park	Middlecombe	137
Pheasants Restaurant	Sherborne	505
Pickwick Inn	Beaminster	458
Plumber Manor	Sturminster Newton	506
Poacher	Portishead	43
Poachers Inn	Piddletrenthide	507
Portman Lodge	Durweston	513
Priory House	Bath	96
Priory Steps	Bradford On Avon	290
Purbeck House	Swanage	406
Queens Head Inn	Broadchalke	344
Redwood Lodge	Bristol	44
Rest & Be Thankful Inn	Wheddon Cross	186
Restaurant Du Gourmet	Bristol	53
Retreat (The)	Shaftesbury	513
Riverside Close	Laverstock	353
Rose & Crown	Huish Episcopi	250
Royal Hotel	Avonmouth	53
Royal Huntsman	Williton	138
Royal Oak Hotel	Withypool	188
Royal Oak	Winsford	187
Royalist Hotel	Stow On The Wold	45
Rudleigh Inn	Easton In Gordano	54
Rudloe Hall	Box	97
Salterns House	Poole	407
Shell Bay Restaurant	Studland	412
Shurnhold House	Shurnhold	291
Sign Of The Angel	Lacock	292
Silver Plough	Pitton	345
Simonsbath Hotel	Simonsbath	189
Slab House	West Horrington	250
Snooty Fox	Warminster	346
Spinney	Curland	146
St Michaels G. House	Bristol	46
St Vincent Rocks	Bristol	54
Stag Cottage	Zeals	242
Ston Easton Park	Bath	98
Stourcastle Lodge	Sturminster Newton	508
Sturford Mead Farm	Warminster	354
Summer Lodge	Evershot	509
Sunfield House	Minehead	146
Swallow Royal Hotel	Bristol	47
Tarr Farm	Dulverton	192
Tarr Steps Hotel	Dulverton	190
Thatch Lodge Hotel	Charmouth	453
The Fox	Corscombe	458
Thornhill	Holt	412

Index to Selected Venues

Three Crowns Inn	Whaddon	347
Three Elms	North Wooton	514
Three Horseshoes	Bradford On Avon	299
Three Horseshoes	Powerstock	459
Three Horseshoes	Wiveliscombe	139
Toxique	Melksham	293
Truffles Restaurant	Bruton	243
Tudor Hotel & Rest.	Bridgwater	147
Uphill Manor	Weston Super Mare	140
Walnut Tree Hotel	North Petherton	141
Walnut Tree	West Camel	514
Wayfarers Restaurant	Sherbourne Causeway	515
Westwood Hse Hotel	Dorchester	459
Whatley Manor	Malmesbury	294

White Hart Hotel	Wells	244
White Hart Inn	Axbridge	251
White Hart	Ford	295
White Lion	Broadwindsor	460
White Lodge	Warminster	348
Wiltshire Kitchen	Devizes	300
Wine Vaults	Shepton Mallet	251
Woodbridge Inn	North Newnton	349
Woodcoate Stud	Abbotsbury	460
Woodcroft Tower	Bournemouth	408
Woolpack Inn	Beckington	100
Woolverton House	Bath	99
Yew Tree House	Burnham On Sea	142

I would like to thank all those who helped me to write this guide, whether it be with research, reading my work through or simply by giving encouragement and being patient with me. In particular all those at Kingsley Media, especially Nicola Miles; the staff at the Exmoor National Park Authority, especially Dave Gurnett; the many Tourist Information staff and those from individual attractions who have given freely of their time, of whom Mrs Cross at Wimborne Minster particularly comes to mind. Also Bernard Shaw, Philip and Rowan Griffiths, Dr Julia Boffey, Lauren, Clarissa, Naomi, Thomas and Eleanor, Anthony and Angela Wiltshire, Stella Sale and the Congdon family. I must also thank my mother and late father for giving me an enthusiasm for Wessex in the first place.

Simon Harrington

Dear Reader

I hope you enjoy reading and using this guide as much as I have enjoyed compiling its contents.

To help make future editions even better, I would appreciate it if you would suggest suitable venues and places to visit for possible inclusion. In return I will be happy to send you a complimentary copy of any one of the other publications in this series. (Subject to availability).

I look forward to hearing from you.
Yours sincerely

Nicola Miles

I would like to thank all those involved in the production of this guide, especially Valerie for her support, Jonathan for his help and encouragement, Paul Bugge and Leigh Walsh for the technical advice, Ian Pethers and Sharon Bradley for the illustrations and all the staff at Kingsley Media Ltd for their hard work and enthusiasm.

Nicola Miles

ISBN 0-9526555-2-7
The Discerning Visitor *(A Four Seasons Guide)*
Published by Kingsley Media Ltd - Plymouth, Devon
Copyright - Kingsley Media Ltd
All Rights Reserved
British Library Catalogue-In-Publication Data
Catalogue Data is available from the British Library

Origination and typesetting by - Paul Bugge and Leigh Walsh
at TYPEstyle, Ivybridge, Devon
Printed & bound in the United Kingdom by Devonshire Press, Torquay, Devon
Concept by - M Willcocks PhD • Editor - Nicola Miles

Introduction

This FOUR SEASONS DISCERNING VISITORS GUIDE gives an introduction to the regions of Wessex and Exmoor. The counties of Bristol, Somerset, Wiltshire and Dorset are covered in their entirety, while just over a quarter of the Exmoor National Park lies within Devon. We start in Bristol, moving down the Bristol Channel Coast, through Somerset to Exmoor, then returning north to the remainder of Somerset and Wiltshire, before finishing in Dorset.

As well as a fairly comprehensive collection of the region's tourist attractions, the main text includes potted history, possibilities for leisure activities, personal reflections, and a few anecdotes to help the journey along. No less importantly the guide also offers a diverse selection of places to eat and stay so that you can decide where to dine or stay in each part of the region.

As with the rest of this series, the names of places, when mentioned for the first time, are given in bold capitals (e.g. **TAUNTON**). Attractions and buildings of interest are in capitals (e.g. SALISBURY CATHEDRAL) and telephone numbers are provided wherever possible. In addition some useful Internet website addresses have been included, where you will be able to access current details and news of events, opening times etc. While there are a huge number of websites available which cover the ground of this guide I have only included those which seemed particularly useful, and it should also be borne in mind that in these relatively early days of mass Internet use, addresses do change and new sites come and go with frustrating rapidity at times.

In an area rich with attractions, as well as events and leisure facilities for the visitor, it would be impossible to cover every single possibility in the text and still leave room for any discussion of them. As a result there is an extra Glossary at the back of this guide listing places for which there was unfortunately insufficient space in the main pages. This has been done to give you as wide a choice as possible, and to create as comprehensive a body of information as can be held in a single book. As well as this you will also find the standard Glossary, with an alphabetical listing of all place-names covered in the text.

So what of Wessex and Exmoor? I thought I knew them fairly well until I came to write this book, but even having lived in the area for quite some time as well as having travelled it extensively, could not prepare me for the full range of what I found. From the ancient monuments of Avebury and Stonehenge to the magical atmosphere of Glastonbury Tor, the centre of this region is steeped in a very tangible sense of antiquity. The edges too, with the dramatic coastlines of Purbeck and Exmoor, and splendid beaches from Christchurch and Bournemouth to Weston-Super-Mare, have a fantastic amount of variety and dramatic scenery to offer. There is modernity as well, with Swindon, Bristol, Salisbury and Taunton offering quality shopping and facilities of which any tourist area would be proud. Added to this there are the buildings of the region. Salisbury Cathedral, Sherborne Abbey, Longleat House and the Priory Church at Christchurch are just the first few that spring to mind; there are many, many others.

Yet I do not think it is any of this that will sufficiently summarise Wessex and Exmoor for those who are familiar with this part of the world. To the north are the Cotswolds and the Forest of Dean; famous areas of beauty much used for an escape from modern suburban and urban life. To the south and west lie Devon and Cornwall, the traditional resort of the vast majority who charge in this direction each summer looking for some sun, sand and rural scenery. Yet in between lie sights that once seen will never be forgotten. The stark beauty and mystery of Glastonbury Tor looking over its own natural amphitheatre of green; the chalk cliffs of Purbeck seeming ready to crumble at any moment into the sea; the improbable and unique Bristol Channel coast at Kilve and East Quantoxhead; again these are just the start. Who can ever forget their first view of Stonehenge, dominating the emptiness of Salisbury Plain? Where else could you hope to find a panorama so powerful and memorable as that from Dunkery Beacon, across the multi coloured moors and farmland of Exmoor.

Some areas of Wessex are undergoing rapid change. Swindon and Bristol, and even Taunton and Bournemouth are busy swallowing up much of what recently lay independently around them. But there are still villages near to these very same places where nothing much seems to have happened for a very long time, except perhaps the arrival of cars and motorised hedge trimmers. There are towns too, that live a quiet life now compared to their historical heritage, often developed many centuries ago.

Of these, Malmesbury is the place that I will remember with the most affection from my research for this book. This quiet little town in North Wiltshire sums up much of what you can expect to find to delight you in Wessex. By-Passed by the multitudes who travel east to west just a few miles south of here on the M4 motorway, Malmesbury is a beautifully quiet place, full of solid stone buildings which have aged with a robust rather than elegant charm. The town was quiet enough for me to find a parking place on its main, steep High Street on my first visit; I had never stopped here before. A short walk up the remainder of the hill and I had discovered yet another place in Wessex which will stay in my heart and imagination; Malmesbury Abbey. Like so many of the historic Castles and Abbeys of Wessex, this one is a ruin of what once stood overlooking the town some five hundred years ago. Yet its story is one of an unlikely survivor, kept alive by the diligence of the local community even to this day, when it supplies the volunteer guides who will eagerly tell you so much about this lovely place. The flying monk, a steeple taller than that of Salisbury Cathedral, but which came to a sudden, dramatic end, and much more, all ready to be discovered in this single building. But I bet that if you have heard of Malmesbury in recent times it will have been to do with none of this, or even its history as a medieval wool and cloth town. Rather you will have heard tell of a daring escape which took place nearby, and a desperate hunt which took many more days than was originally expected. This was not a prison break, at least not of the human kind, but rather the tale of two pigs, whose plight captured the imagination of the entire nation, as they tried to establish themselves in the wilds of Wiltshire.

They were eventually unsuccessful, but the romance of the tale was undeniable. A triviality? Maybe, but if you want to visit places where things still happen, where communities still have the cohesion and identity to create massively impressive and memorable events such as the Bridgwater Carnival, then Wessex is the place for you. The past and the present really do coexist here. There are examples of this everywhere, another is the village of Avebury, where relatively modern, but still picturesque cottages are built amongst a ring of stones from much more distant and pagan times than the neighbouring Saxon church.

It seems to me that Wessex and Exmoor are at last getting the visitors and the attention they deserve. Even the television schedulers seem eager to help the cause, with a whole series of programmes very recently about Longleat; the adventures of some doctors based at Minehead, and a wonderful production of 'Tess of the D'Urbevilles' using the modern version of Hardy's Dorset to give glorious cinematic reality to his writing. I am not at all surprised that the producers and camera crews flood in this direction as soon as the words 'Jane Austen' or 'period drama' are mentioned. There is simply no part of England with so many varied scenes of rural beauty full of fabulous period architecture and landscaping.

I hope some of this may have whetted your appetite to read on, but if you want to make the most of Wessex, and perhaps even more so of Exmoor, then you really need to go there. Like me, you will then make new discoveries of your own, and take back memories that will raise a quiet smile and make you want to go back for more, just as soon as you possibly can.

The next time I am likely to get the chance for a fresh look at Wessex will be on my way to another enchanting and varied area of open landscapes and countless opportunities for the visitor. If you wish to find out how I get on, then look out for the Four Seasons Discerning Visitor Guide to The Cotswolds, Thames & Chilterns which will be available in 1999.

Simon Harrington

Aaron Lodge	Bristol	48
Almondsbury Interchange	Almondsbury	33
Alveston House	Alveston	34
Anchor Inn	Ham Green	49
Arches Hotel	Bristol	49
Berkeley Square Hotel	Bristol	35
Black Horse	Clapton In Gordano	36
Cambridge Arms	Bristol	50
Downlands House	Bristol	37
Dundry Inn	Dundry	50
Failand Inn	Failand	51
George & Dragon	Pensford	38
Harveys Restaurant	Bristol	39
Heatherleys	Bristol	51
Henbury Lodge	Henbury	52
Highbury Vaults	Bristol	40
Howards	Hotwell	52
Hunstrete House	Hunstrete	41
Innlodge	Yatton	42
Poacher	Portishead	43
Redwood Lodge	Bristol	44
Restaurant Du Gourmet	Bristol	53
Royalist Hotel	Stow On The Wold	45
Rudleigh Inn	Easton In Gordano	54
St Vincent Rocks	Bristol	54
Swallow Royal Hotel	Bristol	47

Chapter One:
Ship Shape and Bristol Fashion
Bristol & Surrounding Area

Think of Wessex and Bristol is not among the first places that will spring to mind. By far the largest place covered in the whole of this book, with a population of over a third of a million, it is not one you would immediately think of as a tourist resort either, or even as a desirable place to visit as part of a holiday. Yet there is everything here, from historic docks to a zoo, a cathedral, more Georgian buildings than any other British city can offer, as well as high quality shopping, entertainment, leisure and other facilities galore. As the outlet for the goods of Wessex to a trade area greater than those achievable over land, Bristol has always been an important place to the west of England, despite any aloofness the modern, thriving city might seem to have from what lies around it. Important enough in modern terms to be given its own county (after belonging uncomfortably to several others) Bristol is the modern tourist's gateway to Wessex, for the simple reason that the vast majority of those travelling south west will use one of the two motorways which meet just to the west of the centre of this ever expanding city to get to what lies south of here. With more than 15,000 full-time students at the city's two universities (the University of Bristol and the University of the West of England), Bristol is bound to be a place full of life, with an abundance of leisure and social facilities.

Medieval Bristol was overcrowded, simply because of the restrictions which kept it within the city walls, but it seems the only things likely to stop it taking over much of the west country in its expansion now are the boundaries created by the motorways, and in the case of Clevedon, Avonmouth and Portishead even the M5 seems to have failed in this task. Yet there are still a few places between the north of this metropolis and the Gloucestershire Cotswolds. These are where we will start, for Wotton-Under-Edge, Tetbury and what lies above them is geographically claimed by the ridge of hills which gives the Cotswolds their name, although even these can be seen as very much under the strong influence of the massive city to their south. Thornbury and what lies around it have no such protection, and have long become part of that largely indefinable being, Greater Bristol.

A very unlikely attraction is the first you will meet if you follow the River Severn's Estuary south away from the Cotswolds region. Near **OLDBURY-ON-SEVERN** the OLDBURY POWER STATION (01454 419899) offers free tours around its buildings, giving a 'nuclear power packed day out', much as Hinkley will offer a little further to the south and west (see Chapter 3). You can see the huge turbine hall, overlook the reactors, and visit the control room, but presumably without access to any big red buttons. That you are still very near to the wildfowl sanctuary of Slimbridge, a much more traditional tourist spot to the north, is emphasised by the power station's nature trail, which includes the chance to see peregrine falcons, kestrels and other wildlife. While the Oldbury trips are primarily meant to be educational, there is nothing wrong with taking some leisure time out to see some of the more unfamiliar aspects of how the modern world works, even if you are someone who is usually more interested in exhibits about the past.

Also north of the M4 and near the Severn Estuary, is a completely different place, the OLDOWN COUNTRY PARK (01454 413605), west of **ALVESTON**. There is a nature trail here too, as well as a 'forest challenge' for those with some excess energy to burn off, including such questionable delights as rope bridges, nets to scale, and a fireman's pole. The eighty acres of ancient woodland have much more to do with the Iron Age than the nuclear age though, with the site of a hillfort near the view point from which you can get some excellent pictures of the Severn Bridge.

Nearby **THORNBURY** has its own castle, originally constructed in the early 16th century, and stayed in, while it was still quite new, by Henry VIII and later his daughter, Queen Mary. The Duke of Buckingham, Edward Stafford, who had the castle built in 1511, was not around to see his royal visitors in 1535, as King Henry had him beheaded at some point during the intervening years. At least this was for suspected treason rather than for any inadequacies as a host! The castle can be visited now, but only if you are intending to be a guest, as it is a hotel. The Outer Court of what was actually an unfinished whole when Buckingham was executed, is now home to a vineyard.

The centre of Thornbury, to the south of the castle, still has enough 15th century buildings to demonstrate the town's medieval prosperity, but like many other places it was by-passed by the Turnpike Roads, and fell into decline in Tudor times. Recently (since the 1970s) its population has more than tripled, as it became a fashionable place to live for those working in Bristol. Perhaps this is a sign that we really cannot go any further towards Bristol without feeling its magnetic influence. Giving into this force, let's start in the middle of the city and work outwards, rather than resisting its importance any longer.

Just where is the centre of **BRISTOL** (Tourist Information 0117 926 0767) these days? I suppose for most visitors it is likely to be the GALLERIES SHOPPING CENTRE (www.the-galleries.com/shoppingcentre). Opened in 1991, and with three floors containing more than one hundred different shops it also has the far from negligible bonus of its own car park with nearly a thousand bays (although not usually many free spaces). Bristol city centre is not the easiest to navigate, and the phrase 'port in a storm' somehow seems particularly appropriate. This indoor centre is bright, spacious, and often very busy. The top floor is dedicated to the 'World of Food', and it is a good idea to leave this until you have worked up an appetite, and need a rest, as it wonderful to sit and watch the thousands below you scurrying like ants in a nest which has been in fresh receipt of a child's probing stick.

The Galleries are in BROADMEAD, which with its pedestrianised areas so close to a massive one way system and the expanses of BOND STREET might seem to be the very middle of the city. Historically it is certainly not, and was some distance outside the original boundary walls. For many who only venture to Bristol for a bit of shopping, perhaps coming down from the Cotswolds or up from Exmoor to remember what it is they are getting away from, Broadmead may be the only part of the modern city they visit on foot. This is a real shame, especially as there is so much else to see within a walk of twenty minutes or so towards the Cathedral.

There can be few more ironically named places than BROAD STREET. Some of the main roads through Bristol must be the widest to the south of Birmingham and west of London, making Cheltenham's Promenade, for instance, look decidedly old fashioned by comparison. Yet here is a comparatively narrow, cramped thoroughfare where one way traffic is a desirable inevitability rather than a nuisance; it is anything but broad in today's terms, amongst such near neighbours. In this setting you can see, and walk through, the only remaining opening in the ancient city walls, at ST JOHN'S GATEWAY.

Bristol; A Gateway into the Old City

There were already about three thousand inhabitants of the city at the time of the Norman invasion of 1066, between this northern gate and the natural defences of the River AVON to the south. So much has changed in Bristol since then that it is extremely difficult to see how the medieval maps of the city can be of the same place that you can visit today, making the stonework and open Norman arches of St John's all the more important a relic. Perhaps this is not so surprising when you consider that the rivers FROME and Avon, between which the settlement was first established, were sealed off as long ago as 1809 so that Bristol could have a non tidal, or 'floating' harbour. With the second highest tides in the world, the Avon in particular was just proving too hazardous for the masses of shipping which wanted to get right into the heart of Bristol. The phrase 'ship-shape and Bristol fashion' originally applied to the robust craft built to withstand as many of the twists and turns of the river as possible, even in the worst conditions.

Most of what stood inside the city walls was lost much later, and more tragically, during the blitz of the Second World War. The arches which marked the entry to the old city seem dwarfed and almost lost amongst so much modern building now, but the walls stood as barriers to expansion, to some degree, until the Dissolution of the Monasteries in the 16th century, when the religious orders who owned much of what lay outside finally lost their power to repel all comers. Yet this was where Queen Elizabeth entered the city 1574, riding through St John's Gate, seated upon a white horse. You wouldn't even fit the photographers in this space if our present queen, and Bess's namesake, were to choose to do the same now.

There is quite a bit known about life in medieval Bristol, and it is worth stopping to think what it would have been like here all those years ago, before moving on from the most significant reminder of the shape of the city in those long gone days. Although the walls kept the population hemmed in, this was a good place to be, even during turbulent times such as the 15th century, when the conflict with France was so soon followed by the drain on the country's resources caused by the Wars of the Roses. By 1500, the population had increased to 10,000, and most of these were involved in the one thing that had always been Bristol's economic lifeline; trade.

Bristol traded with just about everywhere, merchants such as the aptly named John Shipward setting up regular routes to all parts, even Iceland! The houses of prominent merchants such as William Canynges and Alice Chester were huge stone affairs, with enormous cellars attached to them, where merchandise could be stored. None of this came about suddenly, the natural situation of Bristol as a port had been carefully nurtured during the previous centuries, when the city was among the first to establish Bye Laws, as well as city rules which included a daily curfew at 8.p.m. There were even street cleaners within the city, called 'rakers', who were paid eighteenpence a week, and Bristol had one of the best piped water supplies in the country, thanks to the Friars of St Johns.

From such times there are bound to be romantic stories, too far lost in history to have every detail verified. So it is that we know Bristol was a centre of the eagerness to find a new land far to the west across the Atlantic, in this same 15th century. The good old U.S.A. gets its name from Amerigo Vespucci, surely, but not perhaps if you are a Bristolian. JOHN CABOT, one of Bristol's most famous figures, arrived in New England on 24th June 1497, the first recorded landing on mainland America. One of his chief backers was allegedly a Mr Richard Amerycke (or Ap Merrick), and so we can but speculate as to the true source of America's name. But even this venture was not really in the sense of true, selfless romance for exploration. Giovanni Cabotto was looking for more trade routes (to the Far East) rather than simple glory, and as his full name might suggest, was not a native Bristolian either.

If Cabot was an import, a freelance Italian navigator (now there's a job title) then he too is part of a trend in the city. Inventors, great men and historical figures have come here to use Bristol as a base, a centre for their work. BRUNEL, perhaps the most famous of them all, was not from Bristol either, but the city benefited immensely from his work, especially in economic terms. In more recent times, the supersonic project of the 1960s and 1970s, resulting in Concorde (which seems to have become a rather forgotten wonder of the world these days) had much of its impetus in Bristol. Even now Bristol welcomes visitors who want to use the city, even if it is to change it into fictional Holby, in order to provide millions with a bit of blood and drama on a Saturday evening, in the form of BBC's CASUALTY. To add contrast, Bristol is also home to the makers of Britain's most regular modern Oscar winners; WALLACE AND GROMIT.

Of course Bristol has also had its share of home grown figures of importance, such as Samuel Plimsoll, whose efforts to have standardization and enforcement of cargo levels saved untold numbers of sailors from joining the many who had already perished around Britain's coasts due to the greed of shipowners who packed ships so full that they were known as 'coffins'. The Plimsoll Line became part of Merchant Sea law in 1876, a surprisingly and shamefully late date.

So we are no nearer deciding upon the central place in this city. It is not an easy job. Bristol's name is first recorded, in late Anglo-Saxon, as *'Briycgstow'*, literally the place of the bridge. The bridge at the end of BALDWIN STREET, near the Tourist Information Office, is the nearest to the site of this original crossing, but as we have already seen the rivers have been changed, and even the whole nature of the city, so that this has little of the importance it once held.

One contender for the symbolic centre of the city must be the four 'NAILS', outside the 18th century EXCHANGE in CORN STREET. These squat bronze pillars were where many a deal was sealed, as the merchants would literally put their money 'on the nail', and they predate the mid 18th century Exchange by more than 150 years. But if the old city is to claim the centre then you must travel a long way to see the true, original marker, for Bristol's HIGH CROSS is now in Stourhead, Wiltshire. In medieval times it stood at the meeting of the four main thoroughfares; Wine, Corn,

High and Broad Streets. From here public exclamations and announcements were made, kings and queens were received, and public whippings made another sort of spectacle. So this focal point has gone from modern Bristol, but at least it still exists, unlike the city's first important building, the Castle built for Geoffrey of Mowbray, a Bishop who was placed in charge of Bristol by William the Conqueror. The city had not fought against the Normans, and its potential was quickly seen by the invaders. An inland port defended by miles of muddy river and treacherous estuary, this had been no easy place for the Danes to get to, and had developed without the troubles of many a Saxon settlement. The castle is no more, although the CASTLE PARK at least makes you aware of where it once stood. King Stephen was kept captive here by his sister Matilda, and it was still an important stronghold during the 14th century struggles between Edward II and his wife, which ended so dramatically at Berkeley Castle to the north west of here.

Our search for a central point is an unfruitful one, and so we must turn to the most logical of starting points in the systematic exploration of any city; its cathedral. More than any of the others covered by this book, BRISTOL CATHEDRAL (0117 926 4879) is the work of many different ages. Not that this matters when you look south from COLLEGE GREEN, just to the west of the old city, and see the powerful lines of its length, straddled by three monumental square towers, making such an impressive whole. Despite its fragmentary architectural history, this building is, from the outside, extremely imposing, almost intimidating. With battlements along much of its length, and in the keep like proportions of its towers to the main rectangular structure of the building, it is not unlike how you might have imagined the long lost castle to have looked. There is also enough about the exterior to remind you more of Tewkesbury Abbey than Salisbury Cathedral, and this is no coincidence, as Bristol Cathedral started life as an Augustinian Abbey.

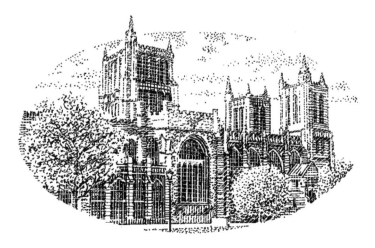

Bristol Cathedral

14

Robert FitzHarding founded this Abbey, then in the manor of Billeswick, outside the city walls, in 1140. He was a powerful man, Reeve of Bristol, and supporter of Matilda, who was then staying in Bristol Castle with her son, soon afterwards to become King Henry II. His support of the rebellion against King Stephen paid FitzHarding well when King Henry was crowned in 1154. The titles and wealth given to him allowed more building, including the CHAPTER HOUSE in 1165, which survives as the oldest remaining part of the Cathedral.

Next (of what you can see now) came the ELDER LADY CHAPEL in 1220, conspicuous for the many carvings of birds and animals, especially monkeys, for some unknown reason! Although there were other additions, such as the EASTERN LADY CHAPEL and CHOIR in 1330, the two main periods of rebuilding were the 16th and 19th centuries. Only three years passed between the Abbey's Dissolution in 1539 and the complete rebuilding of the Nave, which marked its transformation into a cathedral. This is probably why there is such a sense of continuity about this place, and Bristol's first centre of worship was lucky not to go the same way as those in Glastonbury and Shaftesbury. Advertised as 'an oasis of solitude in the bustling city', this is a quiet place, even when the 300 year old organ adds to the atmosphere with its sombre tones.

The Cathedral has survived, enlarged by the Victorians and still used as an active place of worship. Bristol's docks, on the other hand, just a short walk to the south, are now closed for trade, as the city has given over to the inevitable and let Avonmouth, Royal Portbury and Portishead, to the west of the M5, become its trading ports. What the merchants have lost, the tourist has gained. As in Gloucester, there is much restoration, advertised as a 'renaissance' for Bristol's dockside area, and the whole area is busy with pleasure cruisers and floating restaurants, with clubs and galleries lining the banks. The docks are busy once again, although not quite as the poet Alexander Pope saw them more than two hundred and fifty years ago, when he commented that he could see:

> *"hundreds of ships, their masts as thick as they can stand by one another.....*
> *a long street, full of ships in the middle and houses on both sides,*
> *looks like a dream."*

While much of the modern development is centred around the NARROW QUAY and ST AUGUSTINE'S REACH, there are ferry points dotted around the whole dock area, and the blue and yellow boats of the BRISTOL FERRY BOAT COMPANY (0117 927 3416) will take you across from one point to another or on a forty minute trip right around the docks (the ferries are also strongly recommended as a way of avoiding the bridge bound traffic jams which do plague this part of the city). We will return to what is on the Quays to the north of the river later, but if you go down to the stop which is south west of the Cathedral, a short trip will take you straight across to one of Bristol's most famous attractions, and one which has gone through a more complete restoration than that of the Cathedral, although it was not even in existence until 1839. The S.S. GREAT BRITAIN (0117 926 0680) looks utterly different to the rusty hulled carcass greeted by cheering crowds on her return to Bristol in 1970. But even now her appearance can never be as impressive as it was at her first launch, on 19 July 1843 (four years to the day after work was started), when she was the first iron steamship in the world, and the biggest of any type, with a 205 foot keel (322 feet total length). Prince Albert launched her, showing that she was considered something very special, even by royalty.

The early 19th century had not been a good time for the prosperity of Bristol, involved in much contention over the Slave Trade, which was eventually abolished in1833. One success of the time was the Great Western Railway, linking London to Bristol, and the engineer Brunel gave the same company the idea of expanding the line just a little further to the west; to the U.S.A. The first link was made in 1838, when the GREAT WESTERN was launched from Bristol Docks. A wooden hulled steamship, she crossed the Atlantic, but Brunel started the real revolution when he went one further, by making the material from which the ship was constructed, as well as the method of propulsion, something quite new.

For a true idea of just how much these inventions changed the life of the sailors of the world take a look at some of the work of Joseph Conrad, writing half a century and more after the S.S. Great Britain left Bristol on its maiden voyage to New York. The craft of seamanship was changed irrevocably and forever, the gradual world-wide redundancy of the clippers and other sailing ships making the decline of the canals look very insignificant by comparison. Conrad writes superbly about the bitterness felt by those who could not but admit the undying efficiency of the new monsters, no longer reliant on the winds. Stories such as 'Typhoon' emphasise just how much these ships were changing the world, and his knowledge was first hand, as he was a merchant sea captain. The Great Britain may not be the most romantic of Bristol's relics and attractions, put into this context, but it is certainly the most globally significant and momentous.

Ironically this dock's most famous moments also spelt the beginning of their own end. Great Britain had trouble negotiating the narrow locks of the exit to the Severn Estuary, and the bigger steamships would not get this near to Bristol again. Liverpool, and the Cunard company won the contract to carry mail to the United States, and the Great Western was broken up in 1857, two years before Brunel died. The Great Britain carried on, as a luxury liner carrying passengers to America and Australia, then becoming a troop carrier for the Crimean War, before ending her first life as a cargo ship. One and a quarter million sea miles later she ended up abandoned in 1886, about as far away from Bristol as possible, in the Falkland Islands.

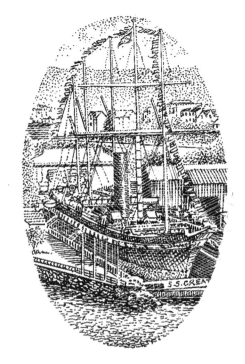

SS *Great Britain*

Far from remaining 'Ship Shape and Bristol Fashion', as she had been built, Great Britain was fortunate to finish up somewhere so far from the scrap yards and breakers of the more heavily inhabited parts of the world, so that her hull survived intact long enough for nostalgia and good business sense to demand her restoration. Since 1970 there have been more than three million visitors to the ship, each contributing to the charity which is restoring her to that original 1843 appearance. From the outside the job may look complete, with the hull, containing 60,000 rivets, shining as bright as black and red can, while the steam stack, or funnel, nestles amongst spars and masts, kept as insurance much as early cars which had electronic ignition still carried a starting handle. The heart is missing though. The romantic appeal which is running at present means that a contribution of £20 will allow you to have your name inscribed on a heart displayed on the Bell Deck, once enough money has been raised to replace the engine from which came the beat of life on board the S.S. Great Britain.

As well as being able to walk around the restored ship, you can stay for a meal, if you have a party large enough to make a booking in the completely restored DINING SALOON (0117 922 5737) worthwhile. The setting is quite splendid, and the recent release in Britain of the film Titanic will surely make this venue even more popular.

17

This was also one of two locations used for the recent episodes of the drama 'Casualty' covering the wedding between the characters Charlie and Baz, so it may well look strangely familiar. Next to the ship is the MARITIME HERITAGE CENTRE, first opened in 1985, which features shipbuilding and exactly what was involved in the construction of the ship leading up to 1843, as well as much more about the history of the other shipping which used these docks.

Now that we are south of the Docks let's see what else this area of the city has to offer. Further east along the same bank which holds the Great Britain is the INDUSTRIAL MUSEUM (0117 925 1470) in a converted 1950s warehouse, which focuses on the history of Bristol at work. It has everything from a mock up of the flight deck of Concorde to models of some of the ships which came here long before Brunel was born, as well as a fascinating collection of Rolls Royce aero engines from 1918 onwards, also made in Bristol. South from here, and across the River Avon are the suburbs of **SOUTHVILLE** and **BEDMINSTER**. At the city end of Bedminster Parade is MONTY'S MUSEUM (0117 966 5693) which concentrates on memorabilia, on a wider range than Opie's museum in Gloucester, but not perhaps in quite such quantities.

Back north of the Avon is **REDCLIFFE**, with its splendid spired church of ST MARY (0117 929 1487), paid for by merchants throughout the two hundred years during which it was built. These are very much Bristol's inner suburbs, but Redcliffe was a rival to the city in the 13th century, which is why such an ornate perpendicular church, with a spire rising almost 300 feet, exists so relatively close to the Cathedral. With its forest of slender pillars, roof bosses and the beautiful Gothic carvings in the hexagonal North Porch, it was still important enough in the late 16th century to warrant a visit from Queen Elizabeth, who famously called it: *"the fairest, goodliest and most famous parish church in England."* Everyone has their favourite church, and whether this was a political compliment or a personal opinion of the monarch or her speech writer is not important now, but as a contrast to the Cathedral, and for its own merits, St Mary's is still very much worth a visit, despite much 19th century alteration and restoration. Samuel Taylor Coleridge was married in this church.

Redcliffe is now central enough to be adjacent to Bristol's main railway station, at TEMPLE MEADS. An atmospheric place, now over 150 years old, some of the departure and arrival screens and other technology looks most odd in this building, which can feel almost subterranean in its darkness at times. A section of the oldest part of the station, designed by Brunel, is now the home of the EXPLORATORY (0117 907 9000 or www.exploratory.org.uk). Britain's largest 'hands on' science centre is another one of those places we might pretend is visited for the education and entertainment of our children, but is really of universal appeal. There are more than 150 exhibits, and if you are tempted to go inside do not expect to escape again for some time. The STRADIVARIUM sound and music gallery is particularly fascinating, with the world's biggest guitar and a keyboard so large that you can get your whole body rather than just your hands on it, and walk along the scales.

Signs from here will take you on a pleasant walk to the north, back to Broadmead's pedestrianised shopping streets. Amongst these is another important religious building, although of a very different type to those visited so far. JOHN WESLEY'S CHAPEL (0117 926 4740) is the oldest Methodist building in the world, founded in 1739. Services and recitals are only held here occasionally now, but with the living quarters above the chapel and the deceptive quiet around the staircased double pulpit from which the greatest reform movement of 18th century Britain got a start, this is a very atmospheric, intriguing place. Wesley set out to evangelize Britain from here, while his companion, Francis Asbury, set off for America, but even their start was doubtful at times. The rear doors of the Chapel were left to be accessible from the pulpit with good reason, as the populace of Bristol occasionally provided a heckling mob which would invade this quiet chapel and a quick escape then became essential. The third nameplate on the tiny rooms upstairs, adding to those for Wesley and Asbury, is that of Charles Wesley, the great hymn writer, and John's brother.

The chapel was built simply because John Wesley was banned from preaching in the vast majority of parish churches because of his non conformist views. This was nothing new in Bristol, for in the 17th century the Quakers had a meeting hall in Broadmead (now taken over as Council Offices), and one amongst them, William Penn, went on to become the founder of Pennsylvania, in the U.S.A. These men were motivators, believers in action, and so it is fitting that even the 'New Room' Chapel is only quietly beautiful. Much of what was said here was the antithesis of the complacency sometimes shown by the merchants who spent so much money on St Mary's Redcliffe, the Cathedral and other churches, to make a more ostentatious show of faith.

The quiet of the chapel could not be a greater contrast to the often teeming streets outside, but if you want a little more time for reflection and quiet in the open air, then a walk in Castle Park will prove surprisingly rewarding. If you head south west this will take you towards the old city and the docks through ST NICHOLAS MARKETS, where the original 18th century wares have long been replaced by antiques, fresh produce and jewellery. NEPTUNE'S STATUE, made of lead and erected in 1723, seems a very appropriate point at which to start an exploration of the older part of the city. The King of the Sea stands at the head of the Harbourside Leisure Area, which is constantly developing, and full of restaurants and galleries. He is less lonely and more accessible than the famous Mermaid of Copenhagen, and a great deal further from the open sea, but somehow there is a similar feeling of strange incongruity about him. The most famous of the ventures he looks down upon is ARNOLFINI (0117 929 9191) for modern art and other media, housed in a converted 1830s tea warehouse, which has as its neighbour the ARCHITECTURE CENTRE (0117 922 1540). Opposite them lies the WATERSHED (0117 927 6444), with cinemas, galleries etc focusing on the contemporary arts, in another warehouse complex.

I think it is fair to say that this area is still finding its final character, but like the Docks in Gloucester, and even the Barbican area of Plymouth, the idea of quality shopping on streets lined by water rather than cars seems a very popular one, and this is already a thriving success. From PRINCE STREET, along THE GROVE, and then WELSH BACK (which takes its name from the importance of the trade with Wales from here), this is one of the best walks in the city, even more so if you add the variety of cobbled KING STREET, with buildings from many periods in Bristol's history. Amongst these is the OLD VIC THEATRE (0117 949 3993), originally the Theatre Royal, which was opened in 1766, and is the oldest theatre in Britain still in use (although there have been occasional breaks in the historical continuity, notably during the Second World War). The top hatted figure of Brunel has the bronze statue here, more glamorous than Neptune's lead, and probably more readily recognised by most non pagan Bristolians!

Bristol Docks

The gorgeously half timbered LLANDOGER TROW is the real visual highlight of King Street, even though there is not much chance of seeing a flat bottomed 'trow' or barge around here these days. Neither are you very likely, as far as I am aware, to see a journalist making a deal with the victim of a natural disaster, offering to make him famous, as long as he can change his name and most of the details of the man's story to create a marketable fiction, billed as real life. This is supposed to have happened here, and the journalist concerned was not a modern hack with Dictaphone and lap top computer, but rather the 'father of the English novel', Daniel Defoe. As far as we know Alexander Selkirk, who Defoe is alleged to have met in the Trow, was never as heroic a figure as the legendary Robinson Crusoe he was to become, and with Defoe's ability to write racy tales such as 'Moll Flanders' and 'Roxanna' this must have been a energetic, lively encounter. I wonder if the author met up with Selkirk again before writing the second and third parts of his adventures, much less read and hardly ever found in print these days? A shame the same cannot be said for many modern sequels, although time will probably put that right.

Although the Trow looks Tudor, the half timbered buildings of King Street are mostly late 17th century, and the immense QUEEN'S SQUARE, which lies to the south, is only slightly more recent in much of its construction. Named after Queen Anne, the best of this is made up of splendid merchants houses, and the statue this time is of William III, who dominates the traffic from his horse, set in the middle of the Square. One local ghost legend has it that this popular Dutchman rides around the Square in the quiet of the night, although he must find it increasingly harder to get a suitably tranquil moment in which to set off on his travels.

There is more architectural variety along ST AUGUSTINE'S PARADE, just to the north west, where you can find two of Bristol's main venues for entertainment, the HIPPODROME THEATRE (0117 929 9444) and the COLSTON HALL (0117 922 3686). The latter is a strange place in some ways. I have been to music events in many venues over the years, but the Italian Gothic frontage and interior of this Hall, in a 19th century style known as Bristol Byzantine, has to be one of the most unlikely. One wonders what on earth Edward Colston, who has other buildings and institutions in the city named after him, as well as his own bronze statue in Colston Avenue, would have thought of all this. He was a philanthropist and merchant of the late 17th century, and lived most of his life in his London, being returned to his birthplace of Bristol to be buried. His name is an ambiguous one in the city's history; a man who established charities which still exist and yet lived partly on money gained from the Slave Trade, Mr Colston lived in a world very different to our own.

Around the corner from the Hippodrome are the HARVEY'S WINE CELLARS (0117 927 5036). The medieval cellars of number 12 Denmark Street have been storing wine since William Perry first started his wine merchants business here in 1796. It was not a good time for such a venture, as the various conflicts with Napoleon were tearing Europe apart and were not conducive to stable trading. Perry imported mostly from Spain and Portugal, and was among many competitors trying to make the most of Bristol's docks and trading facilities. He had two advantages; excellent cellars and a location close to the quays. Wheeled traffic was not allowed at dockside, and all cargo, even the massive tuns of imported wine, had to be dragged by sled to its next destination. At least for Perry's delivery men this was not a long trip.

Perry had a partner by the name of Thomas Urch whose nephew came to work with the company as an apprentice early in the 19th century. Luckily his name was John Harvey rather than Urch, or perhaps the brand of sherry his family perfected would not have remained quite so popular! Harvey only came to Denmark Street because he suffered from seasickness, and so could not easily follow in the footsteps of his ancestors, who were seafarers. His descendants, on the other hand, chose wisely to develop the wine business their father had by now become quite successful in. The story is that in the early 1860s John Harvey's sons, John and Edward, were busy blending a new type of sherry when an aristocratic lady who was visiting the cellars was invited to taste first Bristol Milk, a dark rich sherry, and then to sample the new blend. Her verdict was that: "If that is the Milk, then this must be the Cream". So Bristol Cream got its name, and the firm finally took the title of 'Harveys' just a few years later, in 1871.

Many other companies produced Bristol Milk, but Harvey's wisely made the term Bristol Cream a registered trademark, and things kept improving towards the end of the 19th century, with the granting of a Royal Warrant as a supplier of fine wine to Queen Victoria in 1895. This still continues, and supplies are regularly delivered to Queen Elizabeth II. The 20th century brought new times of good and bad fortune for the company. They were the first Wine Merchants to use any form of advertisement, and after the end of the Prohibition in the U.S.A. in 1933, volumes of business expanded extremely rapidly. The Second World War made importing wine from the usual sources completely impossible, and with stocks running low things got worse when the extensive bombing of Bristol claimed Harveys' Offices as one of its victims. The cellars survived intact. The Denmark Street headquarters were rebuilt after the War, but in the 1950s the bottling operation and other aspects had to be moved to larger premises on the outskirts of the city. So the museum was able to be born in what had become redundant, although 12 Denmark Street is still the centre of the Wine Merchants operations, led by John Harvey, the fifth generation of the family to have run the business.

The displays in Harveys Wine Museum include one of the country's finest collections of 18th century drinking glasses, antique decanters, corkscrews, cellar equipment, silverware and furniture. There is also a collection of Bristol Blue Glass, another of the city's foremost trades in the 18th century. Part of the revival of this trade can be noticed in supermarkets and off licences throughout the country, as Harveys have recently reverted to this most attractive way of getting their products noticed. Drink the contents and keep the bottle, but didn't we all do that with Matteus Rose, until there were more bottles than candles? Every visitor of a legally acceptable age will get a free glass of cream sherry as part of the tour of the cellars, and surely few of you will prefer the less immediately appetizing idea of "enjoying the Harveys experience on CD Rom" as one advert so temptingly puts it.

Opposite the BRISTOL ICE RINK (0117 929 2148) further along Park Street is another museum at number 7 Great George Street, inside the GEORGIAN HOUSE (0117 921 1362). Every detail of this house's construction and decoration was overseen by the merchant for whom it was built at the end of the 18th century. John Pinney was rich, but there were many others in Bristol over the centuries who were just as well off, though their residences have not survived so completely and beautifully as this one.

The slim red Gothic tower of 1897 which rises from Brandon Hill can be seen clearly from here. Brunel has his statue, so do Neptune, Colston, and even William of Orange, but this is CABOT'S TOWER, built to celebrate the four hundredth anniversary of his trip to the west. Other explorers left Bristol and returned more often than the unfortunate Italian, who disappeared on his second American adventure, but it is this man who has stayed in the imagination of the Bristol populace longest of all. If you climb the one hundred feet or so of his memorial you can see far enough to make your own new discoveries, with virtually the whole city laid out before you. To the west the open spaces of the CLIFTON DOWNS, with 400 acres of trees and open grasslands, give you more natural opportunities to take in similar views, as well as those down to the Suspension Bridge and Avon Gorge, of which more shortly. To the west you can see right across the Severn Vale to South Wales.

The CITY MUSEUM AND ART GALLERY (0117 922 3571) is a little further north west out of the central part of the city, towards **CLIFTON**. This has permanent exhibitions of glass, porcelain and fine art, as well as temporary displays, and is as impressive as you will by now be expecting from the main official museum in a place of this size.

This part of the city is Bristol's WEST END (0117 921 3695 for information). As a shopping area this is the perfect complement to Broadmead. There is everything from Department stores to the tiny independent traders of the CHRISTMAS STEPS, with some of the superior feeling of the University, whose Wills Memorial Tower looks down over this area, seeming to have rubbed off on many places. Look in particular for the shops at the top of the steep seventeenth century alleyway that is Christmas Steps, and those on neighbouring Colston Street and Perry Road. MONTPELLIER too, with PICTON STREET and others, has more to offer in terms of unusual and original shops.

Amongst all this is another preserved house, older still than that in Great George Street. The RED LODGE (0117 921 1360) has some superb Tudor interiors, and it is amazing to think that domestic life could be lived in such a grand setting more than four hundred years ago; providing you had the money of course. The carved panelling of the Great Oak Room is particularly sumptuous and must cost a fortune in expensive furniture wax to maintain! If merchants could live like this it is no wonder that Bristol was among the first places to look after its poor, exemplified by Colston's Almshouses in the old city. Before we move west to discuss Clifton at more length, let's add a bit more about what there is to do in modern Bristol. We are not moving away from the city completely, for that is no quick task, but while still near the centre it is worth summing up a little more of what it has to offer.

One of the best ways to see much of the city, which is really too large to explore on foot, is the BRISTOL OPEN TOP GUIDED BUS TOUR (0117 9926 0767 for information). These start from outside the Hippodrome Theatre, and run all day with the important bonus that you can hop on and off as many times as you like, simply picking up a later tour bus when you want to carry on. There are other, ambitious ways to see the city, perhaps none more so than BRISTOL BALLOONS (0117 963 7858) who fly their passenger hot air balloons throughout the year, weather permitting.

Bristol is home to the GLOUCESTERSHIRE COUNTY CRICKET CLUB (0117 924 5216) where crowds have been entertained brilliantly by Jack Russell and Courtney Walsh, among others, over the last few years. To emphasise the unique modernity and pure size of Bristol, compared to much of the rest of the territory covered in this book, the city has two well supported, famous professional football clubs; BRISTOL CITY (0117 963 0630) and BRISTOL ROVERS (0117 977 2000). Mind you Swindon Town are more than a league above both these teams at time of writing, so perhaps Wiltshire's upstart is looking to outpace the old city in more than rates of population growth. This would be particularly ironic, as Swindon probably owes its very existence to a certain Mr Brunel, not unheard of in Bristol (see Chapter 6). I am not partisan in either direction, but cannot see Bristol's soccer clubs struggling for long; they have too much going for them. City's home at Ashton Gate is a welcoming place, and a fine ground, but I must admit I have not yet had the chance to go to Rovers' brand new stadium in Filton Road.

The local rivals are Bath and Gloucester if you are a follower of BRISTOL RUGBY FOOTBALL CLUB (0117 908 5500), but if competition is not something you are after, and a bit of peace and quiet around the water appeals, then the AVON ANGLING CENTRE (0117 951 7250) will probably be of more use to you. Tourist Information in the city has details of cycle hire and routes in the area (Bristol has many cycle paths) as well as a series of leaflets outlining walks around the attractions and places of interest. Here too you can expand on the range of information about evening entertainments already offered, with details of Bristol's many cinemas, theatres, comedy clubs and music venues.

There are various festivals and annual events held in the city too. The BRISTOL BALLOON FIESTA, held each summer, is one of the most prominent, being the biggest event of its kind held in Europe. Although these are of the hot air variety, so many balloons are launched at this event that from a distance you would be forgiven for thinking that an overloaded seller of hand held balloons had tripped and let his wares float to the sky. A beautiful sight, from near or far. Again Tourist Information has details of the full list of Bristol's annual events, including those held on the waterfront. There are many held in and around the Floating Harbour, notably the annual LLOYDS BANK HARBOUR REGATTA. Nearby in King Street, there is an annual JAZZ ON THE STREET FESTIVAL.

Clifton is where you will find the majority of Bristol's surviving Georgian buildings, particularly in the streets of CLIFTON VILLAGE, next to the River Avon. ROYAL YORK CRESCENT is claimed to be the longest Georgian Crescent in Britain, and it is not too surprising to hear that this was a place of many important visitors from the late 17th to early 19th centuries. The main reason for Clifton's popularity amongst the rich and influential may appear more unlikely, for Hotwells Road, which runs along the edge of the Avon Gorge, takes its name from Clifton's Spa, first renowned as a cure for kidney troubles and diabetes. Sheridan, Pope, Cowper and many other literary figures came to take the waters, but Clifton had the unfortunate reputation of being a last resort, if you will pardon the pun. Some of the rows of Georgian houses, which took in visitors became known as 'death row' because of the number of incurables who spent their last days by the Avon. The Pump Room has long gone, but the atmosphere of affluence and a slightly serious way of doing things still pervades Clifton. So it is that we must dispel it, with the unlikely help of Samuel Taylor Coleridge. You might expect to hear a frivolous anecdote about the caperings of Sheridan or Pope, albeit verbal ones, but it was the romantic poet who could allegedly be seen rushing around DOWRY SQUARE under a more energy inducing form of intoxication than the fashionable laudanum he was known to favour. Sober looking houses, and usually a sober personality, but Coleridge was taking part in medical experiments at the house of Humphrey Davy, who was looking into the efficacy of Nitrous Oxide as an anaesthetic. Romantic poets on laughing gas, whatever next? From here the B3124 will take you directly to Brunel's 'first child'. The labour was obviously a very difficult one, for the birth, which started in 1831 with some winning designs, was not complete until 1864, five years after Brunel's death. To get the best view of this remarkable being now you are best to take a longer route down to the side of the Avon Gorge from the village, and then along to the north west until you are right underneath it. The CLIFTON SUSPENSION BRIDGE spans the gorge with most of its 702 foot length, at 245 feet above the river, without touching the bottom of the gorge, a feature which was not in the plans offered by Brunel's competitors. It is estimated that 150,000 people attended its official opening in 1864, a truly amazing and telling figure.

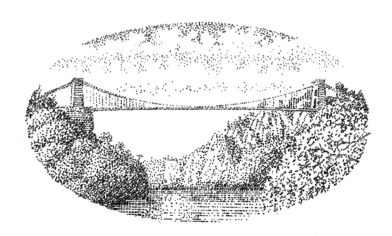

Clifton Suspension Bridge

The thing about the Suspension Bridge is that it still looks so new, so utterly right for the task it was created for, and this, above all else, makes it a real wonder of 19th century engineering. It is also much more attractive, in my opinion, than its neighbour at Avonmouth, both in setting and design. One mystery does tax the mind though. To extend a commercial route from London to Bristol by rail, and even further to America by steamboat makes obvious economic sense, but why on earth join the two sides of the Avon Gorge in such a wonderful but expensive and grand fashion? The answer is not an easy one to find, the bridge looks as if it should be between two huge centres of population or industry, rather than Clifton and Leigh Woods. Perhaps that is why it took so long to be built, with a ten year gap during which the funding had run out. Whatever the truth of the matter, this is a fabulous sight. Inevitable stories about the bridge involve those who have chosen to jump from it. The slightly morbid history of Clifton's Spa might fill you with pessimism, but the tale of Sarah Ann Henley has a happy ending.

If the cameras of any of the 'lifesaver' or 'escape' programmes so popular on today's mid evening television schedules had been at Clifton in 1885 then I am sure we would have been seeing the clips of Sarah's fall at least once a week ever since. As it was she lived long enough to have been familiar at least with the idea of television. Apparently it was because of a lover's quarrel that she used Brunel's bridge as a springboard for a very long dive to the mud below, but her landing was made slow and gentle by the opening of her parachute. No rip cord was pulled though, as Sarah's petticoats billowed in the breeze to give her own impromptu version of the pilot's safety device. One wonders whether she felt frustration or relief as the air filled her light garments to slow her descent to the pace of a falling leaf in Autumn. She later married and lived to the age of 85. A bizarre story, somewhere between the macabre and the pure absurd, but with a sentimental edge. Come to think of it, the nearest equivalent on film might well involve Julie Andrews holding an umbrella and rising rather than falling, as Mary Poppins.

Further away from the river Clifton is home to the BRISTOL ZOO GARDENS (0117 973 8951) which have undergone massive improvements in recent years. The emphasis, as with all British zoos, is turning towards conservation, but there is still the huge variety and favourites that you would expect to find in one of the largest collections of its type in the country. Clifton has its own cathedral too, but do not search the skyline for a suitable spire or tower, for the Roman Catholic Cathedral of ST PETER AND ST PAUL has nothing so ordinary. It does have a central structure which climbs to the sky, but this building defies description in the usual terms of church architecture. A mere twenty five years old, it looks ready to step freshly into the next millenium, with its bright white square lines and lack of any external decoration on its massive stone structure making it elegant in a very new kind of way.

Clifton Village is a very different place to much of Bristol, with its Georgian houses and architecture suggesting prosperity even now. Reflecting this, it is the local place to shop for antiques, arts and crafts, designer clothing and delicatessen foods. The WEST OF ENGLAND ACADEMY and the VICTORIA ROOMS are particularly worth seeing for their design, and perhaps the added fact that both Charles Dickens and OscarWilde performed readings in the latter.

If you continue out from the centre of Bristol on the road through Clifton, resisting the lure of the A4 for now, the A4018 will take you through **WESTBURY-ON-TRYM** to **HENBURY**. Westbury resisted the growth of Bristol until the 19th century, and was a parish long before the Normans came to England. Now it has succumbed, while Henbury has another attraction which has become part of the list attributed to the greater area of the city. BLAISE CASTLE HOUSE MUSEUM (0117 950 6789) is a grand 18th century house, itself built on the site of an Iron Age hillfort. There would not be too much room for camping out or digging earthworks around here these days. Every day life in bygone times is the theme of the museum's exhibits, but the gardens and house are just as much of a draw as the nevertheless fascinating collection of odds and ends from the 18th and 19th centuries.

Even crossing to the west of the M5 it does not feel as if you are really quite leaving Bristol behind, and with the best will in the world this area, seemingly constantly featuring delaying roadworks, is not among the most attractive in the south west. Industrial **AVONMOUTH** is a far cry from the undeniably charming old floating harbour of the city which used to handle this side of Bristol's life.

PORTISHEAD is less uninviting. Visitors were not always encouraged, and the Point was fortified against the Spanish in the 16th century, and later against the potential threat posed by Napoleon. By 1849 its character had changed, with villas, hotels and a pier. There are still some quiet places around the churches here and in neighbouring **PORTBURY**, and this is the beginning of a stretch of coast that will give many delights, none the less for being on the banks of the Bristol Channel rather than the open sea.

Our last stop on this brief visit to the Severn coast in this chapter is at **CLEVEDON**. More Gothic Victorian villas illustrate that this was another resort, still just about free of the industrial spread from the north and east. The town's three miles of quiet shoreline are almost a necessary barrier between what has just gone and what is to come to the south at Weston-Super-Mare. To move from the greys of Avonmouth straight to the golden sands of Weston would just be too much of a shock. Like its southern neighbour, Clevedon grew extremely rapidly in the first half of the 19th century, which is why the majority of the buildings present such a uniformity of style and atmosphere. By 1880 it was at the height of its popularity and had the biggest swimming baths in the west country, as well as the largest ice rink outside of London. Unlike Weston, the present century has seen a steady flow of visitors rather than a seasonal torrent.

27

The town's most visited building is much older than all of this. Parts of CLEVEDON COURT (01272 872257) were begun in the 13th century, its exterior completed to what you can see now by 1570. The light grey stone used has become mellow and quite lovely over the centuries, but the lines seem to combine the solidity of a castle with the subtlety of a church porch, yet all within a whole which is recognisably residential. From the Tudor fireplace and windows of the Great Hall to the collection of 18th and 19th century Nailsea Glass in the Justice Room, the house is full of remnants of the years which have passed here.

The kitchen also has some Eltonware, a type of local experimental pottery which was the work of Sir Edmund Elton, who also designed Clevedon's Jubilee (1897) Clock Tower. One note of caution. Be wary of entering the chapel if you value your hairstyle. Mass removals of the middle section of a head of hair are known to take place in this part of the house, with up to ten unfortunate victims at a single time. The last recorded instance of this tonsuring was that conducted by Bishop Drokensford in September 1323, so you can probably afford to relax.

In reality none of the geographical area covered by this chapter is totally free of the influence of Bristol, but some of the towns to the east of Clevedon, and the M5 have retained more individuality than those nearer the centre of the city. **NAILSEA**, as we have already heard, is famous for its 18th and 19th century glass. The best place to see a variety of the wares now is in the various antique shops in and around Bath, although three companies with outlets in Bristol itself have now revived the local art.

Much of **YATTON** belonged to Wells rather than Bristol Cathedral in medieval times, and the marshy land surrounding it belongs to the River Yeo rather than the Severn. Its finest buildings are the church and what surrounds it, particularly the 15th century rectory and 17th century almshouses. The church is very much of the Somerset style, of fine grey stone, but the vastly increased population it has served in the last thirty years or so was brought here by the accessibility to Bristol rather than anywhere to the south or east. **CONGRESBURY** too has borne a population explosion since the 1960s, with much new building to accommodate the newcomers. This place was settled in the very distant past, with archaeological finds linking this site to Glastonbury Tor and Tintagel, two names which immediately provoke a sense of mystery. The Romans were here too, and later King Alfred was given Congresbury's Abbey as a gift in 880.

To the south of Congresbury lie the Mendip hills, which we will visit in Chapter Three, but a couple of the villages on their northern edge show that it is still possible to have a rural settlement in what used to be Avon. **BANWELL** has winding streets around a church which has been called 'the cathedral of the Mendips', a castle and an Abbey, as well as a cave beneath the edge of the hills, in which a vast array of bones from prehistoric times (mostly of animals) were discovered in the 19th century. The church of ST ANDREW (mostly the work of the 15th century) is splendid both inside and out, and the one hundred feet of graceful spire seem to state that this is very much a place with its own identity, which may be used to live in for those who want to work in the city, but is definitely not prepared to become a suburb. Unfortunately the 'bone cave' is no longer open to the public.

A little to the east from here, near **BURRINGTON**, you may feel suddenly optimistic and roused, in a spiritual way. The overhanging rocks of Burrington Combe provided shelter for the Reverend Toplady during a storm. As such, this narrow two mile cleft in the Mendips, with the village of Burrington at its northern end, was the inspiration for the hymn 'Rock of Ages'. Now it is more likely to entice you south, and onto the Mendips themselves.

North from Burrington the influence of Bristol is undeniably close by. **WRINGTON** is very close to the city's AIRPORT (01275 474444), although its roots were as part of the estate of Glastonbury Abbey. So far south of the main ridge of the Cotswolds, probably the last thing you will be expecting to come across is another place made prosperous by the medieval wool trade. Yet this is what established **CHEW MAGNA**, as the church of ST ANDREW with its hundred feet of tower, complete with gargoyles, bears witness. By the churchyard's gate is the 16th century CHURCH ALE HOUSE. A strange combination? Even more so when you realise that ale was indeed often brewed by the church, to be consumed by the villagers on feast days; mind you proceeds did go to the parish funds. Could be a tradition well worth reviving at a few church fetes these days!

Staying with things of a religious nature, beware of getting too excited by any country or line dancing music while visiting to the east of Chew, or you might end up staying in **STANTON DREW** for rather longer than you had intended. We will meet the devil and his works several times in Somerset and Dorset, but the ancient stones surrounding the village here are said to be wedding guests who got carried away and led into dancing on a Sunday, tempted by the sound of His Satanic Majesty playing the fiddle. You are quite welcome to draw your own humorous connections between the legend attached to these neolithic monuments and the relatively nearby Burrington Combe, Reverend Toplady and 'Rock of Ages', if you so wish!

What lies east and south east of Bristol soon becomes the environs of Bath, and so we will leave Keynsham and the rest until our next chapter. All that is left for us are more suburbs of the city, but some with enough green space and history, or both, to be worth seeing for themselves. **LONG ASHTON**, for example, is surrounded by several golf courses, including Pitch and Putt at the ASHTON COURT ESTATE (0117 973 8508). John Smyth was responsible for the original construction of the house itself, (later added to in the 16th and 17th centuries) using the money made from trading in wool, leather, wheat and wine, but not bitter, as he came from the Forest of Dean rather than Yorkshire. Ashton Court also hosts an INTERNATIONAL KITE FESTIVAL each year, usually in July (Tourist Information Bristol for current details).

To the north of the city **PATCHWAY** and **FILTON** have become part of the greater city, while **MANGOTSFIELD** no longer looks like part of the Royal Forest it once was. Filton and Patchway were once the suburbs of **ALMONDSBURY** rather than Bristol, as the former lay on the main route from Gloucester to Bristol, having its own market from 1285. Perhaps more than anywhere else this inconspicuous place, with its own fine houses such as KNOLE PARK and OVER COURT, suffered from the comings of the motorway. The massive junction of the M5 and M4 has split the original parish in half, and swallowed up much of its farmland.

Even the most used of places in recent times, such as **AUST**, with its services at the base of the Severn Bridge across to Wales, have their roots in the distant past. the name does not come from a corruption or dialect for 'east', but rather the 'Trajectus Augustus' a river crossing used by the Roman legions. Another twist of fate or chance means that Aust's character is undergoing yet another change since the building of the Second Severn Crossing has taken away much of the congestion which it suffered for what seemed so long, but was really only a brief interlude in its longer history.

YATE, on the other hand, does sound like the geographical location after which it is named, even though the town itself was only actually formed in 1966. This was a gate, and entrance into a Royal Forest in medieval times. Now you might assume this was to the north, as the country opens out that way, but this was the Forest of **KINGSWOOD**, to the south. Now there is still a forest, but of housing, factories and urban life rather than trees and deer.

We started in Bristol by looking for a central point, perhaps in a vain attempt to give the city a single character. More than anywhere else in the south west this city has become much too large and varied for that. There is little room left between Bristol and her eastern neighbour, but as we move onto Bath the contrast could not be greater. Both places have history, but while Bristol is cosmopolitan in its design, attractions and even regions, Bath has a single definable feeling, a style that is unique in such a big place. Yet the two complement each other in a unique way. Bath is undeniably more picturesque, even it its dramatic history full of single characters full of eccentricity and glamour, such as Beau Nash, but Bristol has a harder, more real edge. This is not an unattractive thing, especially if you like a bit of real, vibrant city life. What you can have from Bristol you will not get in Bath, and vice versa.

There are other cities in the area covered by this book, but here at the start is the only one that those used to London, Birmingham, Manchester or the larger cities of other countries will recognise as having the bustle and range of facilities they will expect and want from a place taking that name. Bristol's nearest rival in this way is not Salisbury, with the bigger, more splendid Cathedral, or even Gloucester with its own docks, but rather a recent, dramatic upstart with a reputation for growth and modern industry ironically started by the same man who has contributed so much to the fame of Bristol, Isambard Kingdom Brunel. But we have a long way to travel and much to see before we can compare the merits of Bristol to Swindon (Chapter Six), the home of the Great Western Railway.

Meanwhile Bristol will have left you with a collection of memories. Perhaps not least will be those of trying to navigate your way around its outskirts for the first time, or surprise at just how long the suburbs run for, but these will not be all. Once the centre is reached Bristol is a rewarding place, with the history of past times largely covered by modern amenities, without being completely supplanted or forgotten. There is a justifiable pride taken in the city by its inhabitants, nowhere more obviously apparent than in the trouble and effort that has been taken to restore its flagship the S.S. Great Britain, brought home to become an antiquity in the very place where it was once a very modern wonder.

ALMONDSBURY INTERCHANGE HOTEL
Gloucester Road
Almondsbury
Bristol
BS12 4AA

Tel: 01454 613206
Fax: 01454 618305

The position of the Almondsbury Interchange Hotel only five hundred yards from Exit 16 by the Almondsbury junctions of the M5 Motorway with A38 (North), makes it an ideal place to break your journey travelling North to South or East to West. It provides an excellent base for those wanting to stay awhile to explore the magic of historical Bristol and the incredible beauty and architecture of nearby Bath as well as the many interesting smaller towns and villages within easy distance. The coast is less than half an hour away.

People who stay here have found that, despite the fact that it is quite large, with fifty bedrooms, it is nonetheless an independent hotel run on friendly, informal but very professional lines. It came into being in 1967 and is still run by the founding family. Guests have a choice of fifty bedrooms, all ensuite with satellite television, trouser press, tea and coffee facilities, hair dryer and telephone. The restaurant has an extensive A la Carte menu and wide selection of wines whilst light meals and snacks are available in the lounge bar.

Because of its situation the Almondsbury is a popular venue for business meetings and conferences. Conference rooms are available for meetings of between two and eighty delegates and the hotel provides a detailed conference package providing all the information required to plan your meeting and includes a selection of hot and cold menus, room plans and booking procedures. Equal care and attention is given to Wedding celebrations which can be arrange by the hotel's experienced wedding co-ordinator, who is on hand to give advice and help to ensure that the special day is a day to remember. The Almondsbury Interchange is a versatile hotel where caring for the guest on leisure or business is synonymous with the efficient manner in which everything is run.

USEFUL INFORMATION

- OPEN: All year
- WHEELCHAIR ACCESS: Limited
- GARDEN: No

- CREDIT CARDS: All major cards
- ACCOMMODATION: 50 ensuite rms
- RATES: Sgl from £73 Dbl. £83.
  Special weekend rates

- RESTAURANT: A la Carte menu
- VEGETARIAN: Always a choice
- BAR FOOD: Light meals/snacks in
  Lounge bar
- LICENSED: Full On
- CHILDREN: Welcome
- PETS: No

ALVESTON HOUSE
Alveston
Thornbury
Bristol
BS12 2LJ

Tel: 01454 415050
Fax: 01454 415425

AA***RAC Hospitality Merit Awards
RAC 75% Quality + Rosette for Restaurant

Alveston House has to be the perfect venue for anyone wanting to be close to Bristol or amidst some fascinating countryside complete with stately homes and near the coast. One can visit Slimbridge Wild Fowl Trust and the unique Westonbirt Arboretum. Soak up the history of the Roman City of Bath and Berkeley Castle, one of England's most historic homes. Play golf at Thornbury or enjoy a golfing break at Cotswold Edge Golf Club. There is horse racing at Bath, Chepstow and Cheltenham and there are the famous Badminton and Gatcombe Park horse trials. Access to Bristol city centre is simple and it is easily reached from the M4/M5. Once at the hotel Alveston House is surrounded by charming gardens and the period house has a graciousness that is both welcoming and tranquil. From the moment you arrive, the friendly staff will make you feel at home.

This 'feel at home' factor is enhanced in the tastefully decorated bedrooms with all modern facilities provided. A shower or bath in your ensuite bathroom is a perfect way to unwind from a journey and make one ready to come down the elegant stairs ready to appreciate a superb dinner in the award winning Quincey's restaurant. The room has a very special ambience and a quiet restfulness that makes it the perfect place to dine. The menu is a mixture of English and Continental dishes complemented by fine wines from the carefully selected list. Many business people come out from Bristol to entertain their guests, others bring their friends to have a memorable evening. It is ideal for any occasion.

Private function rooms are available for special occasions whether business or pleasure. Enjoy a pre-dinner apéritif and the views in the gardens relaxed in the knowledge that the food, wine and service will be superlative. If you would like a menu specially created for you the chef will be delighted to do so.

USEFUL INFORMATION

· OPEN: All year

· WHEELCHAIR ACCESS: Yes
· GARDEN: Tranquil & charming
· CREDIT CARDS: All major cards
· ACCOMMODATION: 30 ensuite rms
· RATES: Sgl from £79.50 B&B
  Twin/dbl. from £94.50
  Weekend breaks 2nights between
  Thurs & Sun: £47.50pp.pn D.B&B

· RESTAURANT: English & Continental
· VEGETARIAN: Always a choice
· BAR FOOD: Light meals available
· LICENSED: Yes
· CHILDREN: Welcome
· PETS: By arrangement

THE BERKELEY SQUARE HOTEL
15 Berkeley Square
Clifton
Bristol
BS8 1HB

Tel: 0117 925 4000
Fax: 0117 925 2970

Highest Graded *** in Bristol. 4 Crowns

Whilst you cannot be promised a 'Nightingale singing in Berkeley Square', you will certainly find this attractive, Georgian Square, which overlooks the park, tranquil. It was the Square used for the BBC's 'House of Elliott' series. At Number 15 is the gracious Berkeley Square Hotel, part of the Clifton Hotel Group, rebuilt after the bombing in World War II. It has the feel of a Country House Hotel about it, in spite of it being so near the centre. You literally walk down a hill and there you are. It is ideal both for the visitor and those who come to Bristol on business. The management are skilled and professional and this reflects on the staff who are always friendly and helpful.

There are twenty four singles, twelve doubles and six twin-bedded guest rooms, all of which are ensuite. All the rooms are decorated and furnished delightfully, in a manner in keeping with the tranquillity and the Georgian ambience of the hotel. Television, direct dial telephones and a hostess tray are there for your use. Non-smoking bedrooms are available. The cosy, well-stocked bar is a regular meeting place for people and on warm days it leads to a small patio. Great care and attention is given to food served in the pretty restaurant and in the bar, both of which are open to non-residents. The chef is imaginative and his menu includes traditional English fare but with a French link. In the bar you can get a delicious light lunch or snack. The wine list has been carefully chosen to complement the menu and has both full and half bottles from around the world, at sensible prices.

The houses in Berkeley Square were originally built for wealthy merchants at the time when Bristol became a major seafaring port. Clifton was one of these areas and it has become world famous, being a favourite area often described by John Betjeman. One of the most noticeable buildings built in this period, Cabot Tower, stands on Brandon Hill, commanding views over Berkeley Square and the whole of Bristol. It was built to commemorate the anniversary of John Cabot's voyage on the Matthew during which he discovered America. To the North of the square lies the vast Gothic University Hall and the lightly Baroque City Museum. Both of these buildings were built by the Wills family who donated many fine civic buildings to the City.

USEFUL INFORMATION

· OPEN: All year	· RESTAURANT: English/French link
· WHEELCHAIR ACCESS: Yes	· VEGETARIAN: Limited choice
· CREDIT CARDS: Visa/Master/	· BAR FOOD: Light lunches
Diners/AMEX	· PETS: Yes
· ACCOMMODATION: 42 ensuite	· LICENSED: Full On
· RATES: £86sgl B&B £107 dbl. B&B ·	CHILDREN: Welcome

THE BLACK HORSE
4 Clevedon Lane
Clapton in Gordano
NR Bristol

Tel:01275 842105

This is a genuinely atmospheric inn that has changed little over the years - always a comfort to the regulars and ensuring a great atmosphere for those who walk through its welcoming portals for the first time. The partly flagstone and partly red-tiled main room has winged settles and built-in wall benches around narrow, dark wooden tables and pleasant window seats. The walls are full of amusing cartoons and photographs of the pub and there is a crackling log fire with stirrups and bits on the mantelpiece. A window in an inner snug is still barred from the days when the room was used as a jail house. The high-backed settles, one with a marvellous carved and canopied creature and another with a copper insert which reads 'East, West, Ham's Best. Everywhere there are mugs hanging from the old beams. It is both a fascinating place to visit and an excellent hostelry. Good, quickly served bar food is available every day at lunch time except Sundays, from a simple sandwich to one of the two Daily Specials. The Courage Best and Wadworth 6X on hand pump or tapped from the cask and an excellent farm cider are well kept. There is a simply furnished children's room and a little flagstone front garden full of flowers in summer with tubs, hanging baskets and flower beds. Rustic tables and benches provide the seating which extends around the side of the car park. Live music on Monday evenings. Children's play area.

USEFUL INFORMATION

· OPEN: 11-3pm & 6-11pm Fri/Sat 11-11pm	· BAR FOOD: Simple pub fare with Daily Specials at lunch time. Not Sunday
· WHEELCHAIR ACCESS: No	· VEGETARIAN: Always a choice
· GARDEN: Yes	· LICENSED: Full On
· CREDIT CARDS: None taken	· CHILDREN: Welcome
	· PETS: Yes on leads

DOWNLANDS HOUSE
33 Henleaze Gardens
Westbury on Trym
Bristol BS9 4HH

Tel/Fax:0117 9621639
mjdownlands@compuserve.com

RAC Acclaimed AAQQQ
ETB Commended.
Frommer & Which Hotel Guide

Downlands House is the home of Michael and Jane Winterbottom who have returned here after spending 30 years running hotels in Kenya and the West Indies. Their assured touch has brought new life to Downlands, an elegant Victorian town house with gracious rooms and a welcoming atmosphere. It is situated close to the city centre, theatres, cinemas and restaurants, two minutes walk from the downs and the Zoo is nearby as well as the stunning Clifton Suspension Bridge. Clifton Village is a favourite area for shopping. Bristolians frequent the pretty shops in search of that special gift and to admire the splendour of the Georgian and Regency Terraces. Not to be missed in Bristol is the SS Great Britain, as well as special events such as the Bristol Regattas and the Balloon Fiesta. Harvey's Wine Museum which also includes a stunning restaurant, the Art Gallery, the waterfront, the cathedral and endless other places of interest always enchant the visitor.

Within the house which has retained the charm and atmosphere of a large family house, there are nine attractively furnished and decorated bedrooms, most with ensuite shower and toilet facilities. Each room also has colour television, hair dryer and tea/coffee hospitality trays. Downlands House is a delightful place to stay where you will be quietly cared for and feel a person rather than the anonymity that pervades many modern hotels. An excellent Continental or full English breakfast is available each day from 7.30-9am. The full breakfast, freshly cooked, is delicious with bacon, sausage and tomato and a choice of eggs. One starts with fruit juice and cereals and there is always plentiful toast and preserves and freshly ground coffee as well as piping hot tea which includes herbal teas. Special requests are also catered for. There is a small lounge with cable TV and video. No evening meals but with such a wide choice of eateries within easy reach, this is not a problem.

USEFUL INFORMATION

- OPEN: All year except Christmas
- WHEELCHAIR ACCESS: No
- GARDEN: No
- CREDIT CARDS: Master/Visa/Delta
- ACCOMMODATION: 9 rooms
- RATES: SQL £30-39 Dbl. £45-52 Children to 5 yr. (sharing with parents) £5. under 15 yr. £15

- DINING ROOM: Full English.
- VEGETARIAN: On request
- LICENSED: No
- CHILDREN: Yes
- PETS: By arrangement

THE GEORGE AND DRAGON
High Street
Pensford
Bristol
BS18 4BH

Tel: 01761 490516

The George and Dragon is an historic Coaching Inn built in 1760 and is situated in the pretty, old mining village of Pensford. The now disused viaduct dominates the village of small stone built houses where the River Chew flows slowly through the village. There are a lot of beautiful walks along the river. Stanton Drew is nearby where medieval stones were recently uncovered and which is fast becoming a major tourist attraction. Next door to the pub is the original Round Stone Prison Cell where prisoners were held overnight before being executed up on the hill behind the George and Dragon.

The beautiful Chew Valley Lake is close by, much loved by fishermen and those who like to mess about in boats. The world famous musician and larger than life character, Acker Bilk lives in the village and is often to be seen at the bar. The incomparable city of Bath is within easy distance and so too is Bristol and many other places. The George and Dragon is the ideal place to stay whilst you explore or set forth on business in the area. Owned by Anna Henderson and Lionel, it is one of the friendliest places imaginable and oozes the atmosphere built up over the centuries.

The food is cooked by joint owner, Lionel Seigneur, who combines both English and French cooking. Food is served between 12-2pm and between 6.30-9pm. The menu covers three courses including Goats Cheese Salad and Prawns for starters and the main courses include steaks, salmon and trout. The menu is changed regularly and hot filled baguettes are also always available at lunch time.

There is a very pretty patio at the back where you can relax in quiet surroundings. Once a month on Saturday evenings, the bar resounds to live music. There are three letting rooms, one double and two twin-bedded served by one bathroom with shower. There are also TV and tea and coffee making facilities in each room.

USEFUL INFORMATION

- OPEN: Mon.-Sat 11-11pm Sun:12-10.30pm
- WHEELCHAIR ACCESS: Yes
- GARDEN: Yes
- CREDIT CARDS: Not at present
- ACCOMMODATION: 2tw.1dbl 2 bathroom, 2 showers
- RATES: £45 per room inc. B&B

- RESTAURANT: Good home-cooked fare
- VEGETARIAN: Yes
- BAR FOOD: Traditional
- LICENSED: Full On
- CHILDREN: Welcome

- PETS: Yes

HARVEYS RESTAURANT & WINE CELLARS
12 Denmark Street
Bristol
BS1 5DQ

Tel: 0117 927 5034
Fax: 0117 927 5051
www.harveysbc.co.uk

Belonging to the rich wine heritage of John Harvey & Sons stretching back two hundred years, Harveys Restaurant not only offers the very best in contemporary cuisine and service but also the finest wines, ports and sherries from its famous medieval wine cellars. Since it opened in the 13th-century cellars beneath 12 Denmark Street in 1962, Harvey's has consistently held the reputation as one of Bristol's best loved attractions.

The original medieval cellar setting makes Harvey's Restaurant unique in Bristol. Historic surroundings complement the simple, crisp lines of the table settings whilst the whitewashed brick-lined cellar walls serve to highlight works of art by contemporary west country artists. High quality glassware, cutlery and crockery have been carefully chosen to match the classic and distinctive presentation of the food.

Harvey's is run by a Frenchman, Daniel Galmiche. Daniel believes that eating out is one of the great pleasures in life and invites all customers who visit the Restaurant to share his passion. The Fixed Price A La Carte menu is available both at lunch time and in the evening £33.95 for two courses, £39.95 for three courses. Harvey's also has a Business Lunch Menu - £14.95 for two courses, £17.95 for three courses. The Restaurant Wine List is one of the finest and most complete in the country, with over 300 wines, and is supplied by Harvey's Wine Merchants, also located at 12 Denmark Street. An added bonus for customers visiting the Restaurant is the opportunity to wander through Harvey's original medieval wine cellars which contain a unique collection of rare glassware, antique silver and Georgian furniture.

Harvey's Restaurant has retained it's Michelin Star for the fourth year in succession.

USEFUL INFORMATION

- OPEN: Mon.-Fri.: Lunch 12 noon-2pm Dinner: 7-10.45pm Sat: Dinner only
- WHEELCHAIR ACCESS: No
- GARDEN: No
- CREDIT CARDS: All major cards
- RESTAURANT: Contemporary cuisine
- VEGETARIAN: Always a choice
- LICENSED: Yes
- CHILDREN: Welcome
- PETS: No

HIGHBURY VAULTS
164 St Michael's Hill
Cotham
Bristol
BS2 8DE

Tel: 01179 733203
Fax: 01179 744828

Egon Ronay Recommended

This Real Ale Pub has quite a gruesome history! Prisoners condemned to death were given their last meal here before being hanged outside. Such horrible happenings are definitely things of the past, and today Bradd Francis, the landlord, runs one of the most congenial hostelries in Bristol. Situated close to the Universities, the General and Children's Hospital, it is a pub much in demand and the regulars create an excellent atmosphere which radiates out to visitors who soon find themselves being treated like a local. It has a pleasingly not modernised yet timeless atmosphere and character with an intimate snug at the front leading to a bigger but equally cosy bar. One of its modern day charms is the secluded floral trellised heated garden which means that apart from streaming wet or intensely cold days, one can always take a drink outside. Conversation is an encouraged art form here. Juke Boxes, fruit machines, pool tables are not permitted and Bradd will tell you that he has declared Highbury Vaults a World Cup 98 Football free zone! Egon Ronay recommended the pub for its atmosphere and he should also have added the efficiency of the friendly service.

The Highbury has always had a well deserved reputation for selling a Nation-wide range of hand-crafted ales much appreciated by the regulars and visitors alike. Alongside the choice of traditional ales there is a wide selection of bottled beers, lagers and soft drinks.

Good pub fare is on offer every day both at lunch and in the evenings from Monday to Friday and at lunch time on Saturday and Sunday. The Menu consists of dishes like chillies and curries, casseroles and bakes and vegetarian dishes, all under £3. The portions are generous, the dishes tasty and definitely no fried food. Sandwiches, Ploughman's and other snacks are also available.

USEFUL INFORMATION

- OPEN: Mon.-Sat 12-11pm
  Sun: 12-10.30pm
  Food : 12-2 &5.30-8.30pm Mon.-Fri.
  Sat & Sun 12-2pm only
- WHEELCHAIR ACCESS: Yes
- GARDEN: Secluded & heated
- CREDIT CARDS: None taken

- BAR FOOD: Chillies,
  Casseroles

- VEGETARIAN: Always a choice
- CHILDREN: Welcome
- PETS: No

HUNSTRETE HOUSE
Hunstrete, Pensford
NR Bristol BS39 4NS

Tel:01761 490490
Fax: 01761 490732

3AA Red Stars & 3 AA
Rosettes for cooking.
'Best Hotels of the World' award in 1997

This beautiful 18th Century house set in ninety two acres of deer park at the edge of the Mendip Hills, justifiably won 'Best Hotels of the World' award in 1997. The standard it sets is second to none and at the same time it makes people feel they are actually staying in a private house, a sense heightened by the drawing room and library, both beautifully furnished with antiques, original paintings and collections of fine porcelain. Hunstrete House is Georgian and has exciting and beautiful gardens which in the front of the house are conventional, much like other country houses but on the other side Hunstrete conceals what 'Homes and Gardens' described as 'a gardening treasure - an old walled kitchen garden which has always been a priority as the source of food for the kitchen, flowers for the house and the enjoyment of visitors. Within the grounds one can swim in the outdoor heated pool, play tennis or croquet. By arrangement one can try one's hand at Laser/clay pigeon shooting or endeavour to master the skill of archery. Everywhere you wander the sense of 'God's in his heaven and all is right with the world ', pervades the atmosphere. A place for relaxation, to be away from 20th century stress and at the same time aware that the outside world is easily accessed.

Hunstrete House has twenty three bedrooms and suites, each room superbly appointed and with private facilities. One suite has a magnificent four-poster. In the Terrace Room you will be fed on beautifully cooked and presented food, produced by innovative chefs who specialise in modern English cooking and use every bit of fresh produce they can get from the kitchen garden. The result is a wonderful meal whether it is at breakfast, lunch or dinner. The accompanying wine list has wines from around the world. There is a private dining room for special occasions. Much sought after as a venue for small conferences, Hunstrete House has 3 conference rooms. There are delegate rates and the most modern up to date equipment is available upon request. The largest room has a capacity for twenty four people seated boardroom style. With the airport eight miles away and railway stations at Bath, six miles and Bristol Temple Meads nine miles and the M32/M5 Motorway ten miles, M4, Junction 18, fifteen miles, Hunstrete could not be better situated.

USEFUL INFORMATION

· OPEN: All year	· THE TERRACE ROOM: Superb food Modern English cuisine
· WHEELCHAIR ACCESS: Yes	· VEGETARIAN: Always a choice
· GARDEN: 92 acres	· LICENSED: Full On
· CREDIT CARDS: All major cards	· CHILDREN: Yes
· ACCOMMODATION: 23 bedrooms & suites	· PETS: No
· RATES: Sgl. from £120 Dbl. From £130 Suite from £260	

INNLODGE
North End Road
Yatton
NR Bristol
BS19 4AU

Tel: 01934 839100
Fax: 01934 839149

Innlodge at The Bridge is only fifteen minutes from the ever growing Bristol Airport with world-wide connections daily. An ideal place to stay whether you come to Bristol for holidays or pleasure or even your honeymoon. There are opportunities for leisure pursuits while staying at Innlodge. Within easy reach are the ancient cities of Bath and Wells with its splendid cathedral. Then there is Wookey Hole, Weston-Super-Mare Sea Life Centre, Waverley Steam Paddle, the Mendip Hills, Avon Riding and Skiing Centre, Cheddar Caves, Mendip Outdoor Pursuits, SS Great Britain, Longleat, Motor Museum, Clark's Village at Street and of course, historic Bristol itself with its great maritime traditions. You could spend time playing golf on a pay-as-you-play course minutes from the hotel - with a driving range and lessons from teaching professionals. There is an adventure play for children in the grounds of The Bridge. Fishing in nearby lakes teaming with Carp and bird watching at the famous Chew Valley Lakes also potholing, quad biking, archery, riding and skiing all close at hand.

There are twenty nine spacious bedrooms, everyone with a full bathroom ensuite, queen size (5ft) double bed or twins, colour satellite TV, radio and dial direct telephone plus hair dryer, trouser press and tea and coffee making facilities. You have a choice of three categories:- Standard Rooms - also for single occupancy and offering exceptional value for money with extra beds or cots available. Executive Suites - with separate lounge area and dedicated line for PC or fax. Luxury Suites - The spacious Bridal Suite features a Jacuzzi and is furnished in that extra luxurious style, suitable for honeymooners or that very special occasion. Non smoking rooms and a room for the disabled are also available.

For good food and a warm and welcoming atmosphere, you'll find a direct link to The Bridge Inn, one of the areas best known pub and restaurants with a wide ranging reputation for good food with an emphasis on value for money. Innlodge also offers, outstanding business, banqueting, conference, training and interviewing facilities.

USEFUL INFORMATION

· OPEN: All year	· RESTAURANT: In The Bridge Inn
· WHEELCHAIR ACCESS: Yes	· VEGETARIAN: Yes
· GARDEN: Yes. Play area	· BAR FOOD: In the Bridge Inn
· CREDIT CARDS: All major cards	· LICENSED: Full On
· ACCOMMODATION: 27 ensuite rooms	· CHILDREN: Welcome
· RATES: Week day from £44.95	· PETS: No
Weekend from £37.50	
Cots or extra beds are available at £7 per night	

THE POACHER & SPOONS RESTAURANT
106 High Street,
Portishead BS20 6AJ

Tel: 01275 844002

Portishead has grown from a village into a town but it still has just one main street, the High Street, with the Poacher, a large single room pub, in the centre. It is an attractive grey-stone building with a large car park and frontage, set in the midst of shops and offices.

The first licence was granted in 1683 when it was known as the Blew Anchor. During the 1720's, a widow lady, Mary Whitwood, ran the pub and had stocks and whipping post outside with which to dispense justice! The pub has changed its name several times; in 1850 it became the Gordon Arms, to appease the local squire; a little later it was renamed The Anchor and in the 1900's it became The Blew Anchor once more and remained so until 1971 when it was renamed The Poacher - Spoons Restaurant is an addition. Mr and Mrs Hazelton are the present landlords. They are a convivial couple whose aim has always been to make people welcome. They have achieved a wonderful atmosphere which not only attracts customers but their caring attitude has meant also, that the staff have stayed with them over the years.

The food is excellent whether you have it at the Bar or in the attractive Spoons Restaurant which opens in the evenings offering an a la carte menu. For the bon viveur Spoons Restaurant also arranges regular Gourmet Evenings and Wine Tasting. The pub caters for all types of clientele and during lunch time you will find it a popular pub with the local retired population. One of the nice things about The Poacher is its gentle ambience whilst catering for both the older generation and the younger ones with regular quizzes.

USEFUL INFORMATION

· OPEN: 11-2.30pm & 6-11pm	· RESTAURANT: A la carte in the evenings. Gourmet evenings Wine Tasting
· WHEELCHAIR ACCESS: Yes	· VEGETARIAN: Yes
· GARDEN: No	· BAR FOOD: Wide range
· CREDIT CARDS: Euro/Visa/Delta	· LICENSED: Full On
· CHILDREN: Not allowed	· PETS: No

REDWOOD LODGE HOTEL
Beggar Bush Lane, Failand,
Bristol BS8 3TG
AA***RAC

Tel:01275 393901
Fax: 01275 392104
www.marketsite.co.uk/redwood

Set in sixteen acres of wooded countryside, Redwood Lodge is an out of the ordinary hotel. You will find it by taking the B3129 from the A369 just by Gordano Services on the M5. It has a remarkable history and once was the Garden House and Chapel of the Ashton Court Estate. In the early 1960's John Ley acquired it and it became the Ashton Court Country Club, a popular haunt for Bristolians and when Snooker became fashionable, the venue for many tournaments attracting major names. During these years the ethos of a Businessman's Country Club gradually expanded to include a sports and leisure complex together with restaurants, dance floors to suit different age groups, a casino, and extensive outdoor tennis courts etc. It rapidly became the 'In' place to be and to see Stars of Stage, TV and Radio for cabaret on Saturday evenings.

Redwood Lodge has had several owners over the years and has never been in better hands than today when it has become one of Bristol's leading hotels. One of its newest facilities is a one hundred and seventy five seat cinema auditorium, featuring all the latest films on Saturdays and Sundays. Every one of the one hundred and eight ensuite bedrooms is attractively furnished in a stylish modern manner, and equipped with colour television, direct dial telephone and a hospitality tray as well as many other extras for your comfort. The restaurant is open to non-residents and a popular place for diners who enjoy the ambience and the excellence of the food produced by a team of talented chefs. There is a wide choice and caters for every taste. In the friendly bars people gather just for a drink or to have an aperitif while they study the menu. Bar meals are also available. Redwood Lodge offers a whole range of special breaks throughout the year. It is a great place to stay whether on business or leisure. So close to the centre of Bristol and yet in a rural setting, it gives the visitor the best of both worlds. Bristol is an exciting city with much of interest and the surrounding area has just about everything from Stately homes to beaches.

USEFUL INFORMATION

· OPEN: All year	· RESTAURANT: Wide choice
· WHEELCHAIR ACCESS: ramp etc.	· VEGETARIAN: Yes
· GARDEN: 16 acres	· BAR FOOD: Yes
· CREDIT CARDS: All major cards	· LICENSED: Full On.
· ACCOMMODATION: 108 ensuite rooms	· CHILDREN: Welcome
· RATES: Sgl. room £85 Dbl. room £100	· PETS: Guide dogs only
SPECIAL OFFER BREAKS	
details on application.	

THE ROYALIST HOTEL
Digbeth Street
Stow-on-the-Wold
Gloucestershire
GL54 1BN

Tel: 01451 830670
Fax: 01451 870048

AA** ETB 3 Crowns Commended

The oldest inn in England of Saxon structure (A.D.947) when it was a hospice for travellers, was rebuilt in the 15th and 16th centuries. It is arguably the most prestigious building in Stow-on-the-Wold, certainly it is one of the most fascinating, full of old beams, uneven floors, nooks and crannies and a never ending source of legends, some with little substance and some mere fantasy but making excellent story telling and each one adding to the undoubted atmosphere of The Royalist Hotel. In addition to the stories of hidden tunnels, ghosts, priest holes and witches, one legend seems rooted in fact. Sir Jacob Astley the commander of the King's Army at the Battle of Stow, the last one of importance during the Civil War, formally surrendered in what is now the hotel dining room - hence the name. Whatever the stories, whatever the age of the building, today's owners, Graham and Marie-France Clark, have a love and understanding of this ancient hostelry and in the short time they have been there have revitalised the whole. The ambience is terrific, informal and relaxed, the furnishings tasteful but not plush, in fact everything has been done with an eye to the age of the building. It truly is a great place to stay and a perfect centre with easy access to Stratford, Oxford, Cirencester and Cheltenham as well as allowing the opportunity to explore the quaint towns and villages and the rolling countryside of the Cotswolds on foot, on horseback or by cycle.

Most of the twelve ensuite bedrooms are contained within the Jacobean part of the hotel. They are full of character and charm, beautifully furnished and complete with television. The Bar has been restored to its original glory with oak beams and frame and exposed stone walls. The Jacobean Restaurant has a high ceiling and an impressive fireplace at either end. The bare wooden tables and place mats are just right for the setting and from the a la carte menu you will dine in Royal style. The menu is described as English produce a la sauce francaise with an emphasis on seafood and game. The wine list matches the excellence of the fare. The bar offers a lunch time buffet as well as traditional hearty dishes of diverse origins. There are also vegetarian options.

USEFUL INFORMATION

· OPEN: All day	· RESTAURANT: English fare with a French influence. Emphasis on seafood & game
· GARDEN: Yes	· VEGETARIAN: Always a choice
· CREDIT CARDS: All major cards	· BAR FOOD: Buffet/Trad dishes
· ACCOMMODATION: 12 ensuite	· LICENSED: Full On
· RATES: From £30 pp B&B	· PETS: Yes
Winter breaks -3 nights price of 2, 5 for 3	· CHILDREN: Welcome

ST MICHAELS GUEST HOUSE
145 St Michael's Hill
Bristol
BS2 8DB

Tel/Fax: 0117 9077820

Built at the turn of the 19th century St Michael's Guest House is full of character as are so many in this part of Bristol. It is no distance into the centre of the city with all its attractions from the waterfront to the theatre and concert hall, wonderful shopping areas, university and splendid Georgian architecture. People come here to stay because of the casual manner in which the house is run, it is unpretentious and great if you prefer an atmosphere of honest working people. The Guest House is probably better known for its Cafe serving one of the largest breakfasts you will find in Bristol, feeding people all day up to 7.30pm on a wide range of tasty fare at sensible prices. The Cafe specialises in Vegetarian food.

There are fifteen standard bedrooms, none of which are ensuite but they have colour television, cable TV and a generously supplied hostess tray. All sorts of people come to stay here because it does feel like a home from home and has no petty restrictions. It is central for anyone working in the city and further afield. The visitor on a discovery of Bristol will be pleased to find that not only is it close to the centre but to the elegant Clifton area as well. It is close to the Suspension Bridge, built by Isambard Kingdom Brunel and still one of the world's great engineering feats. Another example of his work is the Iron ship, the SS Great Britain which one can board in the docks. There are many good walks on the outskirts of the city and golf courses not too far off.

USEFUL INFORMATION

- OPEN: All year

- WHEELCHAIR ACCESS: Cafe only
- GARDEN: Yes
- CREDIT CARDS: All major cards
- ACCOMMODATION: 15 rms not ensuite
- RATES: £25sgl £35dbl

- CAFE: Super, very large breakfast Open to public 7.30am-7.30pm
- VEGETARIAN: Specialises
- LICENSED: No
- CHILDREN: Yes
- PETS: Guide dogs only

THE SWALLOW ROYAL HOTEL
College Green, Bristol
BS1 5TA

Tel:0117 925 5100
Fax: 0117 925 9951

****Luxury 2AA Rosettes for Food
in Palm Court Restaurant

Swallow Royal Hotel is a splendid example of Victorian architecture and one can only be thankful that it was not completely destroyed by German Bombers in World War II. Much damage was done and that has led to the rebuilding which has kept the stately mid-19th century air and at the same time allowed discreet modernisation. It could not be in a better position in Bristol, right in the centre, next to the Cathedral, overlooking College Green. The handsome interior, with its marble floor, chandeliers, shining brass and polished mahogany spells out a welcome that both cares for the traveller and at the same time with a degree of friendliness that is sometimes missing in a big hotel. To reach the Swallow, the nearest Motorway is the M4/junction 19. At the end of M32 keep right and follow signs for the City Centre. The hotel has a private car park.

There are two hundred and forty two luxuriously appointed bedrooms with twenty four hour room service and a full valet service. All are equipped with colour television and direct dial telephones. Several suites overlook the inner harbour. The public rooms are equally gracious and superbly furnished. One feels as if one has stepped back in time whilst taking Afternoon Tea in the graceful drawing room. Many people gravitate towards the Cocktail Bar for a pre-dinner drink and to meet friends or merely unwind after the exigencies of the day before going into dine in the award winning glass-roofed Palm Court, or relaxing in the less formal Terrace Restaurant overlooking Cathedral Square. Wherever you choose to eat the food is superb, prepared by experienced and talented chefs. The wine list is extensive and has half and full bottles from around the world. There is a Public Bar as well and here Bar Snacks and lighter meals are available every day. The Swallow has excellent conference facilities, on four floors, brilliantly planned and well equipped with state-of-the art technology, but have traditional comfortable furniture. A satellite link gives access into world-wide conventions. The Swallow Leisure Club has a spectacular pool, spa facilities, a fitness room and beauty salon. There is good golf nearby and Bristol has excellent theatres.

USEFUL INFORMATION

- OPEN: All year

- WHEELCHAIR ACCESS: Yes
- GARDEN: No
- CREDIT CARDS: All major cards
- ACCOMMODATION: 242 rooms
  & suites
- RATES: £135 sgl &
  £155dbl pp.pn. B&B

- RESTAURANT: Award winning
  Palm Court Restaurant &
  The Terrace Restaurant
- VEGETARIAN: Yes
- BAR FOOD: Yes in Public Bar
- LICENSED: Full On
- CHILDREN: If prepared for a
  formal atmosphere
- PETS: Guide dogs only

AARON LODGE
425 Fishponds Road
Fishponds
Bristol
BS16 3AP

Tel/Fax: 0117 965 3132

If you have business in Bristol or you have come here to explore this fascinating historic city, you will find that Aaron Lodge in Fishponds is an ideal place in which to stay for several reasons. It is conveniently situated close to the city centre with its new shopping mall at Lodge Causeway. Isambard Kingdon Brunel's famous ship the SS Britain is moored not far away and so too is his fabulous Suspension Bridge which swings across the Avon Gorge leading into Clifton and on to the city centre. The Maritime Museum interests people enormously and there are many art galleries. There are theatres and concert halls as well as cinemas. The waterfront attracts thousands of visitors and here you can find floating restaurants, good hostelries and a lot of fun.

The well built Victorian house has light, spacious rooms and off street parking - a great boon in Bristol. Mr and Mrs Palmer are the resident owners and they work hard to ensure the comfort of their guests. Every room is tastefully furnished and decorated with the emphasis on warmth and comfort. In the Dining Room you will be served a substantial traditional full English breakfast or a lighter Continental meal if that is your preference. Evening meals are available upon request although many people enjoy sampling Bristol's many eateries offering all kinds of food from around the world.

There are nine guest bedrooms, with two doubles, two singles, two twin-bedded rooms, all ensuite, and a further twin and two single rooms sharing a bathroom. All the rooms have colour television with remote control, and satellite TV as well as a well-supplied hostess tray. Aaron Lodge has a residential licence which allows one to enjoy a drink in the evenings at the end of a busy day.

USEFUL INFORMATION

- OPEN: All year
- WHEELCHAIR ACCESS: No
- GARDEN: Off street parking
- CREDIT CARDS: None taken
- ACCOMMODATION: 9 rooms
  most ensuite
- RATES:- Dbl./Twin £36 to £45 prpn.
  Single £23 to £29.
  All with breakfast. Reductions for children
  on application. Discounts for block bookings.

- DINING ROOM: Full English breakfast
- VEGETARIAN: Catered for

- LICENSED: Residential
- CHILDREN: Welcome
- PETS: No

THE ANCHOR INN
Ham Green
North Somerset

Tel: 01275 372253

This latest addition to the Upton Inns Group continues to uphold the fine standards established by Mike and Joyce Upton over the last twenty years. Its nautically-themes interior offers two bars and a separate dining area, while the cosy lounge delights in the warmth of a real open fire.
Ideally situated, from the front The Anchor overlooks that quintessentially English scene, the village cricket ground while the back garden, (including the children's play area) offers splendid views across the valley. Diners will appreciate the inn's good value, down to earth pub fare, from sandwiches and jacket potatoes to hot meals. A 10oz rib-eye steak will set you back just £6.50, or choose from home-made Steak and Kidney Pie at £3.75 and the ever popular Sunday lunch at just £4.95. There is also a Children's menu, as well as a selection of salads and ploughman's. For the beer buffs a great pint of draught Bass or Courage Best awaits you.

USEFUL INFORMATION

- OPEN: All day every day Food: 12-2.30pm & 6-9.30pm
- WHEELCHAIR ACCESS: Yes
- GARDEN: Yes & Play area
- CREDIT CARDS: None taken
- CHILDREN: Welcome. Play area & Menu

- BAR FOOD: Great value, wide range
- VEGETARIAN: Always a choice

- LICENSED: Full On
- PETS: Well behaved on leads

ARCHES HOTEL
132 Cotham Brow
Cotham, Bristol
BS6 6AE
Tel/Fax: 0117 924 7398
ETB 1 Crown Commended

Arches Hotel an early Victorian house built in the Georgian style and set back off the road, providing quiet, comfortable surroundings just one hundred yards from the main A38. Inside a Victorian stained glass window illuminates the hall and some of the original mouldings have survived. In the dining room the original window shutters were discovered behind hardboard and have been restored to working order. This all adds to the ambience of the non-smoking Arches Hotel, owned and run by Mr & Mrs Lambert. There are nine, centrally heated bedrooms decorated individually in subtle shades of pink, apricot and green.
Every room has a wash basin, remote control colour television, hairdryers and a hostess tray with herb teas on request. Two bedrooms have an en-suite shower room. An added touch is the placing of an Ioniser in every room which removes dust and pollen to aid a good nights sleep in the comfortable beds. Included in the tariff is a Continental Breakfast. In addition there is a choice of six cooked breakfasts with traditional, vegetarian and vegan tastes catered for. No evening meals are provided as there are many diverse, traditional and vegetarian restaurants within a two to ten minute walk.

USEFUL INFORMATION

- OPEN: All year except Xmas & New Year

- WHEELCHAIR ACCESS: No
- CREDIT CARDS: All major cards
- ACCOMMODATION: 9 rooms 2 ensuite
- RATES: From: sgl £22.50 dbl. £39.50 twin £42
  Family £52.50 all inc. continental breakfast

- DINING ROOM: Continental Breakfast inc. in tariff + 6 choices of cooked breakfast from £2-£3.25
- VEGETARIAN: Yes & Vegan
- NON-SMOKING HOTEL
- LICENSED: No

- CHILDREN: Welcome
- PETS: With prior notice

THE CAMBRIDGE ARMS
Cold Harbour Road
Redlined, Bristol
BS6 7JS
Tel 01179 735754

Just 200 yards from the famous Whiteladies Road and close to the hotels, shopping area and five minutes from the centre of Bristol the Cambridge Arms is one of Bristol's most popular pubs. It is surrounded by famous listed buildings but has a unique quality of its own. The proprietor also owns the excellent hostelry, The Prince of Wales, in Westbury on Trym in which he has a Royal theme. This ideal he has copied at the Cambridge, with maps and memorabilia pertinent to the university. He has a knack of creating atmospheric and happy establishments and this is certainly true of The Cambridge which is run by Val and Rod Duckett. The sporting instinct is very apparent here with football, cricket and local charity events. The pub attracts a wide range of people, both for its ambience and its excellent Real Ales and wines. On Monday nights there is always live music from local bands. Every day there is a good range of traditional pub fare with a touch of international cuisine added to it. The emphasis on home cooking comes over every day, but is probably strongest on Sundays when it would be very hard to fault the traditional Sunday roast, complete with Yorkshire Pudding, crisp roast potatoes and a choice of fresh vegetables. Children will be happy here but in the garden only, where there are slides, a Wendy house, climbing frame, bouncy castle and an undercover barbecue area.

USEFUL INFORMATION

- OPEN: Mon - Sat 11-11pm
  Normal Sunday hours
- WHEELCHAIR ACCESS: Yes
- GARDEN: Large, with BBQ area
- CREDIT CARDS: All major cards
- CHILDREN: Garden Only

- BAR FOOD: Home cooked
  Sunday lunch
- VEGETARIAN: Always available
-
- LICENSED: Full on
- PETS: Dogs on leads

THE DUNDRY INN
Church Road
Dundry
Bristol
Tel: 01179 641722

No one coming to Bristol should be allowed to leave without visiting Dundry, a well known beauty spot. It looks right out over Bristol and is dominated by the tower of the church which was built with money donated by the Merchant Ventures of Bristol and provided a Navigational point for ships in the Bristol Channel and those entering the safety of the City Docks. Legend has it that The Dundry Inn is as old as the tower which seems highly probable, although there is no firm evidence to support the theory. What is fact is that this pub is everything one dreams of. Its age gives it a wonderful feeling of stability, the walls seemed to have soaked in the history of the centuries and the local people who use it are not so different from their ancestors - maybe in dress and hairstyles, but the conversation is still topical, fun to listen to and, for the stranger, an instant welcome. Real ale is of prime importance and beautifully kept, as is all the beer. The food is good, wholesome pub fare with a range of dishes that allows for everyone's palate. Every day, in addition to the general menu, there are several very tasty daily specials, cooked freshly and sensibly priced. Children are very welcome if they are accompanied by well behaved parents. There is a family room but, in the summer months, the large garden is particularly popular with parents and their children.

USEFUL INFORMATION

- OPEN: All day

- WHEELCHAIR ACCESS: Yes
- GARDEN: Large, with seating
- CREDIT CARDS: All major cards
  except AMEX

- BAR FOOD: Wide range of good
  wholesome food
- VEGETARIAN: Always available
- LICENSED: Full on
- CHILDREN: Welcome

FAILAND INN
Clevedon Road
Failand
NR Bristol

Tel: 01275 392220

Just fifteen minutes from Bristol City Centre, this lovely old Victorian coaching inn oozes character and charm. There are two main bars and a large garden which seats up to forty people and is perfect for small parties, wedding receptions etc. The extensive menu offers everything you'd hope for from an Upton Inn, plus an ever changing specials board featuring such delights as a medallion of pork fillet with a provencal sauce, new potatoes and vegetables at £5.95 or salmon steak in a white wine and tarragon sauce. The wonderful sweets board meanwhile, promises raspberry pavlova, fruits of the forest, cheesecake or banoffee pie, all home-made by the resident chef. The traditional roast on Sundays at £5.95 is very popular. This is a friendly, efficiently run hostelry keeping up the high standards of Upton Inns which Mike and Joyce Upton have fostered over twenty years.

USEFUL INFORMATION

- OPEN: All day every day Mon-Sat 11am-11pm
  Sunday 12-10.30pm
- BAR FOOD: Great value home-cooked fare
- WHEELCHAIR ACCESS: Yes
- GARDEN: Yes
- CREDIT CARDS: None taken

- PETS: Well behaved on leads
- VEGETARIAN: Always a choice
- LICENSED: Full On
- CHILDREN: Welcome

HEATHERLEYS
93 Lower Redland Road
Redland
Bristol
B56 6SW
Tel: 0117 9744497

Heatherley's is to be found in a rank of shops dating back to the turn of the century in an area known as 'Redland Village'. It is a friendly restaurant owned by Linda James who runs it with a willing and efficient staff. The emphasis is obviously on the provision of good food; you will not be disappointed in the dishes that come to table, but one of the most memorable things about Heatherley's is its beautiful toilet which always invites comment. Customers who visit first always send their dining companion upstairs to see for themselves! The restaurant still has its original frontage and you sit in an attractive room with a rear window that looks over the pretty garden. When the restaurant opened locals were wary about the noise that late night diners might make but they themselves are now regulars and delight in the exciting culinary addition to the area. The menu offers half a dozen starters and eight or so main courses. The sweets are delectable - try the white chocolate cheesecake with blueberry topping if you get the opportunity. At lunch time you can pop in for something as simple as a jacket potato or a baguette or something slightly more sophisticated like tagliatelli with smoked salmon and spinach and cream cheese tart. The wine list is well chosen and like everything else at Heatherley's, it is sensibly priced.

USEFUL INFORMATION

- OPEN: Lunch Tues.-Sun 12-2pm Dinner Tues.-Sat 7-11pm
- RESTAURANT: Delicious food at sensible prices
- WHEELCHAIR ACCESS: Yes. Upstairs toilet
- GARDEN: Not at present
- CREDIT CARDS: All major cards except AMEX

- PETS: No
- VEGETARIAN: Choice
- LICENSED: Restaurant
- CHILDREN: Welcome

HENBURY LODGE
Station Road, Henbury
Bristol BS10 7QQ
Tel: 0117 950 2615 Fax: 0117 950 9532
AA Rosette for Food   AA***RAC ETB ****

Aptly described as the 'Country Hotel in the City', Henbury Lodge is in close proximity to the Centre of Bristol but lies in the heart of an area of outstanding natural beauty. There are two highly regarded golf courses nearby and there is trout fishing at Blagdon and Chew Valley lakes as well as salmon fishing on the river Wye. Within walking distance of the Hotel special sites of historical interest include Blaise Castle and Mansion House, a 12th century village church and Blaise Hamlet, a unique collection of 10 cottages designed in 1810 by John Nash the world renowned architect. Henbury Lodge dates back to 1600 since when there have been various additions culminating in the conversion during the 1760's to its present Palladian Georgian Mansion Style. It is a small family run hotel which prides itself on its' friendly service and warm welcome. In addition to offering a personal and efficient service they also provide luxurious surroundings with all the standards you could expect from a three star establishment, including sauna and solarium. There are 20 beautifully appointed bedrooms, television, direct dial telephones and generously supplied hostess trays are there for your comfort and enjoyment. The restaurant has recently been awarded an AA rosette for food. Henbury Lodge caters for weddings, parties and functions for up to thirty five for a sit down meal, or seventy for a stand up buffet. Without doubt it is a happy place in which to stay.

USEFUL INFORMATION

- OPEN: All year
- WHEELCHAIR ACCESS: Yes
- GARDEN: Yes
- LICENSED: Restaurant & Residential
- CHILDREN: Welcome
- RATES: Mon/Thurs.Dbl.£88.50.prpn
  Sgl.£78. Fri./ Sun. Dbl.£62.prpn. Sgl.£41. Children £8. Sharing with adult.

- RESTAURANT: Award winning/non-residents
- VEGETARIAN: Always a choice
- CREDIT CARDS: All major cards
- ACCOMMODATION: 20 ensuite rooms
- PETS: By arrangement

HOWARDS
1A-2A Avon Crescent
Hotwells , Bristol
BS1 6XQ
Tel: 0117 9262921   Fax: 0117 9255585
AA Good Food. Egon Ronay. Michelin

Howard's is a restaurant with a great reputation which has been built by Chris Howard since he first opened the doors in premises in Kingsdown in the seventies. Already successful, his reputation grew in stature when he moved to Avon Crescent which is not only pleasanter but is easy to park - a definite plus in Bristol. Furnished and appointed in a charming, relaxed manner it is a delightful place to eat. The menu is a mixture of modern English and French. Chris Howard is an inspired chef who has an instinctive regard when it comes to flavouring sauces. Imagine fried king scallops in a puff pastry case or deep fried crab pancakes with tomato and chilli sauce as a starter. Then one might have lamb perfectly cooked, nicely pink and extremely tender, or breast of guineas fowl, stuffed with crab and sweetcorn mousse. One doubts if you would have room for dessert but if there is a little corner, the desserts are delectable. The wine list is well chosen with a choice of anything from the Napa Valley to France. It is always advisable to book but at weekends it is essential. Smoking is permitted. There is no problem with disabled access and above all dining at Howard's is value for money whether you come for the set three course lunch at £13 or dinner from Monday to Friday at £15 or choose the a la carte or blackboard specials..

USEFUL INFORMATION

- OPEN: Lunch: Mon-Friday12-2pm Dinner: Mon.-Sat 7-11pm
- RESTAURANT: English/French cuisine
- VEGETARIAN: Blackboard choice daily
- LICENSED: Restaurant
- CREDIT CARDS: Visa/Master/AMEX/Diners

- WHEELCHAIR ACCESS: Yes
- GARDEN: No
- PETS: No
- CHILDREN: Welcome

Restaurant Du Gourmet
43 Whiteladies Road
Bristol

Tel: 01179 736230
Fax: 01179 237394

For twenty six years this attractive restaurant with an elegant frontage has been under the same professional and sympathetic management of Serge Francolini and his partner Lucien Parussina. In all these years they have had the talented and creative support of the same chef. This must be quite a record and no doubt accounts for the unchanging standards of The Restaurant du Gourmet which is not only renowned in Bristol but has a world-wide following. These two restaurateurs are accomplished chefs in their own right and trained in Switzerland. They are more than capable of taking over in the kitchen and frequently do, but what they enjoy most is being in the front of house, caring for their clientele and delighting in the pleasure the food brings to diners. It is not only food that is good here; the wine list is extra special. There are some 120 wines on the list, each carefully selected. Frequently the restaurant hosts wine tasting. The menu is a pleasure to read and the choice of thirteen starters makes it difficult to decide. Each dish is tempting. An equal number of dishes for the main course makes the choice even more difficult. Perhaps one would start with a Salad de Concombre au fromage de Chevre, French style cucumber salad with goat's cheese and walnuts and follow that with Filet Mignon de Porc Parisienne - slices of pork tenderloin, white wine sauce, diced bacon, shallots, mushrooms. The delicious desserts are equally tempting. This is a memorable restaurant.

USEFUL INFORMATION

- OPEN: Mon.-Fri.; 12-2pm & 7-11.30pm Sat; 7-12.30am
- RESTAURANT: Wide choice plus daily specials
- WHEELCHAIR ACCESS: Level & Toilets
- GARDEN: No
- CREDIT CARDS: All major cards

- VEGETARIAN: Always available
- LICENSED: Restaurant
- CHILDREN: Very Welcome

THE ROYAL HOTEL
28 Gloucester Road
Avonmouth, Bristol   BS11 9AD
Tel: 0117 9822847   Fax: 0117 9592236

Gone are the days when The Royal Hotel served the needs of the docks from manual workers to Sea Captains and their crews of the transatlantic liners sailing for America. It was not unknown for passengers to refresh themselves here before embarking as well. Built at the end of 1897 it has always catered for an itinerant population but at the same time never wavered from its popularity as the watering hole of locals. This is very apparent today when you find the bars full of local characters who add to the appeal this hostelry. Pub fare is served every day and can be anything from steak and chips to a freshly cut sandwich. The bedrooms, some of which are ensuite, all have television. There is fun to be had in the two bars with Happy Hours on Monday, Tuesday and Thursday between 5pm and 8pm and on Sundays from 1pm-6pm. Play traditional pub games including skittles or just sit back and enjoy the friendly chatter whilst drinking well kept ale. You will find The Royal Hotel five miles outside Bristol and about half a mile from Junction 18 on the M5. The Railway station is three minutes walk from the hotel making it very convenient for seeing the attractions of Bristol without having to use your car. This is an unpretentious busy locals public house, with all the bawdy rancour and humour you would expect to find in such an establishment, to stay here is an unforgettable experience, and not for the faint hearted.

USEFUL INFORMATION

- OPEN: All day, every day 12 noon-11pm

- WHEELCHAIR ACCESS: In bars only.
- BEER GARDEN: New in 1998
- CREDIT CARDS: None taken
- ACCOMMODATION: Yes, some ensuite rooms
- RATES: £25pp p.n.

- RESTAURANT: Good pub fare. Great value for money
- VEGETARIAN: No
- BAR FOOD: Many Daily Specials
- LICENSED: Full On
- CHILDREN: Welcome
- PETS: No

ST VINCENT ROCKS HOTEL
Sion Hill, Clifton
Bristol   BS8 4BB

Tel: 0117 973 9251 Fax: 0117 923 8139

The first thing one sees as one crosses Isambard Kingdom Brunel's magnificent Suspension Bridge into Bristol, is St Vincent Rocks Hotel. It dates back to the early 19th century and is part of a traditional Regency terrace. It is very conveniently situated for anyone who has business in Bristol and is an excellent base for those wanting to enjoy a holiday or a break which includes the exploration of Bristol. Here there is a wealth of history, fine architecture, a stunning cathedral, museums, art galleries, theatres, concert halls and an exciting waterfront . A little further afield you can visit Glastonbury Tor, Wells Cathedral and many other places of interest. The hotel has forty six ensuite bedrooms, many of which have views of the Avon Gorge and one room has a stunning four-poster. Every room has direct dial telephone, colour television, radio/alarm and a generously supplied hospitality tray. There is limited guest parking. The attractive restaurant is open to non-residents and has a reputation for high quality cuisine based on traditional English fare with a Continental influence. The comprehensive wine list has a fine selection of wines from around the world and at sensible prices.

USEFUL INFORMATION

- OPEN: All year
- WHEELCHAIR ACCESS: No
- GARDEN: No
- CREDIT CARDS: All major cards
- ACCOMMODATION: 46 ensuite rooms
- CHILDREN: Welcome
- RATES: Dbl./Twin £85. Single £75. Both room only on week days .Fri to Sun inclusive Dbl./Twin Two persons £80. Prpn. B/B. Single £49. B/B. Special break prices on application.

- RESTAURANT: High quality cuisine
- VEGETARIAN: Always a choice
- BAR FOOD: Light meals
- LICENSED: Full On
- PETS: No
- PARKING: Limited

RUDGLEIGH INN
Easton in Gordano
NR Bristol

Tel: 01275 372363

The longest established of the Upton Inns, the Rudgleigh has a well deserved reputation for its fine food and warm welcome. An extensive menu includes at least ten daily specials and a variety of hot and cold food, all prepared on the premises. The Sunday lunch at £5.25 is always popular and along with the special children's menu can be enjoyed in the large garden during the summer months.

This traditional-style pub also includes the trademark Upton's garden room seating up to 50 and caters for families with children. Perfect for watching the cricket in summer while working your way through the Rudgleigh's large selection of real ales. Especially popular is the Marstons Pedigree or the large selection of wines from around the world.

USEFUL INFORMATION

- OPEN: All day every day

- WHEELCHAIR ACCESS: Yes
- GARDEN: Large
- CREDIT CARDS: None taken
- CHILDREN: Welcome & Menu

- BAR FOOD: Daily specials and a range of hot/cold food
- VEGETARIAN: Yes

- LICENSED: Full On
- PETS: Well behaved on leads

Apsley House	Bath	81
Bath Lodge	Norton St Philip	82
Bath Spa Hotel	Bath	83
Bell Inn	Buckland Dinham	101
Combe Grove Manor	Monkton Combe	84
Cottage Garden	Compton Dando	85
Eagle House	Bathford	86
Eden Vale	Beckington	87
Frome Way	Radstock	88
Green Lane House	Hinton Charterhouse	89
Haydon House	Bath	101
Hinton Grange	Hinton	90
Holly Lodge	Bath	91
Homewood Park	Hinton Charterhouse	92
Irondale House	Rode	102
La Bisalta	Frome	102
Limpey Stoke Hotel	Lower Stoke	93
Lodge (The)	Standerwick	94
Manor Lodge	Keynsham	103
Paradise House	Bath	95
Priory House	Bath	96
Rudloe Hall	Box	97
Ston Easton Park	Bath	98
Woolpack Inn	Beckington	100
Woolverton House	Bath	99

Chapter Two:
The Circus is Always in Town
From Bath To Frome

A city of unity and architectural beauty, on a scale you will not find in many other places in England. The approach to Bath promises much, the whole place sitting most comfortably in its gap between the hills, marking the southern end of the Cotswold Hills, and the break between Bristol and the Wiltshire towns to the east. The temptation is to take you straight there, and to revel in the history of the Romans, the Baths, buns, biscuits and Jane Austen; Beau Nash, Ralph Allen and John Wood, as well as a Circus which is always in town.

Unlike Bristol, Bath will surely never expand much from where it is. Even if it were to spread to the east, for example, Bradford-on-Avon will never submit to becoming a suburb of anywhere, it has too much history and identity of its own. Geographically Bath is a unity too, and if it were to try and infiltrate the countryside of Wessex, the surrounding hills would provide an effective barrier. So we cannot say that the whole of this chapter is about Bath or those that live from it, and there are other places, particularly amongst the southern Cotswolds, which you will wish to visit on your way to the main attraction.

Coming south out of Gloucestershire on the A46, a right turn just over the border will take you to **HILLESLEY**. The village is sheltered under the edge of the escarpment of the hills, but a trip up onto them will take you straight to somewhere from which you can see much of what lies to the north, as well as a great deal in any direction you choose to take next. The SOMERSET MONUMENT was not named in order to make yet another county claim to these 'in between' lands, but rather to commemorate the courage in action of Lord Somerset, who served with Wellington at Waterloo. The railings near the top of this thin grey needle of a tower declare that it can be climbed. Views from here reach to the main body of the Cotswolds above Wotton-Under-Edge, and on to much of Somerset in the south. Nearest the monument in this direction is the village of **HAWKESBURY**, with a lovely church paid for with local wool money, giving it a clear allegiance to the Cotswolds region.

Following the lanes a little further south will bring you to **HORTON**, with the National Trust property of HORTON COURT. In the gabled style so familiar to the north, even the stone roof tiles of this Norman Hall look a much lighter grey than those of Tetbury and the rest of the Cotswolds, without going away from the common rough-edged style which lasts for centuries, yet looks ready to crumble into dust at any moment. The Court lies east of the rest of Horton village, and nearer the A46, which we must return to briefly so that we do not miss what lies between it and the

Wiltshire border. The village of **DUNKIRK** has a name which might well catch your attention, but this one reflects the influence of Flemish weavers rather than the events of the Second World War.

To the east of the main road there are two villages, not so different in size as their names of **GREAT BADMINTON** and **LITTLE BADMINTON** might suggest. Neither is this area's claim to fame though, for that lies with BADMINTON HOUSE and the THREE DAY EVENTS (horse trials) held in its park each Spring. This is the oldest competition of its kind in the world, and has a reputation of being an extremely exacting test for both horse and rider.

So near to Wiltshire, Badminton is another of the great houses built in the 17th century, with some of its 15,000 acres landscaped by Capability Brown, who seems to have spent a good deal of his life in the region just to the east. Just as there are two villages, so Badminton has two claims to sporting fame, as the title of the game of the infuriating shuttlecock also comes from here. The grounds are quite superb, and the House too, but you will have to check with local Tourist Information (Bath or Chippenham) about opening times, as they are not always accessible to the public.

Back on the main A46, the next two villages which are signposted will raise a smile. **LITTLE SODBURY** must be an excellent place in which to bring up children, while **OLD SODBURY** should be a great retirement destination. Naturally the real explanation of the place-names is not quite so entertaining, as 'Soppa' was apparently a Saxon important enough to have three settlements named after him. The third is **CHIPPING SODBURY**, which although by far the largest, is also the youngest.

Having said that, Chipping was a market place on the main London to Bristol road (via Oxford) by the early 13th century. The centre of Chipping Sodbury is something of a mixture, with signs of prosperity in buildings from both the 15th and 18th centuries, reflecting its placement between the wool towns to the north and the cloth towns to the east. There has been much construction on the outskirts in recent decades too, but the oldest site in the area is the earthwork of SODBURY HILLFORT. Unlike many of Wessex's Iron Age hillforts, this one remained in use right up until Saxon times, and had a brief revival when Edward IV camped his forces here on the way to the Battle of Tewkesbury which effectively marked the end of the Wars of The Roses. The ramparts are still very visible and show just how long this sort of defence can last for. These days this is a good place for a circular walk and some fresh hill air, but such places do have an atmosphere all of their own, empty now, but once full of men taking a last night's rest before a battle which would change their lives, and in many cases end them.

Any further south and the A46 becomes entangled with the southern sections of the walkers' Cotswold Way (which has taken in the Somerset Monument, Horton Court and Sodbury Hillfort), but a more solid thoroughfare runs west to east; the M4.

It does not take long to get away from this busiest of modern Wessex roads, and the lay-bys and turn offs full of cars parked for the day while their owners save fuel by doubling up for a trip to work, mostly in London.

The Cotswold Way then heads south west, straying far enough from the main road to approach DYRHAM PARK (0117 937 2501). This massively impressive National Trust House is big enough to fill a large section of the otherwise tree lined horizon. Sometimes modern terraces or detached houses have been built with access to both back and front, usually so that garages or car parking areas can be reached without going right around to the front door. Occasionally the back door becomes the more regularly used, and the other entrance becomes virtually redundant as the whole layout of the house becomes reversed. Dyrham is the grandest archetype of this you are ever likely to see. Originally built to the desires of William II's Secretary for War, William Blathwayt, this was unintentionally planned for in advance by the use of two separate architects, who each built one front of the house, only ten years apart.

The first to be built is quite a regular affair (west front), built with local stone, while the second is much more ornate and unorthodox, with Tuscan pillars and a huge Orangery. The designer of the second stage was an assistant to Sir Christopher Wren, and he also planned the gardens, with fountains and cascades on this, the eastern side of the house. By the beginning of the 19th century the landscaping was a little out of date, and the Gloucester to Bath road had been moved. The solution, get Repton in to design a whole new set of gardens to the west and simply make the front the back, if you see what I mean.

The inside of the House is worth some exploration, simply because hardly anything has been removed or added since the late 17th century. The same can be said of the grounds really; Dyrham means 'deer enclosure' in Anglo Saxon, and there are still fallow deer roaming the park. A climb up from the house, so that it lies 130 feet across its width in the foreground below you, gives some views right across to the Welsh Mountains in the far west.

Things have certainly changed more in the village of **DYRHAM** itself since its most famous hour. Whether King Arthur was a 6th century defender of Wessex or not (see chapter five and Glastonbury for much more) he was probably not here for one of the definitive Saxon victories which tightened their hold on Wessex. Here in 577 Cirencester, Gloucester and Bath were handed over to the invaders and three of the Kings of the Britons were killed in battle. Amazing how such a quiet place, with a sprinkling of 17th and 18th century stone cottages, should have been the site of a crucial victory in the past, which finally divided the Britons in Wales from those in Cornwall, their last two strongholds. Another case of history being covered completely by passing time, something that is very unlikely to occur in the future at our next stopping place.

It is impossible to get much nearer to the seven hills around **BATH** (Tourist Information 01225 477101) without falling under the influence of what must be the most unique city in Britain. Your first view of it is likely to be from above, with the brightness and quantity of local Bath Stone (and its modern crushed limestone equivalent) dazzling on a sunny day, and looking comfortable on a grey one, the whole gorgeous collection nestled snugly in between the green slopes which surround it. The architecture of the whole city centre, which is more residential than most, is compelling, unified and tantalising, and made all the more fascinating when you realise that it was designed to be like this by a small band of those who lived here in the 18th century. There are more than three thousand Georgian houses in Bath, all built between 1712 and 1789.

You may grow to love the terraces and crescents of square lined, pale stone buildings with their columns, stone carvings and panelled windows, or you may find it all a bit claustrophobic and relentless after a while, but either way you will never forgets these streets. Bath is not an easy place to get to know thoroughly, or to summarise satisfactorily in a few sentences, but what is here now, as well as what has been in the past are worth hearing about and experiencing, as there is, quite literally, nowhere else like this.

From the Peat Moors Centre near Glastonbury (chapter five) to the Iron Age Homestead near Dorchester (chapter eleven) this book has many examples of that often compelling idea of the 'Living Museum'. Outside the area covered in this volume, but just to the north of here, many of the Cotswold villages, from Guiting Power to Lower Slaughter, Chedworth to Bisley, have so little added to them that they too are a sort of living monument to life in centuries gone by. But none of this has the scale or grandeur of Bath, which is a museum lived in by many more than any other in Britain. In its entirety Bath has been declared a WORLD HERITAGE SITE by UNESCO since 1987. This is not to say that Bath is only an exhibit, where people live out the existence of the Romans or the 18th century gentry for the benefit of Tourists. On the contrary, Bath's tourism is amazingly inconspicuous and low key for such a beautiful place, although its use of premium rate information lines would suggest that the city still expects its visitors to be of a high calibre, at least in terms of disposable income.

I first got to know the city when I spent the best part of a year working here. My job entailed much travelling around Bath, finding individual addresses, and hopefully those who lived within them. Every day I did this there was at least one occasion on which I found a new building, or row of houses, which threatened to take my breath away. It is amazing how small you can feel walking up to the front door of one of these residences, be it in the streets around The Circus, or one of the terraces up in Lansdown. Yet who lives in all these glorious houses? Many of them are divided into flats, which is not apparent until you notice that there are three or four doorbells by that imposing front entrance. The inhabitants are ordinary, as much as any city's can be called such without any hint of uniformity. The houses may all look the same, and the number of dwellings effectively tripled by slicing them into flats, but despite the appearances there are students, shop assistants, civil servants and musicians, Bohemians, recluses, and all other varieties of modern woman and man living behind the historic facades of light Bath Stone. Yet in many other towns just one such building would be singled out for attention, made into a museum or opened for visitors, to show what a prosperous and elegant past the place had.

So Bath's population live in history, rather than parcelling it up for those who come to visit, but even this is nowhere near the whole story. There are very few Elizabethan buildings left in the city, and even less of what came before that, but an Anglo Saxon King was crowned in Bath, and this was *Aquae Sulis*, a holiday resort for the Romans in Britain. Sulis was a Celtic God rather than Roman, and the springs, which bring a quarter of a million gallons of hot water to the surface each and every day at the constant temperature of 116 degrees Fahrenheit (46.5 Centigrade), had been discovered long before the birth of Christ. Let's have a look at the most popular of the legends about the beginnings of the city, recognised in the carvings of acorns and oak leaves found everywhere from the houses of The Circus to the front of the Grand Pump Room.

The Roman Baths and Bath Abbey

The story has it that young Bladud was a handsome lad, son of a Celtic King of the region over 2,500 years ago. With maturity he developed less becoming looks, not due to acne, but leprosy. Exiling himself to rural pastimes, he became a swineherd. One day the pigs started to show sores too, and poor Bladud was horrified. The pigs caught sight of a nice patch of acorns, and seconds later were cavorting in a warm spring; from then on they started to recover. Bladud bathed too, and was cured. Returning to his heritage he then built a palace over the healing waters of the Springs, and so Bath was born. Bladud went on to be a master of many sciences, but apparently not that of unpowered flight. Unlike Brother Elmer of Malmesbury (see chapter six) he did more than break his legs when his homemade wings failed, and the springs could not save him this time. Still, it could have been worse, he could have experienced problems with his granddaughters if he had lived, as his son went by the name of Lear, a King whose family problems are so tragically celebrated in Shakespeare's play.

The Romans arrived to find something that was a very pleasant reminder of home, amongst the misty islands and swamps of Somerset that were not all as romantic as Avalon, especially if you were trudging in full armour, expecting slingshot to rain down on you at any moment. They took on the local Celtic traditions to the extent of dedicating the Baths to Sulis, the Celtic God of healing, as well as Minerva, their own equivalent. I have seen some fairly unlikely looking doctors in my time, but the likeness of Sulis, as interpreted by the Romans, beats the lot. With Gorgon like snake hair, staring eyes, and a curved moustache looking as waxed as stone can, he is quite disconcerting; perhaps hypnosis was his main healing technique. You can make your own judgement at the ROMAN BATHS MUSEUM (01225 477785) in the first version of the 18th century Pump Room. The Roman Baths lasted four hundred years, double the time so far enjoyed by their successors.

This is a good place at which to start your visit to modern Bath, not just because these are amongst the oldest remains. The Baths and Pump Room are themselves in the grounds of another of the city's historic buildings, BATH ABBEY (01225 330289). Bath's Abbey does not have the age or length of history of those at Tewkesbury and Sherborne, or the awesome antiquity of what remains at Malmesbury, but it is a brighter building than some of these, and in its simple perpendicular style has a grace and elegant atmosphere all its own, especially considered in its setting.

The present Abbey only just made it in time to be decimated by the Dissolution of the Monasteries in 1539. There was an older building, in which King Edgar was crowned in the year 973, and the Benedictine Monks had much power in Saxon Bath. Bath declined steadily as a religious centre in the 13th and 14th centuries, so that churchmen could only dream of better days. One did so more literally than most, and the figures of those climbing to heaven depicted in stone on the present building come from the dream vision of Bishop King, who had the Abbey completely rebuilt at the beginning of the 16th century. Work was barely finished, and the Bishop in his grave, when King Henry VIII's agent declared that one of the monks had ten mistresses, and none of the others fewer than eight. I can only assume that the agent's descendants now work for the tabloid press. The Abbey lost all its lead, glass and bells in the stripping by Royal Command which followed upon this contrived scandal, and by the time Elizabeth I visited Bath the building was in a sorry state.

Sir John Harington, god son to the queen, and a man whose descendants must surely have gone on to better sorts of writing, judging by his surname, summed up the situation by suggesting that if the church could not protect its occupants from water coming in from above then how could it hope to save them from the fire below. The rain carried on getting in through the roof a little longer, but repairs were soon made as the 17th century proved a better one than the Abbey's first.

From this time come the solid stone doors, their heraldic designs originally carved as a single piece to fit the arched doorway precisely. There is a compactness about the inside of the Abbey, despite its size, and the long views given by the unusually open Nave, with no divisions to break your line of sight along its entire length. You can quite happily spend an afternoon just looking at the multitude of different memorials in here, including many to those who frequented the nearby Baths at different times, but had to end up here rather than in the Pump Room. Underneath the Kingston Pavements on the south side of the Abbey, you can also visit the BATH ABBEY HERITAGE VAULTS (01225 422462), with artefacts from the whole of the Abbey's history presented in these 18th century cellars.

Where the Abbey is not austere, it does have the expected restraint of furnishing that you will not find in its neighbour the PUMP ROOM (01225 461111 extn 2785), just a few yards further from the edge of the River Avon. To talk about the resurgence in Bath's popularity as a healthy holiday resort, as well as much else, we have to move forward another century to the one that will surely continue to dominate this city's history for the rest of recorded time. 18th century Bath was a phenomenon the like of which has not been seen again in British society. The most respectable men of letters, such as Dr Johnson, Fielding, Pope and Sheridan, Oliver Goldsmith and later Charles Dickens came here to relax and to socialise, to take the waters and to be entertained. Yet just a few decades before women and men cavorted naked together in the open bathing areas, and the Methodist reformer Wesley called the city the Devil's stronghold and headquarters. By the time Bath itself got its most famous literary treatment in the work of one of its least enamoured guests, Jane Austen, the city had already experienced a century of being fashionable. Her dislike for its frippery does not hide the vibrancy Bath still held at the beginning of the 19th century, and by then most of what you see today, minus the cars and other clutter, was already firmly in place throughout the city.

The efforts of a few men dominate the early stages of this relatively rapid rise to long lasting fame and popularity. Considered as a group they make an unlikely mixture; the infamous Beau Nash alongside the humble Ralph Allen, the model for

Fielding's Squire Allworthy in 'Tom Jones', with the unendingly ambitious architect John Wood thrown in for good measure. Yet these men had an immense impact on Bath.

Nash wore a cocked white hat around the city, to show that he took the post of Bath's Master of Ceremonies with a strong mixture of dashing, pride and dedication to a new cause, to add to his long term favourites of gambling and womanising. The hat also helped to give him his unofficial title as the 'King of Bath'. Although he was no architect, so that unlike Wood and Allen there is little of actual substance left to remember him by, this man gave Bath the impetus it needed, before the new phase of building even started. He brought in Bath's new vogue as a centre for genteel manners, but with a decidedly humorous edge. More practically he brought in a new orchestra to the city, and made sure that visitors got good treatment, so that numbers started to increase rapidly. He even had Bath's cab fares regulated, although these were of the Sedan rather than modern Metro variety. At least the surcharge for carrying extra passengers would have seemed more reasonable then, as it was meant so literally!

Nash came to Bath in 1705, and by the time Allen and Wood developed their plans for the use of local Bath Stone to bring a new era into British architecture using the city as a starting point, Nash was already a very famous man, and the city was alive again. The building programme finally started in 1726 with the foundations of Queen Square, carrying on until the end of the century. The idea of bringing Roman designs and shapes into Bath again, but this time interpreted by local designers, and using local materials, was a stroke of genius we must always be grateful for. We will meet the most famous examples as we explore out from the centre, but it is essential to know something of what had happened in the city before you enter the Pump Room, built from 1789 to 1799, some years after Nash's death (he had lived to the age of 86, showing that not all the good, or at least lively, die young).

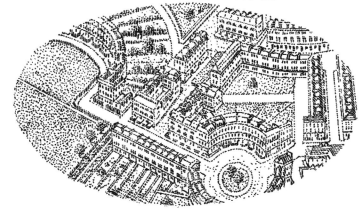

The Georgian Streets of Bath

So Nash never entered this building, but the atmosphere that still presides here today is one he would have relished. Looking down from his stone statue in the Grand Pump Room he is famously a 'bullish' rather than dashing figure. It is as if he is watching to see how the modern visitor looks on a promenade, after following the first part of the daily regime he initiated by rising early and taking three glasses of the iron tinged water (one may be enough for you now though). The furniture, decoration and everything else about these rooms has been perfectly maintained, and they really are a must for any visitor, just as they were then. The atmosphere here is of pure elegance, especially if you get the chance to enjoy a more traditionally flavoured warm drink than the spring water, perhaps accompanied by a Bath bun, and the music of the Pump Room Trio.

The earlier Pump Room, which became too crowded during the 18th century, stands on top of the Roman Baths as we have already said, and is now part of the museum. The complex built by the Romans had more than bathing areas, with spaces for games, exercising and massage. The remaining pools are fascinating, if not quite tempting enough to want to make you take a dip. The atmosphere of the main bath, originally enclosed but now open to the air, is added to in the late summer, when torches are lit in the twilight, the fire rising dramatically from them to cast shapes in the air which appear much more exact in their reflection in the water below. A walk underground to see the hypocaust, the Romans way of heating the complex, gives you some idea of what you are really seeing; a piece of engineering very much ahead of its time, built some 800 years or so before England even had its own common written language. Far from being just a curiosity, these baths are quite humbling in showing how far the civilizations of past empires had advanced two thousand years ago. That our own land was not ready for such things is shown by the fact that the drains clogged with mud soon after the Romans left in 410, and eventually nature took the site back until it was much as Bladud's pigs would have found it. The whole place and story are like something out of Science Fiction, for instance when Charlton Heston stumbles upon the Statue of Liberty lying buried in the sands of a post nuclear beach at the end of the first 'Planet of the Apes' film, suddenly realising that he has gone forward in time, although to a comparatively primitive society. These baths emphasise that civilization does not always advance in straight lines, and so neither does engineering, or applied science.

The Saxons used the ground over the hot water spring as a graveyard, and despite renewed bathing in the KING'S BATH and others in the 17th century (when mixed nakedness was the vogue) the source was not rediscovered until 1755. Even then it was by chance, when workmen were clearing the rubble from the freshly demolished Priory of the Abbey. The 18th century architects of the new Bath, who were so keen to build on Roman lines, were obviously not so worried about restoring any of the original Latin influence, as the remains were largely left untouched until towards the end of the 19th century.

You do not have to go too far from this central collection of buildings to the first of these new building projects to reach completion. You can walk from the Pump Room to QUEEN SQUARE along Westgate, and then Barton Streets, passing the THEATRE ROYAL (01225 448844), which combines the chance to see one of the city's more attractive buildings and to be entertained in the same horseshoe auditorium as so many other visitors have since the 19th century. Major touring companies come here, and the setting is quite splendid, although this was not where Garrick was watched by the multitudes who came to Bath in the 18th century, for the original Theatre Royal is in Orchard Street (now the Freemasons Hall). Yet this was a significant area before the new Theatre was built, as Beau Nash lived, at one time or another, in two of the houses which adjoin it.

The approach to Queen Square is usually busy with traffic, and it is not easy to get a good view of it as a whole without the irritation of cars negotiating its corners and barring your view. It is worth climbing the steep incline and braving the traffic to see the top, north side of the Square, in particular. Even though you do not have much open space to view this terrace from, the effect of the whole is still impressive. Again these are not monuments. It is fascinating to see every day business in solicitors and Building Society offices going on in these gorgeous houses, which do look suitable for the more prosperous side of financial matters to take place in. This was surely a very impressive start, and the six giant central columns, reaching up two complete stories, were enough of a success to convince John Wood that this was a venture worth continuing. Bath Stone had not been a success as a building material until this time; it was considered too soft, and when transported to London proved vulnerable to the acidity of city air. Now a style had been found which made the most of its naturally smooth, pale appearance, in a place where vast quantities were readily accessible. The success of the stone has continued to such an extent that one of its most recent uses can ironically be seen much nearer the country's capital, in the sections of Windsor Castle restored after the fire.

Wood had the money necessary to turn more of his dreams into reality. GAY STREET was designed by him, as well as his son and successor, and the elder architect lived in number 41. But as you walk between the rows of pleasant, almost identical Georgian houses, your eye will inevitably be drawn to what lies ahead of you, for this is THE CIRCUS, without a big top. The long range perspective is breathtaking. A circle fills your view, made up of the same pastel stone houses which lead to it from every direction, the curved lines of each Crescent section between roadways as smooth in their lines as the straight edges of the terraces are sharp. Built in 1754, this was a very ambitious undertaking, each house identical except for fine detail such as the individuality of the small stone figures carved into the frieze between the ground and first floors. Each one depicts a different art, trade or science, with virtually no duplication right around the entire circle of houses. This whole area looks like something out of a dream; perhaps of what a Roman University's Halls of Residence would have looked like, if the Empire had lasted long enough to have such questionable delights. Mind you the houses, no matter how sub-divided, are very different to the boxed, mundane reality of the campus rooms at Bath's University. Some do not like the monotony of the design, and as with many of Bath's houses, these do not look the most comfortable to live a modern life in, but The Circus is still a glorious place, particularly in bright sunlight, when the creamy stone reflects the yellow rays so brightly.

Just off The Circus, in Bennett Street, is the MUSEUM OF COSTUME AND ASSEMBLY ROOMS (01225 477789). In the museum more than two hundred dressed figures help to exhibit the story of fashion since the 16th century with the strongest emphasis on the trends of the 18th century, but again the building itself has much else to offer, especially in terms of its history. The Assembly Rooms cost £20,000 to build, which does not sound a great deal until you realise that this was in 1771. The TEA ROOM, restored after bomb damage in the Second World War, is a grand place from the elegant row of super imposed pillars at one end to the intricate detail of the coved plaster ceiling, but knowing that Dickens, Strauss (the elder) and Liszt all performed for visitors here in the past adds even more to the undeniable atmosphere of grandeur. The BALL ROOM too, more than a hundred feet long and at over forty feet, exactly as high as it is wide, is truly lovely, with the decoration concentrated on the higher parts of the room so that nothing would take away from the colour of the collected dancers and revellers. You can still attend a Tea Dance or Antique Fair in the Assembly Rooms, depending on what the City Council has arranged, but the company you will have is not likely to be as large or quite as spectacular as those which met here around the end of the 18th century. The Costume Museum is downstairs, so if you feel ready to dance pop down and see if they will let you borrow one of those ribticklingly tight corsets first, just to get you in the historically correct, truly breathless, mood.

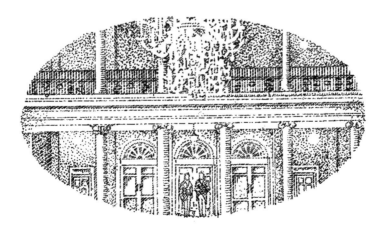

Inside the Assembly Rooms

On the opposite side of Bennett Street, and back towards The Circus, is the MUSEUM OF EAST ASIAN ART (01225 464640). Although this might not seem a natural addition to the more home developed attractions of the city, some of the artefacts are older than anything Bladud could have brought here, with a range of Chinese, Japanese and Korean objects from 7,000 years ago right up to the present century. In nearby GRAVEL WALK you can get to the GEORGIAN GARDEN (information 01225 477000) to see how the outsides of the better kept houses in the area might have looked two hundred years ago.

Crossing The Circus into Brock Street a short walk will bring into view the third of Bath's triumvirate of spectacular collections of domestic architecture. The claustrophobic surroundings of Queen Square and the impressive geometrical confinement of The Circus cannot prepare you for the open grandeur and scale of the ROYAL CRESCENT. This was the first residential Crescent to be built in Britain, yet remains one of the most spectacular, and is claimed to be the longest in Europe. The Crescent represents John Wood the younger's finest hour, and it seems almost incredible that there are only thirty houses in this continuous terrace, framed by 114 giant Ionic columns rising from the first floor to the roof high above. For its setting as well as bright symmetry, this is probably the finest hour in Bath's architectural history too. NUMBER ONE ROYAL CRESCENT (01225 428126) belongs to the Bath Preservation Trust, and has been restored to hold what would have been in such a house in Georgian times. Mind you, not every resident of 18th century Bath would have been able to afford the Chippendale furniture or exquisite glassware this exhibition dwelling now holds. I wonder if there was the equivalent of the modern day 'show house' when the Crescent was new, with an Estate Agent waiting to point out every salient feature? I think not, which is another good example of how civilization has since regressed.

Not all the houses of the Crescent are on show, and the attempts of residents and visitors to park their cars in a line following the curve of the terrace, against the iron railed fence opposite it, are quite amusing. I wonder if this was easier to achieve with coaches? There is an irony in the edges of the shiny metallic vehicles protruding in a very ungainly way, when the plain stone, in place for well over two hundred years, has no such problems. The cars are the uncomfortable visitors, even though the modern world undeniably belongs to them rather than such stately buildings. Some of the more famous residents of Royal Crescent would be amazed to see the city as it is now, buzzing with traffic rather than the gossip from the Baths and Assembly Rooms. Before the Crescent was even completely finished it had its first scandal, when, in 1772, Sheridan eloped with a seventeen year old girl who was living at number eleven. There must surely have been some fine repartee and a couple of hidden screens and closets to make this something like 'The Rivals' or his other fabulously funny plays. There was certainly a duel, in fact two, although the couple did eventually marry a year or so later. A certain Mr Pitman lived at number seventeen in 1844, when his revolutionary system of shorthand was first published for general use.

So you will now have seen the most 'listed' or commonly recommended architectural attractions of Bath. Each will have tested the proficiency of your wide angle lens and each will long be remembered for its own qualities and setting, but it is my guess that you will have found your own buildings to add to the film, hidden amongst the more famous and celebrated. Right next to the Royal Crescent, and on your left as you look up from Royal Avenue to get the best perspective of all thirty houses at once, the MARLBOROUGH BUILDINGS are just one more example of what may have caught your attention; another long, bright Terrace of grand houses, this time framed by the green expanses of the ROYAL VICTORIA PARK which lies behind them. There is still much to see, especially if you are prepared to travel a little way out to LANSDOWN, BATHWICK and the other areas around the city. On a first approach Bath does look very compact, emphasised by its natural setting between the hills, but exploration leads you to find that this is deceptive. Perhaps this is because there is no redundancy; you cannot go to one particular area of the city to 'see the sights' as they are everywhere, especially in the central residential areas, which in other towns and cities would probably be avoided.

Lansdown, from the centre of Bath

Back past The Circus and on the way towards Lansdown, the BUILDING OF BATH MUSEUM (01225 333895) is another attraction in one of the original Georgian buildings, this time the COUNTESS OF HUNTINGDON'S CHAPEL, built in 1775. Selina, the Countess of Huntingdon, was a zealous Methodist, who certainly did not approve of all that went on in late 18th century Bath, and the design of her chapel, with some Gothic elements, makes it a slightly surprising choice in which to hold such an exhibition. However, the Chapel does have the proportions necessary to deal with the large scale model of the city and various 18th century building tools collected here. The model is a great way of finding new buildings to look out for, or for getting bearings back if your explorations have already led you on some unexpected but rewarding wanderings.

Before you head too far out of the centre there are other attractions which should not be missed. A little further towards Lansdown, MR BOWLER'S BUSINESS (01225 318348) tells the story of a local family firm. The exhibition is in the BATH INDUSTRIAL HERITAGE CENTRE, a name which in itself tells you that this is about a slightly later era than that of the Woods and Nash. Jonathan Bowler started his business in Bath in 1872. A good hundred and twenty years ahead of his time he made Britain's original varieties of 'alcopops', with names such as Orange Champagne, Hot Tom, Bath Punch and Cherry Ciderette. The family business also continued making and repairing soda water machinery up until 1969, when the founder's grandson retired, and the site finally closed. This now makes an unusually interesting place to visit because although this was less than thirty years ago, when the factory shut it was still using gas light, and all the Victorian machinery it had started out with nearly one hundred years before. Restoration and preservation became a single, mixed task for those who created the present exhibits, and was definitely worth the effort. The Bowlers turned their hand to just about any job offered, and the machinery they used for mending pony harnesses or beer engines, or making the gas lights used for Queen Victoria's Jubilee are all here to be seen, still looking ready for action. There are other subjects explored too, including a reconstruction of a Bath Stone quarry face.

Back towards the centre of the city the BATH POSTAL MUSEUM (01225 460333) in Broad Street is the place from which the first ever postage stamp was sent, on 2nd May 1840. Even earlier than this the visitors to Bath helped to create a need to develop the stage-coach postal system in Britain, which became a model for the whole of Europe. These were not cheeky cartoon seaside postcards, but I expect a good few lines of scandal and a few 'wish you were heres' left here in a hurry aboard the Royal Mail coaches. A logical place for the mail system to develop really, as many of us still only write voluntarily and without necessity when we are on holiday, bathing in places whose air temperatures are not that far from those generated by the constant heat of Bath's natural Springs.

SALLY LUNN'S REFRESHMENT HOUSE AND MUSEUM (01225 461634) is just around the corner from the Abbey, and is said to be the oldest surviving house in Bath, built in about 1482. There have been excavations revealing Roman and Saxon habitation here, and these can still be seen in the cellar of the building. The name Sally Lunn is bound to sound familiar, as this famous resident of Bath gave her name to the famous buns you can still buy here today. Although there is not that much known of her actual life, it is thought she lived here in the late 17th century, a generation or so before Dr Oliver gave his treatise and developed the Bath Oliver biscuit, the city's other offering to culinary heritage, as well as to the health of the nation.

The guided walks around this area of the city, littered with buildings and other places of local history to see, come highly recommended, with the local guides showing a very justifiable pride in their home city. They have the grand title of the MAYOR OF BATH'S CORPS OF HONORARY GUIDES (01225 477000 Extn 7786) and have their headquarters in the Pump Room. For a guided walk with a more specific theme the brave can try the GHOST WALK (01225 463618), which sets out from the Garrick's Head public house, apparently haunted by more than just the usual regular visitors. The walk lasts two hours and is an evening occasion, presumably so that you stand a greater chance of seeing the ghouls in action.

Something a little more definitely substantial was discovered in 1781 at the house in New King Street which is now home to the WILLIAM HERSCHEL MUSEUM (01225 311342). The planet Uranus was identified here for the first time, with the use of a hand made telescope which was the property of another of Bath's versatile figures. Unlike the Bowlers, William Herschel kept his occupations down to just two in number. As well as a famous astronomer he was a musician and composer who rose to be Bath's director of music. The museum is yet another chance to see what one of these multitude of houses would actually have looked like inside during the 18th century.

Near to the spectacular Pulteney Bridge, but still on the Abbey side of the Avon, the VICTORIA ART GALLERY (01225 477772) has contemporary exhibitions as well as a collection of British and European Art from the 17th century onwards. From here the choice is a simple one, you either head towards the path alongside the shops which form part of the bridge, or finally fall to the temptation of the hills behind you, where Lansdown Crescent makes such an appealing landmark.

There are other landmarks in Lansdown too, notably BECKFORD'S TOWER (01225 338727). We will meet the eccentric writer of 'Vathek' again in Wiltshire (chapter six) when we will see that this fairly plain tower, (with 156 steps and far reaching views if you fancy the climb) was among the least dramatic of William Beckford's architectural and literary projects. So too was the joining of his two houses, one on the end of Lansdown Crescent, the other its neighbour in Lansdown Place, by a habitable bridge, known unsurprisingly as BECKFORD'S BRIDGE. Bath is just the sort of place where such a man could leave his mark feeling that it was likely to survive at least a few hundred years after his death.

Lansdown is full of more splendid examples of Bath's residential architecture, such as the fine uniformity of SOMERSET PLACE, broken only at its centre by a spectacular broken pediment. Yet it is the views which are the best thing here. It is strange; as soon as you get to Lansdown your eye is drawn to what is laid out below, yet once you return to the city the views above will recapture you attention. Perhaps this is the real triumph of Bath's buildings, they really do look superb from distance, collected together in such dramatic formations.

Pulteney Bridge is quite dramatic in itself, especially if seen from below, standing on the path which runs alongside the River Avon. From here the bridge looks rather like a tunnel, or the front of a Victorian railway station, somehow made to hover over the water. The closed in, boxlike design is thought to bear Venetian influences, which seems quite possible, with three wide arches looking just right to produce a gondola from within their dark interior. Somehow it seems right that Bath should not have an ordinary or conventional town bridge, and what makes Pulteney even more notable is the area it leads into. After negotiating Laura Place you are suddenly confronted by another landmark to add to the list; GREAT PULTENEY STREET. This is a hundred feet wide and eleven hundred long, looking fit for the start of a huge fun run or a stage of the Tour de France, except that it is too steep a hill for one, and in the wrong country for the other!

Pulteney Bridge

THE HOLBURNE MUSEUM AND CRAFTS STUDY CENTRE (01225 466669) at the end of this massive thoroughfare, was originally an 18th century hotel but now takes its name from Sir William Holburne (1793-1874), who amassed important collections of everything from the paintings of Gainsborough and Turner to continental silver, porcelain and glass. The setting is quite splendid, and as a hotel this really must have been a fantastic place to stay, although you may feel the need to bring a sleeping bag even now if you are to have sufficient time to see a fair representation of this enormous collection, as well as the Crafts Study Centre, which features the work of 20th century British craftspeople.

Part of the beauty of Bath's setting does come from the river which runs through it, and you can appreciate the Avon's appeal for a few hours or more at the BATH BOATING STATION (01225 466407), another attraction which advertises itself as a living museum. Accessible from the Holburne Museum by heading for the Avon via Forester Road, the quiet surroundings of this Victorian boating station can hardly have changed in the last hundred years. Trees, water, and rusty brown bottomed wooden boats, the atmosphere is lovely to observe, and you can hire a punt or canoe to join the scene and then explore on your own if you wish to. The Avon is just wide enough to be tempting, without the far, branch entangled bank looking more than a short swim away, if you should lose your footing.

This route out of the city soon takes you towards Wiltshire, and to another waterway of which you will hear much more when we come to explore that county thoroughly, the KENNET AND AVON CANAL (see Chapter Six). The course of the water may be narrower, but if the Boating Station has whetted your appetite rather than your feet, then a more sedate cruise can be had from the BATH HOTELBOAT COMPANY (01225 448846), JOHN RENNIE CANAL CRUISES (01225 447276) or the BATH & DUNDAS CANAL COMPANY (01225 722292) who between them can provide everything from self drive cruisers to canoes, or a canal bound function room if you should suddenly decide to party afloat. The last of these is at **MONKTON COMBE**, right up against the border with Wiltshire, while at **CLAVERTON**, on the way back towards the city, the Canal has its own 19th century relic which predates the Boating Station without rivalling its scenic appeal. The CLAVERTON PUMPING STATION (0117 986 7536) links the Canal to the Avon in a more direct way too, as it was from here that water was drawn out of the river up into the Kennet and Avon almost fifty feet above. You can still see the huge water-wheel which harnesses the power of the river to make this unlikely transfer possible, via the beam engine pump, first used in 1813. Also in Claverton is the AMERICAN MUSEUM (01225 460503). Rooms within Claverton Manor, in which the museum has its home, are filled with period furniture and other items to recreate life in America, from the 17th to 19th centuries. Another 'living museum' side-show to the main attraction that is modern Bath.

The city does have its more modern residential suburbs and estates, notably the less immediately gratifying OVAL, which has neither the comparatively compact charm of The Circus or the atmosphere of the cricket stadia at either Kennington, London or Kensington, Barbados! It does have originality though, with hundreds of houses spread in two bands around its gently curving route. Other parts have more age, and some individual dwellings are worth a detour to see. Foremost among these must be the National Trust property of PRIOR PARK, although it is the LANDSCAPE GARDEN (01225 833422) which they welcome the public to, rather than the house once lived in by Ralph Allen. Allen had the superb mansion built to the designs of John Wood the elder in 1735, and even a quick peek at the huge portico of giant Corinthian columns at the front of what is now a school will convince you that this was no less of a project than those nearer to the centre of the city. The gardens were of Allen's design, with the help of a couple of other gentleman of whom you may have heard. One was Lancelot 'Capability' Brown, responsible for so many dramatic landscapes in the 18th century, especially in the county just to the east of here. The other was Alexander Pope, more known for his cutting couplets than his imaginative pruning. A strange combination perhaps, but the results of their temporary allegiance are wonderful. After all the stone laden beauty of the city, the expanses of green come as a pleasant addition, if not a relief, only broken by the water of the lakes, or the elegant lines of the follies and ornamental constructions such as the Palladian Bridge which crosses one of them.

Further south of the city **WIDCOMBE** has much of what is in the centre reduced to a smaller total scale, with a splendid Manor House, Crescent, Terrace and church. Henry Fielding and his sister lived at Widcombe Lodge, which in those 18th century days would have been much more surrounded by countryside and further from the edges of Bath than it is now.

It would be unfair to leave Bath behind without telling you more of what can be found to do here in modern times. Mention the name of the city to a Frenchman and his frown will not be from jealousy or scorn for its architecture, but is much more likely to reflect a bitter taste left very recently when BATH RUGBY FOOTBALL CLUB (01225 325200 / 460588 or www.bathrugby.co.uk) became England's first ever winners of Rugby Union's European Cup with a last minute penalty goal against Brive, on the French team's home soil. Towards the end of the sport's amateur days Jeremy Guscott and his fellows at this club dominated much of England's domestic rugby, and even now they are a team of which the whole region is justifiably proud. Bath has to be different, and how many other towns in the south of the country pull supporters from the surrounding countryside in such numbers for any team sport other than football, or occasionally cricket?

With The Galleries and the rest of Bristol's massive shopping area so relatively close by, Bath does not need to compete in terms of the scale of its facilities for those who wish to buy. Instead the city has a tremendous range of specialist shops, many of which are tucked away waiting to be discovered in alleys and side streets. In particular Bath has more than its fair share of Antique Shops, and these can be found dotted all over the city, as well as in the central, pedestrianised area. The Abbey Green and York Street area has its own Independent Retailers Association, with boutiques, a specialist tobacconist, jewellers, a Lacemakers, and many other, varied outlets. Walcot Street too, with everything from cheeses to hats, is definitely worth a stroll, as are the many side streets off Milsom Street, traditionally the main shopping road, even in Jane Austen's time here. There is a definite feeling of class to the whole of this area, carried on by many excellent and diverse eating places. Milsom Street has some newer Arcades and Malls now, but kept in the style of what is older, and full of unusual shops, but it also has another addition, the HISTORY OF PHOTOGRAPHY MUSEUM (01225 462841). Run by the Royal Photographic Society this has displays of modern work alongside an exhibition of early equipment.

Only a couple of days before writing this I happened to meet somebody who had lived most of her life in Bath. After agreeing that it was a wonderful place she suddenly declared that she would not go back to live there. I was quite surprised, but could understand her reasons when she said that it was 'just too much of a chocolate box'. The phrase implied that everything is laid out nicely, neatly presented and delicate, waiting to be unwrapped; for a price. What this also describes is the ideal place to visit, Bath is literally built to please the eye, while its shops and walks, museums and attractions, are full of delights that are more than enough to leave you wanting more. A city full of surprises, alive and completely in tune with the present, but without leaving the past behind. I really cannot do more than say that there is nowhere else in the country quite like this; Stratford Upon Avon has the atmosphere of past glory and present wealth, London has architectural masterpieces on a greater scale, and more antiquity too, but nowhere has the sense of complete, seamless adaptation from 18th century centre of fashion to modern city that Bath does. It is as if you have entered a completely different world when you descend into its valley, of modern bustle amongst Georgian elegance, of present day rush intruding on the ground of many past intrigues and scandals, now so long forgotten. Any idea that this might be a sleepy little place, as rural in its outlook as the county of Somerset to which it belongs, will last no longer than the negotiation of the first roundabout or crowded set of traffic lights.

Jane Austen did not come to Bath by choice, and is said to have fainted when told that her family were to spend time in the city. In her books this is the place where things happen, the unlikely and unusual. In real life she found the place tiresome, and its glamourous trimmings to be affected and irksome, but used the setting to express social lightness, danger and triviality. What she was so cleverly doing was to suggest that in such an unreal place, where everyday routines were established around regulated pleasures and socialising rather than work, values and morals can become relaxed, creating the chance for what we would term a 'holiday romance'. Whether you consider modern Bath to be romantic or not, after a few hours here, amongst the very same buildings visited in fiction by Miss Elliot, Captain Wentworth, Louisa Musgrove and other of Miss Austen's characters, you will agree that there is a feeling that anything could happen here, given half a chance. Somehow the hedonistic days of 17th century Bath, when such serious figures as Samuel Pepys joined in the communal naturalism have left their mark even now, intermixed with the elegance of the whole central section of the city to make a heady, rich cocktail for the visitor.

Jane Austen found her way around Bath in what is still the best manner for the visitor; she walked. If you want to follow a route constructed to show you as many elements of Bath as she knew it as possible, such as her home in Sydney Place and St Swithin's Church in Walcot Street, where her parents were married then you can find out more about the 'Jane Austen' Walks from Tourist Information, or if you have access to the Internet try www.openworld.co.uk for maps and details of the suggested route.

There are various events in Bath each year, from a LITERATURE FESTIVAL to a SPRING FLOWER SHOW, as well as the main BATH FESTIVAL, when candles are lit in the upper storey windows of Royal Crescent to give the feature even more colour. Contact the BATH FESTIVALS TRUST (01225 462231) for a full list of what is happening during your proposed visit to the city. Bath always seems ready to take on the festival rather than perhaps carnival spirit, and let's hope you finally leave the city with the same feelings expressed by Catherine Morland, of Jane Austen's Gothic novel spoof 'Northanger Abbey':

"Here are a variety of amusements, a variety of things to be seen and done all day long... I really believe I shall always be talking of Bath."

Coming out of the city to the west it really is not far to the ever growing Bristol these days, with **KEYNSHAM** becomingly increasingly squeezed between the two, despite the fact that it once had its own Abbey, some of the ruins of which lie, unexcavated, beneath the very by-pass used by so very many hurried travellers without a thought for the past. Across the Avon to the north of Keynsham is the village of **BITTON**, whose railway station, accessible from the main A431, is the headquarters of the AVON VALLEY RAILWAY (0117 932 5538 / 7296). This is the first of the many steam railways we will find in Wessex, being recreated as Heritage Lines so that generations who have never had the chance to experience the age of steam can share them with those who are old enough to remember at least something of the romance of the pre diesel era. The setting is lovely, and a welcome break from the main roads, as the steam engines will take you on a journey north or south along the green spaces of the Avon Valley. Plans are afoot to extend the line to Bath, which really will make this a great trip. Meanwhile you may feel tempted by your very own chance to emulate 'Casey Jones', on the RAILWAY EXPERIENCE courses (0117 932 5421) run by the railway, when you can learn how to drive a steam locomotive, without any danger of sudden intervention from the 'injuns' or cattle rustlers. Also near Keynsham is the AVON VALLEY COUTNRY PARK (0117 986 4929), another chance to enjoy the scenery around the river.

Heading south the country becomes quieter, and approaching Bath through **PEASEDOWN ST JOHN** you have no idea of what is to come until the suburbs actually start. This is a rural area, and for me combines the best of both worlds for the residents of its scattered villages; peace and space when you need it, but with all the busy beauty of the city so nearby. At **PRISTON** you really know you are in the countryside, with a chance to visit PRISTON MILL (01225 423894 / 460234) which has a water-wheel that has been helping to mill corn into wholewheat flour for more than a thousand years. The villages are Bath's neighbours and do bear the city's historical influence, down to fine details such as the piece of Roman sculpture built into the chancel of the church in **COMPTON DANDO**, which is thought to have originally been part of the Roman temple in Aquae Sulis itself. Some of the other villages have histories linked to stories we will hear more of as we travel south and east of here. Countess Ela of Salisbury performed the ceremonial opening of Hinton Priory at **HINTON CHARTERHOUSE** on the very same day on which she did the same for Lacock Abbey in Wiltshire. Not much chance of a chauffeured driven half hour ride along the A36 between the two either, as this all took place in 1232. Ela was a very determined character, whose story we will hear at Lacock (chapter six), but the

Priory fell in 1539 along with so many others, although ruins of some of the monastic buildings are still here to be seen.

NORTON ST PHILIP was once part of Hinton's property, but even before Ela came here the Coombs family were already part of the parish records. Recent examinations of these records by a member of this family has brought to light an incident which is part of another of the main historical stories of Wessex which will develop as we move on. Thomas Coombs was one of twelve men executed in the village in 1685 for their part in the Monmouth Rebellion. Judge Jeffries and his Bloody Assizes meant that men and women all over Somerset and Dorset were killed in various horrific ways to satisfy royal revenge, but the only clue as to the details of what happened in Norton is that twelve shillings were paid for faggots of wood for the execution. Coombs and his companions were burnt to death. Perhaps the retribution was so horrific because Monmouth had a temporary headquarters in the village pub during the rebellion, and there is apparently still evidence of the fighting to be seen, in the form of a hole made in one of the beams by musket shot, perhaps even intended for the pretender himself.

As with many other sites of the aftermath of the rebellion (as well as the battlefield of Sedgemoor itself) this seems much too quiet and peaceful a place for such goings on, and the more you hear about these bloody times the more eerie present day Wessex can appear in its emptier spots. The golden stone cottages and farm buildings of **WELLOW**, as well as its Manor House, are reminders that this was probably a busier place in medieval times, when the sheep grazing around here gave these places a prosperity seen from the Cotswolds to the Marlborough Downs through the use of their wool. The WELLOW TREKKING CENTRE (01225 834376) gives you a chance to climb the hills on horseback and see more from the many bridleways provided.

It is not until you reach the very close neighbours **MIDSOMER NORTON** and **RADSTOCK** that the modern world really seems to take complete control again. These two towns advertise themselves as a joint shopping centre of some excellence, full of independent retailers as well as department and chain stores. There is not too much elegance here, but this fits with history too, as Radstock was the centre of Somerset's mining area, calling itself the 'powerhouse behind Bath' after the mines started to be developed in the late 17th century, before using the canals and then railways to grow rapidly as part of the Industrial Revolution. This is the recent history, but like Bath itself, there is something earlier. Radstock takes its name from its place by the Roman Fosse Way, while Midsomer Norton was a medieval market town which originally grew up as a northern satellite of Stratton-on-the-Fosse (see chapter five). How time can change things. The last coal mine shut in 1973, but the RADSTOCK, MIDSOMER NORTON AND DISTRICT MUSEUM (01761 437722) shows pride in the industrial heritage of the region as well as what came before.

From Radstock we will carry on south east along the A362, through Frome, until we reach the Wiltshire border. Even in this little triangular corner of land between main roads there are more attractive villages and places to visit, as well as some more history.

In the north east of this corner at **RODE**, are the RODE TROPICAL BIRD GARDENS (01373 830326), where there are free flying birds as well as aviaries. With lakes and woodlands too, this has everything from flamingoes to penguins, as well as insects and butterflies. This might seem about as far as you can go without crossing the county border, but one attraction lies right on that border, sometimes claimed by Somerset and at others by Wiltshire. As I have given Forde Abbey to Dorset in the similar situation in the south (chapter nine), I will redress the balance a little by keeping FARLEIGH HUNGERFORD CASTLE (01225 754026) in Somerset.

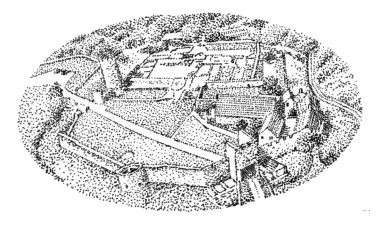

Farleigh Hungerford Castle

The real reason for this is that the remains of the castle are on the western side of the River Frome, where the building had a formidable defensive position against any force approaching from the east, and so protected the edge of Somerset from within its natural geographical boundaries. There had already been a Manor House here for several centuries when the Hungerfords bought the site in the late 14th century. It might surprise you to hear that their next problem was planning permission.

It was not that the Council were dissatisfied with the architect's drawings, and it is hard to imagine the two remaining medieval corner towers being half constructed, with a bureaucrat in a hard hat at the base shaking his head over the plans. The problem was the particular style chosen by the new owners in 1377. Apparently you had to obtain a special licence if you wished to 'crenellate' your property, and so have it fortified. The Hungerfords either ignored this requirement, hoping fairly reasonably that they were well out of the way of any stray court crenellation inspectors, or forgot to apply. The licence was eventually granted in 1383, after the event.

The initial part of this construction was started by Sir Thomas Hungerford, the first person to hold the post of Speaker of the House of Commons, not that this in any way suggests a hint of nepotism or political arrogance in the proceedings!

Somerset does not have many medieval castles; many have fallen into complete ruin and subsequently disappeared forever, others suffered badly during the Civil War, when Wessex was at the centre of much of the fighting. The style of what is left at Farleigh shows how much we are missing, the rounded towers which can be seen again at nearby Nunney (chapter five) looking very like those to be seen in more complete remains in Sussex and Kent.

History has not completely deserted this site though. When the castle was expanded by Sir Thomas's son, the local parish church of **FARLEIGH HUNGERFORD** itself was enclosed within the new walls. Another church was eventually built in the village, and the original became the Hungerford's private chapel, dedicated to St Leonard. This still stands within the largely empty shell of the rest of their home, and is full of memorials to members of the family, including a particularly massive one to Sir Thomas. This is the most substantial part of what English Heritage now preserves for the visitor, and a trip down into the crypt will undoubtedly appeal, but standing amongst the ruins of the main part of the castle you cannot help wondering why it fell into disrepair. The answer is not that guns were fired upon it, as they were at Nunney, or that a siege by either Royalists or Parliamentarians was followed by looting, as at other such places in Wessex, but rather that it simply fell into neglect. By the 18th century a visitor already commented upon its "melancholy picture of fallen greatness". Farleigh did change hands in the Civil War, but without a fight, and it seems even more disappointing that it has fallen so far since when you know this. It also makes you wonder what may have happened to the castles at Corfe and Sherborne, as well as many others, had they not been so violently destroyed by Cromwell's gunpowder. At least they went out with a bang, not a gradual, decaying whimper. Still, the ruins here are lovely in their own right, and the setting in the Frome valley is undeniably superb.

This is now a quiet valley, but there are a still a few signs of its former prosperity in the cloth trade, such as SCUTT'S BRIDGE, a fine packhorse bridge between Rode and **WOOLVERTON**, and the church in **BECKINGTON**, which claims to have the largest surviving, most ornate Norman tower in the county. It is certainly an impressive, solid structure in its square lines, and grand enough to dominate the rural skyline.

To appreciate just how much this past can mix in with the present we must move to our last stop in this chapter. **FROME** (Tourist Information 01373 467271) has more listed buildings than any other town in Somerset. After a hundred years of stagnation the population here has doubled since the 1960s, and you may be surprised to find such an attractive town centre after getting through the modern suburbs.

In common with nearby Wells (chapter five), it was the power of the local water, this time from the River Frome on whose banks the town was built, which helped to establish local industry. Frome was a wool town, giving it much in common with Trowbridge and the other Wiltshire towns just to the east. Like so many other places, Frome also felt the wrath of Judge Jeffries, and twelve local men were hanged for their part in the Monmouth Rebellion.

Frome's centre is not the easiest place to find your way around, and exploration on foot is the best way to appreciate some of the narrow winding streets packed with interesting buildings, although the hills can be a little challenging. The best areas are congregated on each side of the town's main 17th century bridge over the river, itself notable for the buildings which take up one side of it, in an echo of Pulteney in Bath.

To the north of the bridge in North Parade is the FROME MUSEUM (01373 467271), while just around the back in Bridge Street is the BLACK SWAN GUILD (01373 473980), an arts and crafts complex, while in between lies the ROUND TOWER, recently refurbished to house the Tourist Information Office.

Best of all though are the streets climbing to the south of the river, such as the sweeping lines of the pedestrianised CATHERINE HILL. Along with the more medieval buildings of CHEAP STREET and APPLE ALLEY they give the shopping area some real charm. GENTLE STREET too, a cobbled street full of houses from the 16th to 18th centuries, is worth the walk a little further up the hill.

Frome has some unusual events each year, including the FROME CHEESE SHOW on the third Wednesday each September, and ST CATHERINE'S MEDIEVAL FAIR, which takes over the centre of the town on the third Saturday in August. Both have growing and deserved reputations. It is said that in 1720 Frome was bigger than either Bath or Salisbury, now it makes a fitting place to end a chapter dominated by the city a few miles to its north. Frome was a wool town, although originally built around a monastery, and what remains is quaint and picturesque in a way you can find in many different places throughout Wessex which have similar origins. Bath might be more of an attraction, and is certainly more unique, but Somerset has other places too, where the living present does not so obviously give you the past, and where a little exploration will reward you with just as many surprises as in the city with a Circus.

APSLEY HOUSE
Newbridge Hill
Bath, BA1 3PT

Tel: 01225 336966 Fax: 01225 425462
E-mail:apsleyhouse@easynet.co.uk
www.gratton.co.uk/apsley

AA 5 Q's. Premier Selected. ETB Highly Commended. Johansens. Les Routier

Adrian Hobday describes Apsley House as 'Like my favourite wine 'Pouilly Fuisse' unassuming on the outside and sheer delight inside'. An apt description for this elegant Georgian Country House built for the Duke of Wellington in 1830 and set in its own delightful garden. The hotel has been refurbished in great style and every care has been taken to preserve the elegance of bygone days. The magnificently proportioned reception rooms offer both style and comfort, the interior includes many period features the house being furnished with fine antiques and original oil paintings. Owned and run by David and Annie Lanz, Apsley House is one of Britain's finest small hotels. Guests are offered a very warm welcome and personal care, the atmosphere is more in keeping with a private house than an hotel with every discretion given to the comfort and enjoyment of guests. Help is always available if you require information on how best to spend your time in and around the beautiful city of Bath. Located just over one mile west of the city centre, Apsley House offers its own private car park for the use of guests. A leisurely walk to the centre will take just over twenty minutes. Alternatively there are regular bus services from outside the hotel gates Monday-Saturday early morning to early evening or taxis can be booked on request. The hotel has nine delightfully appointed bedrooms, all are beautifully presented, invitingly romantic and are individually styled with sumptuous furnishings, lovely drapery and ensuite bathrooms. Equipped with remote colour tv, satellite, direct dial telephone, radio alarm facilities, hair dryer, trouser press and hospitality tray, they provide every comfort for your needs. Fax, laundry service, iron available on request. Breakfast served in the elegant dining room is a feast with a variety of choice from traditional English to house specialities and vegetarian selection all prepared to order and beautifully presented. Continental breakfast can be served to your room should you require. The drawing room and dining room with their stunning Georgian windows overlook the charming and secluded garden. Apsley House has a residential licence. Drinks are served in the Bar, the Drawing Room, which is non-smoking, or room service is available. Alternatively the garden offers the perfect setting to relax and unwind on a warm summer's day. With over 80 restaurants Bath boasts a wealth of choice from highly acclaimed Michelin 2 star fame to the more rustic Bistro or traditional English pub. There is something for everyone. Recommendations and assistance with reservations are all part of the personal service offered at Apsley.

USEFUL INFORMATION

- OPEN: All year
- WHEELCHAIR ACCESS: No
- GARDEN: Secluded, delightful
- CREDIT CARDS: All major cards
- ACCOMMODATION: 9 ensuite rooms

- DINING ROOM: Delicious breakfast
- VEGETARIAN: Upon request
- LICENSED: Residential
- CHILDREN: Over 5 years
- PETS: No

- RATES: Dbl./Twin from £75 £100 prpn.. Single £55- £75. Family £75 per two people. £18 per extra person. All rates incl. b'fast.
  Mid-week discounts & Seasonal break prices on application.

BATH LODGE HOTEL
Norton St Philip
NR Bath
BA36NM
AA 5 Q's.

Tel: 01225 723040
Fax: 01225 723737

Bath Lodge Hotel is set in a rural location amidst five acres of mixed formal gardens and woodland with its own stream and waterfall and adjacent Deer wood. Sporting activities are readily available including clay and game shooting, golf and riding. Bath Lodge is easily reached from the main A36 which makes for good journey times if you wish to explore the magic of Longleat, Stourhead, Wells, Glastonbury, Avebury, Stonehenge, Bath, Bristol, Lacock and many other delightful places.

Built in 1806 by Colonel John Houlton who was the Lord Chancellor of the time, it was the principal Gate Lodge to Farleigh Manor and Castle, an estate dating back to 970AD. The nearby villages of Norton St Philip and Farleigh Hungerford both witnessed skirmishes in the English Civil War and Farleigh Castle regularly holds Re-enactments of historic interest. Bath Lodge Hotel itself is full of interest with castellation and turrets as well as embattled terraces. The unique nature of Bath Lodge's appearance as a small castle is its strongest single draw. Imagine it, full of nooks and crannies, interesting stairways, rough cast walls, open fires and stone mullions. It is a very special place.

There are eight guest rooms, all ensuite, with family configurations possible. Three of the rooms have Four-poster beds and each room is furnished and decorated uniquely to enhance its features and location in this distinctive property. Each room has television, video, direct dial telephone and a hostess tray. Graham and Nicola Walker the owners have made it their objective to provide high quality AA5Q accommodation with an emphasis on value for money. The atmosphere is perfect and informal but very professionally run with the accent on personal service. Breakfast is a delicious meal, cooked to your choice and on Fridays and Saturdays dinner is available, a Prix Fixe meal of five tempting courses served at a beautifully appointed table with bone china, sparkling crystal and shining silver. A small but well balanced wine list at sensible prices completes the meal.

USEFUL INFORMATION

- OPEN: All year
- WHEELCHAIR ACCESS: No
- GARDEN:
- CREDIT CARDS: Visa/Master/Switch /Delta/AMEX
- ACCOMMODATION: 8 ensuite rooms
- RATES: From £25 pp low season £32.50 high season

- RESTAURANT; Delicious food. Dinner on Fridays & Saturdays
- VEGETARIAN: With prior notice
- LICENSED: Yes

- CHILDREN: 12+

BATH SPA HOTEL
Sydney Road
Bath
BA2 6JF

Tel: 01225 444424 Fax: 01225 444006
E :mail fivestar@bathspa.u-net.com

AA/RAC FIVE STAR. Numerous Accolades

The Bath Spa Hotel is very special, and oddly enough it might never have been if the Health Authority had not been faced with the prohibitive running costs of the building in 1985 and forced to sell. Many schemes were considered for the building but the proposals for an elegant five star hotel won the day. The restoration and refurbishment work took three years to complete at a cost of £22 million, and The Bath Spa Hotel, restored to its former glory opened in January 1990, It is a handsome building in a handsome setting. Nestling amongst ancient Cedars, the elegant Grecian facade can only hint at the warmth that awaits you. Beyond the fine Georgian portico lies a stylish, distinctive interior. It is set in seven acres of mature grounds and there is at once a sense of calm, a tranquil oasis. Panoramic views of the formal gardens, ponds and gentle fountains surround you.

Dining at the Bath Spa is a unique experience with two very different Restaurants and one menu offering a host of international flavours and tastes. In the Alfresco Restaurant, distinctive murals and exotic plants create an informal, vibrant atmosphere. The Vellore Restaurant, the heart of the house, has its own elegant and relaxing style, once host to the season's most dashing debutantes, the revitalised ballroom now echoes to the hubbub of dinner conversation.

Each bedroom is individually decorated providing essential creature comforts and a host of indulgent extras. Bathrooms are luxuriously appointed in mahogany and marble with fine toiletries and large baths to wallow in. Boasting nine majestic suites the Hotel offers the full modern amenities one would expect of not only an RAC Five Star Hotel of the Year, but also the Caterer and Hotelkeeper 'Hotel of the Year', while still retaining the character of a homely country house. You will receive free membership of the Laurels Health and Leisure Spa for the duration of your stay. There are pampering beauty treatments and the Salon can design a hair style to suit your image or indulge a mood. There is a swimming pool, a tennis court and a croquet lawn. Quality golf can be found a mere three iron drive away at Sham Castle and some of the best club rugby in the country is but a five minute walk. The hotel is ideal for conferences with seven meeting rooms providing capacity for up to one hundred and twenty delegates. Above all the quality of the Bath Spa Hotel is based on the staff, people who take pleasure in pleasing you.

USEFUL INFORMATION

- OPEN: All year
- WHEELCHAIR ACCESS: Yes
- GARDEN: Yes. Tennis, croquet
- CREDIT CARDS: All major cards
- ACCOMMODATION: All ensuite
- RATES: From £139 per person per night. Suites from £349

- RESTAURANT: 2 superb restaurants with delicious cuisine
- VEGETARIAN: Always a choice
- LICENSED: Full On. Fine wines
- CHILDREN: Welcome
- PETS: Behaved dogs by prior arrangement

COMBE GROVE MANOR HOTEL & COUNTRY CLUB
Brassknocker Hill
Monkton Combe
Bath
BA2 7HS

Hotel: Tel: 01225 834644
Country Club 01225 835533
Fax: 01225 834961

Named after the large fir groves surrounding the house and gardens Combe Grove Manor was entertaining visitors for 300 years before it became the Hotel & Country Club it is today. The present owners purchased the manor in 1985 and it is their careful modernisation which has updated the estate's facilities, while being careful to preserve its original architectural splendour and decorative elegance. It is in a wonderful position, easily accessible from anywhere in the country. It is an excellent base for exploring the South West. Nearby Bath with its rich historical, architectural and cultural significance, contains all the amenities, facilities and high street names one would expect to find in any large city.

Combe Grove is much more than a hotel and a country club. The estate's generous eighty two acres of gardens, woodlands and meadows provides stunning scenery and the guest with a mini-paradise in which to stroll. It is also perfect, and has the space, to host almost every event you care to imagine. When you stay here you will find the furnishings, fabric and decor in the 9 bedrooms delightful. Two of the bedrooms are luxury suites and have their own sitting room and Jacuzzi bath. All the rooms have stunning views over and beyond Limpley Stoke Valley. Every creature comfort is there for your use including satellite TV, mini-bar, tea and coffee making facilities, dressing gowns, and others you would not anticipate like home-made cookies. The Garden Lodge has thirty one bedrooms with the same degree of comfort but in a more modern style. These rooms have their own sun terrace and spectacular views. There are two restaurants at Combe Grove Manor in which to taste the labours of the award winning chef. Each one has its own distinct atmosphere and style of cuisine. The Georgian Restaurant is a perfect setting for more formal dining occasions and the Manor Vaults Bistro with its low ceilings, gentle lighting and informal menu offers an intimate and casual atmosphere.

Leisure is taken very seriously at Combe Grove Manor. For those who like vigorous exercise there is swimming, aerobics, a fully equipped gym, indoor and outdoor tennis courts, and a demanding two mile jogging trail around the estate. There is a Beauty Clinic, a Spa Complex - in fact all that anyone could wish for.

USEFUL INFORMATION

- OPEN: All year
- WHEELCHAIR ACCESS: Yes
- GARDEN: Beautiful
- CREDIT CARDS: All major cards
- ACCOMMODATION: All ensuite
- RATES: From £99 per room B&B

- RESTAURANT: Superb cuisine
- VEGETARIAN: Always a choice
- BISTRO: Informal. Excellent fare
- LICENSED: Full On
- CHILDREN: Welcome
- PETS: No

COTTAGE GARDEN
2 Tynings Cottage
Fairy Hill
Compton Dando
Somerset
BS39 4LH

Tel: 01761 490421
Fax: 01761 490030

Compton Dando is a small village nestled in the Chew Valley. It is a great place for those who enjoy walking in the countryside; across meadow woodland, and along the river bank The Avon Cycle way passes through the village, so why not cycle? It is a village with a delightful community lifestyle; locals gather in the village pub and the old Norman Church looks quietly on. Here you are within easy reach of the Chew Valley Lakes, Cheddar Gorge, Wookey Hole, Glastonbury, Bath and Bristol. Compton Dando is situated on the historic pathway known as The Wansdyke which is clearly visible for at least a quarter of a mile.

On the edge of the village surrounded by 'set a side' land where many acres of native trees have been planted, stands Cottage Garden, the home of Viv and Spencer Sands, two fascinating people who have any number of interests and are both talented. Spencer worked as an art restorer and now is dedicated to spending his spare time painting and gardening in their acre of naturalised garden complete with pond and moisture garden, whilst Viv is keen on raising plants and creates beautiful hanging baskets. In the summer there are always fresh flowers in the bedrooms, sweet peas, cosmos and roses bringing the smell of the garden into the rooms. There are three guest rooms each individually decorated. One double ensuite, one twin ensuite and a single with a shower opposite. All three rooms are charming, furnished in cottage style and decorated with imaginative paint effects and handmade stencilling. All three rooms have television, hostess trays, hairdryers and toiletries. A delicious breakfast is served every morning in an 'overgrown Conservatory', and Viv will cook an evening meal if requested and preferably with prior notice. This is a great boon for the walkers and cyclists after an energetic day. The village pub only serves food at lunch times but there are plenty of restaurants and local pubs where meals are served, within a couple of miles..

This is a happy house in which to stay and perhaps some it stems from the fact that Viv and Spencer are qualified Reiki Healers (a natural way of healing mind and body). There is a 'Healing' room specifically decorated by their eldest artist son. Hourly sessions can be booked. What a talented family - Spencer and their sons Mark and Corin, reproduced over 1,000 Garter Knight Shields as part of the Restoration Project at Windsor Castle and the middle son Ashley, a wood carver, made one of the decorative bosses, also on that project.

USEFUL INFORMATION

- OPEN: All year except Dec 25th &26th
- WHEELCHAIR ACCESS: No
- GARDEN: Superb
- CREDIT CARDS: None taken
- ACCOMMODATION: 1dbl.1twin. 1sgl ensuite
- RATES: £25pp b&b Children under 5 negotiable

- DINING ROOM: Excellent breakfast. No evening meal
- VEGETARIAN: Yes
- LICENSED: No
- CHILDREN: Welcome
- PETS: No

EAGLE HOUSE
Church Street
Bathford
Bath
BA1 7RS

Tel/Fax 01225 859946
E.mail jonap@psionworld.net

Which Guide.
Good Bath Guide.
4 Crowns

Bathford is a charming conservation village just three miles from the incomparable city of Bath. There is a profusion of interesting places nearby including Castle Combe beloved by filmmakers, the National Trust village of Lacock, the Cotswolds, Longleat House, Avenury and Stonehenge. Within the village Eagle House, an elegant Georgian house, designed by John Wood, standing in one and a half acres of mature grounds, is the home of John and Rosamund Napier. These two hospitable, friendly people enjoy taking care of guests staying in the house. You reach Eagle House from the A4 taking the A363 towards Bradford-on-Avon. Go 150 yards, then fork left up Bathford Hill. Take first right into Church Street; Eagle House is 200 yards on the right.

Eagle House has eight bedrooms, all with private facilities, and each individually furnished and decorated in keeping with the style of the house. All the rooms have colour television, hairdryers and tea and coffee-making facilities. Some of the rooms are especially large and ideal as family rooms. Cots and extra beds can be provided on request. Breakfast is a delicious meal with several choices. No evening meals but John and Rosamund are always glad to help with reservations for tables in one of Bath's many good restaurants. Eagle House has a spacious drawing room, which is frequently used for meetings of up to 12 people. There is also a smaller lounge. For those who wish to be energetic there is a new lawn tennis court.

Set in a walled garden adjacent to the main house is a cottage with two bedrooms, two bathrooms, sitting room and kitchen, which can be occupied for stays of two nights or more. It is completely private and has stunning views across the valley.

USEFUL INFORMATION

- OPEN: All year
- WHEELCHAIR ACCESS: No
- GARDEN: 1 1/2 acres Tennis court
- CREDIT CARDS: Visa/ Mastercard
- ACCOMMODATION: 8 ensuite rooms
  Cottage with 2 bedrooms, 2 bathrooms,
  sitting room & kitchen for 2 nights or longer
- RATES: Sgl. £34-45 Dbl. £44-72

- DINING ROOM: Delicious breakfast
- VEGETARIAN: Upon request
- LICENSED: No
- CHILDREN: Welcome

- PETS: Yes

EDEN VALE FARM
Mill Lane
Beckington
Bath
Somerset
BA36SN

Tel: 01373 830371

Eden Vale Farm was an 18th century Mill house which is the home of the Keevil family. It is a charming house still with the mill chimney of what was once a corn and cloth mill. The situation is a delight. A very rural area by the riverside, fishing, canoeing and walking are among many of the activities available, it is also close to a cycle-way. The farm has lots of free range chicken, geese and ducks, Peacocks strut proudly across the lawns and an abundance of wild life lives around Eden Vale. A stroll along the river bank to the weir in the afternoon will often be rewarded with the sight of owls, woodpeckers and pheasants roosting. The village of Beckington is a ten minute walk away where the village pub provides good meals and real ales, or a short drive will take you to many other good eating places. You would never be bored staying at Eden Vale Farm. There are several golf courses within a twenty minute drive as well as a number of Tourist Attractions including the National Trust village of Lacock with its glorious abbey, Stourhead Gardens, Longleat, Cheddar Gorge, Clarks Village at Glastonbury, Rode Tropical Bird Gardens, Stonehenge, Salisbury with its magnificent cathedral and the incomparable city of Bath.

Barbara Keevil runs Eden Vale with the help of her family. She is a friendly lady who delights in ensuring her guests enjoy their stay. Very much into horses, she invites guests to stable their own horses during their stay, if they wish. The house is warm and welcoming with a nice, open log fire burning brightly in the Breakfast room on chilly days. The three bedrooms are all ensuite. A twin bedroom looks over the garden and the Mill Stream. There is a double ensuite with a bedroom and a room above which can be used as a sitting room. In the Stable unit, which is opposite the house, there is another double bedded room and a small room off it with bunk beds; very suitable for a family. These rooms have their own shower and toilet. All the rooms are individually decorated and furnished with pretty drapes and bed covers, some antique furniture, comfortable chairs , television and hostess trays. An iron, hairdryer and washing machine are available. Breakfast is a true farmhouse meal, freshly cooked to your order and caters for both a full English meal and a Continental one. Vegetarians are also catered for.

USEFUL INFORMATION

- OPEN: All year
- WHEELCHAIR ACCESS: Yes
- GARDEN: Yes & Stabling
- CREDIT CARDS: None taken
- ACCOMMODATION: 3 ensuite rooms
- RATES: From £25sgl & £45dbl

- BREAKFAST ROOM: Delicious, farmhouse breakfast
- VEGETARIAN: Catered for
- LICENSED: No
- CHILDREN: Welcome
- PETS: Yes in 1 room

THE FROMEWAY
Frome Road
Radstock
Somerset
BA3 3LG

Tel: 01761 432116
Fax: 01761 431188
E:- mail to hilary.denning@lineone.net

Situated on the A362 from Midsomer Norton to Frome, the Fromeway is ideally placed to explore the many areas of interest nearby. It is within easy reach of Bristol or to explore the beauty of the Mendip Hills and beyond. The Heritage city of Bath is only a few miles away and the Cotswolds just a little further. The beautiful Cathedral city of Wells and mystical Glastonbury are within easy reach. There are several good golf courses as well as pony trekking available. Walking in the Mendip Hills is popular, taking in Cheddar Gorge and bird watching at Chew Valley Lake. At Midsomer Norton there is an indoor swimming pool and squash courts.

The Fromeway, a Free House with an excellent Restaurant, is in the capable and friendly hands of John and Hilary Denning. John Denning, is the sixth generation of his family in the business. A choice of well kept real ales is available and good food is freshly prepared and served in the bar and a 'non-smoking' restaurant. A separate small room is popular for family functions and special occasions. With a varied menu ranging from home-made soup and a sandwich to a freshly cut prime steak, there is something for everyone. Blackboards provide the daily specials which are an important part of the menu, including vegetarian and fresh fish dishes. Home-made sausages, burgers and home-cooked ham are favourite options for light lunches whilst those with larger appetites may choose a mixed Grill or home-cured gammon steak for an evening dinner. Traditional Sunday lunches are served and it is advisable to book. There is a pleasant garden to enjoy in the summer with children's swings and a climbing frame.

The Fromeway is open all year and offers comfortable en-suite accommodation in three modern twin-bedded rooms with television, and a full English breakfast.

USEFUL INFORMATION

- OPEN: All year. 12-3pm &6-11pm 7pm Sun
- WHEELCHAIR ACCESS: Yes
- GARDEN: Yes
- CREDIT CARDS: Visa/Master/Switch
- ACCOMMODATION: 3 ensuite rooms
- RATES:£45 twin £35 single

- RESTAURANT: Wide range Non-smoking
- VEGETARIAN: Catered for
- BAR FOOD: Daily Specials
- LICENSED: Full On
- CHILDREN: Welcome
- PETS: No

GREEN LANE HOUSE
Hinton Charterhouse
NR Bath
BA3 6BL

Tel: 01225 723631
Fax: 01225 723773

AA QQQQ selected

Hinton Charterhouse is a peaceful village close to the beautiful city of Bath. To reach it you take the B3110 from Bath towards Frome. In the village you turn left after the Rose and Crown Inn which will bring you into Green Lane and to a small, very comfortable Bed and Breakfast establishment, Green Lane House. Christopher and Juliet Davies are the owners of this nice house built in 1725 as three cottages now converted into one. It is furnished in a cottage style with soft floral upholstery and curtains and the living room has a log fire.

Two things make the cottage unusual. First of all you will make the acquaintance of Dessie, the security guard, a huge white Pyrenean mountain dog, who bounds round the garden. Secondly everywhere in the house you will find mementoes from thirty years of living overseas; anything from ebony elephants and rhinos to tribal statues and an ostrich egg. Dessie has not yet been called on to guard them against invaders but you never know!

There are four bedrooms in pairs at opposite ends of the house. All four rooms are decorated in soft water colours, pinks, greens and yellows. There are two doubles and two twin-bedded rooms. One twin and double share a bathroom whilst the other twin and double have en suite facilities. After a peaceful night's sleep you come downstairs to the aroma of freshly brewed coffee and a full English breakfast, which will set you up for the day, whatever the purpose of your visit. No evening meals but there are two pubs in the village within easy walking distance, both serving dinner, copies of the menus are available at Green Lane House. Staying here is a pleasure.

USEFUL INFORMATION

· OPEN: All year	· DINING ROOM: English breakfast
· WHEELCHAIR ACCESS: No	· VEGETARIAN: Upon request
· GARDEN: No	· NO SMOKING THROUGHOUT
· CREDIT CARDS: Master/Visa/Euro/AMEX	· LICENSED: No
· ACCOMMODATION: 4 rooms 2 ensuite	· CHILDREN: No
· RATES: Sgl. £28-£42 Twin/dbl. £40-£54 pppn. B/B.	
Special breaks available on request	· PETS: by arrangement.

HINTON GRANGE HOTEL
Hinton
Dyrham
NR Bath
SN14 8HG

Tel: 0117 937 2916
Fax: 0117 937 3285

Hinton Grange Hotel has a very special significance for many of the guests who stay here. One has only to read some of the appreciative 'thank-you' letters to realise how people feel about the owners John and May Lindsay-Walker and Hinton Grange, which is not a grand mansion but a delightful old stone farmhouse which originated in 1416 as a beamed cottage and was extended in 1740 to make a large farmhouse. There is no rush here. This is the place to relax from the pressures of everyday life or, as a grateful guest put it, 'Hinton Grange means something very special to us in our busy lives and its good to know it's there waiting to restore our sanity with peace and care.'

There is a romantic aura about the whole hotel. The old farmhouse courtyard, stables and barns have been converted into this small, intriguing, friendly hotel to appeal to the romantic in all of us. It has been restored, bringing back all the old character and feeling of a bygone era. Each room, whether bedroom or one of the many lounges, has been individually decorated with period and old furniture. The Lindsay-Walkers are unashamed romantics with an ardent love of antiques and fine old things and they have striven for the ultimate in designing and furnishing all the rooms. They want your room to be home and not just another hotel room. The best and deluxe rooms, most with private exterior entrance and individual terraces overlooking the grounds, have open fires and these you are encouraged to use. The Old Inglenook Restaurant has a large Inglenook fireplace, capturing the magic atmosphere to enhance a romantic, candle-lit dinner. Hinton Grange takes pride in the originality of its menus which are compiled after selecting the finest, freshest produce available from the markets of that day. All tastes are catered for including traditional English, Continental cuisine, Vegetarian meals, and for the more adventurous International delights. A full English Champagne Breakfast is served every day.

Hinton Grange has six acres of grounds to explore with nine holes of Pitch and Putt. Fishing is encouraged and licenses are available. There is a sauna and a solarium and for the energetic activities include swimming. It is the perfect place for a break or a holiday with lovely views across the southern slopes of the Cotswolds and the trout lake from most of the rooms. Shooting, dry slope skiing, motor racing, riding, gliding and golf can be arranged and balloon flights take off from the grounds.

USEFUL INFORMATION

· OPEN: All year	· RESTAURANT: Superb cuisine
· WHEELCHAIR ACCESS: Yes	· VEGETARIAN: Always a choice
· GARDEN: 6 acres	· BAR FOOD: Snacks available
· CREDIT CARDS: All major cards	· LICENSED: Yes
· ACCOMMODATION: De-luxe & Standard	· CHILDREN: Over 14 years
· RATES: From £99 -£195 dbl Sgl from £75	
Spring Leisure Breaks from £54	· PETS: No

HOLLY LODGE
8 Upper Oldfield Park
Bath
BA2 3JZ

Tel: 01225 424042
Fax: 01225 481138
Internet: http://www.scoot.co.uk/holly-lodge/

ETB 2 Crown De-Luxe.
AA QQQQQ.
Premier Select 'England for Excellence' Award

The Victorians built some superb town houses and Holly Lodge, set in its own grounds enjoying magnificent views over the world heritage city of Bath, is one of its finest examples. Twelve years ago the house was almost derelict but in the capable and loving hands of Carrolle Sellick and George Hall it has been reborn, superbly furnished and now boasts seven individually designed rooms, some with queen size beds and others with specially built four-posters. All the rooms have luxury bathrooms, TV and satellite movies, direct-dial telephones, hot drink facilities and a host of extras. Over the decade Holly Lodge has won many accolades including being a winner in 1993 of an ETB 'England for Excellence' Award. You will find Holly Lodge featured in many well-known guide books and is graded 'De Luxe' by the English Tourist Board.

Holly Lodge is a strictly non-smoking house and one in which you can enjoy an imaginatively prepared breakfast in the pretty conservatory breakfast room. In the evenings the beautiful lounge or the floodlit gazebo make ideal places in which to relax and unwind after the exigencies of the day whether it has been pleasure or business. Bath is incomparable and will provide hours of pleasure whether it is exploring the abbey with its glorious windows, taking a look at the Pump Room and the other Georgian features of interest, wandering along Pulteney Street, standing on the bridge and watching the river flow past or indulging in a bout of shopping in the superb shops. There are many nearby attractions as well including Castle Combe, Wells Cathedral, Stonehenge and the Cotswolds.

Although Holly Lodge does not provide dinner, there are so many good eateries of all kinds that this poses no problem. Holly Lodge is somewhere that will happily remain in your memory for years to come and you will assuredly want to return.

USEFUL INFORMATION

· OPEN: All year	· BREAKFAST ROOM; Delicious breakfast
· WHEELCHAIR ACCESS: No	· VEGETARIAN: Catered for
· GARDEN: Yes. Floodlit Gazebo	· LICENSED: No
· CREDIT CARDS: All major cards	· CHILDREN: Welcome
· ACCOMMODATION:7 ensuite rms	· PETS: No
· RATES: From £38 pp B&B	

HOMEWOOD PARK
Hinton Charterhouse
Bath
BA3 6BB

Tel :- 01225 723731
Fax :- 01225 723820

3 Red Rosettes. 1 Michelin Star

On the edge of Limpley Stoke Valley and just six miles from Bath, Homewood Park is a delightful, secluded hotel set in a ten acre estate of woodland and well kept grounds. It is country house living at its best and no wonder that it has been discovered to be the ideal retreat for business people wanting undisturbed meetings. Its situation makes it an ideal base for business or pleasure and those coming here in need of rest and relaxation will find themselves quietly and not being pampered.

Everything about Homewood Park is stylish. The beautifully furnished, elegant reception rooms have big log fires on cool days. The friendly, well-stocked bar is where guests enjoy an aperitif and have the opportunity to make new friends. Drinks are also served in the comfortable Drawing Room. The Dining Room is renowned for the excellent menus and the immaculate service. The medieval wine cellars hold bottles of some of the most exciting wines in the world. Having dined and wined superbly one wends one's way to bed in a room that has its own style and charm, has private facilities and many touches designed for one's comfort. Most of the nineteen bedrooms overlook the gardens in which one can play croquet or tennis.

For business meetings Homewood Park has three designated Board Rooms, one able to seat thirty delegates, theatre style. Excellent presentation equipment with professional support is available. These rooms also make excellent private dining rooms for celebrations or family parties.

Golf, fishing, shooting and riding is available within easy reach. Bath with its glorious abbey, fine theatre and famous hot springs must be visited. There are many more great places of interest not too far away.

USEFUL INFORMATION

- OPEN: All year
- WHEELCHAIR ACCESS: Yes.
  Ground floor rooms.
- GARDEN: 10 acres Tennis. Croquet
- CREDIT CARDS: All major cards
- ACCOMMODATION: 19 rooms, private facilities
- RATES: £135 prpn B/B. D.B/B. £205 for two persons.
  Superior £170 prpn. B/B. D.B/B. £246
  Semi-suites £200 per night B/B. D.B/B £270
  Full suites £245   B/B D.B/B £315
  Single £105 pn. B/B. D.B/B £140.pn.
  £25 per person extra where appropriate.
  £10 per night for cots (child free). Children under 6 yr. free if sharing with parents.

- DINING ROOM: Superb, renowned fare
- VEGETARIAN: Always a choice
- LICENSED: Full On
- CHILDREN: Yes

LIMPLEY STOKE HOTEL
Lower Limpley Stoke
Bath
BA3 6HZ

Tel: 01225 723333
Fax: 01225 722406

Located on the outskirts of Bath, just off the A36 Bath to Warminster Road, Limpley Stoke stands in 3 acres of beautiful private gardens in a delightful village setting overlooking the magnificent Avon Valley, convenient for Stonehenge, Salisbury, Wells, The Cotswolds and the National Trust attractions of Lacock, Stourhead, Bowood and Dyrham Park. It is Traditional Georgian country hotel founded in the reign of King James I, becoming a hyrdropathic health resort in 1860. The Limpley Stoke converted to an hotel after the War and has since become one of the finest in the South West.

The objective of the owners of this privately managed and owned hotel, is that the comfort and well-being of the guests is of paramount importance. The peaceful lounges with roaring log fires are an oasis for the weary traveller either after an exhausting but exhilarating exploration of Bath and its environs, or for the business man after a busy working day. Unwind in the Sportsman's bar equipped with satellite TV and cask ale or perhaps play a game of snooker, bar billiards or table-tennis. If you feel energetic fishing on the River Avon is available on request. Golf, clay pigeon shooting, canal boating and some super walks are all there to be enjoyed.

Limpley Stoke Hotel is renowned for the excellence of its food which makes dining a pleasure especially accompanied by a choice of wine from the extensive list. The extensive gardens and spacious public rooms make the Hotel an ideal venue for your wedding reception or party celebration. With a choice of function rooms for up to two hundred guests and the staff's care and attention, the Hotel prides itself on making any celebration a truly memorable occasion.

All sixty seven rooms have private facilities and are equipped with a hostess tray, radio and colour TV, with the majority enjoying magnificent valleys views in this area of outstanding natural beauty.

USEFUL INFORMATION

- OPEN: All year
- WHEELCHAIR ACCESS: Yes
- GARDEN: 3 acres
- CREDIT CARDS: All major cards
- ACCOMMODATION: 67 ensuite rooms
- RATES: From £34 - £40 pppn B&B
  Children up to 10 years free if sharing.
  £5.00 per day for food.

- RESTAURANT: Renowned
- VEGETARIAN: Always a choice
- LICENSED: Yes
- CHILDREN: Very welcome
- PETS: Yes

THE LODGE
Fairwood Farm
Standerwick
NR Frome
Somerset
BA11 2QA

Tel: 01373 823515

Standerwick is located on the A36. A short distance towards Warminster is the turn off for the B3099. Following this road the Lodge is three hundred millimetres, in which Bob and Molly Brown are still involved in running the farm but at the same time welcome guests for bed and breakfast. It is a very comfortable, non-smoking house, modernised completely in 1994. Here you can relax away from the stress of modern day life and revel in the quiet, peaceful atmosphere around you. It is excellent for walks with several on a private farm track. There are good country inns nearby, serving tempting food. It is 3 miles from Longleat, four miles from Westbury with its White Horse and 3 miles from Rode Bird Gardens. The incomparable city of Bath is only thirteen miles away.

The Lodge has three attractively appointed guest bedrooms, all of them ensuite, with central heating and double glazing. Each room also has colour television and a well supplied hospitality tray. Breakfast is a substantial meal starting with fruit juices and cereals and followed by a full English traditional. Plenty of toast and marmalade, tea and coffee complete the meal which will set you up for a day's exploring. A Continental breakfast is available for those who prefer it. No evening meals are served but that is no problem with so many good pubs in the area.

In addition to those mentioned already there are a plethora of places to visit including the world famous Cheddar Caves and Wookey Hole, the Somerset Steam Railway and the cathedral city of Salisbury with its superb architecture.

USEFUL INFORMATION

· OPEN: February to November	· DINING ROOM: Excellent breakfast
· WHEELCHAIR ACCESS: No	· VEGETARIAN: Upon request
· GARDEN: Yes	· NON SMOKING HOUSE
· CREDIT CARDS: None taken	· LICENSED: No
· ACCOMMODATION: 3 rms all ensuite	· PETS: No
· RATES: £25sgl £36dbl	

PARADISE HOUSE HOTEL
Holloway
Bath
BA2 4PX

Tel: 01225 317723 Fax: 01225 482005
E-mail:paradise@apsleyhouse.easnet.co.uk

AA QQQQ RAC Highly acclaimed Johansens Recommended

Described as 'Paradise in Bath', this elegant Georgian House built of classic honey coloured Bath Stone dates back to 1735. It was later sympathetically extended in Victorian times and now offers a building of true architectural interest being both listed and in a Conservation area. Paradise House is ideally situated in a quiet location on the Southern slopes of the City just 5 minutes walk from Bath Spa Station and 7 minutes walk from the City Centre, Roman Baths and Abbey.

Behind its classic and dignified exterior it conceals more than half an acre of splendid walled gardens where trim lawns, and rose-covered pergolas do their best to compete with the splendour of the city below. Overlooked only by the ancient Magdalen Chapel next door, these secluded gardens are available to guests at all times. Traditional English Croquet or a game of French Boules are provided should the English weather allow! With breathtaking views across the City to the famous Royal Crescent and Abbey, Paradise will afford you many wonderful memories of Bath, not the least the illuminated spire of the Abbey at night a spectacular sight.

Paradise is a small privately owned hotel and guests are offered a very warm welcome and personal care, the atmosphere is more in keeping with a private house than an hotel, with every discretion given to the comfort and enjoyment of guests. Help is always available if you require information on how best to spend your time in and around the beautiful city of Bath.

Paradise offers 8 delightfully appointed rooms, all individually decorated and furnished to offer every comfort for your stay. All rooms have private ensuite facilities and are equipped with remote control colour television, direct dial telephone with radio and alarm, hair dryer and hospitality tray. A delicious traditional English Breakfast is served in the dining room with Continental breakfast available in your room should you require. There is a splendid drawing room which boasts an open fire in Winter and views over the garden where guests are welcome to relax and unwind from their day. Daily newspapers are at hand as well as local information on Bath and surrounding areas. Bath has a wealth of restaurants to suit all tastes, the choice is many and varied and with over 80 restaurants eating out is an adventure and a delight. Recommendations and assistance with reservations are all part of the personal service at Paradise House Hotel.

USEFUL INFORMATION

- OPEN: All year
- WHEELCHAIR ACCESS: No
- GARDEN: Delightful wall gardens
- CREDIT CARDS: All major cards
- ACCOMMODATION: 8 ensuite rooms
- RATES: Sgl from £55. Dbl from £75 prpn.
  Family from £75 (two persons) £18 per person extra.
  All rates include breakfast. Seasonal discounts. Midweek Discounts

- DINING ROOM: Excellent breakfast
- VEGETARIAN: Upon request
- LICENSED: No
- CHILDREN: Welcome
- PETS: No

THE PRIORY HOTEL
Weston Road
Bath
BA1 2XT

Tel: 01225 331922
Fax: 01225 448276

3AA Rosettes

Set in four acres of award-winning landscaped gardens on the edge of the City, the Bath Priory Hotel was built in 1835 as a private residence and remains on the finest example of Gothic architecture of it's time. Now beautifully converted, The Bath Priory offers visitors comfort, peace and privacy as well as the luxurious health spa facilities.

Overlooking the stunning gardens are two restaurants where guests can enjoy modern French and Mediterranean cuisine from Michelin starred Chef, Robert Clayton, with the careful direction of the Restaurant Manager, Vito Scaduto, formerly Head Waiter of the year,1993. Three comprehensively equipped meeting rooms can cater for up to sixty people, which suites can be set up for more private meetings.

Internationally renowned designer Penny Morrison has created the Priory's twenty eight bedrooms. All of which are equipped with ISDN line, voice mail; UK/US modem points; remote controlled T.V. with satellite channels; marble bathrooms, fine antique furniture, traditional British fabrics and objects d'art. The Hotel houses a fabulous collection of original and contemporary paintings from the private collection of it's owner. Andrew Brownsword. All guests have complimentary access to a health club, which features a fully equipped gymnasium, heated indoor and outdoor swimming pools, Jacuzzi, spa, sauna, steam room and solarium.

USEFUL INFORMATION

- OPEN: All year

- WHEELCHAIR ACCESS: Yes
- GARDEN: 2 acres landscaped
- CREDIT CARDS: All major cards
- ACCOMMODATION: 21 ensuite rooms
- RATES: Sgl. £160 Dbl. from £220.
  Junior Suite £310 Four-poster £310

- DINING ROOM: French classical & English cuisine Room service & afternoon teas
- VEGETARIAN: Always a choice
- LICENSED: Full On. Fine wines
- CHILDREN: Over 6 years
- PETS: No

RUDLOE HALL
Leafy Lane
NR Box
Wiltshire
SN13 0PA

Tel: 01225 810555
Fax: 01225 811412
E-mail london@g-p.co.uk

Rudloe is a magnificent Victorian house set in four acres of beautiful grounds with commanding views of the countryside including the world heritage city of Bath, 6 miles away. Rudloe Hall belongs to John and May Lindsay-Walker whose other hotel in the area is the romantic Hinton Grange. Both hotels are run with outstanding professionalism and here the emphasis is on making the visitor feel they are staying in a country house, not an Hotel. Life at Rudloe Hall is not rushed. There are only 12 rooms and the pace is informal and relaxed, with the guests enjoying a warm and friendly service. Open fires are a feature of life here. All the reception rooms and most of the bedrooms have them. Guests take so much pleasure from them; they are in keeping with the house and the romantic atmosphere. Your housemaid will service and tend the fire for you, Victorian style!

The Restaurant, open to non-residents, the food is delicious and the priced sensibly. In the evening there is a three course Table d'hôte at £19.95 as well as an extensive A La Carte menu. Cream teas in the afternoon are delicious and an ideal time to meet friends. The Portland Suite is available for business or for celebrations and can cater for up to one hundred people.

Many guests just want to relax, lounging about the hotel in the lounge or the library but the energetic are really spoilt for choice. There is pitch and putt golf and croquet in the grounds and in the area there is golf, riding, fishing and walking. Bath , Bradford-on-Avon and the National Trust village of Lacock, Castle Combe, England's prettiest village and the totally unspoilt village of Biddlestone are all within easy distance.

USEFUL INFORMATION

- OPEN: All year
- WHEELCHAIRS: restaurant only
- GARDEN: Yes
- CREDIT CARDS: All major cards
- ACCOMMODATION: 11 ensuite rooms.
- RATES:- Single £65 - £87 B/B
  Dbl/Twin £70 - £186 prpnB/B.
  Weekend rates D.B/B £44 - £83 pppn.
  (Minimum two nights).
  Other discounts on application.

- RESTAURANT: Delicious food
- VEGETARIAN: Always a choice
- BAR FOOD: Snack menu. Cream teas
- LICENSED: Full On
- CHILDREN: Over 14 years
- PETS: Yes .

STON EASTON PARK
NR Bath
Somerset
BA3 4DF

Tel: 01761 241 631
Fax: 01761 241 377
email:stoneaston@cityscape.co.uk

Egon Ronay Hotel of the year 1983.
G.H.Guide Caesar Award 1987. GFC.
County Restaurant of the year 1989.
Egon Ronay current rating 88%.
AA Rating 4 Red Stars.2 Rosettes 83%.
Michelin 4 Red Turrets. (Featured in all subjective guides).

Ston Easton Park, family home of the Smedley's, is one of the most elegant country house hotels in England. This immaculately restored, aristocratic Palladian mansion was built in 1740 and is set in a Humphry Repton landscape, resplendent with mature beech trees, old oaks and magnificent limes. The Saloon provides ornament of a high calibre in the handsome Kentian plasterwork and 18th century tromp de l'oeil murals and the Library is lined with mahogany bookcases. Throughout the mansion the rooms have all been furnished with appropriate Georgian mahogany. It is somewhere that spells out comfort and unpretentious luxury. If one were looking for somewhere that had an international reputation for outstanding service, excellent cuisine, based upon the highest quality produce, lightly cooked in an imaginative style, a superb wine list then one is scratching the surface of what Ston Easton offers. It is quite superb and at the same time fascinating. 'Downstairs' illustrates the other side of life in the eighteenth century - the old Servants' Hall, Kitchens, Linen Room and Wine Cellar are open for guests to view. Flowers, fruit, vegetables and herbs come straight up to the kitchens from an impressive four-and-a-half acres Kitchen garden. There is a tennis court, golf course, billiard room, croquet lawn, hot air ballooning and wonderful park land walks with Sorrel, the Springer spaniel. Shoes are shined, car windscreens cleaned.

The twenty one bedrooms, all with ensuite bathrooms, are the essence of comfort. The beds have finest quality Egyptian cotton sheets. Direct dial telephones, television and trouser presses are all there to add to one's well-being. The surrounding area contains many historic houses and famous gardens including Stourhead. Bath is only eleven miles away and Thomas Hardy country half an hour away. Pretty villages, the Cotswolds, Stonehenge, Cheddar and the Cathedral cities of Wells, Salisbury and Bristol are all close by. Perhaps have a picnic by the river with a specially made up picnic hamper or Cycle on the Mendips - Bicycle Hire available.

USEFUL INFORMATION

- OPEN: All year

- GARDEN: Yes. Croquet. Hot air ballooning
- CREDIT CARDS: All major cards
- ACCOMMODATION: 21 ensuite rooms
- RATES:From £185 per night per room

- RESTAURANT: Superb food prepared by a talented chef
- VEGETARIAN: Yes & special diets
- BAR FOOD: Terrace menu
- LICENSED: Full On
- CHILDREN: Over 7 years or babes in arms

WOOLVERTON HOUSE
Woolverton
Nr Bath
Somerset
BA3 6QS

Tel: 01373 830415
Fax: 01373 831243

When Noel and Marina Terry acquired Woolverton House, they set about restoring the early 19th century building which originally was a rectory for the 'United Parishes of Woolverton & Rode'. Meticulous and caring in their approach the house has blossomed into a delightful, elegant English country house. It is set in over two and a half acres of grounds and has superb scenic views over the 'glebe lands'; on which the parson traditionally had grazing rights. Woolverton House is, as the Terry's intended, a retreat from the modern world where the emphasis is on heritage, history and nature. They also own a chateau in Brittany where the same principles have been put to work and an ideal holiday atmosphere produced.

There are twelve bedrooms all charmingly decorated and appointed with private bathrooms ensuite. Each room has colour TV, direct dial telephone, a well-supplied hostess tray, trouser press, hairdryer and mini-bar. Non-residents are welcome in the beautifully furnished restaurant where the menu is imaginative and at times innovative with the end result being a delicious meal. The wines, entirely French have been chosen to complement the food. Both the dining room where one has breakfast - another sumptuous meal to set one up for the day - and the elegant drawing room have log fires in the cooler months and the conservatory bar is pleasant all year.

Woolverton House is surrounded by interesting things to see and do, mostly within a twenty miles radius. The city of Bath is always a joy to explore, Longleat with its world renowned Safari Park, the East Somerset steam railway, Cheddar Caves, Wookey Hole and Rode Tropical Bird Gardens and many more places. To reach Woolverton House from the M4 exit 17 take the A350 and then the A361 to Woolverton.

USEFUL INFORMATION

- OPEN: All year
- WHEELCHAIR ACCESS: No
- GARDEN: 2 1/2 acres
- CREDIT CARDS: Mastercard/Visa
- ACCOMMODATION: 12 ensuite rooms
- RATES: Sgl. £45 Dbl. £55-70

- RESTAURANT: Open to non-residents Excellent menu
- VEGETARIAN: No
- LICENSED: Restaurant & Residential
- CHILDREN: Not under 12 years
- PETS: No

THE WOOLPACK INN
Beckington
NR Bath
BA3 6SP

Tel: 01373 831244
Fax: 01373 831223

2AA Rosettes
Le Routier Award

Beckington, a charming village on the A36 Bath-Southampton Road and on the borders of Somerset and Wiltshire, has recently been by-passed and is now a peaceful place. In its midst is The Woolpack, a small 16th century coaching inn. Legend has it that condemned criminals were allowed a final drink here before being led away to the gallows. Today it is the centre of village life and an ideal place in which to stay if you want to explore this part of Somerset and Wiltshire. There are places to visit nearby in abundance: the Georgian city of Bath, the cathedral cities of Salisbury and Wells, Longleat House and Safari Park, Lacock, the National Trust village, Glastonbury, Stourhead, Cheddar Gorge and Wookey Hole, the stone circles at Stonehenge and Avebury, and the tropical bird gardens at Rode.

The inn is furnished in a style that is in keeping with its age and is redolent of the atmosphere of the past, something that is encouraged by the owners and the friendly staff. On the ground floor is the bar area with its stone floor and open log fire, where fine traditional ale is served. There is also a small, very comfortable lounge in which to enjoy a quiet drink. The food here is renowned and whether you eat in the Oak Room, Dining or Garden Rooms, you will find the menu has a wide choice. Freshly prepared dishes include locally caught game and fish. The chefs are both imaginative and innovative but at the same time they are not unmindful that many people still enjoy traditional English fare.

The Woolpack Inn has twelve guest rooms all ensuite and two of them have splendid four-poster beds. Each room is attractively furnished and appointed and has both colour TV and satellite, direct dial telephone and a well-supplied hostess tray. An ideal place in which to stay whether on business or pleasure.

USEFUL INFORMATION

· OPEN: All year	· RESTAURANT: Imaginative fare
· WHEELCHAIR ACCESS: Yes	· VEGETARIAN: Yes
· GARDEN: Yes	· BAR FOOD: Wide range
· CREDIT CARDS: All major cards except Diners	· LICENSED: Full On
· ACCOMMODATION: 12 ensuite rooms	· CHILDREN: Welcome
· RATES: Sgl. £55pppn B&B Dbl. £65	
Four-poster £85	· PETS: By prior arrangement

THE BELL INN
High Street, Buckland Dinham
Frome, Somerset   BA11 2QT
Tel: 01373 462956   Fax: 01373 452572

Les Routiers

If you catch sight of one of the promotional leaflets issued by The Bell Inn you will see a very fair description of all that this magical, creeper clad village inn has to offer. In it the proprietors, Paul and Lynda Hartley-Nadhar tell you 'Its all Theatre'. Act One opens in the bar, lovers holding hands, groups of friends laughing and chatting. In the Interval, the cast and the audience meet in the bar while in the walled garden Al Fresco eating is enjoyed to the sound of Boules being played. And then there is Act Two. Here the stage is set in the restaurant. Centre stage a group of business folk choose from a menu of classic and Mediterranean dishes, while a group of friends extol the virtue of a well stocked wine cellar. Act Three and the leather clad, motor cycling vicar rides on stage to announce 'Sunday Lunch is served'. This brilliant piece of promotion makes one want to visit The Bell. You will find the 16th century Inn in the centre of the village. It has a competition Boule Court, Walled Gardens and Terrace, and a two acre paddock for events. Inside is the traditional flag stone floor, beamed barn, log fire and the warmth of hospitality from Paul, Lynda and their staff, who are very proud of The Bell. It is an experience visiting The Bell, one that will always be remembered and repeated.

USEFUL INFORMATION

· OPEN: All year 11-45-3pm & 5.30-11pm	· RESTAURANT: Superb food Traditional, exotic, Oriental
· WHEELCHAIR ACCESS: Yes + Toilet facilities	· VEGETARIAN: 3-4 choices
· GARDEN: Yes. Boule Court	· BAR FOOD: Excellent choice
· CREDIT CARDS: All major cards	· LICENSED: Full On
· CHILDREN: If well behaved	· PETS: On a lead

HAYDON HOUSE
9 Bloomfield Park
Bath, Somerset   BA2 2BY
Tel: 01225 444919 Fax: 01225 423751
English Tourist Board Category De Luxe;. AA Premier Selected. Good Hotel Guide
Haydon House is an elegant Town House built in 1904 at the height of the Edwardian period. An oasis of tranquillity, it stands in an attractive terraced garden in a quiet road some 10 minutes from the centre of the incomparable city of Bath, the first World Heritage city in Britain. The owners, Madeleine and Gordon Ashman-Marr, have spent considerable time and effort in ensuring that the standards of the house its accommodation are just the way they, and their guests, like them. No expense has been spared but the money has been invested wisely. Every room is beautifully and thoughtfully furnished and in keeping with the age of the house. The decor is rich, yet not overpowering, the mainly Laura Ashley fabrics charming, and the whole effect created is one of light, warmth and elegance. There are five ensuite guest rooms; three doubles, one twin and one family room, all available for single occupation. Every conceivable comfort is offered, including not only hairdryers, hot water bottles, television, and direct dial telephones, but a generous hospitality tray with sherry and home-made shortbread. At breakfast, the choice is remarkable, including all the traditional fare, with the addition of innovations such as whisky porridge, scrambled eggs with smoked salmon, and eggs Benedict. Haydon House is strictly non-smoking. Well behaved children are welcome by prior arrangement as are well behaved dogs.

USEFUL INFORMATION

· OPEN: All year	· DINING ROOM: Wide choice for Breakfast
· WHEELCHAIR ACCESS: No	· VEGETARIAN: Yes
· GARDEN: Terrace garden	· LICENSED: No
· CREDIT CARDS: All major cards	· CHILDREN: By prior arrangement
· ACCOMMODATION: 5 ensuite rooms	· PETS: By prior arrangement
· RATES: From: sgl. £45-£60 dbl. £65-£85 Family: (3 people) £95-£110	

IRONDALE HOUSE
67 High Street
Rode, North Somerset
BA36PB
Tel/Fax: 01373 830730

AA QQQQQ

The village of Rode was built around the wool trade and the 18th century Irondale House was one of the principal houses in the village situated adjacent to the village green. Today it is the home of Jayne and Oliver Holder, two hospitable people who invite guests to share their house with them. There are wonderful views from the house and with its beautiful walled garden, it is a place of peace and tranquillity. Furnished throughout with a harmonious collection of antiques, the atmosphere is relaxed and welcoming. There are two ensuite double bedrooms, one of which is a self-contained garden room, one of which can be a twin. Both rooms have matching curtains, valences and bed-heads made from some wonderful materials. Crisp polly cotton bedding completes the picture. Afternoon tea is offered on arrival if the time is right, otherwise you will be given a drink before you go out to dinner. Breakfast, served in the Dining Room is delicious, the elegant lounge has a superb ceiling. In summer Melon and Strawberries as well as cereals, fruit juices and a traditional English breakfast are served and in winter the Melon and Strawberries are substituted with a bowl of fresh fruit. Ideally situated for people on business or on holiday, Irondale House cannot be bettered.

USEFUL INFORMATION

- OPEN: All year.
- WHEELCHAIR ACCESS: No
- GARDEN: Delightful and walled
- CREDIT CARDS: Master/Visa/Euro
- ACCOMMODATION: 1 dbl 1 s/c garden suite.
- RATES: From £30pp B&B

- DINING ROOM: Delicious breakfast
- VEGETARIAN: Upon request
- SMOKING; Downstairs only
- LICENSED: No
- CHILDREN: Welcome
- PETS: No

LA BISALTA
6 Vicarage Street
Frome, Somerset
BA11 1PX

Tel: 01373 464238

In a quiet residential road just 200 metres from the centre of the old market town of Frome you will find La Bisalta, a charming Italian Restaurant owned and run by Luigi and Susan Violino. La Bisalta has a high reputation for the delicious food it serves and has a clientele who come here regularly from miles around to enjoy both the cuisine and the relaxed, informal atmosphere created by Luigi and Susan. One of its great features is the Terrace where meals and drinks can be taken in the Spring and Summer in a rural setting surrounded by mature trees and walled gardens. In the winter when one needs the warmth of the elegantly furnished dining room with its cheerful log fire, provides just the right atmosphere and one can still look out onto the garden. The menu is a pleasurable mixture of dishes with the emphasis on Italian cuisine complemented by Italian wines. There are two attractive bar areas, intimate in atmosphere and characteristically furnished with open brickwork in the original walls and beams.

USEFUL INFORMATION

- OPEN: 12-2pm & 7pm until late

- WHEELCHAIR ACCESS Yes
- GARDEN: Terrace for warm weather
- CREDIT CARDS: All major cards
- PETS: No

- RESTAURANT: Delicious Italian food in elegant surroundings
- VEGETARIAN: Always a choice
- LICENSED: Full On
- CHILDREN: Yes

THE MANOR LODGE
21 Station Road
Keynsham
Somerset
BS31 2BH

Tel:0117 9862191

Built in Victorian times in the late 1800's, The Manor Lodge is opposite the train station and with a bus stop close by and as it is only five miles from Bristol and Bath it is an ideal place in which to stay for anyone on holiday or working in the area. The Avon Canal provides fishing, there is a golf course within five miles and all around there are some pleasant walks. The house is furnished in keeping with it's period but all the modern amenities are there. The seven attractive bedrooms are all ensuite, each room has television, direct dial telephones and a hostess tray. There is a comfortable Residents Lounge. No evening meals are served but you will enjoy a first class breakfast cooked to your order. The portions are generous and certainly enough to set you up for the day. There are pubs providing food, and a number of eateries within easy distance of the house.

USEFUL INFORMATION

- OPEN: All year
- WHEELCHAIR ACCESS: No
- GARDEN: Private parking
- CREDIT CARDS: Master/Visa
- ACCOMMODATION: 7 ensuite
- RATES: FROM £25 sgl £40 dbl

- DINING ROOM: Great breakfast No evening meal
- VEGETARIAN: Upon request
- LICENSED: No
- CHILDREN: Welcome
- PETS: Yes

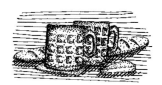

Bason Bridge Inn	East Huntspill	143
Camelot	Blue Anchor	131
Curdon Mill	Williton	132
Fairfield House	Williton	143
Gables	Dunster	133
Globe Inn	Appley	134
Higher Dipford Farm	Trull	144
Home Park Farm	Blue Anchor	144
L'Arivee	Weston Super Mare	145
Langley House	Wiveliscombe	135
Lutteral Arms	Dunster	136
Monkton Inn	West Monkton	145
Periton Park	Middlecombe	137
Royal Huntsman	Williton	138
Spinney	Curland	146
Sunfield House	Minehead	146
Three Horseshoes	Wiveliscombe	139
Tudor Hotel & Restaurant	Bridgwater	147
Uphill Manor	Weston Super Mare	140
Walnut Tree Hotel	North Petherton	141
Yew Tree House	Burnham On Sea	142

Chapter Three:
Of Steam Trains and Cider, Beaches and Cliffs
From Weston-Super-Mare To Minehead

The M5 motorway which divides Somerset in a north to south line carries the vast majority of visitors to the South West straight through the county. Those who do stop in Somerset head for history laden Bath and Wells, or the spectacular Cheddar Gorge, leaving the relatively small area to the West of the main route to the young families heading for Butlins Somerwest World at Minehead or the beaches of Weston-Super-Mare. This leaves an area often quite empty of tourists, but full of real treasures to be discovered, from the remote coastline with the highest sea cliffs in England and the longest "heritage" steam railway line in the country, to the unspoilt beauty of the villages to the east of Exmoor.

Taunton is easily accessible from the motorway, and is a much bigger, busier place than you might imagine. The Bristol Channel coast north of Exmoor is worth a visit too, with an immense variety of shoreline between the sands of Weston-Super-Mare and the pebbles of Porlock. The county boundaries have changed several times to the north of this section, but the M5 seems to claim everything north of Weston as part of the Bristol conurbation, and although Clevedon may officially be part of Somerset, it is at the section of land to the west of Junction 21 that we will make a start.

WESTON-SUPER-MARE (Tourist Information 01934 888800) is often labelled a typical English seaside resort, and to a large extent this is true, even to the causes for its sudden growth in the 19th century. As with Bournemouth, there was little here before 1800, the population in 1811 being a mere 163. You can probably count more people than that in a couple of minutes on the promenade in Summer these days. Both Weston and neighbouring **UPHILL** became fashionable around this time as places for health-giving 'air-taking' if not quite bathing, so famously practised by George III at Weymouth. The sands and air of Weston and the West Somerset coast have always been more attractive than the water, which tends to look a little brown, like cold tea, or something that has been left in a thermos flask for too long, if the dark sands have been stirred by the currents.

What really sealed Weston-Super-Mare's future was the arrival of the railway in 1841. Like so many west country places this marked the town out among its neighbours as the population centre of the future. As a result it is as much a Victorian place in its older buildings as Bath is Georgian. But if you go to Weston then it is the beach which is bound to draw you into the atmosphere, which is unmistakably that of the British at play.

Weston-Super-Mare

Weston-Super-Mare has the modern reputation of being a place for the young, where nightclubs and amusement arcades mark their ownership of the resort. Yet I have often seen many older people enjoying the flat expanses between **WORLEBURY** and **BREAN**. Perhaps this is because most of the noisier activities of the young tend to centre around the Grand Pier, leaving much space for quieter enjoyment.

Maybe, on the other hand, it is simply because Weston has a simple charm which can affect the child in any of us, especially when we are in the right mood to enjoy watching a toddler take his or her first tottering ride on a donkey, or to roll up trousers and walk the shallows, with the noise of thousands of cheery voices easily drowning out the cries of the gulls. The fine curving stretch of the promenade seems to demand a leisurely stroll too, especially in the early evening. Whatever the attraction it is a powerful one, as more than a quarter of a million people come to stay here each year, while six times as many come for at least a day trip.

Among the many attractions at Weston-Super-Mare is the SEA LIFE CENTRE (01934 613361), just to the south of the Grand Pier. As at the attraction of the same name at Weymouth (Chapter Nine), you can learn about the many species represented in a surprising number of ways, including touching some of the tamer rays and other fish. This is one of those places where you can look as if you are merely here for the children, while actually enjoying it immensely for yourself!

Off Regent Street, which leads back into the town from the base of the pier, is the TIME MACHINE (01934 621028) a beautifully maintained museum whose exhibits lead you through the ages; the Edwardian Dentist's Surgery is as scary as you might expect, while the Seaside Gallery provides a more cheerful balance by celebrating the history of the British nation's traditional choice of holiday. The PLAYHOUSE THEATRE and WINTER GARDENS (01934 645544), which has a particularly splendid ballroom, provide shows and activities to make the present day version of a rewarding holiday resort complete. The Weston-Super-Mare HERITAGE CENTRE (01934 412144) has more about the town's history. Three miles from the seafront, near the more industrial **LOCKING**, the INTERNATIONAL HELICOPTER MUSEUM (01934 635227) claims the world's largest collection of helicopters, and also offers pleasure flights.

The middle of Weston, away from the beach, has a good range of shopping available, with the modern indoor SOVEREIGN CENTRE and a pedestrianised, spacious High Street at its heart. From here you can easily get to Weston's various gardens and parks, among which GROVE PARK and the ITALIAN GARDENS are notable for some unusual features such as a fragrance garden and water staircase. Each November there is an illuminated carnival in Weston-Super-Mare, and there are various other events each year, from Kite Flying championships to nights of seafront firework displays (Tourist Information for current details).

Of course if you do tire of being one among very many, then there are quieter beaches to both the north and south, as well as four hundred acres of woods on WOLREBURY HILL, which is also the site of an Iron Age hillfort. WESTON WOODS cover much of the hill of carboniferous Limestone, three miles long and 3/4 mile wide, which juts out into the Bristol Channel, and as Weston-Super-Mare grew in the mid 19th century parts of the original ramparts were eaten into by residential building work and tree planting. Before all was lost two local archaeologists led a group which excavated the interior of the Iron Age defences, in 1851. This was the first full exploration of this kind anywhere in the country, and gave many finds which you can see in the local museums. The fort itself is now a protected ancient monument, and has a spectacular setting on the seaward edge of the hill. The proximity of now empty centres of ancient civilization and busy modern towns is always a compelling one, making you wonder what another couple of thousand years might bring, and is a pattern that we will see repeated many times in Wessex, notably at Dorchester and neighbouring Maiden Castle in Dorset (Chapter Nine).

SAND BAY then gives more beach to the north, before the promontory of SAND POINT, topped by the 15th century version of WOODSPRING PRIORY, makes the right of the two arms which reach out into the sea (Bristol Channel) to protect Weston and make it the ideal setting for a seaside resort. To be surrounded by even less humanity, but more birdlife, you may wish to take a boat trip across to the little island of STEEP HOLM, which is used as a bird sanctuary and also holds some rare species of flora (01934 632307 for sailing information).

The Mendips are mostly to the east of the M5, but the western extremity of the hills comes to a point at BREAN DOWN, which sticks out into the sea to divide Weston-Super-Mare from its southern neighbours, making the other protective arm. The AXE estuary means that Brean Down is quite inaccessible, especially from the north. The views from it are quite fascinating, so a detour through **BLEADON**, a hilltop suburb of Weston, then south to double back through Brean itself, is worth the trouble.

Now a National Trust property, the clifftop is a picturesque place in itself, with sea birds, springy turf, and the sea crashing against its base; a typical west country scene. Yet look left and right, or north and south, and you will be amazed at the contrast. Weston sparkles as only a seaside resort can, especially if the sun is out to help. The other view is a strange one, to say the least. The dunes and sands of Brean are up to three quarters of a mile wide in places, looking almost like a thin strip of desert rather than part of a shoreline. Although there are caravans, there are no camels visible to complete the scene (we will find some of them shortly, in Bridgwater) and the mobile homes are losing out as time progresses to holiday chalets and bungalows. For all the world this looks like a series of temporary encampments, as if the travellers were locked out by the wall of Brean Down from the more permanent civilization of Weston-Super-Mare.

BREAN DOWN BIRD GARDEN (01278 751209) features tropical birds in suitable gardens, and might make a pleasant change if the wind is blowing hard on the clifftops. Many a kittiwake (among other seabirds) has found it impossible to get back to sea after such winds, making this a notorious area for stranding. For another way to enjoy the setting, if not perhaps too many dunes, there is an eighteen hole golf course which welcomes visitors inside the BREAN LEISURE PARK (01278 751595) on the sands. An alternative course can be found at the BURNHAM AND BERROW GOLF CLUB (01278 785760).

The sands of Brean run straight on southwards to become the flats and dunes of **BERROW**, as the strip of land between the coast and the motorway narrows towards Burnham and Highbridge. All in all there are some tremendous stretches of sandy beach running along this coast, reminiscent of the expanses between Christchurch and Poole, with Bournemouth in between. Like the Dorset resort conurbation, Weston and its neighbours are expanding fast, especially in terms of attractions and accommodation facilities for visitors; it is the major industry. But this area has a very different character to that of the south coast.

Horse Riding on the sands of Brean and Berrow

The land behind the coast is not yet completely taken over by modern housing, and the mound of **BRENT KNOLL**, which has given its name to the village below it (as well as to the motorway services area) is a reminder that it has not always been tourists who have camped amongst the Dunes. There was a hillfort here, and it may have been the site of the BATTLE OF BATTLEBURGH, one of King Alfred's most important triumphs over the Danish invaders of ninth century Wessex. We will hear much more of Alfred in Wiltshire, but with the Battle of Sedgemoor dominating local military history (as well as providing the name for the next Motorway services), it is ironic that a battle of even greater import might well have happened here more than twice as long ago, less well documented but equally dramatic, especially in its setting.

The church of ST MICHAEL in the village of Brent Knoll is famous for some carved, medieval bench-ends, which seem to tell the story of a corrupt local abbot who came to a sticky end. We have the substance of the story but not the detail, while the older legend about the creation of the Knoll itself is more straightforward, yet much more fanciful. The devil is supposed to have dug out Cheddar Gorge with an immense shovel, throwing the huge clods of earth out to the west. In this way Steep Holm was made, but perhaps the effort taxed his throwing arm, as the next shot fell short, creating Brent Knoll. When you think of all the tourist revenue made from Cheddar, as well as the military protection allegedly provided by Brent Knoll, it would seem that His Satanic Majesty has favoured the natives of Somerset. I hasten to add that I am sure this was never his intention, or that they have in any way curried favour with him!

Nearby **BURNHAM-ON-SEA** (Tourist Information 01278 787852) adjoins **HIGHBRIDGE** so closely that they virtually form a single town, filling the narrowest part of the gap between shore and motorway. Neither really has either the charm of Weston-Super-Mare or the wilder appeal of neighbouring Berrow and Brean, but do have some places of interest, linked to a history which has had its moments. The most interesting period in Burnham's history revolves around the efforts of the Reverend Davies, perhaps an unexpected source of entrepreneurial wisdom. He it was who dug the wells which made Burnham a spa, giving the early nineteenth century tourist trade a new impetus. This was a costly operation, and he raised the money by building a lighthouse and obtaining permission to charge passing shipping a toll. The lighthouse which you can see at Burnham now was its replacement, built in 1832. The bridge of Highbridge was in fact a dam, and kept the sea back, even when it was at a higher level than the River BRUE, at whose end the town stands.

This might seem like a fairly ordinary and unexciting part of the country, and the smell of the local cellophane factory, if caught when the wind blows ill, might not give much promise to the next town to the south. Whatever else **BRIDGWATER** (Tourist Information 01278 427652) is, ordinary and unexciting it is not. A place of camels and canals, there is something strangely disconcerting about this large town perched at the end of the River PARRETT'S Estuary. There is one day each year when all this and much more is forgotten around here though, when you either enter the party atmosphere or head for the hills to avoid some of the most amazing traffic jams you are likely to meet so far away from the M25. The BRIDGWATER CARNIVAL is the undisputed champion of all those held in Wessex.

If you have not lived in Somerset it is quite difficult to understand the sense of anticipation that builds in local communities, starting late in the summer. Many of the organisations and individuals responsible for the carnival floats work on them all year, but it is the rehearsals and last minute tests of electrics, costumes and dance routines, taking place on farms and in halls in many a backwater which really get the community feeling of celebration going. This is more than a night to pull in some Autumn tourists. Mind you, some of the 120,000 people who flood to the town on the Thursday nearest to November 5th each year must come from further afield than the many youths and adults from Taunton, Chard and other towns and villages of the area who compete so devotedly to make their float the best in its category.

What I really like about the carnivals is the lack of obvious sponsorship; so much of what is done to create the long procession of bright lights, colour and sound is real local effort, not paid for by some national or multi-national company looking for another way of advertising. This is the carnival of all Somerset carnivals, so if you are only going to visit one then Bridgwater is the place for the largest, although some of the settings of the lesser ones (the crowds clinging to the walls around the church for a good view in Ilminster for example) stop it from being the best in every way. The atmosphere of each is unique, and the night, in each town, is really one it would be very hard not to enjoy.

Perhaps something of the spirit of this event stays in the locality through the year, as I have found the BRIDGWATER ARTS CENTRE (01278 422700/1) to be a lively place over the years too. Drama, music and the visual arts are all given space here. This may be a small centre of population in an essentially rural area, but a quiet backwater it is not. Bridgwater has some good shopping too, and is a bigger place than it might at first seem to the casual visitor.

Let's talk about camels. The M5 is not the most joyous of routes to take to work, as I have learnt through personal experience over the years. So it is that any little piece of eccentricity experienced upon it is likely to remain in the collective memory. Several years ago my radio alarm clock woke me up with a lively discussion on Danny Baker's Radio Five morning programme about animals on roads. He was interested in hearing about models rather than real animals; something to rival the concrete cows made so famous by Milton Keynes.

My mind flew straight to Bridgwater, but by the time I had summoned enough consciousness to make my way to the telephone many others had beaten me to it. This was a telling moment. Thousands had noticed the camel, and beheld it with the same affection I had. The camel is perched by the fence at the side of the motorway, on the left as you travel north, in a field empty except for its presence. I am sure I have seen him expelling irrigating water from his mouth too, or perhaps just drainage overspill. Recently I saw him wearing a scarf, garland of flowers and a bright new coat of paint. Apparently he is a relic from a carnival float of the past, unlike Atakor, Tazruk, Tiefet and Seita, who are very much the real thing.

When I heard about these camels of the BRIDGWATER CAMEL COMPANY (01278 733186) at nearby **OVER STOWEY** I immediately telephoned in the hope of finding that there was a connection, thinking that perhaps the idea of running local Camel Treks had been inspired by the motorway sentinel. Unfortunately not, but the real camels have been in the area since the end of 1996 and the day or half day treks take place across the BRIDGWATER BAY RESERVE to the north of the town. Once you are on the sand flats the camels feel quite at home, and if you would like to fabricate a holiday to the Sahara then this might well be the place to get the pictorial evidence with which to fool your friends and neighbours.

Back to more serious matters at Bridgwater. It was from here that Monmouth, in 1685, made the last, doomed decision of his short lived rebellion. Seeing the Royalist approach he decided to leave the town to surprise them to the east. The rest of the story of the actual Battle of Sedgemoor belongs to the east of the motorway which now separates Bridgwater from the site, and so to another chapter, although the rebellion had its effects nearly everywhere in Wessex, an example of which we will soon discover at Taunton. A more lasting hero of Bridgwater pre-dates the ill-fated Duke of Monmouth.

The ADMIRAL BLAKE MUSEUM (01278 456127) is housed in the birthplace of Robert Blake, Cromwell's chosen leader of the fleet at the Battle of Santa Cruz.

He was also Taunton's defender during the Civil War, and a member of parliament, and there is a statue of him in front of the main post office in the town. The museum covers local history from Blake to Sedgemoor and onwards to the time of the canal.

The BRIDGWATER AND TAUNTON CANAL still runs from the docks at Bridgwater to the River Tone at Taunton, crossing the M5 twice before reaching its destination. One way to see the waterway during a day or evening guided cruise is to contact the owners of PEGGOTYTOM and LADY PEGGY (01278 446744 / 0378 750974) two cruising narrowboats based in Bridgwater. Day trips and boats for longer, self-drive hire are available elsewhere too, and the canal is good for fishing, but more of this later, east of the motorway. Built between 1824 and 1827 this remains the only part of the planned Bristol to Taunton waterway ever to reach fruition.

Bridgwater is perhaps Somerset's most successful industrial town, and it started on this path long ago. With pretensions to rival Bristol as a port, the canal built upon Bridgwater's usefulness as a supply line to the coast for Taunton, Yeovil and much of central Somerset. The Parrett has a very muddy estuary, and Bridgwater was the best place to cross. Other industries have been important to the town too, and the SOMERSET BRICK AND TILE MUSEUM (01278 456127) on the East Quay has the last surviving brick kiln in the county. Now there are different industries, from shoes to engineering, not forgetting cellophane, but the most controversial of the area's working places lies a little further west.

How does a 'nuclear power-packed day out' sound? Perhaps you are led to think of Jet Skis, or some contraption with bouncy suspension which will have no trouble outstripping the camels across the sands. The line actually comes from an advertisement for visits to what many will see as the black sheep of the Somerset coast, HINKLEY POINT POWER STATIONS (01278 654700). Whatever you might think of the ethics of four nuclear reactors sitting on the coast half way between the Nature Reserve of Bridgwater Bay and the seaward end of the Quantock Hills, the trip is intriguing, and educational.

If you go expecting to feel as though you are part of a 1970s Science Fiction movie, then in some ways you will not be disappointed. Hinkley is very isolated, it is like going into a whole village, or separate community, and the name badges and white coats worn by some of the staff do make you feel as if Jane Fonda or Donald Sutherland might appear around the next corner carrying a clipboard and looking worried. In all, this is a comfortingly down to earth place, and one surprise is the noise of the generators; for some reason you would expect the production of nuclear power to be an eerily silent process; it isn't. There is no equivalent of customs where you are checked by a Geiger counter on the way out either!

Part of the Visitor Centre at Hinkley is a Nature Trail, and if you wish to see more, the STEART FLAT BIRD SANCTUARY (01278 652426) to the east should be ideal. The often tortuously busy A39 from Bridgwater, which gives access to Minehead and the west, takes you through the village of **CANNINGTON**, best known for its Agricultural College. The College's HERITAGE GARDENS AND PLANT CENTRE (01278 655019) adjoin the much older CANNINGTON COURT, originally a nunnery built in the 12th century. There are five walled gardens here with individual themes, as well as tropical and temperate glasshouses.

A little further west you may suddenly feel thirsty, even if the rain is pouring and the green of the Quantocks to your left suggests that there is *"Water, water everywhere...."* for the unpretentious village of **NETHER STOWEY** is where that very famous line was written. Samuel Taylor COLERIDGE lived in the Cottage now owned by the National Trust (01278 732662) between 1796 and 1798, and 'The Rime of the Ancient Mariner' was composed during this stay. If inspiration was drawn from the world around him then this must have been a much more sinister place two hundred years ago, especially as the disturbing 'Christabel' was also written here. In reality he did get stories of seafaring from nearby Watchet and Porlock, and the disturbing sense of reality mixed with nightmarish fantasy which pervades some of his verse is not inappropriate for some of the coastline around here, especially towards Kilve and East Quantoxhead, as we will soon see. The countryside presumably gave help in the planning of the 'Lyrical Ballads'too, planned by William Wordsworth during his stay at nearby **HOLFORD** on the Quantock Hills. He came here in 1797 to be close to Coleridge. Another, more recent, literary connection can be found on the other, south western side of the range of hills, where the village of **COMBE FLOREY** held the family home of Evelyn Waugh.

For now we will abandon the A39, to return to it later via a much more scenic road, where tyres have no place. Heading back through Bridgwater towards Taunton, there are some detours worth taking from the main A38, which runs parallel to the motorway. FYNE COURT (01823 451587) in the hamlet of **BROOMFIELD** was ravaged by fire at the end of the 19th century, but the gardens remain, as do parts of the building. Various events are held here, by the SOMERSET TRUST FOR NATURE CONSERVATION, whose headquarters it is. These have imaginative themes including dawn birdsong, Narrow Boat art and wild flower identification.

From here you can cut back towards Taunton through **KINGSTON ST MARY** with its fine square church tower, and then **CHEDDON FITZPAINE**, where you will find HESTERCOMBE GARDENS (01823 413923). The restoration of these gardens originally conceived by Lutyens and Jekyll at the beginning of the century has justifiably won awards during 1997. The whole has yet to be completely reclaimed, but the three formal period gardens, Georgian, Victorian and Edwardian are already impressive in season. The landscaping really is on a gorgeous scale, with walls, steps, terraces and curiosities appearing amongst banks of herbaceous plants and shrubs, all lined by trees. Hestercombe is a real triumph of modern conservation and restoration work as well as classic landscape designing, with the Bampfylde Landscape Garden from the

1750s open again in 1997 for the first time in well over a century. The forty acres of lakes and woodland walks are still being restored in full, but this only adds to the attraction, as you can still see aspects of the reclamation taking place.

TAUNTON (Tourist Information 01823 336344) might bring to mind orchards and flagons of cider, but what you will find in Somerset's county town is very far from a rural backwater. The centre is busy, and with an almost incredibly rapid expansion of its population over recent years, Taunton has spread in all directions, with major investment in Leisure and shopping facilities on the previously empty land past CREECH CASTLE leading to the M5 being particularly apparent.

There are still a few things which Taunton does not have which will help to define its character. The lack of a single centralised shopping mall has helped little alleyways like BATH PLACE keep their character, with rows of small specialised shops just a few steps from the main pedestrianised street with its more predictable major stores. No university (although there are some sizeable Colleges of Further Education of which one is linked to Plymouth University) means that the younger population remains pretty much indigenous, and this is quite rare in a place this size. Taunton is getting very big indeed, but it still has a sense of community, stronger than in many smaller places.

With all respect to TAUNTON TOWN F.C. and their many heroics in the F.A. Vase competition, what the town also does not have is a major football team. Why should this matter to the visitor? Spend a few hours in some of the better local Wine Bars and other hostelries and you will most likely hear of other sporting heroes of the fairly recent past, in what is one of the most cricket mad towns in the country.

The County Cricket Ground, Taunton

Whether SOMERSET COUNTY CRICKET CLUB (01823 272946) had such a following before the late 1970s I am not qualified to say. All I know is that the escapades of a certain Mr I.T.Botham and his county colleague Viv Richards, inflated as they undoubtedly have been by much retelling, definitely add something to Taunton. I think it is because you feel that despite its new found size, this is still a place where the individual can make a difference, and where you are more than usually likely to see a stray celebrity walking the town's main streets without the need for a bodyguard. Another cricketing personality from the Southern Hemisphere gave some new gloss and colour to the legends in the later part of the 1980s, when Merv Hughes and his unforgettable moustache came to town.

Taunton Cricket Ground is still a wonderful place, and the cheers can be heard through the unusually empty streets of the town centre when a one day cup match is going well for the home team. The SOMERSET CRICKET MUSEUM (01823 275893) will tell you more of the longer term history of the county's top sport. Television coverage of these events always includes some shots panning across the skyline, where the church spires of Taunton stand out to give beauty and a sense of history, and probably add to the popular misconception of the town as being a quiet, rural place!

There has been a town nestled between the Blackdowns and the Quantocks since at least 710, when King Ine established Taunton in the valley of the River TONE. Over the next few hundred years the town became a centre for ecclesiastical rather than royal power, and eventually gained the reputation of being a place of puritans and dissenters. Cornish rebels entered the town in 1497, and soon after another rebellion, led by Perkin Warbeck, finally collapsed here.

At this very time the tallest of Taunton's spires was being built, on ST MARY MAGDALENE'S. One hundred and sixty three feet of tower, built from the distinctive golden yellow stone of nearby Ham Hill, top one of the finest churches of the Gothic Perpendicular style you will find anywhere. After a period of very active local fundraising the church has undergone extensive restoration in recent years, and benefits from being just off the main shopping streets, accessible yet not overshadowed or trodden down by weight of numbers.

Taunton was a prosperous place, with cloth as its main industry, even managing to get through the Civil War relatively unscathed, despite being a Parliamentary stronghold in a largely Royalist part of the country. The temporary undoing of Taunton and its prosperity started on a day in June 1685, when twenty seven young 'Maids of Taunton' welcomed the Duke of Monmouth with an embroidered crown and twenty seven 'chaste' kisses (one each).

The Duke knew there were discontented subjects throughout England, but his choice of Lyme Regis as a landing place from which to build his attempt to claim the crown was made specifically with Taunton in mind. It was here that he declared himself King (in the Market Place), and so it was here that the retribution after his defeat fell the strongest, comparable with events in Dorset's county town of Dorchester (Chapter Nine).

Before the infamous Judge Jeffries even got to Taunton thirty rebels had been hung in the Market Place by Colonel Kirke. Bodies of many more were dismembered, the heads and limbs sent to be displayed in the villages to spread the royal message. The Bloody Assizes then followed, and although a mere 150 were condemned to death by Jeffries here, as opposed to nearly double that number in Dorchester, the victims were from a more concentrated, local area. Many, many more were transported to almost certain disease and death in the tropics, and the whole episode is a very dark patch in Taunton's history. Even the 'Maids' who had welcomed Monmouth were given by James II to members of his household, and were only returned to their parents for a sizeable amount of money, even though some of them were still several years from being teenagers.

It is said that Taunton was so shocked by all of this that it still remains anti-royalist to this day, although I think this is an unlikely generalisation. Georgian times brought happier days again to the town, and the short road leading to Mary Magdalene's is named after Benjamin HAMMETT, who was instrumental in finding the town replacements for the waning cloth trade. Even today the shirt industry survives on the edges of the town, and others have since joined it, but it is as an administrative centre that Taunton really stands out. The Victorian COUNTY HALL and the nearby CRESCENT emphasise the regrowth of prosperity during the 19th century, but they cannot take the focus away from the real centre of the town, just a couple of hundred yards away.

The SOMERSET COUNTY MUSEUM (01823 320201) is right in the middle of this, on the CASTLE GREEN, accessible through the bulky 15th century gateway which seems to promise so much. Most of the original castle is gone, but the museum has an appropriate home in what is left, and features everything from archaeological remains to a collection of toys and dolls, as well as a history of the Somerset Light Infantry.

Coming back out of the Castle Gateway there are a confusing number of directions in which to take a walk around the shops. If you head left to the bridge over the River TONE, and then turn left again, a walk along the banks past the British Telecom Headquarters leads very quickly to a lovely quiet area. I have spotted some excellent chub and large roach cruising the shallows in summer here, but must admit that I have seldom seen the anglers who line the banks catching many of them. Of course that doesn't really matter if you want to sit and let time slip by as easily and quietly as the passing water. Further along the river, in the other direction, and near the cricket ground, the BREWHOUSE THEATRE (01823 283244) can be found, built inside a 19th century warehouse amongst some more streets full of small shops as well as a glassworks where you can watch the products being blown (01823 333422). As in Bridgwater, this is a centre for the arts which does not always put commercial enterprise first, making it an exciting and often adventurous place.

There are many facilities in Taunton, and the number is growing fast. Some, such as VIVARY PARK are just as they were many years ago, while the VIVARY GOLF COURSE (01823 333875) provides another way to enjoy it. But before we leave the town behind we must go back to where we started, and the single thing most people associate with this town; cider.

The SOUTH WEST OF ENGLAND CIDERMAKERS ASSOCIATION produces a leaflet which features some twenty three locations in Somerset and Devon where presses are still working, and the largest and most famous of these is TAUNTON CIDER (01823 332211) at **NORTON FITZWARREN** on the outskirts of the town. Apparently cider has been made for very many centuries, and perhaps the legends of Somerset being a land of permanently sozzled scrumpy drinkers have something to do with the fact that until the late 19th century it was common practice for farm labourers to receive four to six pints of cider a day as part of their wages! The nearest I have come across to a modern equivalent was while I lived in Taunton. I shared a house with one of the administrative staff from Taunton Cider. Each Friday afternoon he would arrive with a crate full of the latest experiment or brand in bottled cider. Tasting them all was a terrible chore, so I sometimes offered my help.

Cider has become much more fashionable in the last ten years or so, and orchards are being replanted. SHEPPY'S CIDER FARM CENTRE (01823 461233) in **BRADFORD-ON-TONE**, between Taunton and Wellington, gives a chance to taste some of the many varieties, and to see how the presses work. Bradford itself is a pretty little village, with a punishing hill for those of us foolhardy enough to have taken part in the Taunton Marathon (at least I only ran the thirteen mile course), and there are many others surrounding the county town. Most lie east of the motorway and so fall into our next chapter, but others, such as **TRULL** to the south and **MONKTON HEATHFIELD** to the north, should not be missed. Despite both the proximity of the motorway and the non stop expansion of Taunton's housing areas, these places have retained a quiet rural character, and are lovely places to go for a quiet drink or walk on a warm Summer's evening.

Now we have moved to the south let's go as far as the Devon border before turning back. From just about everywhere in this part of Somerset a monument to the Iron Duke, who also gives his name to the town of **WELLINGTON** (Tourist Information 01823 474747), is visible. The National Trust owns a strip of land from the road to the monument, which lies just to the east of the M5, but must nevertheless stay with its home town in this chapter. The obelisk, which is 175 feet tall, was erected by the townspeople to celebrate the Duke's exploits. He took the town's name because it was close to his family name of Wellesley, and Wellington gave him a monument despite any other real connection with it. Sounds like a fair exchange. The views from here are wide ranging, taking in the Blackdowns, Quantocks, Taunton Deane and Exmoor. The town of Wellington itself is a pleasant enough place without being spectacular in any way. The WELLINGTON MUSEUM (01749 673477) tells of its history as a cloth town, a similar industrial story to that of Taunton. By now the west will call, and only a short drive from Wellington the country opens right out, covered with so many little lanes that there scarcely seems room for fields in between them.

WIVELISCOMBE is the largest place in the area between Wellington and Exmoor. If you have been to 'Wivvy' then the term large, even used as a comparative, is likely to make you smile. If ever there was an archetypal country town, surrounded by nothing other than villages, hedges, farms and fields, then this is it. Somehow it has a very distinctive charm, so remote as to remind me of many of the smaller places in Southern Ireland. Wiveliscombe was chosen as a hiding place for many of London's art treasures during the Second World War, to keep them safe from the blitz. A wise choice; even if the bombers knew to head for the town I doubt they would have been able to find it! As if Wiveliscombe hadn't already enough charm, its prime industry is the brewing of excellent beer, just to give you some variety from the local ciders! If you like a narrow, steep High Street with some horribly tight junctions and corners, but without many vehicles around to negotiate them, then this is the place for you. It is also an excellent base from which to explore the west, even right into Exmoor, which is now only a short drive away.

There is no visible border of the National Park, except on the maps, and this is a delightfully quiet area, where the countryside is all. The rolling green farmland of the south east section of the Moor runs straight into that west and south of Wiveliscombe without any further sudden change of character, and the whole region is surprisingly unexplored by the vast majority of visitors to Exmoor. At nearby **MILVERTON** I can personally recommend the carp lakes to be fished at LOVELYNCH FARM, and throughout the area there are other places to stay, fish, ride and generally enjoy the country. In particular there are more lakes, with carp among the fish present, near two of the other villages. Back towards Wellington, at **LANGFORD BUDVILLE**, are the LANGFORD LAKES (01823 400476), while near **CHIPSTABLE**, outside Wiveliscombe, the fishing at OXENLEAZE FARM (01984 623427) is in a particularly lovely setting.

There are many villages too, some extremely difficult to find in the labyrinth of narrow lanes. **TOLLAND** is one of these, and is the location of GAULDEN MANOR (01984 667213). Privately owned since the Dissolution of the Monasteries, this is famous for some tremendous plasterwork, thought to be from the 17th century. A lived in home, Gaulden is also known for its peaceful gardens.

We are now at the edge of the picturesque Vale of TAUNTON DEANE, but in order to appreciate it, and the Quantock Hills, in the most romantic of ways it is first necessary to go back towards Taunton itself. Let's take a trip out of the county town to the north west. As you leave the motorway and then Taunton behind you, the country quietens immediately into a place of lush dark green hedges and rolling fields more reminiscent of Devon than Somerset, yet even now you are just a handful of miles from wild spacious moorland and some of the most unusual and spectacular beaches nature can offer. The diversity of this area is part of its beauty, making it both rewarding and memorable.

Leaving Taunton by the A358, with a passing salute to the armed sentry at the Norton military camp (who usually returns the gesture), you soon arrive at **BISHOPS LYDEARD**. A new venture here is a museum called BLAZES (01823 433964). Using technology as well as displays of equipment and uniforms, it explores the history of fire fighting, and is planning to expand into the only museum in the northern hemisphere to cover all aspects of mankind's relationship with fire.

It will have to go a long way before it can compete with its very near neighbour. The main attraction here is the chance to leave the car and take to the WEST SOMERSET RAILWAY (01643 704996 or website at http://www.wctb.co.uk), which operates through ten stations from Bishops Lydeard to Minehead. For twenty miles of curving railway lines following the contours of the Quantock Hills and then the Bristol Channel coast, you are transported back to the age of steam.

The West Somerset Railway

This is an original part of the Great Western Railway, and every effort has been made to retain the feel of otherwise bygone days. From the first sight of the fearsome black engine entering the station to details such as the original metal advertisements flanking the platforms, you notice the care which has been put into creating an engaging reality rather than a show-case. The carriages are comfortable but not pristine; they too have seen many years service. The buffet is very reasonably priced, the staff are friendly, and the nostalgic atmosphere is undeniable. If you can see a raw beauty in steam railways then this is the place to be. The West Somerset Railway is open from March to January, and is sensibly priced, running a series of family and group discounts, it also hosts events during the year, from "Friends of Thomas the Tank Engine" to a Steam Fayre and Vintage Vehicle Rally. We will use the train route from Bishops Lydeard to see what else the area has to offer.

The sense of an exploratory adventure is immediately established as the train climbs slowly out of Bishops Lydeard through rich forest edged in the colours of the season. First stop is **CROWCOMBE HEATHFIELD**, a small rural village ideal to use as a starting place for a walk on the Quantocks, always with the chance to see a vibrant wild stag roaming the countryside below. The Hills get their name from a Celtic word meaning circle or rim, and this is the shape they form, running for thirteen miles from Quantoxhead on the coast to **THURLOXTON**, halfway between Bridgwater and Taunton. A walk along the ridge in the middle of this route is to be recommended. This broken path has had many uses, even carrying coaches in the early 19th century if the lower roads became impassable. In fact it has been here a good deal longer than any of the major roads of the region, being a prehistoric route dotted with barrows, cairns and beacon mounds. Iron and Bronze Age earthworks look down from the ridge onto more recent, but equally peaceful villages. Notable examples are DOWSBOROUGH HILLFORT above Holford, and the cattle enclosures of TRENDLE RING overlooking **BICKNOLLER**. The whole area has been designated an Area of Outstanding Beauty, and the Forestry Commission has created a Nature Trail near Over Stowey which runs for about two and a half miles. With open spaces of bracken and heath, as well as wooded combes, wherever you choose to walk on the Quantocks your views will be varied, but quite breathtaking.

Back near to Crowcombe Heathfield is HALSWAY MANOR FOLK CENTRE (01278 446189), home of the West Somerset Morris Men who meet each Thursday from September to April. Next comes **STOGUMBER**, as the surroundings start to change, opening out and leaving most of the trees behind. This village houses BEE WORLD (01984 656545). A popular place for families to visit, the exhibition of the honey collecting process, as well as the chance to observe working hives in action gives it more to appeal to adults than most farm attractions. If you do use the train to visit Stogumber and the Bee World an extra discount is given by both, a welcome sign of the move towards public transport as a more ecological way to access the countryside. The walk through exhibition is packed with information about bees, hornets and wasps, and has been built up over the last few years with obvious loving attention by the beekeeper and his family. Don't worry though, the glass screens which separate you from the many thousands of live bees appear quite secure! After you have watched the bees in action, their delicious honey can be bought from the farm shop on the way out.

The next train station at **WILLITON** has been beautifully restored to its original 1860s appearance, and it is from here that the railway line turns to the West, leaving the Quantocks and following the coastline towards Minehead. Williton bills itself as the largest village in the country. Among the crafts in the village is the WILLITON POTTERY (01984 632150) which has a workshop as well as an exhibition gallery and showroom. An unusual attraction is the BAKELITE MUSEUM (01984 632133) which has the honour of being Britain's first museum of vintage plastics.

To the east of here lies some most surprising and spectacular coastline. The beaches between **WEST** and **EAST QUANTOXHEAD**, and especially that at **KILVE**, were once described to me by a child as being a lunatic giant's attempt at crazy paving. Vast slabs of slate and rock form uneven terraces which step into the sea, waves constantly crashing against the bottom-most platforms. You will need a good pair of walking boots rather than flip-flops to explore these shores, as crazy angles filled with seaweed and rivulets of sea water divide each section at random.

It is possible to walk from East Quantoxhead to Kilve along the edge of what are some of the highest sea cliffs in England, or if you are feeling brave then a rock climb along the beach can be attempted. Either will leave you inspired by the power of nature's display, and personally I find the rugged lines of this area quite beautiful in their own unique way. Kilve itself is a quiet village, and The Hope Arms, a lovely, peaceful pub, is ideally sited next to the path leading down to the shore. East Quantoxhead has an exquisite little duck pond at its centre, and even the walk from here across suddenly rough country to the shore is a memorable one.

Away from Williton in another direction, through **MONKSILVER** to the south, lies the COMBE SYDENHAM COUNTRY PARK (01984 656273), right up against the edge of Exmoor. This has ten miles of marked woodland walks, nature trails, fly and coarse fishing as well as the 16th century Manor House at the heart of the Estate. This started life as a monastic house, improved upon in 1580 by the father of Elizabeth Sydenham, the heiress who married Sir Francis Drake five years later. The West Wing of the House has been restored, including the Court Room, and there is a also a working bakery to see.

Meanwhile, the railway line continues on from Williton through the holiday village of **DONIFORD** to reach the sea at **WATCHET,** a small harbour town. This is probably one of the quietest periods in this pretty town's history. From raiding Vikings to optimistic Iron Ore miners, Watchet has seen them all come and go over the last millenium and more, without looking flurried by the experience. Another man is supposed to have left here for an unfortunate meeting with an albatross, as the central figure of Coleridge's most famous poem, the aforementioned 'Rime of the Ancient Mariner'. One wonders what the poet would make of the town's more recent role as a base for the exporting of tractors to Portugal!

The MARKET HOUSE MUSEUM (01984 631345) will tell you much more about the history of Watchet as a seaport, be it through fossils from the local cliffs or the coins left behind by Saxon and Norman civilizations.

As the train chugs along the coast towards **WASHFORD** it is easy to forget that this vast expanse of water is not the Atlantic, but rather the Channel between England and Wales, although on a clear day the Welsh town of Barry is clearly visible in the distance. A fifteen minute walk from the station at Washford lies CLEEVE ABBEY (01984 640377). Founded for Cistercian monks at the end of the 12th century, this site is one of the few of its era to have survived with a complete set of cloister buildings. These date from the 13th Century, the Abbey's most prosperous period. As you pass the secluded gate-house, there are few clues to what awaits inside the monastic quarters. Among the most memorable details are a 15th Century wall-painting, and the beautifully tiled pavement of the Refectory, as well as an open arched timber roof which has already lasted seven hundred years to look as stout as any modern construction. It is hard to believe that the monastery was dissolved in 1537, and yet so much has survived through the intervening years. When the Abbey surrendered to Henry VIII's forces there were fifteen monks in this idyllic setting. One of them at least had not seen the end of the wrath of the King's family. John Hooper went on to become a protestant Bishop of note, eventually burnt alive outside his own Cathedral in Gloucester, on the orders of Henry's daughter, Queen Mary, in 1555. 1998 is the 800th anniversary of the Abbey, with some special events about Monastic life being held late in June to celebrate the occasion.

For another cider tasting, 'straight from the barrel', the TORRE CIDER FARM (01984 640004) is a little further from Washford, as is the TROPIQUARIA (01984 640688), where the only thing that might slip down as easily is a snake from a branch. The town also houses the SOMERSET AND DORSET RAILWAY MUSEUM (01984 640869 / 01308 424630) at the Washford Station. This commemorates a more local railway enterprise than the Great Western we have been using to travel on, namely the SOMERSET AND DORSET JOINT RAILWAY, although membership of the Trust that runs the Museum will also give you the considerable bonus of a year's free travel on the West Somerset Railway too. Among the exhibits is a Railway Coach built in 1886 at Highbridge, which later fell into use as a Cricket Pavilion. Somehow this seems appropriate for part of the equipment for a line which ran from Bath to Bournemouth until its closure in 1966.

A traditional and popular sandy beach can be found at the picturesquely named **BLUE ANCHOR**, before the train makes its penultimate stop at **DUNSTER**. DUNSTER CASTLE AND GARDENS (01643 821314), form an imposing break in the gently sloping land, with immaculate lawns framing a sweeping drive, leading to the symmetrical grey castle perched on a large crag of dark rock.

It is possible to approach the castle from either the gardens or the village of Dunster, but if the weather is pleasant the former is an excellent choice. Now belonging to the National Trust, the gardens were mostly planted by the late Mrs Alice Luttrell in the 1920s. The castle was the home of the Luttrell family (now resident at East Quantoxhead) for some 600 years (1375-1976), although originally built by the Mohun family, who were granted Dunster after the Norman invasion of 1066. The garden is virtually frost free, and tender plants flourish on its south facing slopes. Apparently the century old lemon tree even provided fruit in 1995, albeit somewhat sour. There is a calm, secluded beauty to these gardens, cool even in sunshine, bushes and tropical trees providing shade as you walk between them in a route of your choice.

There are many winding paths to explore, some leading across a stream to the working DUNSTER WATER MILL (01643 821759) built near the site of another mill mentioned some seven hundred years previously in the Domesday Book. That was the Upper Mill, while this lower site was certainly used in medieval times too. Rebuilt almost completely from 1779 to 1782, its setting by the River AVILL is quiet but beautiful. Inside you can still see wheat being turned into flour, as it has been with only brief periods of disuse, since the 18th century, which is also when the lovely stone MILL BRIDGE was built. The water driven machinery inside the Mill is open to be seen at close quarters, and is impressive in its silent solidity. This really is a very peaceful spot, and ideal for a break in your walk around the castle grounds.

The castle proper is surrounded by smaller lawns and decorative battlements added as part of the remodelling of both exterior and interior by the Victorian architect Antony Salvin in 1870-1. Originally used as a fortress for the defence of Exmoor and what was then the port of Minehead, the few remaining Tudor elements include plasterwork and the main staircase. The Victorian design helps to make you feel as if you have visited an elegant country house full of intricacies rather than anything with military significance. Dunster Castle is home to various events during the year, from special tours to exhibitions of Wessex lace making. Leaving the castle by the gate leading to the village provides a sharp contrast to the gentle approach from the south. The HIGH STREET dives down to the cluster of dark buildings nestled below, and then turns a corner into the aptly named STEEP. The village breathes antiquity; you already sense that this place has stood much as it is for centuries past, without the need to hear any of its history.

The preservation of much of Dunster has occurred because of the virtual collapse of the local economy in the 18th century. As you look at the Yarn Market and other remnants of the cloth industry which built up the town from the 13th Century onwards, it is strange to realise that it was a failure in this same trade which has saved so much for us to see now, as further success would without doubt have led to modernisations and change.

On a rainy day the High Street can be quite a forbidding place, with rain driving in from the sea. You might then find yourself taking shelter in what at first appears to be a very large octagonal bus shelter, covered with a wooden roof. This structure, built in 1590, and restored in 1647 after damage in the Civil War siege (look carefully for the hole made by a cannonball through one of the main beams), is the site of the DUNSTER YARN MARKET. It is easy to imagine that this was built for the protection of the traders and their wares, but as the market has run from at least 1222 one wonders what the shelter was like for the first three hundred years and more! For many years Tourism has become one of Dunster's most important modern industries, and there are apparently no less than twenty three Tea Shops here, a phenomenally large number for such a small place. Amongst the picturesque shop-fronts Dunster has a DOLLS MUSEUM (01643 821220) in the Memorial Hall.

There is also a sandy beach, which claims to be the only one in Somerset onto which you can drive (information 01643 821296). I have memories from not too long ago of driving onto the beach near Weston-Super-Mare, but perhaps this is another county boundary problem. Dunster used to have a harbour too, but it is now a peaceful inland lake, the channel into the sea silted up for ever more. The stillness of the water is quite eerie when you consider how comparatively recently it was subject to the tides.

It is also well worth a walk from the centre of Dunster through PRIORY GREEN to the remains of the Priory, especially the Cloister garden and the Dovecote. This last circular brick building is much more romantic than a modern barn for mass produced chicken, although there was some similarity in use. The eight hundred nesting boxes so cleverly crammed into its structure were not tended to keep birds to fly messages, but rather to supply the kitchen with the essential ingredient for fresh pigeon pies. The Dovecote can be found behind the church of ST GEORGE, which has a magnificent Rood Screen. Dunster has a COUNTRY FAIR each July and the DUNSTER SHOW in August. Later in the year the tradition of DUNSTER-BY-CANDLELIGHT is worth remembering if you happen to be around here at the beginning of December. Despite any cold weather, there is music and dancing in the street, and the houses along the main streets are lit up by candlelight. During any season the views from the top of Dunster are quite lovely; as with many fine settings this one is almost as good to look down from as it is to look up to, as you cross the level land approaching the sea, whether by train, car or bicycle.

Drawing into Minehead station at the end of your train journey, it suddenly feels as if you have been, understandably with reluctance, dragged back into the present age, and the questionable pleasures of urban bustle. **MINEHEAD** (Tourist Information 01643 702624) is a popular resort for families during the summer. BUTLINS SOMERWEST WORLD (01643 703331) dominates the eastern end of the seafront, and as tempting as the funfair rides and external flumes from the swimming pool might appear, the overall impression from the outside is of a functional collection of modern buildings, cut off from the rest of the town by a perimeter fence. The open stretches of sandy beach opposite this look all the more inviting for their lack of such boundaries.

Minehead does have another side though. A left turn out of the railway station takes you away from the sea and into the main shopping streets. During the summer these are decorated with hanging baskets and tubs of flowers, and you can understand how this part of the town helped to earn the Britain in Bloom award in the very recent past. Look in particular for BLENHEIM GARDENS, between the main shops and the Quay.

The more attractive parts of Minehead, architecturally, are to the west. The Quay, Harbour and Higher Town still have enough evidence of the town's past, when the cargo landed at the port was of more importance to the local economy than the tourists from inland, to make them worth the extra walk from the centre. The winding slopes leading to the wooded NORTH HILL, with their thatched, cob cottages and many side lanes and alleys are a feature of the area known as HIGHER TOWN, where the light grey church of ST MICHAELS dominates the skyline. From the front of this plain but imposing 15th century building you can look down on Minehead as a whole.

What a place of contrasts it is too. The harbour is much as it was when constructed by the Luttrells of Dunster Castle in the 17th and 18th centuries, when smuggling was rife, and there are seafarer's cottages, which have survived up to three hundred years of storm and flood. The Esplanade is on a completely different scale, and can look particularly huge and almost sinister on a wet evening. Add to this the row of Amusement Arcades and trinket shops which line up against it, with the lights of a funfair too, and you really do have a bit of everything.

It is difficult to sum up such a diverse town, where you can see more of what a centuries old harbour would have looked like than in most places, and yet where you are also able to buy more varieties of personalised T-Shirts, Cyber-Pets and Candy Floss than anywhere else for many miles around. What can be said is that the elements seem not to mix, and the fences around Butlins could be moved to include much of what is opposite the Esplanade without many complaints from those who visit to enjoy the other side of the town. If the various communities of natives and visitors do have a coming together, and a point popular to all, then it is the beach, the real centre of any seaside resort.

Butlins is due to expand, but will not be the only part of Minehead to alter in the next few years. A £12.7 million project to bolster the town's sea defences is ahead of schedule, and is expected to conclude by 1999, including the raising of the level of the beaches with tons of sand and gravel. Looking at the vast expanses of the seafront the scale of the work must seem quite awesome even to those who have planned it.

However, some traditional events in the town are not likely to change, such as the strange procession of the Hobby Horse, which takes place early each May. This whirling figure, looking a little like a dragon from a Chinese carnival, was meant to scare off Scandinavian pillagers. If you get too close he can still be a pretty fearsome creature, especially if a sudden lurch to the side by one or more of those who control him makes you step back in alarm.

From Minehead you can take a trip on the last sea-going Paddle Steamer in the world, THE WAVERLEY, built in 1947. The pleasure steamer BALMORAL is also used, the last remaining member of the great WHITE FUNNEL FLEET of steamers which have taken holiday-makers around the Bristol Channel for almost the whole of this century (01446 720656 for information on cruises). Several of the fleet were lost after saving thousands of lives at Dunkirk, but the loss of another of Minehead's features during the Second World War was in stranger circumstances.

The Waverley Paddle Steamer, Minehead

Minehead used to have a pier. It was demolished during the war, apparently to stop German submarine captains simply pulling up alongside it and hopping off onto shore (see Bridport in Dorset for such an alleged incident). Eminently sensible idea? Maybe, but why would a U-Boat have travelled around Penzance and up the Channel to Minehead when there were piers everywhere from Bournemouth to Margate, none of which were destroyed! Perhaps this strange mystery could be solved by Arthur C Clarke, surely the most famous native of Minehead to be born this century.

So we have reached the end of the line, for the heritage railway and for this particular chapter. Minehead and Dunster are on the very borders of the Exmoor National Park. Venturing any further along this fascinating coast will mean an inevitable interruption, not from a border guard or sign declaring that this is land under a different jurisdiction, but rather because that is one of the traditions forever linked to Porlock and its famously steep hill. Apparently it is just as hard to remember dream visions from a sleep induced by the taking of laudanum. It is said that Coleridge was interrupted after such a slumber by "a visitor from Porlock", destroying his concentration even as he was writing his dream vision down as verse, thus leaving the poem 'Kubla Khan' tantalizingly unfinished for all time. So it is with Western Somerset, its story is not quite told, but we must take a break to give the remaining area, linked so inextricably with a portion of Devon, the close attention it deserves and demands.

Somehow it also seems appropriate to end with Minehead, the only place in this strip of land west of the M5 which bears any real resemblance to our starting point at Weston-Super-Mare. What has come in between them has been diverse and spectacular in many ways, with the beach near Kilve, in particular, being a truly unique place. I once drove up to the completely deserted coastline very late on a weekend evening. Armed with a strong torch I still only dared move a few yards from the landward edge of the rocky beach, as the empty darkness, filled only with the sound of the sea crashing against those impossibly patterned rocks, was overpowering and very daunting. Finding a dry, safe perch I sat and listened to it all for half an hour or so, although time was quite meaningless in such a wonderfully contemplative setting. Yet just a few miles away in either direction the nightclubs of Butlins to the south at Minehead, and the Pier at Weston-Super-Mare would still have been open, and teeming with collected humankind. This is the beauty of West Somerset; its resorts are unpretentious and jolly in a way that somehow seems almost like a cheeky Victorian postcard, but its emptier places are as remote and beautiful as anywhere you can find in the whole South West of England.

CAMELOT GUEST HOUSE
Carhampton Road
Blue Anchor
Minehead
Somerset
TA24 6LB

Tel: 01643 821348
E Mail:D.Thrush@btinternet.com

Camelot Guest House is a friendly house owned and run by David and Rita Thrush who came to Minehead in recent years and eventually intend to retire here, but in the meantime they thoroughly enjoy looking after their guests and do so with a deal of informality which masks the efficient manner in which Camelot is run. Camelot is situated two minutes walk from the sea at Blue Anchor Bay, it is close to Dunster, Minehead and the access roads to Exmoor, the Quantocks, Brendon Hills and other places such as 'Lorna Doone Country'. It is a quiet, peaceful place but if you have sporting inclinations you will find you can fish off the foreshore, hire boats at Watchet and Minehead, play golf at Minehead and there are several riding stables within fifteen to twenty minutes drive.

The house is furnished and decorated in a comfortable and light manner. The six bedrooms all with central heating and hot and cold running water, also have colour TV, tea and coffee making facilities, clock radios and a hairdryer. Four of the bedrooms have en-suite shower and WC., and there is a public bathroom with full facilities. All the front bedrooms contain a double and single bed, and two are big enough to provide ample accommodation for a family of four. Two of these rooms are ensuite. Facing to the rear are two double bedrooms, ensuite, and one single.

Breakfast is served in the attractive dining room and it is a delicious, freshly cooked meal. Evening meals are by arrangement. The well-stocked bar is a meeting place for newly found friends at night and there is also a 'dry ' lounge/TV room for the use of guests.

USEFUL INFORMATION

- OPEN: All year
- WHEELCHAIR ACCESS: No
- GARDEN: No
- CREDIT CARDS: None taken
- ACCOMMODATION: 6 rooms 4 ensuite
- RATES: From £16pp - Premium on sgl occupancy in high season. Children Sleeping with parents £8 1st night £6 thereafter

- DINING ROOM: Great breakfast Evening meals available
- VEGETARIAN: Upon request
- LICENSED: Residential/Restaurant
- CHILDREN: Welcome

CURDON MILL COUNTRY HOUSE & RESTAURANT
Lower Vellow
Williton, Taunton
Somerset
TA4 4LS

Tel: 01984 656522
Fax: 01984 656197
Email:www.curdonmill.@compuserve.com

Curdon Mill was one of the first venues in West Somerset to be licensed for Civil Marriages and since then many couples have taken their vows in the Millers Room and enjoyed a reception in the dining room or a Marquee in the garden. Having been to Curdon Mill one can well understand why it appeals. It is enchanting and not only for weddings and other romantic or celebration occasions but as a place simply to relax. The warm ambience of Curdon Mill is welcoming to everyone. It creates an atmosphere conducive to party giving - the special Birthday, Anniversary, Christening or Retirement - a meeting point after a treasure hunt, or maybe for a cream tea. Frequently there is a marquee in the garden, a Barn Dance in a real barn, a Summer Ball, a barbecue or Winter Extravaganza - so many permutations. Just one mile off the A358, Taunton to Minehead road, in the hamlet of Vellow, this old sandstone water mill is waiting to greet you. It is somewhere to take time perhaps to amble around the garden, to see the mill stream and the bridge of oak tree roots sturdily spreading over it, to smell the roses, admire the view and maybe sip a Pimms on a rustic bench. The traditional country cuisine cooked in the Aga of a farmhouse kitchen provides Millers award winning restaurant with gastronomic delights using fresh local produce, much of it from Curdon Mill's own gardens. It is open for lunch Tuesday-Friday inclusive, for Sunday Lunch and for dinner every evening except Sunday. Curdon Mill is renowned for its talent and ability as Outside Caterers. They say they can entertain you, anywhere - riding on a steam train perhaps, in a glass house, a factory or even a marquee in the middle of Exmoor! It does not matter to them whether the occasion is large or small - the result is always perfection.
There are six pretty bedrooms, all ensuite and all appointed with everything one needs including colour television and tea and coffee making facilities. Some guests come for dinner and stay the night, some come for a night and stay for a week. Whatever you do and for whatever reason you come, you will want to come back.

USEFUL INFORMATION

· OPEN: All year

· WHEELCHAIR ACCESS:
  Limited. Shallow steps in restaurant
· GARDEN: Large & beautiful Heated
  swimming pool Croquet Lawn. Skittles
· CREDIT CARDS: All major cards
· ACCOMMODATION: 6 ensuite rooms
· RATES: From £30-40 per person per night B&B
  Short breaks minimum two nights Sun-Thurs inc. dinner from £52 per person

· MILLERS RESTAURANT: Excellent chef
  Delicious, traditional country cuisine

· VEGETARIAN: Always a choice

· LICENSED: Full On
· CHILDREN: Over 8 years

THE GABLES
33 High Street
Dunster
Somerset
TA24 6SF

Tel: 01643 821 496

ETB 2 Crown Highly Commended

This small hotel with a charming tea-room stands in a prominent position in the High Street just above the famous Yarn Market, in the beautifully preserved medieval village of Dunster, often referred to as the 'Jewel of Exmoor'. The village has a fine castle, dolls museum, dovecote, and a working water mill. Dunster Country Fair is held in July, Dunster Show in August a Flower Festival in the church in August and Duster By Candlelight in early December. There are also many beautiful walks, riding and fishing and driven tours of Exmoor. Once a private merchant's house with large open fires, the 'Gables' were added at the turn of the century and are now the guest bedrooms (one of which has been known to be visited by a friendly ghost about 3am). The front rooms view the High Street and Yarn Market and the back rooms look toward Grubbiest Hill where the Victorian writer, Mrs Alexander, is reputed to have written the hymn 'All things bright and beautiful'. She was also the wife of the Vicar of Duster. The facia of The Gables is in cream limewash and the paint-work is bottle green linseed paint - the original colour and materials.

This relaxed and friendly non-smoking house is run by the owner, Penny Groves, with occasional help from her son Ben. There are five guest rooms all ensuite. Each is individually decorated and furnished with co-ordinating bed linen. Comfortable seating, television, a full selective beverage tray make the rooms a haven away from home. Ironing equipment and hairdryers are available on request. The Guest Lounge area has luxurious seating, waxed pine furniture and some delightful antique ornaments. Chocolates and mints, an honesty bar and a profusion of magazines are there for your enjoyment. Penny produces a delicious and very substantial breakfast starting with a selection of fruit juices, cereal and fresh fruit and followed by a full English traditional. Wholemeal and white toast, a full range of savoury and sweet preserves together with freshly made coffee, tea and hot chocolate, completes the meal. A special Veggie Breakfast is also on the menu. The Tea-room with its home-made fare is only open in the summer months. From November to March there is a Special Break price. Three nights for the price of two including an evening meal.

USEFUL INFORMATION

- OPEN: All year
- WHEELCHAIR ACCESS: No
- GARDEN: Yes
- CREDIT CARDS: None taken
- ACCOMMODATION: 5 ensuite rooms
- RATES: From £22.50 pppn Children £10
- STRICTLY NON-SMOKING

- DINING ROOM: Delicious breakfast
- VEGETARIAN: Catered for
- TEAROOM: Summer only
- LICENSED: Residential/Restaurant
- CHILDREN: Well behaved + babies
- PETS: No

133

THE GLOBE INN
Appley
NR Wellington
Somerset
TA21 0HJ

Tel: 01823 672327

On the Somerset/Devon border in beautiful rolling countryside is the little village of Appley and in its midst is the Globe Inn which has been dispensing hospitality for five hundred years. It has remained unspoilt and has a delightful, old world atmosphere with beams, two inglenook fireplaces and a bar to be found in a brick floored passage way. People come here to enjoy themselves in the beautiful countryside and the well kept ale as well as the friendly chatter at the bar. Much used by locals, the inn has a reputation that stretches well beyond the confines of nearby Wellington. People know it is a good place to come out to, spend some time in the bar and perhaps take a walk along the well signed footpaths.

Andrew and Liz Burt together with Roger and Janet Morris bought The Globe Inn ten years ago. It was already a well loved hostelry but they have done so much to improve it, not least in the food department. Andrew is the main chef but they are all capable of taking their turn in the kitchen if need be. Andrew's menu is made up of many time-honoured favourites. Seafood Pancakes, Fresh Salmon, a large bowl of home-made fish soup, strips of garlic battered chicken, strips of rump steak, scampi, Vegetarian dishes, Children's dishes, salads, sandwiches; the choice is vast. On Sunday at Lunch-time Roast Topside of Beef served with Yorkshire pudding and all the trimmings, is very popular. Food is served both in the dining room and the bar at lunch and evening. Two Real Ales are on tap and there is always a Guest Ale and the other is Cotleigh Tawny Bitter. Farmhouse Cider is available in the summer months.

USEFUL INFORMATION

- OPEN: Weekdays 11-3pm & 6.30-11pm
  Sun: 12-3pm & 7-10.30pm
- WHEELCHAIR ACCESS: No
- GARDEN: Yes
- CREDIT CARDS: None taken
- CHILDREN: Welcome
- DINING ROOM: Good pub fare
- VEGETARIAN: Always a choice
- BAR FOOD: Wide range
- LICENSED: Full On
- PETS: On leads

LANGLEY HOUSE HOTEL
Wiveliscombe
Near Taunton,
Somerset
TA4 2UF

Tel:01984 623318
Fax: 01984 624573
Internet:http://www.johansen.com/j1301

2 AA Good Food Rosettes, Michelin 'Red M'.
Good Food Guide County Restaurant of the Year

Nestling in the folds of the Brendon Hills, the country town of Wiveliscombe lies on the edge of some of the most picturesque and history laden countryside in England. Langley House has been a part of this history, as the house dates from the 16th century. Additions and alterations during the early 18th century left a mark of Georgian elegance that has been maintained in this small country house hotel. Hidden away from the crowds within a private garden Langley House is both charming and tranquil something that the Chef/Patron Peter Wilson and his wife Anne have striven to achieve - and succeeded - since their arrival in 1985. It is set in 4 acres of award winning gardens and on the edge of Exmoor making it a very special place to stay for a break or a holiday in order to explore the stunning countryside and coast. Some of England's most famous gardens are just a short journey away: Knighthayes, Bicton, Stourhead, Dunster Castle,Montacute and Hestercombe amongst many.

Langley House is famed for its food. The award winning restaurant is open to non-residents and has a regular clientele from many miles around all eager to sample Peter's eclectic menus based on prime quality cuts of meat, fresh fish from Brixham, and freshly harvested herbs and vegetables - many from Langley House's own kitchen garden. There is also an impressive wine list featuring over two hundred and forty wines, chosen with knowledgeable care.

The emphasis is on comfort and informality, and much attention to detail in all the interior decoration resulted in Langley House winning the Wedgwood/British Tourist Authority Interior Design Award. The house is furnished with traditional fabrics, and fine antiques and paintings, creating an aura of understated elegance and discreet good taste. All the bedrooms, two of which are non-smoking, have been individually decorated and furnished and enjoy the convenience of a private bathroom, direct-dial telephone, television and radio. The majority overlook the gardens. Included are the little things that make guests feel cosseted, such as fresh flowers, reading books, mineral water, sewing kit, hairdryer, and in winter hot water bottles.

USEFUL INFORMATION

- OPEN: All year
- WHEELCHAIR ACCESS: Yes
- GARDEN: 4 acres, award winning
- CREDIT CARDS: AMEX/Visa/Master
- ACCOMMODATION: 8 ensuite rooms
- RATES: Sgl from £75 low season
  £82.50 high season
  Dbl. from £90 low season
  £127.50 high season. Children £15

- DINING ROOM: Award winning fare
- VEGETARIAN: Daily changing menu
- LICENSED: Full On
- CHILDREN: Welcome
- PETS: Yes £4.25 per night

LUTTRELL ARMS HOTEL
32-36 High Street
Dunster
Somerset
TA24 4SG

Tel: 01643 821555
Fax: 01643 821567

*** Star

Dunster is one of the prettiest small towns in Somerset and nestles on the edge of Exmoor. It has a splendid castle, a working mill, a fine old church and a trip on the Steam Railway is not to be missed. In the bustling High Street is The Luttrell Arms Hotel which dates back to the 15th century and is a delightful place in which to stay and especially if you want a good base from which to take advantage of all that Exmoor, the North Devon coast and other interesting places within easy reach, have to offer.

The Luttrell Arms is beautiful outside and that continues in the atmospheric interior in which the lounge has an original hammer beam roof and four of the pretty bedrooms have four posters. It is also blessed with a beautiful split level garden with spectacular views of the castle. It is the most relaxed of places whether you are having a drink in one of the bars, or listening to the busy chatter of the regulars who come to enjoy a pint or two of well kept ale and to talk over the happenings of the day. The relaxed atmosphere no doubt has been acquired over the centuries but much has to be said for the caring management and the well trained friendly staff who make sure that everyone enjoys visiting The Luttrell Arms. The restaurant is always popular and its reputation for good food is known far and wide. The menus are based on traditional English fare with some interesting Continental and Eastern dishes added for good measure. In the Bar, light snacks are served every day.

The twenty seven ensuite bedrooms are charmingly appointed with pretty drapes and covers, comfortable beds and many other little luxuries like direct dial telephones, colour television and hospitality trays. Excellent breakfasts are served every morning with a choice of traditional English or Continental. Short Breaks are available at special prices for a minimum of two nights, Dinner, Bed and Breakfast.

USEFUL INFORMATION

· OPEN: 11-11pm Mon-Sat 12-10.30pm Sun	· RESTAURANT: Traditional English fare
· WHEELCHAIR ACCESS: No	· VEGETARIAN: On request
· GARDEN: Split level	· BAR FOOD: Wide range
· CREDIT CARDS: All major cards	· LICENSED: Full On
· ACCOMMODATION: 27 ensuite rooms	· CHILDREN: Welcome
· RATES: Sgl £75 room only dbl. £95 room only	
Children 75% off normal rates up to 16 years	· PETS: Yes £10 per stay

PERITON PARK HOTEL
Middlecombe
NR Minehead
Somerset
TA24 8SW

Tel: 01643 706885
Fax: 01643 706885

AA** 76% 2 Red Rosettes

Periton Park Hotel has been described as a place 'where time stands still' The explanation is apt. Once you climb the winding drive through the woods, rhododendrons and azaleas to this Victorian country house hotel on the edge of the Exmoor National Park, you come into a quiet world of enchantment. The hotel is a perfect retreat for country lovers with Exmoor on the doorstep and miles of varied, unspoilt territory with breathtaking landscapes to explore. Riding is available from stables close to the hotel and shooting is also available in season. Sea and river fishing can be arranged. There are two golf course in close proximity. Dunster Castle and Gardens, Kinghtshayes, Rosemoor, Selworthy and Arlington are within easy reach.

Richard and Angela Hunt are the owners of Periton Park and it is their innate understanding of the needs of their guests that makes this such a special, caring place in which to stay. It is run in a professional yet relaxed and informal manner. All the rooms are spacious and well proportioned, enlivened with warm autumn colours to create a restful atmosphere. There are four double and four twin ensuite bedrooms, beautifully appointed and furnished with a mixture of antique and traditional pieces. Every room has colour television, direct dial telephone and a hospitality tray. Three of the bedrooms are strictly non-smoking. The wood panelled restaurant with its double aspect views over the grounds, is a restful place and the food is delicious. Succinctly one would say it is modern British, Country House style. All the ingredients used are of the highest quality, the vegetables are fresh and as much local produce is included as possible. A well chosen wine list complements the meal.

USEFUL INFORMATION

- OPEN: All year
- WHEELCHAIR ACCESS: Yes
- GARDEN: Yes
- CREDIT CARDS: All except Diners
- ACCOMMODATION: 8 ensuite rms
- RATES: Dbl. £100 per room per night

- RESTAURANT: Country House style cooking using the very best of ingredients
- VEGETARIAN: Yes
- BAR FOOD: Not applicable
- LICENSED: Yes
- CHILDREN: Over 12 years
- PETS: One room only

THE ROYAL HUNTSMAN
7 Long Street
Williton
Somerset
TA4 4QN

Tel: 01984 632441
Fax: 01984 634869
E-Mail:leighton.timms@virgin.net

The general opinion of people who have been lucky enough to stay and sample the hospitality of The Royal Huntsman, is that it is to be highly recommended for its warmth, its welcome and the unstinting service offered by the owners and staff. Something to live up to but the proprietors, family members Barbara and Leighton Timms and Harriet and Wayne Jordan have the knack of keeping the inn running on oiled wheels and at the same time creating a relaxed atmosphere. The Royal Huntsman is a 17th century coaching inn which in time has welcomed hundreds, if not thousands, of weary travellers who must have been so pleased to get here. It really is no different today except that travelling is a little more sophisticated!

The welcome is just the same, the low ceilings, the beams, the open fireplaces have not changed nor has the hospitality. The bar is a cheerful, warm friendly place and the restaurant serves delicious fare. The menu is extensive with some eleven starters including hot baby Brie wedges with cranberry sauce or whitebait followed by sizzling mussels in a home-made tomato and basil sauce or white wine and cream sauce, or a Huntsman Steak Platter. There are Sizzlers, Vegetarian dishes and much more to tempt the palate. The bar also has a good menu with everything from light bites to basket meals or toasted sandwiches to Pizzas. The food is excellent and it is all value for money.

The attractive guest rooms provide visitors with a very comfortable night. There are six ensuite rooms; one family room, three twin-bedded rooms and two double rooms. All of them have colour television and a hospitality tray. Breakfast is a memorable meal which will set you up for the day whether you have business to attend to or are simply here for a holiday. If you enjoy a game of skittles, darts or pool, the facility is there for you to use. A great place to stay.

USEFUL INFORMATION

- OPEN: Winter 10.30-2.30 & 5-11pm
  (All day Fri & Sat) Summer All day
- WHEELCHAIR ACCESS: Yes
- GARDEN: Yes. PETS: Yes
- CREDIT CARDS: Master/Visa/Switch
- ACCOMMODATION: 6 ensuite rooms
- RATES: From £18pp B&B
  £2 single supplement Children: 5-12 £10

- RESTAURANT; Excellent menu
- VEGETARIAN: Yes
- BAR FOOD: Wide menu
- LICENSED: Yes. Full On
- CHILDREN: Welcome

THE THREE HORSESHOES
Langley Marsh
Wiveliscombe
Somerset
TA4 2UL

Tel: 01984 623763

Star rated Which Good Pub Guide.
AA Guide. Egon Ronay etc.

Langley Marsh is a peaceful small village close to the old town of Wiveliscombe. It is a delightful rural area and in the midst of the village with farmland views all around, is The Three Horseshoes, a traditional village country pub, where John and Marella Hopkins are the landlords. These two cheerful and friendly people run the pub with the help of their family and some local girls who wait table. The Three Horseshoes has been a hostelry for over three hundred years and in this century there have been only four landlords, always the sign of a good pub. It is as attractive inside as it is out and much of the internal decor has not been changed. Everywhere you look there are vintage motoring photos and memorabilia. There is an uniqueness about The Three Horseshoes which strikes everyone who comes here. Much frequented by locals it also attracts a clientele from miles around. All sorts of things go on here; Folk music, Quiz nights on alternate Sunday evenings and Morris dancing sessions. You can sit on rustic seats on the veranda or in the sloping back garden with a fully equipped children's play area.

The no-smoking dining area has antique settles and tables and benches and it is here you can feed on genuinely home-made food; anything from pigeon breasts in cider and cream, daily fresh fish , a delicious home-made steak and kidney pie and many other tempting dishes. One can have filled rolls, soup, pizzas and a variety of vegetarian dishes as well. The lovely puddings tempt even the strongest willed. You will never find chips or fried food here and many of the vegetables come from the garden. Recently there has been a new addition - an external, well equipped skittle alley which is great fun and much in use for parties. The lively front room has sensibly placed darts, shove-half'penny, table skittles, dominoes and cribbage. It is a thoroughly enjoyable pub with a friendly welcome.

USEFUL INFORMATION

· OPEN: 12-2.30pm & 7-11pm	· DINING AREA: Excellent home-made fare
· WHEELCHAIR ACCESS: Yes.	· VEGETARIAN: Yes
· GARDEN: Yes. Play area	· BAR FOOD: Wide range. No fried food/chips
· CREDIT CARDS: Visa/Master-	
card(Not Switch)	· LICENSED: Full On
· CHILDREN: If well behaved	· PETS: No

UPHILL MANOR
3 Uphill Road South,
Uphill
Weston-Super-Mare
Somerset
BS23 4SD

Tel: 01934 644654
Fax: 01934 624603

This must be one of the most unusual urban hotels in the country. Built in 1806 with later additions it stands in nineteen acres of delightful grounds with a walled garden, lawns, woodland and paddocks and yet it is just three minutes from the town centre, two minutes from the beach and two minutes from the golf course. Add to all this its striking architecture complete with towers and you have something very special. Craig and Tina Kennedy are the owners and they describe Uphill Manor as warm and comfortable, elegant but not grand. This is an apt description but for someone coming here for the first time the architecture is outstanding. Much of the original has been retained. The Gothic Entrance Hall has intricate stencilling, the drawing room is grand with its Gothic style, vaulted ceiling and great historical interest - you can read about this fascinating house in the fine Library, whilst you are there but just to let you know a little, it has been described as 'the most complete Pugin-inspired Crace scheme in existence, with the exceptions of Anbey Hall near Manchester and Eastnor Castle in Herefordshire'.

The Kennedys run the hotel with that degree of informality which only comes from professional people who know exactly how to achieve their purpose. Every room is furnished with a happy mixture of antique, traditional and modern pieces. The Library is a gem with many interesting records to peruse. An 'Honesty Bar' is open all day for the benefit of guests and after an excellent night's sleep in a very comfortable, well furnished bedroom you will come down to breakfast in the elegant dining room, to a meal that is both delicious and plentiful. Evening meals are not available but Weston-Super-Mare is full of eateries of every kind, taste and price. Each bedroom is ensuite and has television, hair dryers, trouser press and a well supplied hostess tray.

USEFUL INFORMATION

· OPEN: All year	· DINING ROOM: Great breakfast No evening meals
· WHEELCHAIR ACCESS: No	· VEGETARIAN; On request
· GARDEN: 19 acres	· LICENSED: 'Honesty Bar'
· CREDIT CARDS: Visa/Master	· CHILDREN: Welcome
· ACCOMMODATION: 5 ensuite	· PETS: No
· RATES: £50 B&B sgl £75 B&B dbl.	

THE WALNUT TREE
North Petherton
NR Bridgwater
Somerset
TA6 6QA

Tel: 01278 662255
Fax: 01278 663946

AA***RAC ETB 4 Crowns
Highly Commended
BEST WESTERN HOTEL

The Walnut Tree once was an 18th century coaching inn which must have been a welcoming sight to weary travellers as they pulled into the pretty Somerset village of North Petherton on the A38. Today, the welcoming owners, Richard and Hilary Goulden carry on the traditional values, setting a very high standard throughout the inn. You will find it one mile from the M5 (exit 24), one and a half miles from Bridgwater, 8 miles from Taunton, 12 from the small cathedral city of Wells, thirty miles from Bristol, forty from Exeter and one hundred and fifty miles from London.

Each of the thirty two bedrooms, all of which are quietly located at the rear of the Inn, has superb amenities with private bathroom, sky TV, beverage making facilities and a writing desk. The decor is tasteful and warming, and the four-poster bed suite is a popular choice for those seeking a special or romantic weekend break. Three rooms have been adapted for the disabled. Recently a new guest lounge overlooking a waterfall in the garden, has been added. Everywhere there are fresh flowers and log fires in winter. The reception lounge and bar are friendly, comfortable places. The popular Bar with Cottage grill room will tempt you with real ales, light bar snacks and succulent steaks. For a very special meal there is nothing better for miles around than the beautiful Sedgemoor Restaurant with its soft lighting and warm colour scheme, where you can dine on superb dishes created from Somerset produce, including duck, salmon, lamb and locally grown vegetables. The accompanying wine list of well chosen wines enhances the meal.

Upstairs, the newly refurbished air conditioned Quantock Suite provides conference and seminar facilities and weddings for up to one hundred and twenty. The Walnut Tree is a memorable experience and one you will want to repeat.

USEFUL INFORMATION

- OPEN: All year
- WHEELCHAIR ACCESS: Yes
- GARDEN: Yes
- CREDIT CARDS: All major cards
- ACCOMMODATION: 32 ensuite rms
- RATES: From £56sgl B&B
  Dbl. from £70 -£95
  Executive suite £125

- RESTAURANT: First class, international cuisine using Somerset produce
- VEGETARIAN: Always a choice
- BAR FOOD: Light bar snacks, Steaks
- LICENSED: Full On
- CHILDREN: Welcome
- PETS: No

YEW TREE HOUSE
Hurn Lane
Berrow
Burnham-on-Sea
Somerset
TA8 2QT

Tel/Fax: 01278 751382

Yew Tree House is in a superb situation with the sand dunes just three hundred metres away and then seven miles of sandy beach. At the side of the house are fields - Berrow Nature Reserve and Berrow Animal Farm as well as Brean Bird Garden are there for your enjoyment. For those who enjoy walking the National Trust Brean Down and Brent Knoll are close by. With a Cider Farm, horse riding, golf and fishing locally, you are spoilt for choice with things to do before or after sampling the excellent accommodation and delicious food in the Tea Rooms at Yew Tree House.

Gill and Nigel Crewdson are the owners of Yew Tree House and it is their planning and imagination which has changed it from being a licensed restaurant into the more relaxed and friendly establishment it is today. It is a lovely old house built about 1640 and then extended in 1890 and again in 1920. The country style garden with its flowers and shrubs is enchanting and here you can sit and eat at wooden, pub style seating under big umbrellas enjoying a cream tea that is definitely a diet spoiler.!

When the summer visitors have gone is the time to take a 'get away from it all' short break here. Laze around the house or take a walk on the deserted beach, explore the local countryside with its many villages and out of the way pubs.

There are three ensuite guest rooms. In the 1640 part of the house there is a 5ft verdigris double bed and bunk beds and in the 1920 part two more rooms, one double and the other twin-bedded. They have recently been refurbished and are of a very high standard. Each room has a colour television and a hostess tray. There is also a Guest Lounge with Colour television and an attractive Dining Room, in which you will be served a super breakfast.

USEFUL INFORMATION

· OPEN: January to November	· DINING ROOM: Traditional Breakfast for residents
· WHEELCHAIR ACCESS:	· STRICTLY NON-SMOKING
· GARDEN: Yes. Tea Garden	· TEAROOMS: Home-made cakes, light snacks sandwiches. Cream teas
· CREDIT CARDS: Not at present	· LICENSED: No
· ACCOMMODATION: 3 ensuite rooms	· CHILDREN: Welcome
· RATES: From £17.50 pp B&B Low season	· PETS: By arrangement £2 p.n.

142

BASON BRIDGE INN
East Huntspill
Highbridge, Somerset
TA9 4RL

Tel: 01278 782616

The Bason Bridge Inn has been a popular watering hole for well over a hundred years in which time is has developed a great atmosphere generated, no doubt, by the happy band of regulars who have made it their local over the years and none more so than today in the capable and friendly hands of the landlords, Keith and Ray Hobbs. It has long been known as somewhere that provides amongst its extensive and home-cooked menu, the best king-size home-baked ham rolls in Somerset. All sorts of dishes appear on the menu daily with many time-honoured favourites and frequently the odd surprise or two. The small, intimate restaurant seats twenty.

Whilst the outside is not spectacular to look at the interior of The Bason Bridge Inn is spacious and light and on a cold night very cosy with its open fire roaring away. The bedrooms are ensuite and have television and a hostess tray. A good place to be. There are facilities for small functions and conferences.

USEFUL INFORMATION

- OPEN: Mon-Fri 12-2.30pm &6-11pm
  Open all day Saturday & Sunday
- WHEELCHAIR ACCESS: Yes
- GARDEN: Yes
- CREDIT CARDS: All major cards
- ACCOMMODATION: Ensuite rooms
- RATES: £20pp B&B

- RESTAURANT: Good, home-cooked fare
- VEGETARIAN: Yes
- BAR FOOD: From steaks to sandwiches
- LICENSED: Full On
- CHILDREN: Welcome
- PETS: By arrangement

FAIRFIELD HOUSE HOTEL
51 Long Street
Williton , Somerset
TA4 4QY
Tel: 01984 632636
RAC Acclaimed

Records of this interesting hotel go back as far as 1751 but it is thought that it is far older. It certainly has an atmosphere gleaned over the centuries and is enhanced by the modern day but traditional welcome you get from the owners, Judy and Fred Mellor who run the hotel with the help of their daughter and son-in-law, Sarah and Steve Ashby, when they are busy. It is always cheerful and warm within its welcoming doors and whether you go for just a meal or to stay a night or two, every effort will be made to make your stay an enjoyable one. Dining in The Quantock Restaurant in intimate surroundings with just 20 covers is delightful. The menu offers a wide choice of well-cooked and well presented home-made fare with anything from a Starter of Chilled Melon and Black Grape Cocktail followed by a delicious Fisherman's Pie made to the Fairfield recipe with Cod, Haddock and Prawns in a Cheese sauce, topped with mashed potato and finally a delectable home-made dessert, or maybe a more robust, perfectly cooked steak with or without Diane Sauce. Every day there are Daily Specials - many of them time-honoured favourites. Stay here a night or two and you will sleep in one of five ensuite rooms in the greatest comfort and come down in the morning to a hearty breakfast which will set you up for the day.

USEFUL INFORMATION

- OPEN: January-December
- WHEELCHAIR ACCESS: No
- GARDEN: Yes
- CREDIT CARDS: Visa/Delta/Euro
- ACCOMMODATION: 5 ensuite
- RATES: From £23.50 B&B £37 BB&D
  SPECIAL 3 DAY BREAKS: (available throughout the year)
  Bed/Breakfast/Dinner £105pp Bed/Breakfast £67.50pp Phone for details

- RESTAURANT: Delicious home-cooked fare, wide choice
- VEGETARIAN: Own menu
- LICENSED: Restaurant
- CHILDREN: Welcome 10+
- PETS: No

HIGHER DIPFORD FARM
Trull, Taunton
Somerset
TA3 7NU

Tel: 01823 275770 Fax: 01823 257916

Oak framed Somerset longhouses are becoming a rarity. Higher Dipford Farm dating back more than six hundred years is a fine example (the name itself goes back to the 14th century). The owners Maureen and Chris Fewings have done a splendid job of modernising this Grade II Listed house. Not an easy task when you are determined not to lose the character of the centuries. The many exposed elm beams and inglenook fireplaces remain. It has been done beautifully and they are also in the process of converting another Grade II building, an old barn which is attached to one end of the house. The bedrooms are delightful. There is one double, and one twin-bedded with a magnificent gold-plated shower room and the other with a private bathroom and another bedroom in the Hayloft. They are warm and comfortable, relaxing and restful. Each room has Colour TV with Sky and a selection of teas and coffees on a hospitality tray. Home cooking is the speciality of the house with fresh produce from the farm and garden all helped down by a jug of cider. A happy house in which to stay and only two and a half miles from Taunton.

USEFUL INFORMATION

·	OPEN: All year	·	DINING ROOM: Specialising in home-cooking with fresh produce from the farm
·	WHEELCHAIR ACCESS: Yes	·	VEGETARIAN: Yes & Vegans
·	GARDEN: Yes	·	LICENSED: Restaurant
·	CREDIT CARDS: None taken	·	CHILDREN: Welcome
·	ACCOMMODATION: 3 ensuite		
·	RATES:From:£25pppn Children under 8 half price under 11 25% discount		

HOME PARK FARM & TEA ROOM
Blue Anchor
Minehead
Somerset
TA24 6JS   \

Tel: 01984 640817

Home Park Farm with its attractive Tea Room is a delightful place to visit. You have a choice of taking a farm tour which will both entertain and inform you followed by a visit to the tea room or simply go directly to the tea room to enjoy a light lunch or a delicious cream tea. There is a charge for the farm tour of £3 per adult and £2 per child or a family ticket for two adults and two children at £9.50. No charge is made for direct entry into the tea room. The tour is designed to show the general public how their food is produced and is arable with cattle, sheep and pigs. The situation is glorious just one hundred yards from the Bristol Channel and the Sea front and within five minutes walk of the West Somerset Steam Railway. In the Tea-room light lunches are available - try the home-produced, dry cured ham salad, the ham is the best you will ever taste. Home Park Farm is also famous for its Farmhouse Cream Teas and home-made cakes.

USEFUL INFORMATION

·	OPEN: April- September	·	TEAROOM: Delicious home-cooked fare. Light Lunches. Farmhouse Cream Teas
·	WHEELCHAIR ACCESS: Yes + Toilet	·	VEGETARIAN: Yes
·	GARDEN: Yes for teas etc. + 20 acres of farmland	·	LICENSED: No
·	CREDIT CARDS: None taken	·	CHILDREN: Welcome
·	PETS: Well behaved dogs		

L'ARRIVEE
75/77 Locking Road
Weston-Super-Mare
Somerset   BS23 3DW
Tel/Fax:01934 625328

ETB 3*** RAC Acclaimed

There are many good reasons for selecting L'Arrivee, a licensed Guest House, as your base for a holiday or short break. The first has to be the very warm welcome you will receive from the owners Caroline and Noel. It is their cheerful, informal but totally professional running of the house that makes every one feel immediately relaxed and at home. Another good reason is the easy access to many attractions. Weston has its own plethora of places to visit including its sea front complete with a little railway that runs up and down the length of the promenade in summer. Superbly kept flower beds along the front always draw comments from visitors. In winter walking along the beach appeals to many people who prefer the quieter times out of season. You can walk to the town centre and the sea front in ten minutes from L'Arrivee. A short drive will take you to Cheddar Gorge, Wookey Hole, the cathedral city of Wells, Glastonbury, Street, Taunton and many more places. L'Arrivee has twelve bedrooms, ten of which are ensuite and there are two rooms with four-poster beds and one with a King-size bed. Comfortable beds, television, video and a hostess tray complete the picture. Breakfast is a substantial, freshly cooked meal and in the evening a delicious home-cooked dinner is available.

USEFUL INFORMATION

- OPEN: All year
- WHEELCHAIR ACCESS: Yes
- GARDEN: No
- CREDIT CARDS: All major cards
- ACCOMMODATION: 12 rooms 10 ensuite
- RATES: £18.50 basic £22 ensuite pppn

- DINING ROOM: Good, English Fare
- VEGETARIAN: Upon request
- LICENSED: Residential
- CHILDREN: Welcome
- PETS: Yes

THE MONKTON INN
West Monkton
Taunton
Somerset
TA2 8NP

Tel: 01823 412414

There are many reasons why one should visit The Monkton Inn but one of the most unusual is to read 'the sayings of Tracy'; malapropisms started by a lady of this name and continued today. Each is written up above the bar making good reading and certainly raising a chuckle! West Monkton is a small village nestling at the foot of the Quantocks and there is no doubt that The Monkton Inn is the focal point of village life. Talk to the regulars who enjoy the well kept beer and you will hear all sorts of fascinating stories including the capture of an Eel in the car park on a stormy night when the river flooded! The Inn is on a Public Right of Way and on many Ramblers maps and is a Mecca for thirsty and hungry souls. It is also a haunting ground for two friendly ghosts who obviously enjoy the friendly and lively atmosphere created by Sue Harris-Searle and her competent staff. The furnishings include many old styles of seating - settles, pews etc. and gives a rustic appearance. The food is good traditional English fare with tried and tested favourites both on the restaurant and the bar menu.

USEFUL INFORMATION

- OPEN: Mon-Thurs:12-3pm & 6-11pm
  Fri-Sat 12-11pm Sun 12noon-10.30pm
- WHEELCHAIR ACCESS: Yes
- GARDEN: Yes. Play area BBQ
- CREDIT CARDS: Master/Visa
- CHILDREN: Welcome

- RESTAURANT: Traditional fare
- VEGETARIAN: Always a choice
- BAR FOOD: Wide range
- LICENSED: Full On
- PETS: Yes, well behaved

145

THE SPINNEY
Curland, Taunton
Somerset TA3 5SE

Tel/Fax 01460 234362
E-Mail: bartlett.spinney@zetnet.co.uk
AAQQQQ Selected ETB 2 Crowns Highly Commended

Ten minutes or so south of Taunton, nestling on the slopes of the Blackdown Hills, in a peaceful location surrounded by beautiful countryside with panoramic views, is The Spinney, the home of Ann and John Bartlett, two people who are quite genuine when they say that nothing is too much trouble when caring for their guests. It is a well-appointed modern, detached house with a warm and friendly atmosphere enhanced by crackling log fires in cold spells. The rooms are delightful, spacious and bright and furnished to a very high standard. It is an ideal base for those wanting to explore. One can walk for miles through woods and fields. John enjoys drawing maps to help guests find their way on excursions. There are 3 ensuite bedrooms, two of which are on the ground floor and upstairs is a family bedroom, large enough to take an additional bed if required. All the bedrooms have delightful views and are equipped with television and a hostess tray. Breakfast is a freshly cooked feast and a traditional English evening meal is optional. The Spinney is non-smoking throughout.

USEFUL INFORMATION

- OPEN: All year
- WHEELCHAIR ACCESS: No
- GARDEN: Yes. Equestrian centre at end of lane
- CREDIT CARDS: None taken
- ACCOMMODATION: 3 ensuite rooms
- RATES: From £22 pp B&B
- DINING ROOM; Delicious breakfast Optional evening meal
- VEGETARIAN: By arrangement
- NON-SMOKING THROUGHOUT
- LICENSED: No. Welcome to BYO
- CHILDREN: Welcome

SUNFIELD PRIVATE HOTEL
83 Summerland Avenue
Minehead, Somerset TA24 5BW

Tel: 01643 703565 - Freephone 0500 600 726
2 Crowns Approved

This is an hotel built at the turn of the 20th century with light, airy rooms and furnished in a modern, cheerful style with plenty of restful colours in the decor, pretty drapes and comfortable furniture. The ideal place for a holiday at anytime of the year, the house is centrally heated. James and Lynda Hatch have been here for over twelve years and they have developed quite a following of people who would not dream of going anywhere else when coming to Minehead. They are a friendly couple who enjoy their guests and work hard to ensure that everyone has a happy and memorable stay. There are eight guest bedrooms, five of which are ensuite and each room has television and a beverage tray. The food both at breakfast and evening meal is of a very high standard and plenty of it. There is a cosy bar which is the Mecca for visitors in the evening having a drink and meeting up with newly made friends. Minehead is a great place for a holiday. It is the Gateway to Exmoor, has good beaches, offers deep sea fishing, golf and some breathtaking walks both short and long. It is twenty five miles from Taunton and for Steam Railway lovers, the Minehead to Bishops Lydeard line runs along a twenty two mile track.

USEFUL INFORMATION

- OPEN: All year
- WHEELCHAIR ACCESS: No
- GARDEN: Not for guests
- CREDIT CARDS: None taken
- ACCOMMODATION: 8 rooms, 5 ensuite
- RATES: Ensuite £19 Standard £15
- DINING ROOM: Excellent food
- VEGETARIAN: Yes
- LICENSED: Residential
- CHILDREN: Welcome
- PETS: Well behaved dogs

TUDOR HOTEL & RESTAURANT
21 St Mary Street
Bridgwater
Somerset
TA6 3LX

Tel: 01278 422093 Fax: 01278 445292

Privately owned and run for over thirty five years by two generations of the Mouzoure family, the Tudor Hotel & Restaurant in St Mary Street, Bridgwater, is a busy friendly place providing both excellent food and accommodation. It is a delightful 16th century Listed building, full of character and charm with low ceilings and beams adding to the atmosphere. Old fashioned service is the hallmark of the staff here and nothing ever seems to be too much trouble. You may have a traditional breakfast in the restaurant or a delicious lunch with regular Daily Specials adding to a wide ranging menu with an a la carte menu at dinner. The emphasis is on good, fresh food and this goes for the excellent fish dishes on the menu. There are two bars and if you haven't time to enjoy the restaurant then a quick meal in the bar will be both delicious and rapidly served. The hotel has sixteen guest rooms all ensuite. Every room is attractively appointed and furnished with a pleasing mixture of antique and modern pieces. Each room has colour television, direct dial telephones and a generously supplied hostess tray. A very enjoyable place in which to stay and an ideal base for those wanting to explore this part of Somerset.

USEFUL INFORMATION

- OPEN: All year
- WHEELCHAIR ACCESS: No Ground floor only
- CREDIT CARDS: All major cards
- ACCOMMODATION: 16 ensuite rooms
- RATES: £39.50sgl £49.50 dbl
- PETS: No

- RESTAURANT: A la Carte + Daily Specials
- VEGETARIAN: Catered for
- BAR FOOD: Wide range
- LICENSED: Full On
- CHILDREN: Welcome

Anchor Hotel & Ship Inn	Porlock Weir	175
Anchor Inn	Dulverton	176
Ashwick Country House	Dulverton	177
Bales Mead	West Porlock	178
Bossington Farm	Appleford	179
Carnarvon Arms	Dulverton	180
Castle Hotel	Porlock	181
Cottage Hotel	Porlockweir	182
Crown Hotel	Exford	183
Downfield	Watchet	191
Heddons Gate	Parracombe	184
Higher Combe Farm	Dulverton	192
Lorna Doone (The)	Porlock	185
Rest & Be Thankful Inn	Wheddon Cross	186
Royal Oak	Winsford	187
Royal Oak Hotel	Withypool	188
Simonsbath Hotel	Simonsbath	189
Tarr Farm	Dulverton	192
Tarr Steps Hotel	Dulverton	190

Chapter Four:
A Royal Forest and Much Moor
Exmoor

Between Minehead and Combe Martin the coast is dramatic, severe and quite awe inspiring in places, with the highest sea cliffs in England. What lies behind these unforgettable shores is equally memorable, and just as varied. Wild, empty moorland mixed with rolling green cultivated farmland, dark ancient forests and ridiculously steep wooded slopes above fast flowing, rocky bedded rivers, all this is just part of what you can find in one of the least celebrated and famous, yet constantly rewarding of Britain's areas of natural beauty. Before we take a trip around the region to discover exactly what there is to see and do, let's briefly consider its history and present status.

The **EXMOOR NATIONAL PARK** (Dulverton Heritage Centre 01398 323841) covers 267 square miles, some seventy one percent of which is in Somerset, to the surprise of many who pair it with Devon's Dartmoor. Since April the First 1997, the National Park Authority has had control of the area as a free-standing body, no longer tied to the local councils. This means that the visitor to Exmoor has even more help and support than elsewhere, as this whole area is run by a group who think very long and hard about how to give the best to their annual influx of about 800,000 tourists, without damaging the local environment. Nature is on their side, for the more of Exmoor's immense diversity you see, the more you will appreciate and respect its beauty. Do you find it ironic that most of us choose to spend our time huddled together in cities and urban areas and yet yearn to spend time in places where we can walk for hours without seeing another habitation, and maybe not another human being? The National Parks Act of 1949 was an early conservation measure, but also an attempt to give the city dwellers and manual workers of post war Britain the opportunity for some freedom in the open air, to the benefit of their health and quality of life.

There are now eleven National Parks in England, and they receive 76 million days of visiting each year, making more than one for every single member of the population (even allowing for overseas visitors). Perhaps you may account for this as being an inevitable side effect of industry, technology and stress, the symptoms of the modern working world, but there is something more essential to the human nature in this choice of pastime than that. Getting away from it all is not a new idea, and the thought of a 'pastoral' escape was certainly known four hundred years ago:

They say he is already in the Forest of Arden, and a many merry men with him; and there they live like the old Robin Hood of England. They say many young gentlemen flock to him every day, and fleet the time carelessly, as they did in the golden world."
Charles, from Shakespeare's 'As You Like It'
Act One, Scene One, Lines 105-109.

Exmoor is not Shakespeare's Forest of Arden, where the love of Rosalind and Orlando eventually flourishes away from the pressures of the court. But as one of the few remaining safe havens in England for our largest and surely most magnificent mammal, the Red Deer, and with a diversity of landscape and scenery bonded only by an unquestionable common beauty, this is as close to 'the golden world' as you are likely to be able to get in modern England.

Unlike the fictional Arden, most of Exmoor is not a forest at all, although you are likely to hear it referred to as such. This is part of the area's history. There were trees on the central moorlands long ago, but for the most part they were felled by Neolithic and Bronze Age peoples as they cleared the land for cultivation more than two thousand years before even the Romans arrived. The central area of what now makes up the National Park was the Royal Forest of Exmoor from the 11th to the 19th centuries, except for a fairly brief period after the Civil War. The name forest was generic to such areas belonging to the reigning monarch. The job of the Warden of the Forest was to keep the deer ready for the summons to the dining table of the king or queen, while grazing land was let out to the surrounding farmers.

You may have noticed that there are not many royal castles or residences in the immediate area, and this has been very good news for the deer over the centuries. Fortunate for the landscape too, which was almost completely untouched , except for the grazing of livestock, during the eight hundred years of royal ownership.

Another easily misleading name in the Park's history is that of the Knights of Exmoor. At first I thought this might have been a chivalric, perhaps quite romantic group of people sworn to protect the deer and countryside against all comers, perhaps at the original instigation of King Arthur himself! While the reality is less fanciful, in some ways it is no less dramatic. John Knight was the man who finally bought Exmoor from The Crown in 1818, when the government finally gave up hope of using it to plant trees for the use of the navy. Succeeded by his son Frederic, he 'broke' much of the land so that it could be farmed more effectively. This was not immediately successful, and many of the first crop of tenant farmers of the 1840s were 'ruined by Exmoor', but eventually the project worked out pretty well, to the extent that now more than half of the area of the Park is farmland of one sort or another.

So what of this area today, now subject to another very different form of governorship? The objectives of the Park Authority are clear and enlightening. Conservation is vital, and so is the duty to make the park accessible and informative to the public, but without adversely affecting the existing communities either socially or economically. The first permanent dwelling place in the Royal Forest was built by James Boevey at **SIMONSBATH**, during his unpopular reign over the area after the end of the Civil War. There are now at least ten a half thousand people living on the larger tracts of land covered by the National Park. Dartmoor might spring to mind as a deserted place, but in comparison it has nearly three times as many residents in a total area less than half as big again as that of Exmoor; Dartmoor also receives almost three times as many visitors each year (based on figures for 1994). No matter how crowded Tarr Steps or Watersmeet might seem, there is still plenty of open space in Exmoor, if you know where to look for it.

A Stag Roaring, Exmoor

In 1810 William Wordsworth spent some time on Exmoor, calling it:

"a sort of a national property in which every man has a right and interest who has an eye to perceive and a heart to enjoy."

Prophetic words, as the park is now run by an Authority whose members include a fair proportion appointed by the nation as a whole, through central government, as well as others elected locally.

So everything looks good for the area we are about to explore in a little more detail. As a nation we have realised that it is of great importance, and are taking it as seriously as it deserves. Yet the Park Authority readily admits that it is facing some great challenges. The population of the area is ageing, as unemployment and high housing costs (partly due to the use of the Park for 'second homes') are driving young people away, although on the other hand tourism does supply jobs. Traffic congestion caused by the vast hordes who want to 'fleet the time carelessly' among the land lived in by the very few, is in danger of damaging the most popular spots.

Exmoor is nothing at all like a Theme Park or commercially run rural attraction. Its diversity and the fact that most of it is still in use, actually owned by the farmers who work it, means that it has a definite character, arguably stronger than that of some of the other National Parks. The National Park Authority will actively encourage you to enjoy and add to this character, but has a delicate and perhaps unenviable job in maintaining it, without letting the whole area become the victim of its own success.

As well as the Heritage Centre at Dulverton, there are other National Park Visitor Centres including those at Combe Martin (01271 883319), Dunster (01643 821835) and Lynmouth (01598 752509). Most of the surviving village stores and Post Offices also act as Information agencies for the area. Whole books have been written about this fascinating area, so while it is impossible to do justice to even half of everything you can do and see in Exmoor in this text, a taste of what you can experience, and an outline of the different areas must be attempted with due humility.

The deserted and open countryside and scenery you might be expecting from Exmoor is most spectacular in its central and western areas, but we will leave the traditional moorland and open inland spaces for now, to continue the journey ended in our last chapter at Minehead, along the south eastern edge of the Bristol Channel.

The coast is not the common starting point for visitors to Exmoor though. In fact there is a very well defined route taken by the vast majority of those who come to the National Park. This follows the A39 through Dunster and then Minehead, followed by a quick visit to Porlock, then onto Lynton and Lynmouth in the west. To keep to the main roads the return journey will probably include a run down the A396 to take in a little of the wilder moor, as well as perhaps a final diversion into Dulverton. If you take this popular and well inhabited path you will see some of what Exmoor has to offer, but by no means a fair, even half complete picture. Taking a few minor roads to enlarge the scope of the drive is not the answer either. The Park Authority's research suggests that the average visitor to Exmoor walks a total of seventeen metres (about fifty five feet) during an entire day, and here lies the answer. More than anywhere else in this book, Exmoor demands that you explore; on foot, cycle or even horseback. You do not have to be a determined rambler or off road cyclist, but if, like so many others, the only air you breathe in during your visit to the National Park is that filtered in through the conditioning system of your car then you really are missing the best of what is here.

You will not need many resources to aid your exploration. There is a wonderful series of leaflets outlining specific walks, published by the Park Authority, as well as plenty of marked routes and pathways. For the more ambitious there is the TWO

MOORS WAY, linking Exmoor to Dartmoor, and the TARKA TRAIL (01837 83399, or e-mail: tarka@tarka.romgroup.co.uk for a guidebook) which follows the trail of the famous otter around the route taken in the stories by Henry Williamson. Some of this last route lies to the west of Exmoor, but the moor is a useful place from which to start. Access to the various parts of Exmoor does vary in its freedom; rights of way are open on the central portion owned by the Park itself, while there are marked paths across privately owned farmland. The best way to tell them apart is to use the Park Authority's 'Bible', the Leisure Series 1:25,000 scale map, which gives a clear picture of the best routes to take. If you only make a single purchase during, or prior to, your visit then this is the one I would recommend. There is one little tip I must add, based on embarrassing and irritating personal experience. The map is two sided, dividing the region east to west. It is also very large and extremely difficult to manoeuvre inside a car, so be sure you have the right side ready to be viewed before you set out, otherwise you may have to reassemble the whole thing on the top of a windy part of the moor, with predictable results.

There are many guided walks and events on Exmoor each year, run by the National Park Authority and other organisations; the Heritage and Information Centres will have the latest details. Public transport is a good option to get you to the parts you particularly want to see, especially as this helps to reduce the wear and tear caused by the vast volumes of tourist traffic. The EXMOOR PUBLIC TRANSPORT GUIDE will tell you what you need to know about bus routes, trains, and times etc, and is available from Tourist Information Centres and Park Information Centres in the area. Recently the various 'Park and Ride' schemes promoted by the Authority have proved particularly popular, and are worth looking out for.

Cycling and Horse Riding are two more effective ways of getting around. There are four hundred miles of bridleways within Exmoor, maintained by the Authority and their Park Rangers, who are happy to give advice on how to proceed, whether you bring your own horse to one of the many stables or farms in the area, or prefer to use one of those which can be provided. Try WEST ANSTEY FARM (01398 341534) or PINE LODGE (01398 323559) near Dulverton, BRENDON MANOR FARM (01598 741246) or CLOUD FARM (01598 741213) near Lynmouth, the DEAN RIDING CENTRE (01598 763565) at Parracombe, the COURT FARM STABLES (01643 831179) or STOCKLEIGH STABLES (01643 831166) near Exford, or the OUTOVERCOTT RIDING STABLES (01598 753341) at Barbrook near Lynton to assess the selection of services available. There are even Horsedrawn Tours available from the WEST ILKERTON FARM (01598 752310) inland from Lynton. One enviable advantage for those on horseback is that Exmoor's Red Deer do not flinch at the sight of a horse, whereas a car or even walkers will usually see them depart rapidly, before you are even aware of their presence. The same goes for herons, dippers and buzzards, so that with the increased accessibility and range a horse gives, this is the ideal way to cover quantities of the Park and increase your chances of seeing some of its rarer inhabitants.

Some of the bridleways combine with other tracks to give opportunities for off road cycling and mountain biking, and the Authority has other routes for cyclists; again contact the Information Centres for current details. TARKA TRAIL CYCLE HIRE (01271 324202) based at Barnstaple, promise up to twenty one miles of level traffic free cycle track, if this particular trail appeals more to you as a two wheeled adventure rather than a pedestrian one. 'Safaris' of the moorland by Land Rover are offered by companies in Dulverton and elsewhere. Try the MOORLAND WILDLIFE SAFARI (01398 323699) at Dulverton, or EXMOOR SAFARI (01643 831166) based at Exford for half or full day details and prices.

Somehow it seems odd for a moor to have a coastline, but in some places there is not a single tree or building between the sheep grazing the grasses of the National Park and the precipices of sea cliffs towering over the Bristol Channel. At times the animals look in need of some mountaineering gear if they have any intention of taking a single step further. There are 34 miles of dramatic coastline to explore, some over a thousand feet above sea level, culminating in the GREAT HANGMAN near Combe Martin. Sea birds such as guillemots, razor bills, kittiwakes and many others are established here, in an extremely important haven and breeding area. Further out there are porpoises, pilot whales and basking sharks in the Bristol Channel, although to see any sign of these you will need to take to a boat.

Our last chapter ended with an interruption; **PORLOCK** (Information Centre 01643 863150). To the west of Minehead, but just this side of the Devon border, it is not only the story of Coleridge's unfinished poem (Chapter Three) which links Porlock to the idea of a break in a journey, be it intellectual or physical. The hill road which drops down to this quiet seaside town will break any trip from east to west if you are tempted to take it, as so very many others are. The higher sections of the hill are relatively gradual, and it is easy to pay little attention to the signs warning that lower sections have a gradient of one in four, and that a very low gear is the best to select. On my last visit the road was just beginning to steepen, in lovely swinging curves when it occurred to me that freewheeling a bicycle down here would be a refreshing and exhilarating challenge. Around the very next bend was a sign stating that all cyclists should dismount, undoubtedly the safer and more sensible option. The lower sections are steep enough to make you feel quite giddy, but the vertical perspective is one that that will make you wonder in many more locations before you leave Exmoor.

Until the 1920s there were only two practical ways of getting back up Porlock Hill. The first was to walk, and the second was by horse drawn coach, as the road was still unsurfaced. Even then the coachman would ask you to walk the steepest sections to lighten the horses load. Apparently ladies over the age of forty were allowed to stay aboard, but it has been suggested that many who were obviously only just past this milestone preferred to walk, rather than produce proof of their date of birth, or even voluntarily admit to their age. This does seem hard to believe. Many passengers of both genders chose to walk the descent too. Perhaps this was because the sliding motion of the coach, produced by the necessity of engaging a metal drag on the rear wheels to slow it down, was more than a little disconcerting. Early cars had another problem. Some had a 'gravity petrol feed', with the result that the only way up the hill was to engage reverse gear. This really must have been good fun, especially as the driver often had to get out and steer though an open window to lighten the load sufficiently to get up the hill at all. As the decades went on it became more usual to see over heated cars and their equally hot occupants taking an unwanted stop at some point, in order to top up the radiator.

A much more vicious and complete interruption than those mentioned so far was made to the lives of the villagers of Porlock in 886, when the Danes landed to loot and fire the place to the ground. It looks as if a further interruption hindered whoever was building the spire of Porlock's church, as its truncated form might suggest that the bills were not being paid, or that there was a dreadful scarcity of materials. Other local stories say that a giant simply snapped off the spire of this church of ST DUBRICIUS, or that it came off in a storm long ago. The break is awfully clean for either of these last two to be true. Whatever the case, Porlock is a delightful little village by the sea, and worth the gearbox straining drive back up the hill. In the High Street you can also find the DOVERY MANOR MUSEUM, with a collection of local artefacts housed in an attractive 15th century building.

St Dubricius Church, Porlock

If you wish to stay near the sea for a little longer, one of the Park Authority's leaflets outlines a walk around PORLOCK BAY which will help you to make better sense of some of what you may have seen on your steep descent. Starting from the main car park this route takes you across to **WEST PORLOCK**, passing what may have looked from above like some irrigation ditches built surprisingly close to a sea that looks ready to flood them at any moment. In fact these make up the original natural drainage system for the DECOYS, a system of ponds built to trap swimming wildfowl. Apparently cygnets often found their way from here straight to the Lord of the Manor's dining table. The area of green rising up from here, known as The Parks, belonged to this same dignitary, and was where deer and rabbits were kept, presumably in order to give his diet some variety.

Further west is the 19th century dock of **PORLOCK WEIR**, built in the fishing harbour to deal with the expected traffic from the Knights' Iron Ore mining operations on the nearby Moor. The proposed railway to Simonsbath was never built, but there was much trade for a while, with sheep and cattle exported from here to feed the miners in South Wales. Some ships from the North Devon coast went much further, and as meat and wool started to arrive from as far afield as Australia the signs were not good for local farmers who relied on the sea trade. There were no turnpike roads along this coast, and no railway until almost the turn of the century, Porlock Hill did not even have tarmac until 1930, when it had to be hammered in by hand because of the steepness of the slope. This made the sea a vital line of supply and communication, and Porlock was not without its dramatic incidents, as we will see shortly. Now Porlock Weir is a good place from which to take a boat trip along some of this very inaccessible, rugged stretch of coast.

Turning back to the east, the route of the walk takes you through the SUBMARINE FOREST, for which you may need a pair of waterproof boots, but not a full set of diving gear. Patches of peat, lying above the local grey clay, have remains of trees which grew here until about seven thousand years ago. This whole section of coast appears to mix the natural with the seemingly synthetic just as spectacularly as that at Kilve and East Quantoxhead back to the east (Chapter Three). From the roads above and inland from Porlock the coast seems edged with a smooth wall of light grey concrete, perhaps coloured by the use of too much pure cement. It is only when you get a good deal closer that this sculpted fortification is seen for what it really is, a natural storm barrier made up of pebbly shingle. This has been here for much longer than man has been using cement, with geologists believing the feature was first caused by the rise in sea levels at the end of the last Ice Age. The bank has stood as it is for at least 6,000 years. Personally I love the sound of the current pulling at these banks of small stones, sucking them all the stronger into the sea as the wind picks up before throwing them back from where they came, but clear days are a must if you wish to explore. Beware of rougher weather, as a storm of Autumn 1996 is reported to have rolled some sections near Porlock up to sixty feet inland. Natural breaches do occur in this barrier in times of severe weather, and an insert presently issued with this particular walk leaflet suggests that to continue along the bank is not wise, or often practicable, dependent on the tides. Of course these are a major factor in keeping the wall looking as smooth as it does, with a tremendous difference of nearly sixty feet between the lowest and highest water levels during the Spring Tides.

Back to the east of Porlock there are more peaceful surroundings at the hamlet of **BOSSINGTON**, where a stream reaches the sea across a harmless looking, pebbly beach. Leaving the Park's walking route, let's turn inland, where the villages start to build the complicated picture of Exmoor as a whole. Heading south around the bottom of BOSSINGTON HILL, the BOSSINGTON FARM AND BIRDS OF PREY CENTRE (01643 862816) provides a chance for you to see the work of wildlife conservation and breeding projects, with a glorious backdrop formed by the dark green and pinky red hilltops to the north.

Much of what lies to the south and east of here is National Trust property, with dotted settlements amongst coombes and larger forested areas. These are naturally very quiet places amongst trees, **HORNER** even gets its name from an Old English word meaning 'snorer', reflecting the peaceful setting rather than any qualities for curing insomnia! Meanwhile the church, with its leering gargoyles, is the dominant feature of nearby **LUCCOMBE**. In the woods between the villages the Red Deer have enjoyed the peace for a very long time, and the very knowledge that they are in there somewhere gives an air of majesty and magic to the whole area. The National Trust has its own leaflet outlining a Horner Hill Wood Walk. There could not be a greater immediate contrast to the scenery on the route from Porlock. No shingle and sea breeze here, or cement greys, but rather a floor deeply carpeted with the leaves of past years, the trees above filling the sky over your head with the colour appropriate to the time of year. Part of a National Nature Reserve, Horner Wood has ancient Oak and large Holly Trees, as well as many other rarities including more than four hundred different species of fungi, of which eighty or so are not commonly found in Britain. Parts of the wood are on steep slopes, and the walk is an ever changing one, full of lovely views and opportunities to see wildlife across the scale from the red deer to woodpeckers, as well a profusion of insects and beetles in the decaying dead timbers which the Trust deliberately leave standing.

A fourteenth century church and Tithe Barn give character to **SELWORTHY**, another peaceful settlement, sheltered by its own SELWORTHY BEACON to the north, with beautiful views of Dunkery to the south. The church is white, lime-washed to match the thatched cottages around it. At nearby **ALLERFORD**, the RURAL LIFE MUSEUM (01643 862529) explores life in the area over the centuries, including a restored Victorian Schoolroom.

Moving our tour on in an anti-clockwise direction, the coastline between Porlock and Lynmouth is largely a very inaccessible one. From **CULBONE** to the lighthouse at **FORELAND POINT** the guillemots and other seabirds perched on the ledges of severe cliffs and around the huge weathered rock formations of SIR ROBERTS CHAIR get the best of the views along the lands around the South West Coast Path, with access to many places that we would find quite impossible to reach. This is remote country, perhaps even more so than the centre of the moor. The expanses around **COUNTISBURY** are country for the dedicated walker, and the National Park's Visitor's Centre at COUNTY GATE (01598 741321), where Somerset meets Devon, is largely dedicated to their needs and interests. If you like dramatic slopes and bare cliffs, then this could be the place for you to explore, but do take advice about weather conditions and accessibility from the Centre first.

Even the main A39 west from here has some extremely dramatic views. To the north there seems to be very little between the oncoming traffic and the sea, hundreds of feet below. A grassy bank, no more than eighteen inches in height in some places, totally obscures your view of any other land. There is an urge to stop the car and investigate. If you can find a suitable place to park safely then it is tempting to approach the bank as horizontally as possible, craning your neck slowly over its flat top to see what is below. If you do, beware any sheep or goats suddenly appearing right in your face as they climb the impossibly steep slopes, which look to be coming up from the sea at a minimum angle of eighty five degrees. Several years ago I followed this pattern, and then climbed down just a few feet from the road, to sit on a grassy ledge surrounded by rocks looking out to sea. I had travelled by car from Taunton, at an average speed of about twenty miles per hour, as the summer traffic had dictated. The relief of the fresh salty air and quiet, less than twenty yards from the main road, was tremendous. The antics of the animals grazing these grassy sea cliffs provided almost comical entertainment, and it was not an easy spot to leave behind quickly. Yet the harshness of this terrain and what is to the east of it puts a very serious piece of Exmoor's history into an almost terrifyingly tangible context.

1999 will be the Centenary of one of the finest hours in Exmoor's history, the OVERLAND HAUL. As we noted at Porlock Weir, local sea routes were essential supply routes to the communities living around the Exmoor coast in the 19th century. Shipwrecks and strandings were not uncommon, and after the 'Home' ran aground off the Foreland in 1868, a church collection provided the money for Lynmouth's first lifeboat. It looked as if her successor, the 'Louisa', could not possibly help the iron ship 'Forrest Hall' and its crew of fifteen when it hit trouble in Porlock Bay during some very inclement weather in January 1899. The winds were just too strong for the boat to be launched. At approximately eight p.m. on the night of the 12th January a large crowd, including the crew, as well as at least a dozen horses, set out to try the only alternative. Looking out today at the coastline between Lynmouth and Porlock what they achieved that dark wind torn night seems simply incredible.

By six o'clock in the morning the lifeboat had put to sea; at Porlock. It is difficult to know what must have been the most difficult, dragging her over Countisbury Hill, or finally holding her carriage back so that the 'Louisa' did not dive down Porlock

Hill in a last tragic, swift descent. At least a mile of the journey involved dragging the boat on skids when the path became too narrow to take the carriage at all, which then had to be taken across the open moor inland to meet up with her later on. One two mile section of the route involved climbs totalling some fourteen hundred feet. By five p.m on the 13th January, having worked for an unbroken twenty one hours, the crew were able to rest in the harbour at Barry, in South Wales, having rescued all aboard the crippled ship.

History is much easier to appreciate in Exmoor than in many other places because so little has changed in the intervening years. As one official at the Park Authority put it to me, it is as if the tarmac roads have been built as a track from which passing humanity and outsiders can view what has been as it is for at least a hundred years, and often much, much longer. Looking out to sea from any perch along this stretch of northern coast the events of that Winter's night, when the community struggled against both weather and terrain with such determined bravery, do seem as if they could have happened a decade rather than a century ago. At the time of writing plans are afoot to stage a full scale reconstruction of the events of the 12th / 13th January 1899 on the occasion of its centenary. The RNLI official I heard discussing these plans commented that he still does not know how on earth the three and a half tons of lifeboat were man-handled up the hills, so it should be an occasion worth braving the Exmoor winter for.

To appreciate the tragic events for which **LYNMOUTH** (Information 01598 752509) is most famous it is necessary to take you far inland, temporarily. In one of the most deserted areas of central moorland, near the Chains, is a fairly flat area about the size of a football field. Incredibly this is the starting point of both the River EXE and the River LYN. There are just a few inches of peat here above the 'Iron Pan' which had to be broken for the cultivation of other parts of Exmoor in the 19th century. As a result much of the rain that falls is held on the surface, and then flows downhill into the tiny channels which soon build into the two rivers. It is only gravity which decides whether the water goes north, on a seven mile trip to the sea at Lynmouth, or south on a seventy mile journey to Exmouth. On one occasion in 1952 a freak nine inches of rain fell in a single day, onto peat which was already soaked from previous downpours. With seventy miles to travel, and across some reasonably flat bottomed valleys, the Exe coped with this strain rather better than the Lyn. Moving back north towards the sea it is necessary to have a look at **WATERSMEET** before you can really appreciate the inevitability of what happened next.

By now the (West) Lyn has grown to a fast running river, splashing down most attractively over the rocks to meet another tributary by the National Trust property of WATERSMEET HOUSE. As with the coast to the east of Lynmouth and Lynton, it is the vertical perspective here that is the most impressive, especially if you stand some way up the steep wooded slopes looking down on the cascading waters below. Above you and in front of you stand the sites of two ancient hillforts, the one to the South West being that at MYRTLEBERRY CLEAVE. It is quite easy to imagine two ancient communities assembled in these settlements, able to communicate with each other by simply shouting across the gorge, if they could make themselves heard over the noise of the water. If this failed they could easily have tried throwing stones across the deep gap, or tried out any new missile weapon, be it spear or ballista.

The river valley is simply like a pipeway with its top open to the sky. The western arm of the system, coming through **BARBROOK**, is scarcely less confined, and all that would happen to an unusual volume of water running through here is that it would pick up pace. Since 1952 other parts of the Lyn have been widened to dissipate the power which struck Lynmouth with its full, tragic force at that time.

As the swollen river waters savaged this area in 1952, the terrible path of destruction became national news. Lives were lost and many homes completely destroyed, and looking at still photographs of the aftermath, there can be few more awesome examples in this country of an 'Act of God'. The LYN AND EXMOOR MUSEUM (01598 752317) in neighbouring **LYNTON** (Tourist Information 01598 752225) is housed in an old stone cottage, and features Exmoor life from its beginnings up to the present day, including an exhibition about the flood. In Lynmouth there is also a FLOOD MEMORIAL HALL (01598 752204) with newspapers and photographs from the time. Now the two small towns, linked by 150 yards of water powered cliff railway, are again busy with people, but quiet in terms of scenery compared to what surrounds them.

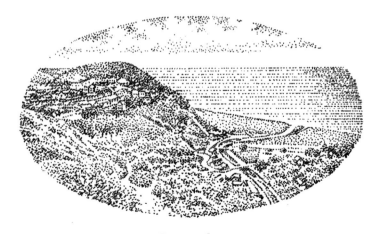

Lynmouth

Instead of acting as a magnetic funnel for flood waters, it is visitors who are drawn together now at Lynmouth, particularly in the summer months. The main road goes right down towards the grey stoned harbour, although it is possible to by-pass the town. Very few choose to do this, and the relatively huge car parks, for such a small place, are usually packed to overflowing in decent weather. It is almost as if the multitudes have been scared by the emptiness of the moor, or the severity of Foreland Point, and gather here for sanctuary before charging off towards the next 'honey pot'. As if to emphasise this, at the top of the Authority's list of most visited places (where numbers can be counted) is the Cliff Railway between Lynton and Lynmouth (01598 753486) the advertising for which declares it to be Devon's top tourist attraction.

It is nothing new for Lynmouth to be a popular resort; well before the Cliff Railway was constructed between 1885 and 1890 it had become known as the 'English Switzerland' and tourists arrived daily by coach and boat, until the more traditional form of railway finally arrived in 1898 (and then met its demise by 1935). I am glad to relate that it was money from one of that eternally generous breed, a publisher, which allowed the engineer Bob Jones to have the link between the two places built. This new Cliff Railway was the first of its kind to be built anywhere, and still continues to work on the very same principles of its original design. There are two rectangular carriages, looking rather like brightly painted metallic enlargements of a traditional garden shed, but each with a small balcony. The two only ever meet momentarily, as the weight of the descending carriage, with its tank full of water, pulls the other to the top along the neighbouring track, but not at a rate which will cause any alarm. The slow ascent is perhaps the best of the two journeys, as you have the chance to see more of the surrounding coastline gradually exposed to your view as you get higher.

Lynton is a quiet little place, without the same volume of visitors as its downstairs neighbour, but both are very much worth the crush of numbers, although if you manage to get yourself here in the quieter months there is certainly more room. With spectacular and well maintained sections of the South West Coast path leading both to the east and west, Lynton and Lynmouth also make a good base from which to see the coast, as well as Watersmeet and the rest of the countryside behind them. Lynmouth is also a popular place from which to take a sea-fishing boat trip. It is also home to the BRASS RUBBING AND HOBBYCRAFT CENTRE (01598 752529) with many up to date local crafts products on sale, a chance to try the ancient art of Brass Rubbing, and a collection of brasses from the last seven hundred years and more.

To the west lies some more superbly unusual coastline, starting immediately as you leave Lynton with the VALLEY OF ROCKS. The valley is a rare geological feature because the rock strata run parallel to the coast rather than along the course of any stream or other course to the sea. What at first look like spectacular piles of unevenly shaped flat rocks, ready to topple at any moment, are in fact solid pillars which show the ages of the rock in the strata which have survived. It is also a valley without a river, as it is thought that the waterway which carved out its shape was redirected as long ago as the last Ice Age.

In a quiet moment here you can imagine you are far away, perhaps on the set of one of Clint Eastwood's Spaghetti Westerns; the long silent 'hands on guns' scene from

'The Good, the Bad and the Ugly' comes to mind. Do not get too carried away by this idea though, as a jumping goat could easily cause you to bite that smouldering cigar in two, as it breaks the silent tension without the slightest warning. Reality will soon come back with a blast of the sea breeze, or the realisation that there is much too much green for this to be in such a scene. I do not remember views of the sea featuring in the film either, so perhaps the comparison was a little facetious, although a quiet scamper up among one of the marked paths among the rocks might bring out the poncho in you.

Chimney Rock and Rugged Jack, The Valley of Rocks

A longer walk around the valley can be taken using another of the Park Authority's leaflets. This begins and ends in Lynton, so expect a little climbing. Among the notable rock formations this passes are the White Lady, Chimney Rock, Rugged Jack, Castle Rock and the intriguingly named Devil's Cheesewring (a sort of press used in cider making). This last is near to the cave home of the witch Mother Meldrum in the novel 'Lorna Doone' (of which more shortly), while in the early 19th century Aggie Norman, reputed to be the real item, spent her summers in a hut right over the sea, next to Castle Rock. This last is my personal favourite, looking like the ultimate folly, a remnant of a particularly insane attempt to fortify a place which nature has already made about as impenetrable to humanity as it could possibly be.

The western extremity of the walking route takes in LEE ABBEY, which was never part of the Dissolution of the Monasteries simply because it has never been an Abbey, although its most recent reinvention is as a Christian Retreat and Conference Centre. The mock Gothic building of red brick which stands here today was built in the mid 19th century, but if you travel a little further, paying for the toll road and car park (in a field) if you are no longer on foot, then **LEE BAY** might give you a chance for some quiet reflection of your own. On my last visit I was the only person on the entire beach of dark sand between more cement coloured rocks; these of much larger dimensions than those making up the barrier at Porlock. This was on a clear, mild day, but in early Spring, before the main influx of visitors hits Exmoor, so I cannot vouch for any chance of such solitude during the summer months. Even so this, and neighbouring **WOODY BAY**, will usually be much emptier than Lynmouth to the east or Combe Martin to the west, and are just as pretty, in their own ways.

These are quieter places in terms of scenery too, although SMUGGLER'S LEAP, above Lee Bay, has a dramatic story to go with its steep precipices. It is said that in the early 19th century a Customs Officer, riding on horseback, chased a smuggler towards this drop at full gallop. Catching up with his prey at the very edge he grabbed the other bridle, only to make both horses rear, sending all four over the cliff to their deaths. An unpleasant little legend, but quite credible in the surroundings. The narrow road west from Lee Bay weaves in and out of the trees, to the extent that it takes all your concentration and attention away from the abrupt edge just to your right. If you do get a chance to glance across the drop to the sea is just as sudden as that east of Lynmouth, and it seems amazing that some of the extremely necessary passing places have been built on this northern side of the road, bringing tarmac even closer to the very last trees, clinging to soil which appears to be almost directly above the sea. If anything the shoreline becomes even more inaccessible the further west from here you decide to go. There are many small coves and inlets, with pasture and cultivated heath ending abruptly above. Nearer to the westernmost point of Exmoor just outside **COMBE MARTIN** the slopes become too steep for grazing, and woodland dominates the coast once more. From RAWN'S ROCKS to HANGMAN'S POINT there is still much to explore here, but only if you are prepared to leave the beaten tracks well behind.

Now we are compelled to turn inland, but what a variety this National Park has already offered. In the far west the countryside is very empty, with the ancient barrows and stones of TRENTISHOE and HOLDSTONE HILL (both National Trust properties) giving some of the very few landmarks. Moving east, we have already seen some of the spectacle offered by the land behind Lynton and Lynmouth at Watersmeet, but there is more of a similar nature in less well visited spots too. If you like your drama to be romantic, then further east, behind County Gate, the church at **OARE** will be of particular interest. This is the heart of DOONE country, and it was in the little church of ST MARY, that Carver Doone shot Lorna in the climax of the action of R.D.Blackmore's novel. Another of the Park Authority's walking routes leads from the Centre at County Gate through much more of the landscape used in the novel. Whether or not you have read the book, the trip through BADGWORTHY WOOD and then out onto more open moorland will show you more of the memorable variety of Exmoor.

Oare itself is also home to the EXMOOR NATURAL HISTORY SOCIETY'S FIELD CENTRE, manned by volunteers, and with exhibits about local landscapes and wildlife. Perhaps the finest things about the south western part of the moor, where sheep graze the grass on the peaty soil, are the views across to the south and east. Much of the rest of Devon is visible from heights such as FIVE BARROWS, with Dartmoor looking particularly inviting, if rugged. There are few villages here, even **PARRACOMBE** looks quite precarious with its steep streets plunging into the contours of the HEDDON VALLEY.

Turning east towards TARR STEPS the boundary between the counties of Devon and Somerset is a fluid one, quite literally, as it follows the windings of the river BARLE at the bottom of its valley. After the bracken, gorse and then deeper woodlands of the ANSTY COMMONS, **DULVERTON** marks the beginning of yet another change in the surroundings, with the BRENDON HILLS beckoning from the east. It was here that I had one of my own most memorable experiences on Exmoor.

After a summer day spent pleasantly in Dunster and then the countryside around Lynmouth I was driving back towards the east in the early evening. As it began to get dark I stopped in Dulverton for a break. The skies had been clear all day, but it was humid, and close. As the sun set a patch of pure black suddenly appeared to the north west over the vast open spaces towards the centre of the Moor. The storm which followed was like none other I have ever experienced.

Whether the landscape here can make a difference to the speed in which such weather can travel, or whether it is simply the stark setting which lends an Exmoor storm its stunning visual power, I do not know. One minute there seemed to be plenty of time before the distant rumblings and flashes could approach, the very next it was as if my car was the focal point for a display of shuddering explosions and bright blue lightning, such as I have never seen before or since. The storm was brief, but the shapes made by the Brendons as they appeared, momentarily lit up against the otherwise pitch black skies, are something I will never forget.

Despite this dramatic picture, you will find Dulverton a quiet, attractive place on most days, although full of visitors in the busiest summer months. If Exmoor has an inland centre then this is it. As the headquarters of the Park Authority you might expect this, but do not look for a metropolis with plenty of supermarkets and evening entertainments. With the river winding through its very centre, and plenty of wooded spaces between the buildings looking down onto the centre of the town, Dulverton is a small, idyllic rural town, whatever its administrative role. A visit to the Visitor Information Centre (01398 323841) can be followed by a stroll down to the medieval BARLE BRIDGE, or if you prefer a longer walk along another of the routes published by the Park Authority then a round trip of five miles will take in much more, including a long stretch following the path of the River Barle and the village of **BRUSHFORD**, with its ancient church. Back in the town, the GUILDHALL HERITAGE CENTRE incorporates a small museum which houses the Exmoor Photographic Archive, as well as a cottage showing living conditions as they would have been one hundred years or so ago. Eventually the Centre may hold an exhibit about 1997, the year in which Dulverton and many of its population appeared in the film 'Land Girls' starring

Anna Friel. The EXMOOR PRODUCERS ASSOCIATION (01398 324383) has its headquarters in the town too. Here you can find out about almost one hundred different producers of high quality goods in the Exmoor region, many of them through traditional crafts.

In some ways Dulverton is between two extremes. To the east is the richest farming land of Exmoor, characterised by verdant coniferous plantations, while to the north and west is the central area, a place where complete solitude and open views can be found. The National Park Authority owns much of the land around Simonsbath, and what was the heart of the Royal Forest. It is surprising how quickly the comfortable surroundings of Dulverton can be left behind in this direction, even on a fairly major route such as the B3223 which cuts between **WITHYPOOL**, **EXFORD** and **WINSFORD**. Before you have time to take in the sudden change the round bank atop WINSFORD HILL beckons as a suitable viewpoint from which to get your bearings.

Coming out of Dulverton you have followed the course of the river a little further, its fast running waters just wide enough to look fit to have their own narrow steep-sided valley, and definitely promise trout rather than chub for any hopeful angler. Now the surroundings are completely and utterly different. A short walk from the parking bay to the actual earthwork gives you a chance to take in some of the air, which has little to stop its progress as it blows across the moor. If you are alone the sound of this wind is likely to be the only thing you can hear from Winsford Hill. The setting is totally peaceful, and suddenly remote. The smell of the heather and gorse covered moor fills you nostrils, and the long views of rolling hills, some cultivated, many left wild, please the eye. Any signs of humanity are likely to be in the form of walkers or those still seated in their cars, for with the exception of an occasional farm building there are no signs of more permanent occupation to be seen anywhere, except in the earthwork, which looks like a discarded, upturned giant cake tin, of the variety used to make an iced ginger cake, in the shape of a ring.

Dulverton is known as the 'Gateway to Exmoor', and this section of open moor, surrounded by farmland, serves as a sort of introduction too, showing some of the variety found elsewhere on a larger scale. To the south west and north east there are much larger open areas, while we have already seen that there are wooded areas larger than the steep coombes lining the Barle to the north of Dulverton. Nearer to Simonsbath the variety continues, with ancient remains such as COW CASTLE and FLEXBARROW above the continuing course of the Barle, and what is reputed to be the highest beech wood in the country at BIRCH CLEAVE. There are more recent reminders of human activity too, such as the ruins of the Cow Castle cottages at WHITE WATER and the long abandoned mines at WHEAL ELIZA.

These last two have a macabre link. Times were hard for the shepherds living in these cottages in the middle of the 19th century. Living on Exmoor was something new, instigated by the Knights from nearby Simonsbath, and the pickings were certainly not easy or rich for those who were the first to try and earn a livelihood here. One William Burgess took desperate measures in 1858, killing his six year old daughter Anna-Maria, apparently in order to save the half a crown a week it cost to keep her. He then threw her body into the flooded mine shaft at Wheal Eliza. Perhaps it is just as well both sites now lay in ruins.

Simonsbath is a small place, where you can find out more about the Knights and their attempts to 'break' Exmoor into farming land. To the north west of the village is the wet country of THE CHAINS, treacherous even in the middle of summer for the walker who unwisely chooses to leave the marked paths. As we have discovered form the disaster that hit Lynmouth, water sits just beneath the peaty surface here, because of the same vein of Iron Ore which provoked investment into optimistic mining operations in the 19th century. The vein is solid, preventing proper drainage, but was not wide enough to be mined profitably. These are some of the loneliest stretches of this or any other National Park. On a sunny day the glorious golds and greens of the moorlands are only broken in the far distance by thin lines of dark green, marking the hedged perimeter of the cultivated lands.

The Knights followed Boevey by basing their operations at Simonsbath, and PINKWORTHY POND (pronounced Pinkery) is perhaps the most mysterious relic of their stay. The calm sheet of water is now termed a 'folly', simply because no-one can be sure of its true purpose. It may well have been purely decorative, but it may have been the start of another project to use the land of Exmoor for some sort of production. What really matters is that the pond now looks completely natural, and gives more colour to what surrounds it as the sun reflects from its glittering surface.

Moving east from property owned by the National Park Authority to that owned by the National Trust, we will go to Exmoor's highest point, more than 1700 feet above sea level at DUNKERY BEACON. It is easy to see why this was chosen as the site for the Medieval fire signal which gave the hill its name. Here the views are just as undulating as those to the west, but with wooded combes and valleys amongst bare moorland hills, the effect is totally different. On a misty morning the hills rise like the humps of sleeping dinosaurs lying in a grey, mysterious sea. Gradually the day will burn off the cover around the rivers and streams, revealing tantalising glimpses of darker greens, until the whole lovely panorama is complete.

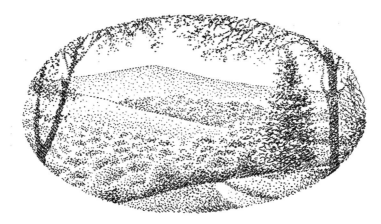

Dunkery Beacon

The National Trust and the Park Authority have combined to try and save the paths around the beacon from further erosion. Conservation is a complex issue on Exmoor. The environment, and various habitats for wildlife are actually man made, despite the wild appearance. The farmland of the Brendon Hills, with reddy ploughed soil, and smaller, patchwork green fields, shows what a 'natural' development of even the grassy, cultivated parts of the moor would bring.

Farmers are compensated for having to use 'traditional' methods, and what is now being preserved is what previous centuries has made, from the Neolithic tree fellers, who left only the inaccessible steep slopes to give us ancient woodlands in some areas, to the pioneer Knights and their successors in the Exmoor farming community. If the thousands of visitors to Dunkery were not considered then its remote setting simply would not be enough to save it. So it is that inconspicuous stone drains have been fitted to the paths leading up towards it, in an effort to remove surface water as quickly as possible, and so reduce erosion. This was part of a three year DUNKERY PROJECT, which has now led onto a more permanent collaboration started in September 1997, the EXMOOR PATHS PARTNERSHIP.

The roads of Exmoor get more than their fair share of work too. Approaching Dunkery in this way, you may end up being delayed by more than the volume of wheeled traffic, as even a single sheep can add to the chaos by deciding to cross the tarmac. A partial answer to this last problem is to leave your car in Minehead or Porlock, and take the bus. Somerset County Council and the Exmoor National Park Authority have even combined to produce a leaflet which gives details of the 285 Service and walking routes around Dunkery. For example one of these takes you from **WHEDDON CROSS** via bridleway, road and footpath to the Beacon, then taking you onto Exford, where you can catch a bus back to base. Other walks linked to bus routes in this series include **TIMBERSCOMBE** to Porlock and another around Dunster.

The idea is a truly admirable one, and has proved extremely popular and successful. You can also get a three day ticket which will allow you unlimited travel around Exmoor.

We have covered all the main aspects of Exmoor, and much of what you may wish to visit, but this is not yet all. It is surprising to hear that the second most visited attraction in the National Park is the WIMBLEBALL WATER PARK (01837 871565, Sailing Club 01278 652146), famous for trout fishing and sailing as well as lakeside walking and sightseeing. This lies in the south east corner of Exmoor. The border with west Somerset, and the quiet villages around Wiveliscombe, is unseen and largely undetectable. Both areas generally seem much emptier of visitors than much of what is to the north.

Wimbleball Lake itself was created in the 1970s by the damming of the River Haddeo, and is well over seven hundred feet above sea level, with a capacity of over four million gallons. There are some 374 acres covered by water, with over 500 of surrounding woodlands and meadows. The dam itself is something to see, at a height of over one hundred and sixty feet (fifty metres). The main bankside facilities of the Water Park are on the western side of the lake, and this an excellent place to start a short walk. Form here the oaks and beeches of WEST HILL WOODS, on the opposite bank, give a lovely backdrop to the expanse of shimmering water, with even more colour when a carpet of bluebells lies beneath the trees in the Spring. The lake is seldom empty, with sailing dinghies and rowing boats, the latter carrying anglers looking for the best spot from which to catch trout. If you then head south into EASTERN WOOD a short walk will bring to the south western extremity of the water, where the dam suddenly comes into view. The wood to the south of the Haddeo here is the Wimbleball, from which the lake gets its name.

This might be a long enough walk for you, with a climb over the stile into the fields approaching the dam itself. If not, then you could carry on along the banks of the river through **HARTFORD** towards **BURY**, which is worth a visit for its delicate little medieval packhorse bridge. In between you will have the chance to see less permanent 'Clammer' bridges of log, spanning the River Haddeo. Nearby BURY LODGE, of Victorian origin despite its Tudor style, has had many uses, including as a Prisoner of War Camp for captured Italians during the Second World War. If you return towards Wimbleball and HADDON HILL across the more open land to the east, you will have a chance to see the Corral used by the National Park Authority for pure bred Exmoor Ponies. The breeding herd is usually only to be found detained inside this in the Autumn.

Haddon Hill, at a height of more than eleven hundred feet, is a superb place form which to appreciate the full setting of the lake, and there are more facilities here if you wish to make this an alternative base for your visit. Here you can also see across to the natural fortress of hills surrounding **BROMPTON REGIS** to the west of the lake. This is where Gilda, the mother of King Harold holed up after the Battle of Hastings, refusing to surrender to her son's conqueror. She built a Manor here (long since destroyed) and was allowed to keep her freedom, such as it was, until her death.

There are many other villages and places worth visiting within the National Park, but our brief tour of some of what Exmoor can offer is finished. Yet we still have to mention some of what lives in the Park. The red deer have pride of place in any discussion of the area's wildlife. If you are lucky enough to get a view of them then their majestic beauty will immediately be apparent to you. It still seems incredible that even the full sets of antlers sported by the largest stags are shed each Spring, to be fully regrown in just sixteen weeks or so.

The ponies are Exmoor's other famous survivors; they have been here longer than man. The nearest thing we have to wild horses, they are sturdy and hardy beasts, so much so that they were used to replace depleted stocks on the inhospitable Falkland Islands after the war there. Fifty years ago there were only fifty or so of the pure bred variety left, and even the present number of around 950 makes them a more endangered species than the Giant Panda, numerically. But these are only two of the thirty one native mammals of the Park, not to mention the 243 species of birds that have been sighted, or the 1751 species of insects! As well as the grand sight of a herd of deer or ponies roaming the moorlands, there are less spectacular but equally rare habitats in places such as the saltmarsh behind Porlock. These SITES OF SPECIAL SCIENTIFIC INTEREST also harbour rare flowers and grasses, and Exmoor's variety is truly immense. You will not see all of this from a car, or even in a day's walking around the Park, there is just too much to cover. The longer you spend here, the more you will find to do and see. If you should wish to try and supply some of your own food while you are here then there is much good fishing to be had on Exmoor too, mostly of the Game and sea varieties. As well as Wimbleball, try the EXE VALLEY FISHERY (01398 234079) for trout lakes.

Because the land is so open, and so varied, there are habitats for endangered species of many types on Exmoor. The lichens of the wooded Barle Valley are particularly rare, as are some much more unlikely creatures. It seems even the dung of Exmoor has its own distinction. Apparently the grubs of the large brown and yellow Hornet Robber Fly live in cow pats, on a diet of dung beetles. For some reason the fly has become very rare, although I have not noticed a decline in the number of malodorous foot traps of this nature around the country. During the Summer of 1997 the fly was spotted on Exmoor, and this was heralded as an important discovery.

All parts of the food chain are important, but you may prefer to take part in a survey about something more traditionally loveable then the Robber Fly. Dormice have had a hard time in Britain during the last century, with up to a fifty percent reduction in their numbers. This has been because many of their habitats have disappeared, but not those on Exmoor. Dormice are nocturnal, so you will be lucky to see them, even if you spend time in the ancient woodlands they inhabit. What you might see are some tell-tale signs of their presence, particularly nut shells. Hazels are their favourites, and the National Park Authority collected data from visitors' observations of empty hazel shells during the Summer of 1997 to establish the numbers still in the region. Let's hope the next project does not involve predators of the dung beetle!

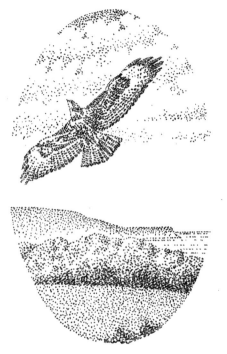

A Buzzard over Exmmoor

Hedgerows are one particular type of habitat that must be protected on Exmoor. Nationally we have lost half the hedgerows that were present fifty years ago, while on Exmoor the decrease has only been one in ten over the same period. Despite the fact that they hold many rare species of plants and wildlife, they have only been protected by national legislation for a couple of years. Some of Exmoor's hedges are very ancient. To establish the approximate age of a particular hedge all you have to do is walk about 30 metres (100 feet) of it, counting the number of woody trees and shrubs living in it. You then have to multiply this number by one hundred to give the number of years that particular section has been in place. Once again this has to be more pleasant than looking for Robber Fly grubs!

We cannot finish with Exmoor without going to one of its very busiest places. We have already heard that huge numbers of visitors are counted annually visiting the

Cliff Railway and Wimbleball, but these are the places where they can be accurately counted, and it would be hard to imagine any of them attracting the size of the crowds at TARR STEPS on a clear summer's day. This ancient 'clapper' bridge of flag stones over the River Barle, between **LISCOMBE** and **HAWKRIDGE** in some ways sums up the paradox of Exmoor. In the middle of much that is empty come thousands to 'fleet the time carelessly' while appreciating the undoubted beauty of the tree-lined river and its bridge. It would be easy to become cynical and suggest that this is the easy, destructive option even, and that anyone with any gumption will get away from the crowds and find the open spaces. Yet you will not find many happier gatherings than the crowds at Tarr Steps or Watersmeet. Exmoor's variety is not only in its scenery and wildlife, but also in the many, many ways in which it can be enjoyed, alone or as part of a crowd of admirers contemplating its beauty.

THE ANCHOR HOTEL & SHIP INN
Porlock Weir
Somerset
TA24 8PB

Tel: 01643 862753
Fax: 01643 862843

AA*** RAC ETB****
Recommended by
Ashley Courtenay, Egon Ronay

This delightful combination of Hotel and Inn, The Anchor and The Ship, is just ten yards from the water's edge of a small picturesque harbour set amidst Exmoor's magnificent scenery. It is the most relaxed and peaceful of places; somewhere that will help you unwind and charge your batteries away from the frenetic 20th century world. It is a perfect base for the exploration of Exmoor where the atmosphere and charm has been unchanged for generations. Exmoor straddles the border of North Devon and West Somerset and is a paradise for the lover of beautiful scenery and open spaces. There are wonderful walks and rides everywhere. Sparkling rivers, sandy coves, picturesque harbours, ancient villages with thatched cottages and medieval churches that will enchant you.

The bedrooms are comfortably appointed. One delightful bedroom has a four-poster which can be reserved. The rooms in the 16th century Ship Inn are smaller than those at the Anchor. Every room has direct dial telephone, television and a hostess tray as well as many other nice touches for your comfort. Breakfast in either the hotel or the inn is a scrumptious, substantial meal to set you up for the day. When you return in the evening the Cocktail Bar of the Anchor or the friendly bar at the Ship are both great places to meet up with newly made friends. The Anchor's Dining Room, looking out directly onto the water's edge, some five yards away, is renowned for its cuisine with the emphasis on Anglo French dishes using many local ingredients with Lobster Thermidor and steak, kidney and oyster pie as specialities. Tasty home-made bar food is always available in the Ship Inn, if you prefer a pub atmosphere.

After dinner, if you do not want to go out or join anyone in the bars, then the peace of the large and comfortable Drawing Room in The Anchor is a super place to be with its deep armchairs and an open fire if the weather is cool.

The owners of these two excellent establishments have a very clear objective and that is to make sure that your stay is relaxed and enjoyable. Prices are kept to a minimum that still enables the standards of food and accommodation that you require to be maintained.

USEFUL INFORMATION

· OPEN: All year & Christmas & New Year

· CREDIT CARDS: All major cards
· ACCOMMODATION: All ensuite
· RATES: Mar-Apr from £43.75 B&B
May-Oct from £47.80 Nov-Feb excluding
Christmas week from £41.75
· CHILDREN: Welcome

· DINING ROOM: Anglo/French
with Lobster Thermidor & Steak,
Kidney & Oyster Pie specialities
· VEGETARIAN: Always a choice
· BAR FOOD: Tasty, traditional

· LICENSED: Full On
· PETS: Yes

THE ANCHOR INN
Oxbridge
NR Dulverton
Somerset
TA22 9AZ

Tel: 01398 323433
Fax: 01398 323808

This 17th Century coaching Inn is in the heart of Exmoor and an ideal place to stay if you want to uncover the secrets of Exmoor. Mentioned in R.D. Blackmore's Lorna Doone, the Anchor Inn is situated on the river Exe on the border of Devon and Somerset and just on the edge of the Exmoor National Park. It is a popular hostelry with a warm welcoming Tom Faggus Bar with its excellent range of cask conditioned real ales along with an extensive selection of wines. You are encouraged to relax over an excellent lunch or cream tea in the picturesque riverside garden. It is ideal for families with a large lawn section set aside for seating and a safe children's play area alongside. Dry and wet fly fishing are available in season at the Anchor itself, year round stocked lake fishing is available locally.

The Stable block restaurant is open throughout the year, offering a full and varied A La Carte menu, supplemented by a Table d'hôte and a once weekly speciality menu. There is a Fish Night every Wednesday when you are invited to enjoy a wide variety of freshly prepared fish dishes. Served between 7-9pm, bookings for this evening are preferred. A Traditional Sunday 3 Meat Carvery offering a choice from six vegetables and two potatoes is very popular. Bar Meals and snacks are available at lunch-time and evenings including the daily specials board and superb home-made desserts. It is a perfect venue for Weddings, Birthday and Anniversary celebrations, Business Functions or Family Gatherings.

To appreciate and discover the beauty of this countryside with over six hundred miles of well sign-posted walks in Exmoor you should stay here in one of the six beautiful ensuite rooms, including a four poster suite for that special occasion. Each room has direct dial telephone, television & a hospitality tray.

USEFUL INFORMATION

- OPEN: All year

- GARDEN: Yes riverside & play area
- CREDIT CARDS: All major cards
- ACCOMMODATION: 6 ensuite rms
- RATES: Sgl £37.50 pp.pn B&B
  Standard dbl. £65 Superior £75
- PETS Yes

- RESTAURANT: A la Carte & Table d'hôte
  Special Fish Nights. Sunday Carvery
- VEGETARIAN: Always a choice
- BAR FOOD: Wide range. Cream Teas
- LICENSED: Full On

- CHILDREN: Welcome

ASHWICK COUNTRY HOUSE HOTEL & RESTAURANT
Dulverton
Somerset
TA22 9QD

Tel/Fax: 01398 323868

AA Red Star Michelin Red House

Chef patron of Ashwick House, Richard Sherwood is a renowned chef who presents quality cuisine using fresh local produce. He is extremely particular about every dish he presents and it is this attention to detail which makes this small charming Edwardian Country House such a special place in which to stay. The house stands in six acres of beautiful grounds above the picturesque valley of the River Barle within Exmoor National Park. Sweeping lawns lead to large water gardens where guests can relax in summer shade amidst the glorious scent of flowers. The emphasis here is on old fashioned hospitality and courtesy wherein the well-being of the guest is of paramount importance. The atmosphere is wonderful, the house is arrayed with flowers in summer and in winter, the cold weather is kept firmly at bay with roaring log fires and the romanticism of dinner by candlelight.

Breakfast is served on the terrace which opens out from the elegant restaurant. Like every other meal served at Ashwick House, it is memorable. At night you sleep in a spacious bedroom furnished with great taste and to a very high standard. All the rooms have ensuite facilities, remote control colour television, movie channel, alarm clock cassette radio, electric weighing scales together with fresh fruit and a complimentary drink on arrival. The Superior rooms, all south facing, are larger and in addition to the other facilities have teletext, a mini-bar and bath robes. The baronial style hall with its long, broad gallery and cheerful log fire together with the comfortably furnished lounge are great places in which to relax, sip a drink perhaps, read a book or do absolutely nothing!

One would never be bored staying here. There are many places of interest nearby including Dunster's Norman Castle and 17th century Yarn Market, Exmoor Forest and many National Trust houses and gardens.

USEFUL INFORMATION

- OPEN: All year
- WHEELCHAIR ACCESS: Restaurant only
- GARDEN: Delightful
- CREDIT CARDS: All major cards
- ACCOMMODATION: 6 ensuite rooms
- RATES: From £48 per person B&B
- RESTAURANT: Superb cuisine
- VEGETARIAN: Always a choice
- BAR FOOD: Not applicable
- LICENSED: Yes
- CHILDREN: Over 8 years
- PETS: Not in house

BALES MEAD
West Porlock
Somerset
TA24 8NX

Tel: 01643 862565

Words are almost inadequate to describe Bales Mead, a Bed and Breakfast establishment extraordinary. Owned and run by Peter Clover and Stephen Blue, you find yourself staying in the home of two exceptionally talented men. Peter is a writer and illustrator and his creative artistry is evident in the lovely paint effects in both bedrooms and luxurious bathrooms with power showers. Stephen is a musician and his Grand Piano graces the elegant and sumptuously decorated lounge. It is a house reflecting tasteful charm and style to be found mid-way between Porlock village and the harbour at Porlock Weir.

The setting is superb. The bedrooms are named after local villages; Bossington and Selworthy have stunning panoramic sea views. Allerford, a third bedroom overlooking the garden surrounded by the wooded hills of Exmoor, can be made available if a larger party is staying and does not mind sharing a bathroom. All the rooms are individually decorated, and include personal touches such as fresh flowers, fruit, fudges, mineral water, a crystal decanter of sherry, pot-pourri in a chamber pot and luxurious toiletries - all pointers to the manner in which guests are cosseted.

The garden is a delight with its mature shrubs and trees and an abundance of colourful flowers in the summer.

Breakfast at Bales Mead can only be described as a lavish feast. In summer, weather permitting, it is sometimes served in the immaculate garden. Fresh fruit salad or fresh fruit compote, freshly squeezed fruit juice and cereal start the meal and then there is a choice of either traditional English or Continental breakfast - a selection of warm pastries, croissants and brioches with preserves. Kedgeree, fish cakes and scrambled egg with smoked salmon sometimes ring the changes.

The house and owners extend an extremely warm welcome to their guests and perhaps the most astonishing factor is the size of the bill - unbelievably inexpensive. You would not find better treatment, service, food or bedrooms in a five star hotel. It is no wonder that Bales Mead is one of the top twenty establishments in the Which? Bed and Breakfast Guide.

If you have the opportunity to stay here, seize it with both hands!

- OPEN: All year, except Christmas and New Year
- WHEELCHAIR ACCESS: No
- GARDEN: Yes
- CREDIT CARDS: None taken
- ACCOMMODATION: 3 Doubles, 2 with private facilities
- RATES: Sgl £44-£48   Dbl. £58

- DINING ROOM: Superb breakfast
- VEGETARIAN: Upon request
- STRICTLY NON-SMOKING
- LICENSED: No

- CHILDREN: Not under 14
- PETS: No

BOSSINGTON FARM & BIRDS OF PREY CENTRE
West Lynch Farm
Allerford
NR Porlock
Somerset
TA24 8HJ

Tel/Fax: 01643 862816

ETB Listed

It is not often one has the good fortune to stay in an enchanting farmhouse and at the same time be on the site of a tourist attraction. This is what Bossington Farm and Birds of Prey Centre is all about. It is situated five miles west of Minehead, one mile from Porlock nestled between the National Trust villages of Bossington and Allerford with views across Porlock Vale to the sea, North Hill and Dunkery Beacon. The mild climate of the Porlock Vale and the tranquillity of its setting, provide the perfect location away from it all for touring, walkers, nature lovers and bird watchers.

Built in the 15th century on an old Saxon site, as an open-hall manor house, complete with its own chapel and three yards of thatched barns and cobblestones with an original arched front door, the house is full of character and charm and has a superb, friendly atmosphere enhanced by the exposed beams, stone fireplace, polished floors and fascinating corners in every room. Country style accommodation is available within the house in beautifully decorated and furnished rooms with comfortable beds, and antique furniture. Each room has a hospitality tray. A delicious, sustaining breakfast is served every morning. Packed lunches are available or if you wish to lunch in the house, a simple, wholesome menu is available. People from many countries and many walks of life have stated in the visitors book that staying at Bossington is 'the highlight' of their visit to this country.

The farmyard is now occupied by rare breeds of sheep and goats and a large collection of owls and birds of prey. Stay in the farmhouse and enjoy an evening Hawk walk or a days Falconry tuition and hunting.

USEFUL INFORMATION

- OPEN: All year except Christmas
- WHEELCHAIR ACCESS: No
- GARDEN: Yes. Bird of Prey Centre
- CREDIT CARDS: None taken
- ACCOMMODATION: Country accommodation
- RATES: B&B From £17.50 pppn £2.50 sgl supplement

- DINING ROOM: Super breakfast. Packed lunches. Lunch menu
- VEGETARIAN: Upon request
- STRICTLY NON-SMOKING HOUSE
- LICENSED: No
- CHILDREN: Over 12 years
- PETS: Yes Dog £2 Horse £10

CARNARVON ARMS
Brushford
Dulverton
TA22 9AE

Tel: 01398 323302
Fax: 01398 324022

One wonders how different is the clientele of the Carnarvon Arms today from 1874 when it was built by the Earl of Carnarvon for passengers arriving by train at Dulverton Station. The Station is long gone, but the hotel goes from strength to strength in the capable hands of the proprietor Toni Jones who has very decided ideas - all good ones - on how a hotel should be run. Today people come here for a variety of reasons. The energetic for hunting' shooting' and fishing' and walkers who revel in the spectacular countryside and others for a rest, a swim in the outdoor heated pool and perhaps to enjoy the National Trust gardens within reach. One can play tennis or croquet in the grounds. Whatever the reason it is a comfortable hotel. The hall is decorated with antlers, trophies and cartoons of the hunt. Two ground floor lounges have different characteristics in keeping with the changing mood of the moor. The main lounge is wood-panelled, with comfy chairs grouped for conversation, a roaring fire and plenty of reading material. The second is a light airy room, perfect for soaking up the sun. Rich red-carpeted stairs lead down to the dining room dominated by an alcove full of wine. The menus offer a wide choice using local produce in both English traditional and other styles of cuisine.

Toni Jones is constantly improving the Carnarvon Arms and each year guests returning find bedrooms have been newly decorated. The ensuite rooms are all slightly different and mostly with splendid views. For example Room fourteen has a grandstand view of the West Somerset Polo Club in action. Room service, a rarity today, is available and replaces the hostess tray but tea and coffee making facilities will be placed in your room if you prefer to make drinks for yourself; Toni's philosophy is that people on holiday should not have to do anything for themselves! Television, direct dial telephones are there for your use. Two ground floor bedrooms are available for those who have difficulty with stairs and there is wheelchair access to the hotel via two ramps. Children are welcome and there are baby listening facilities as well as early suppers.

USEFUL INFORMATION

- OPEN: All year
- WHEELCHAIR ACCESS: Yes
- GARDEN: Yes. Tennis. Croquet
- CREDIT CARDS : All major cards
- ACCOMMODATION: 24 ensuite
- RATES: Sgl pn £45 Dbl. from £90
  Suite £100 Breakfast extra -
  heated pool

- DINING ROOM: Traditional English
- VEGETARIAN: Yes
- BAR FOOD: Snacks available
- LICENSED: Full On
- CHILDREN: Welcome
- PETS: Yes

THE CASTLE HOTEL
High Street
Porlock
Somerset
TA24 8PY

Tel/Fax: 01643 862504

Porlock is one of Somerset's prettiest villages almost on the border of Somerset and Devon and on the fringe of Exmoor National Park making it a super base for anyone wanting to enjoy all that this exciting area has to offer including the sea, excellent walks, pony trekking, sea fishing and many other activities. One could never possibly be bored spending time here and where better to stay than The Castle Hotel in the High Street where the welcome is what one has come to expect in Somerset - warmth and hospitality. There has been a Castle Hotel for many a year but this one was rebuilt after a fire in 1890. It is full of character and the bar is frequented by locals - always a good sign. The bar has beams and open fires creating a delightful atmosphere.

Food is always important on holiday or when one is staying away from home and here people have come to expect a high standard of well cooked, home-made fare. The attractive restaurant has a wide ranging menu. There is always a choice of salads and some tempting desserts. Traditional English Bar Food, prepared on the premises, is served in the Bars as well and there you will find some time honoured Daily Specials. Vegetarians are offered a choice.

Thirteen comfortably furnished ensuite bedrooms are all situated on the first floor. Some rooms contain double and single beds and one family room has a double and two singles. The majority of the rooms are centrally heated. All have television and a hostess tray. Cots are available if required. The Castle is a very happy place in which to stay whether on holiday or business.

USEFUL INFORMATION

- OPEN: 10.30-11pm daily Sun: 12-10.30pm
  Hotel & Rest closed 24th & 25th December
- WHEELCHAIR ACCESS: Yes
- GARDEN: Yes
- CREDIT CARDS: All major cards
- ACCOMMODATION: 13 ensuite rooms
- RATES: £25 pppn b&b single £21pppn b&b double

- RESTAURANT: Delicious home-cooked fare
- VEGETARIAN: Yes
- BAR FOOD: Traditional fare
- LICENSED: Full On
- CHILDREN: Welcome
- PETS: Yes

THE COTTAGE HOTEL
Porlock Weir
Minehead
Somerset
TA24 8PB

Tel/Fax: 01643 863300

Tourist Board, Highly Commended
Johansens Country Houses & Small Hotels

The Cottage Hotel is a small hotel enjoying a big reputation for both its comfort and its cuisine - the latter is available for non-residents on Friday and Saturday evenings. Porlock is renowned for its quaint ambience and for its enviable position almost on the Somerset/Devon border and therefore in close proximity to the grandeur and legendary wild beauty of Exmoor with its ponies and red deer and the home of Lorna Doone - Blackmore's wonderful tale of life on Exmoor. Porlock is also well situated for anyone wanting to go further into Somerset and perhaps explore the excellent shopping to be found in the county town, Taunton. Porlock is a great place to be based for a summer holiday or in the off season periods when the quiet and the spectacular scenery can be enjoyed to the full without the intrusion of the busy holiday times.

Mr and Mrs Baker came to The Cottage Hotel over a year ago and in that time have stamped their own personalities on the business. The house is charmingly furnished with many fine Georgian pieces in keeping with the age of the house which was built 150 years ago and has the imposing presence that all Georgian buildings acquired. There are five double, ensuite guest rooms, each one with comfortable beds, nice linen, pretty drapes and fine furniture. Television and a hostess tray is provided in every room. Not really designed as a family hotel but there is one bedroom suitable for parents and a child. Both the Bakers enjoy good food and wine and they make sure that their guests are fed on delicious food from an ever changing menu which takes seasonal food into account. Breakfast is a sumptuous feast and will set everyone up for a day out in the fresh air. Golf, beaches, walking or riding on Exmoor, its all there for your enjoyment.

On Friday and Saturday the restaurant is open to non-residents between 7-9pm and the food served is well known in the area for its exciting flavours and beautiful presentation. The wine list is small with only 16 different wines available but what it loses in quantity it gains in impeccable quality and has been carefully chosen to complement the food and to be sure that the prices are sensible.

USEFUL INFORMATION

- · OPEN: All year
- · WHEELCHAIR ACCESS: No
- · GARDEN: Yes
- · CREDIT CARDS: All major cards
- · ACCOMMODATION: 5 ensuite rooms
- · RATES: £65 -£110 per room B&B

- · RESTAURANT: Delicious fare Open to non-residents Fri & Sat
- · VEGETARIAN: Catered for
- · LICENSED: Yes
- · CHILDREN : Yes
- · PETS: No

THE CROWN HOTEL
Exmoor National Park
Exford
Somerset
TA24 7PP

Tel:01643 831554
Fax: 01643 831665
Email:bradleyhotelsexmoor@easynet.co.uk

RAC*** + Restaurant Award AA
*** Rosettes. Egon Ronay Recommended

How relieved and grateful weary travellers must have been in years gone by when their coach drew up outside the welcoming doors of The Crown Hotel which was the one of the most famous coaching inns on Exmoor. It has always been a place of great comfort for travellers from all walks of life and from every corner of the globe. It has never been better than today in the skilled, experienced hands of Mike Bradley and his very efficient staff. You will find The Crown Hotel situated in the middle of Exford, one of the prettiest villages on the moor and known as the capital of Exmoor. It is beloved by the locals and very much the centre of village life.

Recently The Crown has been completely refurbished to its former glory and been brought sympathetically into the 20th century. The lounges have deep seated armchairs and sofas encouraging one to relax. The Dining Room presided over by the Head Chef, Eric Bouchet, a master of his craft, is elegant. The meals provide the diner with some of the most wonderfully exciting food on Exmoor. Every bedroom is ensuite, individually decorated, furnished in a similar style, and perfectly appointed with direct dial telephone, colour television and hair dryers plus the bonus of tea and coffee being provided by Room Service. The Superior rooms are very large and have King Size or Queen Size beds. The Hotel has a well equipped meeting room for a maximum of forty people.

The Crown Hotel will happily quote for Riding, Hunter Hire, Hunting, Stabling, Rough/ Driven Shooting, Clay Pigeon Shooting, Fly Fishing and Exmoor Safaris. It is the sort of hotel where you can choose to do everything or nothing at all! The Hotel's Water Garden is a delight. The countryside is glorious. Exmoor has a magic of its own and to stay at The Crown makes a holiday perfect.

USEFUL INFORMATION

- OPEN: All year
- WHEELCHAIR ACCESS: No
- GARDEN: Yes
- CREDIT CARDS: All major cards
- ACCOMMODATION: All ensuite rooms
- RATES: Sgl from £37 Standard Dbl. from £37. Superior dbl. £55pp.pn

- DINING ROOM: Superb food
- VEGETARIAN: Always a choice
- BAR FOOD: Wide range
- LICENSED: Full On
- CHILDREN: Welcome

- PETS: Yes but not in public rooms

HEDDON'S GATE HOTEL
Heddon's Mouth
Parracombe
Barnstaple
EX31 4PZ

Tel: 01598 763313
Fax: 01598 763363
E-Mail:info@hgate.co.uk

With a wonderful position in the isolated, woody Heddon valley, Heddon's Gate was originally built in 1890 as a hunting lodge. It has had many changes and many owners since then but the Victorian graciousness still remains with some more modern additions like the big picture windows which now make it possible to appreciate the stunning views from both the lounge and the dining room. It is a comfortable friendly hotel in which guests feel very relaxed, extremely well fed and very reluctant to leave when the time comes for their departure.

The spacious Dining Room with its spectacular outlook is the ideal setting for unhurried meals. The kitchens are personally run by the proprietor Bob Deville who describes his cooking as being 'modern English with a Mediterranean bias' but he almost always sneaks in a good old fashioned British Pudding like Spotted Dick with lashings of custard. Much effort is put into obtaining prime produce such as West Country Farmhouse Cheeses, locally grown vegetables, Somerset Bacon and non intensively reared poultry. Even the Hotel's water supply comes from a natural spring. Complimentary Afternoon Tea is served as a daily gift to all guests who are invited to help themselves to the home-made scones, cakes and savouries on offer.

No two bedrooms are alike, they vary in size and aspect and are named either according to their original use or to their particular style. Bedrooms for romantics include a magnificent half-tester bed dating from 1840, a four-poster complete with interior lighting and wrap-around drapes, and the Chinese room with strong and rich 'William Morris' colours. About half the bedrooms have a view across the valley, and the remainder look into the woods that surround two sides of the house. Cottages just below the Hotel with magnificent views, offer an alternative choice of accommodation especially for those who desire all the benefits of the Hotel with the freedom of a 'no-cooking' cottage holiday.

USEFUL INFORMATION

- OPEN: Closed early Dec to late Mar/Easter
- WHEELCHAIR ACCESS: Yes
- GARDEN: Yes
- CREDITCARDS: Master/Visa/AMEX /Switch
- ACCOMMODATION: 15 ensuite rooms
- RATES: Sgl from £50 Dbl./four-poster from £95 Suite from £110
  (rates inc. breakfast, dinner & afternoon tea)

- DINING ROOM: Modern English with Mediterranean bias
- VEGETARIAN: By arrangement
- LICENSED: Yes
- CHILDREN: Yes.
- PETS: By arrangement only

LORNA DOONE HOTEL
High Street
Porlock
Somerset
TA24 8PS

Tel: 01643 862404
Fax: 01643 863018

ETB 3 Crowns

The Lorna Doone Hotel not only reminds one of R.D. Blackmore's famous book about Exmoor, its history stems even deeper into the literary world. The poet Lord Byron's family owned the site on which the hotel is built. The first building, an old pub, was demolished in 1886 and today's hotel built in 1888. You will find it in the centre of the village, one mile from the coastal path and an ideal centre for walking or riding on Exmoor. Several Riding Stables are situated within two miles catering for both the expert and beginners. From Porlock it is also easy to visit many fascinating places including Lynton and Lynmouth. Toni and Dick Thornton own and run the hotel with the help of a small, friendly and efficient staff.

The hotel is furnished attractively throughout with a happy mixture of antique and other pieces. The Restaurant is renowned for its good food and imaginative menu. It is open to non-residents. You might choose to start with a Smoked Chicken Salad with a Raspberry Vinaigrette and follow it with Doones Seafood Crumble - a delicious mixture of whitefish, salmon, scallop and prawns in a wine sauce topped with a tangy lemon and parsley crumble. The steaks are succulent, the poultry superb and in season there is always game on the menu. The wine list complements the food with a selection of wines from around the world. For those who choose to stay in this comfortable hotel, breakfast is a memorable meal with several choices including a full English breakfast or Kippers topped with a poached egg. Parties of up to 24 people are frequently and very successfully catered for.

There are fourteen ensuite bedrooms, each charmingly furnished and with colour television and tea/coffee making facilities. Some of the rooms are not in the hotel. For instance The Cottage rooms are across a courtyard from the hotel and have adjoining child's rooms. The Stable rooms are ground level in the courtyard. Cots can be provided. There is limited car parking in the courtyard and a Public Car park located fifty yards from the hotel.

USEFUL INFORMATION

- OPEN: All year, except Xmas
- WHEELCHAIR ACCESS: Yes
- GARDEN: Yes
- CREDIT CARDS: Not AMEX/Diners
- ACCOMMODATION: 14 ensuite
- RATES: From £19.50pp
  Children sharing £9.50pn Cots £5 per visit

- RESTAURANT: Good, imaginative menu
- VEGETARIAN: Min of 5 dishes
- LICENSED: Yes
- CHILDREN: Welcome
- PETS: Yes £2.50 per visit

THE REST AND BE THANKFUL INN
Wheddon Cross
Exmoor
Somerset
TA24 7DR

Tel/Fax: 01643 841222
rbtinn@compuserve.com

***Crown Highly Commended
QQQQ Selected AA/RAC Acclaimed

If one were really looking for the remotest inn you could possibly find, The Rest and Be Thankful would be one of the main contenders. It is at Wheddon Cross as remote as it gets on Exmoor by road. The views are stunning and the sense of peace and tranquillity tinged with the awesome factor of the moor attracts many people for many different reasons. To reach it at all one drives through spectacular countryside and for the dedicated walker or even those who only want to stroll, one could not wish for more superb surroundings. There are views to the sea to add to the enchantment. Twenty minutes by car will take you to Minehead, the nearest town and all around there are places to visit, things to see including the quaint harbour at Watchet, the Steam Railway running out of Minehead. Michael Weaver and Joan Hockin are the landlords and together with their staff they pursue whatever is required to make their visitors comfortable and do exactly what the name says, Rest and be Thankful.

There is an excellent choice of food every day from delicious, freshly cut sandwiches, home-made soup. Ploughman's, to a home-made pate and individual bakers pies. House Specials include a great macaroni cheese and cauliflower cheese, Italian dishes, chicken, fish and steaks, all served with garden peas, fresh carrots and potatoes either chipped, jacket, new or croquette. A salad can be served if preferred. There are several dishes for vegetarians.

The five guest rooms, all ensuite are beautifully furnished with high quality drapes, bed linen and other nice touches including direct dial telephones, television, hairdryers, an honesty bar and a well supplied hostess tray. A great breakfast is served every day. The service is excellent and the whole inn feels welcoming.

USEFUL INFORMATION

- OPEN: 10.30-3pm & 6.30-11pm
- WHEELCHAIR ACCESS: Yes
- GARDEN: Yes
- CREDIT CARDS: All major cards
- ACCOMMODATION: 5 ensuite rms
- RATES: £27 pp.pn B&B
  3 day breaks at £24 per person

- RESTAURANT: Great choice, great value
- VEGETARIAN: Always a choice
- BAR FOOD: Wide choice
- LICENSED: Full + Supper licence
- CHILDREN: Welcome

THE ROYAL OAK INN
Winsford, Exmoor National Park
Somerset
TA24 7JE

Tel: 0164 385455
Fax: 0164 385009

RAC *** AA ***
ETB 4 Crowns
Highly Commended

One of the highlights of anyone's visit to Exmoor is to the picturesque thatched 12th century inn, The Royal Oak at Winsford. The ancient riverside village is on the edge of the Exmoor National Park and anyone staying here has, within easy distance, a host of exciting things to see and do. The owner, Charles Steven will be delighted to arrange many sporting pastimes for his guests, including riding, fishing, hunting, shooting, golf and adventure walking. The hotel also provides a comprehensive sightseeing list covering Exmoor National Park and beyond.

The atmosphere in the Inn is redolent of the past. It reaches out to you as you walk through the welcoming doors into the bars or the well appointed comfortable lounges with open fires, chintz fabrics and oak beams. In the pretty restaurant the tables are set with Wedgwood and fine glassware, conducive to the enjoyment of a delicious meal for which The Royal Oak is renowned. Only the freshest local produce is used to prepare traditional English country recipes to a consistently high standard. Everything is home-cooked whether it is the hams, the pies with their mouth-watering pastry, the pates, the bread or the delectable desserts. A good choice of light meals is available in the bar.

Eight of the charming bedrooms are in the Inn and the other six have been created in the courtyard area. Like every other room, they are furnished and appointed to a high standard . Every room is ensuite and they all have colour television, direct dial telephones and hostess trays. There is a large suite with armchairs and a sofa. Breakfast like every other meal here is sumptuous. The Royal Oak is a super place to visit whether for a meal, or drink or to enjoy the luxury of a pampered stay.

USEFUL INFORMATION

- OPEN: All year
- WHEELCHAIR ACCESS: No
- GARDEN: Yes
- CREDIT CARDS: All major cards
- ACCOMMODATION: 14 ensuite rms
- RATES: SgL from £70 Dbl. from £90

- RESTAURANT: English country fare Everything including bread is home-made
- VEGETARIAN: Always a choice
- BAR FOOD: Wide choice of light meals
- LICENSED: Full On
- CHILDREN: Welcome
- PETS: Owner's discretion

THE ROYAL OAK HOTEL
Withypool
Exmoor National Park
Somerset
TA24 7QP

Tel: 01643 831236
Fax: 01643 831659

Withypool is 7 miles north of Dulverton and is a small village in the heart of the Exmoor National Park, on the banks of the River Barle, surrounded by open moor land where wild Red Deer and Exmoor ponies graze. It is close to many historical sites and only 10 miles from the North Devon coast. Lovely in its own right, the village is enhanced by the presence of the award winning Royal Oak Inn, somewhere that can be best described as a 'Residential Inn and Restaurant'. No one is quite sure about its Royal connections but it was certainly a watering hole for wool traders in the 17th century and it has many historical connections. R.D. Blackmore stayed here while he was writing the immortal 'Lorna Doone' and less than one hundred years later it played host to General Eisenhower whilst he was preparing for the D Day Landings. Appropriately the inn was once owned by the head of MI5 who knew, no doubt, many of the plots that were hatched over a pint of ale.

The aim here is to give guests a memorable stay. This is achieved - how could it not be - with delightfully furnished bedrooms, welcoming bars, superb food and a heart-warming, friendly welcome from the staff.

Great emphasis is placed on the quality of the food; the head chef is a man of enormous experience and imaginative talent who controls an enthusiastic and committed team determined to excel. Sophistication there may be at this level and in the furnishings and accommodation but The Royal Oak maintains its role of Country Inn from which one can pursue riding, hunting, shooting and fishing, all arranged by the friendly, efficient owners and their staff.

USEFUL INFORMATION

- OPEN: 11-2.30pm & 6-11pm
- WHEELCHAIR ACCESS: Not ideal
- GARDEN: Patio for limited numbers
- CREDIT CARDS: All major cards
- ACCOMMODATION: 8 doubles private bathrooms
- RATES: Sgl from £31 Dbl. from £37

- RESTAURANT; English cooking
- VEGETARIAN: Available
- BARFOOD: Various from fish to cheese
- LICENSED: Full On

- CHILDREN: Certain areas only
- PETS: Well behaved

THE SIMONSBATH HOUSE HOTEL
& BOEVEYS RESTAURANT
Simonsbath
Exmoor,
Somerset
TA24 7SH

4 Crowns ETB Highly Commended.
2 Stars with Rosette

Inside the stout walls of this 300 years old house people have been waking up in the morning knowing that it will be to the sounds of the real countryside. The first was James Boevey, a wily London Merchant of Dutch Huguenot extraction, who as Warden of the Forest of Exmoor in 1654, chose a spot where all the tracks across the moor appeared to meet, to build this fine house.

Many people famous, and not so famous and sometimes infamous have enjoyed the hospitality of Simonsbath House in the ensuing years and there will be few who have not enjoyed the experience. Simonsbath means a lot of things to a lot of people. You can do everything, but you do not have to do anything. It is your holiday and the owners just want you to enjoy it. You can ride through the Forest to the top of Dunkery Beacon - Exmoor's highest point and if the day is clear see over a range of one hundred and fifty miles to the Malvern Hills, Brown Willy on Bodmin Moor in Cornwall, from the Brecon Beacons in Wales to the rolling downs of Dorset. There are woodland walks, picturesque thatched inns, serious walking. This is the country of wild Red Deer, the last surviving herds in England, the game bird, the rainbow trout, and the salmon.

When you have had your fill of so much beauty, Simonsbath House awaits you with an afternoon tea of home-made scones, strawberry jam and clotted cream. Boevey's restaurant, a barn conversion, is a completely separate building offering good food during the day . There are three self-catering apartments across from the restaurant. Simonsbath House offers so much that is to be enjoyed.

USEFUL INFORMATION

- OPEN: Hotel closed Dec & Jan
  Boeveys Restaurant closed Dec & Jan
- WHEELCHAIR ACCESS: No

- GARDEN: One acre

- CREDIT CARDS: Master/Visa
  /AMEX/Diners

- ACCOMMODATION: 7 ensuite rooms
- RATES:£48pp.pn B&B Dinner £20 extra

- RESTAURANT: House residents only
- VEGETARIAN: On request Boeveys
  has a Vegetarian menu
- BAR FOOD: Not in hotel. Boeveys
  has a wide range
- LICENSED: Restaurant & Residential
  in hotel.
- CHILDREN: Welcome over 10 years
- PETS: No

TARR STEPS HOTEL
Hawkridge
Dulverton
Somerset
TA22 9PY

Tel: 01643 851293
Fax:: 01643 851218

The approach to the Tarr Steps Hotel heightens everyone's expectancy. You approach it through narrow lanes which wind through overhanging Exmoor woods, creeping up steep gradients and plunging down into valleys with breathtaking suddenness. The final hairpin reveals the eleven room Georgian hotel tucked into the side of a hidden valley, overlooking the River Barle. It is wonderful. The river is just a few yards further along and here you will find the legendary Tarr Steps, the medieval stone clapper footbridge. The setting is superb and when one meets the owners Shaun and Sue Blackmore, you are immediately made to feel part of a friendly house party where you are encouraged to do whatever takes your fancy. There are three and a half miles of fishing for wild brown trout and salmon, five hundred acres of rough shooting, clay pigeon shooting and stabling. Walking is endless and well signpost marked across the hundreds of undisturbed acres of Exmoor National Park. Pretty towns and villages provide hours of enjoyable exploration and the dramatic North Devon coastline is less than an hour away.

The hotel is a rare gem. The rooms glow with well polished and treasured antique furniture, fresh flowers abound and the smell of roaring beechwood fires on colder days make you feel very welcome. The bedrooms are delightful, individually and lovingly refurbished with Sue's eye for country style and comfort. There are direct dial telephones and beverage trays but TV's are definitely not allowed.

The excellent cuisine is English at its best, using home-grown fruit and vegetables from the kitchen garden, fish from the river and only the finest local fresh produce. Home-made scones topped with rich Devonshire clotted cream and Della's mouth-watering raspberry jam taste even more delicious on hot sunny days whilst lingering on the sun trenched terrace spotting rare birds and butterflies. Binoculars are a must!

Whatever your reasons for choosing a country break, you will be delighted with your discovery of this true jewel in Exmoor's crown.

USEFUL INFORMATION

- OPEN: All year
- WHEELCHAIR ACCESS: Yes
  1 ground floor bedroom
- GARDEN: Yes
- CREDIT CARDS: Yes except AMEX
- ACCOMMODATION: 11 rooms 9 ensuite
- RATES: Winter sgl from £58 Dbl. from £60
  All rates are inc. of D.B&B & morning & afternoon tea

- DINING ROOM: Delicious English cooking
- VEGETARIAN: Please advise when booking
- LICENSED: Yes
- CHILDREN: Welcome
- PETS: Dogs & horses

DOWNFIELD HOUSE HOTEL
St Decuman's Road
Watchet
Somerset
TA23 0HR

Tel:01984 631267
Fax: 01984 634369

AA** ETB 3 Crown Commended

Downfield House Hotel, offering views over the town, harbour, steam railway and the Bristol Channel, is one of Watchet's most beautiful buildings. Ian and Margaret Moffat have made the house a place of relaxation and welcoming atmosphere. They came to the area just over a year ago and in that time have made the Downfield a much sought after venue. It is thoroughly enjoyable to book a table here for dinner and have an aperitif in the charming lounge whilst you peruse the menu and then wander into the chandelier lit dining room where the tables are beautifully laid with fresh napery, the glasses gleam and the cutlery sparkles making the ideal environment in which to savour the excellent food. Margaret delights in producing a first class meal, which is always three courses, a fixed price and offers a choice on all courses.

The non-smoking house has been refurbished sympathetically with an eye to its Victorian origins. The six double and twin rooms, all ensuite, are situated on the first floor and charmingly furnished. In the Coach House there are two more bedrooms, ensuite and furnished with pine furniture throughout. Every room has Direct Dial Telephone, Television, and a Hostess Tray. Pets are welcome in the two Coach House rooms only. Watchet is delightful and is surrounded by interesting places to visit including Dunster Castle and Gardens, the West Somerset Steam Railway, the 13th century Cleeve Abbey at Washford and Combe Sydenham Country Park where Sir Francis Drake courted Elizabeth Sydenham.

USEFUL INFORMATION

- OPEN: All year
- WHEELCHAIR ACCESS: Yes
- GARDEN: Yes 1 acre approximately
- CREDIT CARDS: All major cards
- ACCOMMODATION: 8 ensuite rms
- RATES: From: £22 sgl & £44 dbl. Children free if sharing

- DINING ROOM: Exciting food. Open to non-residents
- VEGETARIAN: A daily choice
- NON SMOKING HOUSE
- LICENSED: Restaurant & Residential
- CHILDREN: Welcome
- PETS: Coach House only

HIGHER COMBE FARM
Dulverton, Somerset   TA22 9PT

Tel/Fax: 01398 323616
abigail@highercombe.softnet.co.uk

Abigail Humphrey and Tom Flanagan are your hosts in this exceptionally nice farmhouse. It is one of the highest houses on Exmoor at 1200ft with stunning views. From here you can see Dartmoor and the Devon Coast line. You reach it up a private drive which runs for about a quarter of a mile and it is surrounded by four hundred and fifty acres of private land. You can walk directly onto the open moor land of Exmoor with its abundance of wildlife and Exmoor Red Deer (often seen from the house) Highercombe is close to Tarr Steps with its ancient Clapper Bridge and just 3 miles from Dulverton. It could not be a better place to stay for anyone wanting peace and quiet and the opportunity to recharge their batteries in superb surroundings. It is a real working Exmoor farm and you wake each morning to the sounds of the countryside and activity on the farm. The three guest rooms, all with private bathrooms, are named after fields on the farm -'Saddleback' 'Court Down' and 'Draydon'. They are beautifully furnished and co-ordinated. 'Court Down' is extra large and luxurious with a walk out balcony. Each room has television and a hostess tray. The Farmer's Breakfast is outstanding and delicious, traditional farmhouse fare is served at night. The hospitality is unmatched and the welcome friendly. A great place to stay.

USEFUL INFORMATION

- OPEN: March-November
- WHEELCHAIR ACCESS: No
- GARDEN: Yes. 450 acres of farmland
- CREDIT CARDS: None taken
- ACCOMMODATION: 3 rooms with private bathrooms
- RATES: From £20-£22 pp p.n. B&B 6-12 50% reduction Reductions for 3 nights or more

- DINING ROOM: Delicious farmhouse fare
- VEGETARIAN: Upon request
- LICENSED: No
- CHILDREN: Welcome 6+
- PETS: Yes £2 per dog per night

TARR FARM RESTAURANT & GIFT SHOP
Tarr Steps, Liscombe
Dulverton, Somerset
TA22 9PV

Tel/Fax: 01643 851507

This 16th century Farmhouse restaurant is an eating experience not to be missed and has the added delight of being in a perfect setting alongside the historic, National Monument Tarr Steps. The food is of a very high standard and caters for all tastes. During the day the simple menu has a wide range of light food including baguettes with a variety of fillings and the tea-room provides a delicious cream tea and home-made cakes. At night the highly acclaimed restaurant a la carte menu is exciting, the dishes beautifully presented. There are some 15 starters and 20 main courses including vegetarian dishes. The restaurant seats 40 comfortably but you must book a table for the evening. There are tables outside for eating at during the day. A superb situation with rugged countryside around you , the River Barle close at hand and the famous old Clapper Bridge almost at your feet. The Gift Shop is stocked with all sorts of interesting things enticing you to buy something to take home in remembrance of your visit to Tarr Steps. A place to enjoy from every aspect.

USEFUL INFORMATION

- OPEN:11-5.30pm&7.30-11pm
- WHEELCHAIR ACCESS: No
- GARDEN: Yes
- CREDIT CARDS: All major cards
- CHILDREN: Yes but not in the evening

- RESTAURANT: Delicious,Highly acclaimed
- VEGETARIAN: Yes
- TEAROOM: Great menu Home-made fare
- LICENSED: Yes
- PETS: Yes. Daytime only

Belfield Guest House	Shepton Mallet	244
Beryl	Wells	223
Black Swan	Langport	245
Boltons (The)	Neighbourne Oakhill	224
Bond's Hotel & Restaurant	Castle Cary	225
Bowlish House	Shepton Mallet	226
Box Tree House	Westbury Sub Mendip	245
Broadview Gardens	Crewkerne	227
Cat Head	Stoke Sub Hamdon	228
Cloisters Restaurant	Wells	246
Coxley Vineyard	Coxley	229
Crown At Wells	Wells	246
Farthings Hotel	Hatch Beauchamp	230
Fountain Inn	Wells	247
Franklyns Farm	Chewton Mendip	247
Frog Street Farm	Beercrocombe	248
Gables	East Chinnock	248
Infield House	Wells	231
Kings Arms	Montacute	232
Lamb At Weare	Lower Weare	249
Lana	Westbury Sub Mendip	233
Langford Manor	Five Head nr Taunton	234
Lynch (The)	Somerton	235
Market Cross Hotel	Cheddar	249
Middlewick Farm	Wick	236
Miners Arms	Priddy	237
No 3	Glastonbury	238
Old Stagecoach Inn	Crewkerne	239
Old Stores	Westbury Sub Mendip	240
Pecking Mill Inn	Shepton Mallet	241
Rose & Crown	Huish Episcopi	250
Slab House	West Horrington	250
Stag Cottage	Zeals	242
Truffles Restaurant	Bruton	243
White Hart Hotel	Wells	244
White Hart Inn	Axbridge	251
Wine Vaults	Shepton Mallet	251

Chapter Five:
The Smallest City and the Largest Street
Central and Southern Somerset

The section of Somerset which lies east of the M5 motorway, and south of Bristol, Bath and their environs, looks a little empty of defining colour on many maps. There are few built up areas of any size, and apart from the Mendip Hills, little green shading to denote areas of woodland, or downs. In the middle of this section of the county are the Somerset Levels, some of the flattest country you will find anywhere in Britain.

Yet this area is not dull, far from it. This claims to be the land of King Arthur and his knights, and is most certainly the home of some of the most spectacular underground scenery in the country. The smallest city in England is at the heart of what lies above the ground; a place of beauty and tranquillity, but also bustle and modern life. There is much more too, from places of magic and myth to those with a history all too real and sometimes miserable. Come off the motorway, or away from Bristol, Bath and Taunton, and you will find an area packed with places of interest, the memories of which will stay with you forever, as I already know they will with me.

Let's start in the north west, on the hills which tower above the M5 as you travel south, the MENDIPS. Part of their majesty comes from their setting; from the flat expanses of the Vale of Gloucester to the North West, or the Levels to the south, they provide a horizon of dark green, inviting and secure. On a journey south they take over this role from The Cotswolds, but where the beauty of Cotswold Stone has been quarried and then used for all to behold, the softer lime under the Mendips has left a very different legacy, hidden from all but the brave.

About ten years ago I held the common view of 'potholers' as a strange, eccentric breed who were mad to invite catastrophe by burrowing away under tons of rock and earth. Just a couple of days before writing this I heard a news item about two such in Derbyshire who survived more than twenty fours underground after being cut off by flooding. These days I can understand why they were there.

I only had the opportunity to go caving in the Mendips on four or five occasions, but one in particular was so memorable that I am not sure if I will ever be so overwhelmed by the work of nature again. After a couple of 'safe' trips to accessible caves I had the chance to spend an evening exploring something more dramatic; I think the cave is called G.B.1, but time has blurred that detail. What I do remember is the building excitement of our descent. There were two other 'novices' with me, and two experienced cave guides.

Perhaps you will understand that it was not without some trepidation that I took the first few steps down the vertical metal ladder leading down into the earth from the manhole cover in the middle of a cold, empty field if I tell you that I can get claustrophobic in a Department Store, let alone a lift! The first thing you notice on a trip underground is the temperature. It was winter, and I was expecting it to be incredibly cold, even though I already knew that in theory the temperature underground is constant. Without any wind chill, the result is like an early Spring day, when you cannot quite take any clothes off, but you do not feel any shivers either.

Soon it is the quiet which entrances, and the power of what surrounds you. I remember having to crawl under some four or five feet of hanging rock at one point, through a body tight gap, which is terrifying if you cannot see the end of the tunnel you are entering, even if you know the guide is waiting there for you! There was a short climb down a vertical sheet of rock glistening with water; just half a minute of clinging to a rope, knowing the harness was secure, slipping gently from one toehold to the next. The novelty of the journey did not allow time for anticipation about its end, and so the underground stream and massive open spaces came as a total surprise, a completely bewildering terminus. Everyone felt a sense of elation, and then each of us silently looked about, the formations of limestone and the vaulted roof of the caverns were just too much to put into words.

This may not appeal to you, but if you get any chance to explore under the surface of the Mendips, and you are even slightly tempted, then I can recommend that you take the chance. Among those who may be able to help you realise any such ambition are MENDIP OUTDOOR PURSUITS (01934 820518 / 823666), the BLACK ROCK OUTDOOR ACTIVITY CENTRE (01934 744389) and the MILL ON THE BRUE OUTDOOR ACTIVITY CENTRE (01749 812307). All of these will cater mostly for groups, but if they cannot provide what you want, then they will put you onto the local Caving Clubs, who should be able to help. It almost goes without saying that you should not venture one step underground without expert help, but do not think you will have to be a well trained athlete to take on the caves, the guides will respect your limits.

The Mendips are ideal for many other pursuits, some of which are much less intimidating. The same centres run a range of activities including hill walking, abseiling, archery and Orienteering. Most of you will have already heard of the most accessible caves here too, at **CHEDDAR**. Here you can walk along well lit underground concrete paths to see GOUGH'S CAVE and COX'S CAVE, part of the group of attractions now billed as the CHEDDAR SHOWCAVES AND GORGE (01934 742343).

These caves are spectacular, and must have been even more so to their 19th century discoverers, after whom they are named. They were inhabited in the more distant past too, by cave lions, hyaenas, bats, and man, among others. I have to say that the present day environment is so completely different to that of an even slightly 'wild' cave that this is nothing like caving whatsoever. The lighting and partitioning are necessary to keep the fantastic, cathedral like calcite formations of stalactites and mites intact and fully visible (tights come down is how I was taught to remember the difference), but even if you do not have the time or ability to go to any other caves, try to take up the ADVENTURE CAVING option also available here so that you can get some of the best of both worlds.

The Gorge is definitely worth exploring too, although I do remember that the 300 odd steps of JACOB'S LADDER which climb the side of it are quite a challenge. The Gorge has a height, or depth, of up to 500 feet in places, and the views from its edge are impressive, and quite alarming for anyone who has tendencies to vertigo! From the top of the ladder there is a three mile marked walk around the Gorge, for which you will need to use sturdy footwear. The viewpoint at PULPIT ROCK is particularly awesome, even though it is not the highest point, and you could certainly preach to a good few if they collected below you here. There are also bus rides around the gorge in an open top double decker if you prefer an easier option (during the summer).

The top of the Gorge is a good place from which to get an idea of what the rest of Somerset holds too. The vast expanses of flat land to the south, spread out beneath you like a well laid but randomly patterned carpet, end only in the far distance with the heights of the Quantocks and Exmoor. PAVEY'S LOOKOUT TOWER, at the top of Jacob's Ladder, allows you to climb a little more so that you can see even further.

If you want more from the Mendips, then a trip of just two miles up onto the heights will take you to the village of **CHARTERHOUSE**, from which you can walk through the local Roman Lead Mining area to the giddy heights of BEACON'S BATCH, the highest point on the Mendips, at 1,067 feet above sea level. This is a wild and open area, and you stand a good chance of seeing a peregrine falcon perhaps hunting dormice, or you may catch sight of a raven, black against the fields.

There are many Nature Reserves on the Mendips, from ancient woodlands to the open drama of EBBOR GORGE. But this last is further east, and we cannot leave Cheddar behind without being forced to smile by saying cheese. Yes, this is where the most famous of cheese's got its name centuries ago. The CHEDDAR GORGE CHEESE CO. (01934 742810) has what it calls the 'Real Cheddar Cheese Dairy' but cheddar can come from virtually anywhere now. Cheddar village is a collection of tourist attractions and shops, and the craftspeople collected at this 'Working Village', including a cooper and a spinner, add more to its appeal.

On the eastern edge of the Hills, at **CHEWTON MENDIP**, the CHEWTON CHEESE DAIRY (01761 241666) is another place where you can watch traditional cheese making. The east also has its showcave, just as famous as those at Cheddar.

WOOKEY HOLE (01749 672243) is spectacular in a very different way to the other showcaves. Here it is the setting, with the underground head-waters of the River AXE and the huge GREAT CAVE, which are more memorable than particular fine detail. The cave has had many previous visitors, including the legendary Witch of Wookey, who now, apparently, concentrates on telling her story to modern visitors, as part of the new organisation of Wookey's attractions.

The Witch's Kitchen, Wookey Hole

Wookey also has the last working mill to handmake paper, a reminder that the local economy was not always so reliant on the tourist trade. This mill has been here for four hundred years or more, but with Wookey Hole is now surrounded by some other more recent additions such as a Victorian Pier Arcade, Victorian Portrait Studio, and Magical Mirror Maze. Just two miles from here is the smallest city in England, **WELLS** (Tourist Information 01749 672552). This place has been a personal favourite of mine since the very first time I happened upon it. It is not just the breathtaking West Front of the Cathedral, or the placid moat of the Bishop's Palace that appeal, the whole place has a delicate but sustained balance between its roles as a modern, living and working centre of population and as the home of some of the most delightful architecture of the whole west country.

Unlike nearby Glastonbury, (which is also a great place in its own way), Wells has absolutely no pretensions, and it is quite possible to come to the city for the first time on business, as I did, without knowing anything about the other side of what is here. The city centre (it *is* hard not to refer to it as a town!) is full of winding streets, intersected by wide alleyways. The shops are functional yet tasteful, and this is definitely a city without Tower Blocks. The vast majority of the buildings are two storey, and there always seem to be plenty of local people bustling around the old, uneven pavements.

Park the car and take a walk around these streets, and any route you choose to take seems to end up in the same place, where the tarmac suddenly ends, to be replaced with a open area paved with neat dark stones. A few steps away from the rest of the city and it already seems quieter here. Looking in front of you there are two inviting gateways of light stone, both looking old and important. To the right you know you have found the centre of Wells by the collection of buildings present; the Town Hall, Post Office, Tourist Information and Citizen's Advice Bureau, virtually lined up so that you can take your pick. This is the Market Place, and is a complete contrast to those of the Cotswold and Wiltshire wool towns, where traffic was, and often still is, invited through the wide main street, enlarged to take the market. Wells has a different layout, a quiet square accessible from each of its streets, but separate from them all, overlooked by the splendid timbers of the 16th century Crown Inn.

So which of the gateway's should we take first? The larger and brighter of the two is straight in front, in the middle of the line of buildings at the end of the square, and looks the more promising. As you approach it you may hear cries from your left, where the other gateway makes up a corner. In years gone by these sounds were doubtless meant to tempt newcomers over to this, the PENNILESS PORCH. For this was where, from the time of its construction in 1450, the local poor were supposed to gather if they were to request alms, although on my last visit there was only a single busker providing an interesting modern alternative! Let's give in and start in this left hand corner.

Just a single peek through to the other side of this dusty porch will make you forget for now that there is another gateway waiting for you. On your right the WEST FRONT of WELLS CATHEDRAL (Office 01749 674483) towers up, from this angle seeming to reach to the very sky, while to the left the CATHEDRAL GREEN gives space into which you can step back to get the massive building into a clearer perspective.

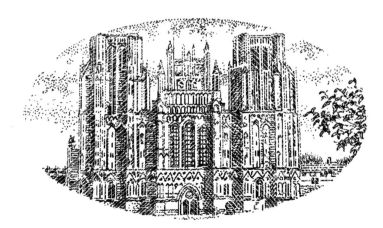

The West Front, Wells Cathedral

What an exterior it is, made all the more daunting by its sudden appearance if you take this approach. It may take time to interpret the elongated stone figures which look down on you, but some say they are part of a panorama representing the last judgement, something it is hard to imagine descending upon Wells! Apparently it is the largest gallery of medieval sculptures in the world and is also described as an illustration in stone of the whole of the Christian Faith.

However you choose to describe and interpret it, the West Front is as beautiful in its square lines and imposing solidity as any building with more delicate tracery or spire could hope to be. It is hard not to make comparisons between Wells Cathedral with its Green and Salisbury Cathedral and the Close, but each is so stunningly original a scene that it must be seen for itself alone. Less than a minute's walk from the centre of Wells' shopping streets and you are in a completely different world, where any residual background noise from the city remains completely unnoticed as you take in what is around you. The inside of the Cathedral Church of St Andrew, which was built between the 12th and 15th centuries, is scarcely less remarkable. Just as you may have strained your neck looking up at the Front as you came through the Penniless Porch, so you may get dizzy again trying to appreciate the height of the Nave, with its delicately decorated vaulting and the 'scissor arches' towards its eastern end. Unlike some other cathedrals and abbeys, the scale of Wells becomes acceptable to the human eye after a while, and you can begin to come to terms with the whole of what you are seeing.

A walk around the interior in an anti clockwise direction will reveal many things you cannot hope to appreciate at first. There is too much to describe here in detail, but I will pick out two or three of my favourites. Towards the eastern end of the Cathedral, still on the right hand side, are some marble tombs, and that of Bishop Bekynton (who had the Penniless Porch built) is particularly unusual. It is on two tiers, with a carving of the Bishop looking at restful ease on the top layer. Underneath is a much more gruesome figure, of a skeleton bearing the remnants of his robes. One wonders if the Bishop chose his own memorial!

Much restoration work has already been done in the programme set out for 1970 to 2020, and perhaps the finest example of what has been done thus far is the Chapter House, on the opposite side of the Cathedral. Up some extremely worn, wide stone steps leading from the Nave, this octagonal room must have made a superb meeting place for the representatives of the parishes whose name-plates are still in their respective places on the walls. Apparently some £650,000 was spent restoring this one room to its original condition, but whatever it cost the results are suitably impressive.

Whoever held the floor from the central pillar of this classical styled meeting place, with only two steps around the perimeter for possible seating, must have felt eyes bearing in upon him from each direction of the compass. It really does appear a good place for a shouting match, and the noise of heated discussion would have had plenty of room to rise up to the roof. Bright and cheerful, even the modern radiators have been made to blend into the walls of the Chapter House, and it would make an excellent, if slightly unconventional, Lecture Theatre today. If the remainder of the restoration work goes as well then this will be an even more impressive place in the future; mind you it is a sobering thought that it costs ten thousand pounds a year just to maintain the lead on the cathedral roof.

Coming out from the Chapter House and down into the main part of the Cathedral you might have the luck and good timing to be surprised, as I once was, by a funny little man striking a bell with his heels. He is part of the 14th century WELLS CLOCK. The noise of his bell made me look in that direction, and the large round face of the clock was immediately apparent, but the sound was coming from somewhere above it. Expecting some sort of pulley mechanism I looked up, but it took a little while to find Mister Jack Blandifer, in his niche high to the right above the main part of the ancient timepiece. He kicks the bell at each quarter, using his hammer only to sound the hour.

I must admit he is such a jolly looking little fellow, almost like a ventriloquist's puppet lounging on a convenient ledge, that he made me chuckle. Part of his charm is the contrast he makes to the more stately nature of the rest of the clock. The face is famous for showing three different pieces of information, one on each of its dials. The outermost uses Roman numerals to give the hour, the next tells you what minute it is, and the innermost has the slightly less immediately useful purpose of telling the lunar month. There is a very useful notice next to the clock to help you decode its messages. It was not just the numerals which drew my eyes to the clock during Blandifer's bells, for there is motion each quarter too, from a roundabout of jousting knights who sit above the clock face. No matter how many times you watch the small figures in their contest, it is always the same one who falls from his horse, defeated every fifteen minutes for more than six hundred years, a sporting humiliation of truly Promethean proportions! The whole effect of the clock is to be totally charming, and fascinating.

When you have exhausted what the interior of the main part of the cathedral has to offer, a turn to the north will take you to the oldest continuously inhabited street in Europe. The VICARS' CLOSE was originally built to house the men of the choir in 1348, and it has been at the centre of the great tradition of music in the Cathedral ever since. Even the organ at Wells sounds better than most, perhaps because of the acoustics of what is a more box like structure than other cathedrals. There are regular lunchtime and supper concerts, along with organ recitals, including some from the pupils of the famous Wells Cathedral School. Try 01749 672773 to book for current events, or 01749 672970 for those run by the Cathedral School.

There is still plenty more to see around the Cathedral. Next to the West Front on the edge of the Green is the WELLS MUSEUM (01749 673477) with much about the Mendips and their Geology, as well as the Witch of Wookey Hole, and the history of the city itself. The CHAIN GATE, CAMERY GARDEN, and restored CLOISTERS are more features of the Cathedral worth looking out for, but even then the beauty at the heart of the smallest city is not complete.

The gateway we abandoned a while ago, back in the Market Place, is called the BISHOP'S EYE. What you will find inside this arch can be reached directly from the Cathedral Cloisters, but as with the West Front the most dramatic approach is that which comes directly from the city.

We all have our favourite memories and the places which go with them, whether they be windswept deserted spots, sun baked beaches or a particular street, building or room. Yet some few places appeal to just about everybody, causing a moment of quite contemplation, usually accompanied by the beginnings of a smile. Such a one is the setting of THE BISHOP'S PALACE (01749 678691) in Wells.

Surrounded by a beautifully smooth moat inhabited by ducks and swans, the red brick edifice looks like the archetypal version of an English Castle, complete with drawbridge and battlements, yet without looking anything like a military or defensive structure at all. Parts of the collection of buildings inside the walls are still used as a residence for the Bishop of Bath and Wells, and have been continuously since the first house was built in the early 13th century, which might make you wonder why the palace has been fortified, with only really the Cathedral as a near neighbour.

This was done in the 14th century, when a Bishop was a very powerful man, often feared and sometimes hated by the general populace (although there is no reason to suppose that even by Elizabethan times he was anything like the "Bishop of Bath and Wells who eats babies before breakfast" so hilariously portrayed in "Blackadder"). Fears about public unrest at that time were not fulfilled, but in 1831 the Drawbridge was raised after rioting in Bristol. It would be hard to imagine a less likely place for any sort of disorder. The walk along Moat Road, then turning left into Tor Street, at the back of the Palace grounds, is superbly peaceful. What I really love about this place is that it has remained so natural, you can walk along here at any time, on any day, and the city will still be next to you, carrying on as usual, but with this whole scene linked to it without the necessity for any fencing, gates or visitors fees.

The swans and their methods of gaining food are justifiably famous. If you are lucky enough to see one of them using its beak to pull the rope attached to the bell near the gateway, which informs those inside that the swans are hungry, then consider yourself privileged. Some leaflets and information suggest that you should not feed them lest they lose the need to ring the bell, but as some five hundred year old glass (at Nailsea Court) depicts the very same scene I think it is safe to suggest that they are unlikely to shake the habit! Apparently white bread is to be avoided, as it is not good for them.

I think a sunny Summer's evening is probably the optimum time to visit this spot. Several years ago I took part in the Wells ten kilometre race, on just such an evening. The route took us around the town twice, with a memorable start as we piled in a single group out through the arch of the Bishop's Eye. The finish was along the Moat Road, and was very dramatic for me. I have never sprinted so fast, as I tried to beat the runner with whom I had travelled the last half of the race. The crowd were cheering, and with a last desperate spurt I won. Only one problem; the crowd was mostly made up of other runners who had long finished 'warming down' and the place I had successfully won was 73rd out of 75. The race was a little out of my class, but the experience was great; even in a contest Wells is a friendly, inspiring place.

Just as much as Cheddar or Wookey, Wells owes its beauty to a feature of nature, in this case the springs from which the city takes its name. They rise in the Palace grounds, and four of them can be seen barely disturbing the reflection of the Cathedral on the surface of the pool which adjoins it, as bubbles rise from the bottom signalling the continuing process which produces an average of 40 gallons of fresh water every second. The springs gave the city more than its name, providing power for the industry for which Wells became famous, the making of paper in mills powered by their water. Now Wookey is the best place to find out more about this part of the area's heritage, although Wells still remains a thriving , if minute, city.

If you have approached the city from Cheddar then you may have been one of the many who have been deceived into thinking that the Cathedral has only a single tower. Wells may be the smallest city, but it has the largest parish church in Somerset, at ST CUTHBERTS. As well as this there are many other architectural treasures hidden in Wells, from a fourteenth century bakery to many splendid Georgian and Victorian shop-fronts and buildings.

East of the city is the WELLS GOLF CLUB (01749 672868), which welcomes visitors at the weekends. Further east these are now the foothills of the Mendips, amongst which lies the former cloth town of **SHEPTON MALLET** (Tourist Information 01749 345258). After the plastic camel of Bridgwater the friendly looking deer calf which looks down on you from one of Shepton's tallest buildings is much easier to account for. This is the home of the Babycham brand, and the statue is set prominently on top of the Showerings factory.

Signs of the town's medieval prosperity, into which it grew from its placement near the Roman Fosse Way, have a familiar ring too. The Market Cross is particularly ornate, like a brighter version of that at Malmesbury (Chapter Six). Unfortunately this was the scene of something much less attractive, as Judge Jeffries' orders led to the public execution of several of the Duke of Monmouth's followers in 1685. A LOCAL HISTORY MUSEUM attached to the Tourist Information Office (also 01749 345258) has more about both the industrial and more remote Roman days of the history of Shepton Mallet.

The ROYAL BATH AND WEST SHOW takes place each year towards the end of May, at a permanent site south of the town. Be wary of the incredible traffic queues which build up for this event, but if you enjoy a mix of produce stalls and exhibitions of agricultural animals and machinery, then this is the event for you. It is quite phenomenal to see the scale of the Show; during the rest of the year the site is rather bleak, and quite remote, but during these few days you can walk for a good ten to fifteen minutes without pause before you have circled the tents and stalls surrounding the Show Ring.

To the west of Shepton Mallet (and south of Wells) the village of **NORTH WOOTTON** is home to the WOOTTON VINEYARD (01749 89359). The Romans first brought Vines to this area, to take advantage of the protection offered by the southern slopes of the Mendips, and 13th century stone carvings on a pillar in Wells Cathedral showing a farmer chasing grape thieves confirms that the process was still around in medieval times. This vineyard was part of a recent revival, originally planted in 1971. There is another at nearby **PILTON**, the PILTON MANOR VINEYARD, as well as the AVALON VINEYARD (01749 860393) in Shepton Mallet. With tasting at all of these as well as the BAGBOROUGH VINEYARD (01749 831146) at **PYLLE** a little further south, be careful not to drive after trying more than a few sips!

Another relatively recent revival in this area took place in 1974, when the EAST SOMERSET RAILWAY (01749 880417) was reopened, with its headquarters at **CRANMORE**, to the east of Shepton. The Victorian style Engine Shed has a collection of tank and other engines which can be visited, and there is a half hour round trip of five and a half miles available along this Heritage line throughout the year, although only at weekends during the winter. To many the prime attraction will be the 140 ton 'Black Prince', the largest working steam locomotive in the country.

The land north of the main road linking Wells to Shepton Mallet and then Frome, is a patchwork of country lanes among which there are many villages worth a visit, hidden in the valleys which run down from the eastern edge of the Mendips. **NUNNEY** has another of the many west country castles to meet its downfall during the Civil War. The bombardment by the Parliamentary forces in 1645 was followed by a looting even more complete than those at Corfe or Wardour, and not a single joist or floorboard was left behind.

Nunney Castle

What is left today is an elegant ruin of the castle walls, with the huge cylindrical towers which make each corner, three of which are almost intact externally, as well as the shell of the central tower. This is quite surprising if you consider the size of the thirty pound cannonballs which were employed against them, one of which is stored in the village church. Also in ALL SAINTS CHURCH, you can see a model of the Castle as it was in the 14th century.

These villages are among the prettiest in Somerset in their own way, and none more so than **MELLS**. Apart from the thatch used on some of the cottages you could suddenly be in the Cotswolds, with grey and yellow stone cottages to be found after an approach through winding roads surrounded by green. In the middle of all this is the church, again as in many Cotswold towns and villages looking very grand for such a small place. Its tower is particularly splendid, although it is not the oldest part of the building. Over a hundred feet tall it boasts a tremendous collection of buttresses, pinnacles and blank and fretted windows. Be wary of going to the wrong village though, as the tower at nearby **LEIGH UPON MENDIP** is so similar that it seems likely that they were designed by the same, now anonymous, person.

Mells was once the eastern boundary of the lands under the control of Glastonbury Abbey, and the local agent, or bailiff in the time of Henry VIII was a certain John Horner. His family is thought to be the source of the Little Jack Horner nursery rhyme, although an exact interpretation is open to speculation! One explanation is that the Abbot sent the Deeds of Mells Manor to King Henry in a pie, as part of an attempt to save the Abbey from destruction in the Dissolution, and that John Horner was the messenger who carried the pie. As every good child knows the errand boy then sat in a corner to remove the 'plum', here meaning that he kept the Manor for himself, and let the Abbey fend for itself!

There are other villages here dominated by superb churches, notably that at **KILMERSDON**. Other places have their own claim to fame, such as **STRATTON ON THE FOSSE**, which has an Abbey at DOWNSIDE that is still in use, and **DOULTING** which is near the quarries that were the source of much of the stone used in the local churches and also Wells Cathedral. **GURNEY SLADE** is home to the MENDIP GOLF CLUB (01749 840570 / 840793). There is much to discover amongst this patch work of lanes without crossing into what we have already covered in earlier chapters, but now we must head south and west back to the M5, to explore some more open country.

The landscapes of the large section of Somerset which lies east of the M5 motorway suggest to me a vast sheet of some corrugated material, with horizontal raised and indented sections running from west to east. The Mendips have formed the northernmost, raised section, while a drive east along the A39 from Junction 23 lets you see the flat expanses of the middle of the county split again to the south by the dark horizon formed by the POLDEN HILLS.

On both sides of the main road are farming country, looking very cultivated and parcelled up by centuries of use. Among the attractions to be found in this area is the SECRET WORLD Badger and Wildlife Rescue Centre (01278 783250) at **EAST HUNTSPILL**. Nearby at **MARK** the rural theme is continued at COOMBES CIDER (01278 641265) where there is a museum as well as the more usual tours of the presses. South of the road is the MOORLYNCH VINEYARD (01458 210393), for even more variety.

Further east the main road begins to join the Poldens, and the expanses to the south, especially those of the KING'S SEDGE MOOR, stretch much further away. It is as if central Somerset has nothing to hide, and has laid out all for you to see. Around this point you will begin to notice a strange, very isolated, break in the horizon, away to the east. From this distance it looks as if some massive earthmoving has been taking place, with the unwanted soil piled up in a great ungainly heap. Yet already there is something magnetic about this focal point, of which the details slowly begin to develop as you travel east.

A little nearer and you can see a tower on its peak, looking only like a little sentry box so far. Gradually you can make out that this is a bigger building, with an open space at is base, making a dark break in its grey colour. By now it is clear that the hill is green, and that any earth that has been moved settled many centuries ago. This is GLASTONBURY TOR, but before you can get any closer to it you will have to negotiate the largest Street in this or many other counties.

Of course **STREET** (Tourist Information 01458 447384) is not a single road, but it does have a pedestrianised shopping area that brings visitors from all over the South West, and the town takes its name from an ancient causeway that joined it to Glastonbury across the River BRUE. Amongst many places with long histories, and very close to the one which claims the most significant in ancient myths and legends, Street is a much more modern success story.

A mere hamlet for many centuries, with only 540 inhabitants in the whole parish in 1801, it was the shoe making of the Clark brothers that saw vast Victorian expansion in the town. With the industrial revolution came the need for mass production of standard quality footwear, and this was one place that could provide what was needed. Clarks have been market leaders ever since, and are still the largest employer in the town. While the massive factories visible from the by-pass are formidable and what you might expect, the CLARKS VILLAGE (01458 840064) has given the town something more than employment and economic stability.

This sells itself as a Factory Shopping Centre, where prices are kept at a discount because the brand name goods come straight from the factory floor. The bargains do include seconds and discontinued lines, but this is still a great place for top quality shopping too. Also in the village is the highly unusual but fascinating CLARKS SHOE MUSEUM and the VILLAGE POTTERY, where you can watch the potter or have a go yourself.

It really is quite incredible how different the two neighbouring towns of Street and **GLASTONBURY** (Tourist Information 01458 832954) are. They are so close to one another that there is scarcely time to draw breath before Street's by-pass meets the roundabouts outside the town of Glastonbury. There is no escaping the eccentricity of this place. A quick look around the shops at the bottom of Glastonbury's main hill, as well as along it reveals names such as 'Man, Myth, and Magic', 'The Crystal Star', 'Anvil Art' and 'Oasis'. None of them seem to sell the everyday goods you would expect in the middle of a medium sized town, but if you are looking for alternative medicines, crystals and amulets, then this is the place for you. Even the local Industrial Estate has the rather romantic, deliberately Arthurian name of 'Avalon', taken from the Isle to which the body of the King was delivered, and of which we will hear much more very soon.

What is normal elsewhere could be distinctly out of place in Glastonbury. I was last there in the middle of winter, but there were still plenty of costumes that you might expect to see only during the summer rock festival time. Extra piercings and dreadlocks are definitely the norm, and there was not a single suit to be seen on the pavements of the High Street. Do not think I am being cynical, for this is a great place. The character of the town is not pretentious because it is so complete and unassuming; as we will discover Glastonbury has an incredibly distinctive and important heritage, to which modern fashions and interpretations can make very little lasting difference. So why is Glastonbury such a centre for those interested in the distant Celtic past and all things mysterious and magical? From the town itself it is not easy to get a glimpse of the Tor, so for now the ruins of GLASTONBURY ABBEY (01458 832267) are a good place from which to start an investigation.

The Lady Chapel, Glastonbury Abbey Ruins

As well as the alleged mystical sources of power, medieval Glastonbury had some very real, tangible social clout centred around what now lies in ruins along Magdalene Road. From the site of the very first Christian church in Britain, supposedly established by Joseph of Arimathea in just 30 A.D. (some legends also add that it was then blessed by Christ himself), an Abbey grew up with power over much of Somerset, in a time when an Abbot could be a very important man. It became such an important place that at least three medieval Kings of England chose to be buried here.

By the time the Abbey was destroyed by fire in 1184 it already had a distinguished history, with William of Malmesbury listing its first Abbot as Saint Patrick, who was said to have died here in 472. It does seem most convenient that it was at the time when the Abbey needed money for rebuilding, and its power and reputation were most at risk, that the bones of King Arthur and Queen Guinevere were suddenly discovered here in 1191, especially as Richard the Lionheart had just declared Arthur of Brittany to be his heir!

King Arthur is a most elusive figure in British history, but not in Literature. Geoffrey of Monmouth started the long tradition with his Latin Chronicle which introduced the basics of the Arthurian legend. The stories were developed over the centuries in both French Romance and Middle English, notably in the alliterative 'Morte D'Arthur' and the work of Wace and Layamon. The definitve version is surely that of Thomas Malory, written in the 15th century. Without demeaning what is a rich tradition it is a bit like the 20th century treatment of a fictional figure such as Batman. For sixty years so far Bruce Wayne's story has been told and retold in many forms, with different details and even main characteristics and events, as well as at least four different actors portraying him in film. Arthur was a cult just as much as the Caped Crusader is today, but the Once and Future King has kept that status, on and off, for about eight hundred years so far, and there is most probably some little trace of reality in his origins.

Arthur may well have been the forerunner of Alfred. King Alfred kept the Danes at bay; Arthur may well have been the one who kept the Saxons back for a while, but did not chronicle his battles so well, with the result that they are lost for all time. He is a legend, and always will be, simply because there is much too much contradictory information for it all to be true. Glastonbury Abbey still claims unequivocally that it has *the* bones of the King and his wife. Perhaps it does, and perhaps Arthur was a fifth or sixth century English King, but then again maybe not. Let's leave him alone until we move to the Tor.

More definitely the stories were given enough credibility for King Edward I and Queen Eleanor to have attended the ceremonial re-opening of the tombs at Glastonbury Abbey in 1278. From then until the Dissolution this was one of the most important religious centres in the country, and the early fourteenth century was the highest point in its prosperity, with sixty monks and sixty servants among those living in the Abbey in 1322. The Abbot never went anywhere without at least one hundred retainers, and the Abbey could entertain up to five hundred 'men of quality' at one time. What took so long to establish, through the efforts of some of the men who shaped the whole social and religious system of this country, such as St Dunstan, was destroyed very quickly. We will return to those dark events a little later, moving now to what is left, and can be seen today.

Not much of what was once a huge building actually remains. Crucially the fragments of the LADY CHAPEL, with their beautifully smooth lines and gaping stone doorways, reputedly stand on the site of the original wattle and daub church, which was certainly here eighteen hundred years ago, and maybe even before that. For this reason alone there is an atmosphere of extreme antiquity about this quiet area of grass from which the last remnants of one of Britain's greatest ever religious centres rise like the broken teeth in a discarded skull. Some of the peripheral buildings have fared better, and the ABBOT'S KITCHEN has survived particularly well.

The scale of this single building gives you some idea of how immense the Abbey itself must have been. Another survivor from medieval times is just behind the Visitor's Centre building from which you gain access to the ruins. The HOLY THORN is a little hawthorn tree which flowers each Christmas, and some say sprung from the staff of Joseph of Arimathea when he arrived here almost two thousand years ago. There are many stories about the Thorn, and the history of its superstitions. The Elizabethans scoffed at it, while 18th century sailors bought sprigs to use as lucky charms while at sea. In the present century George V renewed the ancient custom of accepting a gift of a piece of the Thorn each Christmas, and the reigning monarch continues to receive a new tribute each year.

The ruins of the Abbey are extremely quiet, and a melancholy place in a way. This was once a thriving community, and now there is very little at all. Glastonbury High Street has a little more bustle around other reminders of medieval prosperity. Not least of these is the TRIBUNAL, which is thought to have held the Abbey's Court House. Nowadays this sturdy piece of medieval architecture is home to the Tourist Information Office and the GLASTONBURY LAKE VILLAGE MUSEUM (also 01458 832954).

Instead of more of what you might expect about Arthur, Joseph and the Abbey, this tells the fascinating story of the Iron Age villagers whose remains were discovered towards the end of the 19th century. An interpretation of how these people lived, using canoes and small boats to get around what was then largely the marsh and seas of central Somerset, can also be found at the PEAT MOORS VISITORS CENTRE (01458 860697) near **WESTHAY**, to the north west of Glastonbury. These early settlers were in this area about two thousand years ago, and make an interesting contrast to the legends of envoys sent by Saint Philip or even St Peter to civilize the religion of the area just a few decades later.

There are other impressive old buildings in the main streets of the town, including the church of ST JOHN with its huge tower, while another remnant of the Abbey takes up the corner of Bere Lane and Chilkwell Street. This is the 14th century Abbey Barn, which now contains the SOMERSET RURAL LIFE MUSEUM (01458 831197). Life in Victorian Somerset is the theme explored here, and the museum also holds events and craft exhibitions through the year.

Although it is easy to see from many miles away, Glastonbury Tor is not simple to locate from the town centre. Once you have found the right lane to take you up towards it, you will be close to the other legendary miracle left behind during Joseph of Aramithea's visit, the CHALICE WELL. This was originally a spring, most likely used as part of a ceremonial site by neolithic man, in conjunction with the Tor.

Joseph was supposed to have brought the Chalice of the Lord's Supper here, and made the spring waters run red. Like the Thorn, the powers of the well have been credited on and off for many centuries, at one point giving Georgian Glastonbury a brief 'Spa' status. The waters come from deep under the Mendips, and their healing qualities are still believed in by many. The supply has never been known to fail, and 25,000 gallons flow through here each day.

Now there is only one place left to visit in Glastonbury, and that is the one you most probably saw first, the Tor. In winter it is possible to park your car at the bottom of this hill, but there are only a few spaces in a narrow country lane, so in Summer the walk will be a much longer one. The Tor is now owned by the National Trust, and a concrete path leads up to steps cut into the steeper slopes near its summit.

Such is the shape of this conical mound that from the bottom it looks as if the steps end at the steepest point, presumably leaving you to struggle the last few yards to the top as best you can. Even this is no deterrent, and despite the tangible looks of scorn from the sheep grazing the lower slopes you are compelled to make the climb. The Tor looks even bigger from its base, with the outline of the surviving tower from ST MICHAEL'S CHURCH now clearly defined at its peak. The feeling that this is somewhere very special indeed is one that grows as you ascend.

Once you get to the end of the steps the good news is that the path does start again, swinging to the left to lead around the other side of the Tor. Near the top the sides are steep, and looking down even the few trees clinging to the lower slopes on this side seem to grow almost horizontally to keep their tenuous hold. By the time you reach the Tower, the stone seats inside it are a very welcome sight. The winds blow strong at the top of Glastonbury Tor, and once you have regained your breath and looked around it is easy to see why, as there are absolutely no natural windbreaks for miles.

Some towers, steps and hills are worth climbing for the view, or the particular setting, others are just a challenge which has to be met. Glastonbury Tor is much more, it has a feeling of natural power all of its own. Standing at its summit it feels as if you are in the middle of a vast green amphitheatre, and that if you were to shout the sound would surely carry to the hills which form the furthest barriers of the area making up your captive audience.

As Desmond Hawkins puts it in his excellent book 'Avalon and Sedgemoor':

"If ever a landscape provided its own altar, this is it."

This is also the Isle of Avalon. For in former times much of the low lying green land spread beneath was water, and the mists which hung above it would have given the Tor an even more dramatic outline as it rose from out of them.

Legends say that there is an entrance to the underworld below the Tor, and even though it is easy to be logical about geological formations and the effects of erosion on the softer surrounding clays, you cannot scale this place without feeling some of its mystery seeping into your mind. Avalon was where Arthur was taken at the end of his final battle, mortally wounded:

"'And I will fare to Avalun, to the fairest of all maidens, to Argante the queen, an elf most fair, and she shall make my wounds all sound; make me all whole with healing draughts. And afterwards I will come again to my kingdom, and dwell with the Britons with mickle joy.' Even with the words there approached from the sea that was a short boat, floating with the waves......"

Layamon's Brut, translated by Eugene Mason.

The once and future king could not have had a more appropriate place to spend the time between his first and second comings, and an entrance by Merlin through the gateway of St Michael's tower to declare with much lightning and thunder to the vast open spaces of Somerset that Arthur was about to return would make a fitting ending. But this is the stuff of Hollywood, and even the alliterative 'Morte D'Arthur' put Avalon in a much more real setting, making it the whole area of Glastonbury to which:

> *"The baronage of Bretayne thane, bechopes and othire,*
> *Graythes theme to Glaschenbury with gloppynnande hertes,*
> *To bery thare the bolde kynge, and brynge to the erthe,*
> *With alle wirchipe and welthe that any wy scholde."*

(Then the barons of Britain, bishops and others, proceeded to Glastonbury with terror in their hearts, to bury there the bold King and put him in the earth with all the honour and riches, as indeed they should). This brings us back to the Abbey, appropriately, as the top of Glastonbury Tor was where the work of centuries came to an end. The last Abbot of Glastonbury, Richard Whiting, was dragged up this hill, and then mercilessly hung, drawn and quartered on its summit in 1539, as part of King Henry VIII's Dissolution of the Monasteries. At the very same time the ruination of the Abbey itself had begun, and the screams from the townsfolk must have risen to fill the air as this figure of ecclesiastical power made his final journey, symbolizing the end of a very long era in British history.

What sights there have been over the years from this very spot. The Tor knows the truth; whether it was Joseph of Arimathea or an envoy from second century Rome who first made the Christian church part of Glastonbury and Britain, whether the ghosts of Arthur and his knights do indeed ride around its base each Christmas Eve upon horses shod with silver shoes. Or perhaps the rough and ready military leader of the sixth century stood on this viewpoint to trace the progress of his enemies, ironically the very Saxons who would later be the first to make him into a legendary national hero, but again only the Tor knows for sure.

It does not really matter, for this is such a wonderful place that you can believe as much as you want without feeling any uneasiness; no-one can mock belief in the extraordinary while this fantastic piece of nature's eccentricity is in view. Avalon was not the only island in Somerset, **WEDMORE** too was largely surrounded by water, and seems to have stayed out of the way of much of what has happened since, remaining in the middle of an agricultural area largely untouched by modern industry. **SOMERTON** has also remained away from the crowds, although it was an important town in and before Saxon times, reputedly even the Royal capital of Wessex in the 7th century. Now it is a peaceful and pretty place, particularly the pollarded lime trees of Broad Street and many buildings made from the local blue lias, mellowed to grey with age.

This area is full of quiet little towns and villages. **BRUTON** is famous for its schools, and also has a splendid Gothic parish church, as well as some other notable old buildings. Amongst these are the DOVECOTE, one of the first properties to belong to the National Trust, a lovely PACKHORSE BRIDGE across the River BRUE and the 17th century hospital buildings, named after Hugh Sexey. For a man with such a potentially interesting name he really had the job to go with it, as an Auditor for Elizabeth I. **EVERCREECH** has another splendid church tower, while **CASTLE CARY** has a much smaller building which is bound to arouse curiosity. Only seven feet in diameter, and dating from the late 18th century, this squat cylinder looks like some sort of eccentric storage cupboard, or a statue representing an enlarged policeman's helmet, of the London Metropolitan variety. In fact it was a lock up, similar to the tiny structure you can find in Swanage, Dorset (Chapter Eight). Let's hope it was only ever used for solitary confinement!

To the west there are more islands above the former sea, **HIGH HAM** forms one which must have stood quite isolated at times, nearly three hundred feet above the marshy land below. The village is a quiet one, but worth a visit for the views across the peat moors as well as the detail of the strangely humorous looking gargoyles of its medieval church.

While any certainty is dangerous when talking about the history of King Arthur, with whom we will again be meeting soon, the ridge of land around **ATHELNEY** has a connection with King Alfred which can be made much more securely. The time was 878, and the enemy was Godrum and his Danes. Defeated in Wiltshire (see Chapter Seven), this is where 'England's Darling' and his few remaining men came to lick their wounds. Why here? Because this was another island, difficult for the Danes to attack, but still in the middle of the country from which Alfred could gradually build a new force during the months ahead:

> *"Ond thaes on Eastron worhte Aelfred cyning lytle werede*
> *geweorc aet Aethelinga-eigge; ond of tham geweorce was winnende*
> *with thone here, ond Sumursaetna se dael se thaer niehst waes."*
> Anglo-Saxon Chronicle, 878.

(In this year at Easter King Alfred and his little troop built a fortress at Athelney, and fought with that army from that fortress, as well as in the part of Somerset which was nearest to them).

The language might seem remote and unfamiliar, and there is nothing atop the hill to mark the site of the fortress except a rather plain monument erected at the beginning of the 19th century, but this was a crucial time and place in England's history. Unlike Arthur, who it seems had to give into Saxon invasion eventually, and Harold who was unlucky enough to lose to the Normans, Alfred did succeed in keeping the country united, eventually gaining peace with the Danes. The coming together of 878 marked the first occasion on which men from the different tribes and counties of Western England actually formed a cohesive force, the first real national act of resistance. In some ways this is where it all began, as the march to successful battle at Ethandun followed some seven weeks after Easter (again see Chapter Seven).

The surrounding countryside is much more hospitable than it was then; the *'morfaestnum'* or fen-fortresses have long been replaced with pasture and paddocks, orchards and cultivated farmland. The location of Ethandun may still be in question, even as to its county, but the village of **ALLER** can claim to be the site of another significant event which followed as a consequence of it. In the Saxon church the defeated leader of the Danes was baptised, as part of the terms of peace with Alfred. This was not the end of the trouble, but it certainly marked another important moment in the development of an English national identity, for from this time on Alfred started to rebuild his nation, giving it education, and a written language.

BURROW MOUNT near the village of **BURROW BRIDGE**, is one relic from Alfred's era that has survived. Now owned by the National Trust, it marked one end of his fortifications, and like the Tor at Glastonbury has a ruined chapel to St Michael on its summit. While this site does not have the same power as that of Avalon, you are more likely to find yourself on a modern island here than at Glastonbury.

Looking south, just past the railway Level Crossing you will see a row of houses lining the road which leads off towards the larger estates of **STOKE ST GREGORY**. I once used to make deliveries to some of these houses, and wondered why they seemed so alone, with very few other dwellings off the road, or behind any of them. My answer came when watching the National News during a period of flooding just a couple of years ago. One house that I recognised as being very near to here had been completely inaccessible for almost a month, half of its bottom storey complete underwater. Around the same time I took a rail journey from Bristol to Taunton, and what I saw to the east made me realise just how little it would take for the sea to reclaim the whole of this low lying area.

The ALLER MOOR PUMPING STATION is also at Burrow Bridge, with 19th century pumps and engines showing part of the history of the efforts to keep the local inhabitants above water. At Stoke St Gregory the WILLOWS AND WETLANDS VISITORS CENTRE (01823 490249) has been a centre for traditional basket making since 1819, and has a museum as well as workshops and a craft shop. The River PARRETT runs through much of this lowland area, and the events and walks organised along the RIVER PARRETT TRAIL (01823 356519 for info) give you a good chance to explore in more depth.

Both **LANGPORT** and **HUISH EPISCOPI** have ecclesiastical features of note. The HANGING CHAPEL you may well see on your way through the little town of

Langport sits on top of what used to be the town gate, and its main church also has some excellent stained glass, while the tower of Huish's church completes an elegant exterior. These two are so close together that at the time of the Reformation it was suggested that one of the two should be destroyed as it was superfluous, but fortunately this never occurred.

Despite escaping immediate destruction in the Dissolution, the Abbey at neighbouring **MUCHELNEY** has not been so lucky. After an original settlement of monks was disrupted by the Danes, the Abbey on the 'island' of green was reestablished in the 10th century, and survived intact to be handed over by Henry VIII to the Earl of Hertford, since which time it has gradually fallen into ruin. The remains are majestic, but as with Glastonbury it is the peripheral buildings which have fared better.

The PRIEST'S HOUSE (01458 252621) has undergone complete restoration recently, under the guidance of the National Trust, who now own it. One of the craftsmen who was lucky enough to be involved in this work is a friend of mine, and he says that even in a fairly ordinary dwelling place such as this, the medieval carpenters and masons must have been extremely patient and skilled to achieve such results without the aid of modern tools and machinery, especially in the case of the massive roof timbers.

In the 11th century Muchelney Abbey had two fisheries, yielding 6,000 eels a year. Nowadays THORNEY LAKES (01458 250811) in Muchelney have carp as their main attraction in two lakes of coarse fishing, although I do know of somebody who spent all day after the larger fish, only to hook something very long and wriggly in the twilight. It seems the monks have left more than ruins behind, much to the delight of hopeful *Anguilla* specimen hunters.

MUCHELNEY POTTERY (01458 250324) on the edge of the village is a suitably traditional addition to this mellow village, which seems tucked away far from the main places of modern industry. If Muchelney seems remote then the few spread houses of **ISLE BREWERS**, and **ISLE ABBOTTS** as well as the more regular main housing area of **FIVEHEAD** will put it to shame, as long as you can find them, and then distinguish one from the other!

The ISLE is not the biggest of rivers, but some of its stretches more than make up for it with their unassuming charm, as it winds amongst overhanging trees, the scene occasionally broken by a flash of blue as a kingfisher streaks past. In flood the river is something else. I used to fish the pretty but hardly dynamic section by the bridge on the way into **ILMINSTER**, walking along the western bank towards the by-pass (A303). In late Summer a fight down heavily weeded banks to swims opposite trees which seemed ready at any moment to end their tremendously long life by finally slipping into the river, gave me the chance to spot individual chub before casting to try and tempt them out from under the tree roots, where their home had a ceiling as intricate and decorative as that of many a parish church.

In winter flood the banks are virtually bare, and quiet pools that a few hours ago were ten or fifteen feet below the main path become brown swirling whirlpools which seem ready to tear the very fields down and carry them onwards. Fishing at these times is pointless, but just watching is quite fascinating. The changes are swift, and almost unbelievably dramatic.

Ilminster is a typical Somerset market town, with a square which makes a good meeting place but an awful bottle-neck through which to drive (though it is easily by-passed). The church is set splendidly halfway down the main hill into the town, its grounds ending at SILVER STREET, the main shopping road through which the Autumn Carnival has its route (see Chapter Three: Bridgwater). From here the sparse clump of trees at the top of the other hill protecting the town stand out clearly, and they are part of the HERNE HILL NATURE TRAIL (01460 52149), accessible from what is left of the Ilminster Canal by the main recreation fields. Amongst all the clogged weed of this short stretch of water there are also some nice carp and a good shoal of roach. There are some lovely ancient trees on the Trail, as well as the chance to see wildlife ranging from the nuthatch and woodpecker to the tiny Pipistrelle bat, depending on your luck and timing. From here you can also see across towards the next town we are going to visit.

CHARD (Tourist Information 01460 67463) is the centre of another community which revels in the lights and sounds of the annual Carnival. This is a very different place to Ilminster though. Chard's main street is straight, a hill lined with shops and a particularly contentious modern sculpture. The Georgian Guildhall catches the eye and shows that this unspectacular town has some age, but your gaze will inevitably return to the strange bronze coloured ball covered with handprints and other symbols, and the stream of water which runs down the hill, quietly diverted between new, but open brickwork beside it.

Local opinion is divided about the merits of this recent addition, to say the least. With a wry smile you may hear it referred to as a 'giant Malteser with a Walnut Whip', but it actually commemorates several of the things that make this place of greater historical significance than might first appear. It celebrates industry, not much of which can be seen from the High Street. But take a walk down to the industrialised areas at the bottom of the town and you will be surprised.

Some of the modern products made here are not very glamorous, but Chard has had its inventors, and still has a reputation for excellent engineering. The most celebrated of the imaginative among them was John Stringfellow. He is the reason for the town sign which cheerily declares that you are now in 'Chard, the Home of Powered Flight.' CHARD MUSEUM (01460 654091) towards the top of the High Street tells of his 1847 aeroplane which was exhibited at the Crystal Palace in 1868. Lack of an appropriately refined fuel meant that he remained a man unfortunate to be ahead of his time. Artificial limbs were the other benefit to the wider populace developed here by James Gillingham, whose story is also in the museum.

While the mill on BODEN STREET in the middle of the town is no longer working, HORNSBURY MILL (01460 63317) has a two hundred year old working water mill which you can watch from the restaurant. If you want to see some trout dance in the air for pellets of food, then the lakes here are the place, and those fish must feed well judging by the way they seem to grow each year.

There are some really delightful villages all around Chard. **CRICKET ST THOMAS** itself is overshadowed by an attraction that has undergone a varied recent history. CRICKET ST THOMAS WILDLIFE PARK (01460 30755) is famous for being the location of television's 'To the Manor Born'. The house is not open to the public, but the lakes and woodlands around the collection of animals and birds (including elephants, leopards, flamingoes etc) do make a lovely setting to explore.

Slightly further up this steep hill out of Chard towards Crewkerne the WINDWHISTLE GOLF CLUB (01460 30231) provides a way of testing the name of the hill from which it takes its name, as well as taking in some panoramic views ranging as far as Lyme Bay and the mountains of Wales.

Some of the villages are largely undiscovered; for instance it would be hard to find a prettier and more quaintly set church than that at **CHAFFCOMBE**. If you do find your way here from the main roads you will probably have passed the extremely picturesque CHARD RESERVOIR NATURE RESERVE (info 01460 63073 / 01935 462462 or 01460 63771 for fishing). With open country all around the water itself is surrounded by a band of woodlands, through which there is a two mile way marked walking route, along the reservoir's eastern edge. There are few places anywhere in the county more secluded and tranquil than this.

The road through **WADEFORD** into quiet but charming **COMBE ST NICHOLAS** has some dramatic corners, but to find the extremely remote **WAMBROOK**, surrounded by woodland, is a challenge in itself, as narrow lanes form a maze that can lead in various geometrical patterns, including the circle!

Towards Ilminster, PERRY'S CIDER MILLS (01460 52681) have thatched barns and a museum, as well a tremendous range of farmhouse ciders. Set in the village of **DOWLISH WAKE** this a beautiful place in the summer. A walk around the back of the Mills will take you to some rolling fields which I remember to have a large population of rabbits, their warren running along the line of the hedges. Watching them play in the twilight was a relaxing experience, and that was without any assistance from the fermented apple juice!

Take any turn off the main A358 between Ilminster and Taunton and you will find more tranquillity, as the land rises to the south and west to make the beginnings of the BLACK DOWN HILLS. This is a popular area for horse riding, and there are many good walks. Look out for the woodland paths around CASTLE NEROCHE, once five thousand acres of woodland inhabited in prehistoric times, and then used later as a hunting ground. There are still two thousand acres, which are particularly lovely in the russet glory of the Autumn months.

The BLACK DOWNS are rich, dark hills, and places such as **BLAGDON HILL** and **BUCKLAND ST MARY** have a mixture of farming and commuter communities, both of whom enjoy some glorious surroundings. Look too for an ancient Public House in **STAPLE FITZPAINE**, as THE GREYHOUND is part of my past, but that of very many others too, and when the log fire is roaring in the small 'A' bar frequented by the locals this is an almost timeless place. A little further to the west is the TAUNTON RACECOURSE (01823 337172) and also the TAUNTON VALE POLO CLUB (info 01278 782266) and the whole area is full of those who are riding horses in a less hurried manner.

WEST HATCH is famous locally for the RSPCA WEST HATCH WILDLIFE HOSPITAL (01823 480156), where many lives have been saved after everything from massive oil spillages to post Christmas abandonment. Across the main road and almost at the Motorway, **CREECH ST MICHAEL** is a good spot from which to fish the TAUNTON AND BRIDGWATER CANAL, while a bit further north the MAUNSEL CANAL CENTRE (01278 663160) has boats for day trips, hire, or shorter pleasure excursions.

Turning east again, HATCH COURT (01823 480120) is a splendid Palladian Mansion of Bath stone, making a direct contrast to BARRINGTON COURT (01460 41480) to the east. It is not really very far from **HATCH BEAUCHAMP** to **BARRINGTON**, but the two Houses are different in more than age and design. Barrington has some Gothic features, but generally a more down to earth look than Hatch, yet it is the colour of the two which is significant.

Although just that bit further east, Barrington falls into the area dominated by buildings of golden HAM STONE. Originating from nearby HAM HILL, this gives whole villages a colour equalled only by that of Cotswold gems such as Chipping Camden, but here there is thatch too. **HINTON ST GEORGE** is a particularly picturesque example, but **SOUTH PETHERTON, NORTON-SUB-HAMDON**, and **STOKE-SUB-HAMDON** as well as much that surrounds them positively glow yellow on a sunny day. Slightly further north, **MARTOCK** has some golden buildings form most of the centuries following the 13th, when its annual market and fair were first established. The TREASURER'S HOUSE is among the earliest of the survivors, while The MANOR HOUSE in Church Street shows that the Victorians too could make good use of the local material.

Ham Stone Cottages, Hinton St George

HAM HILL COUNTRY PARK (01935 75272, extn: 2502 for info.) can get quite crowded at its centre in the summer, as walkers climb to take in air and views, to fly kites, or just to join the throng. This is an unusual place, where the erosion of softer areas by nature and quarrying has left a landscape of dunes and crumbling hills more like a sea shore than an inland summit. A walk through the woods or to the eccentrically shaped 18th century folly tower on ST MICHAEL'S HILL, formerly the site of Montacute Castle, will take you away from some of the crowds, and reward you with views for many a mile.

Prominent in these is nearby **MONTACUTE**. Another place of crumbling, dusty yellow, this looks, feels and is positively archaic, but away from the town it is MONTACUTE HOUSE which dominates the horizon. Both this and nearby, but smaller, TINTINHULL HOUSE show that Ham Stone can work just as well on a grander scale than the terraces of Montacute itself. Montacute House is largely sixteenth century, with Elizabethan and Jacobean furniture and art, and its gardens are also open to the public. A huge 'H' of a building, it is contrasted by a more manageable homestead at **TINTINHULL**. There are only four acres of gardens here in comparison to the 300 at Montacute, but they are as pretty as anything you will find in the larger of the two National Trust properties.

Montacute itself was home to a legendary cross, whose healing properties allegedly once cured the Saxon King Harold's paralysis. THE BOROUGH and BISHOPSTON STREET look so completely old that it is easy to believe that some other magic has been at work here, especially as in the middle of the day there are still times when not a single car passes through the centre, for a period long enough for you to become used to a quiet probably greater than that prevailing two to three hundred years ago when these houses were built. Montacute also has a TV AND RADIO MUSEUM (01935 823024) in South Street.

YEOVIL (Tourist Information 01935 71279), like Taunton, has grown rapidly in recent times, and is not the out of the way place you might imagine. It's most famous industry is the manufacture of helicopters at WESTLANDS, made infamous in the politics of a few years ago. With a large central shopping area, including the pedestrianised QUEDAM CENTRE, and facilities such as cinema and theatre (The OCTAGON THEATRE 01935 422884), this is a thriving town. Some of its industries have been here much longer than Westlands, and there has been gloving and tanning at Yeovil since the 14th century. The MUSEUM OF SOUTH SOMERSET (01935 424774) explores local history from its very beginnings.

Despite the modernity of much of Yeovil (its population first rocketed after the railway arrived in 1853) what surrounds it is as unspoilt in other directions as to the west at Montacute. The YEOVIL TOWN TRAIL walk (Tourist Information for details) will take you out as far as the NINESPRINGS COUNTRY PARK, with 40 acres of wooded valleys, grottos, springs and lakes, but there is much more only a little further away from the centre. To the south the roads become empty and peaceful almost as soon as you leave the very centre of the town heading for **BARWICK** and **STOFORD** past Yeovil Junction Railway Station. Around BARWICK HOUSE are some intriguingly named 19th century follies such as the FISH TOWER and JACK THE TREACLE EATER. The latter consists of a spire perched over an uneven Gothic 'umbrello' and is a very curious piece of work indeed. Further south, and on the Dorset border, you can try fishing or just a pleasant walk at the SUTTON BINGHAM RESERVOIR (01935 872389).

Yeovil is also the administrative centre for WILD WALKS (01935 462630) a series of guided informal walks covering much of mid and south Somerset. The town is also the starting and ending point for the one hundred mile circular SOUTH SOMERSET CYCLE ROUTE which has four stages going as far north as Somerton and Bruton, and as far west as Ilminster. You can hire a bicycle at the YEOVIL CYCLE CENTRE (01935 22000), or find out more about the route from Tourist Information if you are bringing your own machine.

CREWKERNE has a splendid 15th century perpendicular church with what looks like much more than its fair share of tall windows. Historically a cloth town, Crewkerne is an unspectacular but pleasant enough place in itself, but again has some great rural areas to explore around it. I can personally recommend the coarse and fly fishing lakes at **NORTH PERROTT**, while the golden Ham stone buildings of **EAST COKER** have an intriguing link with the sea. One of the long thatched houses belonged to William Dampier, who was one of the foremost navigators in the mapping of the Australian Ocean. His other more romantic claim to fame is that he was the one to rescue Alexander Selkirk from his desert island, the inspiration for Defoe's fictional

Robinson Crusoe. **MERRIOTT**'s main claim to fame is that the sails for Nelson's flagship 'The Victory' were made here.

North of Yeovil the attractions have a more modern slant. The FLEET AIR ARM MUSEUM (01935 840565) at RNAS YEOVILTON, near **ILCHESTER** is one of the major aviation museums of the world, with a focus on naval aircraft. There are planes from both World Wars as well as more modern exhibits. Further along the A303, at **SPARKFORD**, the HAYNES MOTOR MUSEUM (01963 440804) has everything from a 1931 DUESENBERG to a SINCLAIR C5 among its more than three hundred vehicles.

You were promised another meeting with King Arthur before we leave Somerset and although these stretches of the A303 look anything but romantic, this area is known to some as CAMELOT, and the castle was supposed to have been at the site of the earthworks of CADBURY CASTLE. Other places have claimed Camelot as well, Cornwall and Wales to name but two. There were certainly some early fortifications at Cadbury, probably from the sixth century, and the outlines of a great hall have been found, but our mythical hero is as elusive here as everywhere else when it comes to hard facts.

By the time you have reached **WINCANTON** (Tourist Information 01963 34063) King Arthur and his rural domain might seem some way behind you. Almost into Wiltshire, you are now indisputably on the main route towards London. But Wincanton itself is another of Somerset's thriving market towns, far enough from the main road to keep its character. Its most famous attraction is of course the WINCANTON RACECOURSE (01963 32344), which is thought to have been the home of some of the very first steeple chases. The town also abounds in old Coaching Inns, for it has long been on the main routes from east to west, as a popular staging post, half way between London and Plymouth. Wincanton also has a nine hole GOLF COURSE (01963 34604) which is open to guests all year, except for race days.

After this last reminder of what Somerset life is like now, it is time to go back and visit one place that has deliberately been left until last. **WESTONZOYLAND** has another of the Pumping Stations used to keep the Levels free of surface water, with an exhibition of 19th century steam engines, but this is not why we have come here now. This typically peaceful Somerset village, with a lovely church, was the nearest habitation to the final battle fought on English soil. The Duke of Monmouth's short lived rebellion against James II ended here one night in 1685, with the BATTLE OF SEDGEMOOR.

If you look carefully you will find a signpost pointing 'To the Battlefield', which is now largely featureless pastureland. Somehow this seems appropriate, for the battle was fought to remove a King who then fell from power just three years later. The more permanent BURTON PYNSENT monument is to the east near **CURRY RIVEL**.

The Duke's night-time ambush from Bridgwater upon the advancing forces of the King was a failure, only sixteen of the King's soldiers received burial here where they fell, as opposed to 300 or so of the rebels; and of course this was just the start. The reprisals have become more famous than the battle, as everywhere from Chard to Shepton Mallet, Lyme Regis to Dorchester lost men and women to the Bloody Assizes of Judge Jeffries. Isn't it ironic that if we can count King Alfred's excursion to Ethandun from neighbouring Athelney as the first truly English force at war on its own soil, then in a way this was the last? All in such a quiet area, seemingly at danger only from floodwaters. Yet even without the legendary stories of King Arthur, Central and Southern Somerset are steeped in more than their share of dramatic history.

BERYL
Wells
Somerset
BA5 3JP

Tel: 01749 678738

Reccomended 'Karen Brown in America'
3 Crowns Highly Commended ETB.
Wolsey Lodges Johansens Guide

Situated just one mile from Wells the smallest Cathedral City in England, 'Beryl' is a gem in a perfect setting, recommended by everyone who has had the good fortune to stay there. It is a small country mansion built in the gothic revival style, containing many interesting architectural and decorative features of its period. It is furnished charmingly and with antiques and other nice pieces with the emphasis on comfort. The house started in 1838 and completed in 1842 was built for a local lawyer and was subsequently used as a hunting lodge by Earl Mount Cashell, but since 1916 has been used as a private residence. Set in original park land of 13 acres with the Cathedral framed between trees completing one of the many vistas of the gardens, it is the home of Holly and Eddie Nowell into which they welcome and care for their guests in a delightfully relaxed and informal manner and at the same ensures that the house is both immaculate and well run. It is the ideal tranquil location for over night stays, West Country Touring, residential meetings or House Parties. There is an outdoor heated swimming pool open from May to September.

Beryl has all non-smoking bedrooms both on the first floor and second floor, some are double, some twin or four-poster rooms and there are single rooms. Every room has either bath, shower, toilet and basin ensuite or shower, toilet and basin ensuite. All the rooms have colour television, direct dial telephones and hostess trays, in fact all the accoutrements of luxury living. A chair lift is available from ground floor to first floor level. An excellent breakfast is served every day in the elegant dining room and a superb dinner is served by arrangement seated dinner party style around a perfectly polished tables, set with gleaming silver and polished glass. It makes for a great atmosphere and enhances the enjoyment of the perfectly cooked food.

There are many interesting and beautiful places to visit in the area including Wells Cathedral, Farleigh Castle, Glastonbury Abbey, The Roman Baths at Bath and many more architectural places. Longleat House, Stourhead, Montacute, Bowood and Wilton House are five of the most beautiful historical houses in the country.

USEFUL INFORMATION

- OPEN: All year
- WHEELCHAIR ACCESS: No
- GARDEN: Large & beautiful
- CREDIT CARDS: Yes
- ACCOMMODATION: Dbl./Twin & Four-posters ensuite
- RATES: Sgl from £50pn Dbl. From £65 p.n. for two

- DINING ROOM: Delicious, home-cooked
- VEGETARIAN: Upon request
- LICENSED: Yes
- CHILDREN: No

- PETS 2nd floor only

THE BOLTONS
SUMACH HOUSE
Neighbourne
Oakhill, Somerset
BA35BQ

Tel: 01761 840366
ETB Listed

Set in half an acre of beautifully maintained, split level garden with ample parking on the gravel drive, Sumach House stands within easy reach of the tourist 'honeypots'.. Owned by Bill and Jill Bolton, the old house has been skilfully and lovingly renovated in the thirty years they have been in residence. Bill is a talented coppersmith and builder and Jill, who is no mean carpenter, has a great eye for colour and decor and between them they have achieved a charming home, highlighting the interesting features such as the two staircases, the arch window and the natural stone wall built to roof level; all in keeping with the age of the property . Bill still works regularly in his workshop in which visitors are welcome to take a look at whatever he is currently making. Samples of his work and their son Zac's handmade glass is on show in the house. Neighbourne is a quiet hamlet in a pretty wooded valley, and because of its convenient situation between the Bristol/Yeovil A37 and the Bath A367 Shepton Mallet, the area affords a wide variety of pursuits, from peaceful walks in the wonderfully luxuriant unspoilt Somerset countryside, to the many gardens, ranging from Stourhead with it's magnificent 18th century landscaped garden with lake, temples and grottoes, to the fascinating private gardens that are open to the public on set days, to the more sophisticated pleasures/activities to be found in Bath with its magnificent Georgian architecture and Roman remains. Glastonbury where the ley lines meet and Joseph of Arimathea planted the crown of thorns, and Wells, the smallest city in the country with it's 13th century Cathedral. It is glorious and beautiful and well worth a visit.

Within the house there are two ensuite, spacious, family size bedrooms and one twin room with a glass panelled door opening on to the balcony with beautiful south views to Ashwick Church and beyond. This room has a bathroom opposite with a sunken bath and a shower. All rooms have television and basins, comfortable beds, duvets and matching curtains and covers. Breakfast is a sumptuous feast including home made bread, jams and marmalade. A light Continental breakfast is available and both vegetarian and Colic diets are catered for. Guests staying at Sumach House are welcome to have tea in the garden, under the willow tree or in the large sunny conservatory, a green oasis in which to relax after your days exertions. There are a large number of country inns close by, serving bar snacks to high quality Cordon bleu.
Most of all it is the friendliness and hospitality which makes Sumach such a good place to stay. Everyone is always welcome in the large country kitchen.

USEFUL INFORMATION

· OPEN: All year	· DINING ROOM: Excellent breakfast including home-made bread & preserves
· WHEELCHAIR ACCESS: Difficult	· VEGETARIAN: Yes + Celiac
· GARDEN: Yes, delightful	· LICENSED: No
· CREDIT CARDS: None taken	· CHILDREN: Welcome
· ACCOMMODATION: 2 ensuite large rooms	
· RATES: £25sgl & £40 dbl. High season 20% discount 3 nights or more	

BOND'S HOTEL & RESTAURANT
Ansford
Castle Cary
Somerset
BA7 7JP

Tel/Fax: 01963 350464

Recommended in all leading subjective guides

For many years Bond's Hotel and Restaurant has gained the approval of subjective guides and with good reason. Kevin and Yvonne Bonds attitude towards hotel-keeping is meticulous and caring and that is why so many people flock to their creeper clad listed Georgian house just off the A371, three hundred yards from Castle Cary station. In coaching days it was known as the Half Moon Inn and one is quite sure that today's travellers are just as happy to reach it as their weary predecessors must have been. True personal service sets the seal on guests well-being. Every room is charmingly furnished with comfortable sofas and large chairs clustered round the fireplace with the Grandfather clock ticking in the background in the smart salon-cum-bar. In the seven period bedrooms, the furnishing and drapes are perfect. Every room is ensuite and has colour television, direct dial telephone, a mini-bar and a hostess tray. The whole house is comfort personified and it is no wonder that there is an ever increasing number of people who want to take over the whole of Bonds for House parties. Kevin and Yvonne see food as one of the major strengths of good hotel-keeping. The reputation they have acquired over the years is phenomenal and the strange thing is that Yvonne, who cooks every day of the week, has had no formal training. She is instinctive in what she prepares and produces and the results are mouth-watering. For the last fourteen years she has risen early to cook delicious breakfasts which might include mango with yoghurt before Eggs Provencal baked and bathed in a rich tomato sauce, followed by nutty brown toast and bite-sized chocolate croissants, and every night splendid dinners unaided for 20 covers. She does take one week off at Christmas! The menu changes regularly and Kevin Bond changes the script on the chalked blackboard outside Bonds commenting at the same time on everything from cricket to politics. For dinner there is a choice of two menus, one for the day and one for the month. The food is very good, possibly more dinner party style than haute cuisine. The starters and main courses tempt and tease the palate and as for the puddings............!!
A thriving kitchen garden supplies fresh vegetables, fruit and herbs, and Kevin Bond has searched the local countryside for producers of quality food. The Bonds are especially proud of their range of English farmhouse cheeses.
Dining or staying at Bond's Hotel is an unforgettable experience.

USEFUL INFORMATION

- OPEN: All year except 1 week at Christmas
- WHEELCHAIR ACCESS: No
- GARDEN: Yes
- CREDIT CARDS: Visa/Mastercard
- ACCOMMODATION: 7 ensuite rooms
- RATES: Sgl from £41 Dbl. from £32

- RESTAURANT: Superb home-cooked fare Light lunches in Lounge
- VEGETARIAN: Always a choice
- NONSMOKING RESTAURANT
- LICENSED: Residential
- CHILDREN; Not under 8 years
- PETS: No

BOWLISH HOUSE
Wells Road
Shepton Mallet
Somerset
BA4 5JD

Tel/Fax: 01749 342022
http://www.theaa.co.uk/region8/5536.html

ETB 3 Crowns Highly Commended
Michelin Red M Good Food Guide 4 + Bottle

Bob and Linda Morley came to Bowlish House more than seven years ago with the intention of turning it into a memorable restaurant with rooms. Their success is now history and this stylish Georgian house is now synonymous with good food and hospitality. Whilst they are always happy to welcome visitors, Bowlish House has become a regular haunt for people living in the area who know that Linda, a talented cook will produce a fixed-price dinner menu that is adventurous without going over the top. In addition on the first Sunday of each month a popular four-course lunch is served. With a two hundred-strong wine list it would be difficult not to find something you will enjoy including a page of carefully chosen house recommendations, and which is affordable.

A typical menu might include Lentil and Apricot Soup with Cardamom, Spinach and Toasted Almond Soufflé Glazed with Cream and Cheese or a warm Chicken, Parsley and Thyme, Mousseline Sausage, with a Creamy Leek Sauce. The main courses are always accompanied by fresh seasonal vegetables loaded with natural flavour. Fillet of Sea Bass with a Basil Butter Sauce or Saddle of Lamb Roasted with Rosemary and Thyme and Herby Just might be your choice. There is a delectable selection of home-made desserts or cheese from the Fine Cheese Co. The whole is a well-balanced, delicious meal with a menu that changes daily.

Stay a night or two and you will have the opportunity to savour the food and the wine and at the same time explore this pleasing part of Somerset with its many places of interest including a number of National Trust Properties. There are three guest bedrooms, each ensuite, charmingly furnished and complete with colour television and hostess trays.

USEFUL INFORMATION

- OPEN: Closed 1wk Winter.
  1wk Spring Lunch Mon-Sat. · RESTAURANT: Delicious home-cooked fare
- WHEELCHAIR ACCESS: No · VEGETARIAN: Always a choice
- GARDEN: Yes · LICENSED: Restaurant Licence
- CREDIT CARDS : Visa/Master/AMEX · CHILDREN: Welcome
- ACCOMMODATION: 3 ensuite rooms · PETS: Yes, well behaved
- RATES: Sgl £48 B&B Dbl. £58 per room B&B

BROADVIEW GARDENS
East Crewkerne
Somerset
TA18 7AG

Tel/Fax: 01460 73424
E-mail: broadgdm@eurobell.co.uk
www.broadgdn.eurobell.co.uk

ETB 3 Crown De-Luxe.
AAQQQQQ Premier Selected
Which Good Hotel Guide and
Bed and Breakfast Guide. Michelin Guide

Broadview Gardens, just three hundred yards from Crewkerne town and with Bincombe Hill to the rear, is set in over an acre of terraced gardens, with all the bedrooms overlooking the gardens. It is an unusual Colonial bungalow built in an era of quality circa 1926 by the Doney family on their return from the colonies. The plot was carefully chosen and it faces south with extensive gardens which are a delight throughout the year. It is a comfortable home with a great relaxed feeling about it. The guest sitting room is of a unique design and overlooks the garden and water wheel to the North. This room also has a ceiling fan, Chinese carpets, antique side table, writing desk for the use of guests and a selection of mature plants. From the south facing sun porch with its netted roof and sun loving indoor plants, there are two stained glass doors which lead into the dining hall, with one large table where guests eat party style together. Fine Wedgwood China and lead crystal glasses enhance the elegance of the table setting. There are three well-appointed bedrooms either en suite or with a private bathroom opposite. Edwardian furniture enhances the comfort and elegance of the rooms which are all interior designed and matching. Lots of nice extras including bath robes and large bath towels, shower caps, hand cream, bath mix, shower gel and hair shampoo as well as colour television and a hospitality tray.

The owners Robert and Gillian Swann run the house themselves. Robert waits at table and mostly entertains the guests whilst Gillian greets guests on arrival and makes them au fait with the house. Cooking is a joint operation. Robert is a master at soup making and vegetarian dishes whilst Gillian prepares the roasts and the home-made desserts. Over the eleven years they have been here Robert has created the garden from a wilderness into the beautiful garden it is today on which everyone comments. The Swann's are an entertaining, welcoming couple who have been offering accommodation for about twenty five years and have many tales to tell of past places they have owned. This is a happy house and enjoyed by everyone who stays here.

USEFUL INFORMATION

- OPEN: All year
- WHEELCHAIR ACCESS: No
- GARDEN: Yes
- CREDIT CARDS: Visa/Master /Euro/Delta (plus 3% charge)
- ACCOMMODATION: 3 rooms ensuite
- RATES:£25-£28. Single occupancy of double room £25-£46

- DINING ROOM: Traditional English home-cooking
- VEGETARIAN: On request
- STRICTLY NON-SMOKING HOUSE
- LICENSED: No. Guests welcome to bring their own
- CHILDREN: Welcome
- PETS: By arrangement

THE CAT HEAD
Cat Street
Chiselborough
Somerset
TA14 6TR

Tel: 01935 881231

This lively, ivy covered Inn is well over a century old and through the years has acquired a contented atmosphere, no doubt born of the many happy drinkers who have frequented its welcoming bars. It is still the haunt of locals today and to their number has been added many visitors who enjoy the relaxed, friendly air which encompasses everyone who walks through the door. The features of yesteryear are still much in evidence including the old flagstone floors and the large traditional fireplace. It is not long since the Inn was acquired by new owners, Mr and Mrs Brian and Mr Fricker who have rapidly become popular with everyone. It is the Brians you will find behind the bar welcoming everyone and serving some of the best beer in Somerset. The garden of The Cat Head is delightful and to this is being added a patio. There is a Skittle Alley, a Pool Room and a Play Area.

Food is available every day of the week both in the Restaurant and from the Bar. The choice on both menus is good traditional fare, home-cooked and using as much local produce as possible. For those who do not have time to eat a full meal, Bar snacks include Ploughman's with crispy bread and generous portions of ham or cheese, freshly cut sandwiches and filled jacket potatoes, which are all readily available. The 2 guest rooms are simply, but comfortably furnished. Children are very welcome everywhere except in the Bar and there is wheelchair access to the Bar and Restaurant.

Easily found, The Cat Head is ideal for anyone wanting a meal after climbing Ham Hill or enjoying one of the many good walks in the area. Local walks are promoted in the Inn and guide packs are supplied for walkers. Yeovil and Crewkerne are five miles away and the old market town of Sherborne with its magnificent Abbey and two old castles is approximately nine miles off.

USEFUL INFORMATION

- OPEN: Mon-Sat 11-11pm
  Sun: 12-4pm 7-10.30pm
- WHEELCHAIR ACCESS: Yes
- GARDEN: Yes. Patio. Play area
- CREDIT CARDS: All major cards
- ACCOMMODATION: 2 rms not ensuite
- RATES: £15 pppn + Standard Rate VAT

- RESTAURANT: Traditional fare
- VEGETARIAN: Yes
- BAR FOOD: Daily Specials
- LICENSED: Yes
- CHILDREN: Yes but not in bar
- PETS: Yes

COXLEY VINEYARD
Coxley
Wells
Somerset
BA5 1RQ

Tel: 01749 670285
Fax: 01749 679708

ETB *** AA***

Unusual to find accommodation in the heart of an English vineyard and add to that a small charming hotel with a distinctly Mediterranean feel about it and you definitely have something out of the ordinary. Coxley Vineyard stands in four acres of vines in the village of Coxley just two miles from the historic cathedral city of Wells. Visitors find no shortage of things to do and interesting places to visit within easy reach. Wells Cathedral and Glastonbury Abbey and Tor are both within five minutes drive, while just a little further afield are the historic city of Bath, Cheddar Gorge and Caves, Wookey Hole, Stonehenge, Clarks Village, Longleat Safari Park, Weston-Super-Mare and Bristol.

The whole of the hotel is quietly and unpretentiously luxurious. Owned and run by Bill Jones and Anita England, together with their friendly, efficient staff, every effort is made to ensure the comfort and well-being of guests. It is an ideal spot for businessman wanting to stay somewhere away from a busy city but with easy access and for visitors wanting to enjoy a relaxed break, be pampered, well fed and certainly offered some exceptional wine. You can choose from one of the ten luxury bedrooms, all on ground floor level and all with en-suite facilities. For special occasions there are two four-poster rooms including one Bridal/Master room. Children are always welcome, and baby-monitoring and cots are provided. Coxley Vineyard can accommodate private functions, weddings and conferences and also offers short-break packages for private fishing and shooting. Bill is the owner of a Peat Works on the Somerset Levels and will be providing fishing and clay pigeon shooting as leisure facilities for hotel guests in the not too distant future.

Dining at Coxley Vineyard is a delightful experience in the refurbished restaurant which is open seven days a week both for lunch and dinner. The talented chef produces the best of modern and traditional English fare using the highest quality ingredients and as much fresh, local produce as possible. At both lunch and dinner there is either a la carte or table d'hôte. Naturally Coxley Vineyards products form part of the wine list. Delicious wines, they are renowned for their fruity flavour. Dining is enhanced in the summer when diners may choose to dine in the open air.

USEFUL INFORMATION

- OPEN: All year, all day
- WHEELCHAIR ACCESS: Yes
- GARDEN: Yes. Swimming Pool. Tennis courts nearing completion
- CREDIT CARDS : Visa/Master/Switch
- ACCOMMODATION: 10 ensuite
- RATES: Sgl from £45 Dbl. from £60 Child from £10

- RESTAURANT: Modern & traditional
- VEGETARIAN: Always a choice

- LICENSED: Full On
- CHILDREN: Very welcome
- PETS: No

FARTHINGS HOTEL
Hatch Beauchamp
NR Taunton
Somerset
TA3 6SG

Tel: 01823 480664
Fax: 01823 481118

2 Star 4 Crown Highly Commended

A quietly elegant and delightful hotel set in three acres of picturesque gardens, Farthings Hotel at Hatch Beauchamp is excellently situated for anyone wanting to stay in this historic part of Somerset either on business or pleasure. It is both an hotel and a restaurant. The restaurant is well known in the area for the quality and imagination of its cuisine and for the impeccable and friendly service. Farthings is jointly owned and managed by Jill and Eddie Sparkes and their daughter Kerry and her husband Eddie Tindall. It is treated very much as a home and this is the nice atmosphere that pervades the whole house. It is easy to get to Taunton from here and Bristol is not that far from Exeter either making it so easy for business people to slip away from crowded cities and enjoy the peace of Farthings. For visitors there is so much to do from walking in the Mendips to sampling the beauty of Wells magnificent cathedral, Glastonbury Abbey and many other places

Jill and Kerry are the chefs and they both have a natural flair for producing interesting, delicious food using top quality ingredients and as much local produce as possible. The menu changes regularly and always accounts for seasonal game and other things. There are three courses with at least five choices at every course and a separate vegetarian menu. The wine list is an exciting collection of over 30 wines from the New World and traditional.

Nine pretty bedrooms are available for guests furnished in a comfortable manner and all ensuite. There are five doubles and four twin-bedded rooms and each has direct dial telephone, television, hairdryers and tea and coffee making facilities.

USEFUL INFORMATION

- OPEN: All year
- WHEELCHAIR ACCESS: No
- GARDEN: Yes. Croquet
- CREDIT CARDS: All major cards
- ACCOMMODATION: 5dbl 4tw
  all ensuite
- RATES: £55pp.pn reduction
  for 3 & 4 nights
- A COMPLETELY NON-SMOKING HOTEL

- RESTAURANT: Imaginative 3 course menu
- VEGETARIAN: Full menu available
- BAR FOOD: Not applicable
- LICENSED: Residential & Restaurant

- CHILDREN: Welcome

- PETS: No

INFIELD HOUSE
36 Portway
Wells
Somerset BA52BN

Tel:01749 670989
Fax: 01749 679093

AA QQQQ

The first thing that strikes you about this Victorian three storey town house is its quiet, tranquil elegance which is apparent as soon as you walk through the front door. Richard and Heather Betton-Foster who became the owners over a year ago have lovingly created a beautiful home with period furnishing and decor and this they share with their guests making sure that everyone who stays is comfortable, warm and contented. People thoroughly enjoy staying here and find that it is very conveniently situated for all that the small, beautiful cathedral city of Wells has to offer with its architectural beauty, a priceless cathedral, the Bishop's Palace and the fascinating Market Square. The town boasts a well equipped leisure centre with a swimming pool, a public golf course is a short drive away and the whole area is excellent for walkers and cyclists. Attractions like Cheddar Gorge, Wookey Hole, the towns of Street, Bristol, Glastonbury and Bath are all easily reached.

Working on the basis that small is beautiful and enables Richard and Heather to give their guests personal attention, there are only three guest bedrooms. Two of them are doubles ensuite, one of which has a luxurious bathroom with bath , shower and bidet, the other overlooks the garden and woodlands beyond. The ensuite twin room at the front of the house, beautifully furnished and decorated as are all the rooms, has a charming button-backed chaise lounge matching the soft furnishings. All three bedrooms have television, clock radios, hairdryers and a hostess tray as well as a selection of books on the locality and attraction leaflets. The elegant dining room is perfectly appointed. The tables are laid with burgundy tablecloths and blue linen table napkins and mats. An a la carte menu is provided both at Breakfast and Dinner. The food is delicious, beautifully presented and imaginative including 5 vegetarian dishes. Infield House is not licensed but you are welcome to bring your own wine.

Short breaks out of season and a three night Christmas or New Year Break are proving very popular. The area has so much to offer that it is as good to stay here out of season as in the height of the summer; in fact many people prefer the quieter time.

USEFUL INFORMATION

- OPEN: All year
- WHEELCHAIR ACCESS: No
- GARDEN: Yes
- CREDIT CARDS: Visa/Master £1 surcharge
- ACCOMMODATION: 3 ensuite rms
- RATES: £24.50 pp 1 night £23. 2-4nights £21. 5+ nights

- DINING ROOM: A la Carte menu at Breakfast & Dinner
- VEGETARIAN: Yes
- LICENSED: No. BYO

- CHILDREN: At Discretion of owners
- PETS: Small dogs £2 per night

THE KINGS ARMS HOTEL & RESTAURANT
Montacute
Somerset
TA15 6UU

Tel: 01935 822513
Fax: 01935 826549

Montacute is a beautiful village in its own right and a fitting situation for The Kings Arms Hotel, an Elizabethan coaching inn. Built of Ham stone like so many of the local houses, it has mellowed beautifully over the years. An inn full of character and atmosphere, many of the original features still remain. There are natural stone walls, mullion windows and uneven floors. The bars, much frequented by local people, are welcoming places where one can just have a drink or in the Pickwick Bar enjoy lunch or supper from one of the extensive menus.

Montacute has one of the most notable stately homes in the area on its doorstep. Montacute House is a gem of Tudor architecture, decorated with tapestries, antique furniture, heraldic glass, plasterwork and panelling. Within easy reach are Brympton d'Evercy, Sherborne Castle and Abbey, Yeovilton Air Museum, Cricket St Thomas Wildlife Park and a Butterfly farm. The coast is only 10 miles away. With so many places to visit it makes The Kings Arms an ideal base for a holiday or a break. The hotel has five twin-bedded rooms and ten double rooms, one with a handsome four poster, all ensuite and charmingly decorated with soft colours and floral fabrics. All the rooms have direct dial telephones, television and a hostess tray.

The Abbey Room restaurant has become synonymous with good food and is a regular haunt for people living in the area. It specialises in traditional English food of the highest quality, cooked with a sure touch and beautifully presented. The a la carte menu includes many firm favourites and seasonal ones too with venison pie served in a port wine sauce, one of the most popular. A carefully chosen wine list complements the excellent food. Served by friendly, efficient staff, a meal here is memorable. In fact the service throughout The Kings Arms strives to make one feel welcome and comfortable.

USEFUL INFORMATION

- OPEN: All year Food: 12-2 & 7-9pm
- WHEELCHAIR ACCESS: Yes
- GARDEN: No
- CREDIT CARDS: Yes except Diners
- ACCOMMODATION: 15 ensuite rooms
- RATES: £53-59sgl B&B £69-75 dbl. £85 four poster

- RESTAURANT: A la carte Mon-Sat.
- VEGETARIAN: By prior arrangement
- BAR FOOD: Lunch & supper menu
- LICENSED: Full On
- CHILDREN: Welcome
- PETS: No

'LANA'
The Hollow
Westbury-sub-Mendip
NR Wells
Somerset
BA5 1HH

Tel: 01749 870635

Heather and Alan Crossey own 'Lana' a modern farmhouse in Westbury-sub-Mendip, a rural village sitting at the foot of the Mendip Hills midway between the small cathedral city of Wells and Cheddar, famous for its Gorge and Caves. This is good walking country and for the daring, potholing and caving are two pursuits. Glastonbury with its famous Tor renowned for its King Arthur Legends, the historic Somerset Levels, Wells with its beautiful cathedral, Taunton, Wedmore and many other places are within easy reach. It is a great place for a break; somewhere to relax and recharge your batteries. What strikes most people who stay here is the easy informality generated by Heather, an Irish lady, with a keen sense of humour and a genuine liking for the human race. She takes great pleasure in ensuring that her guests are comfortable, warm and well fed and will do anything in her power to enhance their stay. It is evident from the number of guests who return regularly that she succeeds admirably.

The house is furnished in a cheerful, tasteful, modern style with comfortable arm chairs and three dormer style bedrooms each with ensuite facilities and central heating. One of the two double rooms has an orthopaedic mattress. All the rooms have beautiful views and television, a refrigerator, hairdryer and that boon to the traveller, a generously supplied hostess tray. Heather's breakfasts are renowned. You start with fruit juice and cereals and then you are offered a choice of a full traditional English breakfast with sausages, bacon, egg, fried bread, beans, tomatoes and mushrooms. Poached and scrambled eggs are also available if you would prefer them. In fact you can choose whatever combination you most enjoy. What is always constant is Heather's home-made Irish bread - a memorable treat. Evening meals are not available but there are many good eateries within easy distance and Heather will happily point you in the right direction.

USEFUL INFORMATION

- OPEN: All year except 22nd-28th Dec inc.
- WHEELCHAIR ACCESS: No
- GARDEN: Yes
- CREDIT CARDS: None taken
- ACCOMMODATION: 2dbl 1tw all ensuite
- RATES: £16 pp low season £17.50 high season £5 single supplement

- DINING ROOM: Excellent breakfast. Home-made bread
- VEGETARIAN: With notification
- SMOKING IN CONSERVATORY OR PATIO
- LICENSED: No
- CHILDREN: Over 3 years
- PETS: Yes. Not in rooms

LANGFORD MANOR
Fivehead
Taunton,
Somerset
TA3 6PH

Tel: 01460 281674
Fax: 01400 281585

This lovely old, 13th-century Grade II* listed Manor house provides every guest with the peace, tranquillity and seclusion most of us long for and seldom find. It is set in 9 acres of gardens and grounds in which guests can enjoy the benefits of the formal gardens, including the croquet lawn, a tennis court, stream and pond with resident ducks and moorhens. They even make their own apple juice and cider from the orchards and serve the juice at breakfast. It really is a very special place and has lost none of its original character. The Tudor staircase, extensive Elizabethan panelling and magnificent mullion windows are superb to look at and a constant reminder of the age of the house. The owners, Peter and Fiona Willcox, have cleverly incorporated modern comforts into the house and every room is spacious and elegantly furnished.

The three elegantly furnished, ensuite double bedrooms are named after colours. The Green Room has a four poster and superb views with a triple aspect predominantly facing south over gardens and paddock. The Blue Room has a wrought iron Gothic bed and the Lilac Room a French half Tester bed. There is a small Nursery Room with 2 single beds but really only suitable for children. Teas-mades, Hair dryers and radio alarms as well as television are in the three double bedrooms. The Drawing Room with its full height mullion windows, large ham stone fireplace with a log fire in winter, a grand piano and knoll sofas is restful and welcoming and it is here that afternoon tea is served between 4.30pm and 5.30pm - a perfect meal, especially after a long journey or a day exploring the Somerset Levels which are steeped in history. Dinner, served in the Elizabethan panelled Dining Room, needs to be booked in advance and is served at 8pm. The food is delicious and much home grown produce is used by Fiona as she creates dishes which are memorable. Her breakfasts are also something guests look forward to. Freshly cooked to order, with several choices, fresh coffee, piping hot tea and not forgetting the apple juice - cider is not on offer!

To stay here is a privilege and add to that the fact that you are splendidly situated to reach the Cathedral Cities of Wells, Bath and Exeter and the Abbey towns of Sherborne and Glastonbury as well as the many stately homes and gardens including Montacute House and Barrington Court, Exmoor, the Quantocks and the Somerset Levels, there can be few better places to stay in Somerset.

USEFUL INFORMATION

· OPEN: All year except Christmas

· WHEELCHAIR ACCESS: No
· GARDEN: Yes. Tennis, Croquet
· CREDIT CARDS: None taken
· ACCOMMODATION:3 ensuite rooms
· RATES: £70 double£50 single includes B&B & Afternoon tea

· DINING ROOM; Excellent breakfast and dinner. Home grown produce
· VEGETARIAN: On request
· LICENSED: No
· CHILDREN; Over 14 years

Publishers note:- This establishment will not offer accommodation during 1999/2000.

THE LYNCH COUNTRY HOUSE
Somerton
Somerset
TA11 7PD

Tel: 01458 272316 Fax: 01458 272590

AA Premier Selected
QQQQQ Karen Brown guide,
Michelin, Which & Egon Ronay

The Lynch Country House is set in the heart of lush Somerset countryside on the edge of the delightful medieval market town of Somerton, the ancient capital of Wessex. This Grade II* listed house is surrounded by an idyllic landscape where two thousand and eight hundred trees have been planted to encourage a wildlife sanctuary. There is a lake which is the home of black swans, numerous exotic ducks and a variety of fish. The Lynch is a perfect base from which to explore a whole range of interesting places including stately homes, famous gardens, museums and other places. It is also an ideal area for walking, touring, hunting and fishing.

The house reflects the feeling of restful tranquillity that surrounds it. The interior has been lovingly restored and refurbished with antiques. It is intimate and very comfortable. The light airy breakfast room where you will be served a delicious, freshly cooked breakfast every morning, overlooks the grounds and lake. No evening meals but there are several places to eat locally, some within walking distance, to suit every taste and every pocket.

There are just five bedrooms, each with bathroom ensuite, colour television and direct dial telephone and each individually decorated and furnished. You may sleep in a room with a Victorian bedstead or in another which has a magnificent Georgian four-poster. Every room has its own character and charm. There is an abundance of magazines, maps, tourist guides etc. in all the bedrooms.

Nearby there is golf, fishing and riding and not far off places of interest such as Bath and Bristol, Cheddar Gorge, Wookey Hole, Dorchester, Glastonbury, Sherborne and Wells. Many Country Houses, including Barrington Court, Lytes Cary, Montacute House, Sherborne Castle, Stourhead House and Gardens and Tintinhull Manor. The Lynch is well situated for those wishing to visit schools at Bath, Bruton, Millfield, Sherborne, Taunton and Wells.

USEFUL INFORMATION

· OPEN: All year except Dec 25th & Dec26th	· DINING ROOM: Excellent breakfast. No evening meal
· WHEELCHAIR ACCESS: No	· VEGETARIAN: Yes
· GARDEN: Yes	· LICENSED: Yes.
· CREDIT CARDS: Master/Visa/AMEX	· CHILDREN: Well behaved
· ACCOMMODATION: 5 ensuite rooms	· PETS: No
· RATES: Dbl/tw from £49-£75 Sgl from £45-£53	

MIDDLEWICK FARM HOLIDAY COTTAGES
Self catering and Bed & Breakfast
Wick
Glastonbury
Somerset
BA6 8JW

Tel/Fax: 01458 832351

ETB 4 keys self catering ETB 2 crowns B&B

Middlewick Farm set in twenty acres, is an early 17th century Grade II Listed farmstead in which Avril Coles, who owns it with her husband Roy, grew up and is the third generation of her family to own it. It is situated in the Mendip area which offers a wonderful blend of history, legend and scenery which together with the Somerset Levels, makes it an ideal base for a holiday or short break at any time of the year. The atmosphere is charming, relaxed and informal and the accommodation second to none.

There is so much to see and do. Wells, the smallest cathedral city in the country is five miles away. Glastonbury is a mere two and three quarter miles. Bath is 23 miles. Some splendid caves are at nearby Wookey Hole and Cheddar, while the sea at Weston-Super-Mare is half an hour's drive.

There are eight attractively named self-catering cottages situated around a courtyard with lawns and garden, sleeping anything from two to six people with a total of thirty people altogether. Every cottage is beautifully appointed and Avril and Roy have painstakingly restored and enhanced the buildings to provide accommodation that is both attractive and sympathetic to the glorious unspoilt countryside of mid-Somerset. Natural stone has been used and old timber in the interiors which are a happy blend of old world charm and country-style decor. Views from the cottages stretch fifteen miles to the Mendip Hills and Cheddar Gorge. There is a luxury indoor swimming pool at the farm. In Meadow Barn which is for Bed and Breakfast there are three en-suite rooms, two of which are double and the third a family room. The same style of furnishing has been used here as well and the result is delightful. All three rooms are en-suite and have television and tea and coffee making facilities. A true farmhouse breakfast is served every morning in the conservatory for people staying in Meadow Barn It is a memorable meal and one which will make sure you set off on your travels or explorations well sustained. Vegetarian breakfasts are also available. Evening meals can be arranged by booking in advance if required, although if you would rather go out the Coles will happily point you in the direction of good pubs and eateries.

USEFUL INFORMATION

· OPEN: All year

· WHEELCHAIR ACCESS: Yes
· GARDEN: Yes
· CREDIT CARDS: None taken
· ACCOMMODATION: B&B 3 ensuite
rooms Self-catering 8 cottages sleeping from 2-6 people
· RATES: B&B From £18.50-£24 pppn. Cottages from £180 -£535

· DINING ROOM: Excellent Breakfast for Bed and Breakfast guests
· VEGETARIAN: Yes
· LICENSED: No
· CHILDREN: Welcome

THE MINERS ARMS
Priddy
NR Wells
Somerset
BA5 3DB

Tel: 01749 870217

Priddy can lay claim to two things - and a lot more, no doubt, but in this instance we are talking about the two thousand years of lead mining which came to an end in 1900 and The Miners Arms, an inn since the early 1800's standing at a turnpike on the old Bristol -Wells road. A team of horses were kept at the inn to 'Double Head' the tiring coach horses as they climbed the hill. The inn would have been welcoming and hospitable then and this tradition is carried on admirably by the present landlords, Bob and Pat Reynolds. There are many things one can do around the inn; walk on the Mendips, cycle on the West Country Way, go horse riding, gliding or fishing. Within eight miles you can visit Cheddar Gorge and Caves, Wookey Hole Caves and the beautiful, man made Chew Valley Lake. Wells, the smallest cathedral city in England is almost on the doorstep and provides the visitor with hour of pleasure. The incomparable city of Bath is no distance, Taunton, the county town of Somerset is a brilliant shopping area. Glastonbury with its myths and legends is easily reached.

Apart from serving good ale, The Miners Arms is known for its food. You can dine here in comfort and in the certain knowledge that the menu will offer something to tempt your taste buds. The charming, non-smoking restaurant, with its low ceilings and glowing fire is a relaxed place in which to enjoy a meal. Pat Reynolds is the experienced and talented chef whilst Bob's love of wine is apparent in the list which includes 60 wines from around the world. There are always 9 starters on the menu including Mendip Snails, Tomato & Rosemary Soup or Crispy Prawn Brochettes. The Main Course offers Breast of Duck with a Peach Sauce or the House Speciality Priddy Oggy with Cider Sauce (Pork tenderloin, smoked pork and herbs wrapped in cheese pastry), and much more.. Vegetarians might choose Spinach and Mushroom Lasagne. The desserts are tempting and for cheese lovers, the board has an excellent selection.

If you would like to stay a night or two, The Miners Arms has three ensuite guest rooms; one twin-bedded room and two doubles. Attractively furnished, the rooms, like the rest of the inn, are warm, comfortable and complete with television and a hostess tray. Breakfast is a substantial, delicious meal with choices and will certainly set you up for the day's exploring.

USEFUL INFORMATION

- OPEN: All year
- WHEELCHAIR ACCESS: Yes
- GARDEN: Yes
- CREDIT CARDS: Visa/Master/Diners/AMEX
- ACCOMMODATION: 3 ensuite rooms
- RATES: £22pp p.n. B&B

- RESTAURANT: Delicious, innovative menu
- VEGETARIAN: Catered for
- BAR FOOD: No
- LICENSED: Full On
- CHILDREN: Well behaved
- PETS: By arrangement. Not in restaurant

No.3.
3 Magdalene Street
Glastonbury
Somerset
BA6 9EW

Tel: 01458 832129
Fax: 01458 834227

ETB **** Highly Commended

Situated in what is probably the best position in Glastonbury, adjoining the Abbey ruins, Number Three is an attractive 18th century Georgian house with historic connections. It was once in the ownership of the Abbey ruins and was lived in by Bligh Bond who was excavating the Abbey ruins in 1912. Winston Churchill's mother, Mrs Randolph Churchill, also lived here. It has a great deal of atmosphere and charm and is furnished with fine antiques, lovely pictures and objets d'art. It is somewhere in which one can go to shut out 20th century life, very private and peaceful with a beautiful, completely walled garden. The owner Mrs Pat Redmond, conscious of the need for security today, has installed security gates and guests have their own tags for opening these gates.

No.3 has four luxuriously appointed guest rooms, each individually designed to a high standard. All the beds have linen sheets, direct dial telephones, colour television and a well supplied hostess tray. Breakfast, served the dining room, is an excellent Continental meal with fresh fruit salad, fruit compote, cereals, toast, hot brioche, croissants and preserves. There are no evening meals but Glastonbury and the surrounding area are full of good eateries to which the Redmond's will happily direct you.

Glastonbury is fascinating in its own right with the Abbey ruins, the Tor and the Chalice Wall and within easy reach there are a plethora of places to visit including the enchanting small cathedral city of Wells just 5 miles away, Cheddar Gorge, the caves and Wookey Hole nearby. Bath is twenty miles, Bristol twenty miles and Street two miles.

USEFUL INFORMATION

- OPEN: February-November
- WHEELCHAIR ACCESS: Unsuitable
- GARDEN: Yes
- CREDIT CARDS: Visa/Master /Euro/JCB/AMEX
- ACCOMMODATION: 4 ensuite rooms
- RATES: Sgl £50 Dbl. £70

- DINING ROOM: Continental Breakfast
- LICENSED: Restaurant Licence
- CHILDREN: Welcome

- PETS: No

THE OLD STAGECOACH INN
Station Road
Crewkerne
Somerset
TA18 8AL

Tel: 01460 72972

This is a delightful port of call for anyone visiting this part of Somerset. The Old Stagecoach Inn could not be better situated for people on business or leisure. It is within easy reach of so many places of interest including Montacute House and several other National Trust properties. The old Dorset market town of Sherborne with its wonderful Abbey is no distance away. The Dorset coast with its many beaches, golf courses which will please the most dedicated players, walks in beautiful countryside and Crewkerne itself is of great interest.

The Old Stagecoach is an old coaching inn built at the turn of the century and has retained its friendly atmosphere and charm. Much of this is down to the attitude of the owners David and Rachida Low who work very hard with their excellent staff, to ensure that people who come to the inn will always want to come again. In this they succeed admirably and you will find both local people and visitors returning regularly. There are thirteen ensuite chalets available, each well appointed with direct dial telephones, television and hospitality trays. Snooker players will enjoy a game in the snooker room where they are likely to be challenged by locals.

The Inn is renowned for its food both in the forty four cover restaurant and at the bar. The restaurant is strictly non-smoking and has an exciting array of dishes from a regularly changing menu. The skilled and talented chef is proud of his daily 'Specials' board which offers simple dishes like Beef and Vegetable Pie as well as a more sophisticated trio of Lamb Cutlets with Stilton Cheese and Celery Sauce or Venison Steak with Redcurrant and whisky sauce. The chef who is an expert on sauces is ably assisted by a 'sweet and cake' lady whose delectable desserts, gateaux etc., tempt just about everyone. Special Theme Nights are held during the year usually at weekends and range from French and Italian to Chinese and Country and Western. Whatever the theme they have a reputation for being great fun, a gourmet treat and above all, the price is right!

USEFUL INFORMATION

- OPEN: All year. Closed on Sunday evenings
- RESTAURANT Delicious Fare
- WHEELCHAIR ACCESS: Yes
- GARDEN: Yes.
- CREDIT CARDS: Visa/Master/Switch
- ACCOMMODATION: 13 ensuite chalets
- RATES: B&B £38 dbl £28 sgl
  Evening meal included in price Fri/Sat stay incl.

- BAR FOOD: Wide range
- VEGETARIAN: Good selection
- PETS: Yes
- LICENSED: Full On Licence
- CHILDREN: Welcome

THE OLD STORES
Westbury-sub-Mendip
NR. Wells
Somerset
BA5 1HA

Tel: 01749 870817
Fax: 01749 870980
E-mail.moglin@aol.com

2 Crowns Commended

One of the great advantages that people who have stayed at The Old Stores many times have found, is the fact that once they have parked their car on arrival, they really do not need it again during their stay, because there is so much to do and see right on the doorstep. The village pub just across the road from The Old Stores is a friendly local and serves real ale and imaginative dishes prepared from fresh ingredients in an acclaimed menu. The church behind the three hundred year old cottage which used to be the village stores, has Norman features and there is a wealth of history from the stone age to the present day within walking distance as well as many tourist attractions including Cheddar Gorge, Wookey Hole and the Cathedral City of Wells (England's smallest city). The coast, Bath and Bristol are within easy reach   Malcolm and Linda Mogford own this charming house and Malcolm has written a book of circular walks all starting from the garden gate.

The Old Stores still has many of its original features relating to its age and history. Every room reflects the past and much of the furniture is period pieces. The essence of the house is its warm friendliness and the real interest Linda and Malcom take in their guests. They are happy to help guests plan their day with the aid of the many local and natural history books available for their use. There are three guest rooms, 1 double ensuite, a twin ensuite and a double with a shared bathroom. They are furnished attractively with colour co-ordinated drapes and bed covers, comfortable beds and all are centrally heated. Each bedroom has a selection of books, television and a hostess tray. The comfortable Sitting Room has an open fire - marvellous for colder days, after an invigorating walk in the spectacular countryside.

Breakfast, served in the beamed Dining Room, is memorable. Always prepared to the wishes of guests it will always include fruit juice, fresh fruit and cereals, plenty of toast, croissants, hot rolls and preserves. The main course is freshly prepared and the outcome is both delicious and sustaining. It would be almost impossible not to relax and enjoy a break at The Old Stores.

USEFUL INFORMATION

- OPEN: All year
- WHEELCHAIR ACCESS: Not suitable
- GARDEN: Yes
- CREDIT CARDS: None taken
- ACCOMMODATION: 3 rooms 2 ensuite
- RATES: £17.50-£19 pppn B&B
  reduced rates for 2nd & subsequent nights. Children £13 depending on age

- DINING ROOM & separate guests' sitting room
- VEGETARIAN: & Vegan catered for
- LICENSED: No
- CHILDREN: Welcome
- PETS: Yes

THE PECKING MILL
A371
Evercreech,
NR Shepton Mallet
Somerset
BA4 6PG

Tel:- 01749 830336

RAC**AA ETB***Commended

This pretty, old world 16th century Inn has maintained many of its original features over the centuries and certainly the wonderful, welcoming atmosphere that has been growing over all those years. In the friendly and capable hands of Reg & Val Jenner the tradition of hospitality, good ale and good food is admirably maintained. You will find it on the A371 between Shepton Mallet and Castle Cary and close to the Royal Bath and West Showground.

The friendly bar reminds one of the age of the Inn with very low ceiling and locally quarried Blue Lias stone-walling. In the cooler weather a villiger glows in the big fireplace which itself carries relics of the past with horse brasses and gleaming copper pans. It is a bar where locals gather to enjoy the beer and chat over local topics. In the oak beamed restaurant with its open log fire, thirty six diners can sit comfortably, relaxed and ready to enjoy the extensive a la carte menu which includes many traditional favourites and specialises in Steak and fine wines. One can also enjoy a meal or a snack in the bar if time is short or you only want something light.

There are six attractively furnished ensuite bedrooms, five doubles and one single. Every room has pretty drapes and bed covers and is equipped with colour television, direct dial telephones, a hostess tray, hairdryer, trouser-press, clock/radio and central heating. An excellent, substantial breakfast is served every morning in the Breakfast Room and the Hotel has a private Lounge for residents for whom there is also car parking.

The Mendip District is Somerset at its best offering a wonderful blend of history and legend. There are enchanting towns and villages to explore and attractions to suit everyone - the magnificent Wells Cathedral, the mystical ruins of Glastonbury Abbey, the grandeur of Wookey Hole Caves and much more. It makes every reason for people visiting the area either on business or pleasure to use this fine old Inn as their base.

USEFUL INFORMATION

- OPEN: All year Rest: 12-2pm & 6.30-9.30
- CREDIT CARDS: All major cards
- ACCOMMODATION: 5dbl 1sgl all ensuite
- RATES: £46 dbl B&B £33 sgl B&B
- CHILDREN: By arrangement

- RESTAURANT: A la carte specialising in Steak and fine wines
- VEGETARIAN: Always a choice
- BAR FOOD: Good choice
- LICENSED: Full On
- PETS: By prior arrangement

STAG COTTAGE
17th Century Old World Tea Room & B&B
Fantley Lane
Zeals
Wiltshire
BA12 6NX

Tel/Fax: 01747 840458

What a pretty place Stag Cottage is - the sort of idyllic cottage one dreams of. Built in the 17th century, it was once three cottages belonging to Zeals Estate, now it stands contentedly with its straw thatched roof and just waits for people to visit. In summer the Tea Garden in front of the cottage draws a lot of visitors either on their way to or after a visit to the many fascinating places in the area. Stag Cottage is only one and a half miles from the National Trust's Stourhead with its wonderful landscaped gardens and a house that is home to the best collection of Chippendale furniture in the whole of England. Longleat Safari Park is 8 miles away and the old town of Shaftesbury with its much filmed Gold Hill, is 7 miles. It is only half an hour from Bath, Salisbury and Yeovil Fleet Air Arm Museum. You can play golf nearby, go to the races at Wincanton or enjoy the simple beauty of a country walk along the many footpaths.

Simple, beautifully cooked food is on offer with Clotted Cream Teas high on the list of favourites. The scones are always freshly baked and the cakes home-made. Scrambled eggs, Cheese, Beans or Sardines on Toast, Toasted Tea cakes and a wide variety of freshly cut sandwiches are part of the food available in the Tea Room. There are cots and high chairs as well as a baby sitting service. For those who would like to stay awhile and enjoy all that this lovely area has to offer, Marie and Peter Boxall who own and run Stag Cottage, have three guest rooms, two of which are ensuite and the third has its own Shower and Toilet room on the landing. Television, hairdryers and hostess trays are provided in all the rooms. All the rooms are charmingly furnished in a cottage style and have individual colour schemes. As one might expect Breakfast is a substantial and delicious meal. Children are especially welcome - Marie was once a Nanny and knows how to please small ones - for instance there are always colouring books and crayons readily available. Stag Cottage is a happy and contented place in which to stay and if you are just calling in for tea or a snack, it is somewhere you will always remember.

USEFUL INFORMATION

· OPEN: All year	· TEA ROOM: Excellent breakfast. Delicious home-made fare including Clotted Cream Teas, Home-made cakes
· WHEELCHAIR ACCESS: Tea-room only	· VEGETARIAN: Upon request
· GARDEN: Yes. Tea Garden	· LICENSED: No
· CREDIT CARDS: None taken	· CHILDREN: Very welcome
· ACCOMMODATION:3 rooms 2 ensuite 1 with separate Shower Room	
· PETS: By previous arrangement	· RATES: From £18pp B & B

TRUFFLES RESTAURANT
95 High Street
Bruton
Somerset
BA10 0AR

Tel/Fax: 01749 812255

2Rosettes AA

Truffles Restaurant is situated in the Saxon town of Bruton, one of the most fascinating places in Somerset with its narrow bridges and home to three private schools and still a centre of Education.. Once Truffles was 2 weavers cottages and part of the original monastic origins. It is such a pretty stone building with Virginia Creeper around the entrance, beautiful window boxes and planters with a profusion of colourful flowers.

The Restaurant is an oasis of tranquillity with just seven tables creating an intimate ambience in which to dine. The tables are perfectly appointed with crisp white linen and large wine glasses. It is smart and stylish with deep blues and gold soft furnishings. Gourmet evenings each month are always looked forward to with keen anticipation. Each month is different. July for example is Thai food and August and September, Lobster Dinners. On normal evenings the menu is a set one, Modern British in content, beautifully presented and using fresh seasonal vegetables. That Denise and Martin Bottrill have achieved a resounding success at Truffles speaks for itself and is evidenced by the fact that it is almost always necessary to book a table in advance. Sunday lunches with 3 courses at £13.95 is great value and combines traditional Sunday dishes with exciting dishes from the monthly menu. The accompanying wine list is comprehensive with well chosen wines from all around the world.

Either before or after a meal, a stroll through the narrow, overhanging streets of this enchanting town is super. The architecture is striking, the stone, mellow and the people of Bruton are welcoming.

USEFUL INFORMATION

- OPEN:Tues-Sat:7-12midnight Sun: 12-3pm
- WHEELCHAIR ACCESS: Yes
- GARDEN: No
- CREDIT CARDS: Visa/Master
- PETS: No

- RESTAURANT: Modern British +Gourmet evenings
- VEGETARIAN: Separate menu
- LICENSED: Restaurant
- CHILDREN: Over 8 years

THE WHITE HART HOTEL
Sadler Street
Wells, Somerset
Tel/Fax: 01749 672056

The charming cathedral city of Wells is home to the elegant White Hart Hotel in Sadlers Street, with views of the cathedral green. The Hotel was originally known as Hart's Head and was first described as an inn in 1497. It is thought to have been the Bishop's guest house. The present owner Peter Ayton has, during refurbishment, discovered many interesting features which have been sympathetically restored. There are thirteen en-suite rooms, with tea and coffee making facilities, colour TV and satellite channels. There is a function suite, overlooking the gothic spires, which holds up to sixty people and has every facility needed for business meetings and conferences. An ideal base for anyone touring Somerset with Wookey Hole and Caves, the City of Wells, Bath and Longleat all nearby. The dining room has an old world charm with its beamed ceilings and is the oldest original example of its kind left in this beautiful city. The menus are prepared by the Head Chef using local produce and are unusual but frequently traditional, including dishes using wild boar, game casserole, quail and venison. The a la carte menu is noted for its fish dishes and delightful desserts, all at very reasonable prices. The bars are cosy and intimate although less formal, the open log fires and exposed beams make you feel very welcome and you can enjoy traditional bar food in these charming surroundings.

USEFUL INFORMATION

- OPEN: 7.30 - 11.30pm
  Lunch 12-2pm Dinner 6-10pm
- WHEELCHAIR ACCESS: Yes
- GARDEN: No
- CREDIT CARDS: Visa/Access/AMEX/Switch
- ACCOMMODATION: 13 rooms All en-suite
- RATES; Dbl/Twin £70 prpn.B/B.
  Single £55 per night. B/B.
- SMOKING; Non-smoking rooms available.

- RESTAURANT: 25 Covers No smoking
- VEGETARIAN: 4-5 choices
- BAR FOOD: A la carte and table d'hôte
- LICENSED: Full on
- CHILDREN: Welcome

- PETS; Yes.

BELFIELD GUEST HOUSE
34 Charlton Road
Shepton Mallet
Somerset
BA4 5PA
Tel/Fax: 01749 344353

RAC Acclaimed ETB 2 Crowns
Belfield Guest House is a mature, grey stone house, standing back from the road in Shepton Mallet and only five minutes from the town centre. It is a well-cared for establishment owned and run by Bob Smith, a retired Army Caterer with hotel and fast food experience. He regards Belfield as his retirement home! Seeing what energy he puts into making it a comfortable and friendly place for his guests, one has to dismiss the idea of retirement! Every room is tastefully furnished and decorated. Each has television and a hostess tray plentifully supplied with coffee and tea. People come here regularly on business and find it a home-from-home and holiday makers rapidly feel at ease. A comfortable Lounge with Television is specially for guests and smoking is allowed in this room only. Breakfast served in the sunny dining room, is freshly cooked and to your order. Bob does not serve evening meals but Shepton Mallet is blessed with many good eateries. Shepton Mallett is the home of the Royal Bath & West Showground with shows, competitions and exhibitions all year round. Cheddar Gorge and Caves as well as Wookey Hole are within easy distance and many more entertaining and beautiful places for the visitor to explore.

USEFUL INFORMATION

- OPEN: Jan 1st-Dec 23rd
- WHEELCHAIR ACCESS: No
- GARDEN: No. Parking at front
- CREDIT CARDS: None taken
- ACCOMMODATION: 2sgl not ensuite 2tw, 1dbl, 1 Family all ensuite · PETS: No
- RATES: B&B £18 pp sgl £39.50 pp dbl.

- DINING ROOM: Traditional breakfast
- VEGETARIAN: If requested
- LICENSED: No
- CHILDREN: Over 8 years

THE BLACK SWAN
North Street
Langport, Somerset
TA10 9RQ

Tel: 01458 250355 Fax: 01458 253905

pullen@btinternet.co.uk

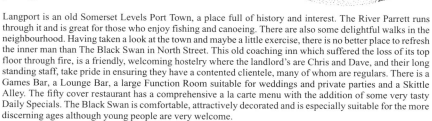

Langport is an old Somerset Levels Port Town, a place full of history and interest. The River Parrett runs through it and is great for those who enjoy fishing and canoeing. There are also some delightful walks in the neighbourhood. Having taken a look at the town and maybe a little exercise, there is no better place to refresh the inner man than The Black Swan in North Street. This old coaching inn which suffered the loss of its top floor through fire, is a friendly, welcoming hostelry where the landlord's are Chris and Dave, and their long standing staff, take pride in ensuring they have a contented clientele, many of whom are regulars. There is a Games Bar, a Lounge Bar, a large Function Room suitable for weddings and private parties and a Skittle Alley. The fifty cover restaurant has a comprehensive a la carte menu with the addition of some very tasty Daily Specials. The Black Swan is comfortable, attractively decorated and is especially suitable for the more discerning ages although young people are very welcome.

USEFUL INFORMATION

- OPEN: 11-2.30pm & 6-11pm
- WHEELCHAIR ACCESS:
- GARDEN: Yes
- CREDIT CARDS: All major cards
- CHILDREN: Welcome

- RESTAURANT: Comprehensive a la carte menu. Daily Specials
- VEGETARIAN: Catered for
- BAR FOOD: Wide range
- LICENSED: Full On
- PETS: No

BOX TREE HOUSE
Westbury-Sub-Mendip, Somerset   BA5 1HA
Tel: 01749 870777
E Mail: doug@willowsys.demon.co.uk
AA QQQQ

Box Tree House, on the A371 just three miles from Wells, lies at the mid-point between Wells and Cheddar. Ideal for the visitor who wants to explore this area from the glory of Wells with its 11th Century Cathedral and the oldest street in Europe, to the mysteries of the caves at Wookey Hole and Cheddar Gorge. Box Tree House is a refurbished 17th century farmhouse in which much of the original features have been retained including inglenook fireplaces, and an Adams fireplace in the visitor's sitting room. Caroline and Doug White are the and both of them clearly enjoy their guests and ensure they have a happy and memorable stay. Caroline has a stained glass workshop in the converted barn where she is delighted to show visitors her work. Doug, amongst his many talents, has a picture framing workshop adjacent to the stained glass. The three beautifully appointed guest rooms, two of which have private bathrooms and the third with ensuite shower also have hostess trays complete with coffee, tea, herbal teas and hot chocolate. The sitting and TV room is a great place to meet other guests. Two particularly nice touches are the welcoming tea and home-made cakes offered on arrival and the second is a great ice-breaker! A large world map on the sitting room wall waits for guests to put a pin in their own home town - a great conversation point. First class breakfast. No evening meal but there is an excellent pub next door with good home-made meals and an innovative chef.

USEFUL INFORMATION

- OPEN: All year
- WHEELCHAIR ACCESS: No
- GARDEN: Yes
- CREDIT CARDS: None taken
- ACCOMMODATION:1fm.1dbl 1tw ensuite or private bathroom

- DINING ROOM: Excellent breakfast. Home-made muffins & breads. No evening meals.
- VEGETARIAN: Catered for
- LICENSED: No
- CHILDREN: Welcome
- PETS: By arrangement
- RATES: £20pp B&B

THE CLOISTER RESTAURANT
West Cloister, Wells Cathedral
Wells   BA5 2PA
Tel/Fax: 01749 676543

The restaurant is set in the cloisters of Wells Cathedral, an architectural gem in its own right with a beautiful vaulted roof and fascinating historic memorials. Wells Cathedral, one of the finest in England, or indeed Europe, is somewhere that no-one should miss. The Cathedral contains many unusual and attractive architectural features, such as the Chapter House - the only one in an English cathedral which is 'upstairs'. The west front, containing nearly 300 carved stone figures, is world famous and much of the stone carving inside is equally fine, as are the embroidered panels in the quire.

Whether you have spent time in these beautiful surroundings or whether you come directly to the cathedral having explored Wells, there is one place you should make for and that is The Cloister Restaurant. Jenny Barnes has been the manager here since the restaurant opened in 1984 and with her supportive and enthusiastic team she provides a first class menu and service.

There is something for everyone amongst the many attractive dishes. Hot dishes of the day might well be Somerset chicken casserole or a spinach and cottage cheese lasagne. There are home-made quiches, freshly prepared salads, cooked meats and ploughman's etc. as well as some good desserts. Cakes, freshly baked scones and cream teas are available all day. Profits from the restaurant go exclusively to the upkeep of the cathedral. The restaurant closes for two weeks each year over Christmas and the New Year. Parties are catered for by prior arrangement.

USEFUL INFORMATION

- OPEN: Mon-Sat 10-5pm (4.30 Nov-Feb)
  Sun 12.30-5pm Closed Good Friday
  and two weeks over Christmas
- WHEELCHAIR ACCESS: Yes
- CREDIT CARDS: None taken
- CHILDREN: High Chairs Mother & Baby room nearby Small portions
- RESTAURANT: Excellent home-made fare
- VEGETARIAN: A choice of dishes
- LICENSED: Wine & Cider with meals

THE CROWN AT WELLS
The Market Place
Wells, Somerset
Tel: 01749 673457 Fax: 01749679792

Wells is, without doubt, one of England's treasures. No one comes here without experiencing the thrill of being among so much history and beauty. The Crown at Wells in the medieval market place, which is adjacent to the cathedral and the Bishop's Palace, is a delightful inn dating back to 1450 and was then a medieval coaching inn. You can feel the sense of history the moment you enter its doors.

Many famous people have been here over the centuries and William Penn, the founder of Pennsylvania, once preached to a crowded market place from one of the hotel bedrooms. Every room, every bar is full of character. If you choose to stay here you will find that four of the fifteen en-suite bedrooms have four posters; naturally they have every modern facility but it is all in keeping with the age of the building. This is a family run business with a charming old world appearance.

There is a private residents and diners bar. The Penn Bar and Eating House is open from ten in the morning until ten at night and serves light meals, morning coffee and afternoon teas. For residents there is an attractive lounge and in the summer the patio area is very popular for those who want to sit and enjoy the surroundings, have a drink or a meal.

USEFUL INFORMATION

- OPEN: All year 10am -11pm
- WHEELCHAIR ACCESS: Yes
- GARDEN: Patio/Terrace for eating & drinking
- CREDIT CARDS: Access/Visa/AMEX
- ACCOMMODATION: 15 rooms, 4 with 4 posters
- RATES: Sgl £35 Dbl./Twin £50 Four Poster £55
  (Prices per room + Continental Breakfast).
- RESTAURANT: Bistro style menu
- VEGETARIAN: 3-4 dishes
- BAR FOOD: Light meals
- LICENSED: Full on
- CHILDREN: Welcome
- SMOKING: Non-smoking rooms

FOUNTAIN INN & BOXERS RESTAURANT
1 St Thomas Street
Wells, Somerset
Tel: 01749 672317

Adrian and Sarah Lawrence have been the proprietors of this very nice establishment for seventeen years and have built up an enviable reputation for food and wine using only the very best of local produce. If you happen to love cheese you will be in your element; they have an award for their selection of West Country cheese. To accompany your cheese, what better than a fine bottle of wine from their great wine selection, of which they have received recognition winning the Mercer award.

The fountain is situated on the junction of the B3139 to Bath and A371 to Sheraton Mallet, just fifty yards from Wells Cathedral, surrounded by many beautiful buildings. After lunch what better pursuit than to wander around the moat to the Bishop's Palace.

The inn was built during the 16th century to house builders working on the Cathedral. Above the bar is Boxers Restaurant, attractively furnished with pine tables and Laura Ashley decor. The pub also has a function room which seats up to 30 people.

An extensive menu is available in both the bar and restaurant. There is a huge selection of delicious home-cooked food, vegetarian dishes and a children's menu, also vegan dishes on request. In addition to the regular menu, the chef's blackboard specials include tempting dishes; Magret Duckling, Venison steak in Cumberland sauce, Mussels or a whole Sea Bass are to name but a few. Sauces accompanying many of the dishes are very interesting and subtle, a little out of the ordinary and look superb.

USEFUL INFORMATION

- OPEN: Weekdays 10.30-2.30 & 6.00-11.00
  Sun 12.00-3.00 & 7.00-10.30
- WHEELCHAIR ACCESS: Yes
- GARDEN: No
- CREDIT CARDS: Visa/Access/AMEX
- CHILDREN: Welcome

- RESTAURANT: Anglo-French using local produce
- VEGETARIAN: 7 Choices
- BAR FOOD: Wide Range as Restaurant
- LICENSED: Full
- PETS: Guide Dogs Only

FRANKLYNS FARM
Chewton Mendip
Somerset   BA3 4NB

Tel/Fax: 01761 241372

2 Crowns Highly Commended

Within easy reach of Bath, Bristol, Cheddar, Wells, Glastonbury, Street, Wookey Hole and Stourhead Franklyns Farm at Chewton Mendip is perfect for anyone wanting a quiet, restful time, staying on a working farm. For those on holiday it provides a wonderful centre and for those on business in the area it provides a quiet retreat after a frenetic day. Set in the Mendip Hills, it has peaceful surroundings, an acre of garden plus a tennis court which you are welcome to use. Another attraction is the nearness of Chew Valleys famous Lake for fishing or boating and several golf courses close by. The ensuite double and twin bedrooms are charmingly appointed, furnished with pine furniture, spacious and have panoramic views. Both rooms have direct dial telephones, television and a hostess tray. Breakfast is memorable. You have the choice of a traditional English Breakfast or the simpler Continental. No evening meals but there are some lovely pubs within easy distance where you will be well fed at sensible prices. Franklyns Farm is just off the A39, on the B3114 Enborough Road. Carry on for about 3/4 mile and you will see Franklyn Farm on your right. There is a sign at the bottom of the drive.

USEFUL INFORMATION

- OPEN: All year
- WHEELCHAIR ACCESS: No
- GARDEN: Yes + Tennis Court
- CREDIT CARDS: None taken
- ACCOMMODATION: 1dbl.1tw ensuite
- RATES: B&B £18pppn Low Season £20pppn High season

- DINING ROOM: Traditional Farmhouse Breakfast or Continental
- VEGETARIAN: Catered for
- STRICTLY NON-SMOKING
- LICENSED: No

- CHILDREN: Welcome
- PETS: £2 a night

FROG STREET FARM
Beercrocombe, Taunton
Somerset   TA3 6AF
Tel/Fax: 01823 480430

Henry and Veronica Cole, the owners of this 15th century award winning, listed Somerset Longhouse, are involved in the world of National Hunt racing and training. They had a second in the Grand National and the Cheltenham Gold Cup and also have young horses and foals in the Stud. They welcome guests into their charming home which you reach down a 'No through road' ensuring that life is peaceful and restful. The Longhouse is surrounded by beautiful gardens. For anyone wanting to take a tranquil break and recharge their batteries, Frog Street Farm has to be the ideal place. There is nothing formal about life here but you will be extremely comfortable, sleep well and be well fed with the emphasis on local produce from the farm and garden. There are three guest rooms, each with a generously supplied hostess tray. Downstairs there is a restful lounge with television and a cheerful dining room in which you will be served a delicious, true farmhouse breakfast complete with free range eggs. Dinner is by arrangement and as Frog Farm is not licensed you are invited to bring your own wine. Vegetarians are catered for by arrangement. Frog Farm is not for children and pets are definitely not allowed. It is also a strictly non-smoking house. Beercrocombe is within easy access of Taunton. The coast is within striking distance and so is the beauty and wildness of Exmoor. Frog Farm is just the place to be based for a break.

USEFUL INFORMATION

- OPEN: All year
- WHEELCHAIR ACCESS: No
- GARDEN: Yes
- CREDIT CARDS: None taken
- ACCOMMODATION: 3 rooms
- RATES: £25 sgl £30 dbl. Reduction 4 days or more

- DINING ROOM: Good farmhouse breakfast Dinner by arrangement
- VEGETARIAN: By arrangement
- LICENSED: No. Bring your own
- CHILDREN: No
- PETS: No

THE GABLES GUEST HOUSE
High Street, East Chinnock
Yeovil, Somerset
BA22 9DR
Tel/Fax: 01935 862237

A happy home for three hundred years, the Gables Guest House situated between Yeovil and Crewkerne, opened its doors to visitors in 1935 and for almost three quarters of a century has been a welcoming haven. Lloyd and Gloria Jones have only been the owners for a short time but they have carried on the warm welcome of their predecessors and added many nice touches of their own for the additional comfort of their guests. They have five guest rooms, two double, two twin and a family room with a cot. Three of the rooms are ensuite with showers. They are all furnished in an attractive cottage style and each room has television and a beverage tray. A super breakfast is served and evening meals are available by arrangement. The Tea-room, which is part of The Gables, serves one of the best cream teas in Somerset. The South Somerset area is a good base for a holiday with opportunities of coast or country touring. There is fishing, sailing, walking on the many footpaths, three golf courses, many gardens National Trust properties and a host of other activities available close to The Gables.

USEFUL INFORMATION

- OPEN: All year except Xmas & New Year
- WHEELCHAIR ACCESS: Limited. 1 ground floor room. Access to Tea-room
- GARDEN: Yes, Cream teas
- CREDIT CARDS: None taken
- ACCOMMODATION: 5 rooms 3 ensuite
- RATES: B&B Ensuite £18pp   Standard £15pp

- DINING ROOM: Excellent breakfast. Evening meal by arrangement
- VEGETARIAN: Yes
- TEA ROOM: Cream teas 2.30-6pm
- LICENSED: No BYO
- CHILDREN: Welcome

THE LAMB AT WEARE
Lower Weare, Axbridge
Somerset   BS26 2JF

Tel/Fax: 01934 732384

This comfortable inn in Lower Weare close to Axbridge, is a popular place with visitors as well as locals who are regularly to be found at the bar enjoying the excellent beer and sometimes dining as well. However the greater number of people who come to eat here come from much further afield including a lot of visitors who have discovered the friendliness, hospitality and good, home-cooked fare on the menu. Hugh and Dee Evens have only been mine hosts here for the last three years or so but they have made a great impact. The locals readily accepted them, and their outgoing, warm personalities have made them firm favourites with the many people who cross the threshold of the Lamb at Weare. Bar food is always available with a traditional menu which includes sandwiches, toasts and a variety of fillings for jacket potatoes. But it is the main menu that is heartily approved of. Succulent steaks, cooked exactly as you requested, home-made pies and fresh fish are always on the menu as well as other tried and tested favourites. You will not only find the food is delicious, the wine list well chosen but above all you will discover that the Lamb at Weare is value for money.

USEFUL INFORMATION

- OPEN: 11.30-2.30pm & 6-11pm
- WHEELCHAIR ACCESS: Yes
- GARDEN: Large garden at rear
- CREDIT CARDS: All major cards
- CHILDREN: Welcome

- DININGAREA: Good home-cooked fare
- VEGETARIAN: Catered for
- BAR FOOD: Traditional
- LICENSED: Full On
- PETS: No

MARKET CROSS HOTEL
Church Street, Cheddar, Somerset
BS27 3RA - Tel:01934 742264
E Mail: afieldhouse@aol.com
AA QQ

This hotel in the centre of Cheddar, was built between 1780-90 and much remains today although substantial alterations were made in Victorian times and again in this century but nonetheless it has the atmosphere of centuries still within its sturdy walls. It is a friendly establishment owned and run by Anne Fieldhouse with a small team of helpers. The bar is small and cosy and consequently does not sell real ales but otherwise is extremely well-stocked. The menu in the dining room always offers two choices and is home-cooked using mainly traditional recipes. Pre-booking is required Sandwiches both toasted and un-toasted as well as other snacks are available in the bar. Vegetarians are catered for but advance warning is required for any other diet. There are three ensuite guest rooms, one double and two family rooms, and three standard rooms, a single, a twin and a double. All the rooms have TV and a hospitality tray. Market Cross Hotel, is a welcoming, unpretentious establishment and could not be better situated for visitors exploring Somerset and the mystery and magic of Cheddar Gorge and Wookey Hole as well as the small city of Wells with its superb 11th century cathedral and boasting the oldest street in Europe. Incomparable Bath is within easy reach and historic Bristol as well as a myriad of other exciting places.

USEFUL INFORMATION

- OPEN: All year
- WHEELCHAIR ACCESS: Possible
- GARDEN: Yes
- CREDIT CARDS: Visa/Master
- ACCOMMODATION: 1dbl 2 family
  all ensuite. 1sgl, 1tw, 1dbl standard
- RATES: From £21.50pp B&B 3 day breaks available Oct-May

- DINING ROOM: Set menu, home-cooked
- VEGETARIAN: Catered for
- BAR FOOD: Snacks, Sandwiches etc.
- LICENSED: Yes
- PETS: Guide dogs only
- CHILDREN: Welcome

THE ROSE & CROWN (Eli's)
Huish Episcopi, Langport
Somerset   TA10 9QT
Tel: 01458 250494

The Rose and Crown, known locally as Eli's is situated at Huish Episcopi near Langport. It was built in the early 1600's. The roof is thatched, there are gothic windows, flagstone floors and roses round the door. Eileen Pattered is the landlady and runs this unique pub with the assistance of her children Steve, Maureen and Trice. Eileen is now 75 and she carries on the tradition started by her grandfather who held the licence for 55 years and as a 'sitting tenant' bought the property from the Duke of Devonshire. When grandfather died his daughter and her husband, Eileen's mother and father Eli, took over the licence for another 55 years until his death in 1978. It was then that Eileen with her husband Jim took over and today she and her children welcome regulars and visitors in the time honoured manner. Eli's has no bar, nor has there ever been one. Regulars congregate in the cellar amongst the barrels and when the family are busy, they serve themselves. There is no electronic till, simply a wooden drawer so prices are to the nearest fivepence. The pub has an apple orchard where Eli used to make his own cider. Eileen remembers their pony Bob, being led around on a long bar in a circle providing power to work the Cider Press. Cider now comes from a local Cider Farm. Good wholesome, traditional food is available including Lamb Hot Pot and Steak and Ale Pie. The surrounding area has many fine walks and the river Parrett is a popular fishing place.

USEFUL INFORMATION

- OPEN: Mon-Thurs 11.30-2.30pm & 5.30-11pm
  Fri-Sat 11.30-11pm Sun: 12-10.30pm
- WHEELCHAIR ACCESS: Yes
- GARDEN: Yes
- CREDIT CARDS: None taken
- BAR FOOD: Good traditional fare
- VEGETARIAN: Always a choice
- LICENSED: Full On
- CHILDREN: Welcome

THE SLAB HOUSE INN
West Horrington
Wells, Somerset
BA5 3EQ

Tel/Fax: 01749 840310

Almost every newcomer to The Slab House Inn comments on its unusual name. It stems from the time of the 'Black Death' when a 3 mile quarantine was imposed around Wells. Cautious farmers and traders would leave food, drink and other produce on a large 'Slab' outside the inn for collection by the inhabitants of Wells. In the last decade Peter and Lynn Owen, the owners, have dedicated their lives to making The Slab House Inn one of the most renowned eating establishments in the area. Once you have been here you will discover how well they have succeeded. The menu is mouth watering, the dishes perfectly cooked and presented and the wine list chosen from around the world to complement the food. As winners of the 'Mendip in Bloom' competition for the last three years running, the two acres of garden and Sun Patio make it a pleasure to eat 'Al Fresco' in the summer, and in the winter there is nothing more conducive to ones well being than enjoying the old world charm in the bars complete with cosy log fires. Definitely an Inn not to be missed.

USEFUL INFORMATION

- OPEN: Mon-Sat: 11-3pm & 6-11pm
  Sun:12-3pm & 7-10.30pm
- WHEELCHAIR ACCESS: Yes + toilets
- GARDEN: Yes & Patio
- CREDIT CARDS: All major cards except AMEX
- Large non-smoking area in the restaurant
- PETS: Bar area only
- RESTAURANT: Superb food
  beautifully presented
- VEGETARIAN: Always a choice
- BAR FOOD: Wide range
- LICENSED: Full On
- CHILDREN: Welcome

THE WHITE HART INN
Old Coach Road
Cross, NR Axbridge
Somerset BS26 2EE
Tel. 01934 732260

The White Hart, an old 17th Century Coaching Inn, nestles at the foot of the southern slopes of the West Mendips and overlooking the Somerset Levels. It is a popular venue for a wide range of people; ramblers, cyclists and walkers; lovers of good food and wines - the pub featured briefly on television in November 1996 when it was held up as an exception to the rule of poor wines in pubs. You will find The White Hart just two hundred yards off the A38 Bristol to Bridgwater road. It is a typical, friendly, country village inn, retaining some of the old fashioned values and traditional pub games; pool, darts, table skittles etc. There is a comfortable Lounge Bar and a cosy non-smoking snug. In the summer the tranquil garden at the rear together with some roadside seating make pleasurable places to drink. A skittle alley and a secluded patio complete the facilities. The food is delicious and all home-made by two experienced and talented chefs. The menu is large and varied and the prices reasonable, ranging from bar snacks to haute cuisine. A wide selection of over forty wines is on offer; either by the glass or bottle. At least three draught real ales are available at any given time. Theme nights with regional specialities are held once a month and about every 5 weeks live music performances are held.

USEFUL INFORMATION

- OPEN: 12-3pm & 6-11pm (7-10.30 Sun)
- WHEELCHAIR ACCESS:
- GARDEN: Yes + Patio
- CREDIT CARDS: None taken
- CHILDREN: Welcome

- RESTAURANT: Excellent International Cuisine. Sunday Roast
- VEGETARIAN: Min of 4 dishes
- BAR FOOD: Wide range
- LICENSED: Full On
- PETS: Yes

THE WINE VAULTS
High Street, Shepton Mallet
Somerset   BA4 5AA

Tel: 01749 342436

This cheerful, friendly pub, attracts many people from far and wide. Built in the 18th century it has a great deal of character and many of the original features have been retained. You are welcome to eat at The Wine Vaults any day of the week either in the twenty four seat restaurant or in the bar. The menu is mainly traditional English with an emphasis on first class steaks and roasts. With a number of visitors just popping in here for a meal whilst they are travelling, attention is given by the owners Brian and Carol Blinman to the need to produce food quickly. Equally if you want to linger over lunch or dinner no one will rush you. In the Bar there is a wide choice of food including the Daily Specials. Simple, freshly cut and well-filled sandwiches, Ploughman's, Jacket Potatoes with a variety of fillings are always popular and the price is right! There is always a Vegetarian choice. For those wanting to break their journey or are inclined to stay a while and discover what this delightful part of Somerset has to offer, including Longleat with its Safari Park and the East Somerset Railways as well as great walking country in the Mendips, The Wine Vaults have three guest rooms, two of which are ensuite and the third is a single. Each room is furnished with pretty drapes, soft decor and pleasing antique furniture. Television and a hostess tray is provided in all three rooms.

USEFUL INFORMATION

- OPEN: All year 10.30-4pm & 6-11pm
- WHEELCHAIR ACCESS: In restaurant
- CREDIT CARDS: None taken
- ACCOMMODATION: 3rooms 2 ensuite
- RATES: £40dbl £20sgl Room only.
- CHILDREN: Over 5 years

- RESTAURANT: Home-cooked traditional fare
- VEGETARIAN: Catered for
- BAR FOOD: Wide range
- LICENSED: Full On
- Breakfast available if required.
- PETS: No

Applegates	Bradford On Avon	283
Beechfield House	Beanacre	284
Bell On The Common	Broughton Gifford	296
Bradford Old Mill	Bradford On Avon	285
Castle Inn	Castle Combe	286
Chilvester Hill House	Calne	287
Clench Farmhouse	Clench	296
Fishermans House	Mildenhall	297
Hermitage	Box	297
King John's Hunting Lodge	Lacock	298
Longhope Hotel	Melksham	288
Lucknam Park	Colerne	289
Midway Cottage	Farleigh Wick	298
Neston Country Inn	Neston	299
Priory Steps	Bradford On Avon	290
Shurnhold House	Shurnhold	291
Sign Of The Angel	Lacock	292
Three Horseshoes	Bradford On Avon	299
Toxique	Melksham	293
Whatley Manor	Malmesbury	294
White Hart	Ford	295
Wiltshire Kitchen	Devizes	300

Chapter Six:

The Old, the New and Raking for the Moon.

Like a great green pincushion holding just a few jewelled pins, there is plenty of space between the attractions in Wiltshire. A solid square of a county, whose barriers have altered less than most, it is unpretentious, straightforward, and beautiful.

The county does not have the greatest reputation as a place that must be visited. Tourists to the West Country head for Cornwall and Devon; they have heard of Dorset and Somerset too, but Wiltshire can be cut through on the M4 or A303 with the minimum of fuss. Yet this county has some of the most famous attractions in the whole of Britain. Many people who have never heard of Wiltshire know of Stonehenge, or Salisbury Cathedral.

Both of those are in the southern half, accessible from the A303. North Wiltshire is bisected by the M4, and this is all that many very temporary visitors will ever see of this area, as they are intent on making their way to or from London, Bristol or Wales. The road has brought growth to the county, and Swindon in particular, but it is quite amazing how close all these people pass to countryside and towns that for the trouble of driving a few extra miles would give them sights they would never forget.

Marlborough, Malmesbury, and Avebury, are just three of the places that will reward those who explore North Wiltshire with beauty, history and such individuality that they should never be neglected.

Wiltshire is known for being flat, how could it be otherwise in a county that includes the expanses of Salisbury Plain. A visit to **MALMESBURY** (Tourist Information 01666 823748) will put this generalisation in its place. A drive from the M4, along the A429 does take you through some level countryside, grazed by sheep, but as soon as you cross the river bridge into Malmesbury (passing the impressive but redundant SILK MILLS) the steep hill of the town centre becomes very evident.

Few towns have immediately impressed me with their elegant antiquity as much as Malmesbury. It is not a major centre of population, and exploration on foot is ideal. A walk up the hill will soon make you aware of this town's crowning glory. Yet MALMESBURY ABBEY (Abbey Office 01666 824226 / 823126) is not as imposing as it once was.

Malmesbury Abbey

Imagine walking up this slope to see a spire thirty feet taller than that at Salisbury Cathedral, making the building six times its present height! Someone must have been in the same High Street when the spire fell and the gilt ball which had looked over the town from its summit rolled unglamourously down towards the river. This was at the end of the 15th century, and by then there had been an abbey at Malmesbury for about eight hundred years. The original parts of the present day Abbey were built in the 12th century. Before that the building was made of wood, which may have made it slightly easier for the flying monk to scale. Elmer managed to fly (or maybe glide) two hundred yards from the roof using home made wings fastened to his hands and feet. This was in the year 1010, a long time before the Wright Brothers, but some distance from Icarus and Daedulus too!

Apparently there used to be a pub named after him, which was supposed to have been built at the point where he fell, but unfortunately it is no more. Perhaps Elmer's fame would have been the greater if he had been allowed to repeat his flight. He insisted that the initial error had been the lack of a tail, and that this would make a big difference, but as he had broken his legs the first time and made himself lame, no-one would listen. Think of him if you happen to see the opening sequence of 'Those Magnificent Men in Their Flying Machines', I must admit the tune was going through my head when I first heard the story.

The hill is a fairly demanding one, but there is a chance to rest at the top before entering the Abbey. What a shelter it is too, as the forty foot high MARKET CROSS dominates the end of the High Street. Flying arches, buttresses, castellations and a miniature spire, the 15th century carved exterior is really something to behold, and looks in good shape too. If you do choose to sit inside for a moment, look down at the worn surface of the stone.

Far from being a mere decoration, this structure was the centre of Malmesbury's life not so long ago, when men would wait here hoping to be hired for work in the local woollen industry. There were so many, and for so long, that they wore the very stone smooth. This seems fitting in a town which oozes antiquity from every building.

Sometimes you enter a building and are struck to silence, giving respect before you have even realised you are doing so. Malmesbury Abbey is such a place, the huge distance to the gorgeous vaulted ceiling made an even more impressive dimension by the foreshortening of the nave at the blank east wall. It looks an awful long way up, even without a spire.

If you ask one of the volunteer guides who are authorities on the history of the building, he or she will tell you that the enclosure of the partly ruined Abbey by this metre thick stone wall probably saved the structure in more ways than one. Apparently the Salisbury spire has the distinct advantage of being made of stone, whereas that of Malmesbury was of wood lined with lead. Do not try such a mixture now, unless you want to make an excellent lightning conductor! Storms weakened the spire, and eventually it came down, ruining much of the remainder of the building.

If the spire had survived another fifty years or so, the lead would have been a tremendous temptation to the looters who implemented the Dissolution of the Monasteries in 1539. What was left of the Abbey was dissolved, but only to become the Parish Church in 1541. The original huge edifice would have been too grand for this purpose, and an immense financial burden on the parishioners. It would probably have fallen into complete ruin instead. It was not until the end of the 19th century that the restoration proper took place, giving much of what you see today. Take a short climb up the narrow winding stone stairs to the PARVISE and you will see some incredible pictures of the Abbey before the work was completed. It really does not look like the same place. Also in the small collection are four splendid volumes of a 15th century manuscript bible.

If it is possible for a single building to be at once romantic and awe inspiring as well as very rugged, then this is the one. The Abbey has been a fortunate survivor, but the privilege is all ours in being able to explore it as it stands. Look for the carvings in the 12th century porch, as well as some lovely stained glass and the tomb of King Athelstan, grandson of King Alfred. It was Athelstan who commissioned the first Abbey on this site. The air is very still and restful in Malmesbury Abbey, and it will take you some time to find the urge to leave its walls.

The same king has given his name to the MALMESBURY ATHELSTAN MUSEUM (01666 822143). For a relatively small place, the town has had its share of famous locals, especially WILLIAM OF MALMESBURY, chronicler of the 12th century. He made the library at the Abbey so good that it is said the Pope borrowed from it. I suspect overdue fines were not charged.

Other aspects of Malmesbury's past are explored at the museum, and the history of local lace making is particularly interesting. In an area where the average male wage was not high, housewives and girls worked with skill and devotion to earn between 6d and 10d (old pence) per yard for material that was so splendid that it was used in the Princess Royal's trousseau in 1912.

More and more of the section of Wiltshire which is north of the M4 has been swallowed up by the growth of Swindon, but there is still enough room between Malmesbury and the metropolis for some countryside. The scenery of this area fits more with the common picture of Gloucestershire and the Cotswolds than that of 'flat' Wiltshire.

From the unspoilt meadow grassland of EMMETT HILL MEADOWS, with orchids and butterflies, to the dragonflies of RED LODGE POND in the BRAYDON FOREST, there are eight Nature Reserves of the WILTSHIRE WILDLIFE TRUST (01380 725670) crammed into this small corner of the county. You will need to contact them first to be sure of access.

It is fascinating to think what this area might be like if Swindon had not become such an important centre for the 19th century railway industry, and at **CRICKLADE**, **HIGHWORTH** (also built on a hilltop), and **PURTON** you can see three examples of north Wiltshire market towns which have grown much less dramatically.

Unlike Malmesbury Abbey, Cricklade's ST SAMPSONS CHURCH still has its tower, a magnificent Tudor effort which dominates the town and countryside around it. At the CRICKLADE MUSEUM (01793 750756) you can find out about local history from the Roman and Saxon eras (Cricklade was a Saxon 'burh' and King Alfred fought many battles in this area) as well as from more recent times. Agricultural history is featured at PURTON MUSEUM (01793 770567). Cricklade was the starting point for a journey which should gain legendary status, at least in my immediate family. Fifty odd years ago, just after the end of the war, my uncle set out with a companion to row to Westminster. His journey began at Cricklade, because it was the northernmost point at which the Thames was navigable. This was not a lazy pleasure cruise though, they went the entire distance by canoe. I wonder if a fortnight's holiday could be spent in the same way today?

To give you some idea of how much **SWINDON** (Tourist Information 01793 530328) has come to dominate this area, there are more than forty people living in the town and its suburbs to every one living in Malmesbury. There have been two bursts of population growth in Swindon, both directly effecting what you will find there today.

The first came after the momentous decision to make it the main junction for the operations of the GREAT WESTERN RAILWAY was made in 1831. New Swindon added forty thousand people to the meagre 1700 who lived in Old Swindon, and in the early 20th century it is believed that the GWR division here employed more people in one place than any other site in Europe. 17,000 were employed by GWR at its height, and work was so easy to come by in wartime Swindon that only restricted entry was allowed into the town for those looking for work in the 1940s.

By 1986 the railway yards were shut, but the second phase of Swindon's rapid growth was well underway. In the 1950s the town was made an overspill area for the population of London, and it has never looked back in terms of numbers of population. Today's Swindon has both the rows of houses built for the railway workers, but also the newer estates built for the 100,000 and more extra inhabitants it has gained in the last forty years or so. No wonder it can claim to be one of the fastest growing towns in Europe.

There could not be a greater contrast to Malmesbury. To get into the centre of Swindon you will have to negotiate miles of suburbs and seemingly innumerable roundabouts. There is no Abbey, or really any central place of historical relevance. But Swindon can offer you much that Malmesbury cannot.

This is the place to come to in Wiltshire for shopping and entertainment. Such a rapidly growing centre of population has had to adapt and learn quickly about the demands of its people. The main shopping precinct is comprehensive and spacious, as well as completely traffic free, with Regent Street and the Brunel Shopping Centre particularly impressive. In 1997 the GREAT WESTERN DESIGNER OUTLET VILLAGE opened in the old railway works, boasting more famous brand names in its one hundred shops than any other outlet village in Europe.

The WYVERN THEATRE (01793 524481) attracts many famous light entertainment acts, as well as orchestras and ballet companies, while the JOLLIFFE STUDIO on the same premises caters for the visual arts and crafts.

As well as the SWINDON MUSEUM AND ART GALLERY (01793 493188) there are also some more specific attractions for those interested in the history of the railways. The GREAT WESTERN RAILWAY MUSEUM (01793 466555) has five locomotives and tells the story of the founding of Swindon's first claim to fame by Isambard Kingdom Brunel.

Incidentally, you may wonder why Swindon, previously such a backwater, was chosen to be such an important centre for the new venture. It is said that it was precisely because there was not much here, unlike further south where the nobility had enough power behind their objections to save their estates from the new iron roads.

Next door to the GWR Museum in Faringdon Road is a Railwayman's cottage which has been recreated exactly as it would have stood a hundred years ago, though some fittings are still originals, such as the range and copper in the kitchen. This simple but effective idea is known as the RAILWAY VILLAGE MUSEUM (01793 466553). I have an uncle (the rower) who, as a child, lived in a house like this, as his father was a railway worker. Even now he is still very much aware of how much the GWR really meant to Swindon.

Security was what the railway offered, and a welfare system which he still enthuses about today. His childhood memories from before the Second World War are of a local community looked after by its employer, with excellent free libraries, regular social events, and a health service which was used as a blueprint for the NHS. Free medicines and hospital care were available at centralised locations, all for a contribution of 6d a week. Today Swindon is very different, but it is still able to offer work in an industrial centre, yet with easy access to some beautiful, much deserted countryside around it. You just have to go out a little further than you used to!

The Victorian railway worker in Faringdon Road would only have had a ten minute walk to his work, but if you follow in his tracks now you can find out about the history, architecture and archaeology of everywhere in the country at the GALLERY, part of the NATIONAL MONUMENTS RECORD CENTRE (01793 414794) situated in the centre of the old railway works (you may want to make some plans about what you are going to research, by seeing what they have to offer at http:// www.rchme.gov.uk).

If you want to see some older trains in action than those which now frequent Swindon, the SWINDON AND CRICKLADE RAILWAY (01793 771615) is at BLUNSDON STATION, just north west of Swindon itself. There is another collection of locomotives and memorabilia here, but with the considerable bonus of four miles of working track restored by local enthusiasts.

Nearer the M4 is the ancestral home of the Bolingbrokes, at the lovingly restored LYDIARD PARK (01793 770401). The house and furniture are mostly 18th century, and are on a grand scale. In direct contrast the neighbouring parish church of ST MARY is minute, but is so full of attractive monuments and features that it is equally worth a visit. Both are surrounded by 260 acres of accessible parklands.

What is left to explore above the M4 is an area of villages, varying in style from those in the north and west, which bear a definite Cotswold influence, to those in the east, which mark the humble beginnings of the River Thames. For an energetic approach there is a section of the WILTSHIRE CYCLEWAY which runs through Malmesbury (contact Chippenham Tourist Information). If you prefer a more pedestrian approach then there are golf courses in both **OAKSEY** (01666 577995) at the very northern tip of the county, and **BRINKWORTH** (01666 510277), which is south of the Braydon Forest.

Of course you will hear much about how Swindon has eaten into the countryside around it. My uncle's father bought a house in **STRATTON ST MARGARET** shortly before the Second World War, and this was a 'move to the country'. Already, during the war, the orchard and Market Garden at the back of his home were replaced with an airfield's landing strip, and when my uncle returned to the house recently an Industrial Estate stood where he had once been able to walk his dog along the small railway line from Swindon to Highworth. Only one train a day used to run in each direction, taking workers to and from Swindon, so the line was safe in between.

One last story typifies what has happened to this part of Wiltshire. From the back garden of this house you used to be able to see a tavern named 'The Plough'. Fifty years ago it was a place of little repute, being only large enough for half a dozen standing customers at a time. My uncle's father used to take his son there for a pint or two, and such an outing was known as a trip to 'the rat trap'. There is now a gleaming, comfortable inn standing in the very same place. Its name? The Rat Trap. So what was local colour has survived, but only through careful adaptation. This is still a comfortable area in which to live, and to visit, because the town planners have been careful with the expansion of Swindon. You can still appreciate the distant perspective of the Marlborough Downs from the flatter expanses of Swindon and its environs, with an essential line of green in between. It is still possible to drive to Chippenham or Cricklade in a short time, and through great scenery, just as you could then.

As much as the M4 is an arbitrary dividing line, it is a very real one. Before you cross it to explore a little further south, do not miss the corner of the Marlborough Downs which has been snipped off above it, where **LIDDINGTON, WANBOROUGH** and **BISHOPSTONE** helped to provide inspiration for RICHARD JEFFERIES, a local naturalist and novelist of the late 19th century. He used to walk into the hills to the south of his home at **COATE** in order to *"breathe a new air and to have a fresher aspiration"*.

The Marlborough Downs, even restricted as they are here by the border created by the motorway, still leave plenty of room for you to walk far enough to be able to echo his further sentiments:

> *"By the time I had reached the summit I had entirely forgotten the petty*
> *circumstances and annoyances of existence.*
> *I felt myself. I was utterly alone with the sun and the earth."*

There is a RICHARD JEFFERIES MUSEUM (01793 526161, Extn 3130) in the farmhouse in the village where he was born, and the COATE AGRICULTURAL MUSEUM is at nearby COATE WATER COUNTRY PARK.

Beware though, for there are mysterious goings on near Liddington. Both above and below the M4, this is a hotspot for mysterious CROP CIRCLES. If you have the chance to enter the name Liddington on an Internet Search Engine you will come up with dozens of articles and pictures about this phenomenon. They are mostly very recent too. If you see any intense looking couples wandering the fields with various devices, they maybe the same that a certain very European sounding doctor speaks about on one of these web reports, saying that a Dutch couple *"borrowed him"* a set of *"drowser's rods"*. The pictures show impressive designs, and I am not a cynic, but the whole subject does seem more than a little bizarre.

Before we get too involved with the mysteries of the downs, let's head west, crossing the motorway on the A429, heading for **CHIPPENHAM** (Tourist Information 01249 657733). So near to so many good things, the town centre of Chippenham is not perhaps as scenic as you might expect. Somehow it reminds me of a town from an old Western film, everything is very open, but looks a bit temporary, despite the fact that this is one of the oldest market towns in Wiltshire.

What does not look at all temporary is the River AVON, and the central bridge over it provides an opportunity to hand feed the ducks and swans just below you. Chippenham Tourist Information provide a couple of good leaflets outlining walks from and around the town, and the CHIPPENHAM AVON VALLEY WALK is definitely worth a look, especially if the season is right for the tree lined river to be reflecting both golds and greens from the leaves above. In one of the most attractive, half-timbered buildings of the town stands the YELDE HALL MUSEUM (01249 651488). This is at the top of the slope, in the Market Place, and features local social history.

The immediate temptation is to head east from Chippenham for the Downs, Calne and Marlborough, but turn first to the west, or you will miss another rewarding corner of the county. SHELDON MANOR (01249 653120) is just out of the town in this direction, and is the oldest inhabited Manor House in Wiltshire. There are no roped off sections here, and the gardens, with ancient yew trees, a specialist collection of old-fashioned roses and a water garden are as welcoming as the beautifully maintained interior of the 700 year old family home. The house is only open on certain days, so check first.

A little further west the village of **BIDDESTONE** with its duck pond and picturesque houses around the village green will give you an appetizer for one of Wiltshire's most famous villages, neighbouring **CASTLE COMBE**.

After being declared 'England's Prettiest Village' in 1962, only four years passed before Combe suffered an invasion from which many places would not have recovered. The BY BROOK, a quiet tributary of the Avon, suddenly had a jetty built alongside it, despite the fact that the sea is some seventeen miles away. All the television aerials were removed from the unusually pointed, steeply sloping roofs of the lovely cotswold stone cottages, and replaced with invisible shared wiring.

Many of the inhabitants were suddenly wearing much more make-up than usual as well, and the final indignity came when a handsome newcomer to the village started to talk to the local wildlife, which had incidentally gained some unlikely additions, such as a llama with two heads.

If you have not guessed yet, the occasion was not military, but the filming of 'Dr Doolittle', and many locals were paid to be 'extras'. Hollywood did not manage to ruin Castle Combe, but its increasing fame meant that visitors increased in number. Now you are asked to leave your car at the top of the shaded hollow in which the village lies, and take a scenic walk down between the trees to the honey coloured cottages below. The Market Cross and the splendour of ST ANDREWS CHURCH bear witness to Combe's first, much more distant, burst of popularity as a centre for the wool trade, although tourism is likely to remain its primary source of income from now on. The CASTLE COMBE MUSEUM (01249 782250) gives you a chance to find out more about both of its incarnations. It is a very beautiful village, and well worth the walk.

However, if walking is not your thing, then why not try a drive in a racing car instead! The CASTLE COMBE MOTOR RACING CIRCUIT (01249 782417) has a Racing School, as well as many events for spectators. The surroundings are somewhat different to those in the village though. There is also a CASTLE COMBE GOLF CLUB (01249 783101) which welcomes visitors only by prior arrangement.

Another, larger centre for the weaving industry was **CORSHAM** (Tourist Information 01249 714660), a short distance to the south. The first thing you will notice here is the stone, the town itself looks like it is made of nothing but stone. Fittingly the UNDERGROUND QUARRY (01249 716288) is just to the south of Corsham, where you can go down 159 steps to see how the Bath Stone has traditionally been mined at this site since 1810. The steps take a little longer to climb on the upwards trip.

Back in the town your appreciation of the row of 17th century Flemish Weavers' Cottages might have been increased by seeing the material from which they are built in its natural, underground setting.

The considerable splendour of CORSHAM COURT (01249 701610 / 701611) dominates the south east of the village. Lancelot 'Capability' Brown landscaped the grounds, but more unusually he also had a hand in the restoration of the building itself. The house has also been used for filming, more recently than Castle Combe though, as scenes from 'The Remains of the Day' starring Anthony Hopkins were shot here (the BBC and HTV have also used it for several recent drama productions).

Corsham Court

Inside the house the State Rooms hold a fabulous collection of paintings, bronzes, statues and furniture. This includes work by Rubens, Van Dyck, Adams and Chippendale. The art gallery is particularly spectacular, with the pattern of the plaster ceiling mirrored in the splendid Madrid carpet below.

Not all the interior of this massive grey stone mansion is open to the public, but it doesn't need to be when these rooms are presented so splendidly. In the same way it seems not to matter that the exterior of Corsham Court is the work of many different architects, each of whom has added something over the centuries. The resultant whole is a monument to the wealth of the clothiers of the 18th century, one of whom (Paul Methuen) had the present structure started to an Elizabethan design.

It seems almost odd to find some of these quite breathtaking houses out in the rural stretches of Wiltshire, but the setting can only help to improve our enjoyment of them. It is not surprising film makers seek out places like this instead of those in more cluttered city areas; Corsham Court looks like it has stepped out of a past that has little to do with tourists, towns and traffic.

Capability Brown was responsible for a couple of unusual features in the grounds which are bound to provoke your curiosity. The GOTHIC BATH HOUSE looks more like an over decorated gate-house, but was part of a medicinal rage for 'cold plunges' which later found its way to Weymouth with King George III.

You might well think thirty seconds is plenty of time in which to walk around a single tree, but you will struggle to beat the stop-watch in a half minute sprint around the Oriental Plane tree planted here by Brown, which now has a circumference of over 240 yards!

Corsham has a flat town centre, but with other impressive 17th and 18th century stone buildings blended into the shopping area, it is certainly not an ordinary place. Look in particular for the Almshouses and the Georgian Town Hall. It is not far from here to Bath, and many more splendid buildings, but there is a little of Wiltshire to the west of Corsham before you reach the border. **BOX** is traditionally 'the last village in the county on the road to Bath', but has a claim to fame that still belongs to Wiltshire.

An unusual name for a place with an unusual feature, a railway tunnel which is almost two miles long, and was the longest in the world when it was built in 1841. It was also the steepest, and is at such an angle that it is said that the sunlight can penetrate from one end to the other, but only very rarely. Rumour says that the most common date for this is April 9th, the birthday of the tunnel's designer, almost inevitably a certain Mr Brunel. Slightly more credible is the local tale that it is most likely to occur on Midsummer's day, at dawn. Appropriately, LORNE HOUSE, which is in the village of Box, was once the home of the Reverend Awdry, creator of Thomas the Tank Engine and his friends. I wonder if he thought of Box tunnel for the prison in which Henry is confined after he refuses to come out into the rain?

You may fancy a quick game of 'stowball' while you are in this neck of the woods, especially if you venture near the hilltop spire which marks the church in **COLERNE**. Apparently it was quite a craze as the turf on COLERNE DOWN was ideal. There is only a couple of inches of fine soil covering the rock, and this made for a bouncy ball, which I imagine would allow it to carry further. Stowball? Apparently a forerunner of what we know as golf. There are some excellent walks around both Box and Colerne, and the land is suddenly much hillier again than at Chippenham and Corsham. Having got a taste for the hills, let's head east for the Marlborough Downs. Between Chippenham and Calne there are no fewer than three more outstanding country houses forming a triangle smaller than many town areas, and a range of attractions which would make any resort proud.

The nearest to Chippenham adjoins LACKHAM COUNTRY ATTRACTIONS (01249 443111) to the south. Lackham House is a fine grey stone mansion, but is now an Agricultural College, and not open to the public. Walled gardens, a superb rose collection and riverside and woodland trails add to the AGRICULTURAL MUSEUM, and with a tremendous range of flowers, vegetables and fruit, you are bound to see something new. The nearby WHITEHALL GARDEN CENTRE (01249 730204) provides an equally comprehensive service as a Garden Centre, so that you can take something home too.

The village of **LACOCK** is within a reasonable walking distance of Lackham. Another place made affluent by the wool trade, its four streets make a hollow square of buildings which are bound to find their way into many a photograph album and holiday video, particularly as there are no modern intrusions amongst them at all.

They have also been used recently for professional filming, notably Jane Austen's 'Pride and Prejudice'. Looking around at the rows of immaculate timber fronted and grey stone buildings, with very little brickwork in sight, it is easy to imagine Mrs Bennett issuing from a shop doorway, a train of her daughters appearing to listen to her every word. Not a single building has been added to the village since the times in which Jane Austen was writing, which makes this a very rare place indeed.

The Village of Lacock

The High Street leads to LACOCK ABBEY (01249 730227), another elegant edifice of light grey. If you have already used your camera in the village, then at the FOX TALBOT MUSEUM OF PHOTOGRAPHY (01249 730459) near the Abbey gates you will find out what you owe to one of the Abbey's most famous inhabitants.

William Henry Fox Talbot took his first picture in 1835, but more importantly he also produced the first photographic negative, and established that prints could be taken from it. Perhaps the museum should be sponsored by the send by mail developing companies, with some of the money they could save by padding out less magazines with their envelopes!

The subject of that first negative was one of the three oriel windows in the Abbey itself. As you look at the octagonal tower and scrollworked chimneys of the building it doesn't seem very ecclesiastical at all, just as Sherborne Castle, with its similar lines, makes for an unusual castle. Like Malmesbury Abbey, Lacock had to change its purpose after 1539, and became a private dwelling. Only the cloisters and Chapter House are from before this time.

Although this is still quite a romantic looking place, there is a sort of sadness in the demise of the nunnery which was established here in 1232. Other older places of worship were established for women by royal relatives, notably Shaftesbury Abbey and the Minster at Wimborne (both in Dorset), but Lacock is unusual in that it was established by a woman, Ela, Countess of Salisbury.

The Countess must have been a strong character, for she was also the only woman to hold the post of Sheriff of Wiltshire. Her life story is one of courage and determination too. After her father died when she was only seven years old, Ela was made the ward of King Richard I, the Lionheart, eventually marrying his stepbrother William. He was reported 'missing in action' in France, and for a long period of time his wife was the only one who insisted that he was still alive, saying that she had her definite knowledge from a dream vision.

Despite many offers from other suitors, she would not take her widows weeds, and was vindicated when William finally made it home to her, alive. The sad irony is that he did not survive long after his return. Some say this was because of the privations he had suffered abroad, others that he was poisoned by one of the disappointed suitors who was none too delighted at the accuracy of Ela's vision.

Whatever the truth, Ela did not remarry, turning instead to the establishment of a nunnery here and a monastery in Somerset (at Hinton Charterhouse). A romantic story, and an agreeable variation on the usual wife as victim tales of many a historic legend. Even the few remaining parts of her work left standing are a tribute to the story of an assertive woman.

BOWOOD HOUSE AND GARDENS (01249 812102) has a shorter and less dramatic history. It is accessible from the road between Chippenham and Calne, lying only just off the A4. There are signposts for Bowood at the M4 junction north of Chippenham, so by now you will be more than ready to see it! Any impatience should not prevent you noticing the village of **DERRY HILL**, clustered around the gates to the great park.

So close to the main road, this is another example of a place that looks almost deserted, as if time had left it behind. The yellow stone cottages and Village Hall, which proudly declares that it was built in 1873, live in the very shadows of the gates and a huge sign to the BOWOOD GOLF & COUNTRY CLUB (01249 822228). The stone perpendicular parish church looks as big as the rest of the village put together, with an ominous sign asking for help in its restoration. Places like this make you realise that there are many villages and hamlets in Wiltshire that have survived somehow, in the middle of much that is newer, but without the good fortune of Castle Combe or Lacock.

Like Corsham Court, Bowood House has had many designers over the centuries, and grounds landscaped by Capability Brown. These are on a very grand scale, as the park and woodlands took up more than a thousand acres, a hundred of which are accessible to visit today. Oxygen was discovered in the Laboratory at Bowood by Dr Joseph Priestley, but the real beauty and grandeur of the building are best seen in the Orangery (used to house an art collection) and on the main terraces, especially in summer. Although there is plenty to see in the House itself, from a flag stone floored Sculpture Gallery to a gorgeous collection of Georgian Costumes, the walks through the grounds will prove equally memorable.

The Terraces at Bowood House

Where Corsham has the Gothic Bath House, Bowood has a Doric Temple, set ideally with dark greens above and lawn below, sloping down to clear water. The Arboretum, Pinetum, Rhododendron walks, lake and cascades might well take more than a single visit to cover. Set amongst the remnants of the CHIPPENHAM FOREST you will also find grottoes, a hermit's cave and more than 160 species of shrubs and trees. So you have had the chance to see several superb houses in a very small geographical area. To the uninitiated this will come as a great surprise, not at all what you would expect from Wiltshire. Yet there are more grand Houses in this area which you will not find signposts to. Neston Park, Bowden Hill and Spye Park; these are not open to the public, but you will be hard put to find such a corner of England packed with so many examples of the more lavish side of domestic architecture, originally funded mostly from the wealth gained in local, rural, industry.

After all of this **CALNE** might seem a little ordinary. Who would imagine that the single biggest slaughter of the civic leaders of this country happened right here, in this inoffensive place, or that in 1900 more than 2,000 pigs a week were turned into sausages and bacon here. No connection intended!

Actually, the death of the *Witenagemot* was probably more of an accident than a deliberate massacre. This body of men was the National Council of Anglo-Saxon England, to whom the King was supposed to listen. At a meeting in Calne in the year 987 all but a single member, the Archbishop Dunstan, were killed when they crashed through the upper floor of a building in the middle of a debate about priestly celibacy. Not quite The House of Commons at Question Time, although one wonders what on earth made them jump so much as to cause the collapse, given the subject matter! Dunstan was suspected by some to have set up the tragedy, but it seems unlikely.

Another dramatic death occurred in Calne in 1638 when a resident died of fright after seeing the local church tower collapse. Yet until 1983 the town was much more dangerous for pigs than humans. The factory here was able to account for up to a 1,000 of their number each day by the time it finally closed down, some 213 years after the Harris family started butchering swine in Calne.

The town was lucky to get a second chance after the woollen industry started to fade here as the River MARDEN was not fast enough to keep up with the demands of the mills. Wander about Calne now and you will find many things that might not appear to be related to bacon. The CALNE FREE CHURCH, for instance, looking old and compact, was actually built by the Harris family, and they looked after the townsfolk, as well as visiting pig drovers, in style.

If you wonder why the little pond is known as THE DOCTOR'S POND this has little to do with swine, as the name commemorates Joseph Priestley, who came here for the water samples he later used to establish the existence of oxygen at his Bowood laboratory. South of Calne you will find the ATWELL WILSON MOTOR MUSEUM (01249 813119).

East of Calne you are into the downlands straight away. The whole area looks a little like a carefully sculpted golf course, any of the rolling indentations could hold a large bunker, but on this western edge there is a real golf course, at the NORTH WILTSHIRE GOLF CLUB (01380 860257).

One of the first sights on the Downs is a White Horse, carved into the chalk near **CHERHILL**. It isn't particularly white now, and not that spectacular, and there is no need to worry if you do not have time to stop, there are five more to see in the county. This one was carved in 1780, to instructions given by megaphone from the side of the road! Like several of the other horses, this one was placed to mark the site of a prehistoric monument, in this case the hillfort of OLDBURY CASTLE, whose ramparts make a good place from which to look east across what is to come.

A note of caution: beware of streakers in the Cherhill area. If anybody should run towards you in a state of total undress then be careful not to turn away with embarrassment, or you might well lose you wallet, handbag or camera. The CHERHILL

GANG are notorious for their nudity, and the savageness of their attacks on passing travellers. Fortunately they haven't been seen much for the last couple of hundred years or so. It is said that they remained naked to help their anonymity. I suppose it does bring several new dimensions to the idea of a 'Photo fit' picture, or indeed an identity parade! Their victims were mostly coach travellers, leaving me to wonder whether they bothered to stop and shout 'Stand and Deliver'; the mind boggles.

After Stonehenge, the most famous ancient site in Wiltshire must be either the AVEBURY STONE CIRCLE or SILBURY HILL. Both of these are within walking distance of the National Trust car park built to keep cars out of the village of **AVEBURY** (Tourist Information 01672 539425) itself. Silbury Hill also has its own car park if you do not fancy the one mile trek. This is a good idea, and you will have seen enough of both monuments to get an idea of their shape before you leave the car at either point. Silbury Hill is easy to describe. Imagine that a giant has returned from a day at the beach with his bucket still full of sand. He turns it upside down and has done an excellent job, with the surfaces smooth and complete, but green. The result is Silbury Hill.

You will form your own idea of the shape (my geometry never was any good), and at the same time you might as well think of your own reasons for the Hill's existence, for these remain a mystery. What is clear is that at 132 feet high it is the tallest prehistoric construction in Europe, and it is estimated that it would have taken a force of five hundred men about ten years to build it out of the packed chalk it contains. This happened around 2750 B.C. The more romantic explanations for its existence include a story that the devil dropped it here on his way to Devizes, so perhaps he was the one who had been to the beach!

There are so many features on the horizon wherever you go around Avebury, that it is as if all the prehistoric monuments had deliberately been collected into a sort of 'theme park'. This must have been a very busy area four or five thousand years ago. You will need a guide or map of the various stones and mounds to make full sense of your surroundings, but a couple more particular features must be mentioned.

The WEST KENNET LONG BARROW is one of the largest burial mounds to have survived from some 5,500 years ago. Apparently the tomb became overcrowded, and so bodies were put out on a rack over the mound, so that when the birds had finished with the carcass the remaining bones would just fall through. This tomb was used for over a thousand years, and is unusual in that you are able to walk around inside and explore the various chambers.

THE SANCTUARY was two rings of stones and five more of wooden posts, where the ritual significance is again unknown, but the mile long avenue of stones called the KENNETT AVENUE, parts of which can still be seen today, led straight to it. Why was it so important to have this line of Sarsen stones leading from Avebury?

Once you have walked from the Avebury car park around the back of the school, the footpath takes you past part of the AVEBURY STONE CIRCLE, the largest ring of Neolithic stones (some weighing more than 20 tons) in Europe. There were two hundred in the Avebury designs alone. As you look across to see bits and pieces of the Kennett Avenue, plus other stones in the distance, you cannot help but wonder about them all.

It occurs to me that part of the mystery is caused by the surroundings. Empty, rolling green downland means that you can see bits of stone sticking up like teeth from behind equally visible mounds and barrows for some distance around. If this was scrubland, or part of a forest, the stones would be hidden. Discovering their path would then be more of a challenge than the irresistible temptation to think what their open patterning might have signified. They almost seem to be a deliberate challenge, taunting us to have yet another guess at their true purpose, which in reality will most likely remain forever unknown.

Many of the stones of the Avebury Circle were taken down in medieval times to be used for local building, and many others became buried, so that much restoration was needed to get back to what you see now. Personally I am not a great fan of the concrete bollards which have been placed between existing stones where the originals are missing. This system does help you to appreciate the size and precision of the complete circle, but somehow the concrete posts look wrong, although it is hard to think of a better way around the problem. False replica megaliths is definitely not a desirable alternative.

The ditch which surrounds the ring of stones is even more impressive when you realise that it is only half its original depth. There is something quite remarkable about its placement. It seems obvious that a ditch in front of a bank would provide a good form of defense, so that the moat and castle wall can be seen as an eventual straight development of this strategy. This is true at most prehistoric sites, but the Avebury ditch is inside the ramparts. Only a ritual significance can be drawn from this, but what?

The stones seem everywhere as you look around the village, especially as there were other megalith designs within the main ring. Alexander Keiller was the archaeologist responsible for much of the restoration of the local monuments in the 1930s, and the ALEXANDER KEILLER MUSEUM (01672 539250) in the village has a very important collection of prehistoric finds. The museum stands between the two buildings which dominate Avebury, the CHURCH OF ST JAMES and AVEBURY MANOR (01672 539388). The WILTSHIRE LIFE SOCIETY'S MUSEUM (01672 539555) is in the large barn belonging to the second of these.

The Manor is an impressive Elizabethan building which is open to the public increasingly often as the restoration work progresses. On my recent visit to Avebury I saw them replacing the stone globes at the head of the tall gate posts, with much

271

evidence of cranes, hoists and workmen. It was not until later that the irony of the fuss that was (undoubtedly necessarily) being made occurred to me. What on earth would they have done with twenty tons of megalith?

The biggest difference between the setting of the Avebury remains and those elsewhere (especially Stonehenge) is the mixture of quiet village, with red brick and whitewashed, thatched houses, and ancient stones. The focus of this mixture is the church. In the middle of a pagan site, there are parts of the Anglo-Saxon Minster surviving in this 19th century version. Most noticeable, and rare, is a 15th century relic, the ROOD-SCREEN AND LOFT.

The rood was a name for the cross, celebrated in the Anglo-Saxon dream vision 'The Dream of the Rood':

"Syllic waes se sigebeam, and ic synnum fah,
forwundod mid wommum."

(The cross of victory was wondrous, and I was stained with sins, sorely wounded with wrongdoings) The rood was Anglo-Saxon Britain's way of accepting the ideas of Christianity into the background of pagan religions, never more evident than in this area.

Most rood screens and the often extremely elaborate crosses they contained were destroyed during the Reformation in the 16th century. Avebury's survived due to some crafty plasterwork which concealed the room until later, safer, times. It is ironic how the tokens of different religions and cultures seem to have survived side by side in this quiet village. The church was very silent when I was there, and somehow appeared much smaller inside than the square lines of the exterior suggested; perhaps it was just the contrast to the very open pagan monuments all around it. Avebury also has a HENGE SHOP, which is fascinating if you want to find out more about the area, and also if you want to see what the other interests of those of us who might be intrigued by a bit of prehistory are presumed to be.

After the emptiness of the Downs, **MARLBOROUGH** (Tourist Information 01672 513989) is suitably elegant for a town in such a wider setting. Approaching from the west you are between the now steeper Downs to the north, and the SAVERNAKE FOREST to the south, following alongside the River KENNET into the town. Another White Horse greets you to the south, this one dug by Marlborough schoolboys in 1804 (not pupils of the famous College).

What an attractive town Marlborough is. MARLBOROUGH COLLEGE is its most famous building, having been at first a castle then an inn before the College was opened in 1843. But it is the general appearance of the town, with its wide, open High Street that immediately catches the eye. This is the result of its status as a market town, although many of the 'penthouses' (those buildings supported by pillars) were destroyed by three fires which ravaged the town during the 17th century.

Marlborough

Marlborough was an important stage-coach town, and until the railways passed it by was a thriving place. This is apparent by the wealth of 17th, 18th and 19th century buildings in its midst, many of which now contain Antiques and Gift shops. Modern Marlborough is an excellent place to use as a base for exploring the surrounding countryside.

There are many ways to appreciate the Downs. Not far from Marlborough you are likely to see racehorses being trained on the open stretches, and there are many Riding Schools and Stables from **WOOTTON BASSETT** and **WROUGHTON** in the north to **STANTON ST BERNARD** and Pewsey in the south, where you can hire a more easily paced way to travel the Downs. Others will provide temporary holiday space for your own horse, so that you can use the stable as a base to tour from. Try the various Tourist Information numbers if you wish to know more, or the BRITISH HORSE SOCIETY (01203 696697), and the ASSOCIATION OF BRITISH RIDING SCHOOLS (01736 69440). More specifically there are numbers for the MARLBOROUGH DOWNS RIDING CENTRE at **ROCKLEY** and **CLENCH COMMON** (01672 63077 / 511411). The Downs are ideal for off road riding.

They are an excellent area for the walker too. Whole books have been written about the RIDGEWAY TRAIL, which starts its run along the ridge of chalk in the Downs, before going on into the Thames Valley to the east. This is one of the oldest roads in the world, dating back at least 5,000 years. The COUNTRYSIDE COMMISSION has marked out eighty five miles of it starting at OVERTON HILL near Avebury, with regular signposts to make sure you know you are still on the right track. Why the Ridgeway? Apart from the fascination of treading such an ancient path, it follows a ridge of chalk, and so keeps you up where you can see around you.

The Ridgeway does not connect towns, villages or even single dwellings of the modern era, so you have the added advantage of being taken to some of the truly remote parts of the Marlborough Downs, where you can walk for miles without seeing a single human habitation. In these circumstances you can see a horizon where the land meets the sky unimpeded, not a common view in modern Britain. On these occasions you will see many a bump against the sky, marking the clear definition of yet another mound or barrow, many of which are much less explored than those around Avebury. The Ridgeway has an Officer who may be able to help you if you are tempted (01865 810224).

Cycling is another alternative, with more sections of the WILTSHIRE CYCLEWAY marked out, try Tourist Information if you wish to know more. The MARLBOROUGH GOLF CLUB (01672 512147), and the SWINDON GOLF CLUB (01672 284217), which is at **OGBOURNE ST GEORGE** both have day hire green fees available. South of Marlborough there is Clay Pigeon Shooting at PARK FARM, SAVERNAKE (01672 512052).

The Downs have areas owned by the National Trust, both NATIONAL NATURE and Wiltshire Wildlife Trust Reserves, as well as Country Parks and picnic areas. There are far too many to list here, but even if you exhaust these there are still forests such as SAVERNAKE and the bluebell filled WEST WOODS to explore. There are more ancient sites too, particularly BARBURY CASTLE and FYFIELD DOWN. Two more White Horses are on the Downs at HACKPEN HILL and near **ALTON BARNES**. If you like a countryside that is accessible, then you will want to spend some time on the Marlborough Downs. To the south of Marlborough the Pewsey Vale rises to meet the Downs. In this chapter we will only go as far south as the Kennet and Avon Canal, which we will use as a dividing line between North and South Wiltshire. Some of the vale, as well as Pewsey lies below this line. The vale is of greensand with underlying clay, and separates the Marlborough Downs from the masses of the next chalk downland, Salisbury Plain.

From TAN HILL you can get a view of the whole of this beautiful valley, lacking only a river running through it. In the distance you can see a spire piercing into the sky like an elaborate stone rocket forever waiting to be launched. Salisbury must have looked even more impressive from here before cars made the journey to the cathedral a shorter one, in terms of time, when the twenty five intervening miles would have been quite a daunting journey, perhaps into the unknown.

Just behind you is another mystery of the Downs which runs for eleven miles west to east towards the Savernake Forest. The WANSDYKE is an earthwork which must have been a defence of some sort, but against whom, and how, will probably never be ascertained. One more relic of the distant past to leave behind you as you go south. The softer lines of the Vale promise a break from such problematical things, an area in which evidence of man's interference just could not hope to last quite so long, or to become so troublesome to the mind used to knowing the purpose of things.

While nature has not provided a waterway to take advantage of the erosion of chalk which has formed the Vale of Pewsey, there is a section of a man made alternative of some proportion. THE KENNET AND AVON CANAL runs from The Thames past Reading in the east to Bristol in the west.

Before we leave North Wiltshire we must make a journey along the canal, taking in the towns which lie above it, as well as those that welcome it through their very centre. **DEVIZES** (Tourist Information 01380 729408) is the biggest of these, and is where we will start.

This is the centre of the legend of the MOONRAKERS. In the 18th century a group of villagers were in Devizes to collect some kegs of brandy, for which no import duty had been paid, they were the spoils of smuggling. Enforcement Officers were heard approaching and the men pushed the kegs into a nearby pond. The officers were only fooled temporarily and came back for a second look a little later.

The villagers were found raking the pond, trying to find out exactly where on the bed the brandy had landed. When asked what on earth they were doing the immediate reply was that they were raking for a cheese they could see in the water. The cheese was the reflection of the full moon on the pond's surface, and so they became Moonrakers.

Some say they got away with this deception, others that they did not, but the term is far from an insulting alternative for the stereotypical image of straw chewing country bumpkins. The Moonraker likes to be the one to make the running, as with the story of the cheese, it is the visitor who has to work out whether what is being said is serious, or a leg-pull which takes advantage of the assumed naivety of the natives.

Be careful not to take on too much of this light hearted attitude to fibbing in Devizes. The MARKET CROSS bears witness to the possible consequences. Apparently a certain Ruth Pierce asked God to strike her dead if she were lying about a corn deal taking place right here in 1753. Presumably she was lying, otherwise God was exercising a particularly macabre sense of humour when she was struck down immediately after making the rash vow.

Devizes has a very different centre to that of Marlborough, despite the fact that they both grew as Market Towns. Where Marlborough's main street is wide, Devizes is a busy, almost cluttered place , but with a large open market place at its centre. The town boasts that no streets have been added to, or taken away from, the layout made when the original Devizes Castle was built over 800 years ago.

There are buildings from every age in Devizes, and some five hundred of them are listed. Everywhere you go there are pleasantly surprising architectural features, take a look, for instance, at the half-timbered, overhanging fronts of the Tudor Houses turned into shops in the little lane off St John's Street, around the back of the 'Wiltshire Kitchen'.

How different they are to the buildings of the WADWORTH BREWERY which dominate the other end of the town, on the corner of New Park and Northgate Streets. These red brick headquarters of Wiltshire's brewery chain cater for no less than eighteen establishments in the town, still using the horse and drays of former times to deliver locally.

THE CORN EXCHANGE, opposite the Market Place, stands out as well, with a statue of Ceres atop its roof proudly declaring that it was erected in the year 1857. While the God of grain and all things corny might have been having a good time in the mid 19th century, they were not particularly positive years for the economic well being of the most famous enterprise to have its centre at Devizes.

Just along the road from the Brewery is a car park which rests at the edge of the reason for the town's prosperity up until that time. The Kennet and Avon Canal did what had been thought of for centuries by joining the Thames and the Avon, removing the need for hazardous sea travel or the slog across land to get an effective trade between London and Bristol.

The Canal building programme received Royal assent in 1794, and it was finished at Devizes with the spectacular section at Caen Hill, of which much more soon! It cut the cost of transporting goods from London to Bristol by half. But the canal boom was a relatively short one, as the railways superseded them completely. Great Western bought out the Canal in 1852, and though they were legally bound to keep the waterway open it became barely navigable and in ill repair.

Doomed to closure, the formation of the CANAL ASSOCIATION in 1952, and then the KENNET & AVON CANAL TRUST saved the canal from extinction. Enthusiasts gradually worked to re-open it (with Caen Hill again being one of the very last sections). The Queen finally declared the canal functional once more on August 8th 1990. The event did make the national news, but if you do not remember it perhaps this is because Iraq had just declared war on Kuwait. The car park is at the wharf, where you will find the KENNET AND AVON CANAL EXHIBITION (01380 721279 / 729489) which can tell you more about the creation and restoration of the waterway. As for enjoying it yourself, there are three basic alternatives; take to the water, use a fishing rod, or walk!

Try WHITE HORSE BOATS (01380 728504) for trips from the wharf, either driven by a guide, or for a day or week under your own captaincy. For fishing try the DEVIZES ANGLING ASSOCIATION (Tourist Information for current details). The KENNET AND AVON WALK can be purchased as a guide book in its own right, with sections of ten to fifteen miles for those who do not fancy the entire trip in one go. The Wiltshire sections include Pewsey to Devizes and Devizes to Bradford on Avon. Towpaths do provide an excellent structure for a walking day or longer holiday, and these stretches mix the chance to see much of the county's industrial heritage with some of the quiet splendour of the countryside.

If you are lucky enough to be at the canal towards the end of March you can witness the start of the annual Devizes to Westminster canoe race. You will not have to go far from the Wharf to see the most spectacular of all the stationery attractions the Canal has to offer, the twenty nine locks of CAEN HILL. The best way to see them is to take the car out of Devizes to the west, and follow the signs to the top of the locks. So, before leaving the town let me mention a few other things it has to offer.

The DEVIZES MUSEUM (01380 727369) is owned by the Wiltshire Archaeological and Natural History Society, and has an exceptional collection of prehistoric material from the Downs and Salisbury Plain. If you enjoyed Avebury then this will be for you. There is much about the more recent history of Wiltshire too.

The present Devizes Castle is a 19th century structure, and is privately owned, but the mound of the original can still be spotted. The WILTSHIRE SHOOTING CENTRE (01380 727282) is based in Devizes, with indoor ranges.

By now you are bound to have at least seen a glimpse of the Caen Hill locks. Take the road out past the Brewery, and just when you think you have gone too far a sign on the dual carriageway sends you doubling back to the right to get a better look at Caen Hill. The approach road to the canal side parking is long and not very well made, so be prepared to exercise a little patience. When you do get to the top, the view alone is definitely worth the trouble.

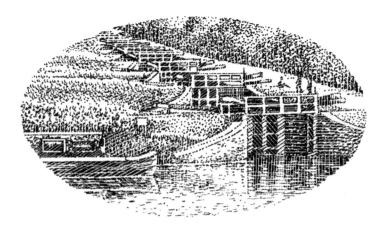

Caen Hill Locks, Devizes.

The twenty nine consecutive locks overcome a rise of 237 feet, and a world record was set here in 1991 when the narrowboat 'Zygnema' completed them in less than two hours and seven minutes. The succession of bright white gateways makes for an excellent chance to test the powers of perspective using a camera or the naked eye. If you take a walk from the car park you are near the top of the run and a footbridge leads on to one of the locks.

Looking down the true size of this remarkable piece of engineering really becomes apparent. Whereas the pictures tend to make the locks look as if they are piled almost on top of one another, the view is a very long one, and it is the narrowness of the empty brick walled locks which impressed me.

It must be very claustrophobic to sit in a narrowboat as it is gradually handed down the hill, from one dark box of brick to another. My morbid imagination somehow came up with the image of a coffin being transported down to the fires without any need for tilting. It is probably not like that at all, but the locks do look quite sinister when there are no boats around.

The CROFTON PUMPING STATION (01672 870300) is another feature of the canal, further to the east, which may interest you. The sturdy red brick station houses two early 19th century beam engines used to provide water for the canal. The volunteers of the Canal Trust run the steam engines on certain days, the centre at Devizes or Tourist Information should have the latest dates.

A little further east again the villages of **GREAT BEDWYN** and **FROXFIELD** emphasise that there were habitations and industries here long before the canal arrived. Great Bedwyn was noted as a reasonably sized place in the Domesday Book, and has some picturesque old buildings, including the church of ST MARY THE VIRGIN which has parts of the original 11th century building intact, and holds the tomb of the father of Jane Seymour, wife number three of Henry VIII's six.

There is also a stone mason's in Great Bedwyn where you can see the craftsmen at work, as well as visiting the collection in the STONE MUSEUM, all this is in Back Lane. In Brook Street there is a basket maker's where you can have goods made to your own specifications.

Froxfield is full of brick and flint cottages, some of which are thatched, with a contrast provided by a quadrangle containing fifty 17th century almshouses. If you should hear some disturbing barking noises from the north it is probably only the Hounds of Hell out on their regular jaunt from LITTLECOTE HOUSE. Do not be concerned, they are not after visitors, but rather 'Wild Darrell' who is said to have murdered a new born baby by throwing it on to a blazing fire. While the name Darrell might suggest he is now in an open youth prison for 'wild' youngsters, the whole event took place in the 16th century, so the Hounds are obviously very persistent as his trail must be quite cold by now. This was in fact Sir John Daryll, who owned Littlecote, and is said to have bribed the Judge by giving him the House in order to save his own life.

The few villages in the hollows at the base of the Savernake Forest make for another pleasant area to explore, especially as the forest contains a herd of red deer, some of whom might be observed by the quiet walker. Nearly at Hungerford we are at the easternmost edge of Wiltshire, though the canal carries on its way.

To the west of Devizes there are still places to visit, adding more variety to the county's northern half. **MELKSHAM** (Tourist Information 01225 707424) used to have its very own canal, linking the Kennet & Avon to the Thames in Berkshire. When the WILTSHIRE AND BERKSHIRE CANAL was built Melksham had a population five times greater than that of Swindon. Mind you Swindon's present count is more than 150 times as great as it was then. This was between 1795 and 1810, and the canal was finally abandoned by an Act of Parliament of 1914. There is a walk around the town section from Melksham Wharf, and it will give you some idea of what a restoration programme will involve, and how much hard work has been put into the Kennet and Avon Canal Trust work over the years. The preservation and improvement of the canal is promoted by the WILTSHIRE AND BERKSHIRE CANAL AMENITY GROUP (01249 652248) if you wish to find out more, or offer assistance.

Melksham is a busy enough place today, but it could have been even more so. It had a spell as a Spa town, competing with Bath, and had some success before eventually admitting failure in the early decades of the 19th century. Some of the attractive houses built for visitors to the Pump Room still remain.

The town was also an important stop on the stage-coach route, and a centre for the wool trade. Wiltshire only really lost its prosperity to its northern competitors in the clothes trade in the 19th century when it failed to compromise its insistence on only producing high quality cloth. Even then there was something of a revival in Edwardian times, when fashion again temporarily favoured the county's wares.

If you visit the Tourist Information Office at Melksham you will pass a relic of those days. Opposite the present building is a round structure which looks rather like a squat version of an oast house. This was where the TIC had its home until a couple of years ago, when it became too small for them. Now the building is used by private companies, but not to dry out fleeces, which was its first purpose. It must be an interesting place in which to work, as it can only take a few seconds to circle the circumference of the whole office. At least you cannot lose anything in a corner.

To the west of Melksham are two more of the houses built as a consequence of the area's former wealth, following down from Corsham. GREAT CHALFIELD MANOR (01985 843600) is a National Trust property with a stream fed moat around the mellow stone of this impressive Tudor Manor House. The place is full of security devices, something perhaps to do with the feudal system it was part of, but I do not mean the hi-tech alarms. Look instead for the spy-holes in the great hall and dining room. The heavy oak doors do not look if they were left open much either.

At nearby **HOLT** the National Trust also own THE COURTS (01225 782340). This was where weavers came to settle their disputes, perhaps making their vows a little more cautiously than Miss Pierce of Devizes! The house is not open to the public, but there are both formal and wild flower gardens which can be visited, as well as an arboretum and a profusion of yew hedges. The last stop on our look at northern Wiltshire is another place where weaving was the making of the town's economy, but there could be few stronger contrasts to neighbouring Melksham than **BRADFORD-ON-AVON** (Tourist Information 01225 865797). Perhaps this is partly because it is nearer to Bath than it is to Melksham. Coming from Bath, Bradford is like a picturesque, semi-rural afterthought; agreeable enough, but not what you originally came to see. Coming from the east its significance to Wiltshire makes it much more, and definitely worth exploring in itself.

Bradford-on-Avon

The town's most notable treasure was lost for well over a hundred years, but the restoration was a very different process to that needed for the canal. The CHURCH OF ST LAURENCE can claim to be the most complete Saxon church in England, with its earliest parts from around the year 700. It is very fitting that the same county to hold the largest collection of prehistoric or pagan religious sites in the country should have this example of the early Christian influence on British culture within its boundaries, albeit far from Avebury and Stonehenge.

From the high ceilinged stone nave you can only wonder at the power the now fragmented cross held over the Anglo Saxons, still to feel the true force of Europe and its more established version of the new religion. The church was lost because of a series of new lives it had taken on, as a charity school, living accommodation and even a storage place for bones from a neighbouring churchyard! It was found due to the efforts of two men, one of whom takes us right back to the beginning of our time in Wiltshire. The other was Canon Jones, who was Vicar of Bradford in 1858, when he spied the outline of the building in amongst the roofs lining the slope down to the river. He knew that there was a Saxon church somewhere in the town thanks to the works of William of Malmesbury, the chronicler of the Abbey to the north.

Other parts of Bradford-on-Avon's past have not survived. There were thirty two working cloth factories in the town at the end of the 18th century, today there are none. But the wealth made in part from the importation of a Flemish workforce has done its job. The honey coloured stone from local quarries was used to make the town look and feel like the last border post of The Cotswolds, even though its loyalties are with the county to the east. Bradford is somewhere to enjoy the only thing our journey through Wiltshire so far has been missing, a picturesque town clustered around and above a majestic river.

Look for the TITHE BARN (01272 750700 for opening times) too, a relic of the 14th century when Bradford was the eastern limit of the lands belonging to Shaftesbury Abbey, and this was its granary; it now contains an Agricultural Museum. The massive timbers of the roof alone support one hundred tons of stone tiles. There are many other buildings, such as the weavers houses, which will catch your attention, as well as less common features including the stone bridges over the river.

Many antique and specialist shops fill the streets, as you would expect from the look of the town, and there are weekly antique, collector and craft fairs. The BRADFORD ON AVON MUSEUM (01225 863280) has at its centre a pharmacist's shop which stood in the town for over 120 years before it was rebuilt here. Not a huge place, Bradford is definitely worth exploring for an afternoon.

When you look back at the range that the first, northern half of Wiltshire has had to offer; from the shops and modernity of Swindon, the elegant but solid age of Malmesbury to the ancient mystery of Avebury, the beauty of the Downs and the many great Houses and buildings scattered throughout, it seems hard to credit that the two most famous attractions of the county have yet to come. Bradford-on-Avon has marked another change in the overall picture, but cannot prepare you for what is further south in the rest of the land of the Moonrakers.

APPLEGATES
32 Winsley
Winsley
NR Bradford-on-Avon
Wiltshire
BH15 2LU

Tel: 01225 723803
Fax: 01225 723804
morris.minor@dial.pipex.com

Applegates is set in over five acres of gardens and woodland with its own duck pond and an abundance of wildlife which always appeals to the visitor. The owners, Liz and Nik Harding assisted by their daughter Sian, run the house. They are an interesting family who thoroughly enjoy meeting people which is basically the reason they welcome guests into their own home. They will tell you that if they did not find it fun and satisfying they would stop immediately. Their guests would be horrified if they did because the welcome is so genuine and everything is done to make them feel comfortable, relaxed and at home.

There are two bedrooms in the main house, one is a double with a shower ensuite and the other a double with a private bathroom. Both are delightfully decorated and furnished and both have television and a hostess tray. There is also a cottage, separate from the main house with a double bedroom, bathroom and shower, its own kitchen, garden, Barbecue Area and also a room with a washing machine etc. The cottage is also furnished prettily and with restful decor.

Breakfast is served in the light, bright dining room and you feast on fruit juice, cereals, fresh fruit, yoghurt, fresh baguettes, when available, as well as a delicious cooked English breakfast.. Plenty of toast and preserves, tea and coffee complete a memorable meal. There are no evening meals but there are many good eateries in the area to which Liz and Nick will be happy to give you directions.

You will find Winsley just over two miles from the beautiful Saxon town of Bradford-on-Avon and a fifteen minute drive from the centre of the Georgian city of Bath, with its many visitor attractions. There are many country walks on the doorstep of Applegates and also many visitor attractions including gardens, pony trekking, Roman Baths, Bath Abbey, Lacock Abbey and much more, all within a short drive.

USEFUL INFORMATION

- OPEN: January-November
- WHEELCHAIR ACCESS: No
- GARDEN: 5 acres
- CREDIT CARDS: None taken
- ACCOMMODATION: 2 rooms ensuite + a cottage
- RATES: From £45 dbl B&B

- DINING ROOM: Super breakfast
- VEGETARIAN: Given notice
- A NON-SMOKING HOUSE
- LICENSED: No

- CHILDREN: Over 10 years
- PETS: No

BEECHFIELD HOUSE & RESTAURANT
Beanacre
Melksham
Wiltshire
SN12 7PU

Tel: 01225 703700
Fax: 01225 790118

Beechfield House is a country house hotel in the small village of Beanacre close to Melksham. It has everything one could wish for in such an establishment. The owners, The Moody family, have spent much time achieving their goal which was to provide their guests with the sort of hotel in which they themselves like to stay. It has been achieved and today their guests come back many times knowing that they will always leave refreshed, well fed and having enjoyed the atmosphere generated by the Moody family and their well-trained, friendly staff. Beechfield has the advantage of being close enough to Bath or Salisbury to make it possible for business people to stay here whilst working in the two cities. It is, for them, the best of both worlds, escaping from the hurl burly of a city at night to enjoy the comfort, the food and the relaxing atmosphere provided by Beechfield House. It is equally well placed for visitors who come here to enjoy all that this part of the country has to offer, including a visit to the National Trust village of Lacock which is stunning. Melksham is also an interesting place. Bath is incomparable and Salisbury Cathedral leaves first time visitors suffering from mental indigestion because of its grandeur and beauty. From Beechfield House you can also go fishing or play golf on one of the several courses within easy reach.

All the twenty one bedrooms at Beechfield House are individually decorated and furnished in a charming, restful manner. Each room is ensuite, some are non-smoking and every one has television, direct dial telephones and a beverage tray. An excellent, freshly cooked breakfast is served every morning. At Lunch or at night you dine in the charming Dining Room on a menu which highlights all that is best about English Cuisine. The menu changes daily and as far as possible only local and fresh produce is used. Vegetarians are catered for and Special Diets given due notice. Lunch is served between 12-2pm and Dinner from 7-9pm. Many people enjoy strolling in the 8 acres of perfectly maintained gardens which surround the Hotel and then wander into the well-stocked bar for a pre-lunch or dinner drink. Children over ten years are very welcome but pets are not permitted.

USEFUL INFORMATION

- OPEN: All year Lunch:12-2pm Dinner 7-9pm
- WHEELCHAIR ACCESS: No
- GARDEN: 8 acres
- CREDIT CARDS: All major cards
- ACCOMMODATION: 21 ensuite rooms
- RATES: From £70sgl & £90dbl B&B
- DINING ROOM: English cuisine
- VEGETARIAN: Catered for
- LICENSED: Yes
- CHILDREN: Over 10 years
- PETS: No

BRADFORD OLD WINDMILL
Masons Lane
Bradford-on-Avon
Wiltshire
BA15 1QN

Tel: 01225 866842
Fax: 01225 866648

Bradford Old Windmill overlooking Bradford-on-Avon is 'a secret waiting to be discovered' and what a discovery! It is not easy to find being well off the road at the end of a private unsigned drive which means when you do eventually get here you can be sure of a quiet stay free from people and traffic pollution, though there are some noisy birds! Peter and Priscilla Roberts own and run this romantic place and in such a manner that once having found this haven, you will never forget your stay and long for more. It is hidden away amongst the trees on the steep hillside above the town and it is the stump of Bradford's one and only windmill which still forms a prominent if rather eccentric landmark. The ornate Victorian spiral staircase, pointed Gothic windows in the four storey Cotswold stone tower and the conical stone tiled roof, are features more reminiscent of a folly, but the restored oak sail gallery is a reminder of the building's origins as a windmill.

Over the years Peter and Priscilla have travelled the world and inside the mill you will find displayed many unusual finds that they have acquired in far flung parts of the world. Masses of books everywhere encourage one to curl up on the sofa in front of the crackling log fire, in the romantically lit circular lounge, formerly the grain store, dipping into books you have long wanted to or meant to read.

After a memorable day one retires to bed in rooms that are special and distinctly different. Try the Queen size waterbed along with its whirlpool bath in the conical roofed Damsel room and wake up to views of the weavers cottages on the hill opposite. The less athletic may prefer a round bed sized for a King in the circular Great Spur room, taking up the floor in the old mill tower which originally housed two pairs of millstones - a large room with space for more than two and a spectacular outlook over Bradford towards Salisbury Plain. The Fantail room together with the Wallflower room form a suite. Children love the Wallflower room with its Minstrel Gallery where they sleep high above you curtained away in a nine foot long box bed. A steep ladder up to the gallery makes the room unsuitable for very young or badly behaved children. The Fantail room, with its old walnut and colourful patchwork quilt, looks out through a pretty gothic window across park land trees to the White Horse at Westbury.

Food at Bradford Old Windmill is delicious as one would expect. Breakfast, like dinner, is a friendly, leisurely, communal affair around a refectory table dominated by a set of grain weighing scales, or alfresco on the terrace on balmy days. Most tastes are catered for at breakfast. Priscilla will cook a splendid, mouth-watering dinner with a little notice and provide anything from an individual soup tray to an ethnic feast. She cooks from recipes she has gathered around the world.

USEFUL INFORMATION

· OPEN: All year
· WHEELCHAIR ACCESS:
  Not suitable
· GARDEN: Yes. Terrace
· CREDIT CARDS: None taken
· ACCOMMODATION: 2 rooms 1 suite
· RATES: From £75 per room. Stand-by-rate after 6pm at door £39

· DINING ROOM: Exciting, delicious fare

· VEGETARIAN: Yes & other diets
· LICENSED: No
· CHILDREN: Welcome
· PETS: No

THE CASTLE INN
Castle Combe
Wiltshire
SN14 7HN

Tel: 01249 783030
Fax: 01249 782315

http://www.hatton-hotels.co.uk
Email: res@castle-inn.co.uk

AA*** 69% Rosette,
Egon Ronay Recommended
RAC*** ETB ** 1AA Rosette

Castle Combe is recognised as one of the prettiest villages in England nestled in a wooded Cotswold valley. Architecturally, little has changed since the 15th century, all properties are listed as ancient monuments. There are no street lights or TV aerials and it is very easy to understand why it has won the coveted 'Prettiest Village in England' award many times. In its midst is The Castle Inn in a perfect setting. It enjoys the simple tranquillity of an age long gone and yet you are only minutes from the M4 Junction 17 and the national communication network. Chippenham is 4 miles away, Bath 9 miles, Badminton 6 miles, Bristol 17 miles and London 70 miles.

Everything about The Castle Inn is stylish, comfortable, welcoming and very friendly. It is furnished, as one might imagine, with a happy mixture of antique and other pieces. In the Bar you experience the unique atmosphere of an old English Inn. There is a fine selection of Ales and if you wish to dine here you may choose from a range of Traditional English dishes and light meals or simply have an aperitif before going into the restaurant for dinner. Oliver's Restaurant was named after Cromwell, who once took refuge from Royalist troops within these walls. The cuisine is imaginative and delicious and the wine list is first class. The head chef will happily prepare special requests or accommodate specific dietary requirements.

The hotel boasts eleven charming ensuite bedrooms, named after trees, all superbly furnished, individual in character and three of which are non-smoking. Five bedrooms have ensuite whirlpool bathrooms, whilst a sixth has a Victorian style slipper bath. Every modern convenience is there with satellite TV, direct dial telephones, radio alarm, hairdryer, trouser press, tea and coffee making facilities, mineral water, fresh fruit, soft towelling robes and luxury toiletries. Nothing is too much trouble for the dedicated staff. The conservatory and patio open for breakfast, morning coffee, light lunches, afternoon tea and evening meals and is also available for wedding receptions and private functions. The conservatory seats up to 40 people.

USEFUL INFORMATION

- OPEN: All year
- WHEELCHAIR ACCESS: No
- GARDEN: Patio
- CREDIT CARDS: All major cards
- ACCOMMODATION: 11 ensuite rooms
- RATES: Sgl from £55 pp.pn B&B Dbl. £90 p.n. B&B

- RESTAURANT: Superb fare
- VEGETARIAN: Yes & special diets
- BAR FOOD: Menu changes daily
- LICENSED: Full On. Fine wines
- CHILDREN: Welcome

CHILVESTER HILL HOUSE
Calne
Wiltshire
SN11 OLP

Tel: 01249 813981/815785
Fax: 01249 814217

Good Hotel Guide Cesar award
ETB 3 crowns highly commended
Michelin Red House. AA QQQQQ
Premier Selected. Which.BTA.

Chilvester Hill House is eighteen miles from Bath and seven miles each from Avebury Neolithic stone circle, Lacock National Trust village. Marlborough, Salisbury and Oxford are within easy reach, as are Hungerford and Tetbury, the home of Prince Charles is in the so called 'Royal Triangle'. On the southern borders of the Cotswolds, it overlooks an OCL stately home, Bowood which is open to the public for much of the year and has an eighteen hole golf course. There are many other houses and gardens open to the public between 10 and 25 miles off. Slimbridge Wildfowl Trust is not too far away and there is racing at Bath, Newbury, Salisbury and Wincanton. With excellent walking country there as well, Chilvester Hill House makes an ideal place to base oneself for a holiday or a break or even on business if you prefer to escape the frenetic bustle of a town or city.

The house is Victorian and built of Bath stone. Its rooms are large and airy and centrally heated. It has a delightful drawing room, a sitting room with television, newspapers and magazines and an elegant dining room. It is here that one dines with other guests at one table in what is always a dinner party atmosphere. Frequently Dr and Mrs Dilley, whose charming and welcoming home it is, join their guests for drinks before dinner or coffee afterwards. Gill Dilley is and accomplished cook who enjoys creating mouth-watering dishes for her guests. Almost all the vegetables and salads are home or locally grown. There is a short but comprehensive wine list. Breakfast is 'what you like'. Most people seem to settle for sometime between 8am and 9am but there really is no rush. There is always a wide choice of cereals, fresh fruit and cooked dishes; various teas and 'real' or decaffeinated coffee; jams, jellies and marmalade - usually home made.

There are three large double bedrooms (double or twin beds) each with en-suite bathroom (with a hand-held shower, but a large shower room is available, for which bathrobes are provided). All the rooms have remote controlled colour television, clock/radio, books, guide books and maps as well as a tea/coffee tray.

USEFUL INFORMATION

- OPEN: All year
- WHEELCHAIR ACCESS: No
- GARDEN: 2-5 acres
- CREDIT CARDS: All except mastercard
- ACCOMMODATION:3 large ensuite rooms
- RATES: Sgl from £50-60prpn Dbl. £75-£90prpn
  Family room £100+ Dinner £20-£25 per person
- DINING ROOM: Delicious home-cooked food
- VEGETARIAN: Upon request
- LICENSED: Residential
- CHILDREN: Not under 12 years
- PETS: Not in the house

LONGHOPE GUEST HOUSE
9 Beanacre Road
Melksham
Wiltshire
SW12 8AG

Tel/Fax: 01225 706737
longhope@aol.com

2 Crown Approved

Melksham is an ideal stopping place for people wanting to visit the incomparable city of Bath with its glorious Abbey, the National Trust village of Lacock where the film Pride and Prejudice was filmed, and many other places including Longleat, the ancestral home of the Marquis of Bath, Stonehenge and Castle Combe. It is convenient for the M4 at Junction 17. Finding somewhere to stay that you will enjoy and be comfortable is all important. Longhope Guest House, is the answer, owned and run by Diana Hyatt and her family, it is somewhere not to be missed. They are welcoming, friendly and sufficiently informal to make everyone feel at home. The house, standing in its own grounds, is Victorian, and as one would expect from a house of this era, it has high ceilings, tall windows, a sense of light and space. The house has been decorated charmingly and furnished throughout with an eye to comfort and using comparatively modern furniture. Its other great virtue is being within walking distance of the town centre.

Six ensuite bedrooms comprising of two twin rooms, two family rooms, one double room and one single are all ensuite with showers and bathroom. The modern beds are the epitome of comfort. Every bedroom has colour television and a hostess tray. A hairdryer is available if you require it. After a good night's sleep you come down to the dining room to enjoy one of the best breakfast's in Wiltshire. Starting with fruit juice and cereal you continue with a full English breakfast. If you prefer something lighter, freshly cooked, fluffy scrambled eggs on toast or baked beans on toast are available. With plenty of toast and preserves, freshly brewed coffee and piping hot tea, it is a meal that is substantial and will set you up for the day whether you are on business or pleasure.

USEFUL INFORMATION

· OPEN: All year	· DINING ROOM; Excellent breakfast
· WHEELCHAIR ACCESS: Yes	· VEGETARIAN: Upon request
· GARDEN: Yes	· LICENSED: No
· CREDIT CARDS: None taken	· CHILDREN: Welcome
· ACCOMMODATION: 6 ensuite rooms	· PETS: No
· RATES: £20pp p.n. B&B	
£40 per room dbl. £50 family	

LUCKNAM PARK
Colerne
Wiltshire
SN14 8AZ

Tel: 01225 742777
Fax: 01225 743536

Lucknam Park, the epitome of an English Lifestyle, is one of the finest and most perfectly run country house hotels in England. It is just 6 miles outside the historic Georgian city of Bath and under two hours drive from central London. The hotel is approached by a mile long avenue of Beech trees through the 500 acres of its listed park land opening out onto broad lawns surrounding the house's elegant facade. Built in 1720 it was sympathetically converted in the 1990s into a hotel.

Enter the house and an aura of tranquillity envelops you as the staff take complete care of your comfort and well being. Every room is perfect in its own right. The Georgian bow-fronted drawing room and wood panelled library are decorated with consummate understanding of the period and proportion of the house. Perfect places for enjoying afternoon tea or quietly browsing through the many books over a fine old Cognac. The elegant dining room, spacious yet intimate, was once the ballroom at Lucknam and boasts a beautiful hand-painted ceiling, crystal chandeliers and fine views across the grounds. It is a wonderful setting for the superb cuisine of exceptional quality: the restaurant has won many awards and delights everyone whether it is a first visit or a returning guest.

Each of the eleven suites and thirty one bedrooms is individually designed with fabrics, antiques and ornaments specially chosen to reflect the character of the rooms. All have marble bathrooms and splendid views across the park or the lovely courtyard. The Leisure Spa at Lucknam offers a complete world of health, beauty and relaxation. At its centre is a splendid swimming pool with whirlpool spa, saunas, steam room and solarium. In the heat of summer the doors open out onto a delightful terrace and walled garden. The Beauty Salon is there to pamper you with five luxurious treatment rooms, where the hotel's own therapists offer a full range of health and beauty treatments. Finally the glorious gardens are therapeutic in their own right enticing guests to stroll through the ancient and beautifully maintained walled garden to the sweeping lawns and surrounding paddocks. Horse riding (Adults) £35 per hour (Children) £20 per hour. Additional £20 per hour for tuition.

USEFUL INFORMATION

- OPEN: All year
- WHEELCHAIR ACCESS: Yes
- GARDEN: 500 acres
- CREDIT CARDS: All major cards
- ACCOMMODATION: 11 suites 31 bedrooms
- RATES: Room Only (based on 2 sharing);
  £200 superior £265 De-luxe £355 Suites
  Leisure Breaks (based on 2 sharing);
  2 Nights - £275 Superior £330 De-luxe £425 Suites

- DINING ROOM: Award winning cuisine
- VEGETARIAN: Always a choice
- LICENSED: Full On
- CHILDREN: Welcome
- PETS: By arrangement

PRIORY STEPS
Newtown
Bradford on Avon
Wiltshire
BA15 1NQ

Tel: 01225 862230
Fax: 01225 866248

Twelve years ago Carey and Diana Chapman decided to leave the London 'rat race' and make their home in the peace of the beautiful old Saxon town of Bradford on Avon, 8 miles east of Bath. It is a decision they have not regretted for one moment and over the years have welcomed many guests into their home. It is definitely a home and not an hotel; there are no locks on the doors, the entire house is furnished with fine antique pieces, lovingly polished. There are flowers everywhere and the atmosphere is redolent of a happy home. Originally it was built as a terrace of Weavers Cottages. There have been many alterations and additions but always trying to retain the old world charm of the house. The views from every room are stunning looking over the town towards the distant hills of Salisbury Plain. You will find the town is an elegant, and remarkably unspoilt old woollen town who reveals her charms coyly. There are tantalising glimpses of secret courtyards and overflowing gardens, narrow alleyways and substantial clothiers mansions. With Bath a short drive away or 12 minutes on a train, it could not be a better spot for a short break or holiday or even if you have business in Bath and like the idea of staying somewhere outside the city.

There are four guest bedrooms and one suite with a sitting room. All the rooms have either bath or bath and shower ensuite. Each room is beautifully appointed, warm and comfortable and has colour television and a hostess tray. Breakfast is served every morning in the sunny dining room. It is a memorable and sustaining meal, more than enough to sustain you for a day's exploration. Smoking is restricted to the Library or the very pretty terraced gardens. Bradford on Avon is blessed with many good eateries but if you prefer to eat in, a set dinner can be served at 7.30pm by arrangement.

USEFUL INFORMATION

- OPEN: All year

- WHEELCHAIR ACCESS: No
- GARDEN: Pretty terraced gardens

- CREDIT CARDS: Visa/Mastercard

- ACCOMMODATION: 2dbl.2tw
  1 suite all ensuite
- RATES: Sgl £52 Dbl. £68

- DINING ROOM: Excellent breakfast
  Evening meal by arrangement
- VEGETARIAN: By arrangement
- RESTRICTED SMOKING;
  LIBRARY OR GARDEN ONLY
- LICENSED: Residential but BYO if
  you wish

- CHILDREN: Not encouraged
- PETS: No

SHURNHOLD HOUSE
Shurnhold
Melksham
Wiltshire
SN12 8DG

Tel: 01225 790555
Fax: 01225 793147

Shurnhold House is a Listed Grade II Jacobean Manor House constructed in mellow Cotswold stone. It has such an air of permanence and tranquillity about it enhanced by lovely old Wisteria creeping along the front of the house and standing in a wonderful, mature garden with many large old trees, one of which is an ancient Yew Tree reputed to be as old as the house which was built in 1640. The peaceful beauty of the house is reinforced by the interior where there are many stone period fireplaces, flagstone floors and large oak beams. Guests staying here will always tell you how rested they feel. Somehow the stress of the outside world is left behind but in fact Shurnhold is only one mile from Melksham and ten miles from Bath. There are many sporting facilities within easy reach including golf, horse riding, swimming and a gymnasium. National Trust properties, lovely gardens are within reach, and exciting restaurants and enticing pubs are within a couple of miles.

The emphasis at Shurnhold is the sense of being pampered in luxury accommodation. All the non-smoking bedrooms are ensuite and have been individually designed, in keeping with the house. There is a choice of four-poster, king size, double or twin beds. There is also a family room. Each room has a direct dial telephone, television, and a generously supplied hospitality tray. The licensed lounge bar has Sky TV, a Video and log fires and the beautifully furnished lounge is the epitome of comfort.. Breakfast is served in the Dining Room which is one of the owner's favourite rooms furnished with fine old tables and elegant chairs. It is a delicious meal with several choices including a Continental breakfast.

USEFUL INFORMATION

· OPEN: All year	· DINING ROOM: Delicious breakfast
· WHEELCHAIR ACCESS: No	· VEGETARIAN: Upon request
· GARDEN: Beautiful garden	· LICENSED: Yes
· CREDIT CARDS: Visa/Master /Euro/AMEX	
	· CHILDREN: Yes
· ACCOMMODATION: Ensuite rooms Four posters; King size, Double or Twin	
	· PETS: At owners discretion
· RATES: From £40-£48 pp Breakfast £5.25 Continental £3.25	

THE SIGN OF THE ANGEL
Church Street
Lacock
Wiltshire
SN15 2LB

Tel: 01249 730230
Fax: 01249 730527

Lacock is a perfect setting, that has changed little over the centuries and is likely to remain unchanged because it is in the hands of the National Trust. People come here just to enjoy strolling through the village and absorbing its beauty and its tranquillity. Those who are lucky enough stay a while or lunch and dine in the 14th century Sign of the Angel where the owners Lorna Lewis and George Hardy ensure that the very highest standards are maintained whether it is in the restaurant or in the beautifully appointed guest rooms. Perfectly furnished, inn-keeping with the style and age of the house, the Sign of the Angel has the added virtue of a delightful garden which wanders down to a gurgling stream.

There are ten individually furnished bedrooms each with lovely antique pieces. Two of the beds are splendid four posters. Four of the bedrooms are in a cottage annexe and the other six in the Angel itself. It is always fascinating to see the way in which such old rooms acquire ensuite facilities. It says much for the owners and for the dexterity of plumbers! All the rooms here are ensuite and there are eight double and two twin-bedded. Every room has the modern requirement of television, direct dial telephones and a generously supplied hospitality tray. In the restaurant, Lunch is served between 12-2pm every day except Monday and Dinner every evening between 7.30-9pm (last orders). The menu has an eclectic selection and incorporates not only traditional English but Continental and a touch of Oriental. Every dish is beautifully presented and only the finest quality ingredients used. The comprehensive wine list has been chosen to complement the food.

Lacock with its superb Abbey and Photographic Museum will give you hours of pleasure but from the Sign of the Angel you can set off to explore Bath, twelve miles away, visit Bowood House or the delightful village of Castlecombe. The River is close and offers fishing and there are Golf Courses within easy distance.

USEFUL INFORMATION

- OPEN: All year
- WHEELCHAIR ACCESS: Yes
- GARDEN: Yes runs to a stream
- CREDIT CARDS: All major cards
- ACCOMMODATION: 10 ensuite rooms
- RATES: From £90. Four-poster & Superior room £105

- RESTAURANT: Delicious menu
- VEGETARIAN: With notice
- LICENSED: Table Licence
- CHILDREN: Welcome High chair avail.
- PETS: Well behaved dogs

TOXIQUE
187 Woodrow Road
Melksham
Wiltshire
SN12 7AY

Tel:01225 702129
Fax: 01225 741773

Good Food Guide:
County Restaurant
of the Year + Hotel of the Year
All major restaurant guides plus
Which Hotel Guide

This award winning restaurant with rooms has a particular charm all its own. It is in a Listed Farmhouse on the outskirts of Melksham with fields at the back and front. The ambience is very special, very relaxed and welcoming which is why so many people make a regular beeline for the restaurant coming from nearby Bath and much further afield.

You dine in two attractive non-smoking rooms, beautifully appointed with crisp white linen, shining silver and sparkling glass. Forty people can dine here in comfortable intimacy both at lunch and dinner. There is a set price meal with £18.50 for lunch and £31 for dinner. The menu, in the Modern English vein, includes a whole variety of very interesting dishes cooked by Helen Bartlett, who together with Peter Jewkes, owns and runs Toxique. Both Helen and Peter have interior design backgrounds which is evident in the delightful manner in which the house is decorated and furnished. Their choice of house wines is selected to reflect the character of their stated grape varieties and, above all, their provenance. They are ideal partners to the food as they are directly flavoured and full of complexity and individuality. The whole wine list will delight wine lovers.

Decorated and furnished individually with the same taste and style as the restaurant and public rooms, the five ensuite bedrooms, are comfortable and restful. All have very large baths and king size beds.

USEFUL INFORMATION

- OPEN: All year
- WHEELCHAIR ACCESS: Yes. One step
- GARDEN: Yes
- CREDIT CARDS: All major cards
- ACCOMMODATION: 5 ensuite rooms
- RATES: Dbl. £160 Sgl £95 PRPN DBB

- RESTAURANT: Modern English
- VEGETARIAN: Options on menu
- LICENSED: Restaurant
- CHILDREN: Welcome
- PETS: No

WHATLEY MANOR
Easton Grey
Malmesbury
Wiltshire
SN16 0RB

Tel: 01666 822888
Fax: 01666 826120

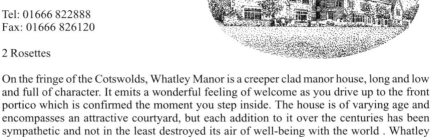

2 Rosettes

On the fringe of the Cotswolds, Whatley Manor is a creeper clad manor house, long and low and full of character. It emits a wonderful feeling of welcome as you drive up to the front portico which is confirmed the moment you step inside. The house is of varying age and encompasses an attractive courtyard, but each addition to it over the centuries has been sympathetic and not in the least destroyed its air of well-being with the world . Whatley Manor stands in splendid, beautifully maintained grounds which stretch down to the River Avon. The pine panelling in the Hall and the oak panelling in the Drawing Room set off the fine antique furniture to perfection and highlight the elegant wall hangings and big bowls of flowers to be found everywhere.

Before one goes in to dine in the stylish Dining Room, drinks are served in the impressive Library. The food is delicious, prepared by a talented and inspired chef who uses every possible fresh ingredient he can to achieve a culinary masterpiece. The emphasis is on English traditional fare with more than a touch of Continental influence and a little Eastern promise. Simple Bar Food is also available. The comprehensive wine list has been well selected and offers a choice from around the world.

There are twenty nine ensuite bedrooms, each individually furnished. Some are in the Manor House or the Tudor and Terrace Wings, others, mostly ground floor, are one minute away in the Court House. Every room has colour television, direct dial telephones. Whatley Manor is very popular for business purposes and has two meeting rooms, both suitable for seminars and conferences, together with a private dining room. Projectors and audio-visual equipment are provided.

The central courtyard houses the old Saddle Room which is now used for snooker and table tennis. Spa rooms are adjacent to the Saddle Room. Outdoors one can swim in the heated pool in summer, play croquet or tennis or simply relax. The Cotswolds offer the visitor wonderful countryside, villages, small market towns and inns to explore. There are many places within easy distance.

USEFUL INFORMATION

· OPEN: All year	· DINING ROOM: Inspired menu
· WHEELCHAIR ACCESS: Yes	· VEGETARIAN: Always a choice
· GARDEN: Superb grounds swimming pool, tennis, croquet	· BAR FOOD: Light meals
· CREDIT CARDS: All major cards	· LICENSED: Full On
· ACCOMMODATION: 29 ensuite rooms	· CHILDREN: Yes
· RATES: From £82-£126 B&B	· PETS: Yes in some rooms
· SEMINAR & CONFERENCE facilities	

THE WHITE HART
Ford, NR Chippenham
Wiltshire
SN14 8RP

Tel:01249 782213
Fax: 01249 783075

2 Star 1 AA Rosette

Although in the countryside and in a valley of natural beauty, nestled by a trout stream, The White Hart at Ford is close to the M4 & M5. The historic city of Bath is only ten minutes away as well as many other delightful and interesting places to visit. Because of its age - the oldest part is the Bar area which reputedly was built in 1553 - and its great character, the Inn has featured in scenes from Doctor Doolittle and more recently in an advertisement for 'Carling Black Label'. Inside the bar the ceilings are low and there is a mass of old wooden beams. Chris and Jenny Phillips are mine hosts. They are experienced innkeepers and this shows in the immaculate way the White Hart is run. The staff are polite and smart, the whole Inn has an air of well-being.

The emphasis here is on ensuring that the atmosphere is relaxed and the customer never feels rushed. It is popular with local people and those who come here to stay will tell you that it feels like a home from home. In the main restaurant where a log fire is the centre of attraction, the wooden beams and an assortment of pictures and guns hanging from the walls creates a perfect ambience in which to enjoy the excellent food. There is a good a la carte menu which includes four or more starters and a wide range of main courses from Beef Wellington to Grilled fillet of John Dory with roasted Langoustine and always a choice for vegetarians. Every day there are tasty specials, hot baguettes filled with beef and horseradish, a ploughman's and sandwiches. Everything is beautifully cooked and presented and it is great value for money. A well chosen wine list with wines from around the world complements the food perfectly. Ales include 6X, Tanglefoot, Pedigree, Smiles Best, Smiles Heritage, Boddingtons, Bass and Spitfire.

There are eleven ensuite rooms with three in the main building and eight in the annexe. Four of these rooms have four-poster beds and are popular with honeymoon couples. All the rooms are decorated in a comfortable, country style and not over frilly or fancy. Every room has direct dial telephone, television and a hostess tray.

USEFUL INFORMATION

- OPEN: All year
- WHEELCHAIR ACCESS: Yes. 4 ground floor rooms
- GARDEN: Yes + swimming pool
- CREDIT CARDS: All major cards
- ACCOMMODATION: 11 ensuite rooms
- RATES: Sgl £50 Dbl. £75 No single rooms at weekends

- RESTAURANT: Wide range, great value
- VEGETARIAN: Yes + Vegans on request
- BAR FOOD: Daily Specials etc.
- LICENSED: Full On
- CHILDREN: Yes. Lunch-time only
- PETS: Yes

THE BELL ON THE COMMON
Broughton Gifford
Melksham
Wiltshire
SN12 8LX

Tel: 01225 782309 Fax: 01225 783327

This interesting old hostelry was built in the early 1700's and its history is recorded since it was purchased by Sir Benjamin Hobhouse in 1780. Today it is the focal point of the small village of Broughton Gifford. It has a warm, friendly atmosphere in the two separate bars. The Public Bar has old wooden tables and benches, stone floor and a large open fire, whilst the Lounge Bar (called the 'Copper Bar') has a copper bar and tables and a plethora of copper and brass ornaments hanging from the walls and ceiling. On one side of the pub is a traditional garden, and on the other side a 27 acre Common. At the rear is the village Bowling Green, and a recent addition is a Boules Court.
There is an attractive Function Room on the first floor, for private parties, small wedding receptions and meetings etc. The food is delicious whether you eat from the A la Carte menu in the restaurant or enjoy a wide range of Bar Food. In either case Daily Specials, which are a happy mixture of time honoured favourites and the occasional more exotic dish, are available. There is a children's menu, a mid-week special, and every Sunday a traditional lunch. Whatever you choose, you can be sure it will be value for money.

USEFUL INFORMATION

- OPEN: Mon-Fri 11-3pm & 6-11pm Sat:
  All day Sun:12-3.30pm & 7-10.30pm
- WHEELCHAIR ACCESS: Not easy
- GARDEN: Large & Beautiful
- CREDIT CARDS: All major cards
- CHILDREN: Welcome. Children's menu

- RESTAURANT: Excellent a la carte Daily Specials
- VEGETARIAN: Yes
- BAR FOOD: Wide choice
- LICENSED: Full On
- PETS: Public Bar only

CLENCH FARMHOUSE
NR Marlborough
Wiltshire SN8 4NT

Tel: 01672 810264 Fax: 01672 811458
AA QQQQ English Tourist Board Commended

This 18th century farmhouse is set in the Vale of Pewsey and surrounded by open farmland at the foot of Martinsell, the highest hill in Wiltshire. Martinsell has an Iron Age fort and within easy reach are Avebury, Savernake Forest, Salisbury with its magnificent Cathedral and the incomparable city of Bath. Not far off is Long Barrow and Silbury Hill, both BC burial grounds. The Kennet and Avon Canal is half a mile away where you can hire a long boat. Wootton Rivers, half a mile away is a very attractive thatched village which has a very good pub. It could not be a more peaceful or relaxed location for anyone wanting to recharge their batteries away from the stress and strife of the 20th century and yet it is close enough to the attractive market town of Marlborough. There are three prettily appointed bedrooms furnished with antiques. One twin-bedded room is ensuite, one double has a private bathroom and the other is ensuite. Clarissa Roe runs the bed and breakfast business whilst her husband works in London. With their three children they have lived here for fourteen years. The garden, where Stan is in charge, produces all Clench Farmhouse's organic fruit and vegetables and Clarissa is helped in the house by Sarah who is her right hand. It is such a friendly establishment. The food is delicious both at breakfast and dinner. Everyone feels at home.

USEFUL INFORMATION

- OPEN: All year
- WHEELCHAIR ACCESS: Yes
- GARDEN: Yes
- CREDIT CARDS: None taken
- ACCOMMODATION: 3 ensuite rooms
- RATES: £25 High Season - £20 Low Season Children £5 - £15 depending in age

- DINING ROOM: Delicious home-made fare
- VEGETARIAN: Yes
- LICENSED: No
- CHILDREN: Welcome
- PETS: Yes

FISHERMANS HOUSE
Mildenhall, Marlborough
Wiltshire   SN8 2LZ
Tel: 01672 515390

Tourist Board - Highly Commended

This wonderful, redbrick house has stood guard on the River Kennet for two hundred and fifty years. To stay here is a privilege and an unforgettable experience. Oxford, Salisbury and Bath are within easy reach. Antique lovers will revel in the shops to be found in Marlborough and Hungerford. Avebury is just ten miles away. Fishermans House is the home of Jeremy and Heather Coulter and they have created perfection within the gracious house. Helped by their innate sense of colour, style and what is right for the house, they have collected some wonderful pieces. Heather happily admits to scouring junk shops for hidden treasures and her finds enhance the furnishings. Heather describes her home as ' like an antique shop'! She is a professional flower arranger and this is evident in the beautiful displays everywhere. In addition to being such a beautiful, perfectly furnished house, it is essentially a home and one in which the Coulters want their guests to feel comfortable and at ease. There is one double bedroom ensuite and three singles sharing a bathroom. Each room is individually furnished and the epitome of country house comfort. Breakfast is, as one would expect, sumptuous.

USEFUL INFORMATION

- OPEN: All year, Not Dec 25th &26th
- WHEELCHAIR ACCESS: No
- GARDEN: Yes
- CREDIT CARDS: None taken
- ACCOMMODATION: 1 dbl ensuite
- RATES: From £55 double £30 single

- DINING ROOM: Sumptuous breakfast
- VEGETARIAN: Upon request
- SMOKERS WELCOME
- LICENSED: No
- CHILDREN: Over 12 years
- PETS: No

THE HERMITAGE
Bath Road, Box
Wiltshire   SN13 8DT

Tel: 01225 744187 Fax: 01225 743447
E-Mail hermitage@telecall.co.uk
AA QQQQ: ETB 2 Crown Commended

Box is a small village just six miles from the historic and very beautiful city of Bath. Here you will find, surrounded by countryside and farmland, The Hermitage, a 16th century house standing in its own grounds with its neighbours the church and Box House all of which were built on the site of a Roman Villa. In the middle of the 1980's an archaeological dig in the garden of The Hermitage, unearthed many Roman remains and even today when Ruth and Paul Best, the owners, are gardening they still find small pieces in the flower beds. It is an enchanting house with five en suite double rooms. Two of these room are situated in the lodge which was once the old stables and has been beautifully converted. Here you have the choice of bed and breakfast or self-catering as both have kitchen facilities. All the bedrooms are delightfully furnished and have pretty colour schemes, televisions and hostess trays. The dining room lounge is a large room with a splendid vaulted ceiling and exposed beams. Here you will be served a traditional English breakfast with several choices, or something lighter if you prefer. The Hermitage is a strictly non-smoking house although smoking is permitted in the 2 Lodge rooms.

USEFUL INFORMATION

- OPEN: All year
- WHEELCHAIR ACCESS: No
- GARDEN: Yes. Heated swimming pool open May-end August
- CREDIT CARDS: None taken
- ACCOMMODATION: 5 dbl. ensuite

- DINING ROOM: Excellent breakfast
- VEGETARIAN: On request
- LICENSED: No
- CHILDREN: Welcome
- RATES: From £35 pp B&B Single £45 double B&B

KING JOHNS HUNTING LODGE
21 Church Street
Lacock
Wiltshire
SN15 2LB

Tel: 01249 730313

Lacock is one of the most perfect villages in England and is in the keeping of the National Trust. It is a restful, serene place in which you feel you have left the traumas of the 1990s behind and retreated to a quieter bygone age. In Church Street, next to the old church is King Johns Hunting Lodge, built in the 13th century, with low ceilings, a wonderful atmosphere and both Tea-rooms and Bed and Breakfast Accommodation. Well known broadcaster, Margaret Vaughan, is the owner of this charming property and has created the sort of sanctuary that King John would have looked for when he made regular use of his Hunting Lodge. The overnight accommodation includes en-suite and with television and tea/coffee facilities. Breakfast is served at almost any time and several village pubs and restaurants can provide evening meals. King Johns Hunting Lodge also has a fine reputation for traditional Cream Teas with local clotted or Jersey creams and home-made scones, jams and preserves as well as home-made cakes, cheese muffins and tea cakes served in the Garden Tea-room or in the secluded garden. During winter the Tea-room boasts a roaring log fire.

USEFUL INFORMATION

- OPEN: All year
- WHEELCHAIR ACCESS: Tea-rooms only
- GARDEN: Delightful tea garden
- CREDIT CARDS: None taken
- ACCOMMODATION: 1dbl &1 family both ensuite
- RATES: £60 & £50 PRPN B&B

- TEAROOM: Delicious home-made
- VEGETARIAN: Upon request
- LICENSED: No
- CHILDREN: Welcome
- PETS: No

MIDWAY COTTAGE
Farleigh Wick, Bradford-on-Avon
Wiltshire   BA15 2PU
Tel: 01225 863932

ETB 2 Crowns Commended AA QQQ. Michelin

You will find this attractive cottage , which is actually a combination of three cottages built in the mid-19th century, on the busy main A363, but one can forget the busy modern world and simply enjoy the delightful surroundings of open farmland with woods and fields all around. Inside the charmingly furnished house the windows have double or secondary glazing so no noise intrudes on the restful, tranquil atmosphere that pervades Sue Lindsay's home. Farleigh Wick was built along the road between Bath and Bradford on Avon to provide much needed accommodation for agricultural workers in the last century and it is on the very edge of the Cotswolds and almost part of Monkton Farleigh a lovely old stone village. There are two double bedrooms and one twin bedded room, all ensuite. Attractively furnished and with very comfortable beds, each room has direct dial telephones, television and a hostess tray. Sue serves a delicious breakfast at whatever time you feel like eating. The meal has been known to be at 6am and 12 noon! Vegetarians are catered for. No evening meals but the 15th century pub next door is renowned for its good food. Staying in this happy house is a pleasure at any time of the year. Its situation makes it ideal for those on business or taking a break.

USEFUL INFORMATION

- OPEN: All year

- WHEELCHAIR ACCESS: 2 steps only
- GARDEN: Yes
- CREDIT CARDS: None taken
- ACCOMMODATION: 3 ensuite rooms
- RATES: £18-19 pp.pn

- DINING ROOM: Delicious breakfast served whenever you wish
- VEGETARIAN: Yes
- LICENSED: No
- CHILDREN: Welcome
- PETS: Yes, by arrangement

NESTON COUNTRY INN
Neston
Corsham,
Wiltshire
SN13 9SN

Tel: 01225 811694 0498 713413

A charming country inn set amongst fields and houses with natural stone wall in a Conservation Area is somewhere that appeals to most people. Neston Country Inn has all those ingredients with the addition of many more. Run by Janet and Ian Tucker and their daughter Tanya, it is one of the most welcoming hostelries for miles around. It has a lovely, homely atmosphere enhanced by two open fires in the bar and the dining room. The Tudor style thatched bar is surrounded by balloons, parachutes and dolls which the family collect. Everywhere you look there is a profusion of greenery all adding to the sense of well-being. Good, traditional pub fare is available seven days a week including some delicious old fashioned puddings. Children have their own menu and every day there are Bar specials and freshly made sandwiches and other snacks. Five newly refurbished ensuite bedrooms are available for those who would like to stay in this beautiful area. A small hair-salon is an added bonus and Children love the play area with its Gypsy Caravan and Pets Corner. The garden is popular in summer with its patio and the soothing sound of a waterfall cascading over stones.

USEFUL INFORMATION

· OPEN: All year	· DINING ROOM: Good traditional pub fare
· WHEELCHAIR ACCESS: No	· VEGETARIAN:
· GARDEN: Yes. Play area. Pets Corner	· BAR FOOD: Wide range. Daily specials
· CREDIT CARDS: None taken	· LICENSED: Full On
· ACCOMMODATION: 5 ensuite rooms	· CHILDREN: Welcome
· RATES: From £45 double room B&B	· PETS: Small pets only

THE THREE HORSESHOES
55 Frome Road
Bradford-on-Avon
BA15 1LA

Tel/Fax: 01225865876

Bradford on Avon, close to Bath, is one of the most delightful towns in England with a Saxon church and Tithe Barn, and yet in spite of the many visitors who come here, has managed to retain a peaceful, tranquil air and for the community a very pleasant way of life. No town worth its salt is without a variety of good hostelries and The Three Horseshoes, in the friendly, competent hands of Richard and Gillian Vestey maintains the tradition of hospitality which has been going on within its walls for the last three hundred years. It has a great deal of charm providing a happy atmosphere in the bar and in the small restaurant, excellent food. The menu is wide ranging with the emphasis on traditional English dishes, in which as much local, fresh produce, as possible is included. Every day there are four or five time-honoured 'Daily Specials' together with six choices for Vegetarians. The bar has its own menu and there are always several choices including jacket potatoes with a variety of fillings, freshly cut sandwiches and substantial, well garnished, ploughman's. On Sundays there is the traditional roast lunch always popular and very good value. In warm weather the attractive patio with forty to fifty seats is a favourite meeting place.

USEFUL INFORMATION

· OPEN: 11-3.30 & 5-11pm	· RESTAURANT: Traditional English fare
· WHEELCHAIR ACCESS: Yes	· VEGETARIAN: 6 dishes daily
· GARDEN: Yes. Patio seats 40-50	· BAR FOOD: Wide range
· CREDIT CARDS: Access/Master	· LICENSED: Full On
· CHILDREN: Welcome	· PETS: Yes but not in eating area

THE WILTSHIRE KITCHEN
11/12 St John's Street
Devizes, Wiltshire
SN10 1BD

Tel: 01380 724840

Egon Ronay 'Just a Bite' Award

Devizes is one of the most interesting and historic towns in Wiltshire and in the main street, opposite the Town Hall, close to the market place is The Wiltshire Kitchen. It is a fascinating area with 15th century overhanging timber-framed houses in the adjacent St John's Alley. In addition to a very nice, well laid out Cellar Restaurant there is a traditional Coffee House on the ground floor. There is also a flourishing Take Home Meals service and a large choice of restaurant meals can be prepared for home entertainment. The Restaurant specialises in freshly prepared and cooked traditional meals using local produce and is open Tuesday to Saturday evenings and Sunday Lunch Time. The Coffee House provides hot and cold drinks breakfast, sandwiches and snacks and home cooked lunches as well as a range of home made cakes. Specials of the day are displayed on blackboards and there is also a good selection of salads, filled jacket potatoes and very tempting hot and cold desserts. Afternoon tea includes fresh scones with lashings of cream. The atmosphere throughout the Wiltshire Kitchen is friendly and welcoming, the price is right and there is something to suit everyone's palate.

USEFUL INFORMATION

- OPEN : All year
- CREDIT CARDS: Visa/Master
- COFFEE HOUSE: Mon-Sat 8.30am-5pm (7pm in Summer) Sun 10am-4pm
- LICENSED: Restaurant licence

- RESTAURANT: Tues-Sat from 7pm Sun 12 noon -3pm
- VEGETARIAN: Always available
- CHILDREN: Welcome

Angel Inn	Heytesbury	333
Belmont	Warminster	350
Bishopstrow House	Warminster	334
Brook House	Semington	350
Crown Hotel	Alvediston	335
Deverill End	South Veny	336
Grasmere House	Salisbury	337
Hayburn Wyke	Salisbury	338
Howards House	Teffont Evias	339
Lamb On The Strand	Semington	351
Les Parisiens	Warminster	351
London House	Pewsey	340
Longwater Park Farm	Erlestoke	352
Mill House	Berwick St James	352
Milton Farm	East Knoyle	341
Morris' Farmhouse	Baverstock	353
Old Manor	Trowle	342
Pembroke Arms	Favant	343
Queens Head Inn	Broadchalke	344
Riverside Close	Laverstock	353
Silver Plough	Pitton	345
Snooty Fox	Warminster	346
Sturford Mead Farm	Warminster	354
Three Crowns Inn	Whaddon	347
White Lodge	Warminster	348
Woodbridge Inn	North Newnton	349

Chapter 7:
The Plain and the Extraordinary.

Southern Wiltshire has both the Plain and the extraordinary. The twist is that one is contained within the other; for no-one could argue that either Salisbury Cathedral or Stonehenge, both within the boundaries of the original area of the Salisbury Plain, are anything other than extraordinary.

What a contrast too. The rugged stones of the Henge and the streamlined architecture of the cathedral are an obvious difference, while the vast emptiness of the Plain and the bustle of the city of Salisbury reflect the true distance between the two attractions in terms of history, use and atmosphere. Stonehenge is a place of mystery, awe, and voices from the distant past; Salisbury Cathedral is a monument to the continuity of the more recent civilizations built upon the Plain, and the beauty they have created and managed to maintain. So that's two places you will not want to miss.

Even these are not all that the southern half of Wiltshire has to offer. The West Wiltshire Downs; Wilton, Mere and Longleat, all of these add to the immense variety of architecture and landscape experienced to the north.

Before we tackle either the West Wiltshire Downs or Salisbury Plain, there is a little unfinished business to tie up in the Vale of Pewsey to the east. **PEWSEY** itself lies just three quarters of a mile south of the canal, just missing inclusion in our last chapter and the small town as well as the villages around it add another dimension to this southern half of the county.

A previous owner of Pewsey, of whom we will soon hear much more, looks down on you from his statue in the town. King Alfred knew this area when things were even quieter, which may seem quite hard to credit, unless you happen to see an Intercity train powering through Pewsey on its way towards or from London.

The tremendous size of the fearsome broadsword the figure of Alfred holds in his right hand looks quite inappropriate to defend such a quiet area, but central Wiltshire was at the heart of the battles with the Danes for control of the whole of Wessex, as we will see later at Bratton.

Statue of King Alfred, Pewsey

Now the southern half of the Vale of Pewsey is a delightful place for quiet exploration. The canal is at its most secluded along the stretch from Pewsey to Devizes, blending into the countryside. In contrast to the twenty nine locks of Caen Hill, there is not a single one for some fifteen miles as it wanders around the contours of the land. If you decide to walk only one section of the Kennet and Avon, then make it this one.

The PEWSEY HERITAGE AND MUSEUM CENTRE (01672 62051 / 62404) has a collection of the various implements and machines man has used to cultivate this green Vale over the centuries, housed in a 19th century foundry building on the High Street. The town also has one of the West Country's most famous carnivals, held each year in September. But as attractive as Pewsey is, with cottages of thatch and timber, it is the surrounding area of peaceful scenery interspersed with delightful villages which is bound to tempt you.

South of Pewsey is the fifth of the six Wiltshire White Horses, taking them from north to south. This one is the most recent of all, having been cut to add to Pewsey's celebrations of King George VI's coronation in 1937. It really is a question of driving or walking around the remainder of the Vale to find your own favourites, as there is so much to choose from, but we will look at a few areas and villages of especial interest.

The WILTSHIRE WILDLIFE TRUST has two Nature Reserves close to Pewsey. JONES'S MILL is an area of fenland to the north east of the town. There are not many fens in Wiltshire, and this one has benefited from the decline of the canal as a working waterway. The resultant diversity of flora is unusually rich, with fourteen species of sedge alone. Wildlife has thrived too, and you can look out for everything from snipe to harvest mice, scarlet tiger moths, and grass snakes.

PEPPERCOMBE WOOD is much further to the west, nearer to Devizes than it is to Pewsey. Another collection of rarities, this small wood has a strip of ancient ash and wych elm woodland. Spring is the optimum season in which to visit, when flowers add to the tranquil beauty.

Do not be drawn too quickly to the west though, as east of Pewsey there is still much before the county border. A drive through the village of **MILTON LILBOURNE** with its old cottages looking down on you from high pavements will take you past the turning to the hamlet of **EASTON ROYAL**, another attractive, out of the way settlement. Next comes **BURBAGE**, with WOLF HALL nearby, where the Seymours (as in Jane Seymour, wife of Henry VIII) had their family home.

So the journey continues, past dozens of equally quiet but likeable villages. Look out for the working windmill on the hill to the east of **WILTON** (not to be confused with the town near Salisbury). This claims to be Wiltshire's only working mill, and appears a suitably traditional way to produce the healthy wholemeal stoneground flour it makes. The village is most picturesque too, with the streams which feed the pond wending their way amongst thatched cottages.

A little further south there are more remains from Roman times, with the unusually curving road known as CHUTE CAUSEWAY, which was part of the soldiers route from Winchester to Marlborough. A drive or short march of your own along this ridge gives you views as spectacular as those from the Wansdyke at the opposite edge of the Vale of Pewsey. The Romans obviously did not mind if they were seen to be on the move. Mind you, this is such a deserted area it is quite possible they could have got away without being noticed if they had desired to.

Of course there are many other ways to enjoy the Vale, from cycling to paragliding. One that has caught my eye for the future is the idea of soaring above the glorious scenery in a hot air balloon. CAMERON BALLOONS (01672 562277) are based in Pewsey and say that they take 'special care' of those making a first flight, so you might happen to share a basket with me!

The PEWSEY VALE RIDING CENTRE (01672 851400) can help if you wish to ride in the area. For those who prefer to stand, but also to fish, there is trout fly angling at **NORTH NEWNTON** (01672 630266). If Avebury has not yet sated your appetite there are more ancient sites to explore too, notably the GIANT'S GRAVE near Milton Lilbourne, another long barrow, or burial mound.

Leaving the Vale of Pewsey behind to travel west towards Trowbridge along the northern edge of Salisbury Plain there are a couple of unusual museums to the south of Devizes which may appeal.

The FIRE DEFENCE COLLECTION (01380 731108) at **POTTERNE** has a fascinating collection of bright red vehicles, from the early hand pumped versions to those with motors. Look also in the village for ST MARYS CHURCH, which has a Saxon font, and the TUDOR PORCH HOUSE.

Further south in **MARKET LAVINGTON** the old schoolmaster's cottage behind the village school houses the MARKET LAVINGTON MUSEUM (01380 818736) which has a restored Victorian Kitchen. I bet the men who were lucky enough to live and work here never had to trouble their heads about the National Curriculum and Statutory Attainments!

Picking up the western limits of the county south of Bradford-on-Avon and the canal there is continuity with the north here too, including more of the many Wiltshire towns which made their names as centres for the wool trade. **TROWBRIDGE** (Tourist Information 01225 777054) is among these, and has its place in the Domesday Book, having then developed into a market town since at least 1200. Another prosperous centre for the manufacture of the cloth 'medley', which was popular from the late 17th to the 19th century, Trowbridge has survived the decline of the mills to become another of modern Wiltshire's successful industrial towns.

Despite being on the western extreme of the county, and much closer to Bath and Bristol than it is to Salisbury or Swindon, this is the county town of Wiltshire. Trowbridge is not one of the most glamorous towns, and has a distinctly practical feel about it, with the modern investments from Ushers Breweries, Bowyers and Unigate replacing the weaving trade.

TROWBRIDGE MUSEUM (01225 751339) is situated on the spinning floor of the last mill in the town, which closed in 1982. For a look at all aspects of the cloth production, from factory floor to home spinning wheel, this is a fascinating place. If you look around the older buildings of Trowbridge you may be able to pick out those which were built for weavers by their large first floor windows. This was usually where the loom was kept, and so maximum sunlight was invited into the workspace by making the windows the largest in the house.

Adding to the already impressive collection of fine Tudor and Georgian Houses north of the Kennet and Avon Canal, is WESTWOOD MANOR (01225 863374) just to the south of the waterway, above Trowbridge. Next to the 15th century church in the hamlet of **WESTWOOD** this is a National Trust property from the 15th and 16th centuries, with some fine Jacobean plasterwork inside, and an unusual garden of modern topiary, or clipped yew, outside.

Even nearer the western extremity of the county IFORD MANOR GARDEN (01225 863146) is an Italian style garden around another Manor House. The House itself is not open, but the terraces, sculptures and views, below some lovely beech woods, make the setting quite special.

The woollen industry has left other reminders of its affluence in the area too, such as the church at **STEEPLE ASHTON**, a particularly good example of the perpendicular style. More recent history has been played out in this area to the south of Trowbridge too. KEEVIL AIRFIELD, between Steeple Ashton and **EDINGTON** was used in the Second World War, not just as a base for the RAF, but also as a camp for many refugees from Poland. Apparently the base is one of the best preserved in Britain, perhaps due to its remote setting, and there are plans to turn it into a museum (try Keevil on an Internet Search Engine for current developments, or if you were stationed here in the 1940s).

EDINGTON PRIORY is another fine perpendicular building, looking a suitably peaceful place of worship despite its huge size for such a sparse parish, and is the centre of a music festival which draws visitors to the village from many parts of the world, each year in August.

Yet on 29th June 1450 William Ayscough, the Bishop of Salisbury and Confessor to King Henry VI, was dragged from the altar in the middle of giving Mass, to be murdered in the fields outside by some of Jack Cade's rebels, who were protesting at the corruption of Henry's court. Apparently the Bishop was stoned to death with local flints; not a pleasant thought. It is not as if Edington is unused to violent death either, depending on which of the many historians of the time of King Alfred have got it right.

Some say that ETHANDUN, the site of his victory over the Danes in 878 was modern day Edington, and that the original White Horse near Westbury was a celebration of the event. If so, then it is believed that the retreating Scandanavian forces took shelter at BRATTON CASTLE, an earthwork now used for its superb views over the Plain and for flying kites.

Whatever the truth, this area looks right for a place in the conflict outlined in the Anglo-Saxon Chronicle, as Alfred trekked across most of the land making up modern day England in order to prevent his kingdom becoming a new Danish colony.

The Chronicle is not consistently poetic in its description of the events, but the cold, blunt sounds of a section from the entry for 878 seem very appropriate in the isolated, wind swept spots lining the Plain:

"Her hiene bestael se here on midne winter ofer tuelftan niht to Cippanhamme, ond geridon Wesseaxna lond ond gesaeton, ond micel thaes folces ofer sae adraefdon, ond thaes othres thone maestan dael hie geridon on him to gecirdon buton tham cyninge Aelfrede: ond he lytle werede uniethelice aefter wudum for ond on morfaestenum."

Translation: In this year he (Godrum, the Danish leader) stole with his army to Chippenham, over twelve nights (from his camp at Cambridge), and overran and occupied the land of Wessex and drove many of their forces overseas. Most of the others were conquered and made subject to him, except for King Alfred: along with a small troop of loyal men he made his way, with great difficulty, through the woodlands and into his fen fortresses.

More than eleven hundred years ago this was where the future of England was decided, because if Alfred had been driven out for good then the area of Wessex would have once again become a series of smaller kingdoms, each ready to be pillaged by invaders at any given time. If the land around here looks grim and a little uninviting on a cold, blustery day, then imagine how it must have felt to be part of an army, marching for miles in the middle of winter, without the benefit of modern roads to make your route any easier.

The Westbury White Horse does not look quite old enough to celebrate Alfred's recovery from such surprise attacks, and this is because the present figure comes from 1778, when the original was rejected as being an unrealistic representation of the equine form. If you want to perform your own act of heroic bravery near the Horse today then you can join the many other hang and para-gliding enthusiasts.

So it is not just Stonehenge and Avebury which give Wiltshire mystery and ancient history. But **BRATTON** and the area surrounding the Horse are at the centre of present day mysteries too. An American tourist by the name of Brian Boldman tells of a visit made to Wiltshire in August 1997 for the specific purpose of seeing some crop circles for himself. The report is on the Internet, connected to those mentioned earlier near Liddington.

He found two 'virgin' circles just over a mile east from the Westbury White Horse car park, and got permission from the farmer to investigate them. Apparently two identical circles were found by a helicopter on the same spot ten years earlier. Whether you think these patterns are made by aliens or freak weather conditions it cannot be denied that they are intriguing, and give something else to look out for among the rural landscapes of Wiltshire.

WESTBURY (Tourist Information 01373 827158) is another market town, a place to return to modern reality if you have been following the trail of mystery and history combining past and present in the surrounding countryside. As well as a supply of wool from the sheep grazing the lands around it, Westbury had the water from innumerable underground springs to use to build its industries.

So why is Westbury any different to Bradford-on-Avon, or Devizes? A railway station. Even now Westbury is on the main route to London, and in the 19th century, when the mills started to fail, the new iron road gave the town a vital head start in the race to stay economically viable.

What this means for today is that much of the rural elegance of other Wiltshire weaving towns has gone, but Westbury does have a long history and some relics from it have survived. Look in particular for ALL SAINTS CHURCH, built in the 14th century on the site of the former Saxon Minster. All Saints boasts the third loudest peal of bells in the world, so be warned! CHURCH STREET has many of the best 18th century houses of the town along its narrow length.

Another more unusual survivor from previous times is the WESTBURY SWIMMING POOL (01373 822891) also in Church Street, which was built in 1887 by a local mill owner. Refurbishment in the 1980s means that the pool is still open for use, and the setting is quite unique, as this is the only remaining indoor Victorian pool in the country. You will particularly notice the difference to modern pools if you relax on your back and look up at the ornate timber beams of the ceiling which make quite a contrast to modern materials.

The land around Westbury is used for an enormous range of leisure pursuits. TRAILBLAZERS (01373 827417) offer everything from Clay Pigeon, Air Rifle and Pistol Shooting to Quad Safaris.

To the north west of the town THE WOODLAND PARK (01373 822238 / 823880) has eighty acres of ancient woodland to explore. Amongst the trees there is a HERITAGE CENTRE dedicated to wildlife conservation. There are many guided walks, and a lake for coarse angling, which is particularly good for carp. After all the tales of Crop Circles, it may not come as a total surprise to hear that nearby **WARMINSTER** (Tourist Information 01985 218548) boasts a tremendously high number of U.F.O. incidents in recent decades.

The last of the wool and cloth towns of West Wiltshire we will visit, it is pinned in between the expanse of Salisbury plain to the north east, and the West Wiltshire Downs to the south west. North of the town ARN HILL is the perfect place from which get an idea of the variety of the scenery around you, either as you walk the marked Nature Trails, or perhaps as you enjoy the views during a leisurely round at the eighteen hole course belonging to the WEST WILTSHIRE GOLF CLUB (01985

213133). Look out for any new bunkers, especially if a green glow emanates from them, you might just end up adding to local statistics!

Light and rural industries have replaced cloth in Warminster, but it has also become a place of some military importance, as home to the SCHOOL OF INFANTRY since 1945, and the workshops of the ROYAL ELECTRICAL AND MECHANICAL ENGINEERS. Conflict has happened here too, but not for some centuries. Warminster changed hands several times during the Civil War, and nearby BATTLEBURY CAMP was a major fort during the Iron Age.

Another place which is ideal to use a base from which to explore what lies around it, Warminster is more attractive in itself than some of its neighbours, and with protected buildings of local stone, many supported on pillars to remind us of the town's importance as a coaching station, it has perhaps more in common with Marlborough than with Westbury or Trowbridge.

The DEWEY MUSEUM (01985 216022) is inside Warminster's main library, and is principally concerned with local history, with particularly good photographic archives. Some of the town's churches are worthy of note too, especially the MINSTER CHURCH OF ST DENYS and the 13th century CHAPEL OF ST LAWRENCE. But it is the land around Warminster which will inevitably draw you away from the town itself, and there really is not far to go.

Right opposite the Tourist Information Office in the Market Place in the centre of the town, a walk along Weymouth Street will take you to the VALLEY OF THE WERE. This is pleasant enough, with lawns and flower beds, a stream and boating lake, all framed by green slopes rising on either side, but continue the walk and you will find the SMALLBROOK MEADOWS, a WILTSHIRE WILDLIFE TRUST NATURE RESERVE (Local info: 01985 840266).

There cannot be many such opportunities to explore water meadows, with marshy grassland and fens, so easily accessible from a sizeable town centre. Look out for Cuckooflower, and ragged-Robin, as well as kingfishers, water vole and dragonflies. If this whets your appetite, several of the paths link to HENDFORDS MARSH and the countryside beyond.

Warminster is also a good place from which to access some excellent coarse angling, with both the HUNTERS MOON COMPLEX and SHEARWATER LAKE (01985 218548) within a couple of miles of the town. The second of these has sailing and walks set in nearly forty acres of coniferous woodlands, contrasting to the surrounding downlands. A third place for coarse fishing, near Shearwater, is the lake which forms a part of probably the most famous of Wiltshire's tourist attractions, barring Stonehenge and Salisbury Cathedral.

LONGLEAT (01985 844400) has become known for its lions as much as its fantastic House. Even this does not give an accurate summary of what is here, with the Dr Who exhibition, a tropical butterfly garden, and what claims to be the world's longest hedge maze, among many other things.

Longleat House

To make a start, let's look at the House itself. Often described as the most magnificent domestic dwelling in England, it started out as a monastic dwelling, passing to Sir John Thynne after the Dissolution in the 16th century, who is said to have paid £53 for the site, about the price of a full family day out to most places these days! Sir John established the main shell of the present building, although at the second attempt after a fire in 1567 ruined the first. Many later additions were made, and the gardens were inevitably the work of Lancelot Brown, whose 'Capability' was a quality first named by Lord Weymouth, who owned Longleat towards the end of the 18th century.

Once you have turned the curve in the drive, the front-on view of Longleat is one which is hard to equal. The grandeur of the great square lines of the golden stone edifice puts me in mind of a building fit for Royalty; but the setting here is so completely different to that of the more accessible Royal dwellings, such as Buckingham Palace. The width of Longleat is quite breathtaking because there is no fence in front of it, or lesser buildings to either side. It is framed by the sky and the lawns, and little else of consequence. The result is three stories of mullioned and transomed windows topped by balustrading, turrets and statues, as well as ornamental chimneys, the whole effect of which is to make you stop and draw breath. There is just so much to see in a single glance, without even approaching near enough to examine any chosen detail.

Longleat has been a private home ever since 1540, and the contents reflect the tastes and interests of its inhabitants over the whole of that time. There is much too much to list in any detail here, but for anyone who has a liking for anything from porcelain to embroidery, books, furniture and silver, time spent inside the house will not be dull. Some of the Venetian ceilings and the tapestries are especially memorable, as is the State Dining Room, with its silver centre piece, which celebrates the end of the Civil War, and apparently weighs 1,000 ounces!

So why has such a splendid stately home taken on wildlife, science fiction exhibitions and so much other external paraphernalia? Many might say that it all spoils the place, but I disagree. Longleat House is such an attraction that those who enjoy such houses cannot seriously be put off by the extras, which only intrude if you want them to (even the lions).

What can happen at Longleat is that children of all ages who come here to enjoy the safari park, or to walk the maze, see the House as an extra; until they have a proper look at it. Many have then returned later with their priorities changed, and with a new interest in domestic architecture.

Are the lions dangerous? Not only lions now, but all manner of wild beasts roam Longleat, including some you can walk among, such as giraffe, llamas, zebra and camels. The only story of danger I have personal knowledge of involves none of these, but instead a man who apparently enjoys a pint of lager.

Trivial this following anecdote may be, but I'm afraid I cannot think of Longleat without smiling, and this is why. A friend and his family were about to visit the Doctor Who exhibition when they noticed the resplendent figure of a 'Cyber-Man' by the entrance (the ones who look as if they have found a particularly comfortable way to be wrapped from head to toe in a soft shining foil). To the family from Somerset this particular enemy of the great Time Lord was affectionately known as the 'Cider Man'. So one remarked to another "I wonder if he drinks cider?"

The ten year old boy of the group was in the middle of laughing at the joke when the Cyberman, thus far believed to be a statue, replied "Actually I prefer lager." The young man ran for cover. It took the family some time to find him, helped of course by the Longleat employee wearing the silver suit. The terrified boy was eventually discovered hiding inside one of the refreshments kiosks, crouched underneath the counter. He refused to come out until the poor 'Cider-Man' removed the top of his costume to show that he was entirely human!

So, if you see a man in a 'Cyber' suit at Longleat today, ask him if he still enjoys a pint, although I would imagine the guilt of his former experience might have made him look for less troublesome employment!

In the end, the fact that most of the facilities and attractions in the grounds of Longleat have very little to do with Wiltshire and its history, or indeed that they could be just about anywhere, is not at all the point. After all, even the natural looking gardens, such as Heaven's Gate are the artificial additions of a landscape gardener, albeit the most celebrated of them all. Longleat makes for a great day out, and it has so much to offer that the often used phrase 'something for everyone' fits here better than most of the places it is applied to. The addition of the CENTRE PARCS (01623 411411) resort within the Longleat Estate suggests that it is attracting more visitors than ever.

Longleat is at the north west tip of the WEST WILTSHIRE DOWNS, which join with the eastern part of the Cranborne Chase to make up the whole of the south west corner of Wiltshire. The whole of this area is safe from local planning policies because of its nationally recognised status as an AREA OF OUTSTANDING NATURAL BEAUTY. There is not a single major town within the huge green section marked out on the map to show the boundaries of the Downs and the Chase. With the latter this is partly because this was where Kings came to hunt (usually based at Cranborne Manor, see Dorset), but in both cases it has left some lovely open land to explore.

Walking or cycling are recommended by the Countryside Commission as being the best way to tackle this area, especially if you wish to find some of the rarer flora and fauna. However, the many remote villages and some of the main attractions of the area are accessible by road, and there other ways of enjoying the Downs too.

The nearest village to both Longleat and Shearwater is **HORNINGSHAM**. Just as the Flemish weavers had houses built for them when Edward III first imported their expertees to the Wiltshire weaving towns, so Sir John Thynne had the MEETING HALL at Horningsham built for the many Scottish masons he had enticed down to help with the building of Longleat. There was no suitable Non-Conformist Chapel in the country, let alone the county, and so this can now claim to be the site of the oldest in the land of the Sasanachs. The present building is from nearly one hundred and fifty years later, having been built in 1700.

Going south along the border with Somerset you will pass GARE HILL, a centre for Game Shooting, before approaching yet another of Wiltshire's famous Houses. As you pass **MAIDEN BRADLEY** the road dives between two hills, with another statue of King Alfred looking down on you from the top of his one hundred and fifty foot tower to the right. The National Trust property around KING ALFRED'S TOWER (01985 844785) is a great place for some views back across to the east, and with the guardian of Wessex seemingly still at his post on the very edge of Wiltshire, everything seems in keeping with the rest of the county. However, this last House is something very different, its setting, in particular, is quite unique.

Near the village of **STOURTON**, in the westernmost part of Wiltshire is STOURHEAD (01747 841152), a Georgian House surrounded by dark green hills and woodland, from amongst which elements of the Italian style gardens peek like the remnants of some long overgrown Roman city.

For once the landscaping is not the work of Mr Brown, but of Henry Hoare, the third of his family to have owned the house after it was bought by his uncle Richard Hoare in 1714. Up until then it had been the home of the Stourtons, created Lords by Henry VI, and who also gave their name to the village. The eighth of those to hold the title was publicly hanged in Salisbury for a double murder in the 16th century, but long before the family mysteriously sold the property to the Hoares.

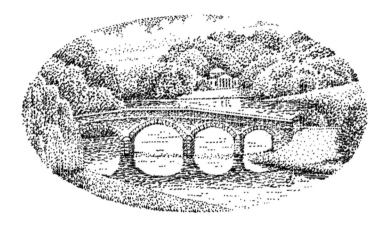

The Gardens at Stourhead

Looking at the obvious influences of contemporary European travel evident in the design of the gardens, do not think that Henry Hoare was anything but a patriot proud of his heritage, as it was he who also had King Alfred's Tower erected. The hilltop is where Alfred was supposed to have set up his standard before moving on to Ethandun to rout the Danes.

A romantic idea; the King with his few remaining bedraggled followers had fled to the "fen fortresses" as the Chronicle told us, now he arrived with fresh men, and new hope. It must have been quite a sight for anyone looking up to see the standard blowing in the breeze, representing unexpected news of a leader whose day seemed to have passed. Of course it may not have been like that at all, the mists of time have well and truly fallen on the details of those events, but it is still great fun to speculate.

History is by no means everything at Stourhead. What the imagination of Henry Hoare has left behind is just as beautiful and accessible today as it was almost three hundred years ago when he started by making the huge three sided lake a centre for the 'focal points' amongst the trees. The idea is that there are various vantage points from which to view the landscapes, and that the classical TEMPLE OF FLORA, GROTTO, PANTHEON and so on, make a semicircle around the lake, each of them clearly visible from at least one of the others.

Whatever the reasons for the choices Henry made, the result is quite unique and magical; no real Italian garden of statues and curiosities could boast such verdant, decidedly English surroundings. The cosmopolitan combination is also reflected inside the house, where the paintings of CLAUDE and POUSSIN which inspired the landscaping take their places amongst Chippendale furniture. As far removed from Longleat as it is from Stonehenge in appearance, Stourhead really does add something special to Wiltshire.

The seasons add plenty of colour to Stourhead, but if you want to take some colour away with you then the STOURTON HOUSE FLOWER GARDEN (01747 840417) can provide rare and unusual home propagated plants, including a wide range of Hydrangeas. The four acre flower garden (next to the car park for Stourhead) is a distinct contrast to the grander scale of the landscapes, and is a way of getting the eye used to operating on a shorter, more detailed focus once more!

As you turn east away from his statue on the hill, you might well be wondering why there has been no mention of King Alfred's most notorious escapade, of a culinary rather than a military nature. Do not worry, for the smell of burning cakes is said to have issued from within the boundaries of the Wiltshire Wildlife Trust Nature Reserve of WHITESHEET HILL, which lies between Stourton and Mere. On the ground you may find field voles and rare downland plants, but looking up your longer focus will again take over, as on a clear day you can see past Stourhead back to the Tower on the next tree lined ridge to the west; if these views are exciting then be prepared for even more at the other White Sheet Hill, some distance to the east.

MERE (Tourist Information 01747 861211) is another of those places which is seen by many more as a name on road signs than actually get to visit the village. Mere is much closer to the A303 than Chippenham or Malmesbury are to the M4, but this makes little difference to the thousands who tear past it each day on their way east (Monday mornings mostly) and west (returning from a week's London work on Friday evenings).

As a watering hole from the days of the stagecoaches, the small town has got used to its role since the 17th century. By now it is not surprising to come across an area with much history and evidence of prehistoric activity just a few hundred yards from an extremely busy link road. Wiltshire accepts the new, but refuses to give up on the old.

Getting close to the borders, features common to Dorset have crept into the history of Mere. William Barnes, the dialect poet from Dorchester, lived in the town here from 1823 to 1835, and Charles II added to the fine collection of inns he stayed in during his flight across the country (see Bridport, Charmouth, Broadwindsor etc) at the George in Mere, which is now the Talbot Hotel. The Charles II trail might make an interesting new way to discover Wessex, although perhaps a little demanding on the liver!

If you prefer a rural base from which to explore the countryside, then Mere has enough shops, and enough peace, despite the nearby traffic, to fit the bill. You are now near the meeting of three counties, indeed I have a friend who lives between **ZEALS** and Wincanton who insists his mail has arrived bearing the county names of Dorset, Wiltshire and Somerset, each with equal success. I am not sure which one is the most correct, and I do not think he is either. From the hill which used to have Mere's castle set atop it, you can see into enough of all three counties to make your own decisions as to whether each has its own characteristics, although in the nearer perspective it is, as usual, hard to follow any signs of a border.

The MERE MUSEUM focuses on local history, and is inside the Public Library in Barton Lane. As well as a good place to start an expedition by foot or bicycle, the town gives access to some of the other ways of enjoying the Downs. The WILTSHIRE AND NORTH DORSET GLIDING CLUB has its base just four miles away in **KINGSTON DEVERILL**, a village where more Sarsen stones mark the spot at which King Alfred was supposed to have met up with more supporters form other counties, perhaps drawn by the odours and smoke from his cooking on Whitesheet Hill.
A drive towards Warminster along the soft contours of the DEVERILL VALLEY, amongst the other villages bearing the Deverill suffix, is another pleasant, quiet experience.

If you drive east from Mere to **WEST KNOYLE**, be prepared for a surprise. Some of the cattle in the fields may look a little fearsome and bulky, but do not book in for an immediate eye test, for these are indeed Bison, from BUSH FARM (01747 830263). They are not part of some Wild West Theme attraction though, for you can actually buy cuts of Wiltshire fed and reared Bison meat, which apparently has only half the calories and cholesterol of traditional beef. If you would rather look than eat, then there are walks around the farm and woodlands, as well as a Gallery of artwork on the subject of American wildlife. Whatever next, although I suppose the bison do look about the right scale of animal to fill some of the open countryside of the south of the county.

To the south east the Downs merge with the Cranborne Chase, giving much greater depth, north to south. Before Wilton there are still no major towns, but plenty more villages and countryside to discover.

To the north of the A303, and running east from Warminster, the WYLYE VALLEY is the northern barrier for the Downs. South of the river itself, and the more major A36 which follows its opposite bank, the B3095 takes you through some of the most idyllic hamlets and villages you could wish for. **SHERRINGTON, TYTHERINGTON, HANGING LANGFORD** and many more, each full of thatched cottages and winding chalk streams amongst the secluded protection of the soft hills which surround them, are sedately beautiful.

By the time you have crossed the A303 again and reached Hanging Langford (named after its location under the hills, rather than any gruesome incident from the past), the steeper slopes to the right, or south, lead up to GROVELY WOODS. As with the GREAT RIDGE to the west, there are no modern roads across this vast area, and as you look down onto Wilton and then Salisbury in the distance, there are few signs of human habitation in between.

If you should hear a shout of 'Grovely, Grovely, Grovely, and All Grovely' from the east then do not worry about being caught up in a pagan ritual, for this is part of the proceedings of OAK APPLE DAY, held in the village of **GREAT WISHFORD** each year on May 29th. On this day the young of the village climb to the wood to claim their right to take firewood back to the village. Mind you, on most other days there do not seem to be many people around to prevent them starting a bit of impromptu deforestation if they so choose.

Another curiosity in Great Wishford is the churchyard wall, which has the history of the price of bread inscribed upon it. The existence of sudden inflation in former times is proved by the fact that between 1800 and 1801 the price of a gallon of local bread rose from three shillings and fourpence to three shillings and ten pence, which I calculate to be about a fifteen per cent increase. Then again it had fallen to a meagre tenpence a gallon by 1904, so inconsistency is not new either! If someone had thought of using chalk and a darker background in Wishford then all this trivia could easily have been lost, and I would not have been reminded that bread was formerly priced by volume rather than weight, much as fishing maggots are nowadays!

There is a road through Grovely Wood, but much older than the ones you will have used to get this far. The road from Bath to Sarum was already well established by Roman times, and is now a bridleway. As such it is an ideal place to start a walk or cycle ride through the blissfully quiet area free of motorised traffic. The Wood also holds the LITTLE LANGFORD DOWN Nature Reserve, rich with wild flowers, and also ant-hills, perhaps in defiance at the invasion of the slightly larger Bison to the south!

The rest of the Downs north of the Cranborne Chase do have some modern roads, although lanes would be a more accurate term for most of them. This is the NADDER VALLEY, an area of fertile greensand set low between the less cultivated areas to the north and south. Around the village of **DINTON**, there is suddenly another crop of great Houses, made of the creamy stone from the quarries at nearby **CHILMARK**. If the stone looks familiar, then this is quite possibly because it was also used for Salisbury Cathedral.

There are four National Trust properties in Dinton alone, with the neo-classical PHILLIPS HOUSE being the largest, but none are regularly open to the public. The link to Salisbury Cathedral is made a little more obvious at **TEFFONT EVIAS**, where the church has a one hundred and twenty five foot spire, fighting for possession of the skyline with nearby cedars, which is most reminiscent of its larger cousin to the east. The battlements on the tower of the Manor House next to the church show that the light stone looks equally elegant when used with squarer lines.

TEFFONT MAGNA has more thatched cottages around a medieval church (ST EDWARD), and miniature stone bridges crossing its stream. Another attraction based in the village has a name which is bound to get the attention. The FARMER GILES FARMSTEAD (01722 716338) does not sound too promising, unless you are looking for some scrumpy and over priced clotted cream, but in fact this is a tremendous celebration of the agricultural, rural life of this area in times gone by.

A working dairy farm, sections of the 175 acre estate use Shire Horses to cultivate the land too, and the Beech belt provides beautiful walks at the right time of year through bluebells and rhododendrons. There's a blacksmith's forge and collection of old agricultural machinery as well, but the real beauty is that with such a collection of villages to explore nearby the whole idea of a look at the history of rural life is placed in an ideal context. As for Farmer Giles himself, I suppose the name is forgivable, as long as they do not start a fast food chain with a straw chewing yokel for a logo.

Moving a little to the west, **TISBURY** is the largest settlement in the Nadder Valley, and has a direct rail connection to London. It also has some more fine stone buildings, including the church of ST JOHN THE BAPTIST and PLACE HOUSE, which stands beside one of the largest Tithe Barns in the country, bearing the small matter of 5,400 square feet of thatch on its 200 feet of roof.

Two characters dominate the history of the area surrounding Tisbury, one of each gender, and the female is buried in the village. During the Civil War, LADY BLANCHE ARUNDELL defended nearby OLD WARDOUR CASTLE (01747 870487) with just fifty men and women to assist her, against a Parliamentary force numbering 1,300. Eventually she was conned into coming out and surrendering the fortress on the agreement that it would be left alone. Cromwell's forces plundered the unusual hexagonal building, and the ruination was completed by Blanche's son, Lord Arundell, during his successful assault to regain the family home a year later.

Old Wardour Castle

This story will sound familiar at Corfe Castle in Dorset, and the odds are similar to the royalist defensive triumph at Sherborne too. Yet the biggest similarity between the three castles is that they all lie in ruins, destroyed not by an invading force, such as the Danes so valiantly resisted by King Alfred and his men, but by an internal war which did untold damage to England's heritage.

In another parallel to Sherborne, Wardour also has a new castle next to the old, which is much less forbidding as a fortress, and is now a Public School. More of the old castle is left than at its two Dorset counterparts, and the tranquil setting above a lake and surrounded by woodlands, makes the old castle seem an unlikely place to have such a history.

The other character from the Tisbury area makes up for any comparative lack of heroism in his history, with more than a double helping of eccentricity. Near **FONTHILL GIFFORD** lies one of the last two remnants of the outlandish life and works of WILLIAM BECKFORD. If you can manage to find the remains of 'BECKFORD'S FOLLY' the small lake amongst the woods cannot hope to give you an idea of what troubles he once went to in this place.

Beckford's architectural dreams started with a wall twelve feet high and seven miles long, built around one of his houses. Next came his dreams for a ruined Gothic Abbey in the garden, and this was Beckford's Folly. William became so fond of it that he left his house to live in the abbey, but the tower kept collapsing as quickly as he could have it built. The other remnant of his life's work is a little more accessible.

A course in Gothic fiction of the late eighteenth and early nineteenth century is the most likely place in which you will hear of William Beckford's *'Vathek'*. There were quite a few 'one off' Gothic Novel authors, who dashed off quite exhilarating stories, and then simply disappeared from the public eye, even if the book was a best-seller like Matthew Lewis's *'The Monk'*. At least with William Beckford we know what else he was up to. Amongst his various and extraordinary projects was the planting of a million trees in a year around the Fonthill villages, and so perhaps a third reminder of his life is all around his former home.

Now we are close to another main road, the A30 from Shaftesbury to Salisbury. A drive out of Dorset to the east along this route helps to define the character of Wiltshire and its Downs. The grass is shorter, there is less undergrowth than further west, and the hills look as if they have been moulded out of fresh clay, perhaps just a few minutes ago. The lines are smooth, as if a gentle sea swell in a tropical ocean had been frozen, and then turned to light green. There are far fewer hedges than in most of Dorset, and the trees are coniferous, with the result that there is a pleasing, distinct contrast between the light green of the ground and the darker shades reaching for the sky.

The section of the A30 south of Old Wardour Castle runs along the other WHITE SHEET HILL. The whole area south of here is fantastic for viewing right down to the south coast and even the Isle of Wight on a particularly clear day. A walk from **LUDWELL** on the main road might lead you across the hills until you are beginning to feel lost. If this is so, and darkness is falling, listen out for the tolling of a church bell. This comes from the little village of **BERWICK ST JOHN**, tucked away beneath the hills. The bell is rung for fifteen minutes at eight o'clock each night in winter, complying with the wishes of the rector who started the custom more than two hundred years ago.

Further south the views are at their very best at WIN GREEN, right on the Dorset border, while **TOLLARD ROYAL** owes its name to a hunting lodge kept here by King John, emphasising that this is now part of his hunting grounds, otherwise known as the Cranborne Chase. Near the village are the LARMER TREE VICTORIAN PLEASURE GARDENS (01725 516228 / 516453) originally laid out by another of Wiltshire's characters, GENERAL PITT RIVERS. The keen archaeologist created these in 1880, with curiosities such as a Roman temple and Indian buildings amongst acres of trees and shrubbery also inhabited by ornamental pheasants, peacocks, and macaws. A similar idea to Hoare's Stourhead, but executed in a different fashion.

From here right across to the villages lining the river EBBLE to the east, this is open country, with the minor roads taking you through the CHALKE VALLEY past more villages, until the Chase comes to an end to the south east of Salisbury. This is another quiet place, ideal for walking or cycling. Each of the valleys of south Wiltshire is considered the prettiest by its inhabitants, and all are worth seeing. Collectively this area has been known as 'General Country' because of the number of army officers who have chosen to retire here. Back on the A30 the hill decorations near **FOVANT** seem quite appropriate with such a background. Regimental badges have been carved into the chalk hillsides, and are maintained by the FOVANT BADGES SOCIETY. During the First World War many regiments were stationed and trained at Fovant, and apparently the first badge was cut by the LONDON RIFLE BRIGADE in 1916.

The detailed work of the badges is quite clearly visible from the main road, although there are special viewing lay-bys with extra information available. I wonder how many near accidents there have been along this stretch, as children in the back seats of a car, surprised by their first view of the badges have shouted out advice to their parents to 'Look at that!' I know that when I was a child the holiday catchphrase, used at first by my mother in reply to such exclamations was 'Not you Dad!' Several trips west were successfully survived in this manner.

If you are heading east with the desire to visit Salisbury and its Cathedral, knowing them to be near the top of the list of what south Wiltshire has to offer, the proud sign on the edge of **WILTON**, declaring it to be 'The Ancient Capital of Wessex' might come as a bit of a surprise. I suppose most of us will have heard of Wilton for its carpets rather than anything more ancient.

Yet Wilton was the capital of King Alfred's Wessex, with a royal palace here in Saxon times, and yes, it is where the entire county got its name. So why has Salisbury taken over? The cause is not so recent as the supposed throwing of a sandwich by Brunel to find the site of his railway centre, which led to the growth of Swindon, but lays in a combination of much older factors. The Danes ransacked the town, as you might expect, but it was the Black Death which really decimated the remains of the Saxon community here.

What Wilton does still have is the oldest Carpet Factory in the country. The WILTON CARPET FACTORY (01722 744919 / 742733) can be visited, and includes a museum dedicated to the subject of weaving. The original carpet making started here in 1655, but until the early 18th century the carpets were not thought to be exceptional. The Earl of Pembroke (of the family still at Wilton House) smuggled two French weavers across the channel to train the locals (allegedly hiding them in a huge wine cask), and the industry never looked back, making a blow to the pride of the xenophobes among us who might have imagined the Wilton brand to be wholly English work right from the start.

A more local importation followed the bankruptcy experienced by the equally famous Axminster carpet factory of Devon in 1835. Hand looms were bought to Wilton, and until 1958 Wiltons and Axminsters were made side by side. Now you can see more modern methods at work in the factory.

Local carpets can also be bought at the WILTON SHOPPING VILLAGE (01722 741211) which has a lovely setting alongside the river. The drive through Wilton is not a long one, but as you leave the town, its greatest attraction grabs your attention from a splendid gateway to your right.

WILTON HOUSE (01722 746720 / 746729) may look familiar if you are a fan of period drama, as this was the location for the filming of the recent production of Jane Austen's 'Sense and Sensibility'. The whole setting of this great House is superb, and dramatic enough to make the use for filming seem inevitable. It comes upon you very suddenly as you drive along the A30, and the glimpses from the road are enough to tell you that this really is something special.

Wilton House

The effect is rather like coming upon Longleat without expecting to, except that the square, grey lines of Wilton House seem to define the term 'stately' in a way that escapes Longleat's more glamorous exterior. If this were a boarding house, then very few could boast such a visitor's book. Shakespeare, King James I, King Charles I, Winston Churchill, Sir Philip Sidney, and Generals Eisenhower and Montgomery; all have spent time within these walls, occupied in different ways.

This was the site of a Benedictine Convent from the ninth century until Henry VIII handed it over to William Herbert in 1544. A fire in 1647 meant much of the house was redesigned by Inigo Jones. As usual there have been additions at various times, but few as spectacular as the State Rooms added by Jones. The interior of Wilton today is packed with treasures. The art collection is phenomenal, one of the finest in Britain, including famous works by Rembrandt, Van Dyck, Titian, del Sarto and Rubens among many others.

The furnishings are superb too. You might expect good carpets in such a location, but the overall effect of places such as the DOUBLE CUBE ROOM and the SMOKING

ROOMS is of a complete splendour of red and gold that does full justice to the Chippendale and other pieces of walnut and mahogany. Although this a much less overtly commercial venue than Longleat, there are now 'living exhibitions' in the TUDOR KITCHEN and VICTORIAN LAUNDRY.

Long after you have left Wilton behind the wall on your right keeps the parklands around Wilton House out of view. There are twenty one acres of landscaped garden to explore, with recent additions such as the Old English Rose Garden and Water Garden to add to more established features such as the Palladian Bridge over the Nadder.

By the time the park wall has been left behind you are virtually into the upstart town of New Sarum, or **SALISBURY** (Tourist Information 01722 334956). The Cathedral is visible from just about everywhere, and does dominate views of the city. If you were to follow the by-pass around the edge of Salisbury and carry on towards Bournemouth, you might think that it was another quiet Wiltshire place, with a particularly spectacular spire as its main attraction. Take on the struggle to find car parking near the centre and you will realise that this is very far from the whole of the story.

There is nowhere else in Wiltshire like this. Swindon has the shops, Malmesbury has the age and elegance, and the architecture is everywhere from Corsham to Lacock, Longleat to Wilton, but nowhere has as much crowded into its streets as the city of Salisbury. Let's start by taking a walk from the very centre, the Market Place.

There is no need to worry about using a map, just look on the skyline for the spire, and take that general direction. As soon as you get into the main city shopping streets you will be impressed by the bright, cheery nature of the partially pedestrianised area. Modern shopping malls mix with lovely Tudor and medieval timbered buildings, and they actually manage to blend in together, which is what many other places have tried to do with much less success than here.

No matter how impatient you are to get to the Cathedral and the Close these streets will give you many occasions to pause. Follow the signs (it is not easy to see even the spire from the narrow streets) and the shops will suddenly come to an end, with the arch of the ancient looking North Gate finally enticing you to your first full view of what is surely one of the finest buildings in Britain.

It is not easy to do justice to what you will see here. If Malmesbury Abbey truly had a spire higher than this then it is no surprise that it fell. You can get quite giddy bending your neck back to appreciate the Cathedral's bright four hundred foot plus pinnacle from the lawn in front of it. Where Malmesbury Abbey is almost eerily majestic, SALISBURY CATHEDRAL (01722 328726) is blatantly, almost gaudily beautiful, even from the outside.

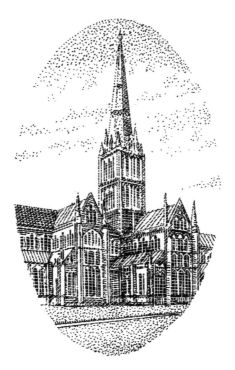

Salisbury Cathedral

Focal point is not a strong enough term for Salisbury Cathedral. Built of Chilmark stone, quarried only twelve miles away (with Purbeck Marble for some of the finer touches), it just looks as if it has been here forever, and yet is fresh and bright in its rule over the whole of the south of the county. If there is one building which forms the architectural centre of Wessex, then this is it.

Built in stages over large sections of two centuries between 1220 and 1380, it looks as if it would take forever to construct with modern methods, let alone in a period when electricity and motor driven tools were yet to come. The inside of the Cathedral is no less awesome. If you were lucky enough to see the live Midnight Mass transmission from the BBC on Christmas Eve 1997 then you already have an idea of just how splendid it can look.

Whether empty or full, the nave and the rest of the interior will make you feel small and insignificant by the pure force of their dimensions and the beautiful simplicity of their design. Further generations have been careful not to lose the lines created by the original medieval architects and craftsmen, even though the beauty of the WEST SCREEN was at first in the colours of red, black and gold, which have now gone without trace. Continuity is so important here, unlike so many of the great houses and castles, and even other places of worship in Wessex, Salisbury Cathedral has retained its original shape without considerable alteration due to fashion, fire, or conflict.

There is too much detail to describe, but for the first few minutes inside the Cathedral it will be enough for you to come to terms with the scale and majesty of your surroundings, and to draw breath before examining any specific features. Amongst what you will find is the oldest working clock in the country, from the late 14th century, which is in the North Aisle, and an original copy of the Magna Carta in the Chapter House. If you should tire of the view from below, then the ROOF TOUR, taking the 120 step spiral staircase up to the PARVISE and TRIFORIUM will give you views along the length of the NAVE (some 230 feet) from another angle. There is almost constant restoration work at the Cathedral, and this may limit your explorations.

The words of GEORGE HERBERT best explain how the interior of Salisbury Cathedral can make me feel. An emotive poet and local clergyman, his tiny parish was at nearby **BEMERTON** from 1630 until his death in 1633. Herbert often came to the Cathedral during these years, but as none of his verse was published until after his death, it is not possible to say when he wrote each piece. Among the most celebrated of them is the shape poem, 'Easter Wings'. The second half of the first verse reminds me of looking up into the heights of the Nave at Salisbury:

"With thee
O let me rise
As larks, harmoniously,
And sing this day thy victories:
Then shall the fall further the flight in me."

If, like me, you are not easily moved to feelings of exultation by ecclesiastical architecture, then be prepared to taken by surprise at Salisbury Cathedral.

No matter how long you spend inside the building, the CLOISTERS will refresh your sense of wonder as you leave. Beautifully and unashamedly Gothic in design, they are both the longest and oldest in any English Cathedral. The buildings of the Cathedral Close, which was first enclosed with walls in the 1330s, are full of other things to see. Starting from the corner of WEST WALK, the first in a series of museums and other attractions is the SALISBURY AND SOUTH WILTSHIRE MUSEUM (01722 332151) in the KINGS HOUSE, a fine Grade One listed building. There is a lot of local history to cover, but the museum rises to the challenge, with everything from the Stonehenge Gallery, to an exhibition about the life and works of General Pitt-Rivers. Most advertisements for the museum show the GIANT and HOB NOB, not a chalk carving and a biscuit, as you might suspect, but the brightly painted, oldest surviving medieval pageant figures in the country.

Next along the Walk comes the MEDIEVAL HALL (01722 412472) with its SECRETS OF SALISBURY, an audio-visual account of local history. The 13th century Hall, with its stark, timbered roof and flag-stoned floor, makes an interesting contrast to the Cathedral.

The REDCOATS IN THE WARDROBE (01722 414536) also known as the ROYAL GLOUCESTERSHIRE, BERKSHIRE AND WILTSHIRE REGIMENT MUSEUM, refers to the original use of the building from 1254. The Wardrobe was actually a store for the Bishop of Salisbury, and the Medieval House makes a fitting setting for the exhibition celebrating the regiment. The Berkshire and Wiltshire collections are kept here.

Around the corner, and near to the HIGH STREET GATE, is MOMPESSON HOUSE (01722 335659). A National Trust property, this is a relative newcomer to The Close, a Queen Anne House built for Charles Mompesson in 1701. The plasterwork and carved oak staircase are highlights, and there are collections of art and period furniture to see as well.

A combination of medieval and later architecture can be found next to QUEEN ANNE'S GATE, at MALMESBURY HOUSE (01722 327027). Originally a 13th century building, later additions were made in the 14th century, and then, notably, by Sir Christopher Wren who added the West Facade. Handel is supposed to have composed part of The Messiah while staying here, and Charles II stopped here during his flight, although it does not seem to be an Inn!

More than half a million visitors come to see the Cathedral each year, and The Close forms an important part of what each one sees. I suspect many go away without visiting the Houses and museums, but not without appreciating the setting the square around the Cathedral gives to the main attraction. It does not really matter if the buildings all become attractions, or change from their original uses, as long as the overall effect remains as pleasing and complete as this does, without a single modern building to interrupt the feeling of an ancient building of tremendous importance surrounded by neighbours it has come to know well over the centuries.

So what else is there to do in Salisbury? Quite a bit. Another trip to the shops could include modern precincts such as the OLD GEORGE MALL, or the collection of independent traders in FISHERTON STREET. Near the latter, and close to the central railway station, FISHERTON MILL (01722 415121) is a Grain Mill from 1880 which is now used to house a series of galleries promoting art, contemporary craft and design.

The Tourist Information Centre in Fish Row runs Guided Walks around the city in both daytime and evening, as well as a third variety known as the Ghost Walks! Salisbury has a LEISURE CENTRE (01722 339966), an ARTS CENTRE (01722

321744), and a PLAYHOUSE (01722 320117) which has classical drama productions and pantomime, musicals and comedies. The CITY HALL ENTERTAINMENT CENTRE(01722 334432) attracts national touring celebrities and shows, as well as providing space for local amateur events and exhibitions.

Around **NETHERHAMPTON**, just to the west of the city, you can find the SALISBURY AND SOUTH WILTSHIRE GOLF CLUB (01722 742645) and the SALISBURY RACECOURSE (01722 326461).

Salisbury has two annual Festivals, the ST GEORGE'S SPRING FESTIVAL in April, which is a unique medieval celebration of England's patron saint, with the inevitable dragon slaying, and the SALISBURY FESTIVAL (01722 323883 / 320333) usually a couple of months later.

At the ENGLISH HERITAGE CENTRE in the city centre you can find out opening times and information about Salisbury's parent, OLD SARUM (01722 335398). Founded about 500 B.C. this massive Iron Age hillfort is a couple of miles north of Salisbury Cathedral. Unlike many other hillforts, such as Maiden Castle at Dorchester, this one was not abandoned after the Romans arrived, or even the Normans, who built a royal castle, palace and cathedral here.

Now it is a huge mound in the middle of the countryside between two contrasting panoramas. To the south there is the spire rising above the city which was started when Old Sarum became too crowded to hold the interests of both the military and church, and to the north Salisbury Plain, which probably does not look that different now to the view a Roman soldier might have had nearly two thousand years ago from the same spot. Even the Norman buildings are in ruins and it is a sobering thought that this place held a thriving community for about three times as long as the ancient Cathedral has stood so far. Complete desolation has followed, something no-one could wish on its successor.

For a local opportunity to compare Old Sarum with an earthwork abandoned after the Iron Age, FIGSBURY RINGS to the north east of Salisbury is convenient, although with Chemical Defence and Microbiological Research Establishments traditionally centred around neighbouring **PORTON**, I should not imagine a wandering tribe would fancy their chances of reclaiming the site now!

South east of Salisbury, PEPPERBOX HILL is National Trust property and another excellent place to see for very great distances. Unlike the intriguing Figbury, there is an obvious reason for the name of this hill. The strangely remote, hexagonal stone building on top of it does indeed look like a pepperbox, although a salt cellar might have done as well. Known as EYRES FOLLY, there are various explanations for this piece of 17th century eccentricity. One suggestion is that it was built as a place from which ladies could follow local falconry, while another says that it was simply so that Gyles Eyres could have the highest tower in the area, at least in terms of feet above sea level at its summit. Either way, it gives an excuse to walk up the hill and breathe in some very fresh air.

Nearby **DOWNTON** is excellent for angling with access to the chalk streams of the Wylye, Nadder and Ebble, as well as the larger Wiltshire AVON, which runs through the middle of the village. There are some excellent specimens of the local catch from the past to be found on the walls of the local hostelry, stuffed of course.

Further into the south east corner of the county NEWHOUSE (01725 20055) near **REDLYNCH** is yet another of Wiltshire's Jacobean Houses, this one containing a costume collection. Still nearer the border the very name of HAMPTWORTH LODGE where the gardens are open, suggests that the New Forest and Hampshire are beginning to take over. How about **NOMANSLAND** as the perfect name for a village on the very border between counties? Apparently the Village shop was built on an angle so as to keep it inside Wiltshire (and therefore simplify the Business Rates) while if you were to look in through the window from outside you would be in Hampshire.

What we have left is back to the north of Salisbury. HEALE GARDEN AND PLANT CENTRE (01722 782504) is more impressive than it might sound, being eight acres of mixed gardens around HEALE HOUSE, which is not open to the public. From snowdrops to magnolias and acers there is something to brighten up each season here, by the Salisbury AVON near **MIDDLE WOODFORD**.

As the Plain takes over and habitations become less frequent, **AMESBURY** (Tourist Information 01980 622833) is nearly the last settlement we will visit in Wiltshire. It is also supposed to have been the last resting place for Queen Guinevere, after her adultery with Lancelot had led to the fall of her husband Arthur's defeat in battle, and removal to Avalon. Malory and most of the other Arthurian chroniclers have the queen ending her days in a Nunnery, and Amesbury claims to be a possible site for it.

What may have confused fact with romance is that Queen Elfrida definitely set up a Nunnery here out of guilt, but for the very real murder of her son, the teenage King Edward, at Corfe Castle in Dorset. An interesting concept in voluntary self imprisonment, and with the Plain to keep them away from further temptation or opportunity from crime, as well as away from the majority of humanity, either Queen chose a good place to perform penance. Amesbury and its satellite towns are not so quiet now, with the military presence on the neighbouring plain spilling over into them, and the long vanished convent was a victim of Henry VIII and the Dissolution.

Salisbury Plain is anything but ordinary. Much of it is often completely inaccessible due to its use for army manoeuvres and as a firing range, but this has helped to preserve the twenty by fifteen mile block of open land. The IMBER RANGE PERIMETER PATH is the best way to make the most of the rare downland flora which has survived in this way, as it skirts for thirty miles around the restricted areas. Try Westbury or Warminster Tourist Information for more details if it appeals.

Back nearer to Amesbury we will end at Wiltshire's most famous attraction of all, STONEHENGE. No matter how many films or pictures of this place you have seen, there is nothing like seeing the monument in its true setting. As a child I would insist that I was kept awake until we had passed it, out of pure fascination. The contrast with the Sarsen ring of Avebury is perhaps a good place to start an attempt to understand the unique feeling to be gained at Stonehenge.

Stonehenge

Avebury has old and new, with stones among a living village. Stonehenge is in the middle of empty, deserted land, and can be seen for miles around. When you first see it, Stonehenge looks quite small, almost insignificant, but conspicuous. As you draw closer the scale of the stone ring starts to make its impression, and even just driving straight past you will be left wondering.

The modern fashion seems to be to belittle Stonehenge. There are older monuments, more discovered every year, and since you can no longer walk freely amongst the stones whenever you like, is it worth all the fuss? Unfortunately the Druidic goings on of Midsummer's Eve have come to give the place some of the horrible media stigma also attached at times to Glastonbury. I like to look at it another way.

Salisbury Cathedral has survived because of its constant use. Malmesbury Abbey is a good example of somewhere that has adapted to survive, shrunk its area to remain viable. So what of Stonehenge, how has it made it through the four or five millenia of its life to the present day? The stones are huge, some from Wales, and others from the Marlborough Downs, and everyone has wondered about how they got here. But they could have been flattened since, and I do not think the army vehicles in the immediate area would make too long a job of it.

No-one would dare to attempt such a thing, the National Trust took over Stonehenge in the 1920s as a result of public demand, and it is now a WORLD HERITAGE SITE, maintained by English Heritage. I think Stonehenge is a monument to the British love of a good mystery, as much as it its to the ingenuity and engineering prowess of the Beaker People or whoever else originally built it.

If we knew exactly what Stonehenge was for, and could see a daily demonstration, perhaps repeated once in the morning and once in the afternoon of how exactly it was used as a calendar, or a place of ritual sacrifice, or a temple, then I am sure many more people would be content to stay at home and watch a video of proceedings, rather than succumb to the urge to have a look for themselves. Isn't it satisfying to be able to have the same reaction as Samuel Pepys, who visited here in the 17th century and said of the stones:

"God knows what their use was."

There cannot be many other places where his observations remain so contemporary and relevant.

I do not have my own theory as to their purpose, but I do think it must have been for something more than just a calendar that up to five hundred men dragged each stone here. The development of our science to the point where we can discover how they were brought here is just far enough for me, I hope their true purpose remains a mystery for all time. There is a mysterious compulsion to get as close to these stones as you can, a power which cannot be quantified or explained.

So this is the extraordinary within the Plain, and perhaps an unconventional place to end. Stonehenge is dramatic enough to take the ending to any tale, and a precedent has been set by the writer most famously connected with Wessex, a fitting man to lead us on into Dorset, Thomas Hardy.

The heroine of *'Tess of the D'Urbevilles'* ends her time on the run here with her lover Angel Clare, captured at daybreak as she sleeps on one of the stones, to be taken away and hung for a murder which every reader of the story must forgive. The choice of scene is symbolic, Hardy makes it clear that Tess is able to find a moment's peace here because she is a heathen, not the aristocrat her father would have liked her to be. The whole passage is moving, but the description of the last moments of freedom, as dawn and the pursuers approach together, capture some of the romance of the extraordinary Stonehenge on the Plain:

"The band of silver paleness along the east horizon made even the distant parts of the Great Plain appear dark and near; and the whole enormous landscape bore that impress of reserve, taciturnity, and hesitation which is usual just before day. The eastward pillars and their architraves stood up blackly against the light, and the great flame-shaped Sun- Stone beyond them; and the Stone of Sacrifice midway. Presently the night wind died out, and the quivering little pools in the cup-like hollows of the stones lay still. At the same time something seemed to move on the verge of the dip eastward - a mere dot."

THE ANGEL INN
Heytesbury
Wiltshire
BA12 0ED

Tel: 01985 840330
Fax: 01985 840931

For three hundred years The Angel Inn has been serving travellers and locals in the most hospitable manner. This tradition is carried on today by the present owners, Tim and Mandy Smith, whose friendly, outgoing personalities reach out to everyone who comes through its old doors. The Inn retains much of the original features and with it the atmosphere generated through the years. It is furnished in a comfortable, cottage style and is a favourite watering hole for people who come from quite a distance to enjoy the well kept ale, the good food and above all the genuine welcome. You can stay here if you wish. Many people do because it is a great base for exploring. Salisbury with its magnificent cathedral, the incomparable city of Bath, Stonehenge, Longleat, the superb gardens at Stourhead and many other fascinating places are all within twenty miles. This also makes it a good base for business people to stay, allowing them to work during the day and return for a peaceful night's sleep and relaxation in the Angel Inn. For the sports minded there is fishing in the rivers and lakes, two golf courses within ten minutes and two riding schools.

There are three guest rooms, all ensuite and furnished in the same cottage style as the rest of the inn. Each room , one of which is a double and the other two, twin-bedded, has television, and a hostess tray. Breakfast here is a meal to remember and the standard is carried on whether you eat in the bar at lunch-time or in the pretty dining room at night. In the Bar you will be offered a traditional, fairly basic bar menu but at night the chef's imaginative dishes have wide appeal. There are some thirty dishes from which to choose including five to eight Vegetarian options. Much use is made of seasonal fare and you will find Game dishes on the menu as well as succulent steaks and other locally produced meat. The vegetables are fresh and the produce is local wherever possible. If one had to describe the food in just a few words, it would be English with an original Continental twist. There is a comprehensive and sensibly priced wine list.

In the courtyard there are picnic tables shaded by unusual wooden parasols - very popular with visitors in the warmer weather..

USEFUL INFORMATION

- OPEN: All year
- WHEELCHAIR ACCESS: Yes
- GARDEN: Courtyard with tables
- CREDIT CARDS: All major cards
- ACCOMMODATION: 3 ensuite rms
- RATES: B&B £37sgl pppn £49 dbl

- DINING ROOM: Interesting, imaginative
- VEGETARIAN: 5-8 dishes
- BAR FOOD: Traditional
- LICENSED: Full On
- CHILDREN: Well behaved welcome
- PETS: By arrangement

BISHOPSTROW HOUSE
Warminster
Wiltshire
BA12 9HH

Tel: 01985 212312
Fax: 01985 216769

EMail:bishopstrow-house-hotel@msn.com

Set in twenty seven acres of beautiful Wiltshire countryside, this classical Georgian home is filled with fine antiques, 19th century oil painting, log fires and fresh flowers which blend together to create a relaxing, informal and welcoming atmosphere. There are many local attraction - Longleat House and Safari Park, Stourhead House and Gardens, Stonehenge and the historic cities of Bath and Salisbury and many more. It is an ideal base from which to explore the Wiltshire countryside and has the additional virtue of extensive beauty and leisure facilities. The Ragdale Spa provides the finest health and beauty treatments. The Health Club offers indoor and outdoor heated swimming pools, indoor and outdoor tennis courts, sauna, steam showers and a high tech gymnasium. The Spa offers Midweek Breaks and they are also included in the hotel's country breaks. There are five excellent golf clubs near the Hotel and to enjoy these there are also Golf Breaks. The River Wylye is one of five superb pure chalk streams in Britain and offers excellent fly fishing for trout. There are three hundred yards of fishing at the hotel and eight beats just ten minutes drive from Bishopstrow House which prompts the hotel to offer excellent Fly Fishing Breaks.

All thirty one bedrooms and suites have satellite television and private bathrooms, some with whirlpool baths and audio entertainment systems. In The Mulberry Restaurant and The Wilton Room delicious traditional English cuisine is served with an accent on healthy eating. Afternoon teas and lighter meals are offered in the Mulberry Bar and Conservatory. Bishopstrow House is the complete escape from the world, even to the extent of having Michaeljohn hairdressing of London and Beverly Hills, within its walls making the pampering and cosseting perfect.

USEFUL INFORMATION

- OPEN: All year

- GARDEN: Super grounds
- CREDIT CARDS: All major cards
- ACCOMMODATION:
  31 bedrooms & suites
- RATES: Inc. Continental Breakfast
  Sgl £95 Dbl. & twin £170
  deluxe £210 Junior Suites £230
  Suites & Oval Room £295
  Children sharing with parents £25 per child

- RESTAURANT: Traditional English with an accent on healthy eating
- BAR FOOD: Yes. Afternoon tea & lighter meals
- LICENSED: Full On. Fine wines

- CHILDREN: Welcome
- PETS: Yes. £5 per dog per night

THE CROWN INN
Alvediston
Salisbury
Wiltshire
SP5 5JY

Tel: 01722 780335
Fax: 01722 780836

The 14th century Crown Inn which has a wonderful atmosphere redolent of the smell of logs burning in the open fireplaces and the ambience built up over the centuries, lies in the middle of the Chalk Valley of Wiltshire, known as the Forgotten Valley. Its peace, its glorious countryside, good walking, riding, fishing as well as its easy access to Salisbury Cathedral, Wardour Castle, Stourhead, Longleat, the quaint Gold Hill at Shaftesbury as well as being within striking distance of Bath, Wimborne, Bournemouth, Blandford and Warminster, makes it the ideal place in which to take a break, stay whilst you are on business, or simply enjoy the life and the friendliness of the inn which not only has good ale and fine wines but has one of the most talented and imaginative chefs in Wiltshire. It is a great place for Shooting parties and in days gone by was a watering hole for Sir Anthony Eden, the Prime Minister at the time of the Suez Crisis. Cecil Beaton lived close by and many famous people have happily entered the portals of this exceptionally nice country inn.

Owned by Nickolas Shaw and Colin Jordan, the Crown Inn has a reputation that goes way beyond Wiltshire. People come for the chit chat over the bar and especially to enjoy the wide ranging menu in the eighty cover restaurant and the exceptional standard of bar snacks. The blackboard menu changes every day and always includes dishes for vegetarians. In fact the chef will produce anything that is asked for given a little notice. The prices for both wine and food are very sensible - even Lobster Thermidor at £19. The restaurant which like the rest of the inn has recently been refurbished, is painted throughout with what is known as 'National Trust Book Room Red'; a colour which is rich, warm and looks great. Throughout the inn there are lots of fresh flowers and other deft touches. There are five guest rooms. One is really a suite and consists of two rooms with bath and can sleep up to a family of five. There are two ensuite doubles and another which also has two single beds and a single room with no facilities. All the rooms have television and are strictly non-smoking. Starting in 1998 there will be some exceptionally good value Short Break deals, you are advised to enquire at the Inn for details.

USEFUL INFORMATION

- OPEN: All year 11am-3pm & 7pm-11.30pm
- WHEELCHAIR ACCESS: Yes
- GARDEN: Yes
- CREDIT CARDS: All major cards
- ACCOMMODATION: 5 guest rooms
- RATES: £45pp B&B
- RESTAURANT: Delicious imaginative fare
- VEGETARIAN: Always a choice
- BAR FOOD: High standard sensible prices
- LICENSED: Full On
- CHILDREN: Welcome
- PETS: Yes

DEVERILL END
Sutton Veny
Warminster
Wiltshire
BA12 7BY

Tel: 01985 840356

ETB Listed

Deverill End is basically a large bungalow but Sim and Joy Greathead have converted it and it now resembles the type of house that one would expect to see in the Southern Cape region of South Africa. The Greatheads have spent many years in Africa. Sim is an ex-South African farmer. They are a jovial, fascinating couple who love entertaining their guests and are always ready to tell them stories of their home country. No one could be anything but happy staying here. Everything about the house is pleasing and the views from the Dining Room and back of the house are stunning, looking out over the rolling Wiltshire countryside. Whilst Joy runs the house Sim now spends a lot of time restoring antique furniture.

The situation of the house makes it ideal for those wanting either a quiet country holiday, walking, fishing or playing golf, or for those who want to explore. Stourhead with its superb gardens is close, so is Stonehenge, Wookey Hole and Cheddar Gorge. It is virtually next to Longleat with its Safari Park and it is in between the incomparable city of Bath with its glorious Abbey and Salisbury with its magnificent Cathedral. Deverill End is surrounded by countryside and you will find cows, sheep and horses coming up to the fence at the end of the garden.

The emphasis on the hospitality at Deverill End is on comfort, relaxation, entertaining conversation and a super breakfast. The three guest rooms, all ensuite, are well-appointed and perfectly furnished. All the rooms have television and tea and coffee making facilities. Evening meals are not available but there are good pubs and restaurants nearby to which the Greatheads will happily guide you. Staying here is an educational, enjoyable and memorable experience.

USEFUL INFORMATION

- OPEN: All year
- WHEELCHAIR ACCESS: Yes
- GARDEN: Yes. Off road parking
- CREDIT CARDS: None taken
- ACCOMMODATION: 3 ensuite rooms
- RATES: £25pp.pn £30 sgl

- DINING ROOM: Excellent breakfast
- VEGETARIAN: Upon request
- LICENSED: No
- CHILDREN: Over 12 years
- PETS: No

GRASMERE HOUSE
Harnham Road
Salisbury
Wiltshire
SP2 8JN

Tel:01722 338388
Fax: 01722 333710

*** Michelin Guide Listing

The City of Salisbury with its magnificent cathedral is blessed with many good hotels but the newest shining star in the firmament is surely Grasmere House, a fine example of a Victorian family residence, set in 1.5 acres of mature gardens laid largely to lawn and with magnificent towering Beech trees and a small woodland copse. Built in 1896 for prosperous Salisbury merchants, Grasmere House is constructed in deep red brick with attractive pointed finials on the roof gables. It has been carefully and skilfully converted and extended into a private hotel, retaining all the features and atmosphere of a comfortable Victorian home.

Stylishly but comfortably furnished throughout, Grasmere House has 20 bedrooms, four located in the original house and sixteen in the new wing. All bedrooms have ensuite facilities, direct dial telephone, radio and colour television with remote control and hospitality tray. Two of the four ground floor rooms are arranged for disabled guests.

Open to non-residents, the Conservatory Restaurant, with spectacular views over Grassmere's gardens and lawns, down to the rivers Nadder and Avon and across to the Cathedral, has seating for forty diners. The food is delicious with the menu featuring a variety of dishes using local produce and changes frequently to reflect the seasons. The Hotel has a successful Dining Club and runs very popular Theme evenings both for members and the hotels many regular guests. The attractive Nadder Bar has its own conservatory with spectacular views as well. Guests can enjoy a Wiltshire Afternoon tea in the lounge or just take a stroll in the gardens or relax on the patio after a busy day. The service throughout the hotel is immaculate and friendly and this includes the excellent attention to detail for those attending seminars or conferences in the meetings centre where one hundred and ten delegates can be accommodated in the main suite and the smaller River Rooms are available as syndicate rooms or for smaller meetings, receptions and private dining. All of Grasmere's meeting rooms have natural light.

USEFUL INFORMATION

- OPEN: All year
- WHEELCHAIR ACCESS:
  Yes 2 ground floor rooms for disabled
- GARDEN: Yes 1.5acres
- CREDIT CARDS: All major cards
- ACCOMMODATION: 20 ensuite rooms
- RATES: Dbl. from £95 Sgl from £55.50

- RESTAURANT: First class cuisine
- VEGETARIAN: Always a choice
- PARKING: For 40 cars
- LICENSED: Yes
- CHILDREN: Welcome
- PETS: By prior arrangement £3 /night

HAYBURN WYKE GUEST HOUSE
72 Castle Road
Salisbury
Wiltshire
SP1 3RL

Tel/Fax: 01722 412627

AA QQQQ. RAC Accredited.
ETB Commended

Salisbury with its magnificent Cathedral and much fine architecture is always a Mecca for visitors and finding somewhere to stay is not always simple. To find somewhere as highly recommended as Hayburn Wyke Guest House is a piece of good fortune. Owned by Alan and Dawn Curnow it is a large, comfortable, Victorian House situated adjacent to Victoria Park and within a ten minute riverside walk to the City Centre and the Cathedral. Going in the opposite direction, the country lane next to the house follows the River Avon to Stonehenge passing by thatched cottages, villages, churches and fascinating pubs.

Finding a house in Salisbury named after a village in Yorkshire is not the norm. This house was so called because in 1898 someone came to work in the Cathedral from there and no doubt assuaged a little home-sickness calling his home Hayburn Wyke. The house has a great deal of style and charm. A beautiful gallery landing is at the head of the staircase lit by stained glass windows. All the rooms are spacious with high ceilings and tall windows. Alan and Dawn have furnished the house with elegance and taste ensuring that every room is both warm and comfortable. There are seven well furnished guest bedrooms, two of which are ensuite and all have basins and hot and cold water. There are 2 public bathrooms where the constant supply of hot water makes bathing simple. Televisions are in all the bedrooms and hospitality trays. Downstairs Satellite television is available. A substantial and delicious breakfast is served every morning with a vegetarian choice if required. The Curnows do not serve evening meals but Salisbury has many good eateries of every kind and they will be happy to direct you.

Hayburn Wyke is ideal for visitors to Salisbury wanting to explore the area and take in the glory of the Cathedral and it is equally good for those coming to the city on business and looking for somewhere, other than a hotel, where they can relax at the end of a busy day.

USEFUL INFORMATION

- OPEN: All year
- WHEELCHAIR ACCESS: Yes
- GARDEN: Yes
- CREDIT CARDS: Master/Visa/JCB/Delta/Switch
- ACCOMMODATION: 7 rooms 3 ensuite
- RATES: £18.50 pp.pn low season
  £23.pp.pn high season.
  Surcharge singles using double
  room depending on season

- DINING ROOM: Excellent breakfast
- VEGETARIAN: Yes
- LICENSED: No
- CHILDREN: Welcome
- PETS: By arrangement

HOWARDS HOUSE
Teffont Evias
Salisbury
Wiltshire
SP3 5RJ

Tel: 01722 716392
Fax: 01722 716820

AA 3 Rosette,
Michelin Red 'Meals' Bibendum

Teffont Evias, one of the most beautiful villages in Wiltshire, is hidden away in the quietness of the lovely Nadder valley. Owned by the same family since Christopher Mayne bought the estate in 1692 and three hundred years later his direct descendant is Lord of the Manor. The family has permitted little change during its tenure and Teffont Evias remains much as it was in the 17th century. In its midst is Howard's House, built in 1623 for Augustus Hayter and added to in 1837 by a member of the family who was impressed by the Swiss architecture during his Grand Tour. The extension and original house were then roofed in the Swiss style. In 1989 the house was rescued by the present owners from years of neglect and after extensive renovations the hotel was reopened in 1990.

Everything about Howard's House is gracious and elegant. The furniture is a happy marriage of old and new offset by superb Designers Guild fabrics. The warm yellows and bold floral prints give the sitting room a feeling of comfort and calm. In summer the fragrance of jasmine wafts in through the open windows from the quintessentially English garden and in winter the warmth emanates from the roaring log fire.

The elegant, award winning Restaurant which is open to non-residents is an eagerly sought venue; Paul Firmin, one of the owners, is a talented chef whose cooking can best be described as 'modern British' using the best local ingredients supplemented with herbs and vegetables from the garden, utilised with flair and imagination. Perfectly appointed tables are complemented by the cool greens and white of the decor. The nine luxury, beautifully furnished bedrooms, all have their own bathrooms, bathrobes, direct dial phone, TV and hairdryer. As in the rest of Howard's House the floral prints and pastel shades combine to enhance the feeling of informality and relaxation. One bedroom has a splendid four-poster.

You have only to read some of the many recommendations from guests to confirm that Howard's House offers a perfect retreat and yet is easily accessible and close to Stonehenge and Old Sarum, Salisbury Cathedral and Wilton House and a little further off the magnificent Stourhead Gardens, Longleat House and Bath. As one guest put it 'So this is where heaven is'

USEFUL INFORMATION

· OPEN: All year	· RESTAURANT: Modern British
· WHEELCHAIR ACCESS: Restaurant only	· VEGETARIAN: With notice
· GARDEN: Beautiful	
· CREDIT CARDS: All major cards	· LICENSED: Yes
· ACCOMMODATION: 9 luxury rooms	· CHILDREN: Welcome
· RATES: From £75 sgl £115 dbl.	· PETS: Yes

LONDON HOUSE RESTAURANT
Market Place
Pewsey
Wiltshire
SN9 5AB

Tel: 01672 564775
Fax: 01672 564785
E Mail: Admin@London House.co.uk

AA 2Rosettes

The Saxon village of Pewsey standing in the shadow of the most famous of the ancient White Horses and located at the head of the Vale, is the setting for one of the finest and most strikingly situated restaurants in the whole of England. London House Restaurant stands in the Market Place, right in the centre of the village, opposite the statue of King Alfred the Great. Swindon is a short journey away situated between junctions 15 & 16 of the M4 which links London and Bristol, with Marlborough and Devizes close by.

London House is the epitome of good taste, superb food and fine wines. It was recently totally renovated but still retains the classical style of the Queen Anne Period. The philosophy at London House is to provide the best cuisine, the finest wines and the most attentive service -to be found anywhere- in an atmosphere of relaxed elegance. The menu has a French flavour and is enhanced by unique monthly specialities featuring authentic examples of European and International cuisine. The Cellar Master cares for a varied and comprehensive selection of fine wines, representing the best from the Old and the New World. There are wines to suit every taste and pocket - and to match every dish. London House provides an unforgettable dining experience.

For extra special occasions, wedding receptions or larger dining parties, the Kennet and Avon Rooms can accommodate from eight to thirty guests, seated in comfort. The rooms are equally superb for meetings and conferences with a choice of two syndicate rooms or one large conference area, fully equipped and furnished. London House can supply conference equipment as required. The standard of excellence that is the hallmark of London House is followed through in every aspect of their operations.

USEFUL INFORMATION

· OPEN: All year	· RESTAURANT: An unforgettable dining experience
· WHEELCHAIR ACCESS: Yes	· VEGETARIAN: Special menu
· CREDIT CARDS: All major cards	· LICENSED: Fine wines
· CHILDREN: Welcome	· PETS: No

MILTON FARM
Milton
East Knoyle,
Wiltshire
SP3 6BG

Tel: 01747 830247

East Knoyle is a beautiful quiet village close to Shaftesbury and in the small hamlet of Milton is Milton Farm, a superb Queen Anne original Wiltshire Farmhouse handed down through the generations. It is truly a picture book house with its stone flagged floor in the entrance hall, a vast farmhouse kitchen with a pine table, and a gun-case beside the gleaming Aga. In the sitting room, which has a boarded ceiling, the log fire radiates warmth from the stone hearth. The old oak furniture, deep chairs, silver and flowers everywhere make it the most welcoming of places. Owned by Janice Hyde and her husband, the farm is a working one with woodland and downs surrounding the hamlet of Milton. It is wonderful walking country and surrounded by many places to visit including Stourhead, Bath, Salisbury, Wardour Castle and Sherborne.

There are two guest rooms, a double with a vast bathroom and a twin-bedded room with a shower en suite. Both rooms, like every other in the farmhouse, are delightfully furnished and have television and a hostess tray. Janice Hyde provides a true farmhouse breakfast but no longer serves dinner, but this is compensated by lovely pubs and restaurants nearby. One little thatched pub within walking distance from the house provides excellent suppers.

Janice Hyde imports beautiful hand painted ceramics from Portugal and they are for sale in an old Gallery in the courtyard next to the farmhouse.

USEFUL INFORMATION

- OPEN: All season March-November
- WHEELCHAIR ACCESS: No
- GARDEN: Yes
- CREDIT CARDS: None taken
- ACCOMMODATION: 1dbl. 1tw ensuite
- RATES: £25. 2 nights or more £22.50 per night

- DINING ROOM: Excellent farmhouse breakfast
- VEGETARIAN: Upon request
- LICENSED: No
- CHILDREN: Yes. Bring your own cot
- PETS: Quiet dogs allowed

THE OLD MANOR HOTEL
Trowle
Trowbridge
WiltshireBA14 9BL

Tel: 0225 777393
Fax: 0225 765443
Email: queen.anne.house@dial.pipex.com

ETB****

The Old Manor Hotel is a delightful five hundred year old Manor farmhouse which for the last seventeen years Diane and Barry Humphreys have renovated with loving care and turned it into one of the nicest small hotels in Wiltshire. It is a super place to stay and so convenient for many places. Lovely little Bradford-on-Avon is just down the hill, entirely built in stone, as is this house. Stonehenge, Salisbury, Glastonbury, Wells and the Cotswolds and especially the incomparable city of Bath are within easy reach. If you don't want to drive into Bath, as it is sometimes congested and difficult to find a suitable car parking space, Diane or Barry will run you to the station for the twelve minute train journey. This is just one of the thoughtful and caring things that the Humphreys do for their guests. They work very hard to make sure everyone's stay is pleasurable.

There are fourteen en-suite bedrooms with lots of original romantic four-poster and half-tester antique beds. Some are in the house and some in the converted three hundred year old barns from the original farmstead. All the rooms are attractively appointed and each has direct dial telephone, television and a hostess tray and some rooms have mini-bars. Diana is a first rate cook -they had a restaurant for fourteen years - and she produces delicious, imaginative food. You can have anything from an onion soup to a full meal with a good choice of pasta, vegetarian or traditional meals, or if preferred a good room service menu. There is a wealth of beams and antiques in the house and the whole site is mostly on ground level. Like the house, the garden has taken years to take shape. It now looks nice with lots of flowers, a new pond and a charming knot garden that Diane and Barry have created.

USEFUL INFORMATION

- OPEN: All year except 4 days at Christmas
- WHEELCHAIR ACCESS:
  Yes 9 ground floor rooms
- GARDEN: Yes
- CREDIT CARDS: All major cards
- ACCOMMODATION: 14 ensuite rooms
- RATES: From £27.50pppn low season
  £55-85 high season Half price for two nights
  - Friday & Saturday Rates per child; £5

- DINING ROOM: Super home-cooked fare

- VEGETARIAN: Yes
- LICENSED: Restaurant
- CHILDREN; Yes
- PETS: No

PEMBROKE ARMS
Fovant
NR Salisbury
Wiltshire
SP3 5JH

Tel/Fax: 01722 714201

ETB Listed & Commended

Fovant is a pretty village at the foot of the beautiful Fovant Downs. The 18th century old coaching inn, Pembroke Arms is at the heart of the village. It was once the shooting lodge of the Earl of Pembroke. Today it is a well loved hostelry, headquarters of the Fovant Badges Society with interesting World War I memorabilia pertaining to the regimental badges carved into the hillside of the Fovant Downs during the war.

Marilyn and Mike Willoughby are the owners. This is their first venture into inn-keeping and they have striven to make it the ideal village inn. That they have achieved their aim is evident by the contented number of locals who drink in the pub and of the ever increasing number of people from a little further afield who have discovered that it is warm, welcoming , provides good food and fun. Log fires in winter, comfortable furnishings and a cosy main bar in which you can enjoy a delicious meal at the right price is a good enough reason for coming here but if you just want a drink you are equally welcome. If you enjoy a game of pool or darts or want to watch Sky television, the adjoining Sports Bar is the place to be. The large, elevated Beer Garden with views of the Downs is very popular in warm weather.

Because of its situation on the main A30 Shaftesbury-Salisbury road, the Pembroke Arms is a convenient place to stay if you want to tour Wiltshire and Dorset with all their superb, varying countryside, historical towns and quaint villages. Pembroke has three guest rooms, two doubles and one twin, all ensuite.. The rooms are attractively appointed with pretty drapes and bedcovers. Each room has television and a generously supplied hospitality tray.

USEFUL INFORMATION

- OPEN: Mon-Fri:11-3pm & 5-11pm
  Sat: 11am-11pm Sun:12-10.30pm
- WHEELCHAIR ACCESS: Yes
- GARDEN: Large
- LICENSED: Full On

- ACCOMMODATION: 3 ensuite rms
- RATES: £20pp.pn B&B ensuite
  £17.50 standard Surcharge £5 single occupancy

- RESTAURANT; Not applicable
- VEGETARIAN: 7 dishes on main menu
- BAR FOOD: Delicious home-cooked food
- CREDIT CARDS: All major cards except AMEX
- CHILDREN: Welcome.
- PETS: Yes

THE QUEENS HEAD INN
1, North Street
Broadchalke
NR Salisbury
Wiltshire
SP5 5EN

Tel/Fax: 01722 784344

This fine old inn has been welcoming and refreshing travellers for centuries and is never more welcoming than today in the friendly and capable hands of Michael and Norma Craggs. It was built roundabout 1465 and whilst the centuries have given it additions and alterations, it still remains the sort of hostelry that one expects to enjoy. It would be hard not to feel good after visiting The Queens Head Inn. Everything is done to make regulars and visitors comfortable and the hospitable Craggs have acquired the knack of mixing their regulars with newcomers successfully, with the result that total strangers leave feeling they have been among friends. This atmosphere is helped by the well-stocked bar and the excellent ale of which Michael is justly proud. Listed by CAMRA and the Good Pub Guide. You are as welcome here for just a drink as for a full blown meal or to stay a night or two.

You find The Queens Head taking the A354 Blandford Road for three miles to Coombe Bissett. Turn right at the sign to Bishopstone and follow the road for 4 miles to Broad Chalke. The Inn is renowned for its food. The chef Adrian Vale has been here for more than nineteen years and produces delectable dishes using the finest and freshest of food - from gourmet dishes to hot and cold bar snacks. Every day there is a tantalising choice of daily specials on the blackboard, often including seasonal game dishes such as pheasant and bacon, jugged hare or rabbit. The Queens Head is also excellent for private functions of up to seventy persons or if you would care to use their outside catering service, the numbers are unlimited.

Off the courtyard, there are four modern double rooms, each with own bathroom and colour TV. They are all centrally heated and have both direct dial telephones and hospitality trays. The rooms are self-contained, motel style so that you are free to come and go as you wish. It is a great place to stay whether you are enjoying a holiday, a break or on business - and the price is right!

USEFUL INFORMATION

- OPEN: 11.30-1500 & 1800-2300
- WHEELCHAIR ACCESS: Yes
- CREDIT CARDS: All major cards
- ACCOMMODATION: 4 dbl ensuite
- RATES: £26 sgl £47.50 dbl. inc. B&B
- PETS: No

- RESTAURANT: Excellent menu wide choice. Daily Specials
- VEGETARIAN: Yes
- BAR FOOD: Hot & cold food
- LICENSED: Full On
- CHILDREN: Yes (well behaved)

THE SILVER PLOUGH
White Hill
Pitton
Salisbury
Wiltshire
SP5 1DU

Tel/Fax:01722 712266

Egon Ronay Pub of the Year 1990

Pitton is a quiet village, with thatched houses and beautiful gardens and in its midst is the award winning Silver Plough Inn, Egon Ronay Pub of the Year 1990. It is very much the focal point of village life and you will almost always find a gathering of local people in the bars enjoying the well kept ale and the lively conversation. Everything about the inn speaks of its well-being. Comfortably furnished it has a collection of antiques hanging from the ceilings in the bar including glass rolling pins which, traditionally, were given as wedding presents, supposedly bringing good luck to the newly weds. The garden of the pub, like many others in the village, is charming and very popular in the warmer weather when people tend to take their drinks and bar snacks outside to enjoy the surroundings.

Food is always important. Everyday the menu has a wide choice of traditional and continental dishes as well as daily specials. The non-smoking restaurant has a great reputation locally and visitors never fail to comment on the service which is both friendly and unobtrusive. Bar Snacks are equally popular with a delicious, fresh home-made soup of the day served with home baked bread and croutons, high on the list of favourites. You can have a bowl of Tagliatelli with a choice of sauces including bacon and mushroom or salmon and basil or a choice of Ploughman's with fresh crusty bread and many other dishes. If you really are hungry try a succulent peppered rump steak chargrilled and served with cajun spice chips. Vegetarians also have a choice of dishes including Feta cheese, walnut and avocado tossed salad.

Many people have discovered how well The Silver Plough runs private functions and others hire the Skittle Alley for parties. It really is a great pub and certainly deserves its Egon Ronay award.

USEFUL INFORMATION

- OPEN: 11-3pm & 6-11pm
  Sundays 12-3 & 7-10.30pm
- WHEELCHAIR ACCESS: Yes
- GARDEN: Yes
- CREDIT CARDS AMEX/ Visa/Master
  /Switch/Diners
- CHILDREN: Welcome.
  No children's menus or highchairs

- RESTAURANT: Wide Choice
- VEGETARIAN: Always a choice
- BAR FOOD: Great value

- LICENSED: Full On

- PETS: Snug Bar only

THE SNOOTY FOX
1, Brook Street
Warminster
Wiltshire
BA12 8DN

Tel: 01985 218100

One might describe the attractive, friendly Snooty Fox, as a country pub in a residential area of Warminster. An odd description but this is what one feels about the atmosphere and furnishings. It certainly does not answer to the name it had in the 1800's - The Poor House. A time when the front, still standing now, was occupied by the Master and Mistress. 4 or 5 rooms were set aside for 'old men and boys' and opposite were similar rooms for the 'old women and children'. It provided for old soldiers and sailors, the deaf and dumb, blind and crippled, orphaned children, as well as being a refuge for the deranged, housing up to a hundred at any one time. Even then it was remembered as a good home where they were well fed and nurtured. That is the only resemblance it has to the Snooty Fox today. Everyone who comes here is well fed and certainly nurtured and cosseted by the landlords, Perry Dunford and Sue Baker.

The whole of the Snooty Fox has an air of well-being. The bars resound to the happy chatter of locals and visitors who have discovered it a short driving distance from the town centre in a village-style setting overlooking a park. The Lounge Bar and Restaurant has overhead beams and its walls are attractively colour washed and stencilled. The upholstered bench seating and polished wooden tables enhance the country feeling. Both Perry and Sue are experienced inn-keepers and Perry's four daughters, Charis, Xanthe, Serena and Tia, with occasional help from Sue's son and daughter, Mitch and Sara, keep the pub a family business and somewhere that everyone is welcome .

Good food has become synonymous with the Snooty Fox. Perry's Starters make a delicious beginning to a meal, then there are Dishy Chick dishes, porky bits, steaks and sauces as well as many more dishes. Each is cooked perfectly and beautifully presented. bar snacks are not forgotten and one can enjoy anything from a sandwich to a salad. The service is excellent and if you are in a hurry, just tell them when you arrive and your needs will be quickly attended to. To reach the Snooty Fox from Longleat or Centre Parks via the Picketpost roundabout taking the A362 for Warminster and to the next roundabout. At the Cley Hill roundabout go straight across still following the A362 for Warminster. On reaching Masefield mini-roundabout, turn right to Broadway. Follow the road to Broadway roundabout and take the second left turning in to Brook Street. The Snooty Fox is approximately two hundred and fifty yards up Brook Street on the right, set back slightly off the road opposite the park.

USEFUL INFORMATION

- OPEN : 12-3pm & 7-11pm all year Except Dec 25th &26th Limited opening lunch-times
- WHEELCHAIR ACCESS: Yes
- GARDEN: Yes. Bouncy Castle. & Aviary. Pets Corner
- CREDIT CARDS: Limited
- CHILDREN: Welcome

- RESTAURANT: Delicious imaginative fare
- VEGETARIAN: Menu on request

- BAR FOOD: Wide range
- LICENSED: Full On
- PETS: No

THE THREE CROWNS INN
Old Southampton Road
Whaddon
Salisbury
Wiltshire
SP5 3HB

Tel: 01722 710211

Lionel Sutton has only recently taken over the Three Crowns Inn in the little village of Whaddon just three miles from Salisbury but with his cheerful personality he has already created a warm, welcoming atmosphere in the bars and restaurant. His background is as a chef in top hotels and in cruise liners so it goes without saying that the food in the Inn is superb. It is an old inn with a sign that has a splendid history. The Palace of Clarendon was a Royal Residence from the reign of Henry 1st to that of Edward III and here in 1357 after the Battle of Poitiers, King John of France and King David of Scotland were the prisoners of King Edward III. The Forest of Clarendon at this time was the scene of the Royal Hunting Party with the three Monarchs riding side by side and this episode became the origin of the sign of The Three Crowns.

The Three Crowns retains all its character with old beams everywhere and an open log fire to add to the warmth of the welcome. The beer is well kept with a selection of Real Ales. Every day you will find locals at the bar enjoying a pint and a chat. Fresh fish cooked in a home-made beer batter is one of the favourite dishes on the menu but there is much more including Daily Specials. Everything is freshly prepared and above all it is value for money. For those who do not want a main meal, the range of Bar snacks provides something to suit everyone's taste and pocket.

For those who would like to stay in this friendly hostelry there are three ensuite rooms which have recently been refurbished and are furnished with an eye to style and comfort. Two of the rooms can be either double or twin-bedded and the third is a family room. All the rooms have television and a hostess tray. Breakfast every morning is a substantial meal with a choice; more than enough to set anyone up for the day whether on business or leisure.

USEFUL INFORMATION

- OPEN: All year
- WHEELCHAIR ACCESS: Bar only
- GARDEN: Yes
- CREDIT CARDS: Visa/Master
- ACCOMMODATION: 3 ensuite rooms
- RATES: £19 pppn low season £22.50 pppn high season

- RESTAURANT: Good pub fare
- VEGETARIAN: On request
- BAR FOOD: Wide range
- LICENSED: Full On
- CHILDREN: Welcome to stay
- PETS: No

WHITE LODGE
22 Westbury Road
Warminster
Wiltshire
BA12 0AW

Tel/Fax: 01985 21238
Pay Phone available
Fax facility on request
bookings@lioncountry.demon.co.uk
Web Site: http://www.lioncountry.demon.co.uk

White Lodge, set in half an acre of garden with ample parking, has a superb position overlooking the beautifully wooded Arn Hill, and adjacent to the West Wilts Golf Club. It is only three quarters of a mile from the Town Centre of Warminster, and conveniently situated for Longleat, Bath, Salisbury, Stonehenge, Stourhead Gardens and Westbury's White Horse. Bath is seventeen miles, Salisbury twenty miles, Glastonbury & Cheddar twenty five miles, Stourhead thirteen miles, Stonehenge twelve miles and the Westbury White Horse five miles.

Built in the 1930's but individually designed, giving it interesting features, including a staircase that winds its way up the turret. The Dining Room and the guest rooms overlook the perfectly maintained gardens which are a riot of colour in summer. Carol Wheeler is the friendly, welcoming owner of White Lodge, which is open to guests throughout the year, except at Christmas. Carol, genuinely enjoys having people staying in her home and works hard to ensure that they have a happy and comfortable stay. It is a strictly non-smoking house, in which there are three attractive guest rooms. There is an ensuite family room with a double bed, a single bed and a Z bed if needed, a twin room and a double room, both with an ensuite shower, but shared toilet. All three bedrooms have colour television and a hostess tray. What is appealing especially about the furnishings at White Lodge, is that much of it is in the Deco style of the 1930's so fashionable when the house was built. The tranquil air of White Lodge, is conducive to a good night's sleep in very comfortable beds, and when you come down to the light, pleasant dining room for breakfast, it will be to a meal that you will long remember. Carol takes a great deal of pleasure and pride in making sure it is delicious. Many of Carol's guests have been coming here for years and those who are newcomers rapidly become friends.

USEFUL INFORMATION

- OPEN: All year except Christmas
- WHEELCHAIR ACCESS: No
- GARDEN: Yes
- CHILDREN: Welcome
- LICENSED: No
- RATES: Single from £25 Double from £36 Child £10

- DINING ROOM: Delicious breakfast
- VEGETARIAN: Breakfast available
- STRICTLY NON-SMOKING HOUSE
- CREDIT CARDS: None taken
- ACCOMMODATION: 3 rooms
- PETS: No

THE WOODBRIDGE INN
A345 North Newnton
NR. Pewsey
Wiltshire
SN9 6JZ

Tel/Fax: 01980 630266

Egon Ronay 'Star' Rated
AA QQ. RAC Acclaimed
Wiltshire 'Pub of the Year'

Make sure you seek out this amazing little hostelry on the A345 at North Newnton, just outside Pewsey. The Woodbridge has to be one of the most delightful pubs in the whole of England. It has been showered with accolades and all of them richly deserved. Owned and run by two friendly, talented people, Lou and Teri Vertessey it is four hundred years old in part and the 'modern' part has been there for two hundred years. Over the centuries it has been a bake house, a brew house and a toll house with a combined annual income of some £39!!. The centuries have given it a warmth and charm which is enhanced today by all that has been achieved by the Vertesseys since they arrived a decade ago. The Woodbridge stands in 41/2 acres of riverside meadow and has stunning, far reaching views over Salisbury Plain. Inside the pub is furnished in a delightful cottage style and everywhere you look you will see something to do with pigs; pig pictures, artefacts, bric-a brac- filling every nook and cranny. Lou and Teri have created a great atmosphere, it is warm, cosy and comfortable and it is no wonder that people from miles around beat a path to its doors. In the summer you can drink outside, play petanque, let the children roam in a great play area. The rolling meadow provides facilities for 30 caravans. One of the many accolades that The Woodbridge has won has been the Corps D'Elite Award from Les Routiers for the well chosen wine list. The Woodbridge is also renowned for its food. Teri is a fantastic cook and her menu, which includes twelve starters, some twenty main dishes and an assortment of delectable puddings and desserts, includes everything from the time honoured traditional English favourites to Thai, Indonesian and Chinese, in which she specialises, as well as Greek, Italian, Indian, Cajun and Mexican. Sunday Lunch is a feast. The pretty restaurant is small and you must book a table beforehand so that you are not disappointed. There are also daily specials and an excellent range of bar meals. For those who want to stay in this beautiful area which is also within striking distance of so many fascinating places, there are 4 double rooms, attractively appointed. Three are en-suite and the fourth has a wash basin. All the rooms have comfortable beds, television, radio alarm and a well supplied hostess tray. Breakfast, like the rest of the food in this super little pub, is a substantial meal cooked freshly to your order. It will be a long time before you find somewhere to beat The Woodbridge.

USEFUL INFORMATION

· OPEN: Mon-Sat 11-3pm & 5.30-11pm Sun:
  12-3pm & 7-10.30pm. Closed Xmas Day
· WHEELCHAIR ACCESS: Yes
· GARDEN: Yes. Petanque. Play area
· CREDIT CARDS: All major cards

· ACCOMMODATION: 4 dbl. rooms 3 ensuite
· RATES: From £17.50

· RESTAURANT: Great menu
· VEGETARIAN: Yes
· BAR FOOD: Large choice
· LICENSED: Yes. Award winning wine list
· CHILDREN: Welcome
· PETS: No

BELMONT
9 Boreham Road
Warminster, Wiltshire
BA12 9JP
Tel/Fax: 01985 212799
monkcom@aol.com
ETB * Crown Commended

Belmont was built as a substantial 'villa' in 1870. A Franciscan Monk lived here at one time and later American Army pilots as well as the American Red Cross Service used the house. Today's owner, Kate Monkcom has brought the house back to its former glory; the kitchen now boasts an Aga cooker and the old walled garden has blossomed in her loving care. Belmont, a non-smoking house, is within easy walking distance of a range of restaurants, shops, and the BR Station. There is a sports centre and pool close by. It is within a few minutes drive of open countryside and interesting walks, for example to Cley Hill, the UFO spotters site. Centre Parcs Holiday village is a ten minute drive away, as is Longleat house, Safari park and ground and the ancient monument of Stonehenge is an easy 20-minute drive. A great place to stay, Belmont is warm and comfortable house, where guests are very well cared for. There are 3 guest rooms; 1 twin, 1 double has a Queen size bed and the other double has a king size bed. The bathroom is always a talking point with an enormous bath, a new shower, and jazzy toilet seat lid. All the rooms are well furnished, have washbasins, colour televisions and hostess trays. Belmont can offer, in addition to Bed and Breakfast, treatments such as Reflexology, Aromatherapy or Holistic Massage. You are advised to book for these treatments in advance.

USEFUL INFORMATION

- OPEN: All year
- WHEELCHAIR ACCESS: Unsuitable
- GARDEN: Yes
- CREDIT CARDS: None taken
- ACCOMMODATION: 1twin.2dbl
- RATES: From £25sgl & £35 dbl

- DINING ROOM: Excellent breakfast
- VEGETARIAN: Upon request
- NON-SMOKING HOUSE
- LICENSED: No
- CHILDREN: Welcome
- PETS: No

BROOK HOUSE
Semington, Trowbridge
Wiltshire BA14 6JR

Tel: 01380 870232

Brook House has only belonged to two families since it was built in 1790 and consequently has that well-loved feeling about it that families create. The present owners, Michael and Tara Bruges have been here for thirty years and it is they who give such a warm welcome to their guests who come from all over the world to enjoy the warmth and comfort, the attractive bedrooms and a superb breakfast for which the Bruges are renowned. Brook House has that spacious feeling about it with high ceilings and large windows. It is furnished throughout with great taste and many period pieces. There are lots of books and a piano for musicians to play. guests are welcome to roam the large garden and orchard complete with brook. There is a swimming pool, tennis lawn and fields for walking as well as the Kennet and Avon Canal towpath which borders the eleven acres belonging to Brook House. You can fish in the brook, enjoy the vast numbers of birds, explore the many attractive villages nearby. Avebury and other Ancient Monuments are within easy reach and Stonehenge, and Glastonbury Tor are not far away.

USEFUL INFORMATION

- OPEN: All year. Not Christmas
- WHEELCHAIR ACCESS: No
- GARDEN: 11 acres. Swimming pool, tennis lawn
- CREDIT CARDS: None taken
- ACCOMMODATION: 1 ensuite double, 1tw, 1fam with adjacent bathroom
- RATES: From £25 pppn Reduction for children under 10

- DINING ROOM: Superb breakfast
- VEGETARIAN: Upon request
- SMOKING DOWNSTAIRS ONLY
- LICENSED: No
- CHILDREN: Welcome

THE LAMB ON THE STRAND
99 The Strand
Semington , NR Trowbridge,
Wiltshire   BA14 6LL

Tel: 01380 870263 Fax: 01380 870815

The tiny hamlet of The Strand can be found midway along the ridge that connects the two villages of Seend and Semington on the northern edge of Salisbury Plain, halfway between Bradford on Avon and Devizes. A kilometre to the north lies The Kennet and Avon Canal around which there are a number of pretty walks culminating in the engineering wonder that is Caen Hill Locks at Devizes. Before it was converted to a pub about 18 years ago, The Lamb on The Strand was a traditional 'drinking house', a working farm where the farmer's wife served beer and cider from the wood to customers seated in her front room. The current owners, Philip Roose-Francis and Sue Smith have furnished and decorated the building in a pub-meets-brasserie style where real log fires meet with the cappuccino machine. Sue trained and ran the restaurant at the Cordon Bleu School in London for three years and that background is reflected in the deliciously original and eclectic menu at The Lamb, complemented by a wine list that includes rarities from Spain and the New World. Certainly somewhere not to be missed.

USEFUL INFORMATION

- OPEN: All year except Xmas Day 11.30-3pm
  & 6.30-11pm Sun: 12-3pm
- WHEELCHAIR ACCESS: Yes
- CREDIT CARDS: Master/Visa/AMEX/Switch

- LICENSED: Yes

- PETS: No
- RESTAURANT; Not applicable
- VEGETARIAN: Always a choice
- BAR FOOD: Wide variety of light
  modern fare + traditional
- CHILDREN: Yes

LES PARISIENS
28 High Street, Warminster
Wiltshire   BA12 9AF
Tel: 01985 217373
2 AA Rosettes for High Standard of Food
AA Best Restaurant Guide 1998

Les Parisiens, a charming restaurant, housed in a traditionally Wiltshire style building dating back to 1740, is conveniently situated in the centre of Warminster (Woolworths is just opposite), and with an abundance of free car parking nearby. The typical Parisian theme created by the owners Nigel and Samantha Snook is immediately evident through the burgundy and cream decor and co-ordinating table linen, the many pictures and posters adorning the walls and the varied collection of French tunes in the background. The restaurant, managed by Samantha, has a very intimate and informal atmosphere with the forty covers split between three rooms, offering smoking and non-smoking dining. As you would expect, the food is also French in its origin. In the morning you can enjoy anything from a simple coffee and croissant, or a croque monsieur and fries, to a three course lunch. In the evening there is a choice from both A la Carte and fixed price menus. Whilst Nigel performs in the kitchen, he also helps to carefully select the wines - all French of course - to complement the menus, and Samantha creates the desserts, although Nigel is 'allowed' to make the tarte tatin and crepes. A blissful harmony which makes Les Parisiens a delightful place to eat at.

USEFUL INFORMATION

- OPEN: Tues-Sat inc. 10-2pm (last orders)
  & 7-9.30pm (last orders)

- WHEELCHAIR ACCESS: Yes
- CREDIT CARDS: All major cards
- CHILDREN: Welcome

- RESTAURANT: Classical, modern French
  food AM: Light snacks & fixed price menu
  PM: Fixed price A la Carte
- VEGETARIAN: Yes
- LICENSED: Restaurant & Supper
- PETS: No

LONGWATER PARK FARM
Lower Road
Erlestoke, NR Devizes
Wiltshire   SN10 5UE

Tel/Fax: 01380 830095
3 Crown Commended: Access Grade 2: AA QQQ

Longwater Park Farm was originally the deer parks in front of Erlestoke House and has a fascinating history which Pam Hampton and her husband will be happy to tell you about. Today it is a one hundred and sixty six acre farm with one hundred and ten acres of grassland, woodland, 8 acres of lakes including one used for coarse fishing. The smaller lake, which Longwater overlooks, is about one acre and has been made into a Waterfowl Conservation Area where eighteen varieties of duck and seven types of geese as well as a whole range of migrating birds always provide the visitor with much to watch. In the wildfowl paddock there are sheep as grass trimmers. They are Castlemilk Moorit, one of Britain's rarest breeds of sheep. It is an exciting place to stay and the atmosphere of the house is so welcoming. It is licensed and the food is excellent. There are two twin, two double and one family room, all ensuite and each has television and a hostess tray as well as a refrigerator. Guests come back here regularly sometimes as many as two or three times a year. It is that sort of house with the facilities of a small hotel but with the comfort of a home.

USEFUL INFORMATION

- OPEN: Early January to 20th Dec
- WHEELCHAIR ACCESS: Yes
- GARDEN: Yes. Coarse fishing
- CREDIT CARDS: None taken
- ACCOMMODATION: 2dbl 2tw 1 family all ensuite
- RATES: From £22 B&B Winter Breaks 2 days B&B £65 3 days B&B £90
- DINING ROOM: Excellent, farmhouse fare
- VEGETARIAN: Yes + any diet by arrangement
- CHILDREN: 5 years and over
- LICENSED: Table Licence
- PETS: Yes

THE MILL HOUSE
Berwick St James
NR Salisbury , Wiltshire
SP3 4TS
Tel: 01722 790331

With a Cross Country walk to STONEHENGE as one of the attractions, it is no wonder that Diana Gifford Mead's Visitors' Book is full of praise for everything about the Mill House. It is delightful and radiates the love Diana has for her home and for Berwick St James. She states that if she could choose where to live anywhere in the world, it would be here. She has lived down by the river in what was the Miller's House for thirty seven years, although the house was built around 1785, and 40 years at Berwick House. It is on an island and can only be approached by bridges. Today with the aid of her schoolmaster son, Michael who lives next door, she runs the Mill House. The rooms are attractively furnished with antiques, ceramics, and pictures, each room has television and a Hostess tray. Breakfast is a meal cooked to your choice. Apart from being a wonderful setting, surrounded by water meadows, wild flowers, fauna and butterflies with 20 mile walks in any direction, the Mill House also has horse trekking and riding nearby, 3 golf courses and fishing which is free in the Mill pool when not in drought. The lovely garden is spectacular with old fashioned roses in summer and bulbs in spring. There is much more to say about the Mill House, not least that it is close to a great pub, The Boot, one of the best in the South and where the chef has won many awards - come and see for yourselves.

USEFUL INFORMATION

- OPEN: All year
- WHEELCHAIR ACCESS: Yes. Must be able to negotiate a few stairs
- GARDEN: Yes
- CREDIT CARDS: None taken
- ACCOMMODATION: 2tw 2sgl ensuite.
- RATES: From £20 low season. Discount for 3 nights or more
- DINING ROOM: Super breakfast
- VEGETARIAN: Upon request
- LICENSED: No
- CHILDREN: Welcome

MORRIS' FARMHOUSE
Baverstock , NR Dinton
Salisbury, Wiltshire
SP3 5EL

Tel/Fax: 01722 716874
Listed and Commended

For total peace and a stay in a charming old Victorian farmhouse, you cannot do better that Morris' Farmhouse owned by Judith Marriott and her husband. It stands some fifty yards back from a B road behind a high hedge in perfect privacy. The house faces south and looks towards the most glorious views which add to ones sense of well-being. No longer part of a farm, the house is a haven of peace and tranquillity and the garden that has been created by Judith's husband is a colourful delight. There are only two guest rooms, both twin-bedded, although one can be made into a double. There is a shared bathroom with lots of fluffy towels and ample hot water. Breakfast is a delicious meal, freshly cooked to your order and served in the south facing conservatory. The traditional English breakfast is a substantial meal but one can choose boiled eggs instead or simply fruit juice, cereal and toast. Morris Farmhouse is ideally situated for anyone wanting to recharge their batteries and enjoy all that this historic area has to offer.

USEFUL INFORMATION

- OPEN: All year except Xmas
- DINING ROOM: Excellent breakfast No evening meals

- WHEELCHAIR ACCESS: Not really
- VEGETARIAN: Upon request
- GARDEN: Yes
- LICENSED: No
- CREDIT CARDS: None taken
- CHILDREN: Welcome
- ACCOMMODATION: 2 twin
- PETS: Yes
- RATES: From £17.00pp Children under 5 free. 5-11 £10

RIVERSIDE CLOSE
1, Riverside Close
Laverstock
Salisbury, Wiltshire
SD1 1QW

Tel/Fax: 01722 320287

Riverside Close is only a mile from Salisbury's magnificent cathedral but it has a definitely rural feel about it, possibly because of tranquillity engendered in the house, something the owner, Mary Tucker, works hard to achieve. She feels her guests need to regard the house as a haven away from the stresses of every day life. Many of her guests are people coming here on business and for them it is great after a busy day but it is equally pleasant and welcoming for her many guests who come from all over the world mainly to see the cathedral and to enjoy the New Forest which is on the doorstep. The house is modern, airy, attractively furnished. There are two ensuite guest rooms, one double and one family. Both rooms have television, hairdryers and a hostess tray. Breakfast is a delicious meal designed to set you up for the day. Mary will cook at night but she does ask for forty eight hours notice.

USEFUL INFORMATION

- OPEN: All year
- DINING ROOM: Great breakfast Evening meals with 48 hours notice
- WHEELCHAIR ACCESS: Yes
- VEGETARIAN: Upon request
- GARDEN: Yes
- LICENSED: No
- CREDIT CARDS: None taken
- CHILDREN: Welcome
- ACCOMMODATION: 2 ensuite rooms
- PETS: No
- NON SMOKING THROUGHOUT
- RATES: £25pp.pn B&B

STURFORD MEAD FARM
Corsley
Warminster
Wiltshire
BA12 2QU

Tel/Fax: 01373 832213

Sturford Mead Farm has quite a history and was once part of the Longleat estate. The present owners Lynn and Jonathan Corp have been here working the farm and building up a great reputation for bed and breakfast, since 1985. They are hospitable people who enjoy sharing their home with guests. The house is a happy one and although the furnishings are of a very high standard with pretty colour co-ordinated curtains and designer duvets in the bedrooms, it is a relaxed and informal atmosphere. Two twin bedrooms are ensuite and a double has a private bathroom. All the rooms have television, a hostess tray, radios and alarm clocks. Breakfast is a splendid meal, as one would expect in a farmhouse. It certainly sets one up for the day ready to explore the glorious countryside roundabout and the many places of historical interest, including Longleat itself. You will find Sturford Mead Farm on the A362 halfway between Warminster and Frome, nestling under the historic monument of Cley Hill (N.T.)

USEFUL INFORMATION

- OPEN: All year
- WHEELCHAIR ACCESS: Not really
- GARDEN: Yes
- CREDIT CARDS: None taken
- ACCOMMODATION: 2tw ensuite
  1 dbl. with private bathroom
- RATES: From £28

- DINING ROOM: Excellent breakfast
- VEGETARIAN: Upon request
- LICENSED: No
- CHILDREN: Welcome

- PETS: No

Alum Grange	Alum Chine	389
Anglebury House	Wareham	390
Ardene	Boscombe	391
Beechleas	Wimbourne Minster	392
Castle Inn	West Lulworth	393
Cleveland Hotel	Westbourne	394
Connaught Hotel	Bournemouth	395
Cromwell House	Lulworth Cove	396
Drusillas Inn	Wimborne	409
Durley Court Hotel	Bournemouth	397
Earlham Lodge	Bournemouth	398
Galley Restaurant	Swanage	410
Gervis Court	Bournemouth	399
Griffs Hotel	Bournemouth	400
Hawaiian	Bournemouth	401
Hemsworth Manor	Witchampton	410
Highways Guest House	Poole	411
Hopewell	Wimborne	411
Hotel Washington	Bournemouth	402
Kemps House	Wareham	403
Kimberley Court	Bournemouth	404
Langton Arms	Tarrant Monkton	405
Purbeck House	Swanage	406
Salterns House	Poole	407
Shell Bay Restaurant	Studland	412
Thornhill	Holt	412
Woodcroft Tower	Bournemouth	408

Chapter Eight:
The West Beckons

Dorset; a county without motorways. This means hours spent on dusty 'A' roads, waiting hopefully for the next suitable passing place. It also means an area with its rural life at least partially intact. Take Dorset at the pace it demands and you will find many unforgettable places, in a county of such variety and beauty that it will always leave you wanting more. If the main roads are tiresome, take a turning and explore the villages; you will not regret it.

A fantastic coastline, some fascinating history, and resorts with facilities and attractions galore, yet Dorset still manages to remain unpretentious and welcoming. This is the heart of Wessex, and the real lifeblood of rural England.

England is at its widest East to West along the South Coast. Even then there are no tremendous distances involved, and four or five hours on the major roads can take you from Sussex to Cornwall. Such a journey provides a cross section, a slice through the heart of this country and its landscape and history. The New Forest is a picturesque and appetizing taster of what is to come in a journey west. Yet its order and relative modernity do not prepare you for the variety and antiquity which greet the traveller to Dorset.

Strictly speaking Wessex is an indefinable area, without true borders, but the National Trust considers Dorset to be its natural Eastern limit, and we will follow this lead.

Entering Dorset through Ringwood, we will travel around the county in a clockwise direction, from Christchurch, Bournemouth and Poole on to Purbeck, then Dorchester and the heart of Hardy's Wessex, before heading north through a multitude of villages, ending up at Shaftesbury.

Following the majestic river Avon due south from Ringwood, the majority of traffic heads along the A338 for the conurbation centred around Bournemouth, the gorse bushes lining the dual carriageway emphasising that you are still near the New Forest, and are approaching a sizeable centre of population more typical of the east than the west; Bournemouth and Christchurch are quite different to the rest of Dorset, and were part of Hampshire until recent times.

Surely the largest resort on the South coast, at first it is hard to establish where one area begins and another ends. Despite this, the towns of Christchurch, Bournemouth and Poole do each have an individual character, and should not be missed.

CHRISTCHURCH (Tourist Information 01202 471780), is an attractive place, full of interest. The town forms the eastern section of this built up area, and takes its name from the magnificent 11th century PRIORY CHURCH, which still towers above the rest of the town. Originally known as Christ's Church it has now passed its 900th anniversary, and its features span the ages, from the unmistakeable round arches of the Norman period forming the breathtaking ceiling of the nave to the 13th century porch and 15th century bell tower. It is the longest parish church in England, and was built on the site of a Saxon Minster by Flambard, William the Conqueror's Chancellor. Dorset will offer you some great churches, but the addition of this one has certainly made its collection richer.

Norman Arches, The Nave, Priory Church, Christchurch.

Christchurch is a pleasant, open town, retaining its Saxon street layout despite extensive modern development. There is much history here, from the immaculately thatched OLD COURT HOUSE, dating from the 15th century, to the 18th century Parish Workhouse, now transformed into the RED HOUSE MUSEUM, (01202 482860) where you can view a varied collection amassed by local historian Herbert Druitt, including Victorian and Edwardian fashion, toys, and dolls, as well as archaeological and geological exhibits.

There are also records of Christchurch life from its earliest times, when it was known as Tweoxneam or Twynham: the place between the waters. True to its original name, the Rivers Stour and Avon will eventually come to dominate any lengthy walk you choose to take around the town.

A more specific collection is housed at the SOUTHERN ELECTRIC MUSEUM (01202 480467), sited in the Old Power Station, Bargates, Christchurch; where early domestic appliances, rare engines and working models help to form one of the country's largest collections of electrical gadgetry. The Power Station was built in 1903.

The middle of the town is marked by the ruins of CHRISTCHURCH CASTLE, and the more intact CONSTABLES HOUSE dating back to the same Norman era. This has one of the oldest chimneys in England, and its five windows would have been an innovation and luxury to the contemporary community, even though they look distinctly cold and lacking in glazing now!

The CONVENT WALK along the Mill Stream, from the ruins on towards the Quay, will take you past PLACE MILL (01202 487626), a restored Anglo-Saxon water mill, which can still be seen at work when the tide assists. The mill was once part of a monastery, but survived the surrender to Henry VIII in 1538 to become part of local smuggling operations in the 18th century, an industry of which you will soon hear much more.

At Christchurch Quay you can appreciate the beauty and power of the Stour and Avon, as the two great rivers meet gracefully to enter the sea. Take a stroll inland along either of these, and crossing Castle and Bridge Street pause to look over into clear waters. There are three Norman bridges spanning the rivers, the Avon has two of these, the Stour one. Most of the other rivers in the county meet the sea as a trickle between eroded chalk or limestone, so this scene has been another welcome addition to Dorset's coastline.

The Quay itself teems with flocks of ducks, geese and swans, giving more colour to an already impressive scene, as anglers fish right in the middle of the town. The ROYALTY FISHERY (01202 591111) can provide day tickets for coarse fishing on The Avon, as well as for salmon and sea trout, although as a rather clumsy fourteen year old I only remember catching eels. Christchurch has a central venue for events and exhibitions in the High St. THE REGENT CENTRE (01202 499148) has everything from regular art and craft exhibitions to ballet, cinema, and theatre performances, as well as collectors markets.

Just over the Stour and Avon is the RIVERSMEET LEISURE CENTRE (01202 477987), which has an eighteen hole golf course attached, while the grandly named KNIGHTS OF CHRISTCHURCH (01202 483777), hold indoor tournaments during the summer months in an 800 seat pavilion at the same location. During the tourist season they also parade through the centre of the town each Monday, at lunchtime. There is also an annual CHRISTCHURCH FESTIVAL, usually held in July.

To the east along the A337 lies **HIGHCLIFFE**, where clean sandy beaches straddle the border into Hampshire. To see a building which is still living out a very chequered history patterned by chance, visit HIGHCLIFFE CASTLE (01425 278807), a grade one listed country house from the reign of William IV, surrounded by fifteen acres of cliff-top woodlands. Just thirty years ago the castle was completely dilapidated, its irreplaceable collection of stained glass from all over medieval Europe in danger of being lost forever.

Despite various efforts the castle was still in a terrible state at the beginning of this decade. Perhaps some sort of ironic justice was being played out, as the original smaller building on this site was apparently funded partly with money found in an attic. James Penleaze had this unlikely windfall: a hatbox stuffed with banknotes in a building he inherited, but it was the Stuart family who ambitiously developed his house into a castle in the first half of the 19th century, their descendants eventually selling the property in 1950. The final twist may be the £2.65 million granted for the building's restoration by the National Lottery Heritage Fund, a much more controlled use of Lady Luck. So far one wing has been opened to the public, containing an exhibition centre. The Castle also has an eighteen hole golf course (01425 272953).

Returning to the main town and looking about at the carefully maintained floral displays, you will not be surprised to hear that Christchurch won the Britain in Bloom competition in 1996, and has already qualified as a 1998 finalist. The sea has made the life of Christchurch, and MUDEFORD QUAY is still the centre of the local fishing industry. This is essentially a peaceful place, but has not always been so. In the 18th century smuggling was rife along this southern coast. It was estimated that two thirds of all the tea consumed in England, in addition to half of the brandy, had escaped the payment of import duties. Such a massive scale of clandestine operations was bound to have its conflicts, and this very place had one so dramatic as to gain the name of THE BATTLE OF MUDEFORD.

On the evening of Thursday 15th July 1784 Master William Allen sailed his Royal Navy sloop *The Orestes* towards Mudeford from Hengistbury Head, the eastern extremity of Bournemouth's beaches, with no idea that the journey would be his last. There were two large smuggling luggers at the Quay. They had unloaded their illicit cargo of spirits the previous day; an operation that one local newspaper suggested had involved upwards of three hundred men. Crime was obviously popular, and it paid!

Some of the Navy's landing craft managed to become stuck in the mudbanks, and while trying to shift them Allen was mortally wounded when the smugglers opened fire from the luggers, as well as from two of the houses on the shore, very close to the present day HAVEN INN.

As was not unusual in 18th century Dorset, the smugglers got away with it, and no witnesses stepped forward despite offers of a reward and the Royal Pardon; perhaps the local community were afraid to shoulder the blame for increasing pub prices throughout the land if the traders were caught.

As you look around you at the most civilised of surroundings it is difficult to imagine such bloody events taking place right here, but the sea does not change, and neither does its potential for prompting both heroism and human conflict. Unfortunately prices and Customs enforcement have altered, and you will not get the cheap brandy as easily these days.

Across the bay from Christchurch stands **SOUTHBOURNE**, and the place with the most ancient history in the area: **HENGISTBURY HEAD**. There is a ferry to it from Mudeford Quay during the summer, as well as to the popular MUDEFORD SANDBANKS which form a thin strip of land directly opposite the Quay. Alternatively a walk to Hengistbury from the nearest car park is worth the quarter of an hour's effort.

This small point of land pushing out into the sea is said to attract too many visitors each year: even those locals who use the location to fly kites have been warned to stay away from the eroding edges. There were both Iron and Stone Age settlements here, and the site is an Ancient Monument, Local Nature Reserve, and Site of Special Scientific Interest for wildlife and geology. Nearly every species of bird on the British List has been recorded here at one time or another.

What hits you first at Hengistbury is the view to the west. Bournemouth and Poole can be seen in a glance, fronted by the golden yellow of the unbroken ribbon of sand which separates them so crisply from the sea. This is the best place to give you some idea of just how big this tourist conurbation has become. To the east and north you can then compare them to Christchurch, and there is a definite contrast, even from this distance.

An aerial view of Hengistbury Head, a fragment of crumbling orange and yellow sandstone between sand banks, leads to you wonder how much longer it can possibly survive, and how on earth it has managed to do so until now.

Hengistbury Head has an OUTDOOR EDUCATION AND FIELD STUDIES CENTRE (01202 425173) for those who wish to explore more thoroughly.

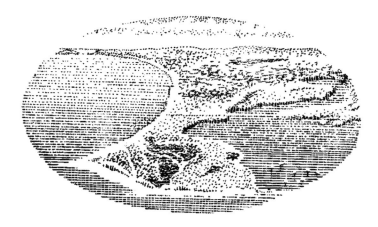

Hengistbury Head, looking east.

Neighbouring **BOURNEMOUTH** (Tourist Information 01202 451700) is a resort through and through. The long, clean sandy beaches, backed by streets full of well established Hotels are a start, yet there is much more to this town. There can be few better places to spend time if you want to be able to walk among pine forested gardens one moment, moving on to golden beaches the next, and still be able to visit the theatre, cinema or a good restaurant in the evening.

The beauty of Bournemouth is that there is so much to do in a compact area, despite the enormity of the town as a whole. Let's start at the pier, and see what there is to offer to the pedestrian.

A walk along the pier itself (not the most attractive of structures) gives you a superb view out to sea. To the west you can see Old Harry Rocks standing like a frail but natural breakwater at the corner of the Isle of Purbeck. To the east you will see the expanses of golden sand broken regularly by wooden breakwaters, dividing the beach into immense sand-pits for children of all ages. Also to the east, on a relatively clear day, your view includes the Isle of Wight, Boscombe pier, Christchurch and Hengistbury Head.

More immediately, you are standing at the point where the River Bourne enters the sea, at the base of the central CHINE, the name given to the pine forested valleys which break into the sandstone cliff shoreline at regular intervals: there are six of these in all. But as you stand looking out to sea, between **EAST CLIFF** on your left and **WEST CLIFF** on your right, do not turn around expecting to see anything like the grand arrival of the Stour and Avon at Christchurch, for the Bourne arrives at the coast as narrow stream, channelled between concrete, and barely noticed.

During the summer you will also see thousands of people from here, giving a kaleidoscopic range of colours to the beaches. Look in particular for some sand sculptors who work at the eastern base of the pier, their work is skilful, and a tribute to the protection offered from the wind by the pier and the raised promenade. Sometimes I have wondered at the painstaking patience of artists and sculptors, but this is a form of art I can imagine being a pleasure in itself, as long as you have plenty of sun block.

It may (and probably will) have taken you some time and effort to get to this place. Crowded suburbs, seemingly endless major roundabouts, and then a struggle to find a parking space anywhere near the front will quite possibly have tried your patience; but once you are here, most of what you will want from Bournemouth is within comfortable walking distance.

The BOURNEMOUTH INTERNATIONAL CENTRE, one of the largest and most modern concert venues and Leisure centres in Southern England, stands as an imposing red brick building above the corner of the promenade on West Cliff, while the 900 seatPIER THEATRE is on the pier itself, and has the PAVILION THEATRE facing it from just a couple of hundred yards back inland. The WINTER GARDENS THEATRE (01202 456456 for all four of these), a regular venue for the BOURNEMOUTH SYMPHONY ORCHESTRA, is just a little further back on the western side and with the RUSSELL-COTES ART GALLERY & MUSEUM (01202 551009) along the promenade on East Cliff, you are really right in the thick of things.

The museum building is a decorated version of an Italiante villa (though actually a late Victorian mansion), with some small but attractive gardens, also in a classical style, overlooking the sea. Although it seems a strangely optimistic site for a museum, with sun worshippers by the thousand all around, it is not a token effort, and won the award for National Heritage Best Fine Art Museum in 1991. It has a fine collection of Victorian and Edwardian paintings, as well as sculpture and furniture.

Bournemouth's sheltered location gives it a surprisingly warm climate, and this helps to make it a superb centre for gardens and parks. In all there are 2,000 acres of horticulture to choose from between the seafront and the edge of the town. Many of these are also immediately accessible from the base of the pier.A walkway takes you under Bath Road, and straight into the LOWER GARDENS. These are fairly formal, with the contained Bourne running along the eastern edge, but feature some excellent floral displays in spring and summer, with varieties of Geranium, Heliotrope, Marigold and Petunia and many others, combined with foliage plants. Begonias and Impatiens are no longer used simply because the multitude of pigeons found them as tasty as they do the many offerings from passers by!

The squirrel population is equally well fed and tame, and will clear any pigeons out of the way whenever they feel the need. There are band performances in the gardens on most summer afternoons, and the FLOWERS BY CANDLELIGHT, when children light 20,000 candles at dusk, is a delightful tradition which takes place late in the summer.

There has to be protection offered to the beds in the form of low fencing, and the paths are as wide as the lawns in some places, since at busy times there are almost as many people here as blades of grass! Despite this the Lower Gardens provide a pleasant way to get to THE SQUARE at the heart of the town.

During the summer months there are free guided walking tours, concentrating on Bournemouth's past, which set out from the VISITOR INFORMATION BUREAU in Westover Road on the right of the gardens.

If you are not ready for the town yet then there are another two miles of garden walks available after you have crossed The Square into the CENTRAL and UPPER GARDENS. At the time of writing the Bourne is being re-routed under the Square to give it further protection.

A short way inland you will come to a wrought iron terrace from Boscombe, apparently moved here to become the PERGOLA, a climbing frame for plants, and a vantage point to look around what are also known as the PARADISE GARDENS, containing a mix of palms, daffodils, crocuses and snowdrops, according to the time of year.

Trees and shrubberies become more dominant in the garden landscapes as you reach the UPPER GARDENS, and there are many unusual and exotic ones amongst them, taking advantage of the clement weather.

Elsewhere in the town there are Italiante and Arid gardens at nearby BOSCOMBE CLIFF, while tropical themes are explored near to Alum Chine. The gardens at BOSCOMBE itself have been in existence for well over a hundred years, and recent landscaping has added more floral beds than ever, as well as three dimensional bedding displays.

The gardens of Bournemouth make a good diversion from the shops, beach and all the other usual facilities of a major seaside resort. The resort won the 1995 Entente Florale award, after a valiant effort by an army of local volunteers, and also the Large City award in the 1994 Britain in Bloom competition.Many of the gardens and walks follow the course of the other chines. These secluded walks exude tranquillity, yet in ALUM CHINE, in 1893, the course of British history was almost changed. A young boy fell off the innocuous footbridge, evading his fellows during a game of chase by attempting to jump to the trees below. He failed, fell, and ruptured a kidney. For the following three days the young Winston Churchill remained unconscious; his recovery is common knowledge.

Historically, Bournemouth is a relative newcomer. Before 1810 it was heathland, until Lewis Tregonwell's villa was built, on the site of the present day Royal Exeter Hotel. He was also responsible for the planting of the first pine trees in the Chines.

The weather has helped Bournemouth (as well as its flowers) to grow, as Victorians and then Edwardians flocked here for rest cures, especially as the newly constructed railway system provided direct access from London after the 1850s.

The romantic poet Percy Bysshe Shelley's son once lived in Boscombe Manor, and the SHELLEY ROOMS (01202 303571) commemorate the poet's life and work. Shelley's wife Mary is buried at ST PETER'S CHURCH, as is the heart of her husband, who drowned in Italy. Mary Shelley wrote Frankenstein, and it can be argued that thanks to Hammer films her fame will be more lasting than that of her husband; though the presence of two such intellects in a single marriage is even more frightening than the doctor's monster!

Whatever else you do in Bournemouth, you will surely not be able to resist at least one walk along part of the six miles of sandy beach, running east to west from Hengistbury Head to Alum Chine. If you include the beaches at Christchurch and Poole, it is possible to walk a full fifteen miles along golden sand with only the brief break at Hengistbury Head. If you wish to do more than walk then there is everything from pleasure cruises to rowing boats, pedaloes to paragliding.

These beaches are maintained with pride and care; each is sifted twice daily, and dogs are banned in Summer, and there are even specific non smoking areas. Families with children are encouraged to use particular, well patrolled stretches, and there is room here for everyone. It is a nice bonus to be able to walk straight from the town centre to the beach without having to cross or negotiate roads by going through the lower parks. Bournemouth has some very open areas, with more space than the rest of the towns in Dorset, and with its own overall atmosphere of a place permanently ready to take on the best of the holiday spirit.

There are a wealth of facilities, including jazz clubs, wine bars, and casinos; there is just about everything you could expect from a resort in this town. The shops range from major department stores to memorable Victorian Arcades. Try Westover Road for quality shopping, or POKESDOWN and BOSCOMBE for antiques.

There are many annual events, mostly concentrated into the summer months, including the BOURNEMOUTH MUSIC FESTIVAL (01202 451718), which boasts an attendance of more than 1,500 musicians from around the world. THE FESTIVAL OF LIGHTS is another noisy affair, with fireworks, lasers and dancing waters. Whatever time of year you find yourself in Bournemouth, it is worth checking with Tourist Information to discover which particular events are taking place.

Since Bournemouth found itself kidnapped into Dorset in the 1970s, it has given the county their only professional football team, at AFC BOURNEMOUTH (01202 395381). There are prestigious annual events in many sports which are held in Bournemouth, from the SNOOKER GRAND PRIX (usually October, B.I.C.) to POWERBOAT RACING, and TENNIS (also 01202 456456).

The tremendous range of other permanent attractions available is emphasised by such novelties as the ALICE IN WONDERLAND PARK (01202 483444) which boasts the South Coast's largest maze, and the BOURNEMOUTH BEARS at the Expo Centre (01202 293544), an exhibition celebrating the history of the Teddy Bear from its origins in 1904. Access to Bournemouth is also possible from the airport at HURN (01202 474115).

Near the airport you can get access to some of the best Coarse Angling in the country on the famous THROOP FISHERIES section of the River Stour (01202 395532). Variety is the key here, with specimen chub, barbel, pike, and bream in many swims along six miles of enchanting riverbank. All of this can be fished on a day ticket.

POOLE (Tourist Information 01202 253253) is dominated by its huge natural harbour, which is the largest in Europe, and the second largest in the world. The whole place has a more practical, down to earth feel than Bournemouth, but has just as many surprises. Some features from Bournemouth just carry straight on; the golden beaches continue west past CANFORD CLIFFS, until reaching a point at the SANDBANKS PENINSULA. Some of the trades follow west as well, Bitman's Chine, now known as CANFORD CLIFFS CHINE, was one of the centres of operations for the man known as the "King of Smugglers", Isaac Gulliver (1745-1822).

As you walk along the seemingly endless heaths and sandy beaches it is easy to see how the corpulent "gentle smuggler" became so successful, especially as Bournemouth had yet to be built. On his death he left a fortune of £60,000 (a modern day multi-millionaire) as well as property in Hampshire, Wiltshire, Somerset and Dorset. He had taken advantage of a Royal Pardon for smugglers in 1782, and become a wine trader. I wonder if his prices were competitive? We will come across more stories about Isaac elsewhere in the county.

As you stand on Poole Quay there is a tremendous contrast between the views to the east and west, emphasising the dual nature of Poole itself. The eastern perspective is dominated by the Sandbanks, in their golden glory looking like a massive pier intended to make Bournemouth feel envious. To the west the cranes and crates of the industrial part of the harbour seem near enough to touch, and it is amazing to think that Poole has the largest onshore oil-field operation in Western Europe, having already produced more than 150 million barrels.

There is certainly a different feel here from your starting point at the base of the pier in Bournemouth, but perhaps the longer history of Poole helps to give it a more permanent, defined character.

There is archaeological evidence to suggest that the harbour was being used as early as 800BC by Phoenician sailors and the ninety plus miles of coastline stretching from the Sandbanks around in a circle to SHELL BAY, must have been a breathtaking discovery for the first mariner who guided his craft through the gap. Poole gets its name from the Old English word "pol" meaning a pool or harbour.

THE WATERFRONT MUSEUM (01202 683138), situated in the Old High Street just off the Quay, is the ideal place to start an exploration of Poole's heritage. As well as features depicting the history of smuggling and seafaring in the area, the museum has items raised from the STUDLAND BAY wreck and a depiction of Baden Powell's first scout camp on Brownsea Island. The same building holds SCAPLEN'S COURT (01202 633558), a restored medieval merchant's dwelling. Reconstructed here are a Victorian pharmacy, school room and kitchen.

Another local industry is celebrated on the quay at the POOLE POTTERY (01202 666200) which has been in existence since 1873. The plain brick exterior, still looking like a Victorian warehouse or factory, actually hides a thoroughly modernised interior, incorporating a pottery museum, working kiln, shops and craft village, and even a 'have a go' area. Some of the products made here are sold in Harrods of London, and Tiffany's in New York, but possibly not those from the 'have a go' area.

The streets around ST JAMES CHURCH are a conservation area, and with such buildings as the GUILDHALL and the CUSTOMS HOUSE help to preserve something of Poole's past. Guided walks around the best of the Old Town are run during the summer, contact Tourist Information (again on the Quay) for details.

As in neighbouring Bournemouth, the sheltered surroundings have led to the development of some truly excellent gardens and parks. COMPTON ACRES (01202 700778) at Canford Cliffs, was originally designed in 1919, and it is hard to credit that you are still in England as you move from garden to garden, from reputedly the only genuine Japanese garden in Europe to more classical Italian arrangements dominated by a stunning array of bronze and marble statues. The peace and sense of escape are so complete that a return to the town comes as a bit of an unpleasant shock.

On the west side of Poole, along the A350, lies UPTON COUNTRY PARK (01202 672625), a much more traditional attraction with 100 acres comprising landscaped gardens, farmland, woodland and saltmarsh, as well as a re-created Romano-British settlement. Poole also has many other unique attractions. At the AQUARIUM COMPLEX (01202 686712), again situated on the Quay, you can see sharks, snakes, crocodiles, spiders and piranhas; while the RNLI MUSEUM (01202 663000) nearby concentrates on the efforts of the lifeboat service over the last 150 years. Two of the less commonly available British sports can be seen here, POOLE STADIUM (01202 677449) plays host to both GREYHOUND RACING and SPEEDWAY.

Much as in Bournemouth, there is plenty to do in this area. TOWER PARK (01202 723770) is a huge leisure complex in **CANFORD HEATH** on the outskirts of Poole, and boasts ten cinema screens, shows, and many other events. The POOLE ARTS CENTRE (01202 685222), which is next to POOLE PARK in the very centre of the town, is first home to the renowned BOURNEMOUTH SYMPHONY ORCHESTRA.

Standing on the Quay it is hard to believe that in less than half an hour you could be walking in the middle of a woodland Nature Reserve, and that you are looking straight at it! A short boat trip (01202 707744) will take you to **BROWNSEA ISLAND**, whose 500 acres contain heath and woodland, secluded beaches, and a disproportionate amount of interesting history for such a small place. The island's three mile circumference surrounds red squirrels, terns, herons and golden pheasants. Brown sea has been owned by the National Trust since 1962, but its inhabitants and owners have been many.

As you approach the island by boat be aware that you may be in the company of ghosts, representing the many others who have made this trip. They are likely to show a great range of emotions in their faces. The anxious Charles II dared not land at all, and was rowed around the island in 1665 because he owed £30,000 to Sir Robert Clayton, to whom Brownsea then belonged.

A party of tradesmen from Poole approached the island with more confidence in 1857. They went to ask Colonel Waugh to represent them in parliament. Unfortunately Waugh's extensive development of the island had brought him money problems. His wife, whose hearing was poor, met the tradesmen and immediately asked them for "time to pay". Waugh fled to Spain shortly afterwards, although the 'sleaze' might seem minimal by today's standards.

Some of these same men had formed part of the 1,000 strong audience ferried across to the island just three years earlier to watch the laying of the foundation stone to ST MARY'S CHURCH at the eastern end of the island. Waugh still had some money then.

St Mary's Church itself holds more than the Victorian exterior would suggest. The treasures inside are imported: the spectacular chapel ceiling dates from 1446 and was originally part of Crosby Palace, Bishopsgate, London, and was in the Palace when its owner, Richard III, was linked with the murder of the Princes in the Tower. Various items were imported from Italy by George Cavendish-Bentinck, who owned the island between 1870 and 1890. These include the ancient well-head which covers his own grave in the churchyard. You cannot fail to notice this piece of what can be seen as either pretension or enterprise, and in some ways this sums up the character of the history of the island. Some projects started here have failed miserably, notably the clay mining, which never produced the quality of goods originally expected. But Brownsea has other claims to fame of a much more lasting nature.

In 1907 twenty boys made the trip to the island, little knowing what an effect they were to have in shaping the lives of the youth of the 20th century in Britain. They were accompanied by Robert Baden Powell, and this was his first experiment in camping with what were to become known as boy scouts. So if there are waves as you cross to Brownsea, be sure to ride the crest of them. There is a commemorative stone celebrating the origins of the scouting movement overlooking FURZEY ISLAND on the southern ridge of Brownsea. It is fascinating to stand and wonder what these young men really thought of the ten days they spent here: tucked away from the rest of humanity in an out of laboratory experiment.

It is this southern half of the island which can be explored more freely today, as the northern, more wooded, section forms the DORSET TRUST FOR NATURE CONSERVATION RESERVE. The walks here take you through 200 acres which are home to about one hundred rare native red squirrels (hard to spot, but there's always a chance), the second largest heronry in Britain as well as deer and peacocks. Guided and self-guide tours are available at set times, contact the warden of the island for details (01202 709445).

Ferries depart to the island every thirty minutes during spring and summer from Poole Quay; there is a charge to land on the island, and no dogs are allowed except guide dogs (details of times etc 01202 631828). There are also ferries from Swanage and Bournemouth.

Returning to Poole by boat, the next area for exploration surrounds you to the west and south; the **ISLE OF PURBECK** which forms the rest of the coastline of Poole Harbour. Studland, in particular, is very close to the Sandbanks, and can be reached by ferry, but for now we will follow the longer but more encompassing route across land.

Leaving Poole by the A351 you can get an idea of some local crafts at the COURTYARD CENTRE (01202 623423), at **LYTCHETT MINSTER**, before heading into more open country.

The gateway to the Isle of Purbeck is the ancient town of **WAREHAM** (Tourist Information 019295 552740), wedged between the rivers Frome and Piddle (or Trent).

Before you get to the town itself the road takes you through the edge of WAREHAM FOREST where a mixture of coniferous plantations and sandy heathlands provide a haven for everything from rare birds to sand lizards and smooth snakes. The dark forest looms with a brooding presence after you have left the sands of Poole and Bournemouth behind, but Purbeck certainly does not live up to any forebodings born here.

Wareham was a thriving port in the Middle Ages, but the silting of the Wareham Channel left Poole as a much better option for trade. Some very old buildings remain, but a fire in 1762 destroyed much of what had originally been here. The conflagration took just four hours to destroy most of the town centre, and only a sudden change in wind direction prevented there being even more homeless refugees in the following months. Just thirty years earlier Blandford had suffered a similar catastrophe, and within two days of the Wareham fire carts of bread and cheese and £73 in cash arrived from the townsfolk of Blandford to help their fairly distant neighbours.

Sizeable monetary relief for rebuilding was a little longer in coming, but like Blandford, the town owes its present collection of Georgian buildings to the need to reconstruct the Town Centre.

Come off the by-pass and spend some time in Wareham and you will find much to see packed into a compact area of narrow streets. There are pleasant surprises amongst the regular criss-cross of streets in the centre of the town, such as JEWELLERY BUY DESIGN LTD (019295 56240), where you can see jewellery being made, just off West Street, near to The Cross.

Wareham was protected by earthworks in the reign of King Alfred, and grass covered mounds surrounding the town on all but the southern side show that they still survive, in part reinforced during the Second World War. Now they work more effectively to keep the old town contained and free from modern development than for any military defense.

The WAREHAM MUSEUM (01929 553448) will tell you much of the town's history, and is centrally placed next to the Victorian TOWN HALL at the Market Cross. Some of the oldest buildings to survive have been churches, including ST MARTIN'S CHURCH, which contains a marble effigy of Lawrence of Arabia, who died locally. The church is in the middle of the North banks, in North Street, and is probably the best preserved Saxon minster in Dorset.

The WALLS WALK, and the TOWN WALK provide a useful way of enjoying the history of the town, by following marked routes. Details are available from Tourist Information, as are leaflets on other walks starting from Wareham, including the PURBECK WAY and the WAREHAM FOREST WAY (which takes you north to Sturminster Marshall).

A trip east, doubling back towards Poole Harbour, will take you to **ARNE** where the dry heathland, bog and saltmarsh provide a remote environment ideal for rare birds. The ARNE NATURE RESERVE (01929 553360) is primarily a bird reserve, which is mostly only accessible with a special permit. But for a view of some unusual countryside, as well as more views of Poole Harbour, try the Nature Trail footpath which starts here and ends at SHIPSTAL POINT. The village also contains the WORLD OF TOYS (01929 552018) at ARNE HOUSE. The museum specialises in antique toys and Victorian music boxes.

Heading south from Wareham further into Purbeck the landscape soon becomes more dramatic. The spine of the Isle of Purbeck is the same chalk ridge that traverses the Isle of Wight, and the spectacular coastline west as far as Weymouth is caused by the limestone which underlies this chalk to the south, in the Purbeck and Portland beds. The geology of the area is particularly apparent at **CORFE CASTLE** (01929 481294).

Man has made use of nature in more than one way here. Most of the buildings of the small town are made from the local grey limestone, as is the castle itself. The knoll on which the ruins of the castle stand has been created by the eating away of the chalk ridge by river water. The resultant mound, perched in the middle of the only gap in the ridge, was an ideal place to build a defensive fortress, which still appears both strong and somewhat sinister, even in its ruins.

Perhaps the darker feelings come from deeds long past: the South-West Gate-house is named EDWARD'S GATE, in memory of the seventeen year old King Edward. He is said to have been murdered on this spot by his step-mother's household on the evening of the 18th March 978.

The event was a national outrage, and his remains at Shaftesbury Abbey were said to be the source of many miracles. It is strange to think that much of what you see today was unchanged more than one thousand years ago when the young king hung from one stirrup of his horse, finally collapsing at the gate to die from the knife wounds in his stomach. Happily the homicide rate in the area has not been unusually high since.

Corfe Castle, Purbeck.

It is also ironic that the fantastic strategic position of the castle was never really tried by any overseas invading forces. The castle was dynamited by Cromwell in 1646 after it had been a Royalist stronghold in the Civil War, and had proved extremely hard to capture.

Corfe Castle was left to the National Trust by Ralph Bankes, in 1981. A walk up the hill will give you the chance to compare what is left of the castle to the model of the complete article (to 1/20 scale) which is in the village below.

The National Trust holds different events here during the year, from an ARCHAEOLOGY WEEKEND to a MEDIEVAL ARCHERY WEEKEND (also 01929 481294). The SEALED KNOT SOCIETY also use the location to stage re-enactments of the Civil War sieges.

About a mile and a half north-west of the castle lies a very different attraction, the BLUE POOL (01929 551408). This is the remains of a 19th century clay pit, now containing water which varies quite spectacularly in colour due to the effects of sunlight on particles of clay suspended within it. The warmer the weather the greener the water, colder weather brings out a shimmering blue. Coniferous woods around the banks make for a relaxing spot, with 25 acres in all, laced with paths leading up to views over the Purbeck Hills.

Five more miles on the A351 will take us to **SWANAGE** (Tourist Information 01929 422885). Alternatively, the newly opened Corfe Castle Station means that the journey can be made by steam, on the lovingly restored SWANAGE RAILWAY (01929 425800). Swanage grew rapidly in the 19th century, particularly due to its success as a centre for shipping stone from the local quarries. Now it is a quiet, peaceful resort with excellent facilities for sailing, fishing and other water sports.

Swanage has some interesting architectural features, many of which were brought from London by the firm of Burt and Mowlem in the 19th century. These include the clock-tower without a clock, originally a monument to Wellington at the south end of London Bridge which was labelled an obstruction by the Metropolitan Police, and had to be moved somewhere! The facade of the 1883 Town Hall is also a piece of salvage, coming from the Mercers Hall in the City of London. It is actually 17th century, and designed by Sir Christopher Wren.

Another curiosity lurks just behind the Town Hall: a tiny square building which looks like a stone store cupboard, but is in fact a lock-up. It has an inscription stating that it is "For the Prevention of Vice and Immorality by the Friends of Religion and Good Order." I wonder if it worked?

Look also for the column on the seafront, celebrating King Alfred's victory over the Danes in 877 (although it was probably the weather which actually defeated the incoming fleet). Does anything look out of place? The cannonballs which top the monument are a slight anachronism, being relics of The Crimean War almost a thousand years later. Swanage, in its innocent beauty, seems an unlikely place for such a deliberate deception! More can be learnt about local features, crafts and industries at the TITHE BARN MUSEUM (01929 423174).

The town's pier is Victorian, and is being restored by volunteers of the Swanage Pier Trust, their efforts including the free SWANAGE PIER MUSEUM (Pier 01929 427058). The Quay and the Pier are both focal points for boat hire, angling and watersports. Try the SWANAGE ANGLING CENTRE (01929 424989) for more about fishing, or MARSH'S PLEASURE BOATS (01929 424152) for trips along the spectacular Purbeck coastline. THE MOWLEM THEATRE AND CINEMA (01929 422239) provides an alternative to the many inns and public houses as a form of evening entertainment.

Views are a prominent feature of this coast, and the hilltop walks around the edges of the town give a chance to see how comfortably the compact resort of Swanage snuggles into a gap in the hills, fronted by a mile of golden beach.

At the eastern end of SWANAGE BAY lies **STUDLAND,** with another popular section of sandy beach, some three miles in length. Following STUDLAND BAY to the north we are at the sea edge of Poole Harbour, only a short distance from the Sandbanks, at the car and foot ferry terminus at Shell Bay.

This point marks the beginning of the SOUTH WEST COAST PATH, running from here right around the South West of England, finally coming to an end at Minehead, on the Bristol Channel. If you have had enough of the beaches by now then how about turning inland to experience some very different terrain, as well as to admire the handiwork of Lucifer!

To the west stretch the wilds of the HARTLAND MOOR NATIONAL NATURE RESERVE (01929 556688), an acid, spongy bog with tracts of heather on the firmer ground, as well as the National Trust property of STUDLAND HEATH, also a National Nature Reserve (01929 556688) which has representatives of all six species of reptiles native to Britain among its residents. The National Trust holds organised walks on the heath, especially in winter to see the departure of migrating birds (01929 450259).

The AGGLESTONE is the biggest of the huge natural boulders which occur on Studland Heath, weighing in the region of 500 tons of solid ironstone. It was long thought of as supernatural, how else could anything so large appear in such a deserted area? Hence the name, as "hagolstan" is the Old English for hailstone, although another local legend says that it was a short-falling shot taken at Corfe Castle by the devil, who was sitting on the Needles Rock, Isle of Wight. Unfortunately there is now a less romantic, geological explanation for its presence. If you hear a cry of 'fore' it is more likely to be a player at the nearby ISLE OF PURBECK GOLF COURSE (01929 44361) than His Satanic Majesty trying to perfect his aim.

The devil seems to have been in evidence quite frequently near Studland, as the name of OLD HARRY ROCKS would suggest. These eroded chalk cliffs at the sea's edge form the easternmost point of Purbeck, lying at the southern end of STUDLAND BAY, to the north of BALLARD DOWN and then Swanage. The main clifftop beside them is also known as OLD NICK'S GROUND, but it is unclear why, unless it is because they are so prone to crumbling that one false step and you could be on your way down a very long way!

Some of these truly spectacular, vertical chalk cliffs are 100-180 feet high, with the sea constantly, if gradually, forming new arches and caves at their bases. An aerial photograph of this section of coast looks like a giant lump of white cheese, with a healthy green mould on top, from which great mouthfuls have been taken, leaving semicircular sets of toothmarks. From ground level the rocks look more like a set of badly kept teeth, with no fillings!

Whatever you like to compare this scenery to, it is certainly worth the walk from Studland to see it, with a good chance of seeing cormorants, black-backed gulls and other sea birds as you do. On a clear day it is quite possible to see The Needles, off the Isle of Wight, the next place where the sea has yet to overcome the chalk. What a contrast this broken line forms to the straight, low beaches of Bournemouth also visible from these clifftops. The setting is a contrast too; the clifftops here are farmed almost to the edges, but there is little other evidence of human interference, unless in the array of boats passing beneath you.

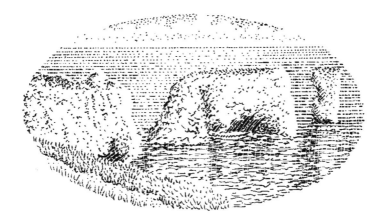

Old Harry Rocks, Studland.

The land of Ballard Down is separated from the main chalk ridge by the geological fault of ULWELL GAP, and as you return towards Swanage you are passing through one of the best sites in Britain for downland butterflies; especially the 'blues', whose caterpillars thrive on the Vetch plants here.

The coast path west from Swanage runs along the edge of the cliffs, from PEVERIL POINT onto DURLSTON and then ST ALDHELM'S HEAD. This section of coast is one you will remember, and is worth a look at in some detail.

One mile's walk from the nearest road, the 260 acres of the DURLSTON COUNTRY PARK NATURE RESERVE (01929 424963) start our journey along the rugged coastline. Yet even here George Burt, of Burt and Mowlem, had his influence. There is a globe on the hillside, weighing some 40 tons; a model of the world made in Portland stone. It is difficult to know what to say about such a surprising find in this location: it is nothing if not unusual, and perhaps typical of the adventurous imagination of the late Victorian era, and in particular that of Mr Burt.

The clifftop walk keeps at least a mile and a half away from the nearest roads for most of this stretch, and the resulting quiet is filled by the noise of the sea, as well as the cries of a multitude of sea-birds. This is the place to be if you are a bird-watcher: cormorants, shags, kittiwakes, fulmars, guillemots and razorbills, each species has its own place on the many ledges.

There have been many other voices here over the centuries. Purbeck marble has been quarried extensively, and used in many famous buildings, including the cathedrals at Salisbury and Exeter. The other main industry along this coast was smuggling. The two worked together at times, as the stone workers helped to unload the boats full of wines and tobacco for which no duty would ever be paid. The underground workings made by the quarrymen proved convenient for the storage of offloaded booty, and have left many names provocative to the imagination: Tilly's Whim, Blackers Hole, and Ragged Rocks among them.

Cries of anguish will have been heard here too, as the East Indiaman "*Halsewell*" crashed against the rocks in 1786, sinking with the loss of more than one hundred and fifty lives. Who can be sure what sounds were heard when dinosaurs roamed here some 100 million or more years ago, leaving footprints in what have now become exposed layers of rock? There always seems to be plenty of time to think about the past in a place where the present is so relaxing and yet so full of visual and aural stimuli.

The villages of **LANGTON MATRAVERS** and **WORTH MATRAVERS** nestle in the hills behind the coast, and the latter is worth a visit for its medieval church of ST. NICHOLAS, and to gaze in wonder at the remains of the quarries on the hills all around you. Behind the church in the centre of Langton Matravers stands THE COACH HOUSE MUSEUM (01929 423168/439372), which explores the heritage of Purbeck stone, and includes reconstructions of quarry working.

KINGSTON too has a similar collection of 18th and 19th century houses made of local stone, and a surprisingly large and spectacular parish church for a fairly small village. The church of ST JAMES was built in the 1870s, and local stone is used to good effect in the black marble pillars inside.

Back on the coast path you will now have passed the DANCING LEDGE, where puffins make their home. During the summer you may even have seen bottle-nosed dolphins surfacing near to the shore.

The next headland has a strange square building on it, with only the plain cross on its summit suggesting its real nature. This is ST CATHERINE'S CHAPEL, at ST ALDHELM'S HEAD. Even the cross is a relatively recent addition; the circular stone in which it is set was originally meant for a beacon, and gives the lie to the use for which the building was constructed.

Various sources say the chapel burnt a light here for centuries before the construction of conventional lighthouses, and that a monk was always inside to keep the fire burning (no pleasant task with only one slit window and walls which are six feet thick); while others say it was built first as a lighthouse in medieval times, by a father who had seen his daughter and her bridegroom drown off the point, as they set off on their honeymoon.

Whatever the truth, this building is typical of the sense of mystery that can pervade the Purbeck coast. Further west there is more geological variety. CHAPMAN'S POOL is at the bottom of a steep sided gash in the cliffs, created by the flood waters of the last ice age, and provides protection for thousands of migrant birds, while the profusion of purple Buddleia attracts exotic butterflies. KIMMERIDGE BAY provides a direct contrast with its low black shale cliffs around a sandless bay covered with rocks containing fossil ammonites.

KIMMERIDGE itself is a quiet village full of stone cottages with thatched roofs. The bay and the village are the places to find information about the PURBECK MARINE RESERVE (01305 264620). This underwater reserve boasts such questionable delights as sea slugs and hairy crabs, but for the marine enthusiast there is much to experience, including nature trails for divers.

If you prefer to stay inland, then SMEDMORE HOUSE lies east of the village, and most of the lands around the village belong to the estate. The impressive house combines Queen Anne, Jacobean and Georgian architectural styles, and the smooth Portland stone edifice is set to great advantage amongst perfect lawns and trees. Again the village of Kimmeridge is the best place to find out about current opening times and events, but the house is certainly worth the short walk for its exterior alone.

At the eastern end of WORBARROW BAY lies **TYNEHAM**, a village which was taken over by the allied forces preparing for the invasion of France, just before Christmas 1943. The residents would have been in danger from shelling, so they were moved, being promised a prompt return. The ruins tell the rest of the story, and one remote location has now been given back to nature.

Worbarrow Bay is another site to please the eye, its long, curving shingle beach framed by massive chalk cliffs in the background, with shorter clay cliffs in the fore. Much of this area of the coast is still used by the military, as firing ranges for the Royal Armour Corps, and as you explore west it becomes increasingly difficult to get to the shore by road without returning inland to the A352, and impossible to gain access to certain areas at all.

LULWORTH COVE is our last stopping place before we head north, as the stream which enters the sea here forms the western boundary of the Isle of Purbeck.

Among all the features of the Purbeck coastline described so far, this must be the most celebrated. This also makes it the most visited, and a very busy place in the summer months. As you descend the road into the village of **WEST LULWORTH** and the cove itself, two chalk ridges hem you in, BINDON HILL on your left (east) and HAMBURY TOUT on your right. These two ridges carry on further than the road, forming the protective arms which stretch out into the sea to protect the sheltered cove on each side.

A small gap in the Purbeck beds of limestone must have let the sea in to begin its work on the softer underlying clay beds. The result is a peaceful circle of cool water, protected from the currents, and providing a popular stopping place for sailing craft as well as tourists. Sitting on the small beach made up of pebble and rock, it is hard to escape the feeling of protection. It seems very natural that so many people should be almost magnetically drawn to this hiding place, with sheer cliffs shielding the quiet crowd from the harshness of both sea and mainland.

A climb up the eastern slope will bring you to the FOSSIL FOREST, where the odd circular fossils formed in the ledge are the remains of the holes made by the trunks of trees from as long as 120 million years ago. Any further east and you come to the edge of the military ranges, walks further along the cliffs here are possible, but the paths are open only at times (weekends, holidays) when guns are not going to be in action.

A climb to the top at one side or the other of Lulworth Cove will give you a better picture of how much protection nature affords here, as you see the ocean in its constant agitation contrasting to the calm of the bay. To learn more about the immediate area try the LULWORTH COVE HERITAGE CENTRE (01929 400587) .

EAST LULWORTH provides access to LULWORTH CASTLE (01929 400510, 400352), the interior of which was gutted by fire in 1929, but is now being restored by English Heritage. You can climb the southeast tower to take in views of the park and its surrounds.

Built in the first decade of the 17th century, after the days of functional, military castles had already past, the castle's corner turret design gave it the appearance of the prototype for all those wooden toy forts so popular among children. A peculiarity of the architecture is that there were no decorative finishing touches to the stone work at all.

From the mid 17th century the castle was owned by the Weld family, and the CHURCH OF ST MARY, which stands nearby, was built to their instructions late in the 18th century. It is not an easy building to spot. It was the first catholic church to have been built after the reformation, and was only permitted by George III (who was a visitor to the castle) on the condition that it be disguised as a house.

The more recognisable church in East Lulworth itself, that of ST ANDREW, houses a permanent exhibition of the life and work of Thomas Hardy, due to his association with the restoration of the building in the 1860s, during his first career, which was that of an architect. More of him later!

To the west from Lulworth Cove are STAIR HOLE, and DURDLE DOOR. Erosion to the cliffs has caused more spectacular rock formations at both of these, and a walk along these couple of miles of coast will provide you with plenty of chances to use up a film or two.

Heading north, the coast of Dorset, from Christchurch to Lulworth, and especially the Isle of Purbeck, will have left you with many memories of sights unusual, powerful, and undeniably beautiful.

I have my own memories of this area, and yet the strongest come from a place which could be equally well situated in any county, in any geographical surroundings. It is not the setting of the BOVINGTON TANK MUSEUM (01929 405096) which has stayed in my mind, but rather the terrifying poignancy of some of its contents. Due north of Lulworth, and past the crossing of the A352, the museum has changed immensely since my first visit to it many years ago. There are now many more structured displays and educational features, yet no amount of background setting and material can hide the fearsome power of the tank, a motorised monument to the wars of the 20th century.

My grandfather fought in the First World War, and I will never forget the eagerness with which I ran towards the flat, box-shaped tank from that period which stood in the open air at Bovington at that time. I wanted to know what it might have been like, even though I knew he had been in trenches, not machines. To clamber over the exterior tracks was a delight for any young boy, but it was the inside of that tank that really stays in my memory. Cramped, uncomfortable and harsh, even to a child, what could it have been like for a man? How vulnerable would he have felt?

The museum is a fascinating place, and will provoke emotions in anyone who has had to learn about war.

Also between **WOOL** and **BERE REGIS** lies CLOUDS HILL (01929 405616) the cottage owned by T.E.Lawrence; Lawrence of Arabia. He came here in 1925, after joining the tank corps at nearby Bovington. Set on the edge of the East Dorset heathlands on a little hill which is covered with rhododendron bushes, the cottage is extremely small, and is another attraction which is subject to overcrowding in the summer months. The interior has been kept much as it was when Lawrence left it for the last time on 13 May 1935. The hero of Arabia was killed as his motorcycle crashed on the return journey from the local post office, when he was just 400 yards or so from home.

The cottage contains very few practical items for everyday living, and the profusion of gramophone records, and books amongst functional furniture says much about the quiet life he was able to have here. The interior of the building, with its exposed beams, brick fireplace and feeling of relaxed ease (typified by the Greek inscription over the door which Lawrence translated as 'why worry?') suits well with the remote setting.

We are now penetrating deep into Hardy country, and at **BERE REGIS**, the parish church contains the tombs of the Turbevilles, used as inspiration for the title family of Hardy's 'TESS OF THE D'URBEVILLES'. The CHURCH OF ST JOHN THE BAPTIST is renowned for its memorable wooden roof, dating from the late 15th century. It has been restored several times over the intervening years and makes a complete contrast to the arched nave of the Priory at Christchurch.

Apart from the Civil War in the 17th century, Dorset has seen little of conflict, and this has meant that many old buildings have had the chance to be maintained through the centuries, and often adapted too. The Bere Regis church typifies this, with features dating from the 11th, 12th, and most other centuries since. Turning east towards the A31, you come across another place which has served more than one role in the life and history of the county. WOODBURY HILL is the site of an Iron Age hill-fort, but also of fairs, both real and fictional. Large fairs were held at this site for hundreds of years until their eventual demise in the 1950s, while Thomas Hardy used the setting for a similar event in 'Far From The Madding Crowd'.

A few miles east along the A31 brings you just north of the suburban edges of Poole and Bournemouth, but **WIMBORNE MINSTER** (Tourist Information 01202 886116) is far enough way, and has a long enough history of its own, to have escaped being swallowed in their growth thus far.

Wimborne Minster from the River Stour

Like many of the small towns of mid and north Dorset, everything here seems to lead to the market square, in this case dominated by the two towers of the Minster, again the product of various centuries. Known as THE CORN MARKET, this square is equally typical of others in the county in giving a distinctive centre to a town with narrow, often bustling streets.

The MARKET HOUSE in the square is home to the EAST DORSET HERITAGE TRUST (01202 888992) from where the legendary smuggler Isaac Gulliver (see Poole) will lead you on a 'stereo walkman' tour of the town. It must be hoped that all appropriate duties for any imported 'walkmans' have been paid!

Wimborne is a market town, and the weekly open and covered markets (01202 841212) are still worth a visit, although no longer dominated by local crafts people. WALFORD MILL (01202 841400), just outside the north of Wimborne, on the B3087, is a permanent craft centre, if you wish to see more of the work by Dorset designers and makers. There are resident designers in the weaving and jewellery workshops, and a programme of various exhibitions through the year.

The character of these mid Dorset towns is quiet and unassuming, but with a community which has not yet been as fragmented by urbanisation as those elsewhere in the country. Time seems to change things more slowly here, just as it has added to the Minster, rather than replacing or discarding it.

The Minster is dedicated to St Cuthburga, the sister of King Ine of the West Saxons, who ruled at the end of the 7th century A.D. There was a monastery and a nunnery on the site at that time, but the earliest parts of the building now standing date from Norman times, after the original edifice was raised to the ground by the Danes, leaving only an oak chest and Saxon stone cross, both of which are still in the current church.

It seems ironic that those who spent so much effort in suppressing and replacing the Saxon culture have unwittingly helped to provide such a splendid monument to a Saxon dignitary. It is believed by some historians that King Alfred was crowned King of England here in the 8th century, and the place still looks worthy of such an occasion. As you approach the Minster its square towers and Norman arches impress with both grace and power, it is a building which immediately commands respect.

The interior is a great place to do your own exploring. There are features from most eras; particularly unusual is the chained library from the 17th century, where each book is literally chained to the shelves.

You can easily spend an informative afternoon discovering your own favourites amongst the seemingly endless diversity here, ranging from a 14th century astronomical clock to a lawyer's tomb embedded in the wall of the south chapel. The minster is so large, and the cross shape has created so many corners and nooks in which interesting artefacts, windows and tombs are hidden, that with the arched roof towering way above you, it really is a place to remember. The minster has an active congregation, and is still very much in use.

Just the other side of the High St from the Minster is the PRIEST'S HOUSE MUSEUM (01202 882533) which boasts ten rooms of local history in addition to an archaeological gallery and a working Victorian kitchen. For a break from history, there are the DEANSCOURT GARDENS (Tourist Information: 01202 886116), still near to the centre of the town. These comprise some thirteen acres including specimen trees, semi-wild areas, and herb gardens. Organically grown herbs are a speciality here. The MODEL TOWN & GARDENS (01202 881924) is in King St, and has over 300 detailed model buildings recreating the Wimborne of the 1950s, as well as miniature shrubs and trees.

MERLEY is a modern suburb of Wimborne, but to the west of it lies MERLEY HOUSE AND MODEL MUSEUM (01202 886533), a restored 18th century mansion housing a collection of model cars, ships and aeroplanes. The house itself has a typically Georgian exterior, while inside there are some excellent Georgian plaster ceilings and an outstanding Lignum Vitae wooden staircase.

North West from Wimborne off the B3082 is the National Trust property of KINGSTON LACY (01202 883402). The 254 acres were left to the Trust by Ralph Bankes, along with Corfe Castle and the rest of his estate, in 1981. This is where the Royalist Bankes family came after the destruction of Corfe in 1646. A first sight of the classical and beautifully placed three storey Restoration house will tell you that it is as different to Corfe Castle as a home could be. This was the choice of the earlier Sir Ralph Bankes, who had the house built between 1663 and 1665 to designs by Sir Roger Pratt, the first architect to receive a knighthood.

Although there were considerable alterations (particularly to the exterior) in the 1830s, the symmetrical house provides a spectacular prospect, especially from the expanse of flat parkland in front of it which could not be in greater contrast to the environs of Corfe. There are 13 acres of lawns here, as well as splendid avenues of limes and cedars. Different seasons provide different themes for walks at Kingston Lacy, and even in February the grounds look splendid, covered in a carpet of snowdrops. There are themes for visits to the grounds organised by The National Trust during the rest of the year too, from a SPRING PLANT FAIR in May to an EVENING GARDEN WALK in August.

Kingston Lacy House

Inside the house is a valuable art collection, including paintings by Van Dyck, Velasquez, Lely, and Rubens. The National Trust rate this as the finest house they have in Dorset, and it is easy to see why as you wander from exquisitely furnished dining rooms and saloons to halls containing marble busts, paintings and examples from the collection of rare Egyptology assembled by the notorious William John Bankes, a friend of Lord Byron, in the first half of the 19th century.

There are items brought from Corfe too, including life-size bronze statues of Sir John and Lady Mary Bankes, the heroine of the Cromwellian sieges upon the castle. Less spectacular, but equally fascinating, is the case containing all the keys to Corfe Castle. Why were they brought here? Perhaps out of sentimentality, or out of hope the family might one day return south towards the coast? Without trivialising the past, I cannot help but think of key-rings holding means of entry to garages not seen in years, and even keys for which the purpose has long been completely forgotten!

The restoration of Kingston Lacy between 1982 and 1985 accounted for £2 million, and many neglected treasures, particularly Egyptian in origin, were found in the grounds of the house, as it seems some of his successors did not quite share William's love of things Egyptian.

Some would have been less easy to lose track of (deliberately or accidentally), such as the PHILAE NEEDLE, a twenty foot high obelisk on a five foot plinth, which was constructed in Egypt in the second century B.C. You would not think another foreign guest would have been neglected either, even though he has long been inside an even older relic: a sarcophagus from the 14th century B.C.

It may seem a strange place to enjoy such things, and extremely different from the British Museum, where you would expect to do so, but Kingston Lacy is made all the more appealing by this collection of artefacts. The National Trust 'Treasure Hunt' through the gardens must really have been quite good fun.

Various members of the Bankes family have had different influences on their home over the centuries. One Henrietta Bankes was distraught to find upon her marriage (1897), that there were no baths in the house. Apparently she had eight bathing places added to the building, by making discreet use of existing space. In one case this was so cunningly done that the bath in the window seat of the west bedroom was not discovered until 1983!

Close to here, in the 1970s, I happened upon the most attractive and truly breathtaking piece of roadway that I have ever seen, running between Wimborne and Blandford. Trees have been planted on each side of the road, their branches touching in the middle to form a leafy roof, or canopy, to a gorgeous tunnel built by nature. The road dips and rises in a straight line, so that an oncoming vehicle will appear, vanish, and then reappear several times before your paths actually cross. A great place to gauge your ability to judge distance and oncoming speed!

I had the advantage of seeing this for the first time in the very early morning, when the mist was rising off the deserted roller-coaster of a road, with its unforgettable lining of pollarded beech trees on each side. It was as if they were a verdant guard of honour celebrating the coming of a new day. Some of the original trees, planted in 1835, have been torn by the winds of several storms in recent years, while others have reached the end of their natural lives, and replacements have been planted, but the effect can still be experienced, especially at sunrise or sunset on a clear day. Various sources will suggest that 365 trees were originally planted (one for each day of the year), or that there are 365 on each side, or indeed 1,000 plus in all. I must admit that I have not counted them myself!

Just off this road (known as BADBURY AVENUE), a short distance past Kingston Lacy, lies another part of the same estate left to the National Trust: the ancient site of BADBURY RINGS.

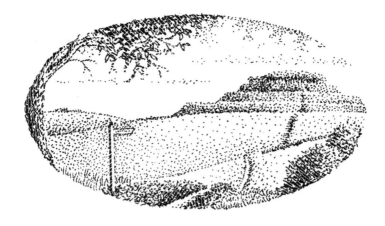

Badbury Rings

The open country around the mound of concentric rings seems suitably empty, giving space in which to consider the significance of the surroundings. The hedge sized banks in the very middle of the mound are the remains of the middle of a Neolithic camp, and date back at least five thousand years.

The main ramparts and ditches are from the Iron Age, built roughly in the middle of the intervening millenia. Unlike many castles and other more ostensibly durable military structures, this one has seen battle. The last occasion was in AD 44-45, when the Romans defeated the Durotrigic people here, going on to conquer the rest of Western England. We will pick up their trail several times, most noticeably at Maiden Castle near Dorchester.

The earthen walls would have been palisaded, made to measure for slingshot warfare, especially as the middle of the fortifications has a mass of ammunition just waiting to be picked from the floor in the form of pebbles. The Romans didn't have an easy time of it here, and as you stand looking across at the raised ground you can visualise the gradual progress of the organised army using spears and swords, while bolts from ballista provided an early form of artillery cover.

The walk up to the ramparts is a memorable one, and as you circle them listen closely for the sounds of a large force of infantry, who are said to haunt the woods to the north east.

Since the National Trust has had ownership of the site, much has been done, both to preserve and tidy it, and there are many local enthusiasts who take pride in this work. There are special events here through the year, including the interesting idea of THE LIGHT FANTASTIC, a moon-lit hunt for glowworms (01202 882493), as well as celebrations of both the summer and winter solstice. Look out also for chances to explore nearby PAMPHILL MOOR, where it is estimated that 3,000 marsh orchids exist in a single large field.

East of Badbury is another place where nature is still in control, a feature of the area known as **HOLT HEATH**. The heath has been declared a National Nature Reserve by English Nature, to provide a refuge for the Dartford Warbler, and to maintain the thin corridor of wild lands still tenuously linking the Dorset heaths with those of the New Forest. It is by far the biggest block of common land in Dorset. Lying on a ridge at the North East side of Holt Heath is BULL BARROW, a Bronze Age burial site.

As you look up at its relatively slight profile against the skyline you may wonder what can make Bull Barrow interesting, but walk up the grassy slope to the barrow itself, and you may be surprised. It is a heather covered, sandy mound, about fifty feet in diameter, nearly five feet high, and dates from about 1800 BC.

The mystery of such a place is tangible and apparent to the most hardened of us, used to the constant presence of man made alterations to the countryside. There is something natural in the curves of the barrow, in its blending with the green slopes around it which leaves you thinking that nature surely had greater power in earlier ages. This type of burial mound has held a sense of menace for many centuries, and you will see very many of them dotted around the hillsides of Dorset.

The Gawain poet, some six to seven hundred years ago, used such a place as the home of the Green Knight, the magical embodiment of the sinister side of the power of nature. Gawain himself travels to the mound and muses what it might hold:

> *"Thenne he bogez to the berge, about hit he walkez,*
> *Debatande with hymself quat hit be mygt.*
> *Hit hade a hole on the ende and on ayther side,*
> *And ouergrowen with gresse in glodes aywhere."*

(Then he approached the mound, and walked around it, debating with himself what it could be. It had a hole at one end, and on either side. It was overgrown, covered everywhere in patches of grass: my translation.) This is the place where Gawain's destiny is decided, where the green knight undergoes a mystical transformation, and where we feel anything could happen. Standing near Bull Barrow, even now, you can appreciate the power such a setting would have on a medieval audience.

Early Christians found the monuments of pagan ages disturbing too, as the church at **KNOWLTON** bears witness. North of Holt, near the B3078, lies the strange sight of a ruined church surrounded by an earthen bank with a ditch. The earthwork is actually a neolithic henge monument, for which the purpose is still not known.

What is known is that the parish church was clearly placed here to assert the new power of Christianity over the more ancient, pagan religions. It is thought provoking to see the relics of both eras standing unused, gradually crumbling to blend in with the contours of the land on which man built them.

After such a dose of land often bare of human habitation, where the power of days past seems stronger than any present day additions, it is refreshing to know that some of the finest gardens in England lie only a couple more miles north east, at CRANBORNE MANOR (01725 517248).

The manor itself is not open to the public, but glimpses of the house, including the original 12th century sections built for the visits of King John, add to the atmosphere while you walk around the impressive planted gardens. Trees separate many of the enclosed sections, as do courtyards, and the river in other instances. Many have natural themes; there is a herb garden, knot garden and a huge range of climbing, rambling and shrub roses. To the north and west lies the Cranborne Chase, where the King came to hunt, and we will explore its many delightful villages and views later.

Between Cranborne and **VERWOOD** is the DORSET HEAVY HORSE CENTRE (01202 824040), where you can see working horses, as well as breeds from giant to miniature. The equine theme is a reminder that you are now close to the Hampshire border, and near Verwood the countryside changes to the browner heathlands which run into the western edge of the New Forest.

Like Verwood, **FERNDOWN** has much modern development. West of Ferndown, near the village of **HAMPRESTON**, are KNOLL GARDENS AND NURSERY (01202 873931). These are informal and compact, but with variety giving colour to each of the seasons.

Also on the outskirts of Ferndown is STAPEHILL ABBEY CRAFTS AND GARDENS (01202 861686) on the site of a 19th century nunnery. There is a mixture here, from a museum depicting rural life in Victorian England to gardens, lakes, waterfalls and a deer park.

All that remains for you to explore in East Dorset is the land between the A31 in the south and the A354 in the north. There are no towns here, but a maze of narrow winding roads amongst a number of small villages. As you descend a steep hill banked by dark green foliage and woodlands it is quite easy to forget just which of the Tarrant or Gussage villages you are about to descend into, however frequently you look at the map. In truth it doesn't matter, as the beauty here is in the setting of a few scattered houses collected in the gaps between the trees and streams, in the inescapable feeling that this is how we should live, rather than in the crowded modern estates growing so quickly just a handful of miles away.

ALUM GRANGE HOTEL
1 Burnaby Road
Alum Chine
Bournemouth
Dorset
BH4 8JF

Tel: 01202 761195

Built as a 'Gentleman's Residence' in the late 1800's, the property was converted to an hotel during the 1950's and called Channel View Hotel. The building still retains much of its original charm with good sized, light, airy rooms, tastefully decorated and furnished. You will immediately feel at home in the easy, friendly atmosphere that surrounds you.

These days, the hotel has a distinct nautical theme. Throughout the building you will find items of nautical memorabilia with the main display being in the Dining Room and 'Captain's Bar'. Intermingled with Andy's collection you will also find items of Barbara's china, most prominent in the Dry Lounge.

In the hospitality trade since 1982, Barbara and Andy have set themselves the highest possible standards of cleanliness and service with the added personal touch to every detail and have built an enviable reputation few can match. All meals are prepared personally by Barbara and Andy using fresh ingredients selected by Barbara daily.

Located just 200 metres from the beach at Alum Chine, the hotel is ideally situated for all the local attractions and as a base for the many and varied activities available within the region.

The hotel has twelve ensuite bedrooms (three of which are on the ground floor) all with television, clock radio/alarms, hairdryer and hostess tray. Some bedrooms are designated as 'non-smoking'. The 'Celebration Room' has a traditionally draped hand crafted four poster bed, balcony with panoramic view of Poole Bay and a luxury corner bath. In short, the Alum Grange Hotel is an hotel of distinction, character and style and combined with Barbara and Andy's special flair and imagination you are assured of a memorable holiday.

USEFUL INFORMATION

· OPEN: All year	· DINING ROOM: Excellent fare
· WHEELCHAIR ACCESS: Ground floor	· VEGETARIAN: Catered for
· GARDEN: Small, very pretty	· BAR FOOD: Snacks can be ordered
· CREDIT CARDS: All major cards	· LICENSED: Yes
· ACCOMMODATION: 12 ensuite rooms	· CHILDREN: Welcome
· RATES: B&B from £19-24pp.pn DB&B £28-£33	· PETS: Yes

THE ANGLEBURY HOUSE
Restaurant with Rooms
15 North Street
Wareham
Dorset
BH20 4AB

Tel: 01929 552988

In 1996 Tim and Jenny Payne achieved a lifetime's ambition when they purchased the 400 year old, Grade II Listed building, Anglebury House. A place that is reputed to have been a favourite of Lawrence of Arabia, and a plaque marks his favourite seat in the Coffee House which is all part of this successful venture. It is one of the few buildings that survived the devastating fire of 1762 which destroyed two thirds of the town. The Payne's have made a charming 36 seat coffee house, an elegant restaurant which seats twenty for private lunches and dinners in which you may choose from either an a la carte menu or table d'hôte. Seven beautifully appointed bedrooms complete the business and of these rooms five are ensuite and two have private bathrooms. It is one of the happiest environments one could wish to be in and for those who stay there it is ideally situated for exploring this part of Dorset. Within easy reach there are a number of historic and fascinating towns such as Sherborne and Dorchester. Poole and Bournemouth are close by and there are miles of golden beaches, beautiful countryside for walking and cycling. Golf players will revel in the fine courses and amongst the many other activities one can sail or go horse riding. Something to suit everyone of whatever age.

Both Tim and Jenny have a keen interest in food and wine which is evident from the menus and the choice of wines. A first class breakfast is served in the Coffee Shop which opens every day from 9 - 5pm although earlier breakfasts are served to residents. Home-made dishes are high on the list of favourites in the Coffee Shop which includes a succulent steak and kidney pie. Fish dishes are also very popular. There are always dishes for vegetarians and for those who have a sweet tooth Anglebury House is renowned for its sweets and puddings. Slightly more sophisticated food is served in the restaurant but wherever you eat you will find the quality unquestionable and the price right.

USEFUL INFORMATION

· OPEN: All year	· RESTAURANT; High quality English fare
· WHEELCHAIR ACCESS: Not really	· VEGETARIAN: Always a choice
· COFFEE SHOP: Wide range	· CREDIT CARDS: Visa/Master
· LICENSED: Yes. Restaurant	· ACCOMMODATION: 7 ensuite rooms
· CHILDREN: Welcome	· RATES: From £25 BB
· PETS: No	

ARDENE HOTEL
12 Glen Road
Boscombe
Bournemouth
Dorset
BH5 1HR

Tel: 01202 394928

Commended

John and Chris Devine who own Ardene Hotel, are the sort of people who know exactly what is needed to care for their guests. Before they came to Bournemouth they had a bar in Southern Spain for a number of years and became to used to entertaining people from all around the world. They came to the Ardene Hotel in 1996 and it says much for them that they already have guests who have stayed more than once and want to come again. Built in 1900 Ardene is an attractive building with ornate ceilings on the ground floor and a splendid stained glass entrance. John and Chris have re-decorated and refurbished throughout in the last two years and in so doing have made sure that everything possible has been done for the comfort of visitors. Every bedroom has Sky television and a video channel as well as tea and coffee making facilities. There is a comfortable lounge where one can relax quietly or watch television and the friendly bar - a great meeting place in the evening for guests who are happy to discuss with newly made friends, the activites of the day, the bar also has Sky TV and a video channel.

This is very much a family run hotel with daughter Louise helping out generally and waiting on table. She also runs the bar occasionally as does John's mother Pat. The Bar incidentally has a games area with darts, push penny, cards, dominoes and other traditional bar games. Chris's brother does most of the maintenance and is always there to help with luggage. They are a cheerful family and the happy atmosphere they create is apparent everywhere.

Food is always important and especially on holiday when one has time to relax and enjoy it. You come down to breakfast in the morning, refreshed after a good night's sleep in a comfortable bed, to find a menu which offers either a full traditional English Breakfast with several choices or a simpler Continental meal if preferred. Chris describes herself as an 'old fashioned' cook and she produces delicious home-cooked evening meals which are always eagerly awaited. She makes sure that children have their own menu.

USEFUL INFORMATION

· OPEN: All year	· DINING ROOM:Good traditional English fare
· WHEELCHAIR ACCESS: No	· VEGETARIAN: Upon request
· CREDIT CARDS: None taken	· BAR FOOD: Sandwiches, Toasties etc
· ACCOMMODATION:Some rooms ensuite	· LICENSED: Residential
· RATES: From £15.50pp B&B £23 Half Board	· CHILDREN: Welcome
· PETS: No	

BEECHLEAS
Poole Road
Wimborne Minster
Dorset
BH21 1QA

Tel:01202 841684
Fax: 01202 849344

AA 2 Red Stars
AA 2 Red Rosettes
RAC Blue Ribbon

Wimborne Minster is a delightful, quiet town in one of the most beautiful parts of Dorset from which you can set out on Thomas Hardy personal guided tours, walk the Purbeck Hills or the New Forest. The spectacular coastline has coves such as Lulworth Cove. National Trust properties abound and include Corfe Castle, Kingston Lacey and Badbury Rings. You can sail out to Old Harry Rocks, Christchurch Bay, the Needles or around Poole Harbour, all arranged for you by local seamen. There is golf at Broadstone, Parkstone, Queens Park, Meyrick Park and Ferndown. Ride in the New Forest or indulge in a shopping spree in Bournemouth and Poole. With so much to do you will not find anywhere better to stay to enjoy all this than Beechleas, a family run hotel which also has an excellent restaurant, well known in the area and frequented by many regular diners.

Beechleas is a beautifully renovated Georgian town house with all ensuite accommodation. You have the choice of Georgian bedrooms within the house, all elegantly furnished, or the cosy beamed rooms in the Coach House with all the atmosphere of yesteryear, together with the added comforts of today. All the rooms have colour television, and hairdryers. A delicious breakfast is served every morning designed to set you up for the day! At night you return to dine in the lovely dining room with its open fire in autumn and winter and in the delightful conservatory in spring and summer. This is genuine English cooking at its best with some French influence, all cooked the traditional way using an Aga oven. Where possible the food is prepared from naturally reared or grown ingredients. Hockey's Farm at Fordingbridge, a well known natural rearing farm, is the supplier. There is a set two course dinner at £16.75 and three courses at £19.75. Everything from the eight starters to the exciting main course and the delectable home-made desserts tempts the most difficult palate. The well chosen wine list complements the food perfectly. Beechleas is a delightful experience and one not to be missed.

USEFUL INFORMATION

- OPEN: Mid-Jan- Christmas Eve
- WHEELCHAIR ACCESS: Yes
- GARDEN: Yes
- CREDIT CARDS: Master/Visa/Delta/AMEX
- ACCOMMODATION: Ensuite rooms
- RATES: Sgl from £69 Dbl from £79

- RESTAURANT: Genuine English with some French influence cooked in an Aga
- VEGETARIAN: Always a choice
- LICENSED: Residential & Restaurant
- CHILDREN: Welcome
- PETS: No

THE CASTLE INN
Main Road
West Lulworth
Dorset
BH20 5RN

Tel: 01929 400311
Fax: 01291 400415

The Castle Inn is a traditional family run thatched village inn which delights every one who comes here. It has the added advantage of being situated in a nice village in the beautiful Purbecks, on the Purbeck Cycle-way and with the famous Lulworth Cove just a short walk away. The scenery is some of the most spectacular in Dorset and there are countless attractions both locally and within easy distance. Walking is always popular through wonderful countryside and along the magnificent coastline. Golf, swimming, boast trips, horse riding, sea fishing, coarse fishing and many other outdoor activities are available including the game of Boules in the Inn's garden. Sometimes there are Morris Men dancing for your pleasure outside the Inn. There are picturesque villages and old towns to explore, Castles and other places of historical interest and a wealth of Museums to help you discover more about this wonderful county.

The Inn which is highly recommended by all subjective travel guides is welcoming, warm and cheerful run by the Hallidays who are genial and very professional hosts and who, with their well trained staff, go out of their way to make sure everyone enjoys visiting The Castle whether it is for a drink, a meal or to stay. The bars are friendly and the candlelit Flambe restaurant on Fridays and Saturdays is a popular haunt. The food is always good with many choices both hot and cold. breakfast at The Castle is renowned and rightly so. You start with fruit juice, cereals, porridge, stewed prunes, apples or other fruit in season and then go on to a huge and beautifully cooked traditional English breakfast which includes egg, bacon, sausage, tomato, mushrooms, black pudding, hash browns and fried bread. You may have fried, poached, scrambled or boiled eggs. Maybe you would prefer kippers or smoked haddock, cold ham or liver and kidneys. With all this there is plenty of toast, rolls, croissants, marmalade, jams, marmite, honey, waffles and maple syrup. If there is anything else you would like you just have to ask! With fifteen bedrooms, twelve of which are ensuite and all comfortably appointed with direct dial telephones, television and videos, a Hostess Tray, sweets, biscuits and a selection of magazines, The Castle Inn is an ideal place in which to stay for a short break or a holiday. For business people it is equally good. There are business and private function facilities, fax and letter writing services and if the day has to start early, a suitable breakfast time can be arranged. Indeed nothing is too much trouble here whatever your requirements.

USEFUL INFORMATION

- OPEN: All year. 11-3pm & 6-11pm
- WHEELCHAIR ACCESS: Yes. 3 ground floor rooms
- GARDEN: Yes. Beer Garden. Boules
- CREDIT CARDS: All except Switch
- ACCOMMODATION: 15 rooms 12 ensuite
- RATES: From £25.00 single £49.00 double Reductions on extended stays
- RESTAURANT: Intimate with good food
- VEGETARIAN: Always a choice
- BAR FOOD: Wide range changing daily
- LICENSED: Yes. Good wine list
- CHILDREN: Welcome

CLEVELAND HOTEL
90 West Cliff Road
Westbourne
Bournemouth
Dorset
BH4 8BG

Tel: 01202 760993
Fax: 01202 760733

John and Margaret Jolly, the owners of the Cleveland Hotel, have made it such a home from home for guests that repeat visits have become very much expected. They work on the premise that nothing is too much trouble when they are caring for visitors, the atmosphere is relaxed and informal but underlying this is the professionalism they bring to the task. Westbourne is a pleasant village just a comfortable flat 3 minute walk away with an array of small local shops. It is one and a half miles west of Bournemouth and four miles from Poole. The walk through Alum Chine from Westbourne to the promenade is stunning and the promenade stretches for seven miles from Sandbanks to Southbourne. Bournemouth is a wonderful holiday centre with endless attractions, good theatres and concerts. In Poole you will find sea fishing available, harbour cruises in season, Poole Pottery and much else.

The exterior of Cleveland Hotel is mock Tudor with parking for six cars and free overnight parking within fifty yards. The house is comfortably furnished with that nice relaxed 'lived-in' feeling and has a lounge which is light and airy with a large bay window and high ceilings. Here you can enjoy a quiet pot of tea and biscuits whilst you plan your next outing. The bar is open from 6.30pm until 9pm where you can enjoy a quiet drink or a bar snack. The breakfast room is a cheerful place in which to enjoy the hearty breakfast cooked by John who simply loves cooking. There are ten bedrooms, some of which are ensuite but they are all well-appointed with televisions and a hostess tray. Currently the rooms are being upgraded. Cleveland Hotel also offers, by prior arrangement, a courtesy car for collection or delivery to Bournemouth International Airport, Bournemouth British Rail Station, Bournemouth Coach Station and Poole Ferry Terminal.

USEFUL INFORMATION

- OPEN: All year
- WHEELCHAIR ACCESS: No
- BAR FOOD: Available every evening
- LICENSED: Residential
- CHILDREN: Welcome
- RATES: High Season £18-£22 B&B pppn Low Season £17-£21 B&B pppn Single supplement £5 (High Season Only) Ensuite £4 per room Children 50% discount when sharing with adult

- BREAKFAST ROOM: Hearty English breakfast
- VEGETARIAN: Upon request
- CREDIT CARDS: None taken
- ACCOMMODATION: 2dbl 1tw, 1fam ensuite 2dbl 2tw 2 amily not ensuite
- PETS: No

CONNAUGHT HOTEL
West Hill Road
West Cliff
Bournemouth
Dorset
BH2 5PH

Tel:01202 298020
Fax: 01202 298028

AA*** 70% RAC*** H.C.R.
ETB 4 Crowns Highly Commended

The Connaught Hotel is described by those who have enjoyed staying there as one of the most elegant hotels in Bournemouth. It was refurbished throughout in 1990 and everything about it is stylish, modern and comfortable. There is an air of well-being the moment you enter the foyer and the ensuing welcome is all one could wish for. Jon and Annette Murray are the owners and their ethos in the running of the hotel is that the guests and their wishes are of paramount importance. Together with their friendly and well-trained staff they ensure that everything is done to ensure everyone enjoys their stay.

The fifty eight ensuite bedrooms, some with balconies are all superbly appointed with comfortable beds, direct dial telephones, satellite television, radio/alarm, hairdryers, trouser presses and hospitality trays. The traditional restaurant offers English and Continental dishes on Table d'hôte and A La Carte menus, using fresh local produce, complemented by wines from around the world. Elegant public rooms include 2 bars, ballroom, and a conservatory lounge opening onto the patio. Alongside is the entrance to our magnificent indoor leisure centre including a 17m pool.

Bournemouth offers so much to anyone on holiday or on business. The beaches and the scenery are superb. A large Sports Centre is available for the energetic. There is an artificial Ski Slope. At the Airport seven miles away one can have flying tuition. Salmon, Trout and Coarse fishing is available and there are two golf courses within two miles. Walking in the New Forest will provide the walker with hours of delight. The centre of Bournemouth has excellent shops, concert halls and theatres. It is impossible to be bored here at anytime of the year.

USEFUL INFORMATION

- OPEN: All year
- WHEELCHAIR ACCESS:
  Full disabled facilities
- CREDIT CARDS: All major cards
- ACCOMMODATION: 58 ensuite rooms
- RATES: £65pp B&B single, £130 B&B pp.pn dbl
- PETS: Yes

- RESTAURANT: English & Continental Fare
- VEGETARIAN: Always a choice
- BAR FOOD: Snacks available. Room Service
- LICENSED: Full On
- CHILDREN: Welcome

CROMWELL HOUSE HOTEL
Lulworth Cove
Wareham
Dorset
BH20 5RJ

Tel: 01929 400253
Fax: 01929 400566

3 Crowns Commended
** AA RAC

High on the hillside overlooking the sea and surrounding hills, and just 200 yards from Lulworth Cove, Cromwell House could not be a better place in which to spend a holiday or a short break. From here you have direct access to the Dorset Coastal Footpath. It is an area of outstanding natural beauty and Scientific Interest especially for geology, flowers and birds. The Hotel was built in 1881 by the then Mayor of Weymouth to promote overnight visits to Lulworth rather than day trippers by his 'ferry'. A quote from the Weymouth Gazette in the Summer of 1881 reads 'Holidays for the more discerning visitor in an hotel equipped with every modern convenience.'

The hotel, run by Catriona Miller with occasional help from her three sons Alex, William and Andrew and other permanent and part time staff, is charming, relaxed and beautifully run. Many improvements have been made since Victorian times but all in keeping with the house. All the bedrooms have recently been renovated, and are ensuite, most have spectacular sea views as have all the reception rooms. In particular three character rooms, one with a four-poster and one with a half tester are very popular with regular visitors. There is a large Family Room again with sea views and on the ground floor there is a comfortably appointed twin bedded room for the less mobile, although without wheelchair access. Every bedroom has television, telephone and a hostess tray.

The elegant dining room with its attractive peach colour co-ordinated tablecloths and linen has thirty five covers and offers a well-balanced a la carte menu as well as an ever changing Table D'hôte menu. Everything is cooked to order and without doubt the specialities are locally caught lobsters, crabs and dived scallops. There are some delectable home-made puddings and if you wish for it a perfect Cream Tea with home-made scones and lashings of cream served either in the garden or in the dining room. The wine list has been chosen from wines all around the world and provides great wine at sensible prices. The service is friendly, efficient and unobtrusive.

USEFUL INFORMATION

- OPEN: 3rd Jan-21December

- GARDEN: Yes. Heated outdoor pool
  May-October

- CREDIT CARDS: Visa/Master
  /AMEX/Euro
- ACCOMMODATION;
  14 ensuite rooms Short Breaks:
  2 days w/e or midweek

- DINING ROOM: Great food. Lobsters,
  Crabs, Dived Scallops Cream Teas

- BAR FOOD: Salads, Sandwiches
  at lunch time

- LICENSED: Residential & Restaurant
- PETS: Dogs only
- CHILDREN: Welcome
- RATES: From £28.50pp BB
  Dinner from £13

DURLEY COURT HOTEL
5 Durley Road
West Cliff
Bournemouth
Dorset
BH2 5JQ

Tel: 01202 556857
Fax : 01202 552455

Built in the late 1800's as a private house, the Durley Court Hotel is now a gracious Grade II Listed building and run on oiled wheels as a hotel by George and Jeanette Biddleston, the owners. It is set in its own attractive gardens, complete with a large car park, on the beautiful West Cliff in an enviable position. George Biddleston spent 29 years in the RAF in the Officers Mess and was awarded an MBE in January 1997 for exemplary service. It is this exemplary service that he and Jeanette bring to the running of Durley Court. The comfort and well being of their guests is always the main criteria and the whole hotel has been furnished and appointed with that in mind. When you enter the doors of the hotel you are immediately aware of the friendly, welcoming atmosphere and from that moment on you know that your choice of hotel was a wise one and could not be bettered. Bournemouth is a great centre and a wonderful place to stay with its superb 7 miles of beaches flying 2 Blue Flags, patrolled by Beach Patrols and Lifeguards. The Victorian Pleasure Gardens are judged to be the best anywhere in the world, shopping is sheer pleasure in the wide pedestrianized boulevards and Bournemouth's four major theatres provide a variety of entertainment all year round.

Durley Court has sixteen delightful bedrooms, thirteen of which, including three family rooms are ensuite. Each room is individually furnished and has both television and video as well as a generously supplied hostess tray. Food is all important at any time but especially so when you are away from home. From the start of the day, after a comfortable night's sleep, you will be served a delicious breakfast in the sunny Dining Room where each table is attractively laid on blue and white table linen with pretty china and sparkling cutlery. At dinner the menu always offer a choice with the emphasis on good, traditional English home-cooking. Diabetics and Vegetarians are catered for. The lounge is a haven of peace and the bar is a friendly meeting place.

USEFUL INFORMATION

- OPEN: All year. Bar standard evening opening
- WHEELCHAIR ACCESS: No
- GARDEN: Yes
- CREDIT CARDS: Visa/Master/Switch/JCB
- ACCOMMODATION: 7dbl, 3 family, 3twin ensuite - 1tw 2sgl not ensuite
- 3 day breaks. Christmas & New Year & Easter. Christmas Shopping

- DINING ROOM: Home-cooked English fare
- VEGETARIAN: Yes
- CHILDREN: Welcome
- LICENSED: Residential
- PETS: No
- RATES: From £27pp

EARLHAM LODGE HOTEL
91 Alumhurst Road
Bournemouth
Dorset
BH4 8HR

Tel: 01202 768223 / 01202 761943

3 Crowns Commended

With just a three minute walk to the Blue Flag beach, Earlham Lodge in Alum Chine, has an enviable position in Bournemouth. From here you can take a delightful walk right along the Promenade into the centre of Bournemouth where you will find it a shopper's paradise. Mick and Lynn Turner own and run this comfortable hotel where guests find themselves rapidly at home and tend to come back year after year.

Decorated throughout in a light, fresh manner, every room is spacious. There are fourteen bedrooms, twelve of which are ensuite with eight doubles, two twins, two family rooms and two singles. One room has a splendid four-poster bed. In every room you will find television. In the non-smoking Dining Room you will be served an excellent breakfast, freshly cooked and with a choice. In the evening the home-cooked meal is essentially traditional English. Vegetarians are catered for. The well-stocked friendly bar is more often than not the meeting place for guests at night, giving them the chance to talk to newly made friends and discuss the day that has been, and what might be on the cards for the next day. Here you can get a snack if you wish. There is a television lounge if you want to sit quietly and watch your favourite programme.

There is no doubt that Bournemouth is a great place for a holiday or a break at anytime of the year. Earlham Lodge stays open all year and its warm atmosphere in winter makes it popular for short breaks of either three, four or five nights for which there are special prices. Many people find the quieter months especially enjoyable. Business people have also discovered that Earlham Lodge offers a friendly, homely place in which one can stay away from the exigencies of the business world.

USEFUL INFORMATION

- OPEN: All year
- WHEELCHAIR ACCESS: Not suitable
- GARDEN: Yes
- CREDIT CARDS: Visa/Master
- ACCOMMODATION: 14 rooms 12 ensuite
- RATES: From £18 pppn B&B or £25 with dinner £15-£22 in low season
  Discounts of 25% or 50% for children sharing with adults

- DINING ROOM: Good home-cooking
- VEGETARIAN: Yes
- BAR FOOD: Snacks available
- LICENSED: Residential
- CHILDREN: Welcome

GERVIS COURT HOTEL
38 Gervis Road
Bournemouth
Dorset
BH1 3DH

Tel/Fax: 01202 556871

Email: enquiries@gerviscourthotel.co.uk
www.gerviscourthotel.co.uk

Centrally located for all Bournemouth's excellent amenities, the Gervis Court Hotel is the ideal place in which to stay at any time of the year. The beach, theatres, shops, pleasure gardens and the International Bournemouth Centre are all within a few minutes walk. The hotel is set on one of Bournemouth's lovely pine tree lined roads and in a Conservation Area. Gervis Court is a Victorian villa built around 1860 and was a private house until the 1930's, the home of a retired major whose brother helped found one of Bournemouth's orchestras. During World War II the house was home to American airmen who were billeted here. Today it is a gracious house, retaining many of its original features and in the capable hands of the owners, Alan and Jackie Edwards, it is superbly run with a degree of informality that hides the sheer professionalism behind the management.

Within the house, where the rooms have all been decorated recently, there is still a Victorian, homely feel and atmosphere. The rooms are all spacious with high ceilings and full of light. The attractive dining room has been converted from the old servants' quarters. One of the features is the servants' bell system which is still in operation today. Each room is linked to a display board in the kitchen. An excellent breakfast is served here every morning. There are beautifully appointed ensuite bedrooms each with television and a generously supplied hospitality tray. Gervis Court is a truly nice place to stay and where you will want to return.

USEFUL INFORMATION

- OPEN: All year
- WHEELCHAIR ACCESS: No
- GARDEN: Yes
- CREDIT CARDS: Visa/Master
- ACCOMMODATION: En suite rooms
- RATES: FROM £18 B&B PP Children £7.50

- DINING ROOM: Great trad. breakfast
- VEGETARIAN: Upon request
- PETS: No
- LICENSED: No
- CHILDREN: Welcome

GRIFFS HOTEL
21 Christchurch Road
Bournemouth
Dorset
BH1 3NS

Tel: 01202 290012
Fax: 01202 311724

Grieves Hotel does not pretend to be a vast establishment but in this instance one is definitely receiving quality not quantity. Everything about Grieves from the public rooms to the bedrooms, the conference facilities to the superb food in the Barracuda Restaurant which is open to non-residents, is of the very highest standard. This has been achieved by a new management team, whose enthusiasm for the hotel is matched by their professionalism. Between them and their well trained staff, every guest for every occasion is superbly looked after. If you come here to stay for a holiday you will immediately feel relaxed and at home. Guests dining in the restaurant which has a Seafood theme, will tell you that the food is delicious, beautifully presented, the service efficient and unobtrusive and the wine list perfectly chosen to complement the food and at the same time at sensible prices. With seafood the speciality of the house, there is nonetheless a wide range of dishes catering for every taste. A comprehensive bar meal menu will delight anyone and is especially designed for those on business who need to entertain clients. People meet in the well-stocked bar and whether you are here on business or pleasure you will find it an excellent venue. Wedding receptions are run on oiled wheels with everything organised for the bride and groom down to the last detail. Conferences are equally efficiently run with equipment supplied if requested, at reasonable rates.

The eight ensuite bedrooms are very attractive. One has four-poster and another a water bed. One room is designed for a family with a double bed and two singles. The rooms all have direct dial telephones, television and a hospitality tray.

Bournemouth is a great place for a holiday at anytime of the year with its Blue Flag, totally safe beaches, its theatres, its shops and many other attractions. Griffs Hotel is the place to stay for those who enjoy being pampered.

USEFUL INFORMATION

· OPEN: All year	· RESTAURANT: Seafood a speciality
· WHEELCHAIR ACCESS: No	· VEGETARIAN: Yes
· GARDEN: Yes	· BAR FOOD: Comprehensive menu
· CREDIT CARDS: Visa/Master/Diner/AMEX	· LICENSED: Full On
· ACCOMMODATION: 8 ensuite rooms	· CHILDREN: Welcome
· RATES: From £35 per night B&B	· PETS: No

THE HAWAIIAN HOTEL
4 Glen Road
Boscombe
Bournemouth
Dorset
BH5 1HR

Tel: 01202 393234

The Hawaiian is a small friendly hotel, built early in the 1900s, situated only 500 yards from safe sandy beaches and just three minutes walk from the pedestrianized shopping precinct. The New Forest with all its mystery and magic, is a short drive away and so too are Christchurch, the old Priory town, Corfe Castle, steeped in history and the glorious Lulworth Cove. The hotel is run by the brother and sister combination, Derek and Dilys Parsons, whose outgoing personalities soon make all their guests feel at home. They work hard to ensure the comfort and happiness of those who stay here and the fact that this is achieved is plain to see from the large number of repeat bookings.

The seven ensuite bedrooms are simply and comfortably furnished. Guests have a choice of bath or shower and one room has a King size bed. Each has television and that boon to the traveller, tea and coffee making facilities. Breakfast is a great meal. You have the choice of a full English breakfast or Continental if you prefer. Fruit juice, cereal, a plentiful supply of toast, butter and preserves and freshly brewed coffee, complete the meal. The portions are generous and it would be virtually impossible to leave the table hungry. A home-cooked three course evening meal is available upon request. The hotel is not licensed but you are very welcome to bring your own wine.

Bournemouth is a great place for a holiday with every kind of activity going on including theatres, concerts and Blue Flag beaches. It is as good in the winter as it is in the summer. In fact many people come here out of season to enjoy the empty beaches and all that the area has to offer without the hurl burly of summer traffic.

USEFUL INFORMATION

· OPEN: All year	· DINING ROOM: Good traditional fare
	Evening meal optional
· WHEELCHAIR ACCESS: No	· VEGETARIAN: Catered for
· GARDEN: No	
· CREDIT CARDS: Yes	· LICENSED: No.
· ACCOMMODATION: 7 ensuite rooms	· CHILDREN: Welcome
· RATES: From £16pppn B&B	· PETS: No

THE HOTEL WASHINGTON
3 Durley Road
Bournemouth
Dorset
BH22 5JQ

Tel: 01202 557023
Fax: 01202 315562

The Hotel Washington is situated ideally for anyone wanting to enjoy all that Bournemouth has to offer from its 7 miles of Blue Flag beaches to the renowned Bournemouth International Centre, theatres and the award winning pleasure gardens which are illuminated at night and make a pleasant place to sit a while, enjoy the flowers and shrubs and plan what you are going to do next.

Built around 1890, it was designed as an elderly gentleman's residence. It became a hotel in 1905 and is a Grade II Listed Building. The external appearance has changed little since the day it was built. It stands in its own grounds with ample parking for everyone, and pleasant garden for guests to sit in. An extension to allow for a licensed bar was added in the 1950's. The hotel is owned and run by Sandra and Dudley Holt, who with their staff, have made it such a friendly, welcoming place that guests return year after year. The food is home-cooked by Sandra, who mixes old traditional English with new ones of her own, producing a menu which changes daily. The Dining Room has covers for forty to fifty people and every table is laid with Irish linen table cloths and napkins. The wine list is small but well chosen and at sensible prices. There is a TV Lounge and a separate bar which is a great meeting place for guests at the end of the day.

Eighteen ensuite bedrooms are all beautifully appointed with varying bed sizes. Some of the bedrooms are strictly non-smoking. All the rooms have television, direct dial telephones and a hostess tray.

USEFUL INFORMATION

- OPEN: All year
- WHEELCHAIR ACCESS: No
- GARDEN: Yes
- CREDIT CARDS: None taken
- ACCOMMODATION: 18 ensuite rooms
- RATES: £30 (High) £25 (Low)
  Child reduction 50% if sharing with parents - Single Supplement £10

- DINING ROOM: Beautifully home cooked fare
- VEGETARIAN: Catered for on request
- PETS: Yes. By arrangement
- LICENSED: Yes
- CHILDREN: Welcome

KEMPS COUNTRY HOUSE HOTEL & RESTAURANT
East Stoke
Wareham
Dorset
BH20 6AL

Tel: 01929 462563
Fax: 01929 405287

4 Crowns Commended, AA Rosette,
Good Food Guide, Good Hotel Guide

Jill and Paul Warren, the owners of Kemps Country House Hotel and Restaurant, have achieved a perfect balance here in what was once a Victorian Rectory. There are those who will sing its praises because of its restaurant, others who will tell you that they enjoy the friendly, attentive staff. Either school is right in its assessment because the food and the atmosphere are worth travelling miles to enjoy and the comfort of the bedrooms plus the warm, relaxed, friendly ambience ensures that anyone who stays here is superbly cared for. Combine one with the other and you have pretty well perfection.

Facing South the Hotel, stands in its own grounds, overlooks the Frome Valley and has delightful views of the Purbeck Hills. Enlarged considerably since its days as a rectory, the additions have all been done with taste and consideration. What was once the old Coach House is now four well appointed en-suite rooms. There are four rooms in the main building and six spacious new bedrooms have been added, all facing the Purbecks. Some have whirlpool baths and one bedroom has a traditional four-poster bed. All the rooms have direct dial telephones, television and a hostess tray.

The charming, non-smoking restaurant has a superb menu with every dish being freshly prepared to order. The chef is insistent on the use of high quality, fresh produce and ingredients, using local produce whenever possible. Everything possible is home-made and fresh bread is baked daily. The Table d'hôte menu changes daily and an a la carte menu is also available. The attractive Conservatory overlooks the perfectly maintained gardens. Kemps specialises in all types of private functions: wedding and parties as well as Conferences.

USEFUL INFORMATION

- OPEN: All year
- WHEELCHAIR ACCESS: Yes
- GARDEN: Yes
- CREDIT CARDS: Visa/Master/Switch
- ACCOMMODATION; 14 ensuite rooms
- RATES: from £40 per person
  - Bargain Breaks Min 2 nights from £88

- RESTAURANT; A la Carte & Table d'hôte Menu changed daily
- VEGETARIAN: Always a choice
- LICENSED: Yes
- CHILDREN: Welcome

KIMBERLEY COURT HOTEL
40 Pinecliffe Avenue
Southbourne
Bournemouth
Dorset
BH6 3PZ

Tel: 01202 427583
Fax: 01202 421061

Situated in a quiet avenue close to the sea, Kimberley Court Hotel is ideal for a carefree relaxing holiday. It is only 2 minutes walk to Southbourne's Blue Flag Beach with spectacular views of the Isle of Wight to the East and Purbeck Hill to the West. Southbourne is renowned for surfing, sea fishing, sun bathing and safe swimming. A five minutes drive to Hengistbury Head will take you to golf, kite flying, walking or wind surfing in Christchurch Harbour. Within walking distance, Natural History enthusiasts will relish all that Hengistbury Nature Reserve has to offer. In fact there are places of interest in all directions and easily reached, including Corfe Castle, Highcliffe Castle, Christchurch Priory, the beautiful old town of Sherborne with its glorious abbey and two castles or Beaulieu National Motor Museum and Poole Potteries to name but a few. Bournemouth itself has something for everyone including super pedestrianized shopping boulevards and four major theatres providing entertainment throughout the year. These theatres attract star names as well as top shows and concerts.
Built as a private house in 1907, Kimberley Court became a hotel in the late 1940's, and has retained a strong family house atmosphere. The rooms are light and spacious and it has a splendid balustrade staircase. Furnished with style and an eye for comfort throughout, visitors feel immediately at home. It is the sort of atmosphere Eric and Sue Dobson, the owners want their guests to enjoy. They are comparative newcomers to the hotel business and the acquisition of Kimberley Court in 1996 was the realisation of a long term dream. From the way in which the hotel is run one would assume it had been their life time's career. They are both enthusiastic cooks. They describe their menus as farmhouse cooking derived from English or American Regional Cook Books. Wherever the recipes come from the result is delicious and has gained the Dobsons a well deserved reputation for good food. Diets are catered for and packed lunches are available upon request.
The eight bedrooms are all large enough to be family rooms. They all have wall mounted remote control television and hostess trays. Three rooms are ensuite and the other five have vanity units and are in close proximity to the bathroom, shower room and toilets. Downstairs the comfortable lounge has colour television and a video. Free newspapers are provided every day and there are several quiet corners where one can enjoy reading. It really is an ideal holiday venue for people of all ages, at anytime of the year.

USEFUL INFORMATION

- OPEN: All Year
- WHEELCHAIR ACCESS: Yes
- GARDEN: Yes, Ponds, BBQ Aviary
- CREDIT CARDS: None taken
- ACCOMMODATION: 8 rooms, 3 ensuite
- RATES: From £20pp BB & EM

- DINING ROOM: Good farmhouse cooking
- VEGETARIAN: Yes & other diets

- LICENSED: Residential Licence
- CHILDREN: Welcome
- PETS: Yes

THE LANGTON ARMS
Tarrant Monkton
NR Blandford
Dorset
DT11 8RX

Tel: 01258 830225
Fax: 01258 830053

Like many of the houses in the pretty village of Tarrant Monkton close to Blandford, The Langton Arms is thatched. It is a tranquil village in which life continues in a leisurely pace and within the walls of the 17th century inn you will always find locals enjoying the ever changing selection of real ales such as Old Speckled Hen, Ringwood Old Thumper and Palmers Tally Ho! It is an inn that has retained its charm over the centuries but nonetheless has moved with the times. Six guest rooms are built in rustic brick, around an attractive courtyard. All are on ground floor level and each has its own entrance and a bay window looking onto the Dorset countryside. Attractively furnished to a very high standard, they all have full en-suite bathrooms, colour television and tea/coffee facilities.

The Inn has a great reputation for its food which is served in both the pub's cosy beamed bars as well as the welcoming family dining room. A separate Bistro restaurant is to be found in an old converted stable and conservatory. It is a relaxed and friendly place to dine. Open Wednesday to Saturday evenings offering interesting quality food and wine at reasonable prices. The chef is both talented and imaginative and delights in using local produce. His Tomato and Herb Risotto or Avocado Salad makes a delicious start to a meal and if you follow that with Supreme Micelle - a tender breast of chicken on a bed of leaf spinach enlaced with a bacon & cheddar sauce or perhaps Prime Scottish fillet steak enhanced by a rich port and stilton sauce, you will have had a meal fit for a King. More simply the daytime menu may well offer you venison sausages, sweet & sour prawn fritters or a choice of fresh pasta and home-made Vegetarian dishes. The choice is wide ranging and it is assuredly value for money. Children are very welcome but not allowed in the main bars.

The village will provide you with a charming place in which to wander and it also makes a perfect base from which to explore the surrounding area, with the ancient Cathedral City of Salisbury and the historic coastal town of Poole just a short drive away. The towns of Blindfold Forum, Wimborne Minster, Shaftesbury and Sherborne are all nearby as well as the many unspoilt and scenic villages which make the heart of Dorset.

USEFUL INFORMATION

- OPEN; Mon-Sat 11.30-11pm
  Sun: 12-10.30pm
- WHEELCHAIR ACCESS: Yes
- GARDEN; Yes. For eating in summer
  Large Children's Play Area
- CREDIT CARDS: Visa/Master/Switch/Delta
- ACCOMMODATION; 6 ensuite rooms

- RATES: per person £39 single £54 double
  (one night-all year) Special rates 2 nights or more

- RESTAURANT; Exciting menu
- VEGETARIAN: Always a choice

- BAR FOOD: Wide range. Great value
- LICENSED: Full On
- CHILDREN: Welcome but not in main bars
- PETS: Yes

PURBECK HOUSE HOTEL
91 High Street
Swanage
Dorset
BH19 2LZ

Tel: 01929 422872
Fax: 01929 421194

The elegant, Victorian Purbeck House Hotel delights everyone who stays here, largely because of its restrained, well furnished Victorian ambience. Every room is furnished with an emphasis on the sort of furniture one might have found in a country house at the turn of the last century. The Victorians were renowned for the spaciousness of the rooms in their houses and the height of the ceilings and windows. Here there are fine examples everywhere. It is fascinating to see the original servants' bells in the hall next to the double faced clock. The Grade II Listed building is set in extensive grounds in the heart of Swanage, itself still enjoying the unhurried life of the last century. From the hotel there are superb views over the Purbeck Hills, Swanage Bay and the beautiful gardens. To wander in the gardens is a great pleasure. Here you have a great willow with its' illuminated pathway and seat and a greenhouse which houses a vine said to be over 60 years old from which until recently wine was made from the grapes. On the lawn in front of the summer house one can play croquet.

Originally the house belonged to George Burt who was christened 'King of Swanage' by Thomas Hardy who often visited him here. One of the most striking rooms is the Thomas Hardy restaurant with its painted ceiling and stunning Carrera marble fireplaces. Here you can enjoy delicious evening meals cooked to perfection by the imaginative and very talented chef who provides both an a la carte and a table d'hôte menu. The tables are laid with fine linen cloths, napkins, gleaming silver and sparkling glass. Slightly less formal is the recently added Garden Conservatory restaurant which leads on to a patio and the gardens. Meals are served here as well as morning coffee and a delectable Dorset cream tea. Before dinner the comfortable lounge bar is a popular meeting place for a quiet drink in front of the Italian marble chimney and fireplace, with George Burt's monograph above. Everywhere you turn there is some reminder of the history of the house which is exciting to explore.

The 18 bedrooms are all ensuite and each individually decorated and furnished with original old pine pieces. They are comfortable and relaxing, warm in winter and cool in summer. Each room has direct dial telephone, satellite and colour television, a hostess tray, hairdryers and complimentary toiletries.
Conferences, functions and wedding receptions are catered for in the Purbeck Room.

USEFUL INFORMATION

· OPEN: All year 11-2.30 &6-11.30pm	· RESTAURANT: Thomas Hardy Room, superb food. Conservatory Restaurant for good meals, Morning Coffee and Dorset Cream Teas
· GARDEN; Beautiful grounds	· VEGETARIAN: Always available
· CREDIT CARDS: All major cards	· BAR FOOD: Snacks and light lunches
· ACCOMMODATION: 18 ensuite rooms	· LICENSED: Yes
· RATES: 2/5/7 night DBB Breaks available	· PETS: Yes
Details on request	· CHILDREN: Welcome

SALTERNS HOTEL,
38 Salterns Way
Poole
Dorset
BH14 8JR

Tel: 01202 707321
Fax: 01202 707488

It is hard to imagine today that Salterns Hotel, was once the site of an Royal Air Force landing base for Flying Boats during World War II. Now it is an attractive hotel with a superb waterside location overlooking Brownsea Island and Poole Harbour with its own Marina home to 300 boats with a waterside patio and manicured lawn. It is a place that is popular with the famous, visited quite recently by Richard Branson, Prince Andrew, Nigel Mansell, Vince Hill and Millicent Martin.

John and Beverley Smith, the owners, lead their experienced and very professional team. The aim is always to ensure their guests are pampered, well fed and want to repeat their visit. The hotel is continually upgraded, is furnished comfortably and attractively. Each bedroom has a theme. For example there is a clown room, a duck room and a bears room. They all have direct dial telephones, television including Satellite TV, Hairdryers, hot water bottle, an Honesty Bar and a hospitality tray with tea, coffee, biscuits and bottled water.

The elegant restaurant over which the renowned chef Nigel Popplewell presides, is a delightful place in which to dine romantically by candlelight in a wonderful atmosphere. The menu is essentially French but there are many innovative variations which appeal to the palate and to the eye - the presentation is superb. John is a lover of good wine and buys for Salterns. His choice is impeccable and covers wines from around the world at sensible prices. For less formal occasions the lively Shellies Bistro is a delightfully relaxed place to eat with the emphasis on seafood from the hotels own catch. There are two friendly bars in both of which bar food is available and for anyone wanting to use this excellent hotel for business, the conference facilities can cater and supply equipment for up to one hundred and twenty people

USEFUL INFORMATION

- OPEN: All year
- WHEELCHAIR ACCESS: Yes
- BAR FOOD: Readily available
- CREDIT CARDS: All major cards
- ACCOMMODATION: 20 ensuite rooms
- RATES: From £76 single B&B & £96 double

- RESTAURANT: French food at its best
- SHELLIES BISTRO: Emphasis on seafood

- LICENSED: Full On. Fine wines
- CHILDREN: Welcome
- PETS: Yes £5 daily charge

WOODCROFT TOWER HOTEL
Gervis Road
East Cliff
Bournemouth
BH1 3DE

Tel: 01202 558202
Fax: 01202 551807

You have only to read some of the appreciative letters from guests to realise that this is the sort of hotel which will always give you the standard of service, care and comfort that you look for on holiday, whether it is just a short break or a longer stay. Mike and Valerie Kemp own and run Woodcroft Tower Hotel and together with their seemingly unchanging staff, they have created a wonderful atmosphere, relaxed and informal but run with a professionalism that makes sure every detail is catered for. Its situation is superb, a quite magnificent sea view lies just a few minutes' level stroll from the hotel and from here you can wander down the zig zag path to the beach relying on the cliff lift to bring you up again! Bournemouth has so much to offer the visitor, whether it is sporting activity or theatrical experiences, concerts or seeking out the many interesting places within easy reach such as the little churchyard near Dorchester where Hardy's heart lies buried or perhaps the pleasant ferry crossing from Lymington to Yarmouth in the Isle of Wight. Throughout the year the Kemps offer a variety of special breaks at very reasonable prices. Every time you come here you will find some improvement made to this already immaculate hotel. The newly refurbished ballroom with its large dance floor provides the perfect setting for the hotel's special occasions like New Year and is used a lot for functions and for conferences. Every bedroom is perfectly and immaculately appointed with either a private bathroom or shower room. Every room has remote control television, telephone, radio, baby listening and tea and coffee making facilities. Stay here for Christmas or New Year and you will feel you are part of a house-party. Beautifully organised, the occasions are the greatest fun. The Restaurant is known for the excellence of its table d'hôte menu, which changes daily. Mike Kemp is an experienced and inspired chef and it is he who personally supervises the kitchens, producing high quality cuisine. Inexpensive bar meals are available at lunch time. The cosy bar leads out onto a sunny patio and there is a separate, comfortable lounge for those who want to be peaceful. The large gardens are perfectly maintained and here you can sit, enjoy a bar snack, take a quiet wander before dinner or tackle the nine hole putting green. There is so much that the Woodcroft Tower Hotel has to offer and this is why a high percentage of the guests are those who have been before and sampled its delights. It is no wonder that a Tourist Board Inspector says that the hotel is a credit to tourism in the Bournemouth area.

USEFUL INFORMATION

- OPEN: All year
- WHEELCHAIR ACCESS: Yes
- GARDEN: Yes. Putting Green
- CREDIT CARDS: All major cards
- ACCOMMODATION: 40 ensuite rooms
- RATES: From £25.00 B&B pp Various rates Bargain Breaks

- RESTAURANT: Excellent fare
- VEGETARIAN: Always a choice
- BAR FOOD: Good & inexpensive
- LICENSED: Yes
- CHILDREN: Welcome
- PETS: No

DRUSILLAS INN
Horton
NR Wimborne
Dorset
BH21 7JH

Tel:01258 840297
Fax: 01258 841222

Voted by readers of local magazine
Pub of the Year 1995

Everyone comments on the delightfully unusual construction of Drusillas Inn. The original building is between two to three hundred years old, thatched on cob walls with brick exterior. Nothing strange about that but add it to the unique circular Tower Room Restaurant and it is somewhere you will always remember especially when you have had the opportunity to taste the food and enjoy the real old world feel of the inn where log fires burn all through the winter creating their own ambience. The restaurant and the bar offer two very different ways of life but each contributes to making this one of the nicest places in Dorset. The restaurant with thirty six covers is attractive, restful and prides itself on the excellence of its fish dishes. In fact Roger Kernan, the owner, will tell you that Drusillas now serves more fish than meat. With an understanding of the needs of local people, mainly from the country and farming, the public bar provides an area of activity and entertainment with two large pool tables, three dart boards, juke box and machines. Salad specialities, sandwiches, hot baguettes, vegetarian dishes and filled jacket potatoes as well as traditional favourites such as steak and kidney pie or lasagne are available in the bar area. Senior Citizens can enjoy their own special lunch time menus from Monday to Saturday at a very reasonable price. The atmosphere is wonderful, the service superb and above all they achieve their motto 'We aim to please'!

USEFUL INFORMATION

- OPEN: 11-3pm & 6-11pm Mon-Sat Open all day Sunday
- WHEELCHAIR ACCESS: Level entrance. No toilets for disabled
- GARDEN: Yes. Playground
- CREDIT CARDS: AMEX /Visa/Master
- CHILDREN: Welcome

- RESTAURANT: Specialises in fish and has an excellent menu. Cream teas
- VEGETARIAN: Always a choice
- BAR FOOD: Good choice
- LICENSED: Yes. Full On

THE GALLEY
9 High Street
Swanage
Dorset
BH19 2LN

Tel: 01929 427299

Nick Storer's converted shop has become one of the most successful and sought after restaurants in Dorset. The Galley, aptly named because of the emphasis on fish and sea food is furnished in a manner in keeping with the sea, with a sea-blue ceiling covered with nets and a plethora of decorative tiles. You will find the restaurant close to the old Stone Quay from where so many of the kitchen's ingredients are sourced. Diners can cross from Poole and Bournemouth to Swanage on the Sandbanks Ferry - many do because this sought after venue has a whole host of regular devotees who eagerly look forward to their visits to The Galley. Dinner starts at 6.45pm each evening and last orders at 9.30pm or by arrangement. You are asked to book. Three courses comprise the meal which is at a set price of £18.50p. It is excellent value for money and the comprehensive wine list matches the standard of the food which may include a starter of Nick Storer's own game and port wine pate or a jug of traditional fish soup with garlic croutons and fresh parmesan. lobsters, oysters, bass, cockles, skate and scallops are usually available or you may choose monk fish fillet or perhaps a venison steak or game pie. Whatever your choice the food will be memorable.

USEFUL INFORMATION

- OPEN: Easter-New Years Eve 6.45pm · RESTAURANT: An eating experience.
  Last order 9.30pm or by arrangement   Seafood & Game
- WHEELCHAIR ACCESS: Yes · VEGETARIAN: Catered for
- CREDIT CARDS: AMEX/Master/Diners/Visa · LICENSED: Yes
- CHILDREN: Welcome

HEMSWORTH MANOR FARM
Witchampton
NR Wimborne, Dorset
BH21 5BN
Tel/Fax: 01258 840216
Tourist Board 2 Crown-Highly Commended

Hemsworth is a family run farm, mainly arable but with cattle, sheep, pigs and various domestic animals. Situated in beautiful countryside with only one other farmhouse in sight it is blissfully peaceful. It is a beautiful old Manor farmhouse in lovely down land countryside and close to the village of Witchampton which boasts a particularly lovely church. The farm is part of the Crichel estate, parts of which were requisitioned during World War II and used as an airfield. Bombers, gliders and other aircraft flew from here on many missions and there is a memorial to those who gave their lives by the old entrance. From time to time veterans, with wonderful stories to tell, return. The area has much to offer in the way of Roman history and there are still signs of old barrows in the fields approaching Hemsworth. Wimborne has a famous Minster and is well known for its Quarter Jack, a fascinating timepiece. You would never have time to be bored if you stay at Hemsworth. Country sports are well catered for and there is golfing, sailing, riding and fishing within easy reach of the farm. Salisbury, Poole, Bournemouth are all within half an hour's drive. Your hostess Bee Tory will look after you splendidly. The four non-smoking bedrooms, three ensuite and one with a private bathroom, are charming and very comfortable. A first class breakfast is served in the dining room.

USEFUL INFORMATION

- OPEN: All year except Xmas · DINING ROOM: Excellent breakfast No evening meal
- WHEELCHAIR ACCESS: Limited · VEGETARIAN: Upon request
- GARDEN: Yes · LICENSED: No
- CREDIT CARDS: None taken · CHILDREN: Over 10 years
- ACCOMMODATION: 3 ensuite 1 with private bathroom
- RATES: From £22.50 per person · PETS: By arrangement

410

HIGHWAYS GUEST HOUSE
29 Fernside Road
Poole
Dorset
BH15 2QU
Tel: 01202 677060
ETB 2Crowns Commended. Brittany Ferries Selected

This warm, friendly guest house situated only one mile from Poole centre, two miles from Sandbanks and five miles from Bournemouth, is the home of June and Ron Bailey, into which they welcome guests. Built in the 1920s, it is beautifully furnished, maintained to a high standard but nonetheless gives visitors the feel of a home-from-home. It could not be in a better position for anyone wanting to enjoy everything Poole, Bournemouth and the surrounding countryside and beaches have to offer. It is also super for anyone working away from home and wanting a quiet haven at the end of a busy day. The five bedrooms are all ensuite with comfortable beds, attractive decor and the added facility of colour television and a hostess tray a great boon to any traveller. Breakfast, served in the non-smoking dining room, is a delicious meal, freshly cooked to your choice and more than generous in portions - you would never leave the table feeling hungry!. Evening meals are available by arrangement although there are many good eateries within easy reach. There is ample parking, and buses for the beach, shops and countryside pass the door. Open all year, the house is fully centrally heated.

USEFUL INFORMATION

· OPEN: All year	· DINING ROOM: First class breakfast
· WHEELCHAIR ACCESS: No	· VEGETARIAN: Yes & Special diets
· PARKING: Ample	
· CREDIT CARDS: None taken	· LICENSED: No
· ACCOMMODATION: 5 ensuite	· CHILDREN: Welcome
· RATES: £20pp B&B	· PETS: No

HOPEWELL
Little Lonnen
Colehill, Wimborne
Dorset BH21 7BB
Tel:01202 880311 E-mail:tony-p@bournemouth-net.co.uk

ETB 2 Crowns Highly Commended

Hopewell is a modern, owner built house which has rapidly acquired a character and charm of its own. It is situated in the village of Colehill, three miles from the historic market town of Wimborne Minster. The owners Esther and Tony Perks chose the site well. It has six acres consisting of garden, woodland and a meadow featuring free range ducks and chickens. It is close to several splendid places to visit including the adjacent Kingston Lacy, Bradbury Rings and Cranborne Chase. There are many golf courses, including Ferndown, wonderful walking country and culture does not go missing with the live theatre at Tivoli, Wimborne. The Perks have created a lovely relaxed and informal atmosphere in their home and are genuinely delighted to welcome guests to share it with them. They have one double bedroom, one twin both ensuite and a single with a private bathroom. Every room is furnished with a happy mixture of modern and antique pieces. Children are very welcome. Breakfast is delicious, starting with fruit juices, cereals and porridge, followed by an English breakfast, scrambled, poached or boiled egg if you would prefer it and local kippers. Plenty of toast, warm croissants and buttered rolls complete a perfect start to the day.

USEFUL INFORMATION

· OPEN: All year	· DINING ROOM: Super breakfast
· WHEELCHAIR ACCESS: No	· VEGETARIAN: Yes
· GARDEN: 6 acres	· STRICTLY NON-SMOKING HOUSE
· CREDIT CARDS: Visa/Master Euro	· LICENSED: No
· ACCOMMODATION: 1dbl 1tw 1 sgl all ensuite ·	· CHILDREN: Very welcome
· RATES: £24pp £2 discount 2 or more days Children 5-15 half price ·	PETS: No

SHELL BAY SEAFOOD RESTAURANT
Ferry Road
Studland
Dorset
BH19 3BA

Tel: 01929 450363
Fax: 01929 450570

Poole Harbour is considered to be one of the largest natural harbours in the world and immediately adjacent with an unrivalled position on the Studland Peninsula overlooking Brownsea Island made famous by Baden-Powell founder of the Boy Scout Movement, is Shell Bay Seafood Restaurant. It would be fair to describe a visit here as a gastronomic experience. The seventy covers are set in a casual dining style with a strong seafood theme and in good weather one can enjoy a superb meal on the waterside terrace. What makes this restaurant so successful is simplicity at every level and especially in the menu where Charles Mumford specialises in cooking all manner of seafood without frills. The menu changes daily according to the best quality available. It is fish at its best and will delight every palate. Charles and his partner Keith Shaw are expert in the art of making their guests welcome. The atmosphere is relaxed and happy and the food superlative. What more can one ask for?

USEFUL INFORMATION

- OPEN: October-Easter Thurs-Sat
  Easter to end Oct Lunch & Dinner
- WHEELCHAIR ACCESS: Yes
- GARDEN: Yes. Waterside terrace
- CREDIT CARDS: Yes not Diners/AMEX

- PETS: No
- RESTAURANT: Specialises in seafood
- VEGETARIAN: With prior notice
- LICENSED: Full
- CHILDREN: Welcome

THORNHILL
Thornhill, Holt
Wimborne
Dorset
BH21 7DJ

Tel: 01202 889434

It is a great feeling to wake up in the morning having spent a comfortable and relaxed night, to a sense of the silence of the countryside only disturbed by the wild life who consider the garden their own. Rabbits, moles, deer and many more creatures are regularly to be seen and buzzards nest in the copse nearby. Thornhill, with its newly thatched roof, will give you that peace and tranquillity and yet you have the village pub, church and shops within easy walking distance. John and Sara Turnbull enjoy having visitors in their strictly non-smoking home, especially those who are keen gardeners and bridge players! John also plays chess. The house is comfortably and attractively furnished. There are three bedrooms, all with wash basins and two bathrooms - one private and one may be shared. Guests have their own sitting room complete with television. A delicious traditional English breakfast is served every day. The large, pretty garden, has garden chairs and guests are welcome to use the hard tennis court.

USEFUL INFORMATION

- OPEN: All year
- WHEELCHAIR ACCESS: No
- GARDEN: Yes. Chairs. Tennis court
- CREDIT CARDS: None taken
- ACCOMMODATION: 1tw.1dbl. 1sgl
- RATES: From £20 Discount for 4 nights or more

- DINING ROOM: Delicious breakfast
- VEGETARIAN: Not applicable
- NO SMOKING
- LICENSED: No
- CHILDREN: Over 14
- PETS: No

Bridge House Hotel	Beaminster	445
Burton Cliff Hotel	Burton Bradstock	446
Casterbridge Hotel	Dorchester	447
Chimneys Guest House	Chideock	454
Devon Hotel	Uplyme	448
Elm Tree Inn	Langton Herring	449
Gaggle Of Geese	Buckland Newton	455
Hotel Alexandra	Lyme Regis	450
Lamperts Cottage	Sydling St Nicholas	456
Manor Hotel	West Bexington	451
Manor House	Piddlehinton	456
Marquis Of Lorne	Nettlecombe	457
Old Farmhouse	Buckland Newton	457
Old Rectory	Winterbourne Steepleton	452
Pickwick Inn	Beaminster	458
Thatch Lodge Hotel	Charmouth	453
The Fox	Corscombe	458
Three Horseshoes	Powerstock	459
Westwood House Hotel	Dorchester	459
White Lion	Broadwindsor	460
Woodcoate Stud	Abbotsbury	460

Chapter 9:
The Heart of Hardy's Wessex

Wessex; the land of the West Saxons. You will probably hear the name just as often in conjunction with that of Thomas Hardy (1840-1928), Dorset's most famous author.

Hardy gave Wessex a new territory to cover, a fictional world based on the reality of 19th century England. Hardy's Wessex was larger than the modern definition used in this book (he also included Berkshire, Hampshire and Devon), yet all save one of his novels are set in his *South Wessex,* which is Dorset.

The south western section of Dorset is the heart of Hardy's Wessex; the action of many of his books takes place here, and Dorchester was his home town. Before he was a writer Hardy trained as an architect, and worked on many of the churches of this part of Dorset too. He lived and travelled elsewhere, but this area was his source of inspiration.

You do not have to read Hardy to enjoy Dorset, but if you have read any of his works then a trip through the places covered in this chapter can only add to your appreciation of them. With gorgeous villages, spectacular coastline and one of the most complete seaside resorts, Central and West Dorset will give you plenty to see and do, no matter who your favourite author might be.

Another writer, not as local as Hardy, but just as famous, also found Lyme Regis (to the west of this section) inspiring, as a read of Jane Austen's "Persuasion" will show. Yet Jane Austen's characters are not defined by their surroundings so much as by their interaction with others, and by their deeds and thoughts. It is because Hardy has left us so many individuals whom we remember against a rural, actual background, be they Tess D'Urbeville or Gabriel Oak, that you cannot travel this part of Dorset without feeling something of his presence.

Picking up the journey west along the A352 from **WOOL** the mostly empty spaces of CHALDON DOWN can be seen to your left, and six rounded mounds are visible on the ridge near to the turning for **CHALDON HERRING.** These will look familiar if you have visited Bull Barrow, and are the barrows known as the Five Maries. It is not clear which is the tomb of the intrusive sixth who spoilt the accuracy of the name!

On the opposite side of the main road is the WHITE HORSE, where almost an acre of soil has been removed to make the prominent white chalk figure of horse and rider. Hardy, in the 'Trumpet Major' suggests this was made in commemoration of the battle of Trafalgar, but more common is the theory that it was dug in honour of George III, after his patronage of Weymouth. In either event it certainly isn't as rude as the chalk figure we will meet at Cerne!

If you wish to make a stop along this road, then try the MILL HOUSE CIDER MUSEUM (01305 852220) at **OVERMOIGNE**. Some of the restored presses and other antique items are impressive, and at the same site you can visit the DORSET COLLECTION OF CLOCKS where the gallery of Longcase, or Grandfather clocks is particularly interesting.

Moving west of the part of the coast used by the military, you can travel towards Weymouth past **OSMINGTON MILLS**. To get here you will need to follow the side road off the A353 close to the village of **OSMINGTON** itself. From the car park on the edge of the low cliffs, the outlook is across WEYMOUTH BAY to the glistening beaches and rows of neat terraced Victorian and Georgian houses of the front at Weymouth, many of which provide welcome as hotels and guest houses.

On a bright day Weymouth looks great from here, and at night the lights of the town and the harbour are equally enticing. Look out for any sign of fire appearing in this view, especially if, for any unlikely reason, you may have neglected to pay a tax bill before leaving home. For centuries fires were lit to warn the smugglers who used this stretch of coast of the presence of revenue officers in the area. Fire and taxes have another link here, if the stories are true.

A prominent smuggler named Pierre La Tour, or French Peter, used to frequent the inn at Osmington Mills, now known as the SMUGGLERS INN. On a particular summer's day he received a rather cool welcome, and realised that he was being warned about the presence of an eavesdropping taxman, apparently hiding in the bottom of the chimney of the large fireplace. Taking the hint, Peter asked for a fire to be lit, and then waited patiently for the inevitable. The blackened figure of the new revenue officer for the coast, a Mr John Tallman, (somehow an apt name for a chimney dweller) eventually appeared, to an inevitable round of jeers.

WEYMOUTH (Tourist Information 01305 785747 or http://www.weymouth.gov.uk) is a delightful resort, partly because the approaches to it from both east and west are so attractive that you are ready to put up with a couple of miles of less appealing suburbs before finding the centre and seafront.

More remote than the Bournemouth conurbation, Weymouth really is the ideal place to make your centre of operations if you are planning to spend some time in West Dorset. It made its name as a safe landing place for any boats in trouble along the treacherous Dorset coast, and is still a haven for many visitors, especially those who arrive by sea and moor their cruisers in the bay.

All the essential elements are here for a seaside resort; golden beaches which run far enough to allow you to walk away from the crowds; a mild, sunny climate; a colourful history; attractions, events and facilities; and access to so much more in the surrounding countryside.

The Esplanade, Weymouth, Looking East.

There were originally two towns here, split by the estuary of the River Wey which makes the present day harbour. Once bridges were built between the two (starting in 1597) it was inevitable that the town would merge, but the larger section, holding the esplanade and the majority of the town centre, was the one to lose its name. Melcombe Regis was no more, but Weymouth was here to stay. Modern Weymouth is a large place, and exploration by foot will take you some time, but is worth the fatigue. Try one of the long stay car parks to the west of the town centre, once you have found your way around the one-way system!

A short walk along the Preston Beach Road will take you to the LODMOOR NATURE RESERVE (01305 778313). The RSPB run the largest area here, with 350 acres inhabited by seamarsh birds, which can be seen from prepared observation hides. On the town centre edge of the site is the WEYMOUTH SEA-LIFE PARK (01305 788255). A collection of hexagonal brown buildings, accessible along a long drive, this does not look the most appealing of places to the newcomer, but do not be put off.

There are the expected shark tanks, but also a variety of less familiar species. Look in particular for the pool of thornback rays. They rise to the top of the water and are tame. To stroke one of these creatures is an act of bravery, but you will not forget the experience easily. LODMOOR COUNTRY PARK makes up the rest of the complex, and has a nine hole golf course, as well as large picnic and woodland walking areas.

A walk along the beach will take you into the centre of Weymouth, and it is difficult to think of a more typical example of a south coast resort, as you walk among bathing huts, amusements and Punch and Judy shows. Yet the beach is so long, and the climate so pleasant, that this is never an intimidating place, as some popular beaches can be. It is also one of the safest beaches in the country, as the shallows go out an unusually long way.

Taking a right turn at the JUBILEE CLOCK into KING STREET, you will come to the KINGS ROUNDABOUT, and a bridge over the WEY. This is called SWANNERY BRIDGE, and crossing it will give you access to the RADIPOLE LAKE NATURE RESERVE AND SWANNERY (01305 778313). Another RSPB reserve, this one is particularly good for waders and warblers, and in summer the flowers and butterflies demand a visit alone, so close to the centre of such a busy town.

Along this far bank of the river lies the NORTH QUAY, and the building known as BREWERS QUAY (01320 789007). Much like the Poole Pottery, a modern centre for education and entertainment has been built inside the shell of a Victorian building; this time a brewery. The TOWN MUSEUM lies within the building, as well as a 'TIMEWALK' exploring Weymouth's history.

The settlements on each side of the Wey grew up from the 12th century, and the Black Death is thought to have arrived in England at Melcombe Regis in 1348. Both sections started to decline as ports in the 17th century, but King George III added fame to the new direction Weymouth was already taking by visiting it for fourteen 'medicinal holidays' at the start of the 19th century. I cannot help imagining a portly king dressed in a striped bathing suit with a crown perched on top of his head, tiptoeing down to the ocean. Brewers Quay has the hardly less eccentric reality of some original bathing machines form the period, and it is a solemn truth that it was along this coast, at this very time, that nude bathing was first exercised as an aid to health. Do look for specified areas before joining the tradition!

Weymouth was given a great boost by the arrival of the railway in 1857, and its future was certain. Perhaps it is because of this that it is such an ideal resort; the whole place is used to its role, and makes life easy for the tourist. Brewers Quay is typical of this: there are more than twenty craft shops on the two floors of the building, and many other displays and facilities, not particularly linked to the theme of brewing!

Around the corner from Brewers Quay is the TUDOR HOUSE (01305 782925/ 788168) which is simply what it says, an early 17th century house furnished accurately to the time, in which you can follow a tour about life in the century which probably had the largest part to play in Dorset's history. This was the house of an affluent person, as the fine stonework front suggests. At the time the Harbour came further inland to the area now known as HOPE SQUARE, and this house would have been much nearer to the water's edge than it now is.

Weymouth was largely on the side of the parliamentarians in the Civil War. Unlike strongholds such as Corfe Castle, and the Isle of Portland, Weymouth changed hands and sides before the eventual victory, and suffered more than once in the conflict.

A walk through the NOTHE GARDENS will take you from here towards the stone pier and main harbour. These landscaped gardens are unspectacular in themselves, but a very agreeable stopping place from which to observe the comings and goings in the harbour. The bare stone pier is much less appealing, but walk out along it and you will have the best view of the surrounding coastline possible without taking to sea. As you stand looking at the calm of Weymouth Bay to the east, save the vision in your mind for a later comparison to the much less tranquil setting of the Cobb, at Lyme Regis.

Perhaps it was the influence of this tranquillity that inspired the irrepressible and extremely funny stories written by Thomas Love Peacock (1795-1866), who was born in Weymouth. With lampoons of the Gothic style occasionally used by Jane Austen, his brilliant "Nightmare Abbey" and "Headlong Hall" are as extreme a contrast to "Persuasion" or even "The French Lieutenant's Woman" as the views from the two sea walls can possibly make.

The NOTHE FORT (01305 787243) makes up the rounded point of this headland. There was considerable fighting here during the Civil War, as this was the obvious place for the town's guns even then. The current building was constructed in the 1860s and 1870s, and was one of PALMERSTON'S FOLLIES, equipped with massive guns which were never used in war. In later times the same emplacements were used for anti-aircraft guns during the Second World War.

The sheer size of this edifice of Portland Stone impresses, every dimension shows the power that it was built to withstand when the massive guns were fired. Test firings of these original 12.5 inch, 38 tonne guns started to destroy the rear windows and doors, which then had to be removed. There are over seventy rooms now in the MUSEUM OF COASTAL DEFENCE inside the fort, with a wealth of information in displays, dioramas and working models etc, but it is the building itself which will leave the most lasting impression.

The harbour at Weymouth is truly cosmopolitan. Fishing boats mix with pleasure cruisers, power-boats, yachts and catamarans, in a lively mix of colour and sound. You can take a trip for fishing, sightseeing or diving from here, and on the esplanade side of the harbour find out more about its history in the DEEP SEA ADVENTURE (01305 760690).

Another adapted building, this time a Victorian grain warehouse, three floors are packed with educational and interactive displays and exhibitions, covering everything from the history of the harbour to the story of the 'TITANIC'. As with

Brewers Quay, this is well organised, comprehensive and full of surprises. If you have the bad luck to be in Weymouth on a rainy day, then the town has made sure there is still plenty to do.

THE PAVILION COMPLEX (01305 783225/6) is a little further along this side of the harbour, and with theatre, shows, music, dancing and exhibitions, provides you with more choices in the middle of the town.

There are many annual events in Weymouth too, especially during the summer months. The range of these is wide: there is a free JAZZ FESTIVAL each June in the Old Harbour, a MILITARY AND VETERANS FESTIVAL (01305 765266) in the same month, and the WEYMOUTH CARNIVAL in August. It is always worth checking with Tourist Information for more events which may cover your individual interests, as there really are far too many in this resort to mention here.

Of the major resorts in Dorset, Weymouth is the most self contained, and the most westerly, and the contrast to the rest of West Dorset could not, in many ways, be greater.

Heading south through **WYKE REGIS**, the A354 takes you to the **ISLE OF PORTLAND**. This is more of an island than Purbeck, but since the first bridge across SMALLMOUTH was built in 1839 there has been no necessity to use a ferry.

The shore between the immense PORTLAND BREAKWATER and the main road to Portland is filled by the expanse of PORTLAND HARBOUR. The breakwater and harbour took more than fifty years in all to complete, and in the early years of this century, when finally finished, formed the largest man made harbour in the world.

The breakwater is one and a half miles of solid Portland Stone. The stone used was that which had proved unsuitable for use in masonry, and had been left on the local hillsides over two hundred years of quarrying. PORTLAND PRISON provided a labour force for the immense task of moving these mountains and reshaping them into the huge sea defences, which were particularly championed by Prince Albert after the Royal Yacht had trouble in a storm off Portland in 1846.

The harbour effectively offered an alternative, deeper safe haven to Weymouth, and became a busy area, particularly for the Royal Navy. This forbidding expanse of stone looks suited to a war zone, and makes an almost shocking comparison to the Esplanade you have just left.

The harbour has seen great acts of heroism, and during a stuka attack in 1940 prompted the actions which later resulted in the first award of the V.C. for off shore combat, when a young rating received fatal injuries as he continued to fire his anti-aircraft gun manually, with the rest of the gun crew lying dead around him. Somehow the sea, even walled in as it is here, seems a fitting memorial to such actions, covering them forever but not letting us forget, as it continues to beat at the breakwaters now exactly as it would have done almost sixty years ago.

Now the navy has left most of this area behind, the six millions tons of local stone which make up the harbour are the subject of discussion, and it seems that the 'Portland Port' will be the subject of a vast maritime project for the future.

Whether you see the island of Portland itself as beautiful or barren depends on your own taste and viewpoint, but a more distinctive landscape than that of this block of limestone protruding out into the sea would be hard to imagine.

The natives of Portland have long considered themselves a completely separate community to that of the rest of Dorset, and at one time only met with the mainlanders once a year, at the NOVEMBER FAIR. Although the event is still held each year, in the lower part of **FORTUNESWELL**, the evening of entertainment remains without the original daytime trading of cattle and sheep. Still, I suspect this might be the more tempting part of the proceedings for most of us.

While we are speaking of Portland and animals, you must be warned about a local custom. A certain small, furry animal exists in numbers upon the grassy, treeless land of Portland, but to mention its name is considered extremely bad luck. So, if you are still in Weymouth you can 'rabbit' on about them to your heart's content, but once you can see Chesil Beach in your rear view mirror you will have to 'burrow' into your imagination to find an alternative.

If Lulworth Castle reminds you of a toy fort, then PORTLAND CASTLE (01305 820539) looks more akin to a modern toy from a plastic mould, set over looking Portland Harbour, as if it were a pool for the use of motorised model boats. The smooth, arced lines of the grey building mask its age. Constructed on the orders of Henry VIII in 1540, its intended purpose was very different to that of Lulworth's castle too.

Portland Castle

Along with the now dilapidated SANDSFOOT CASTLE on the Weymouth bank, these were fortresses to repel any catholic invasion from the south. In the event, the formidable, functional looking castle with walls fourteen feet thick saw conflict only in the Civil War, when it changed hands several times, but held out longer against Cromwell than most. Now it makes an excellent place from which to get an idea of the immensity of the man made Portland Harbour from within. There are tours around the castle too, which has much of its original structure intact.

The PORTLAND MUSEUM (01305 821804) shows that island buildings can be charming rather than just imposing. The thatched house, at the south end of the village of **WAKEHAM**, dates in parts back to 1640, and forms an unusual but picturesque setting for the exhibits telling the history of Portland, as well as the Shipwreck Exhibition and extensive fossil collection. The building is also the inspiration for the cottage in Hardy's tale of 'The Well-Beloved'. Try a walk from here down the set of 153 steep steps cut into the cliff face which will take you to the CHURCH OPE COVE, but only if you are ready for the return trip. The museum also celebrates the famous destinations of some of the stone which has been chipped and blasted away from its place in the island. All around Portland you will see lumps of rock which have been left behind as unsuitable, rejected after all the effort of quarrying, now often overgrown and totally neglected. These are those that remain, others have gone on to long-lasting fame as the building blocks for some of the most famous designs of all, including Wren's ST PAUL'S CATHEDRAL.

The southernmost point of Wessex is PORTLAND BILL. The famous red and white lighthouse can be visited (01305 820495), and there is a new Tourist Information post next to it. A dramatic place to start a coastal walk or to look at the fury of the PORTLAND RACE sea currents, it is also a site of geological interest, and for watching sea birds.

The two lighthouses (that of 1905 is still in use, the 1788 version is now a bird observatory) next to the Ministry of Defence buildings past PULPIT ROCK remind you that Portland, with its cliffs descending steeply into the sea, has been both a defence and a hazard throughout recent history. This rugged spot also seems like it must be at least a hundred miles from the esplanade at Weymouth, or the sands of Bournemouth and Poole. The variety of Dorset really is astounding.

As you travel up the western side of the island, the northern views to the mainland are filled by an unbroken line of shingle, the eight featureless miles of **CHESIL BEACH**, which has claimed more lives than any other stretch of coast in England. Chesil actually starts on the island, and the lower, western section of Fortuneswell is known as Chiswell, or Chesil.

Before you leave Portland it is worth mentioning ST GEORGE'S MEMORIAL CHURCH, which you will pass in the middle of the island if you use the main road. It is a strange collection of buildings, some plain, others almost light heartedly ornate, but the stories told by the gravestones are far from humorous. Among the sailors killed in many shipwrecks lies Mary Way, killed at the age of 21 by a party of marines sent ashore from the mainland on April 1st 1803 to press-gang some of the Portland men into serving in the navy. In this 'EASTERN MASSACRE' only three men were known to be captured, while four residents of the island died, including Mary.

The futility of the gruesome affair is further emphasised by the fact that nine sailors were so mutilated in the fighting that they were of no further use to the navy. Portland can be a hard place, especially when the winds blow off the sea onto its exposed cliffs, and its inhabitants have obviously been stubborn and strong to suit their surroundings.

Chesil Beach does not look so harmful from a distance. The shore appears smooth, and it looks for all the world like a much more attractive, natural version of the breakwaters on the other side of the island. The gruesome facts do not quite match its appearance.

This solid ridge is some 200 yards wide at the bottom, and up to sixty feet high, which means there is no shallows for any vessel driven too close to the bank. There is no opportunity to run aground, and storms can literally throw boats straight onto the rocks. The stones are largest at this end, becoming small, much more shingly pebbles by Abbotsbury, but a ship thrown out of the sea onto Chesil at any point, is usually lost. Escape onto the beach is made harder by the retreating waves, pulling any survivors straight back into deep waters across the slippery pebbles.

The immediacy of any shipwreck here led to some extremely nasty goings on in previous centuries. Organised bands of looters would patrol Chesil during bad weather, waiting for disaster to strike, and some would show false lights to lure ships to their doom. They would then kill survivors for any wealth they held in person, or amongst their cargo. Hundreds of ships have been lost here, and thousands of lives.

Happily, the most common activity on Chesil now is fishing, and for beach casting there can be few better places, although to reach most of the stranded ridge is not easy. The eight mile salt water lake formed behind Chesil, with just the one inlet to the sea near Portland, is THE FLEET, a popular place for ornithologists, with populations of herons, reed and sedge warblers and other species.

As the main roads take you away from Portland and the coast before turning west again, you will have seen the sea in some of its most fearsome settings, ready for the next storm; yet you have also experienced the archetypal seaside health resort of the 19th century just around the corner, safe for swimming, sailing and much else.

The mainland road takes you through **CHICKERELL**, where you will find BENNETTS WATER GARDENS (01305 785150). Norman Bennett first started growing Water Lilies in the disused clay pits here in 1959. If you like garden ponds, then this will be the place for you to see the largest version you are ever likely to find, with over 100 varieties of lilies, as well as enormous specimens of other moisture loving plants. The landscaped setting is ideal for a quiet afternoon spent watching out for the herons and kingfishers which can be seen around the eight acres of water.

The nearest main road to the Fleet runs a couple of miles behind it, taking you towards Abbotsbury through **PORTESHAM**. Hardy lived here too, but not the Hardy of the Wessex novels; this was Admiral Sir Thomas Masterman Hardy (1769-1839), the companion of Nelson, whose name will always be associated with the single "Kiss me Hardy" line, and the innumerable comedy sketches it has spawned.
There are various ancient monuments in the form of standing stones and barrows dotted around the grassy, sheep covered hills which surround the village, but a more recent one is the easiest to spot from distance. HARDY'S MONUMENT looks like a giant chimney with no building underneath, or an abandoned rook left behind at the end of a giant's game of chess, with seventy odd feet of Portland Stone tower on the point of highest elevation in the area.

This is Admiral Hardy's monument, and how different the view is here to that from Nelson's Column in Trafalgar Square, where his compatriot is remembered. There are very few buildings in the immediate area, and no sound of traffic at all. On a clear day you can see from the Devon coastline to the south west to Bulbarrow in the north. With Chesil and the Fleet completing the scene, there are few better places from which to consider the county as a whole, set in an area full of burial places from much earlier times, when perhaps even the middle of London was a very quiet place.

Heading further west along the B3157, a left turn just before you reach **ABBOTSBURY** will take you to the banks of the Fleet, and the ABBOTSBURY

SWANNERY (01305 871858). There are hundreds of swans living here in the only managed swannery in the world, which has been here for nigh on a thousand years.

The best time of year to visit is in the latter half of May and beginning of June, when chicks start to hatch in over a hundred nests, with an average of six coming from each nest. The experience of walking among a carpet of cygnets covering much of the pathways, their fluffy coats so unlike the regal plumage of their parents, is something special, and the compulsion to bend and take a closer look, halting to be amongst them, is quite irresistible.

Swans at Abbotsbury.

In the village of Abbotsbury itself is the TITHE BARN (01305 871817), the last remains of the Benedictine monastery that once stood here. The 15th century storage area is said to be the largest thatched barn in the world, but at over one hundred feet long, is still only half the size of the original structure.

Abbotsbury is one of the most beautiful villages in Dorset, isolated in its own green valley, and the many beautifully thatched, orange stone buildings make for a very agreeable walk. For an equally picturesque interior, try the parish church, of ST. NICHOLAS, another Dorset church with features from many different centuries.

The Swannery is one of the best places to get access to Chesil Beach, and the SUB TROPICAL GARDENS (01305 871387) to the south west of Abbotsbury, are even closer to the shore. These twenty acres of woodland gardens are so well sheltered that frost is an extreme rarity, and this, (much as at Compton Acres, Poole) allows for delicate and rare plants to be grown with success. There are miles of winding walks for you to explore, but the range from Formal Gardens featuring old roses, to the Southern Hemisphere Zone with herbaceous plants, is really quite stupendous. Rare plants are given their own area: the Secret Walk, and streams, ancient lily ponds and tropical trees help to make this a truly excellent place to spend a sunny afternoon.

Abbotsbury is in the centre of some gorgeous countryside, and a trek from the village up onto the surrounding hills, or down onto Chesil, will bring you further panoramas to treasure. CHAPEL HILL, in particular, is worth seeking out. Between these hills and the A35 to the north runs the BRIDE VALLEY, and a drive along some minor roads will take you through a succession of secluded villages such as **LITTON CHENEY, LONG BREDY, CHALCOMBE** and **LITTLE BREDY.** These have many 18th and 19th century cottages, and with the River Bride rushing through the beech trees, the surroundings have suddenly changed dramatically from those at Hardy's Monument just a few miles away.

By the RIVER BRIDE between Litton Cheney and **BURTON BRADSTOCK** there is an OLD FARMING COLLECTION at Bredy Farm (01308 897229), with equipment from processes such as cider making and timber preparation used over the centuries at this farm, which has been in existence at least since the Domesday Book was compiled.

The river goes underground at Burton Bradstock, but the village is still very beautiful, especially in the spring, when its many water meadows fill with flowers. Even the village Post Office is in a building which looks fit to feature in any photograph album, with immaculate thatch over whitewashed stone walls covered in the greenery of climbing plants.

As you approach **BRIDPORT** (Tourist Information 01308 424901) the caravan sites and golf course show that you are returning to the land of resorts, but this is no longer the fishing port it was three hundred years ago.

The nearest coast is at **WEST BAY**, which you can get to first from this direction as it is south east of the main town. There is a shingly beach, but this is a fishing and sailing port first, and any tourist trimmings still look superficial. The HARBOUR MUSEUM (01308 420997) tells much about the history of the bay, and its relationship with the life and industries of Bridport.

Views from the tops of the cliffs here include Portland and Lyme Regis, and there is a good section of the South West Coast Path leading back to Burton Bradstock.

Try a round trip, returning to West Bay in the evening, when the lights of Lyme reflect from the sea like a blaze of fire.

Many is the time I have chosen to take the route through Bridport to travel either east or west rather than keeping to the wider roads further inland, as the journey along this coast is scenic and relaxing, as long as you do not have a tight deadline, or arrival time at Poole to meet!

 ˙ Bridport is pleasant too, a market town with wide pavements and an agreeable lack of tall buildings and modern housing in its main street. So let's bring something dark from the town's past in now, to unsettle you in your otherwise contented exploration of the vicinity.

After the stories of pillage on Chesil Beach, a reference to being "stabbed with a Bridport dagger" will no doubt leave you fearing the worst. This is a traditional, if somewhat black, local euphemism.   The Romans are said to have provided the impetus when they planted the local fields with hemp. By the time of Henry VII all hemp grown within five miles of the town was to be reserved solely for Royal use, mostly for the Navy.

The rope and net industry, which kept Bridport alive when its fishing industry faded, had a darker side too. No-one has been "stabbed with a Bridport dagger" as a means of capital punishment in Britain for several decades now, so you can start to walk easy. Bridport rope was used for the hangman's noose for centuries, a thought which may still cause a slight shudder as you contemplate that slowest of all stabbings!

Hemp is no longer grown here in the age of nylon fibres, but the industry remains, providing everything from catch nets for jet fighters to the nets at Wimbledon, the last somehow making the balance complete and removing any last traces of morbid fascination about the place.

The BRIDPORT MUSEUM (01308 422116) in the centre of the town has a medieval stone porch which intrudes onto the pavement, inviting you to enter and find out about local history and to enjoy displays of local costume, fine art and natural history. The MUSEUM OF NET MANUFACTURE (also 01308 422116) is much more specific, but will require a trip to the north east of the town to the village of **LODERS** if you wish to find out more, and you will need to book at the Bridport Museum first.

A trip in this direction could also take in MANGERTON MILL (01308 485224), a working 17th century water mill with a museum attached. You may also like to add to the day by fishing in the trout lake, or just by following the riverside walk along the MANGER which starts at the mill.

Another local industry might appeal to you more. PALMERS BREWERY (01308 427500) is at the bottom of Bridport's main road, and you will see the visitors car park on your left as you approach from West Bay. It is the only thatched brewery in Britain, and it has been in continuous production for over two hundred years. Tours are available, and you will receive a certificate at the end, as well as a pint or two of the beer, which has earned glowing reports! You would not be alone in enjoying a drink in Bridport. There are many conflicting stories about the time Charles II came to the town to secure his escape to France. What is certain is he did make an attempt from here, and that it failed. One version has it that this was because he incautiously chose to 'hide' in the best inn of the town, and was discovered. An oft repeated mistake, and easy to make.

There is another story about a German U-Boat commander who calmly left his submarine off West Bay in the early months of World War Two, walking into Bridport in civilian clothes to enjoy an evening of jovial hospitality at an inn in South Street before getting a taxi back to the bay. Apocryphal? Perhaps, but this is a very welcoming place even now, and caters for you as a visitor without some of the more glamorous fuss of the major resorts. This is especially apparent during the carnival week, which is usually in August.

Although the methods of making rope have changed out of all recognition over the centuries, the relics of the industry have not gone from Bridport, even to the layout of the streets. The 'Rope Walks' were narrow side streets, with a large elevated hook placed at the closed end. Workers would twist the yarn by attaching it to the hook and walking back towards the main road. Today the streets make for a town centre which has kept its shape better than most, and for many by-ways to explore. There has been little demolition, as existing buildings have been adapted and put to new use, exemplified by the BRIDPORT ARTS CENTRE, near the town museum, which is also the WESLEYAN METHODIST CHAPEL of 1838.

The southern routes out of Bridport quickly become dominated by views of the GOLDEN CAP, with the highest sea cliffs on the whole of the South Coast (618ft). As you may have gathered, this particular part of the coast is one of my absolute favourites, and the orange and yellow topped hill between **SEATOWN** and Charmouth, with its exhilarating views in all directions of the compass reminds me of a phrase from a short story by Saki:

"a joy in life that was not passionate to the verge of being troublesome."

Dorset is sometimes the poor relation of the South West in the eyes of the tourist eager to find Newquay or Torbay, but the comfortable elegance of this county is nowhere better seen than here, where the view from the main road is one which has made many a driver pull over to the next stopping place for an unscheduled but joyful break.

Parts of the county such as this are not "troublesome" because they are not cut up ready for your inspection, unlike some other areas of our country which inspire more "passion" in the multitudes, and inevitably have to be carefully sectioned off to survive the feet of thousands. Yet the gentler beauty of much of rural Dorset has all the more power for being accessible.

The National Trust bought 26 acres including the Golden Cap in 1978, and with investments around Seatown has been building the 'Golden Cap Estate' steadily for more than thirty years. There are many cairns and other ancient burial mounds along the cliffs, presumably placed for the views and prominence afforded to their inhabitants. It is good that their resting places are now being protected for the future, the more so as they have already had three or four thousand years of uninterrupted rest. What would the countryside look like if the tradition had continued?

During that time they will have seen instances at Seatown of that already oft-mentioned Dorset hobby of the past: smuggling. If you go down onto the smooth pebbly beach it is easy to see why this was such an ideal location for the secretive loading and unloading of goods in the 18th and 19th centuries. As you look up to the east the 350 feet of crumbling blue clay named RIDGE CLIFF and then turn to see the even larger Golden Cap to the west, you can appreciate that the houses near where the trickle of the River WINNIFORD enters the sea are hidden from prying eyes about as effectively as dwellings on any shore could be.

The full height of the clay based Golden Cap, with the upper layers of sand that give the cliff its name, is particularly impressive from the beach, as you are standing the full six hundred plus feet below the summit. Now a great place for a bit of peace and quiet, Seatown was home to thirty or forty fishermen in the 18th century. It is said that they alone were responsible for keeping the price of a bottle of brandy in Yeovil to under four shillings for many years. Considerate people, obviously.

A larger, and more popular, beach awaits you to the west, at **CHARMOUTH**. When the tide is out there are two miles of firm sand between Golden Cap and BLACK VENN, the massive landslip to the west. With the River CHAR running into the sea between them, the lower cliffs at the rear of the beach are made of Jurassic Limestone, and have made Charmouth an area of Special Scientific Interest. Over the years the soft rocks erode, subside, and then reveal treasures hidden over millenia: fossils, ammonites, belemnites among them.

The CHARMOUTH HERITAGE COAST CENTRE (01297 560772) runs regular guided fossil hunting walks, and is on the seafront, at the eastern end of the Promenade. The village centre is about a half a mile walk back inland from this point, and is a pleasant place, made much quieter by the recent by-pass, which means that the very steep street through the middle of it has had a massive burden of passing traffic removed. I have particular reason to remember the earlier days, when the harsh gradient gave the final death blow to an ailing vehicle I had the misfortune to own.

LYME REGIS (Tourist Information 01297 442138) has streets which will also test many a vehicle, and as you descend winding hill roads to get to the town itself, you are discovering the final piece in the jigsaw of the south coast of Dorset.

Like Bournemouth and Weymouth, Lyme unashamedly survives through tourism; but perhaps unlike the other two there is one feature here that attracts more people than the rest of the resort, and ironically it is a relic of the town's practical past, rather than anything designed to bring visitors. Bournemouth and Weymouth may have mile upon mile of flat, sandy beach, but Lyme has a grey stone wall of Portland stone which runs out into the bay in a curve. This wall is special; this is THE COBB.

Few cinematic images are imprinted on the collective imagination as clearly as that of the heavily wrapped, dark shawled figure of Meryl Streep standing at the end of this sea wall, as part of the film version of John Fowles' novel 'The French Lieutenant's Woman.'

The Cobb was actually built in the 13th century to form a harbour for Lyme, and though the space inside it may now look much too small to offer serious docking facilities, Lyme was still an important port in the late 17th century. The first structure was made from oak timbers and huge loose stones, the present stone wall was built in the 1820s. By then it was realised that the wall also protected Lyme itself from erosion.

So why is it such a special, magnetic attraction? There are plenty of other sea walls, stone piers and breakwaters, along the south coast of Dorset alone. There is only one way to discover the appeal, and that is to walk along the Cobb, following its surface out into the bay. On a sunny, still day it is like a stroll along a fairly narrow promenade, but with water on both sides.

In rougher, or windier weather, the top of the Cobb becomes slippery with spray from the sea, and eventually from the waters of the waves themselves, then walking along it becomes out of the question. This can happen gradually, and in the early stages of a rainstorm you can find yourself suddenly seeing that wall as much narrower than it was a few minutes ago, when you confidently walked out along it, and the camber feels sharper too.

The Cobb was first linked to the land in 1756, and as you struggle through the summer crowds to get into the flow of humanity which heads for the sea down the steep streets, knowing full well that the climb back up will try you, and that there are emptier beaches to both the east and west, you will not be able to escape the fascination it has exercised on visitors ever since. The history of The Cobb and Lyme's harbour are explored in the MARINE AQUARIUM AND COBB HISTORY (01297 443678) which is in the 18th century warehouse at the landward end of the breakwater.

Lyme has other reasons to be famous, of which at least two are of a more significant nature than the Cobb, without the immediate romanticism. The DINOSAURLAND FOSSIL WORLD (01297 443541), placed on Coombe Street links the modern 'Jurassic' impetus of the films of Steven Spielberg with the exploits of a little girl born some two hundred years ago.

Mary Anning collected small fossils to sell to visitors, and to help her widow mother to provide for the family. Once she had found the fossilised remains of an Ichthyosaur she became a celebrity, and even more so when she unearthed the 30 foot skeleton of a Plesiosaurus a few years later. Just as Portland gave its best stone to London, so these fossils ended up in the British and Natural History Museums in the capital, where they made a tremendous impact.

Since then Lyme, and the coastline leading in both directions from it, has been a vital searchground for geologists trying to piece the distant past together, especially as landslips at Black Venn continue to bring new, fossil rich layers to the surface. There are many examples of their findings in the museum, but the image of a little girl carrying a bag and claw hammer while muddying her feet amongst the cliffs is still the one which will dominate this part of Lyme's history.

Perhaps the displays here and at the PHILPOT MUSEUM (01297 443370) will encourage you to roll up your trousers, or tuck in your skirt and start a fossil hunt of your own. If so, there are information sheets at Tourist Information to help you, and advice about watching the tides!

Views from higher in the town are excellent, and the coast to the west, into Devon, is as attractive as that to the east. But just to the west of the Cobb lies another black place in Dorset's history. MONMOUTH BEACH, with its layers of hard limestone and soft shale exposed in the reefs at low tide, is also the home to some of the oldest of all the fossils found in the area, but its name gives a clue to the source of its true notoriety.

Monmouth and his rebellion, and Judge Jeffries, have their places elsewhere in this book, and indeed this chapter, but this innocent beach marks the spot where the alleged son of Charles II first returned from Holland to try for the crown. That must have been a day of hope for those men of Lyme who became the first recruits to join him on the march north. Three of his ships sailed into Lyme on Thursday, the 11th June 1685. The beach saw hope that day, but Judge Jeffries made sure that the signs of despair were much more permanent. Of the many men executed for their part in the failed rebellion, eleven were quartered and their remains hung in baskets on this beach. This monument to the dangers of treason, and to the humanity of British justice, stayed in place for several years, the remains preserved in brine and dipped in tar. If you are not sure what quartering actually entailed, make sure you are of a strong stomach before researching any further.

I suspect you might prefer to echo the sentiments of Lord Tennyson, who when he first visited Lyme said:

"Don't talk to me of the Duke of Monmouth, show me the exact spot where Louisa Musgrove fell!"

Louisa is the heroine of Jane Austen's 'Persuasion'. Miss Austen came to Lyme to holiday, but collected the inspiration for the most dramatic episode of her last full novel. Back at the Cobb you will have noticed a set of lethal looking steps cut into the stone known as 'Granny's Teeth'.

Even in Jane Austen's elegant prose the drama of Louisa's fall is apparent, especially when you see the Cobb on a windy day:

"There was too much wind to make the high part of the new Cobb pleasant for the ladies, and they agreed to get down the steps....... all were contented to pass quietly and carefully down the steep flight, excepting Louisa; she must be jumped down them by Captain Wentworth. ..... she was safely down, and instantly, to show her enjoyment, ran up the steps to be jumped down again. He advised her against it, thought the jar too great; but no, he reasoned and talked in vain..... she was too precipitate by half a second, she fell on the pavement on the Lower Cobb, and was taken up lifeless!"

If you would like two more literary figures to think about while in Lyme, both in a way the true antithesis to Judge Jeffries, then how about Henry Fielding and Beatrix Potter. Fielding created a scandal at Lyme, when, as a young man, he tried to abduct an heiress by the name of Sarah Andrews. Does this sound familiar? If you know of the book 'Tom Jones' then you will have heard of another young heiress called Sophia Western. So 18th century Lyme inspired comic genius just as it later inspired drama. Lyme has also figured in children's literature, as it was the inspiration for the lovely but sinister 'Tale of Pig Robinson' by Beatrix Potter.

Lyme Regis played its part in military history during the Civil War, when the women of Lyme showed the same sort of heroism for the Parliamentarians during the 'Siege of Lyme' as Lady Bankes had done for the Royalists at Corfe Castle. But Lyme now is a peaceful place, and a walk among the older streets in the middle of the town, especially during the quieter parts of the year; or along the cliffs in either direction from the bay, will make a fitting end to your enjoyment of the south Dorset coast.

North of Lyme Regis, the borders between Devon, Dorset and Somerset become so confusing that you are never quite sure which county you are in. Even from LAMBERTS CASTLE, an iron age hill fort with long views from its 842 foot summit (which made it an ideal medieval beacon site), you will be hard pushed to distinguish between the three. This National Trust land is nevertheless a good place to get your bearings from, and it is surprising that the area holding the least green you can see from here, to the immediate south west, is actually part of Devon. I lived in this area for some time, and heard many long arguments about the correct county ownership and address of various villages, roads and even specific buildings. One Public House even has the distinction of having the Devon / Dorset border running through the middle of it, so that you can buy a drink in one county and drink it in another without purloining the glass!

So it is that FORDE ABBEY (01460 221290) comes to have a Taunton area postcode, a Chard telephone code, and yet is in West Dorset! If anyone tries to impress with local knowledge, you may wish to test their authenticity with these details.

It is not surprising that two or more counties might wish to fight over the ownership of this magnificent building and its gardens. The front of the Abbey manages to combine the appearance of a two storey castle with that of an ecclesiastical building, as well as a home.

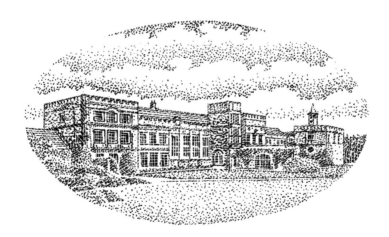

Forde Abbey

So how did such an imposing structure come to be built in such an out of the way place? In 1141 twelve monks were returning through this area to their home in Surrey. These Cistercians had attempted to set up an abbey in Devon, but had given up hope, until they were offered a slightly more easterly opportunity, in the shape of the manor of **THORNCOMBE**.

433

The only parts of the original twelfth century monastery which still survive are the present day chapel and the dormitory range behind it. The Abbot's Hall and cloister date from the 16th century, when the Abbey survived the dissolution of the monasteries by becoming a dwelling. Perhaps its remote location also helped to put Henry VIII off the looting scent!

Inside the Abbey you will find some exquisite furnishings, art, and plasterwork. As a whole the interior is as impressive as that of Kingston Lacy, although perhaps in a slightly less sumptuous style.

The gardens at Forde Abbey are superb, considered even by the locals to be worth frequent revisiting. There are many imported plants, including Asiatic Primulas, Meconopsis and others from the Himalayas in the BOG GARDEN, but it is the natural landscaping which gives the gardens their grace and power. Lakes, stocked with carp for the monks in years now gone, are amongst a fantastic variety of trees, herbaceous borders and shrubs. Add to this millions of seasonal daffodils, bluebells or crocuses, and even the occasional native orchid, and you begin to get a picture of the range covered. There can be few other places where you will find a combination of man made structure and natural setting as attractive and memorable as that at Forde. South East of Forde Abbey, it is not hard to find the highest point in the whole of Dorset; PILSDON PEN (908 feet). This is another National Trust owned Iron Age hill fort, but unlike Lamberts Castle, it has been excavated. As you make the challenging ten minute climb from the car park to the hilltop you can see why here, as at Badbury, the main defensive weapon was the sling.

Also in common with Badbury, this was one of the sites stormed by Vespasian's Romans, in about 45 A.D. It must have been an arduous day for the soldiers from warmer climes, struggling to scramble up the hill in battle dress, with stones flying at their heads.

A lack of trees makes this a tremendous place to see a great distance. Dartmoor and the Mendips can be glimpsed to the west, as can Portland Bill to the south. To the east, central Dorset is spread before you like a huge discarded green bedcover, hedges making a patchwork design on its undulating surface. It is fascinating to think that remains of a Romano-Celtic temple were found in the dig in the 1960s, and that the Celts who first built it in about 200 B.C. could see as much of Wessex in one go as any of us could possibly aspire to today, unless we take to the air!

Just to the east of Pilsdon you will come to the small, and seemingly insignificant village of **BROADWINDSOR**. There seems little more than a crossroads here, but Broadwindsor had a very near brush with lasting fame. Late in 1651, Charles II was still on the run, after his failure to leave the coast from Bridport. He slept in a cottage at Broadwindsor for one night, and the building has a plaque to celebrate this, but it could easily have become his last night of freedom.

A quiet place to stay, well hidden? Usually, yes, but on that particular night a force of troops heading for the last Royalist stronghold of Jersey was in the village. As if that wasn't disturbance enough for the inhabitants, one of the soldiers had a woman with him who gave birth that night. It is said that this event covered the king's tracks, although I must admit I do not exactly see how! On the eastern outskirts of Broadwindsor is the BROADWINDSOR CRAFT & DESIGN CENTRE (01308 868362), with exhibitions and workshops in minerals and crystals, hats, watercolours, and weather vanes; among many others.

The central lands of West Dorset, forming a funnel shape between the A356 and A35 which meet at Dorchester, are real Hardy country. The greens are darker than those of Purbeck, for instance, the hills more gentle in their shape. **BEAMINSTER** definitely feels and looks like it has just stepped out of a Hardy novel, although in fact it does not feature greatly in his work (*Emminster* does appear briefly in 'Tess'). What gives you that feeling is that as well as being a remote, compact village, at the head of the 'hidden valley' of the River Brit, Beaminster has remained largely unchanged, in terms of building, for the last century and more.

Driving around any of this area, you have to imagine what it would have been like before there were cars on the roads. As it is the hills seem to hide most human habitations from view, and with a patchwork of hedges and farming land one minute, and then a group of trees the next, it is easy to imagine the independence one small community could hold from its neighbours in Hardy's time.

Gabriel Oak, in 'Far From The Madding Crowd', loses his livelihood and travels to the nearest market to find employment as a shepherd. The fact that he is able to wander over the hills and make a completely fresh start just a few miles away seems quite plausible in these surroundings, as do the mysterious comings and goings of his rival Frank Troy.

BEAMINSTER MUSEUM (01308 862773/863200) is housed in the Old Congregational Chapel in the town, and has displays about the local buildings, history, and agriculture. Just north of Beaminster are HORN PARK GARDENS (01308 862212). They are only open on certain days, but are beautiful both for their varied content, and for the excellent views across the surrounding countryside. Both the house, built in 1910 by a pupil of Lutyens, and the hilltop gardens make an interesting contrast to Forde Abbey.

The local orange limestone used in nearly all the buildings of Beaminster is also in evidence at PARNHAM HOUSE (01308 862204), less than a mile south of the village. This is a splendid Elizabethan Manor House, with alterations in subsequent centuries which have not detracted from its overall character. Part of the building is now used for furniture making, specifically by the Makepeace Furniture Workshops.

Going east the valleys, if anything, become even more secluded and numerous. MAPPERTON HOUSE & GARDENS (01308 862645) is in one of these. The gardens are open, but tours of the Manor House are only available by prior appointment. The gardens near the house are quite formal, but the trees going down into the valley include an orangery, below which there are two carp ponds, and the walk down into the quiet wooded areas includes some lovely views.

The West Dorset District Council provides a whole series of leaflets outlining cycle rides around its areas of interest, and the Beaminster routes look particularly attractive. Contact the Tourist Information at Bridport or Dorchester if you wish to know more, and have some puff to spare.

As you are drawn gradually south east towards Dorchester, have a look at the tiny valleys and steep hills which surround **POWERSTOCK** , and the church of St Mary which sits on the hill above it. The church, with Norman chancel arch and a medieval doorway with figures in niches is an interesting one, and the terraced grey stone village also gives some superb views across the surrounding area.

From here you will see the iron age hill fort on EGGARDON HILL just to the south east again, and the open spaces of the fort make for another excellent place from which to examine the countryside for many miles around.

There is a chance to find out much more about life in Dorset some 2,000 years ago at the NEW BARN FIELD CENTRE (01305 267463), which is in **BRADFORD PEVERELL** just to the north west of the Dorchester by-pass. At the centre of a twenty acre Nature Reserve containing a multitude of wild flowers, the IRON AGE HOMESTEAD (open in the summer months) is an authentic 'living scene'. Wattle and daub huts show why the many hillforts and settlements are now so barren, just as the turning, carving and weaving explain how we come to have the smaller relics of pottery and cloth from this age in museums around the county, with many more still buried in the soil around undisturbed settlements.

Many of the towns of Dorset have had new roads built around them in the last ten or twenty years, in order to avoid destruction of the town centre (often a single straight street) by the ever increasing levels of traffic. This inevitable and desirable conservation measure has changed the character of some of the towns, and none so obviously as that of **DORCHESTER** (Tourist Information 01305 267992). After the miles of mostly empty countryside, the approach to Dorchester from the north used to be quite distinctive, as you entered the outskirts of the only really major town in central Dorset down a long , straight road, interrupted by a single roundabout before reaching the top of the hill on which the main streets have their place. Hardy's Dorchester was the centre of his real world and Casterbridge (its fictional pseudonym) was equally so in the Wessex of his novels. He thought of it as a self contained place; *"compact as a box of dominoes."*

Now it is harder to get your bearings, as the by-pass will take you right around the town without a real glimpse of it unless you head for the centre itself. Dorchester is still a thriving place, and modern building (such as the football stadium) has stayed far enough out of the centre to be fairly harmless too; it is just that it used to be a town you *had* to go through, and which was more than a name on a road sign to even the most impatient of travellers, and fully justified its status as County Town of Dorset..

The best place to start an exploration of Dorchester is at the DORSET COUNTY MUSEUM (01305 262735), right in the middle of the town. Local history, archaeology and geology are featured, and the museum has one of the largest collections of prehistoric and Roman items in the whole country. 1997 saw the features on Hardy and others revised into the DORSET WRITERS GALLERIES. The Hardy collection, including the largest collection of his original manuscripts (notably 'The Mayor of Casterbridge'), remains the prime attraction.

Further up the same side of High West Street are THE OLD CROWN COURT AND CELLS (01305 252241) where the TOLPUDDLE MARTYRS were tried in 1834. To get to the court you will have to go through the present day Council Offices, but the court was restored by the Trades Union Congress in 1956 as a tribute to the martyrs. The six men were tried for making an illegal oath while attempting to form a trade union for impoverished agricultural labourers. All six were found guilty and transported to Australia. They were later returned to the country and given compensation (see also Tolpuddle).

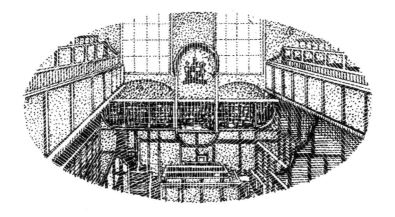

The Old Court House, Dorchester.

Underneath the court, you can take a tour of the cramped cells, always a sobering experience. Both court and cells are said to be exactly as they were in the early 19th century, and the almost ecclesiastical atmosphere makes this a very forbidding place.

This was not the Courthouse used for the darkest event in Dorchester's history. If you look to the other side of High West Street, opposite the museum, you will see an old timber fronted building called 'Judge Jeffries'. One of the oldest remaining buildings in the town, this is now a restaurant, but was formerly the lodgings of the infamous man during the BLOODY ASSIZES.

This was his base of operations during the aftermath of the Monmouth Rebellion. Dorchester was where he condemned nearly 300 people to horrible deaths (accepting bribes quite happily to have sentences reduced, or even in one case £1000 just to have the body buried rather than quartered and displayed), and sent another 800 or so to be transported, again accepting bribes to influence the exact destination! It is always nice to remember that the Judge himself ended up living out his last days confined in the Tower of London, after James II had fled the country, showing that there was some real justice at work amongst all the barbarity of the time.

To complete the gruesome side of Dorchester's history at a single attempt, it is worth mentioning that the town has the dubious distinction of being the location of the last public hanging in England, on August 10th 1858. This took place a little behind the museum, in what is now the prison car park. The condemned was a twenty year old James Seale, convicted of the murder of one of his father's lodgers, twenty three year old Sara Guppy. The Victorians considered the public spectacle to be inappropriate, so the open gallows took its last victim here. It is very likely that an eighteen year old Thomas Hardy was at the execution, and he was certainly present two years earlier when Martha Brown was executed for the murder of her husband in a 'crime of the heart', an event which provided inspiration for the conclusion of 'Tess of the D'Urbevilles.'

From the Court House it is a short walk up to the 'Top O'Town' roundabout, and the KEEP MILITARY MUSEUM (01305 264066) run in celebration of the DEVONSHIRE AND DORSET REGIMENT. The history of the regiments which have combined over the last three centuries to make up the two county force is explored through displays of uniform, medals, weapons etc, but also through the use of modern multimedia and interactive applications. This museum is maintained with particular pride, and is also worth a visit to walk the battlements of the Victorian Keep, from which you can see Dorchester in a wider setting.

Returning down the hill on the opposite side of High West Street, you will have a chance to look at a very different historical display at THE TUTANKHAMUN EXHIBITION (01305 269571). The treasures and mummy are facsimiles, but are fascinating none the less.

If you carry on your walk past the end of South Street towards the lower end of the town, you will find yet another attraction off to the right, the DINOSAUR MUSEUM (01305 269880). This boasts the distinction of being the only museum in the country devoted solely to the subject of Dinosaurs. The advantage of this is that it is not only the scientific and geological aspects of fossils and so on that are explored; there are life size reconstructions of dinosaurs which are made to be touched and approached in a way fossilised remains could never safely be.

Other attractions near the centre of Dorchester include the TEDDY BEAR HOUSE (01305 263200) in Antelope Walk, where you can meet a family of life size teddy bears; and ELDRIDGE POPE & CO. (01305 251251) a local traditional real ale brewery which has guided tours available.

All these attractions are packed into a very compact area, and in between the various museums the High Street has some tidy examples of 18th and 19th century architecture. Of course Dorchester has a much longer history than this would suggest. With the name *Durnovaria* it was the only Roman town in Dorset, and later, when the Domesday Book was compiled (1086), it consisted of 172 houses.

Many of the medieval and Tudor houses of Dorchester were thatched, and a fire in 1613 accounted for about half of the town. The rector of both Dorchester parishes of the time did not lose any time in impressing upon the local inhabitants that such devastation could only be seen as vengeance from God. He was John White, a famous puritan who went on to be a founding figure in the foundation of the Massachusetts colony in the U.S.A.

ST PETER'S CHURCH, on the corner of South Street and the High Street, is the only surviving medieval church, and some features, including the pulpit, are exactly as they would have been in the days when this preacher used a natural disaster to bind the remains of his flock into a new community. The puritanism of 17th century Dorchester was bold, almost revolutionary in its own way, with alms houses, hospices, and even the begins of community health care.

At the end of the north aisle of the same church is a monument to Denzel, Lord Holles, who died in 1679. In full Roman costume, and reclining on a large cushion, with his left hand upon his chest he looks anything but a serious political figure. In fact he was one of the five Members of Parliament who Charles I tried to have arrested in the dramatic events leading to the Civil War. Holles fled the country during the war itself, and managed to return later and be reconciled to Charles II, who made him a Privy Councillor.

Dorchester was considered by the Royalists to be the source of many of the ideas which led to the Parliamentary rebellion, but when the King's forces arrived in Dorset in 1643 the town surrendered without a fight, and John White fled to London. The Royalist fled themselves in 1644, and Dorchester changed hands again, however it is said that Cromwell himself was lucky to escape with his life when an attack fronted by 800 cavalry scattered his troops in the town in 1645, after which Dorchester gradually reconciled itself to the idea of a monarchy.

St Peter's Church was restored by a local architect in 1856, whose 16 year old assistant was a certain Mr Thomas Hardy. Do not be confused, though, by the monument by the doorway, which is dedicated to Thomas Hardye, not a literary man, but the founder of the local Grammar School. The more famous Mr Hardy has a much more prominent statue, by Eric Kennington (as is the figure of Lawrence of Arabia in Wareham) and erected in 1931, which you cannot have missed if you have come through the 'Top O'Town' area.

Lines of trees were planted to replace the Roman walls of Dorchester when the remnants were pulled down in the 18th century. Starting from Hardy's statue you can follow a path around the centre of town, ending up back where you started, using these famous WALKS. Head for the river past the ARTS CENTRE, and they will take you near the thatched HANGMAN'S COTTAGE, before heading south. Here too you can find THE ROMAN HOUSE, which has some splendid geometrical mosaics.

Fragments of the walls do still remain, but for the most part you will have a pleasant, shaded route around the town centre, without having to negotiate any motorised traffic. The other Roman element to the town is now deserted, but MAUMBURY RINGS is where the Amphitheatre stood. Outside the circumference of this walk, on the road towards Wareham, is MAX GATE. This is where Thomas Hardy lived for the last forty three years of his life, in a house he had built to his own designs in 1885. The house is not always open to the public, so check first with Tourist Information if you wish to know the current situation before visiting. Hardy's study, where he wrote novels until 1896, before concentrating solely on poetry, has been recreated in The County Museum, and the rest of Max Gate has been used as a private residence for many years.

Max Gate officially belongs to the National Trust, as does Hardy's birthplace, to the south east of Dorchester at **HIGHER BOCKHAMPTON**. HARDY'S COTTAGE (01305 262366) is hidden away in the THORNCOMBE WOODS to the south of the A35, and is a tiny place. Hardy was sometimes known to be reticent about his humble upbringing, which was quite ordinary in comparison to his later fame, but he also talked with affection of this simple cob, brick and thatch home built by his great-grandfather in 1800.

Hardy's Cottage, Higher Bockhampton, near Dorchester.

Hardy returned here as an adult to write his early novels, saying in later life that he was helped by being in the middle of the places and people he was attempting to describe. The cottage is a real insight into Hardy's Wessex; it lacks ostentation, which suited the times when Dorset's agricultural workforce was the worst paid in the whole of England. Yet as you walk through the woods, maybe continuing into PUDDLETOWN FOREST, or taking up one of the signed Nature Trails, it is easy to see how the countryside became as much of an inspiration as the hard lives of those around him.

Hardy was famous for his agnosticism, but loved the church at **STINSFORD**, again on the eastern outskirts of Dorchester. His parents, sister and first wife Emma were buried here, and he used to cycle from Max Gate to visit their graves. For his own death Hardy made unusual arrangements. His ashes are in Westminster Abbey, but his heart is buried here with Emma.

Some morbid humour from local folklore says that the undertaker's cat actually got hold of the heart, and that the cat was then strangled and placed in the urn so the heart would be where its owner had wished. Another version has it that it was the doctor's cat, and that it only did a little bit of damage. With such easy material for horror there were bound to be some gruesome stories. Whatever the truth, it is fitting that some part of the great author should remain in the land he loved and brought such lasting fame to.

A few hundred yards from Stinsford, and just off the A35, you will find KINGSTON MAURWARD PARK (01305 264738). The huge classical Georgian house is now an Agricultural College, and is not open to the public, but the extensive gardens around it are. With 35 acres of lawns, water gardens, lakes and woodlands of specimen trees, these are well worth a visit. The impressive exterior of the house puts the 'jardin anglais' style of sweeping lawns and parklands down to the lake in an ideal perspective.

Let's end this journey through the heart of Hardy's Wessex by visiting a site which was here long before he was ever thought of, and was here before the Romans first created *Durnovaria* which became Dorchester, which also became Casterbridge.

MAIDEN CASTLE has the distinction of being the largest Iron Age hillfort site in England, with its four concentric ramparts enclosing some 45 acres within the one a half mile inner circumference. Climb to the top, where the first remains suggest habitation more than 5,000 years ago, and you can see down onto the by-pass and over Dorchester itself, but the space is empty, very empty.

Between two and two and a half thousand years ago it was Dorchester that was empty, and this was the heart of a thriving community, quite probably one of the largest in the whole country. Maiden Castle, inhabited by the Durotrige people, flourished right up until Vespasian and his troops arrived in approximately 45 A.D. Much as at Badbury and Pilsdon, the Romans were victorious, but only after a considerable fight. The spine of one of the defenders can be seen at the County Museum, with a Roman arrowhead still embedded in it.

This was the most important victory for the Romans though, and the structure of Maiden Castle, imposing today despite its complete isolation, helped them to win it. Apparently it was all to do with Pythagoras' Theorem. Until the Romans arrived, the hillfort had proved a more than adequate defence against other tribes, with the usual slings, and spears being most effective when hurled down the slopes from behind the earthworks surrounding the summit. Unfortunately the Romans did not have to storm the hill until they were good and ready, because their siege catapults were most effective at the range of 300 yards. From the bottom to the top of Maiden Castle is 200 yards, and the mechanics of a squared triangle, as the great Greek theorised, make this the perfect distance at which to put your crude artillery.

As you stand on the barren green of the enclosure, which now looks like no more than an empty speedway stadium, imagine what it must have been like to be here on that fateful day. You had pardonable confidence that you would never be defeated; after all you were in the best fortress in the land. Then the Romans arrive, and instead of storming the hill, or shouting threats and war-cries, they parade around the base of your encampment, in a show of order and organised force you would be amazed at.

You prepare to give them the treatment that has worked for so many others, sling shot at the ready; and then the heavy rocks start to fall amongst you, crushing some, and scaring all. The Romans can still not be reached, and by the end of the day the world of Dorset has been changed forever.

Of all the fascinating places in the county, this is hard to beat, for this was the centre of a civilization, and now it is completely deserted, and were it not for our curiosity about the past, could be levelled and forgotten forever, to become another bulge in the green blanket of land which guards the outside of Dorchester's by-pass.

THE BRIDGE HOUSE HOTEL
Beaminster
Dorset
DT8 3AY

AA***

Bridge House is scheduled as an Ancient Monument, at first sight it might appear to be an oddly planned Tudor House, the stone mullion windows are certainly of that period (1560-1600). But the fact that they are all of different sizes and in some cases at different levels seems to suggest that they were inserted in Tudor times to convert an older building into an ordinary dwelling house. It is a fascinating place and makes a delightful hotel. The original coach house was restored and converted to bedrooms in 1988 and in 1991 an extension to the newer wing was built providing five new bedrooms.

From the log fires crackling in the centuries-old inglenook to the candle-lit pastel panelled Georgian dining room, the objective of this privately owned hotel, from the very beginning, has been to create a comfortable, country home of a hotel. Books by Thomas Hardy and baskets of dried flowers nestle in the corners of this 13th century priest's house, providing a natural backdrop to the well being of every one of its guests. Character has not been sacrificed for comfort - though comfort there is in plenty.

At the heart of the Bridge House is the food. Whether you are taking a light lunch in the conservatory, or dining from a menu where the combination of simplicity and fine materials makes every meal a new experience, you are benefiting from a rare attention to detail that makes special use, wherever practicable, of fresh produce from the local farms and fishing ports.

Every bedroom is charmingly and individually decorated incorporating all that is required by the modern day traveller. All the rooms are ensuite, have colour television, direct dial telephones and a hostess tray. Some of the rooms are at ground level making them popular with guests who find stairs difficult.

The character old market town of Beaminster is most convenient for touring, walking and exploring the magnificent West Dorset countryside. There are many places of interest and fine houses and gardens within easy reach by car, as well as several golf courses, fresh and salt water fishing, horse-riding, sailing and sea bathing.

USEFUL INFORMATION

- OPEN: All year
- WHEELCHAIR ACCESS: Yes
- GARDEN: Beautiful, walled
- CREDIT CARDS: All major cards
- ACCOMMODATION: All ensuite rooms
- RATES: Dbl from £65 -£107 Sgl from £58 -£76 Getaway Breaks available

- DINING ROOM: High quality using fresh local produce whenever possible
- VEGETARIAN: Always a choice
- LICENSED: Yes
- CHILDREN: Yes

BURTON CLIFF HOTEL
Cliff Road
Burton Bradstock
Bridport
Dorset
DT6 4RB

Tel: 01308 897205
Fax: 01308 898111

ETB 3 Crowns Commended

Burton Cliff Hotel occupies a unique cliff top position overlooking Lyme Bay and is surrounded by Heritage Coast and National Trust countryside. It lies roughly halfway between Lyme Regis and Weymouth and is situated just above the ancient fishing village of Burton Bradstock with its many thatched cottages. Because of its position the hotel is well known as a centre for Nature and Landscape photography and is the home base for a very active Bridport Camera Club. Ramblers walking the Coastal Footpath also find the hotel a welcoming overnight stop. Visitors will find the steps to the Coastal Footpath and to the beach lead from the hotel. There is so much to do in this interesting and historic part of Dorset and Burton Cliff Hotel makes an ideal base.

The Hotel has 18 attractive bedrooms plus a small children's bunk-bedded room. Five doubles and seven twin rooms are ensuite. Each room has direct dial telephone, television and a hostess tray. Pets are permitted but in ground floor rooms only. The hotel happily accommodates wheelchairs with 5 rooms on the ground floor and a gentle ramp at the entrance. One ground floor room has an English Tourist Board category 1 rating for wheelchairs, whilst others are often suitable depending on the degree of disability. There is a comfortable lounge and a cosy bar. Many people enjoy the sheer beauty of the sea from the Cliff top lawn - a delightful spot in which to enjoy a pre-dinner drink.

Slightly unusually the hotel is owned and run by David and June Barnikel, who do so with consummate professionalism but the difference is that all the catering is conducted as a separate business by Judy Stamford and her family. The food is excellent. Breakfast is a generous feast of your choosing. There is an a la carte and a table d'hôte menu in the evening and lunches, bar meals and children's meals are available daily. Sunday lunch is traditional. Vegetarian and Vegan are specially catered for.

USEFUL INFORMATION

- OPEN: Not open at Xmas
- WHEELCHAIR ACCESS: Yes
- GARDEN: Cliff top, sea views
- CREDITCARDS: Visa/Master/Switch/JCB
- ACCOMMODATION: 18 rooms
  12 ensuite
- RATES: From £20 pp B&B
  Short breaks 2days B&B £37-£54

- DINING ROOM: Good, traditional fare
- VEGETARIAN: Yes, and vegans!
- BAR MEALS: Yes. Wide range
- LICENSED: Yes

- CHILDREN: Welcome

- PETS: Yes. Ground floor only

THE CASTERBRIDGE HOTEL
49 High East Street
Dorchester
Dorset DT1 1HU

Tel: 01305 264043
Fax: 01305 260884

ETB ** Crown Highly Commended
RAC Highly Commended
Good Hotel & Which Guides, Michelin,
Fodor, Frommer, Lonely Planet etc.

In the centre of the historic county town of Dorset and named Casterbridge by Thomas Hardy, this Georgian residence with its concealed courtyard annexe combines to provide a peaceful haven behind the bustling street. The owners Rita and Stuart Turner now own and run the business started by Stuart's grandparents. Both are Dorset born and bred and have a great love and knowledge of the county which they are happy to share with their guests. They will plan routes for you, arrange days out, book restaurants and generally do anything they can to ensure your stay is a happy one.

Some eighteen years ago Stuart and Rita, paying particular attention to the period features of the building, added ensuite bathrooms and many other requirements relevant to the comfort of discerning guests today. The result is an immaculate, charming hotel with its original flagstone entrance, furnished with choice antiques, fresh flowers everywhere and a conservatory complete with a fountain where breakfast is served every day. All the rooms are ensuite and some have King size beds and the others Queen size, whilst some of the singles have 4ft beds. Every room is furnished in period style with high quality fabrics and drapes. They all have direct dial telephones, television, and a hostess tray. The cosy bar and library have an honesty bar whilst the comfortable lounge is always there for anyone wanting to sit quietly.

Stuart and Rita have cared for people for years and this is apparent here in The Casterbridge where the atmosphere is very much that of a country house. They are in partnership with John Turner who cares for The Priory Hotel at Wareham, another delightful place which affords a high degree of luxury for the more affluent guest.

USEFUL INFORMATION

- OPEN: All year except Dec25th & 26th
- WHEELCHAIR ACCESS: Yes
- GARDEN: Walled courtyard
- CREDITCARDS: Visa/Master/AMEX/Euro/Diners
- ACCOMMODATION: 14 En suite rooms
- RATES: Sgl from £38 Dbl. from £64
  Winter week-ender 2 nights @ £29 per night 3 nights @ £25 per night

- DINING ROOM: Superb breakfast
- VEGETARIAN: Excellent buffet
- LICENSED: Residential
- CHILDREN: Welcome
- PETS: No

THE DEVON HOTEL
Uplyme
Lyme Regis
Dorset
DT7 3TQ

Tel: 01297 443231
Fax: 01297 445836

3 Star Highly Commended RAC ***
Merit Award for Hospitality & Service

This historic Manor House began as a monastery around 774AD and the stone flagged cellars and catacombs from that time are still there. It is an atmospheric house with an ornately carved oak chimney breast in the reception area originating from the Parish Church. The dining room is magnificent with ornate panelling, sixteen foot fireplace and hammer vaulted ceiling bearing heraldic shields.

The Devon Hotel is run with the needs of the guests being paramount. Towards that there are some excellent week-end courses between October and March including Fitness for the over fifty, Ladies health and beauty and one on developing your dramatic skills. Once during the low season there is also a Murder Mystery Weekend.

The hotel stands in its own landscaped gardens and is the epitome of warmth and comfort. All the bedrooms are ensuite and complete with television, telephone and tea/coffee making facilities. The food served in the Ethelston Restaurant is superb. There are speciality evenings including medieval banquets and French, Italian and Caribbean evenings. The pool is normally open from mid-May to mid-September. Sunday membership of the pool includes a traditional Sunday lunch in the historic Jacobean restaurant. Uplyme is a picturesque village and is only five minutes drive to the coast. Lyme Regis close by is beautiful in its own right and the setting for many novels including Jane Austen's 'Persuasion' and John Fowles 'French Lieutenant's Woman'. It would be hard not to enjoy the Devon Hotel.

USEFUL INFORMATION

- OPEN; All year
- WHEELCHAIR ACCESS; Yes
- GARDEN; Beautiful. Heated swimming pool. Putting Green, Solarium, Gymnasium, Games Room
- CREDIT CARDS; Visa/Master/Amex
- ACCOMMODATION; Ensuite bedrooms Short Breaks; specialist weekends
- RATES: £35 B&B £45 DB&B Children free if sharing with parents Food charged as taken

- RESTAURANT; Open to non-residents. Superb food
- VEGETARIAN; Always a choice
- BAR FOOD; Wide range of food available daily
- LICENSED; Yes. Full On
- PETS; Yes £2 a night
- CHILDREN; Welcome

THE ELM TREE
Shop Lane
Langton Herring
NR Weymouth
Dorset
DT3 4HU

Tel: 01305 871257

This must be one of the nicest pubs in Dorset. It is situated in beautiful countryside close to Chesil Bank and Fleet Lagoon with its nature preservation. The village quietly nestles away from the hurl burly of modern living and yet it is just 15 minutes from Weymouth or Dorchester. The Elm Tree, built in the 16th century, was once a famous haunt for smugglers and a fisherman was once hanged from a ship's mast. Barnes Wallis, the designer of the famous Dam Busters bomb, used to lunch here when the bomb was being tested on Chesil Beach. More recently spies Harry Oughton and Ethel Gee used the inn whilst passing on information to the KGB. Younger members of the Royal family have called in here and it is not unusual to see famous actors enjoying a drink or a meal whilst they are 'resting' in Dorset.

Roberto D'Agostino and Lorraine Horlock own and run The Elm Tree and it is their hard work and instinctive feeling that makes it such a success. Roberto is a classically trained chef and produces exquisite food. Both he and Lorraine believe in ensuring that the service is good and they have succeeded, the waiting staff are all in classic black and white and the male bar staff always wear ties. The country pub ambience has been retained and the food is worthy of any high class restaurant. Roberto and Lorraine will tell you that people come here for the food and the hospitality not to dress and impress!

USEFUL INFORMATION

- OPEN: 10.30-3pm & 6-11pm
- WHEELCHAIR ACCESS: Yes
- GARDEN: Yes

- CREDIT CARDS: None taken
- CHILDREN: Welcome

- RESTAURANT; Superb food
- VEGETARIAN: Exciting & unusual
- BAR FOOD: Extensive menu. Continental flair
- LICENSED: Full On
- PETS: Outside only

THE HOTEL ALEXANDRA
Pound Street
Lyme Regis
Dorset
DT7 3HZ
Tel: 01297 442010
Fax: 01297 443229
E:Mail: alexandra@lymeregis.co.uk.
Internet: http://www.lymeregis.co.uk

RAC ***AA ETB****Highly Commended.
Ashley Courtenay, Egon Ronay

Lyme Regis appeals essentially to those who, on holiday, look for peace and quiet amongst surroundings of interest and beauty. To compliment this need, to pamper, to provide delicious food at every meal, there can be no more charming place to stay in Lyme Regis than the Hotel Alexandra, the epitome of all that a small, high class hotel should be. From the beautiful grounds in which it stands, a private gate opens into The Langmoor Gardens, through which a short walk brings you to the beach and the famous Cobb. In the summer months one can simply sit and gaze out to sea if one wishes, watching the small craft which fill Lyme's quaint old harbour, or look at the Cobb made world famous by local author John Fowles in The French Lieutenant's Woman or Jane Austen's Persuasion. The Hotel was built in 1735 and was the home of the Dowager Countess Poulett and later the Duc du Stacpoole. It became a hotel at the beginning of the century and even now the charm and dignity of a former age may still be felt. There are twenty six bedrooms, all with private bathrooms, colour television, direct dial telephone, hairdryers, individually controlled thermostatic heating, tea and coffee making facilities, radio and baby listening. The majority of the rooms command superb sea views over Lyme Bay and The Cobb. The Sitting Room is a truly relaxing room, ideal for quiet evenings by the fire, reading or playing board and card games from the games chest. The south facing Conservatory with views across the lawn, is a much appreciated sun-trap in the spring, autumn and winter months where guests may enjoy informal lunches and afternoon tea. The Hotel Alexandra is known for the quality of its food. The elegant restaurant is perfectly appointed and the menus prepared by an imaginative and talented chef are classical French with traditional English cooking. As the perfect complement the cellar has bottles and half bottles of specially selected wines from the celebrated regions of France and other wine-producing countries of the world. Informal lunches are served every day from 12-2pm in the bar, conservatory or the garden. Packed lunches are available and a delicious Dorset Cream Tea complete with freshly baked scones, jam and lashings of clotted cream, tempts many people to return to the hotel early. Special Spring and Autumn Breaks are available and throughout the year when people stay seven nights, the seventh night is free.

USEFUL INFORMATION

- OPEN: All year
- WHEELCHAIR ACCESS: No
- GARDEN: Yes
- CREDIT CARDS: All major cards
- ACCOMMODATION: 26 ensuite rooms
- RATES: Sgl from £50 B&B Dbl from £84 Children £15pn. No charge under 2 Special Breaks Spring/Autumn

- RESTAURANT: Classical French and traditional English cuisine
- VEGETARIAN: Always a choice
- BAR FOOD: Informal lunches & teas
- LICENSED: Full On
- CHILDREN: No

- PETS: Yes £4 per night

THE MANOR HOTEL
West Bexington
Dorchester
Dorset
DT2 9DF

Tel:01398 897616/897785
Fax: 01308 897035

The Manor Hotel is a delightful and popular hotel set in rural surroundings with a garden that is just 300 yards from the sea. It is delightful to stay in for a holiday or a short break and a very pleasant place for non-residents to dine. Richard and Jayne Childs are the resident owners and their ethos is that the comfort and well-being of their guests is paramount.

Every room is furnished with a harmonious mixture of traditional and antique pieces in keeping with the age of the house. There are thirteen bedrooms all ensuite and with either bath or shower. Each room has pretty drapes and bedcovers, colour television, direct dial telephone and a hostess tray.

At night there is a first class dinner of two or three courses - residents staying on Dinner, Bed and Breakfast terms are entitled to a three course meal. There are fourteen delicious starters from which to choose and an equal number of perfectly cooked and presented main courses followed by the sweet or cheese board. The cosy bar is open daily and here you can get a light meal or snack.

West Bexington is an ideal base. From here one can look for fossils on Chesil Beach, walk along the cliff tops, go fishing, take a look at the world famous Abbotsbury Swannery and Gardens as well as the many National Trust houses and gardens within reach. The nearest golf course is at Bridport seven miles away.

USEFUL INFORMATION

- OPEN: All year Bar 12-2pm & 6.30-10pm
- WHEELCHAIR ACCESS: Restaurant & Conservatory only
- GARDEN: Yes
- CREDIT CARDS: All major cards
- ACCOMMODATION: 13 ensuite rooms
- RATES: Sgl £52 pppn B&B Dbl £44 pppn B&B

- RESTAURANT: Delicious fare open to non-residents
- VEGETARIAN: Yes
- BAR FOOD: Yes
- LICENSED: Full On. Extensive wine list
- CHILDREN: Welcome
- PETS: No

451

THE OLD RECTORY.
Winterbourne Steepleton
Dorchester
Dorset DT2 9LG
Tel: 01305 889468 Fax: 01305 889737
E.Mail: trees@eurobell.co.uk.
http://homepage.eurobell.co.uk/trees/Welcome.html
2 Crown Highly Commended (ETB)

When a visitors book reads so appreciatively as it does at The Old Rectory with remarks such as 'quite delightful, perfect for reducing the pulse-rate' or 'what a magnificent house - thank you very much for a very pleasant stay! We will be back.' with hundreds of other entries running in a similar vein, then this has to be the place to stay for those who enjoy a relaxed, informal atmosphere, good food, good company and superb service. The Old Rectory is a Victorian Country House Bed & Breakfast situated in a quiet hamlet surrounded by breathtaking countryside. Rectories have occupied the site for hundreds of years as evidenced by a certified Yew Tree planted during the Civil War and the present building was solidly built with Caen stone imported in 1850 for the construction of Little Bredy Church. Queen Elizabeth signed the deeds releasing the house from the Church Commissioners and in 1989 it was opened to guests by the owners Captain and Mrs Tree. This ex-mariner and his French wife have travelled extensively and understand well the needs of their many guests. This is reflected in the provision of a quiet comfortable nights sleep in well appointed bed rooms with welcoming toiletry baskets, as well as coffee and tea making facilities. A copious English, Vegetarian or Continental breakfast is served in the garden room which overlooks the beautiful courtyard enclosed by the flower bedecked outbuildings of the old tack rooms, coach house, stable and Sunday School. Eggs are fresh laid organic and free range from the owners chickens and the bread home made, as well as the extensive range of organic jams traditionally made by Mrs Tree from the garden soft fruit of strawberries, raspberries, blackcurrants, blackberries supplemented by apple, plum, peach, pear, damson and cherry trees. Incidentally the organic jam can be purchased from Mrs Tree. The Crystal Room is available for special celebration dinners and Cordon Bleu cuisine served with full silver service for those special occasions and by prior appointment. The superbly appointed guests lounge caters for the most discerning music ear with concert fidelity audio equipment and a wide music selection ranging from classics and opera to jazz, swing and the blues. Alternatively guests can relax and delve into a wide selection of good books and guides to Dorset and its hidden treasures. The well appointed grounds of one acre offer guests the opportunity to play English croquet on manicured lawns or to relax and enjoy themselves on a separate six hole mini golf lawn. Golfing facilities are close by and Mountain bikes are available. Covered or secure parking enclosed within electronic gates is also available. The hamlet of Winterbourne Steepleton is close to the historic Roman town of Dorchester and the sandy beaches of Weymouth and has a wide selection of local restaurants and pubs, one of which is in walking distance and also caters for the very young.

USEFUL INFORMATION

- OPEN: 1st Jan-23rd December
- WHEELCHAIR ACCESS: No
- GARDEN; 1 acre, croquet, mini golf
- CREDIT CARDS: None taken
- ACCOMMODATION: Well appointed bed rooms
- RATES: From £19 per person B& B

- DINING ROOM: English & Continental breakfasts
- VEGETARIAN: Yes
- LICENSED: No
- **Strictly non-smoking house**

- CHILDREN: Welcome
- PETS: No

THATCH LODGE HOTEL
The Street
Charmouth
Dorset
DT6 6PQ

Tel/Fax: 01297 560407

ETB Three Crowns Highly Commended AA**
74% Two Rosettes Johansens Recommended

Dating back to 1320 Thatch Lodge Hotel is quite perfect. Naturally it has a thatched roof, pink cob walls, hanging baskets, oak beams, a conservatory with a 200 year old vine and extensive walled gardens where you can relax and unwind in a smoke-free environment. Grade II Listed it has been lovingly restored by its present owners, Christopher and Andrea Ashton-Worsfold. The environment is peaceful enhanced by antiques and unusual artefacts. It makes a perfect base from which to explore West Dorset with Golden Cap, the highest cliff on the south coast, to the east, and to the west Lyme Regis, with its romantic Cob which featured both in 'The French Lieutenant's Woman' and Jane Austen's 'Persuasion'. There is the Thomas Hardy Trail, the Dorset Heritage Coast, Abbotsbury swannery and sub tropical gardens, Montacute House (NT), Golf tennis, riding, fishing, bird watching, walking and World renowned fossil collecting on the beach at Charmouth itself.

Each of the seven bedrooms (one on the ground floor) have their own character having been sympathetically and individually decorated - some have Four poster and Half tester beds. Luxury toiletries, crisp sheets, a comprehensive courtesy tray, television and thoughtful extras add to your comfort. The principal bedroom has outstanding views of Charmouth and Golden Cap beyond, other rooms have picturesque front or rear garden views.

An outstanding feature of the 'Thatch' is the fine Inglenook Restaurant. Andrea, a qualified and talented Chef, creates mouth watering imaginative delights, cooked to order, using only the freshest seasonal produce (fruit and herbs from the garden). The result is a meal that will delight the eye and excite the palate. Awarded two AA Rosettes for outstanding cuisine. A comprehensive wine list compliments the experience. The 'Thatch Breakfast' is the extra special way to start your day with a selection of juices, cereals and a full English cooked breakfast.

USEFUL INFORMATION

- OPEN: All year except mid January, February open mid March
- WHEELCHAIR ACCESS: No
- GARDEN: Large garden
- CREDIT CARDS: Most major cards
- ACCOMMODATION: 7 ensuite rooms
- RATES: From £30-£50pp B&B

- RESTAURANT: By prior reservation only
- VEGETARIAN: By arrangement
- **NO SMOKING PERMITTED**
- LICENSED: Residential
- CHILDREN: Not accepted
- PETS: Not welcome

CHIMNEYS GUEST HOUSE
Main Street
Chideock
NR Bridport
Dorset
DT6 6JH

Tel/Fax: 01297 489368

The owners of this enchanting, 17th century thatched cottage, Jenny and Trevor Yerworth, fell in love with it when they stayed here for their first wedding anniversary and from that moment on they were determined it would be theirs. Happily for the many satisfied guests who stay here, they were successful. The cottage is full of character, and the guests lounge has a remarkable beamed ceiling comprising 16 compartments. Several other rooms also have exposed beams. The Yerworth's have created a delightful relaxed, informal atmosphere in which their guests can unwind and enjoy a peaceful break. There are four ensuite bedrooms and 1 not ensuite. One bedroom has an old four-poster and they all have hospitality trays. Two rooms also have television. Breakfast offers a choice of fruit juice, cereals, grapefruit segments, followed by a choice of kippers, eggs, bacon etc. with plenty of toast and marmalade. Chimneys is licensed and there is a selection of bottled beers brewed by the local Palmers Brewery in Bridport. Chideock is just one mile from the unspoilt beach at Seatown, well known for its fossils and dramatic Coastal walks. Quaint villages, iron age hill forts, beautiful countryside all make for a great holiday if you are based at Chimneys.

USEFUL INFORMATION

- OPEN; All year except Christmas
- WHEELCHAIR ACCESS; Not suitable
- CREDIT CARDS; None taken
- ACCOMMODATION: 5 rooms 4 ensuite
- RATES: Discounted stays 3 or more nights (except Bank Holidays) £20-£30 per night pp

- DINING ROOM; First class traditional breakfast
- VEGETARIAN; Upon request
- LICENSED; Yes
- CHILDREN: Over 5 years

- PETS; No

GAGGLE OF GEESE
Buckland Newton
NR Dorchester
Dorset
DT2 7BS

Tel: 01300 345249

Egon Ronay Good Pub Guide.
'Which' Pub Guide.
CAMRA Good Beer Guide

The Gaggle of Geese is the epitome of a good village inn. It is a free-house and for the last 10 years has been in the capable hands of Trevor and Jan Marpole. Everything about the pub is right; it is off the beaten track in the heart of 'Hardy' country and set in 5 acres with a stream running through the grounds. There are many delightful walks roundabout which are very popular with ramblers. The Marpole's have a Caravan Club site as well, in a spacious and secluded spot. For nature lovers there is badger and wildlife 'night watching' within half a mile of the pub and the Gaggle of Geese is just 10 miles from the historic Abbey town of Sherborne and Dorchester. The pub acquired its name when a former landlord started breeding geese as a hobby. Now the pub holds two 'Goose auctions' a year when country people come from miles around to buy and sell breeding stock. The Gaggle of Geese has a great atmosphere with several local characters to be found regularly at the bar enjoying Trevor's excellently kept Real Ale. Jan does the cooking and she is renowned for food which is delicious, innovative and sensibly priced. The 40 seat non-smoking dining room entices people to dine here by candlelight at attractively laid tables. Customers enjoy the Skittle Alley most nights of the week, and the Quiz Nights on Sundays.

USEFUL INFORMATION

- OPEN: 12-2.30pm & 6.30-11pm
- WHEELCHAIR ACCESS: Yes
- GARDEN: Yes for sitting & eating Large Car Park
- CREDIT CARDS: Master/Visa /Switch/Delta/Euro/Electron/JCB
- CHILDREN: Yes, if well behaved

- RESTAURANT: Good food, dine by candlelight
- VEGETARIAN: Always a choice
- BAR FOOD: Wide range. Good value
- LICENSED: Full On. Real Ale
- PETS: Well behaved on lead

LAMPERTS COTTAGE
Lamperts Cottage
Sydling St Nicholas
Dorchester , Dorset DT2 9NU
Tel: 01300 341659   Fax: 01300 341699
AA QQQ

Nicky Willis, over the years in which she has been welcoming bed and breakfast guests to Lamperts Cottage, her delightful, thatched 16th century home, has made sure that they are both very welcome and well entertained. The cottage is on the edge of the pretty village of Sydling St Nicholas, with fields on three sides and a chalk stream running at the front and back. Its situation is ideal for touring , the beaches are twenty minutes by car and the walking superb. In addition there are fascinating day trips which one can make to places such as Athelhampton Manor House, Lulworth Castle, Kingston Lacy, a beautiful National Trust house. Thomas Hardy's Cottage is on the A35 two miles east of Dorchester and Abbotsbury with its unique swannery (the last of its kind in England) is easily reached. Bath and Bristol, Honiton and Exeter will also provide the visitor with interesting and exciting days out.
Within the cottage which is attractively furnished, the dining room has a huge inglenook fireplace with a bread oven and beams. The three bedrooms have dormer windows and are set under the eaves. Each room has a washbasin and there are two bathrooms, one with a shower, shared between the three rooms. breakfast is a feast. You will find Nicky is a friendly person who looks after your every need but doesn't fuss over you. The atmosphere and the ambience is great and it is a pleasure to stay here.

USEFUL INFORMATION

· OPEN; All year	· DINING ROOM; Excellent breakfast
· WHEELCHAIR ACCESS; Not suitable	· VEGETARIAN; Upon request
· GARDEN; Charming	
· CREDIT CARDS: None taken	· LICENSED; No
· ACCOMMODATION: 3 rooms not	· RATES; From £20 per person
ensuite **Restricted smoking**	· CHILDREN; Over 8 years

THE MANOR HOUSE
Piddlehinton, Dorchester, Dorset
DT2 7TE
Tel: 01300 348754
West Country Tourist Board
2 Crowns Highly Commended
Approached along a private drive and river bridge from the pretty conservation village of Piddlehinton, the Manor House is set in secluded grounds with the River Piddle flowing through them. It is right in the heart of Hardy country, ideal for exploring Wessex and is also within easy reach of the coast. The house, originally thatched, was rebuilt in the 19th century and many features of the period remain, including a delightful flag-stone kitchen with its AGA and a huge dresser. An earlier annexe to the house contains a massive inglenook fireplace and a large copper boiler. The whole house has a wonderfully friendly and welcoming atmosphere; Bob and Susie Curtis take particular care to ensure that their guests have a memorable and comfortable stay. Bob is a retired service officer who has travelled widely. He is now a qualified West Country Tourist Board Guide, leading regular walking tours in the area and is happy to share his considerable local knowledge with guests or help them plan a visit to suit their requirements. The two guest rooms are particularly spacious and fully equipped with colour television, hostess tray, and easy chairs. Both have their own large bathroom, complete with thermostatically controlled power shower. Breakfast is delicious with either a full English or Continental meal available. Within 300 metres of the Manor House and further along the river, is the thatched Thimble Inn, praised by the Good Pub Guide for its hospitality and excellent food.
USEFUL INFORMATION

· OPEN: All year except Christmas	· DINING ROOM: Delicious breakfast
· WHEELCHAIR ACCESS: No facilities	· VEGETARIAN: Upon request
· GARDEN: 1 acre	· CREDIT CARDS: None taken
· LICENSED: No	· ACCOMMODATION: 2 guest rooms
· CHILDREN: No facilities	with private facilities
· RATES: From £22.00 per person 10%	
discount 3 days or more	· PETS: No

THE MARQUIS OF LORNE
Nettlecombe, Bridport
Dorset   DT6 3SY
Tel: 01308 485236 Fax: 01308 485666
E-Mail ian_barrett@compuserve.com
AA QQQQ-Selected. Good Pub Guide-Licensees of the Year 1996
CAMRA (Wessex) Pub of the Year 1996

Dorset has so many beautiful hidden places and Nettlecombe is surely one of the prettiest with the added bonus of having The 16th century Marquis of Lorne as its local. It is quite an adventure to find it. Take the A3066 Bridport -Beaminster Road, turn off in an easterly direction approximately 1.5 miles north of Bridport. Pass 'Mangerton Mill'. Go through the village of West Milton and for a further mile until you reach a 'give way' junction. Go straight across towards Nettlecombe and the pub is up the hill approximately 300 yards on the left. It is more than worth the effort to get here. Ian and Anne Barrett have achieved a perfect balance. They have a genuine village pub and at the same time acquired a wonderful reputation for their food and the comfort of the accommodation which brings people from far and wide to enjoy the hospitality. Good beer comes locally from the Bridport based Palmers Brewery. The ever changing menu always has many home-made favourites plus grills, some exotic foreign dishes and a choice of fresh fish from what is available. The wines are well chosen and sensibly priced. All the pretty bedrooms are immaculate and ensuite. In summer the garden is ablaze with flowers and very popular. Special short winter breaks (Nov-March) are available. Ring for details

USEFUL INFORMATION

- OPEN: 11-2.30pm & 6-11pm (6.30 Winter) Sundays 12-3pm & 7-10.30pm
- WHEELCHAIR ACCESS: Not really
- GARDEN: Yes. Lovely floral displays
- CREDIT CARDS: Visa/Master/Switch
- ACCOMMODATION: 6 ensuite rooms
- RATES: £58.bed and breakfast 10% discount for 3 night stay or longer

- FOOD: Always a good choice of well cooked fare on offer, served in bars & dining areas.
- VEGETARIAN: Catered for
- LICENSED: Full On
- CHILDREN: Over 10 years
- PETS: No

THE OLD FARMHOUSE
Buckland Newton
Dorchester
Dorset   DT2 7DJ
Tel/Fax: 01300 345549
Two Crowns Commended

In the heart of Hardy country, Buckland Newton lies between Dorchester and Sherborne and situated on the outskirts of the attractive village, which has a church, a pub, post-office and garage, is The Old Farmhouse, the home of Clare and Alan Phipps who offer a genuine and very warm welcome to their guests. Within this 200 year old Grade II listed Longhouse with its own spring water, the atmosphere is relaxed, comfortable and informal.. The sitting room has a splendid large inglenook fireplace which is commandeered in the colder months by the four resident Burmese cats. There are two large double rooms each with ensuite bath and shower, and one twin room with ensuite shower. The rooms have recently been attractively decorated and each has television, hair drier as well as a generously supplied beverage tray. A freshly cooked, hearty breakfast is served every morning. There are many places to visit within easy reach including two beautiful gardens, Sticky Wicket and Domineys, both in Buckland Newton. Slightly further afield is the historic town of Sherborne with its Castle and Abbey, the coast is not far off and almost on the doorstep of the Old Farmhouse is the Dorset Gap and many beautiful walks.

USEFUL INFORMATION

- OPEN: All year excluding Christmas
- WHEELCHAIR ACCESS: No
- GARDEN: Yes
- CREDIT CARDS: None taken
- ACCOMMODATION: 2dbl 1tw ensuite
- RATES: From £22.00 pp

- DINING ROOM: Delicious breakfast No evening meals.
- VEGETARIAN: Special diets catered for
- LICENSED: No
- CHILDREN: Over 12 years
- PETS: No

PICKWICKS INN
4, The Square
Beaminster
Dorset
DT8 3AS
Tel: 01308 862084

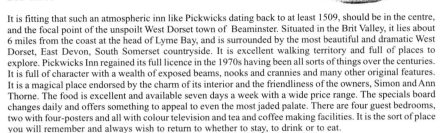

ETB Listed

It is fitting that such an atmospheric inn like Pickwicks dating back to at least 1509, should be in the centre, and the focal point of the unspoilt West Dorset town of Beaminster. Situated in the Brit Valley, it lies about 6 miles from the coast at the head of Lyme Bay, and is surrounded by the most beautiful and dramatic West Dorset, East Devon, South Somerset countryside. It is excellent walking territory and full of places to explore. Pickwicks Inn regained its full licence in the 1970s having been all sorts of things over the centuries. It is full of character with a wealth of exposed beams, nooks and crannies and many other original features. It is a magical place endorsed by the charm of its interior and the friendliness of the owners, Simon and Ann Thorne. The food is excellent and available seven days a week with a wide price range. The specials board changes daily and offers something to appeal to even the most jaded palate. There are four guest bedrooms, two with four-posters and all with colour television and tea and coffee making facilities. It is the sort of place you will remember and always wish to return to whether to stay, to drink or to eat.

USEFUL INFORMATION

· OPEN: All year 10.30am-11pm	· RESTAURANT: Good home-cooked fare. Wide
· PETS: Yes	choice. Daily Specials
· WHEELCHAIR ACCESS: Yes	· VEGETARIAN: Always a choice
· CREDIT CARDS: All except AMEX/Diners	· BAR FOOD: Good choice
· ACCOMMODATION: 4 guest rooms	· LICENSED: Full On
· RATES: £20pp per night Children 1/2 price under 14	· CHILDREN: Welcome

THE FOX INN
Corscombe, Dorchester
Dorset   DT2 0NS
Tel/Fax: 01935 891330
Good Food Guide. 'Dorset Dining Pub of the Year 97. Good Pub Guide

Quite difficult to find, out in the sticks at Corscombe, this enchanting inn is thatched and has a stream running by. It was an old Drovers inn where the sheep were washed in the stream, the weir is still there. Built about 1640 it has stone floors and a slate topped bar. Martyn and Susie Lee, together with their black Labrador Bramble make sure everyone is welcome and well cared for. Stay here in one of the pretty, ensuite guest rooms, well appointed with some fine antique pieces and you will have the opportunity to relax or be energetic - the choice is yours. From The Fox Inn there are some splendid walks, you can hunt, fish, shoot, go-kart, ride or take off for the coast which is just 10 miles away. The garden, looked after by Tim Dorey, has over one hundred roses and is always a talking point. Tim will willingly chat and give you garden pointers. In the five different rooms in which you can eat, the tables are set with gingham cloths and the food prepared by brilliant chef, Will Longman. The menu offers a wide choice of starters and main courses, mainly English in origin but with eastern flavours and dishes thrown in for good measure. Something you will never have here is chips and there is no Microwave. The Fox Inn is full of atmosphere and is a very happy place to be whether for a drink, a meal or to stay.

USEFUL INFORMATION

· OPEN: 12-2.30pm & 7-11pm	· RESTAURANT: 5 pretty rooms in which to eat
	excellent food
· WHEELCHAIR ACCESS: Yes	· VEGETARIAN: Always a choice
· GARDEN: Yes	· BAR FOOD: Wide choice
· CREDIT CARDS: Master/Visa/Delta/Switch	· LICENSED: Full On
· ACCOMMODATION: 1tw and 2dbl ensuite	· CHILDREN: Well behaved welcome
· RATES: Sgl £40 Dbl £60-70	· PETS: No

THE THREE HORSESHOES
Powerstock
NR Bridport
Dorset   DT6 3TF
Tel: 01308 485328

1AA Rosette

A friendly village pub with a small intimate restaurant, The Three Horseshoes is mainly an 18th century building with a great deal of charm and an immediate welcoming atmosphere. The unusually thatched bar is the meeting place for many local regulars who enjoy the well kept ale and the amusing chit chat. Visitors find they are often rapidly drawn into the conversation. The stunning views from the back restaurant and the pretty garden are reasons in themselves why one should come here. Renowned for its good food, which is available at lunch and in the evenings every day, the menu is wide ranging, changes regularly and always produces some exciting dishes. 9 Starters can also be had as 'Small Eats' and range from Leek and Potato Soup to grilled Cornish Scallops. Fresh fish is always on the menu and one of the most popular of choices is Fillets of John Dory baked with sea salt and lime juice. The steaks are succulent, the Rack of Lamb cooked to perfection. For those with a sweet tooth there are usually nine or ten choices with anything from an old fashioned and delicious Bread and Butter Pudding to Pear poached in red wine and cinnamon with vanilla ice cream. A good hostelry, run by good innkeepers and one not to be missed.

USEFUL INFORMATION

· OPEN: All year 12-3pm & 6-11pm	· RESTAURANT: Excellent food. Fish a speciality
· WHEELCHAIR ACCESS: Yes	· VEGETARIAN: Always a choice
· GARDEN: Large, stunning views	· BAR FOOD: Wide choice
· CREDIT CARDS: None taken	· LICENSED: Full On
· **SMOKING IN BAR ONLY**	· CHILDREN: Welcome
	· PETS: Yes

WESTWOOD HOUSE HOTEL.
29 High West Street
Dorchester, Dorset   DT1 1UP
Tel: 01305 268018 Fax: 01305 250282
ETB: 2 Crown Commended, AA Selected 4Q, Logis 2 Fireplaces

Westwood House is a grade II listed Georgian building, believed to have been built in 1815 as a coaching house for Lord Ilchester. You will find it in the centre of Dorchester, a county town, rich in history and home of the author Thomas Hardy. There are many sites of local interest including Roman remains, Maiden Castle and Maumbury Rings. The County and Military Museums are a few minutes walk away and further afield the countryside is beautiful and the coast dramatic - ideal for walking or touring. Angela and Tom Parsley have owned Westwood House since October 1996 and created a relaxed and informal atmosphere in which flexibility is all important. For example there are no rigid times for breakfast. Their ethos is that the welfare of their guests is paramount and they believe very strongly in personal and efficient service. There are seven bedrooms, each room, individually furnished and ensuite, has a name. You might stay in Abbotsbury, a double room with a five foot bed and an ensuite Luxury Whirlpool Spa Corner Bath, or Stinsford, a double bedroom and separate small sitting room with ensuite shower room. Each room has colour television, hairdryer, direct dial telephones, radio, tea/chocolate/coffee making facilities. Breakfast, served in the light and airy, non-smoking Conservatory, is delicious starting with grapefruit, prunes, fruit salads, cereals, fresh fruit and yoghurts and followed by a traditional meal with local supplied bacon, eggs, sausages, fresh tomatoes and mushrooms and croissants and toast. A Continental breakfast is also available.

USEFUL INFORMATION

· OPEN; All year	· BREAKFAST ROOM; Delicious, traditional breakfast
· WHEELCHAIR ACCESS; No	· VEGETARIAN;Yes
· CREDIT CARDS; Visa/Master/AMEX	· PETS; By arrangement
/Switch/Solo	· LICENSED; No. Small complimentary bar
· ACCOMMODATION; 7 ensuite rooms	· CHILDREN; Welcome
· RATES; Special breaks during Low	
Season 2+ nights, reduced rates High Season £31-£37	

WHITE LION INN
The Square, Broadwindsor
Dorset
DT8 3QD
Tel: 01308 867070

The White Lion Inn in the pretty village of Broadwindsor, stands opposite the cottage where King Charles I took refuge after the Battle of Worcester in 1651. Built at much the same time as the cottage it has catered for the needs of locals and travellers over the centuries. Recently it has undergone a complete restoration and refurbishment and to quote a piece we read somewhere 'it has undergone a magical metamorphosis'. It has always been a homely place but today the judicious removal of some interior walls has produced one warm welcoming room. Upon entering the White Lion you are greeted by the tastefully appointed decor beautifully set off by some charming plates and other paraphernalia, with the black beams and huge canopied fireplace all adding to the ambience. Mike and Stephanie Snowdon are the licensees and it is Mike who is rapidly gaining a reputation for the excellence of his food and about to be recognised in the Good Food Guide. He is as adept at Vegetarian dishes as he is with seafood; you cannot fail to enjoy the cockles and mussels and the North Atlantic prawn platter. For the very hungry the White Lion mixed grill is sumptuous and very filling! The prices are very reasonable and the wine list offers wines from around the world. Well behaved children and dogs are welcome but bad language is definitely out of order. There are no noisy fruit machines and everything about the White Lion invites one to relax and enjoy oneself.

USEFUL INFORMATION

- · OPEN: 12-2.30pm & 6.30-11pm
- · WHEELCHAIR ACCESS: Yes
- · GARDEN: Tables in courtyard
- · CREDIT CARDS: None taken
- · ACCOMMODATION: No
- · RATES - on application

- · DINING AREA: Super food at sensible prices
- · VEGETARIAN: Always a choice
- · BAR FOOD: Daily Specials. Sunday Lunch
- · LICENSED: Full On
- · CHILDREN: Well behaved welcome
- · PETS: Yes

WOODCOATE STUD
East Farm.
Abbotsbury, Weymouth
Dorset   DT3 4JN
Tel: 01305 871363

This 17th century farmhouse offers some of the best bed and breakfast accommodation in Dorset. David and Wendy Wood together with their daughters Sam and Nicky are your hosts who genuinely look forward to having you stay in their cosy and warm home. The farm has been in the family since 1729 and is still a working farm with a Dairy Herd and Horses. Both Sam and Nicky are keen Show jumpers. There is a resident pig called Gertie, dogs, cats, chickens and ducks. Altogether a delightful environment in which to spend a holiday. Abbotsbury itself is enchanting with its famous Swannery and beautiful buildings - a setting which has many times been used by film-makers including 'Far From the Madding Crowd', in which Grandfather Wood played the butler to Peter Finch and in which part of the location filming was done on the farm. The comfortable, charmingly old world well furnished bedrooms, two doubles and a twin non-smoking, will provide you with a restful night's sleep and in the morning you will come down to a traditional English farmhouse breakfast. Cream Teas are served through the Summer months from 2pm-5.30pm with home baked cakes, scones and clotted cream either in the Farmhouse or the pretty Cottage Garden.
Pony Trekking is provided for Visitors and Guests at £10 per hour with superb, scenic rides through the village lanes and surrounding countryside.

USEFUL INFORMATION

- · OPEN; All year
- · WHEELCHAIR ACCESS; Can not accommodate
- · GARDEN; Pretty Cottage Garden. Cream Teas
- · CREDIT CARDS; No
- · ACCOMMODATION; 3 rooms all **non-smoking**. Not ensuite
- · RATES; £32 per double room

- · DINING ROOM; Farmhouse breakfast. Cream Teas
- · VEGETARIAN; Upon request
- · LICENSED; No
- · CHILDREN; Over 14 years
- · PETS; No

IAN PETHERS

Acorn Inn	Evershot	489
Bennett Arms	Semley	490
Crown Hotel & Restaurant	Marnhull	497
Eastbury Hotel	Sherborne	491
Grange Hotel	Sherborne	497
La Fleur De Lys	Shaftesbury	498
Newton House	Sturminster Newton	498
Old Bank	Marnhull	499
Old Brew House	Langton Long	499
Pheasants Restaurant	Sherborne	492
Plumber Manor	Sturminster Newton	493
Poachers Inn	Piddletrenthide	494
Portman Lodge	Durweston	500
Retreat (The)	Shaftesbury	500
Stourcastle Lodge	Sturminster Newton	495
Summer Lodge	Evershot	496
Three Elms	North Wooton	501
Walnut Tree	West Camel	501
Wayfarers Restaurant	Sherbourne Causeway	502

Chapter 10:
North Past the Giant and a Multitude of Villages.

Thatch, whitewash, honeysuckle and golden yellow stone; these are some of what man has added to the beautiful setting nature has given to the villages of Dorset. This last third of the county is geographically the largest, but without any very major towns, or a coastline, at first glance there might not seem much to offer in the North of Dorset. Do not be easily fooled, as far too many visitors are, missing the real heart of the county in a rush to the resorts.

While it is true that there is not perhaps anything of the same mass appeal as the spectacle of the Purbeck coast, or the sands of Bournemouth, Poole or Weymouth, a closer look at the map will show that there is still a great deal to experience, in a quieter, and often less crowded setting. Other counties have resorts and spectacular coasts, but few have so many lovely villages and hamlets, and none has such a variety as you will find in Dorset.

There is a band of green running through the middle of North Dorset, from the western half of the CRANBORNE CHASE in the east of the county to the hills surrounding the River FROME in the west, with the BLACKMOOR VALE above them. This is an area full of delightful surprises worth seeking out, including a fearsome, famous giant. Of the towns in North Dorset, Sherborne, Blandford and Shaftesbury are the largest and most noticeable.

Each has a very different character, with Sherborne in particular being somewhere you will not want to miss. By the time you reach Gold Hill, or the Park Walk in Shaftesbury at the end of this chapter, you will have a complete picture or Dorset in your mind, as you look down upon the county sprawled out below you. Without the northern section this picture would not be a whole, and would miss some of the colour of the lasting impression this area full of history and beauty is sure to make upon you.

Picking up where you left off in Dorchester, heading east towards Blandford you come first to **PUDDLETOWN**. The many unusual place-names you will meet to the east and north of here do have a connection with water, though not perhaps the one immediately suspected. The river TRENT, which reaches the sea at Wareham, has two other names, PIDDLE and PUDDLE.

These are the source of the many aquatic sounding villages in the vicinity, with Piddletrenthide managing to combine two of the alternatives. The name Trent gained popularity in Victorian times, because the alternatives were considered vulgar. Just think of all the jokes this might have saved in modern times; the car journey would be so much duller.

Puddletown is the *Weatherbury* of Hardy's 'Far From The Madding Crowd', and the best part of the village is off to the left of the main road, around the church, which itself dates from the 12th through 15th centuries. Look in particular for the alabaster effigies, and brasses of the Martyn family, one of whom (Sir William Martyn) was responsible for the building of Athelhampton House, of which more shortly.

To the east of Puddletown is ILSINGTON HOUSE (01305 848454), which is open to the public at restricted times during the summer. Built in 1690 the interior has period furniture and an art collection, but the exterior was changed dramatically in the 19th century, and has lost some of its former glory. The gardens are formal, featuring unusual irises and peonies, and are a good place from which to view the house, which was also the home of the illegitimate grandson of King George III.

Further east of Puddletown you will find ATHELHAMPTON HOUSE & GARDENS (01305 848363). Sir William Martyn was Lord Mayor of London when the building of this Tudor edifice was started in 1493, but it was well into the next century before the task was completed by his heirs. The gardens at Athelhampton are bound to stop you from making a bee-line for the house itself. The twelve TOPIARY PYRAMIDS, glimpsed to the right on the approach to the front of the house, will draw you over to the hedge dividing you from them in this direction, and make you wonder what other surprises there are hidden in the Great Court they form part of. Looking at once almost artificial and yet the ultimate in skilled hedge trimming, the green, smooth pyramids are a work of symmetry and grace, which really is a good way to sum up everything you will find in both the gardens and the house at Athelhampton.

Athelhampton House & Gardens

The main gardens are filled with features: sparkling fountains, pavilions, a terrace; all adding to the natural shape of the enclosed area given by the River Piddle, which runs alongside it. The gardens are mature and well maintained, having been, in essence, as they are now for over a hundred years. There are seasonal variations here too, well practised and defined, be it clematis, roses, tulips or lilies.

Around the back of the house stands a circular dovecote, some five hundred years old. Its original purpose was to provide plump fodder for the kitchens to use in their pigeon pies, but the elegance of the structure is none the less evident. There was a fire here in 1992 which affected the inside and contents of Athelhampton more than the external structure, but the house and its contents present a whole which seems more natural and easy than its parts from many different ages would suggest possible.

As you stand in the magnificent GREAT HALL, looking up at the curved and moulded timbers of the roof above, then across to the contrast between the powerful stone arch and the fragile heraldic glass of the oriel window it frames, the whole effect is so easy, imposing yet graceful, that even the huge candelabra seem in keeping, and far from extravagant in this setting. Take a look around the restored Library, Dining Room and State Bedroom, and Athelhampton will stay in your memory as a Tudor House kept with pride and care to remain as authentic to the era of its origins as it can.

TOLPUDDLE is the next noticeable village along the A35 heading east. It is not a remarkable place in itself, but the story of its six martyrs has guaranteed this small settlement its own permanent, and significant, niche in history. Whether you have visited the Old Court House at Dorchester or not, the TOLPUDDLE MARTYRS MUSEUM (01305 848237) will tell you more of their story, and direct you to the other historical sites in the village, such as the cottage in which the labourers met to try and defend their rights by making an agricultural labourers union.

Driving from the by-pass around Dorchester you will have passed through PUDDLETOWN FOREST, and the dark coniferous trees make an immediate contrast to the country you are now exploring. Tolpuddle is in the middle of an area that to this day still looks so typically agricultural. The fields are green, hedged, but fairly small. The farms are mostly hidden from your 'main road' view, and the whole atmosphere is of a sleepy place, where the living to be made from the land would be a slow but satisfying way to pass your days.

If the area has not changed much in the last 165 years or so, then the words of George Loveless, at his trial in 1834, come as a nasty jolt as you contemplate the beauty of his home area:
"we were uniting together to preserve ourselves, our wives and children from utter degradation and starvation.

The martyrs were not doing anything illegal in attempting to set up a Trade Union, it was the taking of an oath of loyalty which was deemed an offence, and an infiltrator into the group gave the evidence which would condemn them to seven years transportation. Only one of the six, James Hammett, chose to stay in the village after they were returned from Australia in 1837, and his gravestone can be found at the church of ST JOHN THE EVANGELIST.

Does their emigration seem ironic, lessening the poignancy of their original sentence? Not if you look at some of the conditions prevalent in 19th century transportations. They went to Canada as free men, paying their own passage; on the way to Australia they were chained to the other prisoners, with the cat 'o' nine tails, branding or strait jackets waiting for any who dared to question their gaolers. While waiting to be transported they were confined below decks on a rat infested, disease ridden prison hulk, permanently chained at the waist and ankle. Perhaps their second emigration reflected disillusionment with the state of the country in which they were born; if so, it surely would have been justified.

The triangular block of land between the A354 to Blandford and the A31 to Wimborne, is remarkable first for its emptiness. Several of the **WINTERBOURNE** villages fall into this area, many of the others spread further to the north west. There are fourteen place-names in all with this prefix, which means a stream (bourne) that only appears in the winter, when the chalk downs become saturated.

If you take a left turn from the A31 after you have passed Bere Regis, you can explore these quiet villages, set amongst gently rolling hills and grassy fields. Look out for the towering chimneys of the Jacobean Manor at **WINTERBORNE ANDERSON**, barely visible from the road, and unfortunately not open to the public, which is reputed to be one of Dorset's finest buildings. The medieval church at **WINTERBORNE TOMSON** is also worth stopping to see, particularly as its remote location helped it to escape 19th century modification, with the result that the 18th century box pews are still intact.

The CHARLTON DOWN stretches between these and the route into Blandford, and with no road across it we will return to the main roads and follow them to **SPETISBURY**. Here you will find CRAWFORD BRIDGE spanning the River STOUR. This sturdy but attractive bridge is partly medieval, with nine stone arches, and is part of a road which winds between the villages towards Blandford, virtually joining Spetisbury to **CHARLTON MARSHALL**.

SPETISBURY RINGS, at the south end of the village, is an Iron Age hillfort, but not on the scale of Maiden Castle. More than eighty skeletons were found here when railway building in the 19th century led to some excavation, and the presence of a Roman shield suggests this was another place where the Durotrige culture was overcome by Vespasian and his men, the best part of two thousand years ago.

The railway went in the Beeching cuts of the 1960s, giving the site back to the graves of Romans and Celts. At some point there must have been woodpeckers here too, as the Anglo-Saxon words *speht* (woodpecker) and *byrig* (fort) have given Spetisbury its name.

Before the by-pass was built around Blandford, this road was surely one of the most overcrowded in the county. The otherwise quaint villages looked dwarfed by the lorries pounding through them, and **BLANDFORD ST MARY**, in particular, seemed doomed to choke in fumes and dust. Now it has some of its life back, and the approach to Blandford itself is less oppressive.

The route into the town from the south is the most picturesque, with the Stour crossing the road at the bottom of West Street. Add to this the dominating presence of the 18th stone gateway to BRYANSTON HOUSE (now home to the public school of the same name) and you are prepared to enter a grand, stately town. While this is not quite the case, it is good that the villages of St Mary and **BRYANSTON** still maintain their own identity, keeping Blandford itself contained, and fairly compact.

Bryanston School is a huge country house of the neo-classical style from the late 19th century, and is not the building for which the splendid gateway was originally built. Those lucky enough to attend the school have a fantastic setting in which to pass their youth; the grounds to Bryanston are superb. A walk to the west, along the wooded edge to the Stour is highly recommended, although you will only get glimpses of the Bryanston Estate itself. I remember walking this route one New Year's Day when there had been a heavy fall of snow, and seeing the laden branches of the trees hanging over the sparkling, swelling waters of the bubbling river was something I will never forget.

If Dorchester is the heart of Hardy's Wessex, then **BLANDFORD FORUM** (Tourist Information 01258 454770) deserves to be known as the heart of rural Dorset. It is much smaller than the county town with less than 10,000 inhabitants, and lacks much of Dorchester's glamour, but has nevertheless developed slowly and steadily into a place of undeniable character and charm.

The longer version of its name is apparently still the correct one, but in my years of association with the town I have noticed that the 'Forum' suffix is being used less and less. It would be dangerous to assume that this is purely a chronological inevitability; the local train station was called Blandford for one hundred years after its opening in 1863, and renamed Blandford Forum only for the last three years of its active life. This was never a Roman town as the name might suggest, Forum being used here as a Latinisation of market, or meeting place.

In Elizabethan times the town had a third name: 'Chipping Blandford', a reference to its preeminence as a centre for markets and fairs. The prosperity of Blandford had only one enemy; fire. The streets full of wooden buildings were ravaged several times before 1731, when a conflagration even more serious than that at Wareham destroyed virtually the whole town in just five hours. Written accounts of the day of the fire have survived, and are poignant in their descriptions:

"the stones spit and flew and so fervent was the heat that the church bells dissolved and ran down in streams."

The unlikely sounding saviours and rebuilders of the town were the Bastard brothers, William and John. They were architects and surveyors, and in thirty years built much of what you will find in the town centre today. The brothers had a clean slate to work from, and took the opportunity to re-align some of the narrower streets, so that they are directly responsible for the 'Historic Georgian Market Town' slogan that you will often find used to describe modern Blandford.

Wherever you start from in Blandford, you are likely to end up at the centre of their work, the Market Place. The Georgian influence is obvious, but the splendour of these buildings is made somehow greater by their still being in constant use, very much part of the present day community's life.

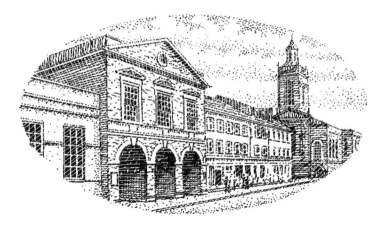

The Market Place, Blandford Forum

Right opposite the Church and Fire Monument you can visit the BLANDFORD FORUM MUSEUM (01258 450388) in Bere's Yard, which features local history, and the industries of button-making, wool spinning and brewing which survived the town's period of rebuilding. Around the small square at the back of the church you will also find the CAVALCADE OF COSTUME (01258 453006), in another attractive Georgian structure, the LIME TREE HOUSE. This collection of outfits spans the last three centuries and represents the life work of Betty Penny MBE.

Before we leave Blandford town centre it is worth exploring the claims that this is the 'most complete Georgian town in England' with the perfect street layout etc. If you take a walk along East Street, or up the hill along Salisbury Street, you will find straight lines of modern shops, much like those in a thousand other towns. If you go down the hill, taking West Street to the large car park by the road bridge over the Stour, the town has a different, open character. All in all, Blandford is most memorable for the compact nature of its centre, and the accessibility of its main features, especially the many distinctive Georgian buildings, but it is no show town, and I think this adds to its impact.

Blandford is also the centre for an annual event of international renown, the GREAT DORSET STEAM FAIR (01258 860361 Show Secretary 1997) which attracts a staggering 200,000 visitors each year. The event is held at an immense 500 acre site adjacent to **TARRANT HINTON** to the north east of the town, and is usually held in the late summer.

The aim of the fair is to give an insight into life at the turn of the century, when steam power was at its most influential. You can easily lose sight of this though, content with marvelling at the colours, grandeur and sheer raw power of the largest gathering of steam tractors and stationary engines held in the world. This is definitely an occasion to look out for.

Blandford has also had military neighbours in this direction for some time, at BLANDFORD CAMP. The camp is now home to the ROYAL SIGNALS MUSEUM (01258 482248), celebrating the history of military communications. The story of the development of radio equipment from its earliest days to modern satellite equipment is particularly interesting.

THE MID DORSET GOLF CLUB (01258 861386), with an eighteen hole course, provides a different way to get to know some of the Blandford area.

Travelling north east of Blandford, you are now in the area known as CRANBORNE CHASE, simply because this is where the kings who visited Cranborne Manor (Chapter 10) used to come to hunt. This Area of Outstanding Natural Beauty, as it has now been designated, spreads over three counties in all, Dorset, Hampshire and Wiltshire. The sections north of the A354 are among the least inhabited areas of Dorset, and the views across the rolling grass plateau are long and restful to the eye.

Nevertheless the optimum way to explore the grassy chalk downs and forests of the Chase is either to walk or take a bicycle. There are many marked footpaths, or if you decide to use two wheels details of the NORTH DORSET CYCLEWAY can be found at the Tourist Information office in Blandford.

One of the few villages in this vicinity is **CHETTLE**, near which you can find CHETTLE HOUSE (01258 830209) a sturdy example of a Queen Anne House, built in the Baroque style to the designs of Thomas Archer in 1710. So why should such an edifice be built out here? The seclusion, as well as the excellent hunting, induced the Chaffin family to move to Chettle in the 17th century. Perhaps they were not among the most popular people in Dorset, as it was a Chaffin who had led a troop of horse against Monmouth's forces at Sedgemoor, where many a Dorset man perished amongst the rebel forces.

If it was a quiet life they were after, it didn't always work. George Chaffin, the man who commissioned Archer to build the present house, was such an avid hunter that he even challenged a neighbouring Member of Parliament from **TARRANT GUNVILLE** to a duel to settle a dispute on the subject. His grandson, William, found other problems in the area and his book 'Anecdotes and History of Cranborne Chase' features stories about the conflict between gamekeepers and deer poachers. He also had the dubious distinction of accidentally shooting a woman the very first time he went out with a gun!

You should manage to spend a suitably peaceful day here now though, with five acres of gardens containing rare herbaceous plants and shrubs, as well as a vineyard. The house also has an Art Gallery which can be visited.

To the north east you are getting near to the borders with Wiltshire and Hampshire, but a story from **SIXPENNY HANDLEY** has echoes from earlier in our travels through Dorset. Isaac Gulliver, of smuggling notoriety, married innkeeper's daughter Betty Beale in the parish church here in 1768. Although thirty miles from the coast this proved another effective base for his highly profitable operations, and a safe one too.

A Blandford paper reported the events of a certain night in the year 1770. The excise men raided a cottage in Sixpenny, recovering tobacco, tea, and brandy. A dangerous trip back to Blandford saw the contraband safely stored in the Exciseman's house, but only until a force of one hundred and fifty armed horsemen arrived later the same night. The goods were given back without a fight, and local industry near the county's inland borders continued unabated.

Why the name Sixpenny Handley? Yes, there is a signpost that declares the distance to *6d Handley* too, so perhaps it cost half a shilling to enter the village, or to get a chance to 'handle' the contraband! Oh well, it was worth a try; the reality is that *Saxpena* and *Hanlege* meant 'Saxon Hilltop' and 'high clearing' in medieval times. Still, if you wish to concoct your own story about the size of the village being in direct ratio to a pre decimalisation coin, or some more devious explanation, then an unwitting newcomer to the area is unlikely to see through the joke straight away, and the place-name is tempting, isn't it?

The National Trust owns sections of the Cranborne Chase, including FONTMELL DOWN and CLUBMEN'S DOWN. Running almost up against the

A350 between Blandford and Shaftesbury, these comprise 282 acres of chalk escarpment which help to form the western boundary of the Chase. Most of the grass has never been farmed, or treated with any chemical fertilisers, and is therefore full of the flora of the chalk downlands. The FONTMELL DOWN NATURE RESERVE (01305 264620) is also a haven for butterflies, particularly the chalkhill and adonis blues, silver-spotted skipper, and Duke of Burgundy varieties.

From here the views west past **FONTMELL MAGNA** into the Blackmoor Vale are quite breathtaking. Yet Clubmen's Down takes its name from another event in the human history of Dorset, perhaps unsuited to such a beautiful spot.

On 25 May 1645 three thousand men rallied on this hill, under the leadership of the Reverend Thomas Bravell. They became known as the clubmen of Dorset, their numbers swelling to almost four thousand by the time they reached Badbury Rings a few days later. It is suggested that this name, given because at first clubs were their only weapons, brought the term club to mean a group gathering with a common interest.

Their particular common interest was to complain at the hardship suffered by ordinary folk under the seemingly unending conflict of the Civil War. They presented a petition to both sides; King Charles listened to their pleas, but the Parliamentary Army eventually brought an end to their continued protests after an attack on 300 clubmen camped on Hambledon Hill. Twelve were killed, the rest were made to disband. A less famous and successful attempt by the ordinary folk of Dorset to be heard than that started at Tolpuddle, but equally worthy of mention.

The site of the Clubmen's last stand can be found just to the west of the A350, near the village of **CHILD OKEFORD**. HAMBLEDON HILL is a National Nature Reserve (01929 556688 / 01202 841026), and the archaeological remains are protected as a Scheduled Ancient Monument. The situation of this Iron Age hillfort makes it more impressive in some ways than even Maiden Castle. The ramparts are visible for many miles around, encircling the whole of a spur of the chalk downlands. This really is a dramatic place, the landscape's rugged lines making the slopes of the hill look pretty daunting to the pedestrian now, let alone to any ancient invading force. What it does have in common with Maiden Castle, Lamberts Castle, Badbury Rings, and the multitude of other ancient sites in the county is its emptiness.

Funnily enough we cannot even claim full responsibility for the present day state of these places abandoned so long ago; we've ruined many other ancient sites by fire, rebuilding or wear and tear, but leaving them alone doesn't necessarily work either. The sheep you see grazing the slopes today have been the main guardians of Hambledon. While inviting a group of our woolly friends into your garden to crop the lawn might not seem ideal, for the preservation of both the ecological and archaeological heritage of Hambledon they have worked wonders.

The turf has remained tight and the grass short, and this is the key. While cattle have kept the flatter areas free of trees and scrub, the sheep have dealt with the slopes. Delicate wild flowers and fine grasses would not have survived the development of any undergrowth, and by keeping the ground cover tight the foraging animals have also stopped the archaeological remains from simply eroding away into oblivion. Aesthetically and economically they must also be acknowledged as superior in such a setting to man; there is no room here for the modern charioteer seated upon his Council lawn-mower!

In the final analysis the initial clearing of the trees from these sites, in this case some 5,000 years ago, and the subsequent use of them as grazing area for livestock by succeeding civilizations has made all this possible. So, unintentionally perhaps, this is a man made phenomenon after all. A similar process has taken place just a mile to the south at HOD HILL. Another huge hillfort, this one is not quite as spectacular as Hambledon in its setting, although the range of flowers and rare butterflies is particularly impressive during the summer.

If Blandford can claim to be the heart of rural Dorset, then the lanes running out into the countryside around it are like arteries and veins, seeming to spread themselves in increasingly finer patterns, especially to the west. There really are a multitude of villages here, of which a few must be mentioned, and as many visited as you have time for, as a lifetime could be spent finding new favourites.

One such is nearby **IWERNE COURTNEY** or **SHROTON** as it also known. Far enough away from the main A350 to retain its individuality, and yet more readily accessible than most of the picturesque villages, this is where the remaining clubmen were brought after the defeat on Hambledon Hill, to be locked overnight in the church.

Despite some more recent development in the village, including a new green, the overall character is set by Dorset Reed thatched, stone cottages and the Gothic style of the church into which the three hundred prisoners were packed. A wide, tree filled valley gives this place a feeling of tranquillity; quite an achievement so close to the busy road. If anything, Shroton has become a quieter village in the last hundred years, losing the great fairs full of side-shows that used to be held here, at one of which Thomas Hardy recalled seeing 'a woman beheaded', perhaps a vertical forerunner of sawing a lady in half!

Travelling south west the country is either largely under the plough or canopied by forest, but between **OKEFORD FITZPAINE** and **TURNWORTH** the National Trust properties of RINGMOOR and TURNWORTH DOWN provide some more open spaces. Turnworth is a very rural, remote hamlet, and its 19th century buildings are dominated by the church, which has Thomas Hardy to thank for some of the architectural features, added when it was redesigned in the 1860s.

For a real feeling of the Dorset countryside and the part villages can play in it, take a walk up to the north end of Turnworth to the car park, and follow the footpath to Ringmoor. A further trek to the north towards Okeford will take you past Roman earthworks, and across open downland, but with nearby chances to wander through some lovely woods of ash and oak, with coppiced hazel.

A drive or walk as far as Okeford will show how two neighbouring Dorset villages can be attractive in completely different ways. Twenty five of the 18th century buildings of the village are listed, and the thatched cottages of local red brick, with some timber framing, look ready for use in a whole range of jigsaw puzzles or postcards.

Both of these villages are charming for their sense of being suspended in time; we are used to seeing metallic painted cars parked outside the quaint cottages, to be driven off before any picture for a chocolate box cover is taken, and even the ubiquitous modern window units can be disguised to be in some character with the rest of the building. You wouldn't think this was an area in which any drastic changes were likely to take place; but that has not always been so.

Somewhat over two hundred years ago an entire town was exterminated near here, on the whim of a single man. **MILTON ABBAS,** full of cob cottages, thatched and whitewashed, looks at first like another village which has grown slowly over the centuries. There is something unusual about this place, something almost eerie in the equal spacing between the dwellings, and the regimented alignment of their gardens, as they line the one road which makes up the settlement. There is a place near Keston, in Kent, where the road takes some very sudden, sharp curves. When I first learnt to ride a motorbike they were quite a challenge, and I remember returning home to complain that they were unreasonably placed on such a major thoroughfare. My father offered me, by way of consolation, the knowledge that the road had to be built like this to avoid the home of William Pitt, the Prime Minister at the time of the construction. I used to think this was quite unreasonable, until I heard the story of Milton Abbas. Joseph Damer, Earl of Dorchester, lived in the new mansion next to Milton Abbey, and was not keen on the local town, so he had it demolished in 1770. Completely wiped out; except for one, isolated cottage.

The town was on his land, and the Earl did have a 'model' village built to replace it, which is why the present Milton Abbas is so uniform, but the story is still quite extraordinary. Various motives have been given for this drastic measure. Some say he couldn't tolerate the smell and noise of the town, others that those who built his mansion had omitted to inform him that it would overlook the houses as well as the wooded countryside. Either way, Joseph Damer will never go down in history as a tolerant man.

At least the forty or so identical houses of the single street of Milton Abbas are a more attractive legacy than 'Pitt's road'. Damer's House and MILTON ABBEY now stand in perfect isolation as he apparently required, but if his ghost haunts the house, I wonder what the Earl thinks of its present occupants? At least advertisements for the Milton Abbey School for boys state that they celebrate individuality, a sentiment he might have agreed with, as long as he couldn't see, hear or smell any celebrations from his windows!

The Abbey was built in the 14th and 15th centuries on the site of an earlier version which was founded by King Athelstan five hundred years earlier. The Abbey has many features, including some excellent stained glass. In all seriousness, the demolition of the market town which surrounded it has left us the old building in suitable grandeur, set in grounds landscaped by Capability Brown. Look for some small gates leading to a set of grass steps, looking like a frozen green escalator. These lead out of the grounds to ST CATHERINES CHAPEL, now mostly a Norman structure, but built on top of another of Athelstan's buildings, where he is said to have had a vision of victory.

HILTON, just to the north west, shows how a less 'planned' hamlet can take advantage of a very similar setting to that of Milton Abbas. Wooded hills frame the village, but this time with the church still at its centre. The flint structure of ALL SAINTS CHURCH stands out, and does provide a focal point. Inside you will find twelve panels painted in the 15th century with pictures of the apostles; these were originally in Milton Abbey.

Hilton gets its name from the Anglo-Saxon word for tansy, the yellow plant you can see growing on the hills to the north. This was used as a cake flavouring in former times. All in all this is a typically remote, picturesque Dorset hamlet, where you feel protected by the slopes which surround you, closing the little world overlooked by the church into a safe hollow in the countryside.

A couple of miles north from Hilton is a very different place, where your view is as wide and good as anywhere in the county. BULBARROW HILL is over 900 feet high, and can be quite a bewildering place. As you stand looking out across Dorset, the choice of which direction to follow is the problem; everything looks so tempting from here. On foot there are more woods to explore, as well as plenty of more open spaces for walking or riding. In the larger perspective, each point of the compass will coax you to take its own direction next.

To the north and north west the misty Blackmoor Vale and the valley of the River Stour, to the north east the village of **IBBERTON**, tenuously clinging to the steep side of the hill, to the west and south west yet more tiny villages and hamlets set amongst hills and woodlands, and to the south patchwork farmland. This has to be the best place to get an ideas of the splendid variety of scenery available in inland Dorset, and from a vantage point so much in keeping with the beauty of the whole area.

474

We will continue west for now, heading for another large presence in the Dorset countryside, but stopping briefly to look at more of the multitude of villages around him. Running north from Puddletown, the river Trent (or Piddle) runs alongside a series of places whose names alone provoke the curiosity: **PIDDLEHINTON, WHITE LACKINGTON**, and **PIDDLETRENTHIDE**, with **PLUSH, ALTON PANCRAS**, and **BUCKLAND NEWTON** just beyond its reaches.

Each has its individual features too, from the horrifying gargoyles under the battlements of the church at Piddletrenthide to the ancient hollow oak at Piddlehinton. These are set in a valley of fertile farmland, while Alton Pancras marks the source of the river (Anglo-Saxon *Awultune*) as well as a church dedicated to the same saint as a very different place, now known as part of the Kings Cross Station in London.

Plush sounds like part of an advertisement for a 'top of the range' sofa, but is actually the tiniest of these places, incredibly remote and attractive in its downland setting. Buckland Newton is the northern most of those I have chosen, and has been used as 'a typical Dorset village' before, by the BBC. There is such variety among the smaller centres of population in the county that this is a difficult term to apply or quantify. All that can be said is that Buckland is a gentle place, amongst meadows and rounded hills, with its dwelling scattered liberally amongst pastureland.

It is strange how the word 'fertile' managed to creep into my descriptions of this area, as we moved closer to **CERNE ABBAS**. Perhaps I was falling under the spell of its most famous occupant, or maybe he really does have the power to bring life. Now is not the time for the faint hearted or shy amongst us, for this is the land of the giant, and his anatomy is part of his purpose and must be discussed.

The 180 foot figure overlooking Cerne Abbas from TRENDLE HILL is undeniably male, as no-one could ignore the thirty feet of phallus which so blatantly declare his masculinity, although some Victorian writers managed to! The CERNE ABBAS GIANT, carved in the chalk hill, makes an alarming contrast to the other chalk figures of Wessex, be it White Horses or regimental badges (as at Fovant).

The Cerne Abbas Giant

He was either meant to be Hercules, or Cernunnos, the Celtic lord of the animals, depending on who you believe carved him first. The trenches which give the giant an outline are no more than two feet across, and no matter how much locals might have found him an embarrassment over the years, someone has always taken the time to keep the chalk scoured enough to save man and club.

Other features have not survived, but can be detected under the surface by modern archaeologists; there was a nose, Celtic in style, which means that it had the shape of the phallus and testicles, inverted, rather in the Graucho Marx impersonator style. There was also something hung over the outstretched arm; a lion's skin (Hercules) or a snake (if Cernunnos) perhaps.

There used to be a maypole set on top of this hill, and this reinforces the symbolic power of the Giant: fertility. Sitting on the phallus is said to be a cure for human infertility too; though if you are considering attempting this a summer evening might be better than mid winter, and do watch out for the fences which surround him. Mind you, there are further legends which insist that to maximise your chances of falling with child you should visit on the shortest day of the year, and only sit when completely naked. There is another action which is suppose to enhance your odds, but I'll leave that to your imagination.

He is certainly a fearsome figure, and naturally there are many other legends as to his purpose and origins. The strange shape of the 120 foot club has suggested to some that he is a carving of an alien who landed here thousands of years ago; the local folk tale is that he is the drawing of a giant who ravaged the Vale of Blackmoor, only to be pegged to the ground here to die, and then have an outline carved around his body. If this last were true, then perhaps the giant set the precedent for all those modern films where the murder victim's last position is drawn on the floor with chalk!

Whatever the truth may be, the giant of Cerne is not easy to forget, and is an intriguing anachronism, even amongst the antiquities of rural Dorset.

Unlike Milton Abbas, Cerne continued to flourish into the 19th century, but paid a higher price after the dissolution of the monasteries, as very little now remains of its 10th century Abbey. The next enemy to the town was the new railway system, which left Cerne alone, with the result that its prosperity faded. Today you can see a mix of housing styles here, with rare survivors from about 1500 in Abbey Street and stone cottages of the 17th century in Long Street among the best.

To the north of Cerne at **MINTERNE MAGNA** you can find the MINTERNE GARDENS (01300 341370), with rare trees, shrubs, lakes, cascades and streams all set in flourishing, landscaped valley gardens.

Another particularly scenic drive will take you south west from Cerne on the road to **SYDLING ST NICHOLAS**. If the route is worth taking for the views into the valley of the SYDLING WATER, then the village at the end of your journey comes as an extra delight. In its own way, this is another of Dorset's finest.

Lines and patterns on the hillsides overlooking the village are the only remaining signs of settlements that were here long before the Romans invaded, and even some of the vegetation is ancient, with the yew trees in the vicarage gardens estimated at a thousand years of age.

It is probable that as farming tools became stronger the people of the area moved down into the protection of the valley, and Sydling itself was formed as they now had the ability to cope with its sturdier soil. There are cottages of yellow ham stone and flint, covered in climbing rose and clematis, and plenty of rich, golden thatch. The village church suffered much during the Civil War, but the enormous font survived, and is thought to be made of material of Roman origin and over a thousand years old itself.

The church of St Nicholas also has a small but poignant moment in the history of cinema and the work of Thomas Hardy, as it was used as a location for the filming of 'Far From The Madding Crowd' in the 1960s. After Frank Troy discovers that his first love, Fanny Robin, and their infant child have died he shows that he is not the completely cold hearted man he has so far shown himself to be by finding bulbs to plant at their grave. One of the most moving moments of the novel is when the rain pours from the gargoyles on the church roof and destroys this man's one act of true love, while he sleeps helplessly nearby. There are real gargoyles on the church here, and the setting was a fine choice.

A little further south the village of **GODMANSTONE** boasts the smallest pub in England, with a royal connection too. THE SMITHS ARMS is in the old thatched forge of the village, and the story goes that King Charles II asked the blacksmith for a glass of porter. When he was told that the forge did not have a licence to sell such a thing, the King replied to the effect that it did now!

The Smiths Arms, Godmanstone.

Dorset does seem to have made good use of the King, his exploits keep cropping up all over the county. Alcohol seems a common theme too, but perhaps this just reflects the ultimate marketing skills of the licensing trade, getting in first to sell beer on the back of a local Royal legend. Not that there is anything wrong with the beer, far from it.

Between here and the border with Somerset lie many more villages worthy of exploration, varied in their buildings, size, and style, as well as setting. **MELBURY OSMOND**, for instance, has stone, thatched cottages which lie along a winding slope leading down to a paved ford with a footbridge. In contrast **EVERSHOT** has a 19th century urban look, although it is a small place, and is one of the very highest of Dorset's villages, being 700 feet above sea level. Continue to drive among the lanes, and you will find much, much more.

As we turn towards Sherborne, consider the bravery of a man who lived in what is perhaps one of the less glamourous of these places, **YETMINSTER**. Benjamin Jesty lived in a time when smallpox was rife, and in 1774 his family were in immediate danger, as others steadily died of the disease all around them. He made a connection between smallpox and cowpox. If you had contracted the latter you recovered, but seemed not to catch the deadlier form.

Benjamin particularly noticed that milkmaids appeared immune to smallpox. Eventually he decide to take a drastic step; he deliberately infected his wife and children with cowpox, as he had already been through a bout of the disease. At first things looked bad, and his wife became very ill. She recovered, but Benjamin was apparently seen as a crank and a foolhardy man by the community around him, despite the fact that he had stumbled upon the principle of vaccination, and none of his family suffered in the smallpox epidemic. They are buried in Worth Matravers, and the gravestone for Jesty's wife shows that she lived to the age of eighty four.

SHERBORNE (Tourist Information 01935 815341) seems like quite a metropolis after our journey through the villages. It is also one of the most aesthetically pleasing towns you could wish to find anywhere. With its grandiose Abbey Church and Castles, this is as far from Blandford, in character, as you could get. The town centre, full of shops offering hand crafted, local wares and quality tourist shopping including antiques, fine art and fashion, has many very old buildings helping to give its mellow, unhurried atmosphere. Sherborne is not a particularly large place though, and its centre is especially compact, making it an ideal place to explore on foot. Before you get there, your eyes are bound to be caught by the two castles, separated only by the lake and landscaped lawns designed by Capability Brown in the 18th century, in order to fill the hollow between them.

Sherborne Castles, Old and New.

The newer SHERBORNE CASTLE (01935 813182) was built in 1594 by Sir Walter Raleigh, whose family lived in Sherborne while he sought the gold of El Dorado. It is certainly an unusual building, and another which seems perhaps unsuited to the title of castle. The hexagonal turrets and rendered walls look far more decorative than functional, and the interior has much more in common with the splendour of Kingston Lacy than the austerity of Portland Castle.

It was built as Sherborne Lodge, because the older castle was still in use, and the rest of the name only came later. Raleigh had made an attempt to make the older building habitable for his family, but the medieval stone structure was more practical than comfortable, as the Civil War would go on to show.

Looking up to the ruins of the old castle, there is a marked contrast between the two, emphasised by the lack of any warmth about the stark ruins in comparison to the homely, if a little eccentric, design of the new, with its many ornamental chimneys sticking like needles into the sky.

When Raleigh was taken to the Tower of London after the succession of James I, the new castle was taken over by Sir John Digby, later made Earl of Bristol. The Digby family still owns the property, and that is why the interior has collected such a number of beautiful rooms, which have changed gradually and only for the better over the centuries. Look in particular for some superb furniture and paintings.

The old castle is impressive, even as merely fragmental ruins. It was constructed in the beginnings of the 12th century by the Bishop of Salisbury. By now, as we have heard the tale of Dorset's history, you can probably make a good guess as to the time of its downfall, especially if you think of Corfe.

The Digbys (who had both Sherborne castles at this point) were prominent Royalists, and the older castle became a stronghold for the King. It was besieged by forces vastly superior in number to its garrison in 1642, but only eventually fell right at the end of the Civil War, in 1645. That the 1642 force of six thousand men failed to take this castle is a great tribute to its design, and it is no wonder that Cromwell called it:

"a malicious, mischievous castle"

Now it looks sad, and deserted, and by the strong lines of what does remain you cannot help but feel sorry that it has not survived to provide an even more impressive backdrop to the newer building and landscaping.

To find what is probably the most important piece of architecture in Dorset to have survived the Civil War, and much else besides, you will have to go into the town centre of Sherborne. SHERBORNE ABBEY was a cathedral for three hundred and seventy years, until William the Conqueror moved the title to Salisbury in 1075. Sherborne still feels like a place of importance, and it is fascinating to speculate what might have been if it had retained its status as a cathedral city.

The present day Abbey is actually the Church of St Mary and was built in the 15th century, after fire ravaged the older buildings. Its most famous and beautiful feature is the stone, fan-vaulted ceiling. The intricacies of this are astounding, and grandeur does not seem a powerful enough term to give to the character this amazing piece of stonework gives to the building.

There are, apparently, 115 bosses in the high vault of the nave alone, and mirror trolleys are provided so that you can gaze upon their beauty and variety without having to live with a stiff neck for days afterwards.

There is a great deal more to see in this unforgettable church and it is also the best place to start from in a walk around this historic town. On the south western edge of the green outside the church is the ALMSHOUSE OF ST JOHN, a splendid looking medieval building in itself, which was given Royal Licence by Henry VI in 1437 to provide succour for the old and impoverished of the town. It must have been a luxurious setting in which to spend your final days, but then again you were expected to give up all your possessions before entering.

On the other side of the green you can get to SHERBORNE MUSEUM (01935 812252) in the Abbey Gate House. This has displays about the abbey, almshouses, castles, and many aspects of local life, including the public school for boys, which can claim to be the eldest in England and has its main building just north of the Abbey.

If the school looks at all familiar, though a little colourful, it could well be that you are remembering it from one of the best black and white films for a good bout of sentiment: 'Goodbye Mr Chips', which was filmed here. The Second World War scenes, with news of various ex-pupils' death in action have particularly stayed in my mind.

Cheap Street is the main thoroughfare of Sherborne, with shops built of the same local yellowy stone which gives the rest of the town its soft, pastel, almost dusty appearance. There are buildings from the 16th century onwards, and a few 19th century shop-fronts have remained unchanged.

The surrounding roads are worth exploring too, as the character of Sherborne is maintained outside of its main shopping street, in Newland Street and Long Street in particular. Even on a drive in or out of the town you will see many stone houses, with red brick window surrounds and arched doorways, which are good to look at in themselves, and make for unusually pleasant suburbs. Sherborne really does appear to have aged from the middle outwards, as each ring of estates gets more recent as you travel out from the centre.

Sherborne has kept its appeal because of what it does not have, as much as what it does. There are no modern eyesores here, and no recent rapid expansion of the shopping areas, as at Yeovil, for example. The shops are in attractive buildings because that's pretty much all there is here, which makes it a lovely place to spend some time.

With a LEISURE CENTRE (01935 814011) and an ARTS CENTRE (01935 813433), the town provides somewhere to come to after spending the daytime exploring the surrounding villages and countryside too, or perhaps to end a day spent at the SHERBORNE GOLF CLUB (01935 812475).

A trip out, just to the west of Sherborne is WORLDLIFE (01935 74608), a conservation centre around COMPTON HOUSE. As well as the butterflies for which it is famous, this also incorporates the LULLINGSTONE SILK FARM, which declares itself the only silk farm in Britain, providing silk for the Royal Wedding dresses of both Lady Diana and Elizabeth II.

The production of the silk is fascinating, and with gardens with both tame and wild animals (and humans too!), the adaptation of the centre to become a fundraiser for conservational charity has been a success and a pleasure to visit. The small area between Sherborne and the border with Somerset has another attraction in **SANDFORD ORCAS**. This little village was in Somerset until 1896, but will remind you of other Dorset places, with leafy lanes and small, hedged, fields and straggling houses following a stream down the valley. Another intriguing place-name, the suffix Orcas is an abbreviation of the unpalatable Orescuilz, the Norman who once owned the manor.

SANDFORD ORCAS MANOR HOUSE (01963 220206) was built from the increasingly ubiquitous golden Ham Hill stone in the 1550s. Not as big or splendid as some of the other houses you may have visited, this has other qualities. Only three families have owned the Tudor Manor since it was built, and the Medlycotts have been the residents for the last two hundred and fifty years. You can see some of their excellent Queen Anne and Jacobean furniture, but the difference here is that you will be guided around the house by the owners, and the emphasis is on the house as it is now; lived in rather than preserved.

Now we must head east, to complete our journey through Dorset at Shaftesbury. The most direct route from Sherborne would take us in and out of Somerset, and would also leave out some more villages and towns which should not be missed. So it is that we quickly regain rich pasturelands around the CAUNDLE villages. **STOURTON CAUNDLE** is probably the most attractive; the land is noticeably flatter than that encountered in most of Dorset, and with lots of willows and alders is reminiscent of Northern France. Mind you, that is probably not a good thing to say in these parts.

When Roman Polanski filmed his version of Hardy's 'Tess' some twenty years ago, there was an outcry in these parts of Dorset because he chose to film in France. The film is excellent, I feel, even as an adaptation of Hardy, but perhaps that is despite the French countryside and the choice of a young Polish actress to play the young Dorset maiden of the title, rather than because of the strange choices.

This is definitely still the heart of Dorset. **BISHOPS CAUNDLE** is the subject of a long poem by WILLIAM BARNES, Dorset's dialect poet. His work is not easy to follow for the uninitiated, but the mood of the celebrations he describes can be caught, and gives the village a cheerful enough epitaph:

> *In Caundle, vor a day at least,*
> *You woudden vind a scowlen feace,*
> *Or dumpy heart in all the pleace."*

Perhaps the biggest surprise to the modern visitor is that he could find enough people congregated here to justify his words, for these villages are quiet places now. The poem was written at the celebrations of victory at the Battle of Waterloo, so perhaps it was not quite a typical scene, even then.

STALBRIDGE is a busier, everyday place, with a Ham stone Market Cross which has survived in a county where so many others perished during the Civil War. If you have reason to take the northern road out of the town you may wonder what the immensely long wall (five miles of it in all) by the roadside once encircled. All that remains now are two stone gate pillars, topped with carved lions.

There was a house here, known as Stalbridge Park, which was eventually demolished in 1822. It has two claims to distinction, though the more credible is not necessarily the more fascinating.

Robert Boyle lived here in the 17th century. You may not have heard of him, but you have undoubtedly felt the benefits of his legacy, for Boyle was the first to show how air could be compressed, starting the process which led to production of the modern tyre. Strange to think how many thousands of these are now impelled on their way past the empty site of his home, by drivers who are mostly completely ignorant of his efforts.

The other story concerns the figure of a blazing woman, said to haunt a certain room of the building each day at five o'clock in the afternoon. The legend says that this was the ultimate mother-in-law; she had deliberately set fire to her son's wife, and then blamed the horrific death on an accident. Confessing to the son on her deathbed, she then haunted the building, consumed by the fires of guilt. Strange story; not least because such apparitions are usually nocturnal. Perhaps she roamed later during British Summer Time, to make her illuminating presence of more practical use. Are ghosts aware of the clocks going back?

STURMINSTER NEWTON is another place with a character all its own, individual, yet hard to define. This is where the poet William Barnes went to school, and Sturminster is still very much a rural, agricultural centre, traditionally known as the capital of the Blackmoor Vale.

It is also a labyrinth of tiny streets at its centre, the newer, residential and industrial estates are on the outskirts. More like Blandford than Sherborne, the shop-fronts here are quite old, especially around the market place, but the shops are more practical than decorative. In a way Sturminster is the most old fashioned of the Dorset towns, empty every week day except Monday, which is market day. It is not necessarily a romantic place, but it is very real, without deserving the label of being down to earth. The locals call it 'Stur', but without any allusion to the slang term for a spell in prison.

The junction of the A357 which takes you to the town from the main Blandford road is distinctive for the immediacy with which you then cross the Stour, which flows to the south and west of Sturminster. This gives you little time to notice the fine bridge across the river, or to look for the mill, which is a shame.

STURMINSTER NEWTON MILL AND MUSEUM (01747 854355) lets you see the working water mill in action, as well as looking at local history. Two hundred yards along from the bridge, the mill of 18th century brick is an unpretentious box of a building, but set on the Stour it cannot fail to look romantic as it fulfils its purpose of harnessing the power of the wide waters. The coarse fishing here is especially good, but beware damaging the bridge as the sign still declares the penalty to be transportation to Australia! Perhaps you might get lucky and receive a mitigated modern sentence; watching Australian television programmes in this country, for instance.

A mile or so down river there is another, smaller mill at **FIDDLEFORD**; this one has been quiet for some time, but its setting, with the building reflected in the stillness of the mill pond, is memorable. Also by the majestic Stour is one of the oldest manor houses in Dorset, FIDDLEFORD MANOR. Go in and look up, and you are bound to think back to Sherborne Abbey. The ceilings of the hall and solar wing at Fiddleford is of wood rather than stone, but is just as fascinating nevertheless. These heavy, vaulted timbers have been here for more than six hundred years, and look ready to survive well into the future.

While this is area is not as conventionally picturesque as some in the county, without the golden Ham stone of the west, or the Purbeck stone and marble of the south, there are many bits of the past which will make you stop and look. Another such is the Pack-horse bridge just to the west of **FIFEHEAD NEVILLE**. This is made of stone with two pointed arches, which look ready to provide an exact fit for a canal barge passing underneath. It is an incidental addition to your travels, but sights like this piece of medieval craftsmanship are what makes Dorset such a fascinating place in which to make new discoveries.

Despite Polanski's choice of setting for his film, Hardy's 'Tess of the D'Urbevilles' was written about this area, and the heroine's birthplace and home were at *Marlott*, which, in the real world, is **MARNHULL**, to the north of Sturminster.

I must admit to this book being my personal favourite among his works. It also has a great deal to say about life in rural Dorset, without any romanticising.

Early in the book Hardy describes the Blackmoor Vale, see if it fits with your appreciation of it today:

This fertile and sheltered tract of country, in which the fields are never brown and the springs never dry,.......... the fields are mere paddocks,...... their hedgerows appear a network of dark green threads overspreading the paler green of the grass. The atmosphere is languorous.... arable lands are few and limited; but with slight exceptions the prospect is a broad rich mass of grass and trees, mantling minor hills and dales within the major. Such is the Vale of Blackmoor."

I think 'Tess' is such a convincing tale because of its very double-edged ending; there is no temporarily satisfying but ultimately unrealistic, sugary sentiment in it, and the hard lives of the characters are reflected in what you see around you, even now. Hardy shows it how it is, the countryside is beautiful, but this is not a utopia. In the same way, Marnhull is a long, straggling place, not easy to familiarise yourself with, but rewarding all the same.

This is not to say that the area is a miserable one, and as if to prove this beyond doubt one of the ultimate exponents of humour in a rural setting was brought up at nearby **EAST STOUR**. Henry Fielding lived here in the 18th century, and though most of what he knew as a child has gone, the surrounding countryside still looks like plausible hunting ground for Parson Adams and Mr Partridge, or their wards Joseph Andrews and Tom Jones. Still, perhaps it is fair to say that the bawdy, roistering picture of rural England that Fielding entertained with was partly what Hardy had to replace with starker reality, though still with a very human touch. For the real Fielding addict (guilty as charged) it is worth adding that he came back to East Stour after his marriage, and that his daughter Amelia was born here in 1735. 'Amelia' is also the name of Fielding's least famous novel, which is a great read nevertheless.

Before turning to our last destination, Shaftesbury, you can get another look at local history in **GILLINGHAM**, at the GILLINGHAM MUSEUM (01747 822173 / 823176). The town used to be in the middle of a forest, but it has been completely cleared, leaving Gillingham a rather bleak edge to the Blackmoor Vale. The new museum has interesting exhibits on the surrounding villages, as well as Gillingham itself, including a manual fire engine from 1790 which is apparently the only one of its type to have survived.

By now Dorset would seem to have exhausted its supply of variety and beauty, but as you approach Shaftesbury, looking down at you over its surrounding hamlets and villages, there is an inkling that there is yet more to come. As you enter the town there seem to be more colours to add the Dorset spectrum, as stone buildings aged with moss give dark greens, browns and greys. More than any other town in the county **SHAFTESBURY** (Tourist Information 01747 853514) exudes age from every crevice of its centre.

If you hear imaginary music near the town centre it is likely to be an extract from Dvorak's 9th, New World, Symphony. You might also start to think of a boy toiling up a steep, cobbled hill, pushing a bicycle. GOLD HILL is Shaftesbury's most famous street, and it used to be a great surprise to many to realise that its cobbles were not further north in the country, as the 'Hovis' commercials for which it was so famous might have suggested.

Gold Hill, Shaftesbury.

At risk of courting controversy, I would argue that Gold Hill is not perhaps all you might expect. It is certainly picturesque, with gorgeous views across the surrounding countryside, and it is accessible too, just around the back of the Parish Church of St Peter and the Council buildings right in the middle of the town.

The hill curves dramatically away from you, and it is the way in which the houses have been built to follow the contour of the slope which makes the street so attractive. However, take a short walk down to the first bend and, horror of horrors, the exquisite cobbling, with lines of green where the grass tries to grow in between the stones, ends suddenly, giving cars access to all but the top twenty or so houses.

Perhaps I am a little cruel to suggest that Clovelly, in North Devon, is the place to see a better example of a pedestrian only, steep cobbled hill, which runs right down to the sea, and makes an exhausting round trip. But if Gold Hill may not quite live up to its billing (the famous advertisement followed the bike *up* the hill, so the best section was always in shot) then just a few steps away is a place which I think more than makes up for it.

As you walk down Gold Hill it is only the left hand side of the road which has houses, the right has a huge buttressed wall, looking old and strong, not surprisingly considering what used to be behind it. This was where Shaftesbury's Abbey had its grounds, and signs direct you to the remaining ruins past the top end of the wall. The first impression if you take this path into PARK WALK, is of a promenade with no seafront.

Looking south there is an ocean of green laid out beneath you, with hardly a human habitation in the further perspectives. The walk is broad, running in front of the Abbey ruins to the north, with a narrow garden border keeping you from the fenced precipice in the opposite direction. Even on a gloomy day the views are such that is nigh on impossible to resist the benches, and to pass without sitting to soak in a little more of the panorama, as your eyes search among the uplands of the Cranborne Chase, with Melbury Beacon providing a central focal point.

Once you have seen enough, a turn at the War Memorial, which is at the end of the broader section of Park Walk, will take you into ABBEY WALK. The abbey has gone, only the footings remain, outlined in the lawns. A short walk around THE TRINITY CENTRE, which is what was the 19th century Holy Trinity Church, and you are back where you started, by the Town Hall. Incredible to think that six hundred years ago this town had the largest population of any town in Dorset.

The Abbey was founded by King Alfred in 888 for his daughter, Aethelgifu, who was the first abbess. The nunnery was the centre of an increasingly prosperous Shaftesbury, especially after the bones of Edward the Martyr, who was murdered at Corfe Castle, were brought to the abbey. They were thought to work miracles, particularly in the healing of the sick.

In medieval times such relics were the biggest draw a town could have. Holidays meant single days, pretty much exclusively, and the pilgrimage was the closest thing to the modern day tourist industry. Chaucer's General Prologue to the Canterbury Tales shows how this worked, with the collection of character portraits reminding us of a present day coach outing.

It is thought that Edward's bones were among those recovered in an excavation of the abbey remains earlier this century, but the fact that the famous relics were in an unmarked box shows how far the industry had declined by the 16th century, when the nunnery fell to Henry VIII's dissolution of the monasteries.

At its height the Abbey's estate was huge, reaching as far as Bradford upon Avon in Wiltshire. Not much of it is left, even the Abbey stone was quarried and purloined for other buildings, some in the town itself. At the top of Gold Hill you can find out more about local history at the SHAFTESBURY ABBEY MUSEUM (01747 852910). The town did make an economic recovery in the 17th and 18th century, as a centre for coaching and button making, but the industrial revolution effectively ended Shaftesbury's second period of prosperity.

There are other things to see in Shaftesbury, such as the Pump Court in St James, a delightful courtyard with a water pump at its centre; but somehow Park Walk seems the best place to start and finish your visit to the town. Of all the views in Dorset, it has to be one of the very best.

If you wish to end in a quieter place then the village of **ASHMORE**, to the south east of Shaftesbury, and right up against the Wiltshire border, is the highest in Dorset, and has more of the best views.

For a time of quiet reflection there can be few more suitable places than this, a settlement formed in Roman times around the pond which is still at the centre of the village. There is a local custom which says that when the pond dries up cakes must be eaten while you sit on its dried up bed. Apparently this doesn't happen very often, so I would not recommend home baking in your preparations for a visit.

From the village, and from vantage points around it, you can see west and south for many miles, even to the Isle of Wight on a good day, but the beauty of Dorset lies at your very feet, and by now it will surely have charmed you. Despite the undoubted attractions of Dorset's resorts and coastline, increased since it gained Bournemouth and Poole, it is the rural heart of this county which can make the longest impression. The longer you look down upon it, the more beautiful it will seem.

THE ACORN INN
Evershot
Dorchester
Dorset
DT2 0JW

Tel: 01935 83228
Fax: 01935 891330

Recently acquired by Martyn Lee this village inn is in the process of being refurbished although to go there at the moment would give anyone pleasure. Evershot is one of those beautiful Dorset villages which have so often been used for films. Tess of the D'urbevilles in Thomas Hardy's book stopped here at 'The Sow and Acorn'. It is a delight with its lovely houses, fine old main street and a complete sense of its own worth. The Acorn fits in perfectly with its air of well-being, stability and ambience which is enhanced by the furnishings and the nooks and crannies. It is a Free-house and such has a wide range of ales and beers as well as a comprehensive wine list.

The pretty restaurant seats 30 comfortably and provides diners with a restful atmosphere in which to enjoy the beautifully cooked food which is mainly traditional English. The main bar is a lively place and here you can get any number of Bar Snacks all fresh and home-cooked. The Skittle Alley is another much used place and can be booked for parties which are great fun.

There are nine ensuite bedrooms, two rooms have four-posters and there are two spacious family rooms. One of the beds is a splendid six footer with Edwardian marquetry headboard and base. The rooms are attractively and comfortably furnished and each has direct dial telephone, television and a hostess tray.

Beautiful walks in the surrounding area, ancient woodlands, drovers tracks, lovely hills and lakes as well as the sea at West Bay within ten miles, make The Acorn Inn a great place to stay for a holiday or a break.

USEFUL INFORMATION

- OPEN: All year 11.30-2.30pm
  & 6.30-11pm
- WHEELCHAIR ACCESS: Yes
- GARDEN: Yes
- CREDIT CARDS: All major cards
- ACCOMMODATION: 9 ensuite rooms
- RATES: Sgl £40-60 B&B Dbl £80-120
  Children in same room £10

- RESTAURANT: English home- cooking.
- VEGETARIAN: A daily choice
- BAR FOOD: Extensive choice
- LICENSED: Full On & Supper licence
- CHILDREN: Welcome

- PETS: Yes £10 (refundable)deposit

THE BENNETT ARMS
Semley
Shaftesbury
Dorset
SP7 9AS

Tel: 01747 830221
Fax: 01747 830152

The Bennett Arms was built as a hostelry four hundred years ago and has stood on the village green, overlooking the church and surrounded by common land, ever since. It is that air of permanence that strikes you when you walk through its welcoming doors to be greeted by Joe Duthie, who has been mine host here since 1976. His welcome, like the rest of his staff, is genuinely warm-hearted and their great desire is to ensure everyone, whether regulars or visitors, enjoy being in the pub. It maybe you will just call in for a drink as the locals do; they are great conversationalists and you will always hear a lot of sport talk especially golf and cricket. Maybe you will come to stay a while either on business or pleasure, or possibly you will have heard how good the food is and make a beeline for The Bennett Arms in the certainty that you will have an excellent meal which may be in the restaurant or in the bar.

Joyce James was the cook here even before Joe arrived and her meals are legendary. The wife of a farmer, she believes that everyone should be well fed. Her dishes are very varied. You may start with a simple, delicious home-made soup of the day, Moules Mariniere, Avocado with Grand Antipasto or a Greek Salad, and that is just a few of the choices. Main Courses are equally exciting. For example, Joyce produces one of the best Bouillabaisse's you will ever taste , Stincotto - half shank of Italian Pork roasted and served with Soya and Ginger Sauce - if you have simple tastes there is always fresh grilled fish available and tender, perfectly grilled steaks. With the exception of ices, all the delectable sweets are made on the premises. The range of bar food is equally varied from a sandwich to smoked salmon.

Staying in the guest bedrooms, one of which has a four-poster and all are ensuite, centrally heated, have television and a hostess tray, allows you to enjoy the delightful atmosphere of The Bennett Arms to the full and because it is so well situated there are endless places to visit from Longleat to Salisbury Cathedral, Gold Hill in Shaftesbury, Stourhead with its wonderful gardens and the best collection of Chippendale furniture in England, and Stonehenge.

USEFUL INFORMATION

- OPEN: All day except Dec25 &26
- WHEELCHAIR ACCESS: Difficult
- GARDEN: Yes
- CREDIT CARDS: All major cards
- ACCOMMODATION: 5 ensuite rooms
- RATES: From £31 pp B&B

- RESTAURANT: Exciting menu
- VEGETARIAN: Always a choice
- BAR FOOD: Wide range
- LICENSED: Full On
- CHILDREN: Welcome
- PETS: Yes

THE EASTBURY HOTEL
Long Street
Sherborne
Dorset
DT9 3BY

Tel: 01935 813131
Fax: 01935 817296

*** AA & RAC. 4 Crowns
Commended. Johansens

The Eastbury Hotel and Restaurant, an elegant Georgian town house hotel with fifteen delightful en-suite bedrooms, all named after traditional English flowers. Each room has bathroom en-suite, tea and coffee making facilities, fresh flowers, colour television, hairdryer and direct dial telephone.

The Hotel is charming, beautifully furnished with a mixture of antiques of the period and other pieces. It has a welcoming tranquillity which has been fostered by the owners, Tom and Alison Pickford. These two, very professional and friendly people, together with their Staff, strive always to ensure the comfort and well-being of their guests. The award winning Conservatory Restaurant and Terrace overlook an acre of walled gardens. The Restaurant is open to non-residents and serves delicious traditional English and French fare both at lunch and dinner. The wine list complements the food with an interesting, and affordable, selection from around the world. In the cosy bar one can enjoy a drink and if you are peckish or in a hurry, they serve freshly cut, well filled sandwiches. It is a super place to stay and one recommended enthusiastically by those in the know.

Sherborne with its magnificent Abbey and two Castles is one of England's most delightful towns. Everything about it is gracious and it has the added benefit of being close to many interesting places including Montacute, a beautiful stately home. Dorchester is not far away and in the opposite direction are Shaftesbury and Salisbury. Within the town itself there is much to see and do including the local Sports Centre and the superb Castle Gardens. Those who enjoy sporting activities will find Clay Pigeon Shooting, golf courses and horse riding as well as good walks.

USEFUL INFORMATION

- OPEN: All year.
  Lunch 12-2pm Dinner 7.30-9.30pm
- WHEELCHAIR ACCESS: No
- GARDEN: Yes
- CREDIT CARDS: Yes. Not Diners
- ACCOMMODATION: 15 ensuite rooms
- RATES: Sgl £49.50 Dbl from £39.50

- RESTAURANT: Beautifully presented traditional English/French
- VEGETARIAN: Yes
- BAR FOOD: Sandwiches & snacks
- LICENSED: Yes
- CHILDREN: Welcome
- PETS: No

THE PHEASANTS RESTAURANT WITH ROOMS
24 Greenhill
Sherborne
Dorset   DT9 4EU

Tel: 01935 815252

AA 2 Rosette. AA QQQQ Selected.
Good Food Guide. Michelin

Sherborne is a town full of architectural and scenic beauty with its two castles, public schools and the Abbey -'the most architecturally significant building in Dorset'. Adding to its distinction both architecturally and gastronomically is The Pheasants Restaurant, built early in the 1800s. It is a place of charm and elegance with the decor in relaxing pastel colours enhancing the Ham stone and beams. It has become a favourite with the lovers of good food in Sherborne and quite a distance away. It is not only the excellence of the food and the exciting wine list that brings people here - it is much more. The atmosphere is redolent of well-being and simply encourages diners to relax from the moment they walk in. The friendly bar and lounge make ideal meeting places for friends to gather, enjoy a drink and peruse the menu which incidentally has set prices depending on whether you have three or four courses at dinner or two or three at lunch.

The restaurant with its attractively laid tables and sparkling glass seats forty in comfortable intimacy. The dinner menu which changes frequently offers 8 'Introductions' which may include bacon, chorizo and black pudding Salade Tiede, smoked haddock with caviar or a delicious cream of watercress and cucumber soup. As a 'continuation' the choice is superb with possibly Saddle of Venison en Croute or sea bass with saffron or a fillet steak enfolding stilton cheese, wrapped by smoked bacon cooked in the oven until just pink and presented with a port and tarragon cream sauce. Equally the chef will be pleased to serve a fillet steak plain or with any preferred other sauce. The 'conclusion' offers delectable desserts or a substantial selection of five English and French cheeses served with grapes, celery and crisp apple slices. At luncheon the menu is slightly more restricted but the choices will tempt any lover of good food. The wine list offers some of the best house wine you will find anywhere and wines that will excite the palate of any wine buff and with every wine on the list well described, the choice is made simple for those who enjoy wine but maybe have no great knowledge. The service is delightful, efficient and unobtrusive.

There are six ensuite rooms at The Pheasants, each individually furnished and extremely comfortable with television. An ideal place in which to stay whether on business or pleasure. It is also ideal for a small conference of not more than twenty five people.

USEFUL INFORMATION

- OPEN: Mid January-end December;
  Lunch: Sat & Sun 12-2pm
- Dinner: Tues-Saturdays 6.30-10pm
- WHEELCHAIR ACCESS: Yes
- BAR FOOD; Not applicable
- CREDIT CARDS: Visa
- ACCOMMODATION: 6 ensuite rooms
  - Open 7 days
- RATES: Single £40 Double £55

- RESTAURANT; Superb food
- VEGETARIAN: Always a choice

- LICENSED: Yes Restaurant Licence

- CHILDREN: Welcome
- PETS: No

PLUMBER MANOR
Sturminster Newton
Dorset
DT10 2AF

Tel: 01258 472507
Fax: 01258 473370
plumbermanor@btinternet.com

ETB 4 Crowns Highly Commended
AA 3 stars Restaurant 2 Rosettes

Plumber was built by Charles Brune in the early 17th Century and has remained a family home for the Prideaux-Brunes. In 1973 Richard, Alison and Brian turned their home into a restaurant with bedrooms under the careful management of the family. Set in the midst of Hardy's Dorset and surrounded by the Home Farm this imposing Jacobean structure built from local stone stands well back in its extensive lawns under the shade of fine old trees. The Divelish stream, tributary of the River Stour runs through these grounds of peace and seclusion. The manor is splendidly situated as a touring centre for the unspoilt countryside of Dorset, the picturesque villages of Milton Abbas, Cerne Abbas, the Piddle Valley and the coastal towns of Lyme Regis, Lulworth and Abbotsbury. The historic splendours of Kingston Lacy, Athelhampton, Montacute and Stourhead are close at hand. The coast is less than 30 miles away, several golf courses, coarse fishing on the Stour, riding and clay pigeon shooting are all available nearby. Free stabling on a do it yourself basis is available to guests wishing to hack or hunt with local packs (Blackmore Vale, Portman, Cattistock and South Dorset). A full livery service is available nearby.

The superb restaurant is the mainstay of the business. Brian Prideaux-Brune's cooking long since recognised by all the major guides provides a balance of imaginative and traditional cuisine using the finest of fresh ingredients and is well supported by an extensive wine list. The restaurant is in three rooms where guests may dine in an informal yet elegant ambience, private parties especially catered for.

In the main house there are six very comfortable bedrooms all with private bathrooms facing south and west, they are approached from a charming gallery hung with family portraits. For guests there is a sitting room and a bar with a residential licence. In 1982 a natural stone barn lying within the grounds was converted adding a further six very large bedrooms all with window seats overlooking the stream and garden. In 1990 the courtyard was completed giving four more spacious individually furnished bedrooms.

USEFUL INFORMATION

- OPEN: March -January
- WHEELCHAIR ACCESS: Yes
- GARDEN: Yes. Tennis & Croquet

- CREDIT CARDS: All major cards
- ACCOMMODATION:16 ensuite rms
- RATES: From £45-70sgl Dbl £95-140

- RESTAURANT: English/French cuisine
- VEGETARIAN: Always a choice
- SMOKING DISCOURAGED BUT NOT FORBIDDEN
- LICENSED: Yes
- CHILDREN: Welcome
- PETS: Yes

POACHERS INN
Piddletrenthide
Dorset
DT2 7QX

Tel: 01300 348358

3 Crown Commended.
AA QQQ

Nine members of the Fox family take an active part in running this excellent hostelry, in the lovely Piddl;e Valley and just six miles from the historic county town, Dorchester. Having made your base The Poachers Inn you might well set forth to discover the Roman Ampitheatre 'Maumbury Rings' on the southern edge of Dorchester or a little further on the Iron Age Hill Fort of 'Maiden Castle'. It was in Dorchester that the infamous Judge Jeffrey held what has become known as 'The Bloody Assize'. The Old Crown Court in High West Street was the trial venue for the Tolpuddle Martyrs. Thomas Hardy lived and worked in Dorchester and his home Max Gate is open to the public. The seaside town of Weymouth is nearby and there are many sporting activities to keep you busy including sea angling.

The reputation of The Poachers has reached out far and wide and many guests return to stay here regularly, looking forward to enjoying not only the warmth and hospitality of The Poacher but also the excellence of its food, wines and well kept ale. The Restaurant with its attractively laid tables, has an extensive a la carte menu with tasty Daily Specials, many of them time honoured favourites. One can also eat in the well stocked bar from a menu which includes a lot of interesting dishes or something as simple as a well filled, freshly cut sandwich. The Riverside Garden attracts many people in summer and is complete with a heated outdoor pool, sun beds and other garden furniture. If you decide to stay here you will find the ensuite bedrooms are beautifully appointed, some with four posters and there are also ground floor rooms. Every room has colour television, a hostess tray and telephones.

USEFUL INFORMATION

- OPEN: All year. 11-11pm Summer only
- WHEELCHAIR ACCESS: Yes
- GARDEN: Riverside with pool
- CREDIT CARDS: Master/Visa
- ACCOMMODATION: Ensuite rooms
- RATES: Short breaks 1st Oct-30 April
  2 nights DBB £66 3rd night DBB free
  excluding Bank Holidays.
  Daily Rates from £25 BB

- RESTAURANT: Good menu
- VEGETARIAN: Always a choice
- BAR FOOD; Wide range. Specials
- LICENSED: Full On
- CHILDREN: Welcome

- PETS: Yes £1 per night

STOURCASTLE LODGE
Gouge's Close
Sturminster Newton
Dorset   DT10 1BU
Tel: 01258 472320
Fax: 01258 473381
AA QQQQ

Even if Stourcastle Lodge were not the fascinating house that it is, Jill and Ken Hookham-Bassett, the owners would make it very special. They are people who have a keen interest in everything they do and that is manifested in the excellent manner in which they care for their guests. Stourcastle Lodge is situated just off the Market square in Sturminster Newton, tucked away down the quaint stone walled Gough's Close leading to the River Stour. It has been a family home since the beginning of the eighteenth century. Originally a thatched farmhouse known as 'Orchard Farm Cottage', it has been renovated in the traditional style over the last 300 years and recently Jill and Ken have completed extensions to the house which have added to its charm. The famous and sometimes notorious Dashwood family owned the house and each bedroom bears the name of one of its past inhabitants. Hence you may well find yourself sleeping in Elizabeth's or Thomas's room. It is such a relaxing house in which to stay. The cottage style gardens are home to some fascinating sculptures and you'll find Henrietta and her seven piglets if you look carefully. At night time there are frequent visits from the resident hedgehog family. In the warmer months it is a sheer pleasure to relax on the south facing terrace. For chilly evenings you can laze around the blazing log fire in the cosy sitting room.

The elegantly decorated bedrooms, some with whirlpool baths all with ensuite facilities, look over the gardens and beyond into Sturminster Newton. In keeping with the tradition of the house the bedrooms have brass bedsteads and an atmosphere charged with the fragrance of dried flowers and spices. It would be difficult not to enjoy a good night's sleep and in the morning you will come downstairs to enjoy a perfect farmhouse breakfast- brown free range eggs, crusty home-made bread and local preserves. It is served in the pretty dining where many of Ken's collection of antique kitchen pieces from early Victorian rolling pins to herb hachoirs is a delight to see. Jill and Ken have also discovered many local artists whose pictures adorn the walls throughout the house. Smoking is permitted in the sitting room only. Jill is an accomplished chef and she cooks on the old fashioned Aga which generates a special warmth throughout the kitchen. Jill produces many traditional dishes using only the best local ingredients and often offers dishes unique to the Lodge created with the use of herbs and flowers grown in their own garden. She also caters superbly for vegetarians and individual dietary needs. At the end of a day exploring Dorset you return for a delectable four course dinner which will remain in your memory long after you leave Stourcastle Lodge, as indeed will the hospitality offered by the Hookham-Bassetts.

USEFUL INFORMATION

- OPEN: All year
- WHEELCHAIR ACCESS: No
- GARDEN: Cottage style
- CREDIT CARDS: Visa/Master/Euro
- ACCOMMODATION: Elegant, ensuite rooms
- RATES: From £26.50pp sharing
  Short breaks: 5% discount on 3 night stay 7 nights 10%
- DINING ROOM: Delicious, innovative food
- VEGETARIAN: Yes & other diets
- LICENSED: No. Bring your own
- SMOKING: Sitting room only
- PETS: No

SUMMER LODGE
Evershot
Dorset
DT20JR

Tel: 01935 83424
Fax: 01935 83005

RAC Blue Ribbon for Excellence
AA *** & 3 rosettes

Unless one has had the good fortune to visit Summer Lodge, it is almost impossible to appreciate what it has to offer. Suffice it to say that it is enchanting, beautifully run, has food that is renowned, immaculate gardens, a heated outdoor swimming pool and an all-weather tennis court. It is obvious, once one has been there why 60% of their business is repeat and 27% on personal recommendation.

Built originally in 1789 by the 2nd Earl of Ilchester, Summer Lodge formed part of the Ilchester estate. In 1891, the house was extended under the supervision of Thomas Hardy, who was then working as an architect in Dorchester. Almost a century later it was sold for the first time, to the present owners Nigel and Margaret Corbett, who turned it into one of the finest country-house hotels in England. Run with a degree of informality which permits the wearing of jeans, except for dinner, everything about the house has a relaxed atmosphere. The 17 ensuite bedrooms with mostly King-sized beds, are individually furnished with top class fabrics and many thoughtful extras for your comfort including Molton Brown toiletries, bath robes, radio, television, direct dial telephones and a generously supplied hospitality tray.

Head chef Timothy Ford is a talented man who, with his team, produces superb food at every meal. The cooking, based on local produce is imaginative and endlessly tempting. Breakfast starts the day off superbly, lunch can be a feast or something light, Afternoon tea is served, buffet style, for residents in the drawing room between 4 and 5pm with a range of freshly baked scones with cream, and home-made cakes. The four course dinner each night is memorable. Naturally the extensive wine list complements the food perfectly.

Superbly situated in the middle of Cattistock country, mounts can be arranged for those who hunt. There is excellent shooting, coarse, fly and sea-fishing available nearby. The glorious rolling hills and woodland of Dorset lend themselves to walking. Most of all the pretty village of Evershot will conjure up memories of the many times it has been used by filmmakers, most recently Jane Austen's *Emma* and *Sense and Sensibility*.

USEFUL INFORMATION

- OPEN; All year to guests & non-residents
- WHEELCHAIR ACCESS; Level entrance
- GARDEN; Delightful with heated swimming pool, croquet and all weather tennis court
- CREDIT CARDS; All major cards
- ACCOMMODATION; 17, spacious ensuite rooms
- RATES: From £125 B & B single £165 double D,B & B from £160

- DINING ROOM; Superb food at every meal
- VEGETARIAN; Always a choice
- LICENSED; Yes. Fine wine list
- CHILDREN; Welcome

THE CROWN HOTEL AND RESTAURANT
Marnhull
North Dorset

Tel: 01258 820224

The Crown Hotel with its attractive, intimate restaurant, is the epitome of a quiet country inn built in the 16th century and retaining much of the original features. It is redolent with a welcoming atmosphere created over the centuries and carried on today by the present tenants Nigel Dawe and Jill Collins. It is a busy place offering some of the best food in the area both at lunch and dinner and in the afternoon a delicious home-made cream tea is served, frequently in the pleasant large garden in warmer weather. The Crown caters for functions of up to 80 people and there are also the traditional pub pastimes of skittles and pool. The Crown has a devoted following of people who come from distances to savour its food, wine and hospitality. You can stay here if you wish. Its situation makes it ideal for anyone wanting to visit Salisbury or enjoy the Dorset coast just forty five minutes away. The four guest bedrooms are attractive furnished in a country style with colour co-ordinated drapes and bedcovers. Each room has colour television, Alarm clocks and a hostess tray. Children are very welcome and dogs too by prior arrangement.

USEFUL INFORMATION

- OPEN: All year Food: 12-2pm & 7-9.00pm
- WHEELCHAIR ACCESS:
- GARDEN: Large
- CREDIT CARDS: All major cards
- ACCOMMODATION: 2dbl 1tw 1fam
- RATES: From: £18pp p.n. B&B Under 5 free under 16 half price

- RESTAURANT: Good home- cooked fare
- VEGETARIAN: Yes
- BAR FOOD: Wide choice
- LICENSED: Full On
- CHILDREN: Welcome
- PETS: By arrangement

THE GRANGE HOTEL & RESTAURANT
Oborne, NR Sherborne
Dorset   DT9 4LA
Tel: 01935 813463 Fax: 01935 817464

3-4 Star

This peacefully situated 200 year old country house is just far enough away from Sherborne to make you feel you are in rural Dorset but it is close enough to the Abbey town to allow you easy access for exploring its glorious architecture and the magnificent Abbey around which the life of the town is concentrated. Here at the Grange you can enjoy the beautiful and perfectly maintained gardens with tennis court overlooking open country. A charming place in which to stay, lunch or dine and run by a family whose head is Italian and a Monte Carlo trained chef with a gift for producing inspired dishes especially Italian and French as well as more traditional English fare.

Guests always comment on the friendliness and beautiful bedrooms of the Grange Hotel. Everyone is made to feel not only welcome but important. The service is excellent and whether on holiday or business the way in which this hotel and restaurant is run will make your stay in Dorset memorable and relaxing. There are nine en suite bedrooms, five with balconies overlooking the garden and four are on the ground floor. Each room is charmingly appointed, has colour television and direct dial telephone as well as a hospitality tray.

USEFUL INFORMATION

- OPEN: All year
- WHEELCHAIR ACCESS: Yes
- GARDEN: Yes. Tennis
- CREDIT CARDS: All major cards
- ACCOMMODATION: 9 ensuite
- RATES: Double £65-£70 Single £49-£50 Child £10-£20 Weekend Break special rate on request

- RESTAURANT: Italian, French & English
- VEGETARIAN: Adaptable menu
- LICENSED: Restaurant Licence
- CHILDREN: Welcome
- PETS: No

LA FLEUR DE LYS
25 Salisbury Street
Shaftesbury
Dorset
SP7 8EL

Tel:01747 853717

2 AA Rosettes. Good Food Guide. Michelin Guide

Shaftesbury has some fascinating buildings and La Fleur de Lys in Salisbury Street is one of them. Once an old coaching inn it still has a picturesque cobbled alleyway. The restaurant on the first floor, which has been charmingly converted, was once the Hayloft and the kitchen no longer resounds to the sound of the Smithy, where it is situated, but to the excitement of preparing and serving some of the best meals in the modern French style, to be found in Shaftesbury. Here you will find the candlelit atmosphere intimate, the tables appointed with gleaming silver, sparkling glass and crisp table linen. The staff are attentive, efficient and courteous with their main aim, apart from serving superb food, to make guests feel relaxed and contented. They succeed admirably and the added bonus is the glorious view over the Blackmore Vale which can be admired by diners. There is also a very pretty small conservatory and courtyard. Dietary needs are catered for with prior notice.

USEFUL INFORMATION

- OPEN: 12-2.30pm & 7-10pm
- WHEELCHAIR ACCESS: No
- GARDEN: Courtyard & Conservatory
- CREDIT CARDS: Master/Visa/AMEX /Delta & Charge cards
- SMOKING: In Conservatory at all times. Restaurant after 10pm
- RESTAURANT: Delicious Modern French
- VEGETARIAN:+ always other diets with notice
- LICENSED: Yes. Restaurant
- PETS: No
- CHILDREN: Welcome if well behaved

NEWTON HOUSE
Sturminster Newton
Dorset
DT10 2DO

Tel: 01258 472783 Fax: 01258 473859

On the A357 Blandford to Sherborne road which runs through the village of Sturminster is Newton House, a fine Georgian Grade II Listed village house, L-shaped and with a thatched wing, the pillared front porch is decorated with Wedgewood style Medallions. It is essentially a family home and Margie Fraser together with her family make sure you are very welcome and do everything in their power to make your stay both comfortable and enjoyable. Everything about the house is attractive including the south facing patio and the partly walled formal garden in which a collection of old David Austen roses are lovingly nurtured.

Furnished in keeping with the house and in a manner which is gracious and elegant but essentially a home. There are five bedrooms, one ensuite double, one double with private bathroom, a twin and two singles sharing a bathroom. Each is attractively furnished and restful. There are never more than six guests staying at any one time. There is television in the Snug where, like the hall there is an open, welcoming fire in winter. Breakfast is delicious, substantial and traditional, it includes orange juice, fresh fruit and cereals as well as freshly cooked free range eggs and locally produced bacon and sausages.

USEFUL INFORMATION

- OPEN: All year except Christmas
- WHEELCHAIR ACCESS: Not really suitable
- GARDEN: Delightful, formal garden
- CREDIT CARDS: None taken
- ACCOMMODATION: 2dbl ensuite 1tw. 2sgl with shared bathroom
- RATES: From: £20.00
- BREAKFAST ROOM: Traditional English breakfast
- LICENSED: No
- PETS: Not encouraged

THE OLD BANK
Burton Street
Marnhull
Sturminster Newton
Dorset   DT10 1PH
Tel/Fax: 01258 821019
Tourist Office Rating: Commended List

Delightful in its own right, The Old Bank is situated in a wonderful spot which must appeal to all those who want to stay somewhere within easy reach of all the Blackmore Vale has to offer. It is an area steeped in rural history and still thankfully relatively undiscovered by the holiday making hordes. It is still pretty much the same Blackmore Vale that Hardy wrote so movingly about in his 'Tess of the D'Urbevilles'. There are miles of well-marked and scrupulously tended footpaths criss-crossing the countryside. Stately homes and gardens abound - Stourhead, Kingston Lacey, Montecute and Longleat are but a few. Quaint villages, character-filled pubs, sparkling streams, tiny patchwork fields and hedgerows bursting with birdsong and country fruits are balm for souls, frazzled by the pace of modern urban living.
A warm Dorset country welcome awaits you at The Old Bank. Built in 1730 from the warm, butter-yellow local stone, the house and barns are set around an attractive courtyard leading to a pretty garden. It is a comfortable home-away-from-home, with its delightful double, twin and family bedrooms, complete with hostess trays. Breakfast is first rate and both Sarah and Robin Hood, your hosts, together with their friendly cat and Labrador dog will make you extremely welcome.

USEFUL INFORMATION

- OPEN: All year except Christmas
- WHEELCHAIR ACCESS: Not suitable
- GARDEN: Yes
- CREDIT CARDS: None taken
- ACCOMMODATION: 2dbl 1tw
- RATES; From £18.00 per night
- FARMHOUSE KITCHEN: Delicious breakfast
- VEGETARIAN: Given warning
- LICENSED: No
- CHILDREN: Welcome
- PETS: Yes

THE OLD BREW HOUSE
Langton Long
Blandford Forum
Dorset   DT11 9HR
Tel: 01258 452861 Fax: 01258 450718

Located in the peaceful hamlet of Langton Long, referred to in the Doomsday Book, the Palladian style Old Brew House was completed in 1831 and designed by architect Charles Cockerell as part of the Langton Estate, country seat of James Farquharson. Today the Old Brew House has retained the Pleasure Grounds to the original Langton House and all the rooms have garden or park land views. Currently undergoing restoration, retaining many of its original features including a cupola and column loggia, one has the choice of self-catering or bed and breakfast accommodation. Whichever you choose the rooms are attractively appointed, warm and comfortable. There are two apartments. The first floor has a double bedroom, sitting room (which can be used as an additional twin or single) bathroom, kitchenette and own entrance. The ground floor apartment has a spacious double or twin room, small dining hallway, kitchen, bathroom and own entrance. In the house there are twin and double rooms, and all the rooms have television, alarm radio, hairdryers and bathrooms with power showers. Breakfast is a sumptuous affair and the house radiates a cheerful, friendly, efficient, relaxed and informal atmosphere. There is parking for five cars. Plenty of places of interest to visit within easy reach. Ideal spot for a holiday or a short break.

USEFUL INFORMATION

- OPEN: All year excluding Christmas
- WHEELCHAIR ACCESS: No
- GARDEN: Yes
- CREDIT CARDS: Not as yet
- ACCOMMODATION: ensuite rooms self-catering apartments
- **NON SMOKING HOUSE**
- RATES: From £30.00pp Under 12 50% reduction
- DINING ROOM: Sumptuous breakfast
- VEGETARIAN: On request
- LICENSED: No
- CHILDREN: Welcome
- PETS: No

PORTMAN LODGE
Learning and Natural Therapies Centre
Durweston
Blandford
Dorset DT11 0QA

Tel: 01258 452168 Fax: 01258 450456

Portman Lodge and its gardens forms part of a designated area of outstanding beauty, making it an ideal place in which to stay to absorb the calming influence of the therapies on offer. It has a peaceful and friendly atmosphere, is warm, comfortable and easily accessible. The village of Durweston has a children's playground and tennis court and two miles away is the Georgian town of Blandford Forum, full of historical interest and many good restaurants. The facilities at Portman Lodge include Bed and Breakfast with ensuite rooms, a library-sitting room with open fireplace and TV, board games and snooker. Whilst you stay why not take advantage of workshops, other therapies and activities which include Acupuncture, Alexander Technique, Aromatherapy, Craniosacral Therapy, Cutting the Ties that Bind, Dr Bach Flower Remedies, Emotional Counselling, Healing-Shiatsu, Homoeopathy, Metamorphic Technique, McTimoney Chiropractic, Reflexology and Reiki. You will enjoy the peace, the fascinating countryside and leave rejuvenated and recharged, once again ready to cope with today's hectic world.

USEFUL INFORMATION

- OPEN: All Year
- WHEELCHAIR ACCESS: Difficult
- GARDEN: Yes
- CREDIT CARDS: None Taken
- ACCOMMODATION: 3 Ensuite Rooms
- RATES: From £20.00 pp - Children from £12.00 pp

- DINING ROOM: Great Breakfast
- VEGETARIAN: Upon Request
- LICENSED: No
- PETS: By Arrangement
- CHILDREN: Welcome

THE RETREAT
47 Bell Street
Shaftesbury
Dorset SP7 8AE
Tel: 01747 850372/854198

Shaftesbury is a charming Saxon hill-top town which is situated on the edge of Cranborne Chase and is an ideal location for exploring the beautiful countryside and historical places of interest in the Dorset area. Undoubtedly the focal point for visitors to Shaftesbury is Gold Hill. Featured many times in films and television advertisements, the hill has great character and provides a superb backdrop to the countryside beyond. 'The Retreat' is a large Georgian town house dating back to the early 1800's and is situated in a quiet, yet central location, off the main high street. The house was bought by the present owners, Linda and Philip Adams in 1995 at a time when it had been derelict for 4 years following a major fire. The Adams embarked on an 18 month project to restore virtually everything and return the main building to its former glory. This included the main staircase, doors, coving and cornices etc. The result is stunning and today visitors enthuse about the warm and friendly atmosphere that the owners have created. Every room has en-suite facilities, television and hostess tray. Other attractions close to Shaftesbury include Stourhead House and Gardens, which is the National Trust's second most visited property. English Heritage's Wardour Castle and Stonehenge are both within fifteen to forty minutes drive from Shaftesbury. Salisbury and Wells Cathedrals, Glastonbury, Sherborne and Bath are also within thirty to ninety minutes drive, as is the beautiful coastline of Dorset.

USEFUL INFORMATION

- OPEN: All year
- WHEELCHAIR ACCESS: Yes
- CREDIT CARDS: Master/Visa
- ACCOMMODATION: 10 dbl./family rms ensuite
- RATES: From £20pp Children from £10.

- DINING ROOM: Good, traditional breakfast
- VEGETARIAN: Upon request
- LICENSED: No
- CHILDREN: Welcome
- PETS: No

THE THREE ELMS
North Wootton
NR Sherborne
Dorset   DT95JW

Tel: 01935 812881

A beautiful, rural inn set overlooking the Blackmoor Vale and with superb views towards Bulbarrow, the highest point in Dorset. Eileen and Howard Manning arrived here in 1986 and have spent the ensuing years creating a hostelry that is recognised as one of the nicest in Dorset. The Three Elms has been featured by the Daily Telegraph in their Eat Out column and is regularly featured in the Egon Ronay Good Pub Food guide as well as many other publications. Certainly they have combined the traditional with the contemporary to provide the best in food and drink and in so doing have delighted their regulars and surprised many a first time caller. Camera recognises The Three Elms for its range of traditionally brewed beers and for lovers of good food, the mixture of traditional, local and more exotic dishes on the constantly changing menu, meets with approval from everyone who dines here. If you enjoy your meal and are tempted to dally on your way the inn has three comfortable bedrooms for guests, including one with a four-poster. All the rooms have colour TV and tea/coffee making facilities. Close to the historic Abbey Town of Sherborne with its two castles, within easy distance of the coast and amid some splendid walking countryside plus a golf course, The Three Elms is a great place in which to stay and in which you will be welcomed warmly by the Manning's and their friendly staff.

USEFUL INFORMATION

- OPEN: Mon-Sat 11-2.30pm &6.30-11pm
  (6pm Fri & Sat) Sun: 12-3pm & 7-10.30pm
- WHEELCHAIR ACCESS: Yes. Small step
- GARDEN: Yes
- CREDIT CARDS: Visa/Master/Switch etc.
- ACCOMMODATION: 3 rooms
- RATES: Doubles £35 Singles £20

- BAR FOOD: Wide range, home-cooked Traditional, local and exotic
- VEGETARIAN: Large selection
- LICENSED: Full On
- CHILDREN: Welcome
- PETS: Yes

THE WALNUT TREE
West Camel
NR Yeovil
Somerset   BR22 7QF
Tel/Fax: 01935 851292
Egon Ronay Food & Bedrooms 1995/96/97/98

West Camel is just over the border from Dorset. The village is delightful and in its midst stands The Walnut Tree, an inn as popular with the locals as with the many visitors who make a bee line for its welcoming doors either to enjoy a drink, a meal, a bar snack or maybe stay in one of their beautiful en-suite bedrooms. Using The Walnut Tree as a base one can enjoy some excellent walks in splendid countryside, for the golfer there are six courses within the area and plenty of places to visit including the Fleet Air Arm Museum at Yeovilton, Haynes Motor Museum at Sparkford and the historic town of Sherborne. It is easy to reach the old Dorset coastal towns of Weymouth and Lyme Regis. In the attractive Restaurant or in the Bar, the home-made food is exciting and delicious. The specials change regularly and includes fresh Tuna fillet with a peppered sauce or Guinea Fowl Breast with roast potato, shallot and mushroom sauce. There is an a la carte menu with a separate Fish Board. You will not be able to resist Brandy Snap Baskets filled with fresh fruit ice cream and a fruit coulis. Staying here is the most relaxing and restful experience. Every room has a direct dial telephone, Sky television, hair dryer and a hostess tray, a special feature must be the garden bedrooms with their own patios.

USEFUL INFORMATION

- OPEN: 11-3pm & 5.30-11pm
- WHEELCHAIR ACCESS: Yes. 3 Ground flr rms
- GARDEN: Yes & for eating
- CREDIT CARDS: All major cards except Diners
- ACCOMMODATION: 7 ensuite rooms
- RATES: Sgl £46 Dbl £69.95 Four Poster £80 dble

- RESTAURANT: Everything home-made
- VEGETARIAN: Yes
- BAR FOOD: Wide range
- LICENSED: Full On
- CHILDREN: No
- PETS: No

WAYFARERS RESTAURANT
Sherborne Causeway
Shaftesbury
Dorset   SP7 9PX
Tel: 01747 852821
2 AA Rosettes in 'Best Restaurants 1998'

Wayfarers Restaurant, 2 miles west of Shaftesbury and heading for Sherborne basks in the totally unspoilt beauty of the Blackmore Vale. Stately homes, Stourhead with its lakes and gardens, equestrian sports, shooting and stunning walks are all here for the visitor to enjoy. To make any expedition more enjoyable, good food is an essential ingredient and within the beauty of 18th century cottage buildings with interiors adorned by exposed beams, natural stone wall and a deep inglenook fireplace, this is exactly what Wayfarers has to offer. For decades the premises has been a venue for diners. The menu is progressive, creative modern English/Continental with inspiration drawn from England and France's premier chefs. The A La Carte menu changes regularly to accommodate the seasons and the freshest local produce. There is a Bistro menu which changes weekly and offers a cheaper set menu which is excellent value for money. The fine wines are carefully chosen and are nicely balanced between the top of French wines and the outstanding ones from the New World. Everything about the Wayfarers is enjoyable. The round tables are tastefully furnished with light primrose top cloths on white damask. Fresh flowers from the garden in summer, accompany sparkling glassware and cutlery. The bar area where apéritifs are served enjoys the wide inglenook fireplace and boasts a real fire in the winter months. Good food, fine wines, super service in delightful surroundings makes the Wayfarers a must for anyone lucky enough to be in the area.

USEFUL INFORMATION

- OPEN: 2nd week Jan - Christmas Day
  Lunch bookings Tues, Fri & Sun 12-1.30pm
  Dinner: Tues.-Sat 7pm-9.15pm Superb food
- WHEELCHAIR ACCESS: Yes
- GARDEN: Yes, lovely courtyard
- CREDIT CARDS: Master/Visa/AMEX/Delta

- RESTAURANT: 35 covers
  Superb food.

- VEGETARIAN: Yes
- LICENSED: Yes. Food only
- CHILDREN: Lunch, yes.
  Dinner over 8 years

503

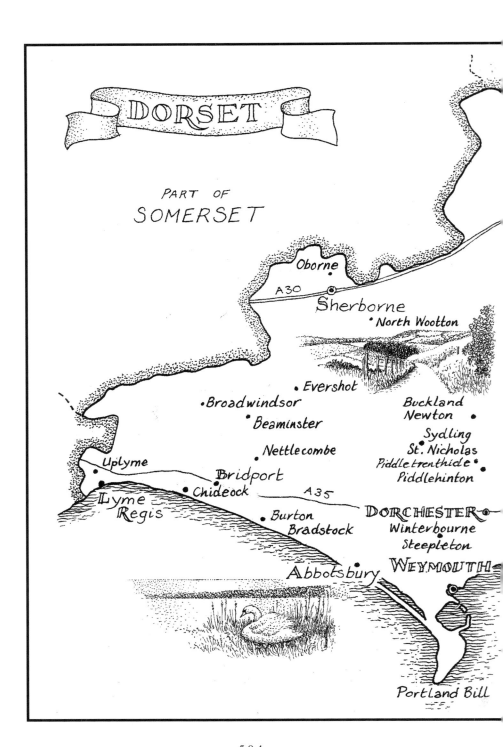

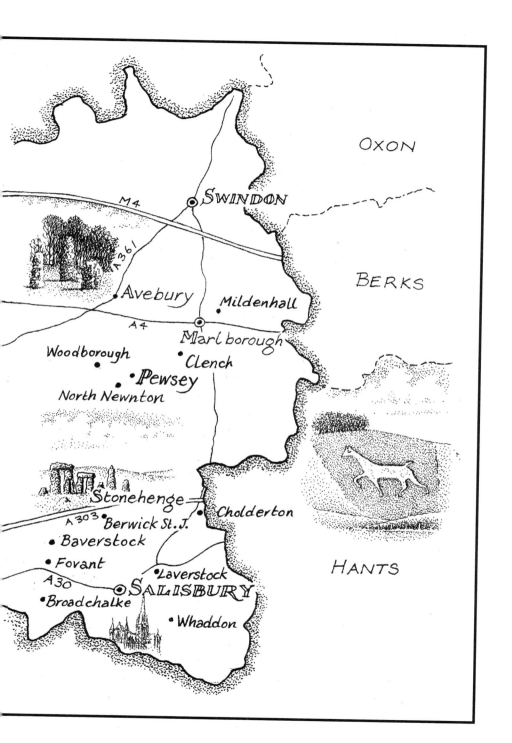

OXON

M4

BERKS

SWINDON

A 361

Avebury

•Mildenhall

A 4

Marlborough

Woodborough

•Clench

•Pewsey

North Newnton

Stonehenge

A 303 •Berwick St. J.

•Cholderton

• Baverstock

• Fovant

A 30

SALISBURY

•Broadchalke

•Laverstock

HANTS

• Whaddon

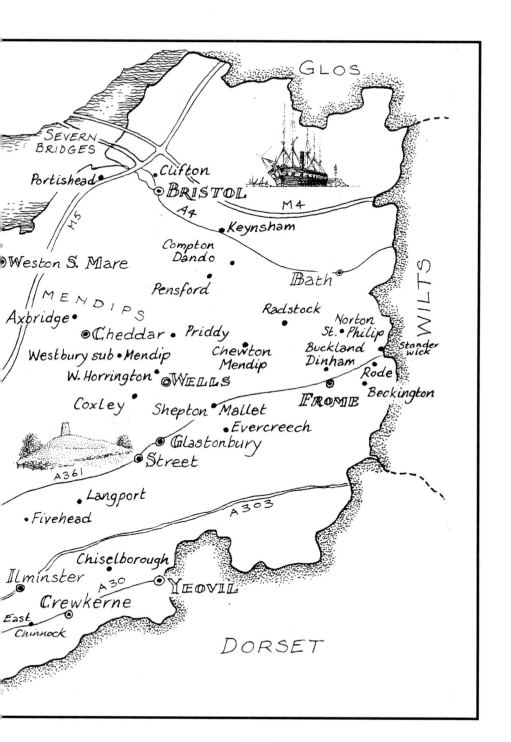

GLOS

SEVERN
BRIDGES

Portishead •

Clifton •
⊙ BRISTOL
A4
• Keynsham

M4

WILTS

Weston S. Mare

Compton
Dando •
Pensford •

Bath ⊙

MENDIPS

Axbridge •

⊙ Cheddar • Priddy

Radstock
•

Norton
St. • Philip

Westbury sub • Mendip

Chewton
Mendip

Buckland
Dinham

Stander
wick

W. Horrington •

⊙ WELLS

Rode •

Beckington •

Coxley •

Shepton • Mallet

• Frome

Glastonbury ⊙

• Evercreech

• Street

Langport •

A361

A303

• Fivehead

Chiselborough

Ilminster •

A30

⊙ YEOVIL

Crewkerne ⊙

East
Chinnock •

DORSET

507

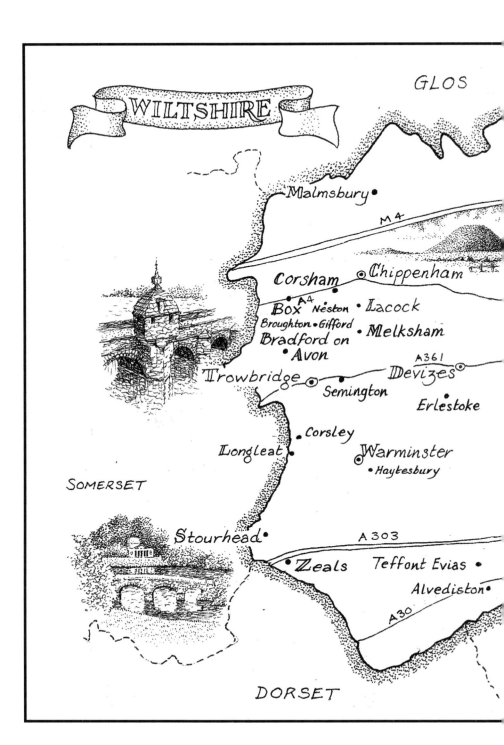

GLOS

WILTSHIRE

Malmsbury •

M 4

Corsham • ◉ Chippenham

Box • ᴬ⁴ Neston • Lacock

Broughton • Gifford • Melksham
Bradford on
• Avon

Trowbridge ◉ • Devizes ◉

Semington A361

Erlestoke

Corsley

Longleat • Warminster ◉
• Haytesbury

SOMERSET

Stourhead • A 303

• Zeals Teffont Evias •

Alvediston •

A 30

DORSET

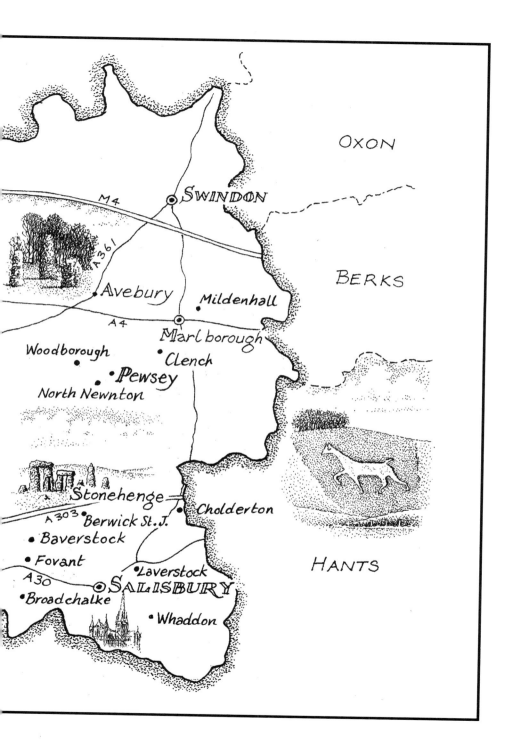

OXON

M4

SWINDON

BERKS

A361

Avebury

Mildenhall

A4

Marlborough

Woodborough

Clench

Pewsey

North Newnton

Stonehenge

Cholderton

A303

Berwick St.J.

Baverstock

Fovant

HANTS

A30

Laverstock

SALISBURY

Broadchalke

Whaddon

509

Index

Abbotsbury 424, 460
Aller 214
Allerford 159, 179
Almondsbury 30, 33
Alton Barnes 274
Alton Pancras 475
Alum Chine 389
Alveston 10, 34
Amesbury 328
Appley 134
Ashmore 488
Athelney 213
Aust 30
Avebury 270
Avonmouth 27, 53
Axbridge 251
Banwell 28
Barbrrok 162
Barrington 218
Barwick 220
Bath ....
... 57, 81, 83, 86, 91, 93, 95, 96, 98, 101
Baverstock 353
Beaminster 435, 445, 458
Beanacre 284
Beckington 79, 87, 100
Bedminster 18
Beercrocombe 248
Bemerton 325
Bere Regis 379
Berrow 110, 142
Berwick St James 352
Berwick St John 320
Bicknoller 122
Biddestone 262
Bishops Lydeard 121
Bishpstone 261
Bitton 76
Blagdon Hill 218
Blandford 513
Blandford Forum 467
Blandford St Mary 467
Blue Anchor 124, 131, 144
Boscombe 391, 401
Bossington 159

Bournemouth 362,
.... 395, 397, 398, 399, 400, 402, 408
Box 97, 265, 297
Bradford Peverell 436
Bradford On Avon ... 280, 285, 290, 299
Bradford On Tone 119
Bratton 308
Brean 108
Brent Knoll 111
Bridgwater 112, 147
Bridport 426
Brinkworth 260
Bristol 10, 39, 46, 47, 50, 51, 52, 53
Broadchalke 344
Broadwindsor 434, 460
Brompton Regis 170
Broomfield 115
Broughton Gifford 296
Brownsea Island 368
Brushford 166, 180
Bruton 213, 243
Bryanston 467
Buckland Dinham 101
Buckland Newton 455, 457, 475
Buckland St Mary 218
Burbidge 305
Burnham On Sea 111
Burrington 29
Burrow Bridge 214
Burton Bradstock 426, 446
Bury 170
Calne 268, 287
Canford Heath 368
Cannington 115
Castle Cary 213, 225
Castle Combe 262, 286
Cerne Abbas 475
Chaffcombe 217
Chalcombe 426
Chaldon Herring 415
Chard 216
Charlton Marshall 466
Charmouth 429, 453
Charterhouse 197
Cheddar 196, 249

Index

Cheddon Fitzpaine 115	Doniford 123
Cherhill 269	Dorchester 436, 447, 451, 459
Chettle 469	Doulting 206
Chew Magna 29	Dowlish Wake 217
Chewton Mendip 197, 247	Downton 328
Chickerell 424	Dulverton 166, 177, 192
Chideock 454	Dundry 50
Child Okeford 471	Dunkirk 58
Chilmark 318	Dunster 124, 133, 136
Chippenham 262	Durweston 513
Chipping Sodbury 58	Dyrham 59, 90
Chipstable 120	East Chinnock 248
Chiselborough 228	East Cliff 408
Christchurch 358	East Coker 220
Clapton In Gordano 36	East Huntspill 143, 206
Claverton 73	East Knoyle 341
Clench Common 273	East Lulworth 378
Clevedon 27	East Quantoxhead 123
Clifton 35, 54	East Stour 485
Coate 261	Easton In Gordano 54
Colehill 411	Easton Royal 305
Colerne 289	Edington 307
Combe Florey 115	Erlestoke 351
Combe Martin 165	Evercreech 213, 241
Combe St Nicholas 217	Evershot 478, 502, 509
Compton Dando 76, 85	Exford 167, 183
Congresbury 28	Exmoor 151
Corscombe 458	Failand 44, 51
Corsham 263	Farleigh Hungerford 79
Corsley 354	Farleigh Wick 298
Cotham 40, 49	Ferndown 387
Countisbury 160	Fiddleford 484
Coxley 229	Fifehead Neville 484
Cranmore 204	Filton 30
Creech St Michael 218	Fishponds 48
Crewkerne 220, 227, 239	Fivehead 215, 234
Cricket St Thomas 217	Fonthill Gifford 319
Cricklade 258	Fontmell Magna 471
Crowcombe Heathfield 122	Ford 295
Culbone 159	Foreland Point 159
Curland 146	Fortuneswell 421
Curry Rivel 221	Fovant 320, 343
Derry Hill 267	Frome 79, 102
Devizes 300	Froxfield 278
Dinton 318	Gillingham 485

Index

Glastonbury	207, 238
Godmanstone	477
Great Badminton	58
Great Bedwyn	278
Great Wishford	317
Gurney Slade	206
Ham Green	49
Hampreston	387
Hanging Langford	317
Hartford	170
Hatch Beauchamp	218, 230
Hawkesbury	57
Hawkridge	173, 190
Henbury	27, 52
Hengistbury Head	361
Heytesbury	333
High Ham	213
Highbridge	111, 143
Highcliffe	360
Higher Bockhampton	441
Highworth	258
Hillesley	57
Hilton	474
Hinton Charterhouse	76, 89, 92
Hinton St George	218
Holford	115
Holt	280
Holt	412
Holt Heath	386
Horner	159
Horningsham	313
Horton	57
Horton	409
Huish Episcopi	214, 250
Hunstrete	41
Ibberton	474
Ilchester	221
Ilminster	215
Isle Abbots	215
Isle Brewers	215
Iwerne Courtney	472
Keynsham	76, 103
Kilmersdon	206
Kilve	123
Kimmeridge	377
Kingston	30, 376
Kingston Deverill	316
Kingston St Mary	115
Lacock	265, 292, 298
Langford Budville	120
Langport	214, 245
Langton Herring	449
Langton Long	512
Langton Matravers	376
Laverstock	353

Lee Bay	164
Leigh Upon Mendip	205
Liddington	261
Liscombe	173, 192
Little Badminton	58
Little Bredy	426
Little Sodbury	58
Litton Cheney	426
Locking	109
Long Ashton	29
Long Bredy	426
Lower Weare	249
Luccombe	159
Ludwell	320
Lulworth Cove	377
Lyme Regis	430, 450
Lynmouth	161
Lynton	162
Lytchett Minster	369
Maiden Bradley	313
Malmesbury	255, 294
Mangotsfield	30
Mark	206
Market Lavington	306
Marlborough	272, 296
Marnhull	484, 510, 512
Martock	218
Melbury Osmond	478
Melksham	279, 288, 293
Mells	205
Mere	315
Merley	382
Merriott	221
Middle Woodford	328
Midsomer Norton	77
Mildenhall	297
Milton Abbas	473
Milton Lilbourne	305
Milverton	120
Minehead	126, 137, 146
Minterne Magna	477
Monksilver	123
Monkton Combe	73, 84
Monkton Heathfield	119
Montacute	219, 232
Muchelney	215
Nailsea	28
Neighbourne Oakhill	224
Neston	299
Nether Stowey	115
Netherhampton	327
Nettlecombe	457
Nomansland	328
North Newnton	306, 349
North Perrott	220

Index

North Petherton 141
North Wootton 204, 514
Norton Fitzwarren 119
Norton St Philip 77, 82
Norton Sub Hamdon 218
Nunney 204
Oaksey 260
Oare 165
Oborne 510
Ogbourne St George 274
Okeford Fitzpaine 472
Old Sodbury 58
Oldbury On Severn 9
Osmington 416
Osmington Mills 416
Over Stowey 113
Overmoigne 416
Oxbridge 176
Parracombe 166, 184
Patchway 30
Peasedown St John 76
Pensford 38
Pewsey 303, 340
Piddlehinton 456, 475
Piddletrenthide 475, 507
Pilton 204
Plush 475
Poole 366, 407, 411
Porlock 156, 181, 185
Porlock Weir 158, 175, 182
Portbury 27
Portesham 424
Portishead 27, 43
Porton 327
Potterne 306
Powerstock 436, 459
Priddy 237
Priston 76
Puddletown 463
Purton 258
Pylle 204
Radstock 77, 88
Redcliffe 18
Redlynch 328
Rockley 273
Rode 78, 102
Salisbury 323, 337, 338, 345, 347
Sandford Orcas 482
Selworthy 159
Semington 350, 351
Semley 503
Shaftesbury 486, 511, 513
Shepton Mallet 203, 226, 244, 251
Sherborne 479, 504, 505
Sherborne Causeway 515

Sherrington 317
Shroton 472
Shurnhold 291
Simonsbath 152, 189
Sixpenny Handley 470
Somerton 212, 235
South Petherton 218
Southbourne 361, 404
Southville 18
Sparkford 221
Spetisbury 466
Stalbridge 483
Standerwick 94
Stanton Drew 29
Stanton St Bernard 273
Staple Fitzpaine 218
Steeple Ashton 307
Stoford 220
Stogumber 122
Stoke St Gregory 214
Stoke Sub Hamdon 218
Stourton 314
Stourton Caundle 482
Stow On The Wold 45
Stratton On The Fosse 206
Stratton St Margaret 261
Street 206
Studland 373, 412
Sturminster Newton ....
.... 483, 506, 508, 511
Swanage 372, 406, 410
Swindon 258
Sydling St Nicholas 456, 477
Tarrant Gunville 470
Tarrant Hinton 469
Tarrant Monkton 405
Taunton 116
Teffont Evias 318, 339
Teffont Magna 318
Thornbury 10
Thurloxton 122
Timberscombe 169
Tintinhull 219
Tisbury 318
Tolland 120
Tollard Royal 320
Tolpuddle 465
Trowbridge 306, 342
Trull 119, 144
Turnworth 472
Tyneham 377
Tytherington 317
Uphill 107, 140
Uplyme 448
Verwood 387

Index

Wadeford 217
Wakeham 422
Wambrook 217
Wanborough 261
Wareham 369, 390, 396, 403
Warminster ....
.... 309, 334, 346, 348, 350, 351
Washford 124
Watchet 123, 191
Watersmeet 161
Wedmore 212
Wellington 119
Wellow 77
Wells ....
.... 198, 223, 231, 244, 246, 247, 250
West Bay 426
West Camel 514
West Cliff 395, 397
West Hatch 218
West Knoyle 316
West Lulworth 377, 393
West Monkton 145
West Porlock 158, 178
West Quantoxhead 123
Westbourne 394
Westbury 309
Westbury On Trym 27, 37
Westbury Sub Mendip 233, 240,245
Westhay 210
Weston Super Mare 107, 145
Westonzoyland 221
Westwood 307

Weymouth 416
Wheddon Cross 169, 186
White Lackington 475
Wick 236
Widcombe 74
Williton 123, 132, 138, 143
Wilton 305, 321
Wimborne Minster 380, 392
Wincanton 221
Winsford 167, 187
Winsley 283
Winterborne Anderson 466
Winterborne Tomson 466
Winterborne Steepleton 452
Witchampton 410
Withypool 167, 188
Wiveliscombe 120, 135, 139
Woody Bay 165
Wool 379, 415
Woolverton 79, 99
Wootton Bassett 273
Worlebury 108
Worth Matravers 376
Wrington 29
Wroughton 273
Wyke Regis 420
Yate 30
Yatton 28, 42
Yeovil 220
Yetminster 478
Zeals 242, 316

THE FOUR SEASONS
DISCERNING VISITOR GUIDE Series.

Titles currently available in this series are:-

DEVON & CORNWALL	£6.95
WESSEX & EXMOOR	£7.95
EAST ANGLIA	£7.95

AVAILABLE FROM LEADING BOOK SHOPS.

Titles in the series for the Millennium..

COTSWOLDS & THAMES & CHILTERNS.
THE HEART OF ENGLAND.
THE MIDSHIRES.
SOUTH & SOUTH EAST ENGLAND.

Also available from Kingsley Media Ltd.

HEALTHY OPTIONS   £9.95
A book that no health conscious person should be without.

To order any of the above titles direct from the publisher, please add £3.77. post and packing, and send you order to:-

ABA BOOKS, 138 ALEXANDRA ROAD, FORD, PLYMOUTH PL2. 1JY.

You may use postal order, cheque, or Visa.(Please do not send cash via the post)

Your can also order via the Internet, please **e-mail: kingsley@hotels.u-net.com** When ordering on the Internet please remember your Visa number, it is fully protected.

READERS COMMENTS

Please use this page to tell us about venues and places of interest that have appealed to you especially and to suggest suitable establishments to include in future publications.

We will pass on your recommendations and approval, and equally report back any complaints. We hope the latter will be few and far between.

Please post to:
Kingsley Media Ltd
Freepost PY2100
The Hoe
Plymouth
PL1 3BR

Name of Establishment:

Address:

Comments:

Your Name: (Block Caps Please)

Address:

Glossary of Places To Visit

ABBOTSBURY

ABBOTSBURY OYSTER FARM (01305 788867).
Overlooking Fleet Lagoon. Watch oyster men at work, guided tours bookable in advance.

CHESIL BEACH CENTRE AND NATURE RESERVE (01305 760579),
Chesil Beach. Displays, regular guided tours etc. Britain's second oldest nature reserve.

GLASS BOTTOMED BOAT (01305 773396).
'Fleet Observer', trips in boat from which life above and below the Fleet Lagoon can be seen.

AXBRIDGE

KING JOHN'S HUNTING LODGE (01934 732012).
National Trust Property. Early Tudor merchant's house; museum.

BATH

APPROACH GOLF COURSE (01225 331162).
Adjoins Royal Victoria Park. 12 hole and 18 hole.

BATH ANTIQUE MARKET (01225 337638).
Sixty dealers each Wednesday. West Country's longest established Antiques market.

BATH GOLF CLUB (01225 463834). 18 hole course.

BOOK MUSEUM (01225 466000).
Memorabilia of authors who lived in , or visited Bath. Jane Austen, Charles Dickens etc.

CITY OF BATH BACH CHOIR (01225 463362 for tickets).
Performances through the year at varying Bath venues.

ENTRY HILL GOLF COURSE (01225 834248). 9 hole, hire available.

GUIDE FRIDAY (01225 444102).
Two hour bus tour includes Stonehenge, Wilton House (optional), Old Sarum.
Chance to try dowsing!

LANSDOWN GOLF CLUB (01225 422138). 18 hole course.

NORWOOD FARM, Norton St Philip (01373 834356)
Rare breeds and Organic farming. Walks, display areas etc.

PADDINGTON AND FRIENDS (01225 463598). Mini museum about Paddington Bear, shop.

THE RONDO (01225 448831). Small theatre, local amateur and smaller professional shows.

BERE REGIS

EAST DORSET GOLF CLUB (01929 472244). 18 hole lakeland and 9 hole woodland courses.

BLANDFORD

RARE POULTRY, PIG, AND PLANT CENTRE (01258 880263),
Milton Abbas. Family run farm attraction.

Glossary of Places To Visit

RINGROSE POTTERY (01258 455570), Blandford St Mary. Studio and shop.

BOURNEMOUTH

BOURNEMOUTH FLYING CLUB (01202 578558).
Light aircraft flights over Dorset, based at Hurn Airport.

BOURNEMOUTH GOLF RANGE AND PARLEY GOLF CLUB (01202 593131 / 591600).
9 hole pay and play course. 23 covered floodlit bays or practice off grass.

BOURNEMOUTH WATER SPORTS (01202 575553 / 575871).
From the pier and East beach. Water-skiing, jet-ski hire, power boat courses etc.

DORSET BELLES PLEASURE CRUISES (01202 558550).
From Bournemouth Pier, to Brownsea, Poole, Swanage, Purbeck, Isle of Wight.
Coastal and evening Cruises too.

DORSET CRAFT GALLERIES (01202 429644). Demonstrations, exhibitions, crafts.

GREEN MACHINES (01202 593733), Bear Cross. Cycle hire.

QUEENS PARK GOLF COURSE (01202 396198). Mature championship course, superb setting.

SOLENT MEADS GOLF COMPLEX (01202 420795),
Hengistbury Head. 18 hole course, clubs for hire. Driving range.

SURF CHECK (01202 434344). For conditions, run by Bournemouth Surfing Centre.

BRADFORD-ON-AVON

LOCK INN COTTAGE (01225 868068). Towpath Trail, Canoe and Cycle hire.

SALLY BOATS (01225 864923). Luxurious narrowboats for hire.

BREAN

UNITY FARM PONY TREKKING (01278 751235).

BRIDGWATER

CANNINGTON GOLF CLUB (01278 652394), Cannington. 19 hole, visitors welcome.

ENMORE PARK GOLF CLUB (01278 671519). Visitors welcome.

BRIDPORT

MOORES DORSET BISCUITS (01297 489253),
Morcombelake. Family business, since 1850. Shop, gallery, and bakery to visit.

BRISTOL

ATLANTA HELICOPTERS (01275 474456),
Bristol International Airport. Scenic tours, including Bristol Channel, Somerset Levels.

BALTIC WHARF SAILING SCHOOL (0117 952 5202).

Glossary of Places To Visit

BIKE (0117 929 3500), Clifton. Cycle Hire.

BRACKENWOOD GARDEN CENTRE AND WOODLAND WALK (01275 843484), Brackenwood, near Portishead.

BRISTOL CLIMBING CENTRE (0117 941 3489).

BRISTOL PACKET BOAT TRIPS (0117 926 8157), Wapping Wharf, by SS Great Britain.

DAUPHINE'S (0117 955 1700). Theatrical and historical costume collection. Group bookings only.

MUD DOCK (0117 929 2151). Cycle Hire.

QEH THEATRE (0117 925 0551), Clifton.

REDGRAVE THEATRE (0117 974 3384), Clifton.

ROYAL WEST OF ENGLAND ACADEMY (0117 973 5129), Clifton. Fine Art etc.

ST WERBURGH'S CITY FARM (0117 942 8241).

SHOW OF STRENGTH THEATRE COMPANY (0117 987 9444), Quaker's Friars.

WILDSCREEN FESTIVAL (0117 909 6300).
Annual festival of natural history film, TV and multimedia. Largest of its kind in the world.

WILLSBRIDGE MILL (0117 932 6885), Willsbridge.

WINDMILL HILL CITY FARM (0117 963 3252),
Bedminster. Working farm, discovery trails etc.

BROADWINDSOR

SOMERSET CYCLING AND WEST SAXON SADDLES (01308 867686).
Many different themed cycle routes, such as The Apple and the Grape, Celtic Kingdoms and Iron Age Forts; off road routes etc.

BURNHAM-ON-SEA

ANIMAL FARM COUNTRY PARK (01278 751628), Berrow. Rare breeds, childrens activities.

MIDDLEMOOR WATER PARK (01278 685578), east of M5. Water ski, jet ski etc.

BURROWBRIDGE

DEVON AND SOMERSET BALLOONS (01823 698757).
Hot air balloon flights, for groups or individuals.

CALNE

BLACKLANDS LAKE COARSE FISHING (01249 813672).

CALNE ANGLING ASSOCIATION (01249 814516).

Glossary of Places To Visit

CASTLE CARY

COTTAGE BREWING COMPANY (01963 240551),
Lovington. Real ale brewery, can be visited by prior arrangement.

HADSPEN GARDEN (01749 813707). Walled garden, wild flower meadow etc.

CHARD

FERNE ANIMAL SANCTUARY (01460 65214), Wambrook. Rescued animal centre.

CHARMOUTH

HIGHER POUND RIDING CENTRE (01297 678747),
Monkton Wylde. Hacks through Charmouth Forest, no roadwork. All abilities.

CHEDDAR

BLAGDON AND CHEW VALLEY LAKES (01275 322339 / 01761 462567),
Blagdon. Fishing permits.

CHEDDAR VALLEY VINEYARDS (01934 732280).

CHIPPENHAM

THEATRE IN THE DOWNS, THE OLYMPIAD (01249 654970). Local Theatre Company.

CHRISTCHURCH

CHRISTCHURCH SKI AND LEISURE CENTRE (01202 499155),
Hurn. Ski shop, workshops, floodlighting, ski bobbing, snow boarding, recreational skiing
or lessons; all in edge of New Forest setting.

CHRISTCHURCH MOTOR MUSEUM (01202 488100),
Hurn. Opportunity to drive a vintage car (booking needed).
Hands on exhibits, collection of vehicles and memorabilia.

MACPENNYS (01425 672348).
Exotic, unusual plants. Four acre woodland garden planted in the 1950s, nursery attached.

STEAMER POINT WOODLAND (01425 272479).
Twenty acre woodland site, conservation events and guided tours. Spectacular clifftop view points.

CLEVEDON

CLEVEDON CRAFT CENTRE (01934 515763).

CLEVEDON PIER, TOLL HOUSE GALLERY (01275 878846), and Information Centre.

CREWKERNE

CLAPTON COURT GARDENS (01460 73220).
Three miles south of town. 10 acres of beautiful gardens.

Glossary of Places To Visit

DEVIZES

CANALFEST (01380 721279). Annual event on Kennet and Avon Canal.

DEVIZES BIKES (01380 721433). Cycle hire.

ERLESTOKE SANDS GOLF CLUB (01380 831027 / 830507), Erlestoke.

MILL FARM TROUT LAKES (01380 813138), Worton.

STERT VINEYARD (01380 723889).
By appointment. Reputedly on site of Roman vineyards, replanted in 1977, English country vineyard.

DORCHESTER

ASHLEY CHASE ESTATE (01308 482580),
Litton Cheney. Produce farm, famous range of cheeses. Tours of cheese house etc.

CAME DOWN GOLF CLUB (01305 812670 / 813494).
18 hole downland course, visitors welcome, green fees.

DORSET ACTIVE LEISURE (01300 345293),
Buckland Newton. Clay pigeon, pistol shooting, archery, quad bikes etc. Off road tracks.

DORSET SAFARIS (01305 250685).
Advance booking needed. Guided routes around Dorset, minibus and walking.

DORSET TOURING COMPANY (01305 250685).
Minibus, car on walking; guided tours. Specialities include Hardy, coast, country pubs.

WATCH (01300 345293),
Buckland Newton. Purpose built hide for badger, owl, fox watching.
Hourly or nightly hire, room for twelve, booking needed.

WEST DORSET GUIDED WALKS (01305 267992). Blue badge guides, all areas.

EAST HUNTSPILL

SOMERSET CYCLE HIRE AND SALES (01278 792777),
part of Secret World Badger sanctuary site. Routes across the levels, including the Bluebell trail.

EXMOOR

BURROWHAYES FARM RIDING STABLES (01643 862463),
West Luccombe. All abilities, escorted rides; Horner Valley, Dunkery, Selworthy, open moor.

EXMOOR STEAM RAILWAY AND GARDENS (01598 710711),
half size narrow gauge railway. Two mile journey through extensive gardens.

HAWTHORNE RIDING AND LIVERY STABLES (01643 831401),
Withypool. One to three hour rides, escorted, across open moorland. Horses and ponies.

HORNER FARM RIDING STABLES (01643 862456).
Escorted or unescorted rides through Horner Oak Woods and across to Dunkery Beacon.

Glossary of Places To Visit

HUNTSCOTT HOUSE STABLES (01643 841272),
Wootton Courtenay, near Minehead. Access to open moor. Quality horses for experienced riders.

MILL POTTERY (01643 841297),
Wootton Courtenay, near Minehead. Handmade Stoneware,
ancient buildings used as workshops in countryside, waterwheel, kiln etc.

PERITON PARK RIDING STABLES (01643 705970),
Middlecombe, Minehead. Escorted riding in woodland and moor, from one hour to full day.

SIMONSBATH POTTERY AND GALLERY (01643 831443).
Pottery and other crafts made on premises.

FROME

CITY CYCLES (01373 451166). Bicycles for hire.

FROME GOLF CENTRE (01373 453410). Visitors welcome.

MERLIN THEATRE (01373 465949).
Purpose built theatre, everything from childrens shows to classical recitals.

ORCHARDLEIGH GOLF CLUB (01373 454200). Visitors welcome.

GLASTONBURY

PEDALERS (01458 831117). Bicycles for hire.

HIGHBRIDGE

ALSTONE WILDLIFE PARK (01278 782405). Red Deer, camels, llamas, owls, emus etc.

COOMBES CIDER (01278 641265), Mark. Cider making, sampling. Museum.

WOODCRAFT (01278 781007), Watchfield.

HIGH HAM

STEMBRIDGE TOWER MILL (01458 250818).
National Trust property. Last thatched windmill built in England, worked from 1822 until 1910.

ILCHESTER

ILCHESTER MUSEUM (01935 841247), Town Hall.

ILMINSTER

WAREHOUSE THEATRE (01460 57294) Small theatre, occasional productions.

LANGPORT

HEAVEN'S GATE FARM (01458 252656), West Henley. More than 300 animals to see.

KELWAYS (01458 250521). Cottage gardens and plant centre. Orchid house.

Glossary of Places To Visit

LANGPORT AND RIVER PARRETT VISITOR CENTRE AND CYCLE HIRE (01458 250350).
Ideal for starting walk or cycle ride around this lowland area.
LULWORTH

LULWORTH EQUESTRIAN CENTRE (01929 400396).
All abilities welcomed. Rides through countryside, pub rides etc.

LULWORTH MARINE (01929 400445). Boat hire and trips along the coast.

LYME REGIS

LANGMOOR AND LISTER GARDENS (01297 445175). Large public gardens near seafront.

MARINE THEATRE (01297 442394). Dramatic coastal views from auditorium.

LYTCHETT MATRAVERS

BULBURY WOODS GOLF CLUB (01929 459574). Visitors welcome.

MARLBOROUGH

DAYS OUT (01672 564075).
Personalised guiding service. People Carriers used to Explore archaeological, historical Wessex etc.
Stonehenge, Glastonbury, Avebury and so on.

RENTALL (01672 513028). Cycles for hire.

RIDGEWAY BIKES (01672 841555), Ogbourne St George. Cycles for hire.

MARTOCK

BURROW HILL CIDER (01460 240782),
Kingsbury Episcopi. Home of the Somerset Cider Brandy Company.
Cider making to be seen, as well as the brandy, which is 42% proof!

MENDIPS

AVON SKI CENTRE AND MENDIP RIDING CENTRE (01934 822383), Churchill.

MENDIP MODEL MOTOR RACING CIRCUIT (01934 750861).

MINEHEAD

HOME FARM (01984 640817),
Blue Anchor. Traditional farm, guided tours, also access to Brendon Hills and woodland walks.

MINEHEAD AND WEST SOMERSET GOLF CLUB (01643 702057).
Part links, part parkland, visitors welcome.

POMPY'S (01643 704077). Bicycle hire.

MUCHELNEY

ALMONRY (01458 250003).
Converted barn and agricultural buildings, facilities include a gallery and gilders workshop.

Glossary of Places To Visit

PEWSEY

CHERRY CRAFT (01725 519462). Luxury narrowboats, moorings etc.

CHISENBURY PRIORY (01980 70406),
Chisenbury. Medieval priory with displays of unusual plant species.

LOWER FARM HOUSE (01672 562911), Milton Lilbourne. Seven acre landscaped gardens.

MANNINGFORD GARDENS AND NURSERY (01672 562232),
near Manningford Bruce. Display gardens and box maze.

PEWSEY VALE CHARTER CRUISES (01703 266200).
Narrowboat cruises on Kennet and Avon Canal.

RUSHALL FARM SHOP (01980 630335), Rushall. Organic produce farm. Bakery etc.

SHARCOTT MANOR (01672 563485). Five acre garden with water.

UPAVON GOLF CLUB (01908 630787), RAF Upavon.

POOLE

BROWNSEA ISLAND FERRIES LTD (01202 66226).
Poole Quay, also trips to Wareham, private charter etc.

CANFORD MAGNA GOLF CLUB AND THE GOLF ACADEMY(01202 59301 / 591212),
Canford Magna. Two 18 hole courses, pay and play, also six hole beginners course.
Turf and covered practice facilities. Short game area.

CONDOR FERRIES (01305 761551). Express day trips from Poole to Guernsey or Jersey.

COOL CATS (01202 701100). Sailing and quality bike hire. Sailing tuition. Sandbanks.

FRENCH CONNECTION WATERSPORTS (01202 707757).
Hire and tuition available , equipment for windsurfing, water-skiing, boarding etc.
Poole Harbour / Sandbanks.

GREENSLADES ISLANDS CRUISE (01202 669955 / 622152).
Ferries to Brownsea, cruises to Wareham, private charter, winter bird-watching trips etc.

MOUNTAIN BIKE HIRE (01202 383898).
Full or half day hire, or longer. Delivery and collection service. Open all year.

POOLE HARBOUR BOARDSAILING (01202 700503). Learn to windsurf in Poole Harbour.

POOLE YACHTS LTD (01202 672155), Hamworthy. Day or weekend sailing trips.

PORTLAND

PARRYS DIVE CENTRE (01305 821261).
Full range of courses. Guided snorkelling, Scuba, equipment supplied.

SUNSPORT (01305 770494). Sailing, windsurfing, canoeing.

Glossary of Places To Visit

WINDMILL STABLES (01305 823719), Weston. Trekking centre, coastal rides.

SALISBURY

A S TOURS (01980 862931).
Minibus tours, including Stonehenge, Avebury, Arthurian country etc. Fully guided and accompanied.

DOWNTON CUCKOO FAIR (01725 510646),
Downton. Annual fair (spring) with morris, maypole, line dancing, 250 plus stalls.
Rural craft demonstrations, etc.

EDWIN YOUNG COLLECTION (01722 410614),
Public Library. Collection of water colours, drawings and oil paintings of local scenes.

ENLIGHTENED TIMES (01722 415640).
Off the beaten track guided tours, carefully researched, small friendly company.
Major sites of Bath, Avebury, Salisbury, Stonehenge too. Photographic advice.

JOHN CREASEY MUSEUM (01722 324145),
Public Library. Collection of books, manuscripts relating to John Creasey.
Collection of Contemporary Art on show.

HAYBALLS CYCLE HIRE (01722 411378).

OLD SARUM FLYING CLUB (01722 322525). Trial lessons, trips. Microlights available.

SALISBURY AND SOUTH WILTSHIRE WALKING AND CYCLING HOTLINE (01980 623255).

SALISBURY CITY GUIDES (01980 623463).
Professional guides. Walks, garden tours, coach tours.

WESSEXPLORE TOURIST SERVICES (01722 326304).
Walks, coach and car tours all over the south of England.
New speciality is alternative shopping tours: arts, crafts, farms and factories with regional products.

SHAFTESBURY

ARTS CENTRE AND OLD MARKET PLAYHOUSE (01747 854321). Art, Light Opera, Drama, etc.

CAMELOT CRAFT GROUP (01747 851972).
Craft Markets, at least twice monthly. Held in Town Hall at top of Gold Hill.

COMPTON ABBAS AIRFIELD (01747 811767),
Compton Abbas. Trial lessons available. Also fantastic viewpoint, 800 feet above sea level.

SOMERTON

LONDON CIGARETTE CARD COMPANY SHOWROOM (01458 273452).
More than 2500 sets of cigarette and picture cards on display. Shop in different premises.

LYTES CARY MANOR,
Charlton Mackerell. National Trust Property, Manor House with 14th century chapel, other features,
including hedged gardens.

Glossary of Places To Visit

SOUTH PETHERTON

EAST LAMBROOK MANOR GARDEN AND MARGERY FISH PLANT NURSERY (01460 240328).

STALBRIDGE

RED LION POTTERY (01963 363075). Throw your own pots. Showroom, resident potter.

STREET

HECKS FARMHOUSE CIDER (01458 442367). Museum, farm shop.

STREET CYCLE COMPANY (01458 447882). Cycle Hire.

STUDLAND

STUDLAND WATER SPORTS (01929 425345). Dinghies, sailboards, canoes.

SWANAGE

OCEAN ACTION (01929 427600). Mountain bike hire.

PIERHEAD WATERSPORTS AND SEA SCHOOL (01929 422254 / 01202 697326).
Powerboat courses, all levels. Water-skiing, sailing, windsurfing etc, powerboat rides.

PURBECK WOOD CRAFTS (01929 427421),
Knitson. Visit, watch and shop at workshops. Storm damaged woods used.

PUTLAKE ADVENTURE FARM (01929 422917),
Langton Matravers. Have a go at hand milking, feeding animals etc.

QUALITY CYCLE HIRE (01929 425050).

SWANAGE LIFEBOAT STATION (01929 427058),
Peveril Point. Working station, open except during emergencies.

SWINDON

LEISURE CYCLES (01793 432476). Cycles for hire.

PARSONAGE FARM (01793 740204), Chiseldon. Footpaths, cycling and riding routes.

WROUGHTON SCIENCE MUSEUM (01793 814466),
Wroughton. Annexe of the London Science Museum.

TAUNTON

ANTIQUES MARKET (01823 289327) held every Monday, Silver Street.

HOLLYWOOD BOWL (01823 444144) Ten pin bowling etc.

MAKERS (01823 251121),
Bath Place. Contemporary crafts co-operative, jewellery, pottery, etching, wood, leather etc.

Glossary of Places To Visit

QUANTOCK POTTERY AND GALLERY (01823 433057),
West Bagborough. Visit working pottery.

SPINNERS AND WEAVERS WORKSHOP (01823 325345),
Staplehay. Day courses in traditional spinning and weaving available.

STAPLECOMBE VINEYARDS (01823 451217), Staplecombe. Walks, winery, tastings, shop.

TAUNTON ANGLING ASSOCIATION (01823 271194).
Permits for river, canal, lakes, including West Sedgemoor Drain.

TAUNTON DEANE BOWLING CLUB (01823 331991 / 271743),
includes six rink indoor bowling green.

TROWBRIDGE

TRANQUIL BOATS (01380 728504), Semington. Canal boats for day hire.

WESSEX NARROWBOATS (01225 769847). Daily or weekly hire, tuition available.

VERWOOD

UPPER FARM (01725 517784),
Edmondsham. Rare breeds and traditional farm animals in working environment.

WAREHAM

BOVINGTON R.A.C. SADDLE CLUB (01929 403580),
Bovington Camp. Indoor and outdoor school. Hire, hacks, cross country course etc.

HYDE WOODS RIDING CENTRE (01929 471087), Hyde. Hacks and lessons.

MARGARET GREEN ANIMAL SANCTUARY (01929 480474),
Church Knowle. Cares for unwanted, abandoned animals; horses, donkeys, rabbits, birds etc.

MONKEY WORLD (0800 456600) Wool, Ape Rescue Centre.

WAREHAM CYCLETREKS (01929 554188). Cycle hire.

WAREHAM GOLF CLUB (01929 554147 / 554156). 18 hole course, visitors welcome.

WAREHAM RIVER BOATS COMPANY (01929 550688). River cruises from Wareham Quay.

WARMINSTER

BATCHELORS CYCLE HIRE (01985 213221).

WATCHET

WIRELESS IN THE WEST (01984 640688),
in same location as Tropiquaria, mentioned in main text. Radio broadcasting history, more than 100 receivers etc, set in first BBC high power transmitting station in South West.

Glossary of Places To Visit

WEDMORE

ASHTON WINDMILL (01934 712694 / 712260),
Chapel Allerton. 18th century flour mill, last complete mill in Somerset.

ISLE OF WEDMORE GOLF COURSE (01934 712452). Visitors welcome.

WELLINGTON

WELLESLEY THEATRE (01823 666668).

WELLS

CITY CYCLES (01749 675096). Cycle Hire.

WESTBURY

BARNES CYCLE HIRE (01373 822760).

FITZROY FARM COMPLEX (01380 830401), near Bratton. Arts and Crafts centre etc.

WESTBURY CYCLES (01373 822799). Cycles for hire.

WESTON-SUPER-MARE

COURT FARM COUNTRY PARK (01934 822383), east of Weston.

FORGOTTEN WORLD (01934 750841), east of Weston towards M5. Gypsy museum.

WEYMOUTH

OUTDOOR EDUCATION CENTRE (01305 784927).
Offers caving, sailing, climbing, canoeing for all ages.

WESSEX WATER MUSEUM (0117 929 0611),
Sutton Poyntz. Museum in Victorian pumping station in picturesque village.

WEYMOUTH SAILING AND WINDSURFING CENTRE (01305 776549).
Sailing, canoeing, windsurfing in Portland Harbour.

WILLITON

ORCHARD WYNDHAM (01984 632309). Ancestral home and gardens, guided tours.

WIMBORNE

STAR COTTAGE (01202 885130),
Cowgrove. Garden and studio, with work inspired by surrounding plants and flowers.

WIVELISCOMBE

WESTFEST (01984 624326).
Annual beer and folk festival. Walks, talks, tours, 57 different local beers!

Glossary of Places To Visit

WOOTTON BASSETT

QUALITY CYCLES (01793 849369). Cycle hire.

YEOVIL

COMMUNITY ARTS CENTRE (01935 432123). Regular art exhibitions and events.

GARTELL LIGHT RAILWAY (01963 370752),
Yenston, near Templecombe. narrow gauge line, on trackbed of Somerset and Dorset Railway.

SWAN THEATRE (01935 428646) Amateur productions.

TOWN TREE NATURE GARDENS (01935 823203).
22 acres of ponds, waterfalls, weirs. Walks, waterfowl, landscaping.

YEOVIL SKI CENTRE (01935 421702). Dry slopes, facilities, Ski Lodge.

Notes

Notes

Notes

Notes

534

Notes

Notes